OXFORD STUDI
EUROPEAN

MW00824214

General Editors

SIMON DIXON, MARK MAZOWER,

and

JAMES RETALLACK

Imperial Russia, it was said, had two capital cities because it had two identities: St. Petersburg was Russia's "window to Europe," whereas Moscow preserved the nation's proud historical traditions. *Enlightened Metropolis* challenges this myth by exploring how the tsarist regime actually tried to turn Moscow into a bridgehead of Europe in the heartland of Russia.

Moscow in the eighteenth century was widely scorned as backward and "Asiatic." The tsars thought it a benighted place that endangered their state's internal security and their effort to make Russia European. Beginning with Catherine the Great, they sought to construct a new Moscow, with European buildings and institutions, a Westernized "middle estate", and a new cultural image as an enlightened metropolis. Drawing on the methodologies of urban, social, institutional, cultural, and intellectual history, *Enlightened Metropolis* asks: How was the urban environment—buildings, institutions, streets, smells—transformed in the nine decades from Catherine's accession to the death of Nicholas I? How were the lives of the inhabitants changed? Did a "middle estate" come into being? How similar was Moscow's modernization to that of Western cities, and how was it affected by the disastrous occupation by Napoleon? Lastly, how were Moscow and its people imagined by writers, artists, and social commentators in Russia and the West from the Enlightenment to the mid-nineteenth century?

Enlightened Metropolis

Constructing Imperial Moscow, 1762–1855

ALEXANDER M. MARTIN

OXFORD
UNIVERSITY PRESS

Great Clarendon Street, Oxford, OX2 6DP,
United Kingdom

Oxford University Press is a department of the University of Oxford.
It furthers the University's objective of excellence in research, scholarship,
and education by publishing worldwide. Oxford is a registered trade mark of
Oxford University Press in the UK and in certain other countries

First published 2013
First published in paperback 2014

Impression: 1

Published in the United States of America by Oxford University Press
198 Madison Avenue, New York, NY 10016, United States of America

British Library Cataloguing in Publication Data
Data available

ISBN 978–0–19–960578–1 (Hbk.)
ISBN 978–0–19–872288–5 (Pbk.)

To Laurie, Jeffrey, and Nicole

Acknowledgments

This book has been in the works since the late 1990s. My dissertation, completed a few years earlier, had been a study of Russian political and intellectual history in the era of the Napoleonic Wars. For this new project, I wanted to stay in the same period but work on a topic that engaged more directly the everyday experience of average people in imperial Russia. The project took many twists and turns and became far more complex than I initially imagined, and I am grateful to all those who have assisted me along the way.

My research and writing were made possible by fellowships from the National Endowment for the Humanities, the American Councils for International Education (ACTR/ACCELS), the National Council for Eurasian and East European Research, the American Philosophical Society, and the American Council of Learned Societies. I also received generous funding from Oglethorpe University, the Nanovic Institute for European Studies at the University of Notre Dame, and the Institute for Scholarship in the Liberal Arts at the University of Notre Dame.

Parts of Chapter 7 were earlier published as "Urban Encounters: The Estate System in Everyday Life in 1820s Moscow," in *Cahiers du monde russe*, 51/2–3 (April–September 2010): 329–51.

Many people have generously helped me as I worked on this project. I am grateful for their support and their insights; they helped make this a much better book. Portions of the book were read by Christopher Hamlin, Janet M. Hartley, Nathaniel Knight, Olga Maiorova, Donna Tussing Orwin, Alison K. Smith, Susan Smith-Peter, Elena Vishlenkova, Elise Kimerling Wirtschafter, and three anonymous readers for Oxford University Press. My research began in earnest during a semester in Göttingen in 1999, where Manfred Hildermeier and Doris von der Brelie-Lewien made my family and me feel welcome. I had the opportunity to develop my ideas, and learn from colleagues, at conferences and workshops in Perm, St Petersburg, Budapest, Voronezh, and Samara, and in talks that I was invited to give over the years at Stanford, Princeton, Columbia, and the universities of Cologne, Berlin, Bremen, Münster, and Oxford. As the book took shape, chapters were read by the participants of the Midwest Russian History Workshop at East Lansing (2009) and Urbana-Champaign (2010), and, in the History Department at Notre Dame, in the Department Colloquium (2010) and the European history reading group (2011). Several chapters received a critical reading from the Nanovic Institute's interdisciplinary discussion group on Cultural Transformations in Modern Europe—Tobias Boes, Julia Douthwaite, Tiago Fernandes, Robert Fishman, Anita McChesney, Thomas Kselman, Pierpaolo Polzonetti, and Lesley Walker. The book owes much to the intellectual encouragement I received from my fellow editors at *Kritika: Explorations in Russian and Eurasian History*, my friends in the Study Group on Eighteenth-Century Russia and the Southeast Workshop on Russian History, and my former colleagues and students at Oglethorpe University as well as my present ones at Notre Dame. Simon Dixon encouraged me to submit the book to Oxford University Press. To all of them, I am grateful.

In one of the very first books that I read for this project, Blagovo's *Rasskazy babushki*, I made a note on the first page that this was our son Jeffrey's first day in preschool. By now, he is in college. My work on this book has also been a chapter in the life of our family. Jeffrey and Nicole attended school in Germany and Russia and took the train across Siberia. Laurie, when she wasn't dealing with the challenges of family life in foreign countries, became an expert guide to the sights of the Russian capital. She was patient and supportive as "the book" invaded our weekends and vacations, and the quality of the final draft owes much to her skill as an editor. To her, Jeffrey, and Nicole, I dedicate this book in love and gratitude.

Contents

List of Illustrations

List of Maps

List of Tables

List of Abbreviations

ChOIDR	*Chteniia v Obshchestve Istorii i Drevnostei Rossiiskikh*
IMGD	*Izvestiia Moskovskoi Gorodskoi Dumy*
MV	*Moskovskiia Vedomosti*
OPI GIM	Otdel Pis'mennykh Istochnikov Gosudarstvennogo Istoricheskogo Muzeia
OZ	*Otechestvennyia Zapiski*
PSZ (First Series)	*Polnoe sobranie zakonov Rossiiskoi Imperii: Sobranie Pervoe*, 45 vols. (St Petersburg: Pechatano v tipografii II Otdeleniia Sobstvennoi Ego Imperatorskago Velichestva Kantseliarii, 1830)
RA	*Russkii Arkhiv*
RS	*Russkaia Starina*
RV	*Ruskoi Vestnik*
TsIAM	Tsentral'nyi Istoricheskii Arkhiv Moskvy
VE	*Vestnik Evropy*
ZhMVD	*Zhurnal Ministerstva Vnutrennikh Del*

Introduction

In December 1752, Empress Elizabeth of Russia left St Petersburg for an extended visit to Moscow. For the next year and a half, Moscow was once again the seat of the Russian government, as it had been before Peter the Great moved it to St Petersburg. Transferring the government to Moscow was an enormous undertaking. Much of the aristocracy, central bureaucracy, and diplomatic corps accompanied the empress. So did the imperial court, which since Peter's time had grown enormously in scale, refinement, and lavishness of consumption: Elizabeth alone brought 4,000 dresses. Whenever the court went to Moscow, grass started to grow in the streets of St Petersburg because there were hardly any carriages left in the city.[1]

The prospect of the imperial visit sent Moscow officials into a frenzy of activity, because their city was in no condition to host all the courtiers and dignitaries (see Illustration 0.1). The historian Sergei Solov'ev, who was a professor at Moscow University from 1850 to 1875, provides a graphic description of the city's dilapidated state on the eve of Elizabeth's arrival. The Kremlin cathedrals, the crown jewels of Russian sacred architecture, stood surrounded by "rubble, broken bells and other rubbish, such that you could only make your way through with difficulty." The magnificent clock over the grand entrance to the Kremlin from Red Square was in disrepair. The clockmaker responsible for maintaining it had been fired for incompetence and drunkenness, but he had to be rehired because no one else could be found for the job. In the area around Red Square, arguably the premier commercial emporium in all Russia, orders had to be given to remove stinking heaps of dung and dirt from empty shops and clear out the criminals and other rabble squatting in disused wooden shacks. When the imperial party arrived, the heirs to the throne—Grand Duke Peter and his wife, the future Catherine II (the Great)—were housed in an overcrowded, vermin-infested firetrap called the Golovin Palace, the only building in Moscow deemed suitable to receive them. The palace promptly caught fire, forcing the august visitors to relocate to a different building where, Solov'ev writes, "the

---

[1] *The Memoirs of Catherine the Great*, tr. Mark Cruse and Hilde Hoogenboom (New York: Modern Library, 2005), 80, 114, 123, 131; Simon Dixon, *Catherine the Great* (New York: Ecco, 2009), 73–5.

Illus. 0.1. "Red Square, Near the St Nicholas Gate of the Kremlin." Genre scene showing market stalls. Line engraving from the 1790s, after a drawing from the 1760s or early 1770s for the coronation album of Catherine II by Jean-Louis de Veilly and Mikhail Makhaev. Courtesy of The New York Public Library. <http://digitalgallery.nypl.org/nypldigital/id?1215566>.

wind blew freely" through the rotting floors and windows and "bedbugs and cockroaches reigned supreme."[2]

Solov'ev's tone, at once amused and appalled, provides a measure of how much Moscow had changed between Elizabeth's time and his own. Beginning in the eighteenth century, the Russian monarchy had sought to turn Moscow into a refined European city and make its poorly educated, xenophobic middle strata into a class that resembled a Western bourgeoisie and was loyal to the imperial state. Solov'ev (1820–79) embodied the success of these efforts. His father belonged to one of the most insular and anti-Western groups in Russia, the Orthodox clergy, but Solov'ev broke with this tradition: he received a secular education, traveled abroad, and went on to become an eminent historian. A central thesis of his scholarship was that Peter the Great and his heirs had

---

[2] Sergei M. Soloviev, *History of Russia, Volume 40: Empress Elizabeth, Politics and Culture, Approach of the Seven Years War, 1748–1756*, ed. and tr. Peter C. Stupples (Gulf Breeze, Fla.: Academic International Press, 2004), 1–6, quotations on 2, 6.

been right to force Russians out of their isolationist shell, and that Russia's destiny was to be a member of the European community of nations.[3] When Solov'ev described his hometown of Moscow in the reign of Empress Elizabeth, he was looking back across a century of urban modernization that had created the indispensable preconditions for lives like his own.

The defects of mid-eighteenth century Moscow that Solov'ev describes had implications far beyond aesthetics or convenience. Neither the built environment nor the mores of the inhabitants met the regime's requirements in the decades after Peter the Great. Moscow's many wooden buildings were dangerous fire hazards. In one disastrous conflagration in 1737, for example, one-fifth of the city burned to the ground.[4] That Moscow's ubiquitous filth posed a threat to public health, and helped cause the plague outbreak of 1771 that left 50,000 people dead, was obvious even though eighteenth-century medical science still blamed epidemics on airborne "miasmas." The horror of that epidemic, and the government's heavy-handed enforcement of quarantine rules, triggered a mass uprising, which only deepened the regime's conviction that Moscow teemed with benighted riffraff. The regime's control of the city was further subverted by a criminal underworld that became legendary thanks to Van'ka Kain, a notorious gangster immortalized in eighteenth-century Russian pulp fiction for his daring crimes and ability to thumb his nose at the police.[5]

Moscow's troubles were all the more alarming because the city was uniquely important to the empire's long-term domestic and foreign policy. Moscow was universally acknowledged as the Russian heartland's *stolitsa*, a word often translated as "capital" but better rendered here as "metropolis"—a city of exceptional size that dominates a nation's life and imagination. It had been the seat of political and ecclesiastical power in Russia since the fifteenth century, and most Russians continued to think of it as their principal city. It also dominated Russia, otherwise a mostly rural country, by virtue of its size and location. Statistics collected in the 1790s by the political economist Heinrich Storch indicate that only three cities in Russia had over 25,000 inhabitants. Storch evidently arrived at his data by taking the official population count by the police, which formed the basis for most Russian urban statistics, and adding an estimate of the number of migrants and

---

[3] Gary M. Hamburg, "Inventing the 'State School' of Historians, 1840–1995," in Thomas Sanders, ed., *Historiography of Imperial Russia: The Profession and Writing of History in a Multinational State* (Armonk, NY: M. E. Sharpe, 1999), 107–8; Ana Siljak, "Christianity, Science, and Progress in Sergei M. Solov'ev's *History of Russia*," in Sanders, ed., *Historiography of Imperial Russia*, 217–22, 227.

[4] N. F. Gulianitskii, ed., *Moskva i slozhivshiesia russkie goroda XVIII–pervoi poloviny XIX vekov* (Moscow: Stroiizdat, 1998), 36.

[5] On the novel *Van'ka Kain* by Matvei Komarov, see David Gasperetti, *The Rise of the Russian Novel: Carnival, Stylization, and Mockery of the West* (DeKalb, Ill.: Northern Illinois University Press, 1998). The novel is available in English: Mikhail Chulkov, Matvei Komarov, and Nikolai Karamzin, *Three Russian Tales of the Eighteenth Century: The Comely Cook, Vanka Kain, and Poor Liza*, tr. David Gasperetti (DeKalb, Ill.: Northern Illinois University Press, 2012).

transients. According to the police, Moscow had 175,000 inhabitants,[6] but Storch thought a more realistic figure was 300,000 in the summer and 400,000 in the winter. This made Moscow the country's largest city, and its location at the center of European Russia and near the headwaters of its major rivers made it a key commercial and transportation hub. The Russian Empire had two other large cities, but these were in peripheral locations far from the interior of the country. St Petersburg, which by Storch's estimate had 220,000 inhabitants, was built on the Baltic littoral to facilitate contact with the West, but its trade with Russia itself was difficult because the uplands to the southeast obstructed river transport. Bringing food to St Petersburg required fleets of grain barges to assemble north of Moscow and embark on a two-month odyssey down nearly 1,000 treacherous kilometers of rivers, canals, locks, portages, and cataracts.[7] Russia's third city, Astrakhan', had 70,000 inhabitants. Located some 3,400 kilometers downstream from Moscow, where the Volga enters the Caspian Sea, Astrakhan' functioned mainly as Russia's gateway to the East.[8]

Moscow's importance extended to foreign relations as well. Before Peter the Great, Europeans viewed Moscow as representative of the entire exotic country that they called "Muscovy." Peter moved the capital to St Petersburg and renamed Muscovy "the Russian Empire" as part of his effort to break with the past and make Russia a part of Europe. He and his successors wanted to trade, form alliances, and recruit foreign specialists, but Westerners remained hesitant to do business with the nation they continued calling "Muscovites." In 1749, a French adaptation of a British geographic dictionary summed up the conventional wisdom: "Formerly the Muscovites were coarse, of bad morals, ignorant, unfaithful to their treaties, & very superstitious. Since Tsar Peter the Great, they have begun a little to become civilized and communicate with foreign nations."[9]

Russia's large cities provided the yardstick by which Westerners judged the whole country. Cities were considered the locus of refinement and civilization. According to the 1762 dictionary of the French Academy, *urbanité* meant "the politeness that comes from social intercourse," and Dr Johnson's English dictionary of 1768 defined "urbanity" as "civility; elegance; politeness; merriment;

---

[6] Statistics for 1789–93, cited in M. Gastev, *Materialy dlia polnoi i sravnitel'noi statistiki Moskvy, chast' pervaia* (Moscow: V Universitetskoi Tipografii, 1841), 264.

[7] Robert E. Jones, "Getting the Goods to St. Petersburg: Water Transport from the Interior 1703–1811," *Slavic Review*, 43/3 (Autumn 1984), 413–33, esp. 420–2.

[8] S. Janicki, L. Jacquet, and A. Pasqueau, *Improvement of Non-Tidal Rivers: Memoirs*, tr. Wm. E. Merrill (Washington, DC: Government Printing Office, 1881), 27; Heinrich Storch, *Statistische Übersicht der Statthalterschaften des Russischen Reichs nach ihren merkwürdigsten Kulturverhältnissen* (Riga: Hartknoch, 1795), 38, 118.

[9] Laurent Echard, *Dictionnaire géographique portatif*, tr. from the 13th edn. of the English original of Laurence Echard, rev. Monsieur Vaugien (Paris: Didot, 1749), 539.

facetiousness."[10] St Petersburg was built as a showcase for Russia's achievements in this area, but many foreigners doubted the authenticity of what they saw there and looked to Moscow for the true measure of the nation. Giacomo Casanova, who visited in the 1760s, spoke for many Westerners when he wrote that

One has not seen Russia if one has not seen Moscow, and whoever has known only the Russians of St. Petersburg does not know the Russians of the real Russia. The inhabitants of the new capital are viewed here [in Moscow] as foreigners. For a long time to come, the true capital of the Russians will be holy Moscow... Moscow clings to the past: city of traditions and memories, city of the tsars, she is a daughter of Asia and most surprised to find herself in Europe.[11]

Russia's rulers in the eighteenth century faced a dilemma familiar to twentieth-century Westernizers such as Kemal Atatürk or the Shah of Iran. By embracing the West, they antagonized their own people but gained only conditional acceptance abroad, and the foreign ways that were supposed to make Russia richer and stronger were slow to bear fruit because they were rejected as alien by the people. In the terms of the early twentieth-century Italian Marxist Antonio Gramsci, the regime exercised a coercive domination (raw political power), but this domination was brittle because it did not rest on hegemony (a popular consensus supporting the regime's worldview).[12] For Russia to escape from this trap, the culture of the imperial elites had to spread to classes below the nobility, and out of St Petersburg into the provinces. St Petersburg was important as a vector of cultural diffusion, but its location was too peripheral, its architecture too foreign, and its population too cosmopolitan. Only Moscow could anchor European "enlightenment" in the Russian interior.

Reconstructing Moscow as an enlightened metropolis became a priority for the regime in the mid-eighteenth century, especially under Catherine II, in whose reign fundamental policy choices were made that remained in place until the Great Reforms of the 1860s and 1870s. Russia's government and society underwent profound changes in the decades from her accession in 1762 to the death of her grandson Nicholas I in 1855, but in the history of the regime's relationship with the city of Moscow, those ninety-three years form a unified historical era in which Moscow underwent a threefold modernization. It acquired the infrastructure of a European city, for example, a police force, a school system, and streets that were paved and lit. Further, a culturally Europeanized middle class began to

---

[10] *Dictionnaire de l'Académie française* (4th edn., 1762), *The ARTFL Project: Department of Romance Languages and Literatures, University of Chicago* <http://artfl-project.uchicago.edu/node/17> accessed 11 December 2011; Samuel Johnson, *A Dictionary of the English Language* (3rd edn., Dublin: W. C. Jones, 1768), no pagination.

[11] Jacques Casanova de Seingalt, *Mémoires*, 10 vols. (Paris: Paulin, 1833–7), 9:290–1.

[12] Antonio Gramsci, *The Southern Question*, tr. Pasquale Verdicchio (West Lafayette, Ind.: Bordighera, 1995), 19–20, 47. Gramsci's concepts are applied to Russia in Alexander Etkind, *Internal Colonization: Russia's Imperial Experience* (Cambridge: Polity, 2011), 22.

take shape. Lastly, literate people in Russia and abroad learned to imagine Moscow in new ways. A new Moscow was "constructed," both in physical reality and in the collective imagination. Each aspect of Moscow's reconstruction followed a distinct historical trajectory. The interplay between the three areas of change—infrastructure, class, and culture—is the subject of this book.

A spatial and institutional environment similar to Western cities was created in the late eighteenth century. Subsequently, however, the pace of change in Moscow slowed even as it accelerated in the West. In the first half of the nineteenth century, Moscow did not make the transition from oil to gas lighting, replace its watchmen with a professional police force, or build sewer mains to replace latrines and cesspits.

Moscow's social structure also became similar to the West but then diverged again. All Russians belonged by law to a social estate (*soslovie* or *sostoianie*) that determined their legal rights and duties. Through a series of adjustments to the estate system, the government sought to divide urban residents into the three general categories typically found in eighteenth-century Europe: a small aristocratic elite; a middle stratum of clerics, merchants, and officials, who were supposed to develop a culture and way of life similar to a Western third estate; and a mass of petty traders and laborers, most of whom were migrant peasants. The regime's hopes for spreading "enlightenment" in Russian urban society rested with the middle stratum, and as we see in the case of Sergei Solov'ev, the priest's son who became a history professor, these hopes were not disappointed. However, Moscow's estates by the mid-nineteenth century had not evolved into the class system that increasingly prevailed in the West. The aristocracy remained a world unto itself, the various middling estates did not coalesce into a unified bourgeoisie, and a fully urbanized factory proletariat did not appear.

Moscow's social order and urban infrastructure by the mid-nineteenth century seemed archaic because they recalled a European city of the eighteenth century. This had fateful consequences for Moscow's image, because urban life was just then becoming an important theme in Russian fiction, journalism, and memoirs. Russians in the decades after 1850 thought they knew, from personal experience and through the stories of their elders, that Moscow was backward because it had changed little since the long-gone days of Catherine II. That Catherine's Moscow had been dynamic for its time was forgotten, because the era that preceded it had passed out of living memory.

This book is a history of Moscow, its people, and how both were represented in Russian and West European culture. It is indebted to a variety of historiographies and hopes to contribute to diverse areas of historical research.

One historiography with which this book is in dialogue concerns state and society in pre-Reform Russia, indeed in all of Russian history since the rise of Muscovy. The central problem posed by this historiography is the relationship between rhetoric and reality in the functioning of Russia's power structures. On paper, Russia's institutions—from the tsars to the Politburo, from serfdom to central planning—were autocratic and centralized. But is that how they functioned in reality?

Some scholars argue that imperial Russia was a proto-totalitarian regime. According to John LeDonne, Russia was "a huge command structure" in which the state was a tool of class rule by the nobility, and despotic authority was exercised by lords over peasants, men over their wives and children, and local communities over their members, all of it sanctified by the Orthodox faith. In this system, "the tyranny of the superior was accepted because it justified the subordinate's tyranny over his own subordinates, leaving no room for the assertion of individual freedom, economic initiative, and social autonomy."[13] In a similar vein, Alexander Etkind writes that imperial Russia exercised a form of colonial rule over its own people and that its social estates resembled the races and castes into which Western imperialists divided their non-white subjects. Building on a theory by Hannah Arendt, Etkind argues that Russia's "internal colonization" under the tsars laid the foundation for the totalitarianism of the Soviets.[14]

This thesis has not, in my view, become dominant in the historiography, but it helps clarify the interpretation that has prevailed in recent decades and that forms the framework for the present book. Was Russia a "command structure"? Yes and no. Monarchs and serf owners often acted despotically, and as Marc Raeff has shown, the Russian monarchy in the eighteenth century attempted to create a "well-ordered police state" to promote the progress of society through bureaucratic regulation.[15] Still, top-down control over the entire society was out of the question because of what a nineteenth-century wit called Russia's twin afflictions of *duraki i dorogi*, fools and roads: vast distances, slow communications, widespread corruption, and a shortage of competent personnel. Absent the possibility of systematic compulsion, the regime, while autocratic in theory, was in practice oriented toward consensus. Monarchs tried to govern with the approval of the upper classes.[16] Imperial governors ruled their provinces through give-and-take with local interests.[17] Serfdom and the patriarchal family took into account the needs of peasants and women.[18] The system of estates was not an inflexible straitjacket imposed on a reluctant population by the autocracy, but a flexible framework used by both state and society to negotiate their relationship.[19]

---

[13] John P. LeDonne, *Absolutism and Ruling Class: The Formation of the Russian Political Order, 1700–1825* (New York: Oxford University Press, 1991), 17, 143–5, quotation on 17.

[14] Etkind, *Internal Colonization*, 23–4, 93.

[15] Marc Raeff, *The Well-Ordered Police State: Social and Institutional Change through Law in the Germanies and Russia, 1600–1800* (New Haven: Yale University Press, 1983).

[16] Richard Wortman, *Scenarios of Power: Myth and Ceremony in Russian Monarchy*, 2 vols. (Princeton: Princeton University Press, 1995–2000); Cynthia Hyla Whittaker, *Russian Monarchy: Eighteenth-Century Rulers and Writers in Political Dialogue* (DeKalb, Ill.: Northern Illinois University Press, 2003).

[17] Susanne Schattenberg, *Die korrupte Provinz? Russische Beamte im 19. Jahrhundert* (Frankfurt: Campus, 2008).

[18] Elise Kimerling Wirtschafter, *Russia's Age of Serfdom, 1649–1861* (Malden, Mass.: Blackwell, 2008), 6–7, 13–14.

[19] Gregory L. Freeze, "The *Soslovie* (Estate) Paradigm and Russian Social History," *American Historical Review*, 91/1 (February 1986), 11–36.

This line of reasoning suggests that power and initiative in Russian society were more diffuse than a top-down model suggests. It also makes the regime's pronouncements more interesting as discursive constructs, as propaganda, than as descriptions of actual reality. For example, the police never came close to achieving the sweeping control over everyday life that it was assigned by Catherine II's Police Code of 1782; instead, what makes studying that code worthwhile is the ideological conception of the social order that it expresses. By the same token, Russians were not only "a community of believers bound by an intolerant consensus on the validity of the social and ideological order" and thus "incapable of resisting the exercise of arbitrary power," as LeDonne puts it,[20] but also individuals with agency and voices of their own. This approach provides the inspiration for the questions at the heart of the present study. What dynamics governed the interaction between the government, the intellectuals, and the inhabitants of Moscow? How did the regime use urban policy to influence the thinking and behavior of its subjects? How did intellectuals in Russia and abroad engage each other and the Russian regime in a dialogue about the urban order? How did individual Russians make a life for themselves within their country's social system?

In trying to answer those questions, this book draws extensively on two historiographies. One is the intellectual and cultural history of Russian national identity in the transitional phase between the early modern and modern eras. Several strands can be distinguished within this literature. The first studies how symbolic forms of representation, such as poetry, architecture, or the ceremonies of the imperial court, were used to create an image of Russia as a powerful and civilized empire ruled by an enlightened monarch.[21] The second examines how the modern image of Russia as a land and a people with a distinctive national identity was constructed in the nineteenth century by novelists, geographers, ethnographers, musicians, landscape artists, authors of cookbooks, and others.[22] The third concerns the process by which the culture of Russia's metropolitan

---

[20] LeDonne, *Absolutism and Ruling Class*, 177.

[21] Andrei Zorin, *Kormia dvuglavogo orla . . . Literatura i gosudarstvennaia ideologiia v Rossii v poslednei treti XVIII–pervoi treti XIX veka* (Moscow: Novoe Literaturnoe Obozrenie, 2001); Vera Proskurina, *Mify imperii: Literatura i vlast' v epokhu Ekateriny II* (Moscow: Novoe Literaturnoe Obozrenie, 2006); Tat'iana Artem'eva, *Ot slavnogo proshlogo k svetlomu budushchemu: Filosofiia i utopiia v Rossii epokhi Prosveshcheniia* (St Petersburg: Aleteiia, 2005); Wortman, *Scenarios of Power*.

[22] Elena Vishlenkova, *Vizual'noe narodovedenie imperii, ili "Uvidet' russkogo dano ne kazhdomu"* (Moscow: Novoe Literaturnoe Obozrenie, 2011); Willard Sunderland, *Taming the Wild Field: Colonization and Empire on the Russian Steppe* (Ithaca, NY: Cornell University Press, 2004); Christopher Ely, *This Meager Nature: Landscape and National Identity in Imperial Russia* (DeKalb, Ill.: Northern Illinois University Press, 2002); Richard Stites, *Serfdom, Society, and the Arts: The Pleasure and the Power* (New Haven: Yale University Press, 2005); Olga Maiorova, *From the Shadow of Empire: Defining the Russian Nation through Cultural Mythology, 1855–1870* (Madison: University of Wisconsin Press, 2010); Cathy A. Frierson, *Peasant Icons: Representations of Rural People in Late Nineteenth-Century Russia* (New York: Oxford University Press, 1993); Alison K. Smith, *Recipes for Russia: Food and Nationhood under the Tsars* (DeKalb, Ill.: Northern Illinois University Press, 2008).

elites spread to provincial regions and wider social strata; the focus in this instance is not on a binary divide between the elites and the people, but on the intermediary levels of society that connected them.[23] The fourth, finally, is the interaction between Russian self-perception, Russian images of the West, and the portrayal of Russia in the cultures of Western Europe.[24]

The second historiography on which this book draws is urban history. One aspect of urban history that is relevant to this study is the scholarship on the social, economic, and administrative history of Russian cities in the century or so before the Great Reforms.[25] The other is the social and cultural historiography that studies the role of urban living in the development of a modern consciousness in Western Europe, including such aspects as sensory perceptions of the urban environment, the experience of nighttime in the city, and the rise of modern consumerism.[26] A recent and as yet limited body of scholarship studies these questions in the context of pre-Reform Russia;[27] the present study hopes to make a contribution to that historiography.

Knowing a city takes analytical as well as imaginative insight, and an understanding of how things were at a given moment but also how they changed over

[23] John Randolph, *The House in the Garden: The Bakunin Family and the Romance of Russian Idealism* (Ithaca, NY: Cornell University Press, 2007); David L. Ransel, *A Russian Merchant's Tale: The Life and Adventures of Ivan Alekseevich Tolchënov, Based on his Diary* (Bloomington, Ind.: Indiana University Press, 2009).

[24] Franco Venturi, *The End of the Old Regime in Europe, 1768–1776: The First Crisis*, tr. R. Burr Litchfield (Princeton: Princeton University Press, 1989); Larry Wolff, *Inventing Eastern Europe: The Map of Civilization on the Mind of the Enlightenment* (Stanford, Calif.: Stanford University Press, 1994); Martin Malia, *Russia under Western Eyes: From the Bronze Horseman to the Lenin Mausoleum* (Cambridge, Mass.: Belknap, 1999).

[25] Boris N. Mironov, *Russkii gorod v 1740–1860-e gody: Demograficheskoe, sotsial'noe i ekonomicheskoe razvitie* (Leningrad: Nauka, 1990); J. Michael Hittle, *The Service City: State and Townsmen in Russia, 1600–1800* (Cambridge, Mass.: Harvard University Press, 1979), 218; George E. Munro, *The Most Intentional City: St. Petersburg in the Reign of Catherine the Great* (Madison, NJ: Fairleigh Dickinson University Press, 2008); Manfred Hildermeier, *Bürgertum und Stadt in Rußland 1760–1870: Rechtliche Lage und soziale Struktur* (Cologne: Böhlau, 1986); Elise Kimerling Wirtschafter, *Structures of Society: Imperial Russia's "People of Various Ranks"* (DeKalb, Ill.: Northern Illinois University Press, 1994); Alfred J. Rieber, *Merchants and Entrepreneurs in Imperial Russia* (Chapel Hill, NC: University of North Carolina Press, 1982).

[26] Daniel Roche, *Le peuple de Paris. Essai sur la culture populaire au XVIIIe siècle* (Paris: Arthème Fayard, 1998); Alain Corbin, *The Foul and the Fragrant: Odor and the French Social Imagination*, tr. Miriam Kochan, Roy Porter, and Christopher Prendergast (Cambridge, Mass.: Harvard University Press, 1986); Simone Delattre, *Les douze heures noires. La nuit à Paris au XIXe siècle* (Paris: Albin Michel, 2000); Joachim Schlör, *Nights in the Big City: Paris, Berlin, London, 1840–1930*, tr. Pierre Gottfried Imhoff and Dafydd Rees Roberts (London: Reaktion, 1998); Jan de Vries, *The Industrious Revolution: Consumer Behavior and the Household Economy, 1650 to the Present* (Cambridge: Cambridge University Press, 2008).

[27] V. V. Lapin, *Peterburg: Zapakhi i zvuki* (St Petersburg: Evropeiskii Dom, 2007); A. B. Kamenskii, *Povsednevnost' russkikh gorodskikh obyvatelei: Istoricheskie anekdoty iz provintsial'noi zhizni XVIII veka* (Moscow: Rossiiskii Gosudarstvennyi Gumanitarnyi Universitet, 2006); A. I. Kupriianov, *Gorodskaia kul'tura russkoi provintsii: Konets XVIII–pervaia polovina XIX veka* (Moscow: Novyi khronograf, 2007); N. V. Kozlova, *Liudi driakhlye, bol'nye, ubogie v Moskve XVIII veka* (Moscow: ROSSPEN, 2010).

time. Hence this book examines macro-level social forces and structures, but it also tries to evoke the everyday lived experience of the people who inhabited imperial Moscow. It tells the story of Moscow from multiple angles, seeking a balance between chronological continuity and thematic approaches.

Chapter 1 examines Catherine II's views on Moscow and her measures to reconstruct the city's space, administration, and social order. Through her legislation of the 1770s and 1780s, Catherine created the institutional and juridical framework for Moscow society until the second half of the nineteenth century.

Chapter 2 takes us into Moscow as a physical space. The chapter explores the sights, sounds, and smells of the city, and the spatial experience of the inhabitants as they negotiated the urban environment by day and after nightfall. Three issues will receive particular attention: the diversity of Moscow's neighborhoods; the government's efforts to transform a filthy, dangerous, unsightly city into an enlightened metropolis; and how the resulting changes affected the perceptions and lived experiences of its inhabitants.

The next two chapters sketch the early development of an optimistic image of Moscow in Russian and (to a lesser degree) West European culture. In the eighteenth century, innovative ways of depicting Moscow emerged in cartography, statistical and historical studies, and the visual arts. These representations, which mostly celebrated the accomplishments of the autocracy, form the subject of Chapter 3. A sophisticated prose literature about Moscow developed somewhat later, when the European-wide polemics triggered by the French Revolution and the Napoleonic Wars made the successes and failures of Russia's social order into an object of ideological contention. This literature, which was constructed by both Russian and foreign authors, is the theme of Chapter 4.

The following three chapters pivot from the history of ideas to that of Moscow's inhabitants. Chapter 5 is about the middle strata in the early nineteenth century and their relationship with the aristocracy, that is, the wealthy elite that formed the upper crust of the nobility. Chapter 6 examines the traumatic experience of the Napoleonic invasion and the post-war reconstruction. Chapter 7 explores the social history of Moscow in the decades after the war, with particular emphasis on the interaction of the middle and lower strata and on the makeup of different Moscow neighborhoods.

At the end we come full circle and return to the history of ideas, with an exploration in Chapter 8 of the debates about urbanism in Russia and the West from the 1820s to the 1850s. Early in this period, the dominant tone in Russian writings about Moscow was self-congratulatory, even triumphalist. Later, however, a growing anxiety and pessimism crept into the Russian discussion, foreshadowing the crisis of confidence in Russia's institutions that erupted after the death of Nicholas I.

1

The Enlightened Metropolis and the Imperial Social Project

If the imperial regime wanted to bring its conception of order and enlightenment to the heartland of Russia, it had to do so from Moscow. This is what the French *philosophe* Denis Diderot told Catherine II when he visited St Petersburg in 1773–4. He observed to her that St Petersburg, with its cosmopolitan mix of nationalities, would always have "harlequinesque morals," and that a country that had its capital on its periphery was like an animal that had "its stomach at the tip of its big toe." The capital, he urged, should be moved back to Moscow, which was the crossroads of Russia's commerce, near to the estates of the nobility, and secure from foreign attack. Catherine could influence Russian public opinion only if her government had its seat there: "Is it a matter of indifference that Your Majesty, who wants to be heard by her subjects, is preaching where they are not, and is heard only through a speaking-trumpet in the place where they are?"[1]

Russia's rulers were not insensitive to these considerations. They governed from St Petersburg, but their compact with the nation was sealed by their coronation as autocrats in the Kremlin in Moscow (see Illustration 1.1). An imperial coronation entailed a lengthy relocation of the whole court. Elizabeth stayed for eight months in 1742, and Catherine II for nine in 1762–3.[2] It was through the coronation, and the elaborate processions, festivities, proclamations, sermons, speeches, odes, engravings, and so on that accompanied or described it, that Russians were introduced to the guiding myth of the new reign, what Richard Wortman calls its "scenario of power." The reign of Anna (1730–40) had been harsh and repressive. In deliberate contrast, Elizabeth's scenario promised to inaugurate an age of joy and gaiety, and Catherine's, the triumph of reason and humaneness over ignorance and vice.[3]

Moscow was the site of imperial coronations because in important ways, it remained the heart of the country. It was Russia's largest city until the nineteenth

---

[1] Maurice Tourneux, *Diderot et Catherine II* (Paris: Calmann Lévy, 1899), 273–9, quotations on 274, 277–8.
[2] Wortman, *Scenarios of Power*, 1:90.
[3] Wortman, *Scenarios of Power*, 1:89, 111–13.

Illus. 1.1. "Proclamation, on Ivanovskaia Square [in the Kremlin] in Moscow, of the Manifesto about the Date Assigned for the Imperial Coronation of Her Majesty the Sovereign Catherine Alekseevna, Autocrat of All the Russias, in the Month of September 1762." Line engraving from the 1790s by Aleksei Kolpashnikov, after a drawing from the 1760s or early 1770s by Jean-Louis de Veilly and Mikhail Makhaev for the coronation album of Catherine II. Courtesy of The New York Public Library. <http://digitalgallery.nypl.org/nypldigital/id?1215564>.

century, when St Petersburg overtook it, and the principal entrepôt of its inland trade. Wealthy magnates and elder statesmen retired there, and it was where much of the provincial nobility congregated in the winter; for millions of serfs, this made Moscow the seat of an authority that had unfettered arbitrary power over their lives.[4] Moscow was home to Russia's only university, and almost 40 percent of its books were published there.[5] It was a great center of religious life: at the end of the eighteenth century, compared with St Petersburg, it had eight

---

[4] LeDonne, *Absolutism and Ruling Class*, 132.
[5] During the period 1756–75, Moscow presses produced 38.9 percent of all books printed in the Russian language; Gary Marker, *Publishing, Printing, and the Origins of Intellectual Life in Russia, 1700–1800* (Princeton: Princeton University Press, 1985), 72, 77.

times fewer military personnel but six times more clergy.[6] The Russian writer Pavel Svin'in expressed the consensus opinion when he told American readers in 1813 that "Speaking of Moscow, we may in some measure, consider it as speaking of the whole empire, for this capital is the cradle of Russia; the manners and habits of its inhabitants are looked upon as a general law, and influence all minds and hearts."[7]

Unfortunately, Catherine II hated the city. "I do not like Moscow at all," she once remarked.[8] Her coronation festivities included a cavalcade of 4,000 people and 200 floats satirizing stupidity, ignorance, drunkenness, deceit, arrogance, and prodigality;[9] this summed up, more or less, what she thought of Moscow. It was the antithesis of "enlightenment," a term that she and her Russian contemporaries understood to encompass rationality, sincerity, humanitarianism, critical self-reflection, cultural cosmopolitanism, a love of learning, and concern for civic and economic improvement.[10] When Diderot suggested making Moscow the seat of government, she answered that it would not be fit for that role for another hundred years.[11] Her low opinion was of profound historical importance, for it formed the impetus for policies that fundamentally changed the city. The thrust of these policies was twofold: to reform Moscow along enlightened lines, and to launch what this book will call the imperial social project—a complex of laws, institutions, and social and discursive practices designed to create what Catherine called an urban "middling sort" (*srednii rod liudei*) that would share her regime's values and support its policies. Defining the term somewhat more broadly than Catherine did, this book will use the expression "middling sort" for the urban strata that were targeted by the imperial social project.

The remainder of this book will explore how the transformation of the city was experienced by the inhabitants and interpreted by observers. The present chapter sets the stage with an overview of what Moscow represented for Catherine and how she sought to transform it into an enlightened metropolis by reconstructing its space and social order.

---

[6] Wladimir Berelowitch and Olga Medvedkova, *Histoire de Saint-Pétersbourg* (Paris: Arthème Fayard, 1996), 178.

[7] [Pavel Svin'in] Paul Svenin, *Sketches of Moscow and St. Petersburg* (Philadelphia: Thomas Dobson, 1813), 29.

[8] John T. Alexander, "Petersburg and Moscow in Early Urban Policy," *Journal of Urban History*, 8/2 (February 1982), 145–69, quotation on 163.

[9] Wortman, *Scenarios of Power*, 1:120.

[10] Simon Dixon, "'Prosveshchenie': Enlightenment in Eighteenth-Century Russia," in Richard Butterwick, Simon Davies, and Gabriel Sánchez Espinosa, eds., *Peripheries of the Enlightenment*, Studies on Voltaire and the Eighteenth Century 2008:01 (Oxford: Voltaire Foundation, 2008), 229–49.

[11] Tourneux, *Diderot et Catherine II*, 284.

CATHERINE'S CRITIQUE OF MOSCOW

Judging by her memoirs, Catherine's antipathy for Moscow formed soon after she arrived in Russia in 1744 at the tender age of 15. Raised in a modest German princely household, she found Moscow repulsive in a visceral sense. Looking back on her visits of 1749–53, she recalled streets that were icy or muddy, depending on the season, and wretched accommodations in the Golovin Palace. Seventeen women occupied a single airless room next to hers, and to go anywhere they had to pass through her bedroom. Her room "was so full of vermin that I could not sleep," and the whole building—which caught fire during her stay— was infested with an "astonishing number of rats and mice."[12] Such squalor, she thought, both reflected and perpetuated the lack of enlightenment among the inhabitants and was a national embarrassment. Years later, when she was empress and received word that the Moscow magistracy building had burned, she wrote back to inquire whether it had been built of wood: "It is shameful for the metropolis not to have a masonry-built magistracy when in other countries, every last little town has a masonry-built town-hall . . . of course the inhabitants of Moscow should erect such a structure to befit the metropolis."[13]

The bubonic plague that broke out in Moscow in 1771 threw into vivid relief everything that she felt was wrong with the city. The epidemic came from the Danube, where Russian troops had been at war with the Ottomans since 1768. By the time it began to subside in October 1771, over 50,000 Muscovites were dead.[14] Catherine's officials tried to enforce a stringent quarantine, but this caused widespread panic without succeeding in containing the disease. Joint efforts by police and Archbishop Amvrosii to limit contagion by restricting religious gatherings only aggravated matters. In September, a large crowd assembled around a revered icon near the Kremlin and began gathering money for a silver cover that would enhance the icon's sacrality and hence the likelihood of a miracle to end the plague. This popular religious response to the epidemic was incompatible with the rationalist, Enlightenment approach advocated by the authorities. When the police proved unable to control the crowd, Archbishop Amvrosii decided to remove the icon to a nearby church and donate the collected money to the Moscow Foundling Home, a secular charitable institution recently established by Catherine. This attempt triggered a massive popular revolt that lasted from 15 to 17 September. Public order collapsed, crowds sacked the Kremlin, and Amvrosii was lynched. The grisly details of his murder, such as

---

[12] *The Memoirs of Catherine the Great*, 76, 115–16.

[13] "Pis'ma Gosudaryni Imperatritsy Ekateriny II-i k kniaziu Mikhailu Nikitichu Volkonskomu," *Osmnadtsatyi vek*, vol. 1 (1868), 52–162, quotation on 90.

[14] John T. Alexander, *Bubonic Plague in Early Modern Russia: Public Health and Urban Disaster* (Baltimore: Johns Hopkins University Press, 1980), 257–8, 303.

the mutilation of his face and eyes, suggest that the killing carried a conscious symbolism of sacred vengeance.[15] Military force was needed to restore government authority. "They fired at the people with cannons, like at an enemy [army]," wrote a shocked provincial merchant.[16]

The terror that average Muscovites experienced as they faced the disease is something we can only imagine, but how their rulers felt is well documented. Plague was interpreted by the Russian elites as a disease of barbarians, specifically the Turks, and its outbreak in Moscow was proof of the city's civilizational backwardness.[17] The 652-page report on the epidemic that was published by the government's plague commission mentions the revolt only once (on page 96), no doubt to avoid embarrassing the authorities, but it still made clear what officials thought of the people. Moscow, the report suggested, had a narrow upper class that behaved intelligently and deserved respect; the rest were a senseless mob. Count Grigorii Orlov, whom Catherine dispatched to take charge of the crisis, informed the public that those rational enough to follow quarantine instructions had survived the epidemic: "among people of eminent and noble as well as of burgher condition who acted with caution, almost no one became infected." By contrast, "all the more died among the common people because they did not take precautions, and out of blindness or ignorance, and in a manner most sinful before their All-Generous Creator, they blamed fate for what was in fact their own fault, that is, their carelessness."[18]

The plague commission had to be diplomatic because it was writing for publication; in private, nobles were far less inhibited. Few texts articulate more clearly the worldview of an "enlightened" eighteenth-century Russian noble than the memoirs of Andrei Bolotov (1738–1833). Reminiscing at Christmas 1807, Bolotov recalled the plague revolt. His fear and anger and contempt were undimmed by the years. During the plague, so he had heard at the time, the nobles and officials had left the city, and the serfs, Old Believers, and other lower classes who remained grew angry about the quarantine measures because these "were not to their stupid taste." Money-hungry priests added fuel to the fire by organizing illegal processions, "not out of piety and sincere devotion, but purely out of greed." The revolt finally erupted when a soldier and a worker spread word of the icon's miraculous healing powers. "Those miscreants," Bolotov wrote, "just had to think up a miracle and spread the rumor all over Moscow...Primitive and stupid though this fable was, and easy though

[15] Marcus C. Levitt, *The Visual Dominant in Eighteenth-Century Russia* (DeKalb, Ill.: Northern Illinois University Press, 2011), 216–20.

[16] M. M. Tiul'pin, "Letopis'," in A. V. Semenova et al., eds., *Kupecheskie dnevniki i memuary kontsa XVIII–pervoi poloviny XIX veka* (Moscow: ROSSPEN, 2007), 273.

[17] E. A. Pogosian, "Ot staroi Ladogi do Ekaterinoslava (mesto Moskvy v predstavleniiakh Ekateriny II o stolitse imperii)," *Lotmanovskii Sbornik*, 2 (1997), 511–20, here: 513.

[18] [Afanasii Shafonskii], *Opisanie morovoi iazvy, byvshei v stolichnom gorode Moskve s 1770 po 1772 god* (Moscow: Pri Imperatorskom Universitete, 1775), 323–4.

it was for anyone to see that this idiot and fool had thought it up himself, all the same, not only the lower classes believed in it, but even the merchants did."[19]

Bolotov returned to the subject of Moscow's lower classes when he recorded his memories of the Pugachev revolt, the vast popular uprising that had engulfed the southeast of the Russian Empire in 1773–4. In 1774, it looked as though Pugachev's army, which left behind it a trail of pillaged noble estates and lords murdered by their serfs, was going to march on Moscow. "We were all sure," Bolotov wrote,

> that all of the commoners and the mob, and especially all of the serfs and our servants, were devoted to that villain—if not openly, then secretly in their hearts, and in their hearts all of them were rebelling and were prepared, at the least spark, to spread fire and flame. The example of the dreadful [plague] revolt that had recently occurred in Moscow was still fresh in our memories, and not only did we fear something like it, we expected it any minute. We knew only too well the stupidity and extreme irrationality of our common people, and under such circumstances we could not count on the loyalty even of our own servants, whom we considered above all others, and not without cause, to be our greatest and bitterest enemies.[20]

An even harsher assessment of Moscow was rendered by Empress Catherine herself. She exempted no one, including the nobility, from blame for the lack of enlightenment that she thought underlay Moscow's propensity to revolt. She knew full well the iniquity of the city's elites. Beginning in 1756, the noble-woman Dar'ia Saltykova had tortured scores of her serfs to death at her down-town Moscow house, usually maids who had not washed the floors or linens to their mistress's satisfaction. Shielded by corrupt officials who prevented the desperate appeals of her serfs from reaching the authorities, she killed with impunity. Finally, in 1762, Catherine (who had just taken power) intervened. The case was politically fraught because the horror of the crime had to be weighed against the risk of antagonizing the nobility. It dragged on for six years, until the government finally charged Saltykova in thirty-eight deaths and declared her a suspect in another twenty-six that remained unresolved. She was stripped of her nobility, exposed at the pillory, and imprisoned for the remainder of her days.[21]

On 6 October 1771, three weeks after the plague revolt, Catherine wrote to Voltaire, who served as one of her conduits to European public opinion. In this letter, she framed the events in Enlightenment terms as a commentary on humanity in general, not specifically Russia. At once sardonic and defensive, she offered the story of the revolt as "a small supplement to the [*Encyclopédie's*]

---

[19] A. T. Bolotov, *Zhizn' i prikliucheniia Andreia Bolotova, opisannye samim im dlia svoikh potomkov*, 3 vols. (Moscow: Terra, 1993), 3:19–20.

[20] Bolotov, *Zhizn' i prikliucheniia*, 3:143–4.

[21] G. I. Studenkin, "Saltychikha," *RS*, 10 (May–August 1874), 497–546.

article on *Fanaticism*." (That article defined fanaticism as "ridiculous, unjust, & cruel actions" arising from "superstitious opinions."[22]) She described how Archbishop Amvrosii, "a man of intelligence and ability," was killed by a "frenzied" mob, and concluded: "The famous Eighteenth Century really has something to boast of here! See how far we have progressed! But I do not need to speak to you on this score; you know mankind too well to be surprised at the contradictions and excess it is capable of."[23]

In a private paper that was apparently written around the same time as the letter to Voltaire, she addressed more explicitly what she regarded as Moscow's unenlightened character. Moscow was, she wrote, "the seat of sloth," a sprawling city where the nobles learned to

assume the tone and allurements of laziness and luxury: they become effeminate, always driving around with a coach and six horses, and they see only sorry sights capable of enfeebling the most remarkable genius. Furthermore, never has a people held before its eyes more objects of fanaticism, such as miraculous icons at every step, churches, priests, convents, pilgrims, beggars, thieves, useless servants in the houses—what houses, what disorder there is in the houses, where the lots are immense and the courtyards are filthy swamps. Usually each noble has not merely a house, but a small estate in the city. There you have that rabble of a motley crowd, always ready to oppose good order, which from time immemorial has rioted at the least pretext.

She went on to decry "the manufactories of immense size which have been built there imprudently and at which there is an excessive number of workmen," and "the villages that are presently intermingled with the city and where no police rule but which give asylum to thieves and crimes and criminals." Compared with St Petersburg, Moscow was a wasteland. "In forty [years] Petersburg has given more circulation to money and industry in the empire than Moscow has in the 500 years since it was built; . . . the people there [in St Petersburg] are more docile, more polite, less superstitious, more accustomed to foreigners, from whom they continually acquire one fashion or another, and so on."[24]

Part of Catherine's response to the troubles of the early 1770s was repression, but because she wanted to construct a polity built on consensus, she avoided a retaliatory bloodbath. Peter the Great, after the Moscow *strel'tsy* (musketeers) mutinied in 1698 in protest against his reforms, had ordered the execution of 1,182 people. Some were beheaded personally by Peter and his lieutenants, in a calculated slap in the face to traditional sensibilities and to dramatize Peter's godlike will to impose a new order on society.[25] By contrast, Catherine stayed

[22] Denis Diderot and Jean Le Rond d'Alembert, eds., *Encyclopédie, ou Dictionnaire raisonné des sciences, des arts et des métiers*, 17 vols. (Paris: Briasson, David, Le Breton, Durand, 1751–65), 6:393.

[23] Levitt, *The Visual Dominant*, 196.

[24] Quoted in Alexander, "Petersburg and Moscow," 164.

[25] Lindsey Hughes, *Peter the Great: A Biography* (New Haven: Yale University Press, 2002), 56; V. M. Zhivov, "Kul'turnye reformy v sisteme preobrazovanii Petra I," in A. D. Koshelev, ed., *Iz istorii russkoi kul'tury*, 5 vols. (Moscow: Iazyki russkoi kul'tury, 1996–2000), 3:572.

away from Moscow while the rebels were put to death, and although her executions were spectacularly staged, they claimed relatively few victims. On 11 November 1771, four participants in the plague revolt were hanged. Another sixty-two were flogged with the knout, had their nostrils torn with tongs, and were exiled to forced labor, and ninety-nine others were lashed or beaten with rods.[26] On 10 January 1775, Pugachev and his leading associates were executed in Moscow. One of the gawkers that day was Bolotov. Troops were deployed to keep the populace at a distance, but nobles were allowed near the scaffold to savor what Bolotov called this "veritable moment of triumph" of their class. Bolotov garnered a front-row spot to watch when Pugachev's arms and legs were chopped off. He was bitterly disappointed when the executioner, acting on secret orders from Catherine, beheaded the condemned man first, and only then severed his limbs.[27]

Repression was only a minor element in Catherine's strategy for turning Moscow into an enlightened metropolis. Far more significant were her efforts to reconstruct the city's space and social structure.

BUILDING THE ENLIGHTENED METROPOLIS

Catherine regarded the built environment as integral to Moscow's backwardness and irrationality. Steeped in Enlightenment rationalism and accustomed to the geometric layout and harmonious architecture of St Petersburg, she had no use for Moscow's meandering lanes and idiosyncratic buildings. Urban planning in Moscow received important impulses during her reign (Map 1.1).

Moscow had evolved organically since its founding in the twelfth century. Like many Russian towns, it was composed of three concentric zones. In the center was the Kremlin, seat of the government and the church. Then came the *posad*, where the larger markets and wealthier merchants were located. (Moscow's *posad*, across Red Square from the Kremlin, was called Kitai-Gorod.) The outermost belt consisted of suburbs (*slobody*). Some suburbs were privately owned areas where a magnate or church hierarch settled tradespeople for whom he secured special tax privileges; others were home to specialized categories of state servitors, such as musketeers or icon painters; and still others were reserved for particular classes of foreigners. In seventeenth-century Moscow, the Kremlin and Kitai-Gorod were surrounded by about 150 suburbs arrayed in four belts: the White City (*Belyi Gorod*, the area inside today's Boulevard Ring), the Earthen City (*Zemlianoi Gorod*, between the Boulevard Ring and the Garden

---

[26] Alexander, *Bubonic Plague*, 226–7.
[27] Bolotov, *Zhizn' i prikliucheniia*, 3:183–90, quotation on 187; Isabel de Madariaga, *Russia in the Age of Catherine the Great* (New Haven: Yale University Press, 1981), 268.

Ring), the outer suburbs beyond the Earthen City, and Zamoskvorech'e (the area south of the Moscow River).[28]

By Catherine's time, the state's fiscal needs had led progressively to Moscow's administrative unification. To protect the tax-paying *posad* population from unfair economic competition, the law code of 1649 had abolished the tax-exempt private suburbs.[29] Under Peter the Great, suburban autonomy became an anachronism: his reforms abolished the social and professional groups that earlier had their own suburbs, and the growth of manufacturing enterprises in the outer suburbs created a need for direct government oversight. Under the empresses Anna and Elizabeth in the 1730s and 1740s, a customs wall, known (after the agency that collected customs duties) as the *Kamer-kollezhskii val*, was built around the outer suburbs and Zamoskvorech'e, unifying Moscow for the purposes of customs enforcement and migration control. The various jurisdictions within became a single administrative space, although autonomous pockets persisted until late in the eighteenth century.[30]

Within this increasingly unified metropolitan area, eighteenth-century governments sought to reconstruct the built environment. Western elites since the Renaissance had looked for ways to rid their cities of the cramped, fetid squalor typical of medieval towns. The ideal early modern city was supposed to be fireproof, express symbolically the greatness of its rulers, and permit air and light to dispel the miasmas that neo-Hippocratic medical theory regarded as the cause of epidemics. Beginning with Peter the Great, city planning along these lines was embraced in Russia as well.

Two approaches were particularly influential. The first, which was adopted for St Petersburg and which Catherine also favored for Moscow, was the Baroque urbanism of geometric avenues and gardens and grandiose building complexes that was promoted in France under Louis XIV.[31] Various princely capitals of Germany adopted this model, as did the planned cities of Spanish America.[32] Its origin went back to the painters of Renaissance Italy, who held that linear perspective, by arranging objects on a grid in geometrically precise relationships, had the power to reveal deeper truths of reality. Applied to urban design, this logic suggested that the regularity of geometrically designed spaces could mold the consciousness of urban citizens by exposing them to a timeless ideal of aesthetic perfection derived from classical antiquity. This type of urbanism did

---

[28] Hittle, *The Service City*, 29–30; Christoph Schmidt, *Sozialkontrolle in Moskau: Justiz, Kriminalität und Leibeigenschaft 1649–1785* (Stuttgart: Franz Steiner, 1996), 225–7.

[29] Hittle, *The Service City*, 66–7.

[30] Schmidt, *Sozialkontrolle in Moskau*, 226–7; Alexander, *Bubonic Plague*, 65–6.

[31] F. L. Carsten, *The Ascendancy of France 1648–88*, The New Cambridge Modern History, vol. 5 (Cambridge: Cambridge University Press, 1961), 163–4; Berelowitch and Medvedkova, *Histoire de Saint-Pétersbourg*, 21, 144–5, chapter 3.

[32] Mark A. Burkholder and Lyman L. Johnson, *Colonial Latin America* (3rd edn., New York: Oxford University Press, 1998), 184–5.

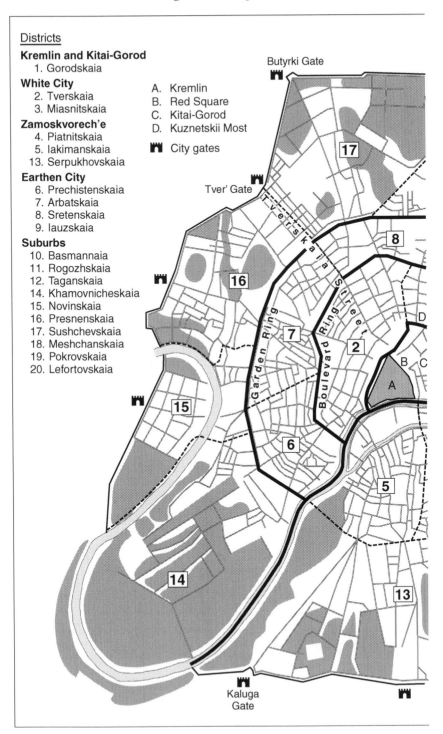

Districts
Kremlin and Kitai-Gorod
  1. Gorodskaia
White City
  2. Tverskaia
  3. Miasnitskaia
Zamoskvorech'e
  4. Piatnitskaia
  5. Iakimanskaia
  13. Serpukhovskaia
Earthen City
  6. Prechistenskaia
  7. Arbatskaia
  8. Sretenskaia
  9. Iauzskaia
Suburbs
  10. Basmannaia
  11. Rogozhskaia
  12. Taganskaia
  14. Khamovnicheskaia
  15. Novinskaia
  16. Presnenskaia
  17. Sushchevskaia
  18. Meshchanskaia
  19. Pokrovskaia
  20. Lefortovskaia

A. Kremlin
B. Red Square
C. Kitai-Gorod
D. Kuznetskii Most

City gates

Butyrki Gate

Tver' Gate

Kaluga Gate

Map 1.1. Map of Moscow in the 1820s (Source: G. Le Cointe de Laveau, *Guide du voyageur à Moscou* (Moscow: Auguste Semen, 1824))

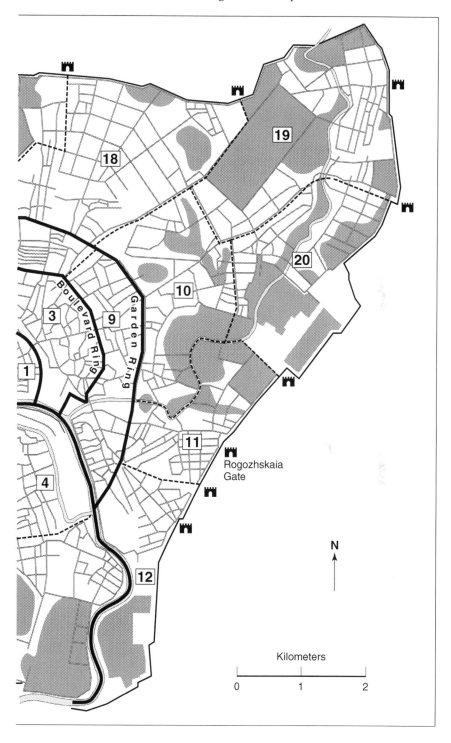

not aim primarily to address the practical challenges facing urban populations, but rather to erect a spectacular stage on which monarchical grandeur could be displayed while the squalor of older neighborhoods and unregulated suburbs was discreetly concealed.[33]

The other approach, which accorded greater importance to the everyday problems of city life, was the proto-Rousseauian notion of urban planning exemplified in the founding of Philadelphia. William Penn, a contemporary of Louis XIV and Peter the Great, was deeply affected by the plague and fire of London in 1665–6. In response, he instructed the commissioners surveying the future site of Philadelphia to "let every house be placed in the middle of its platt as to the breadth of it, so that there may be ground on each side, for gardens or orchards, or fields, that it may be a green country Towne, which will never be burnt, and allways be wholesome."[34] Urban planners in Moscow never made Penn's vision their own, but a belief that Moscow was a city of gardens and embodied the kinds of virtues that Penn saw in his "green country Towne" helped frame how Westerners and Russians thought about the Russian metropolis from the late seventeenth century onward.[35]

Catherine herself took an active interest in urban planning. As a typical European ruler of her time, her priority was to ensure order and stability (of populations, social structures, and economic activities), not to plan for growth or change, and the large sums that she invested in grand public buildings suggest a concern for symbolism rather than practicality.[36] Two main sources informed her thinking. One was the Baroque urbanism of Paris, the premier cultural center of the eighteenth century and thus the gold standard for European cities. French prototypes also served as the model for her reorganization of the Moscow police and her decision to organize welfare services through large state institutions such as the Moscow Foundling Home.[37] Her other source was cameralism, a German theory of government that held that a state needed an interventionist administration to uphold order and morals and to promote population growth and economic development. Cameralists thought that towns ought to be much smaller than Moscow. Confirming Catherine's distaste for Moscow, they argued

[33] Paul M. Hohenberg and Lynn Hollen Lees, *The Making of Urban Europe, 1000–1950* (Cambridge, Mass.: Harvard University Press, 1985), 152–5, 157; Josef W. Konvitz, *The Urban Millennium: The City-Building Process from the Early Middle Ages to the Present* (Carbondale, Ill.: Southern Illinois University Press, 1985), 33–40.

[34] Russell F. Weigley, ed., *Philadelphia: A 300-Year History* (New York: W. W. Norton, 1982), 1; Penn is quoted in William P. Holcomb, *Pennsylvania Boroughs* (Baltimore: N. Murray, 1886), 15.

[35] See, for example, Anna Ananieva, *Russisch Grün: Eine Kulturpoetik des Gartens im Russland des langen 18. Jahrhunderts* (Bielefeld: Transcript, 2010), 97–9, 141–2.

[36] Munro, *The Most Intentional City*, 87–8, 112, 281.

[37] Madariaga, *Russia in the Age of Catherine the Great*, 293; David L. Ransel, *Mothers of Misery: Child Abandonment in Russia* (Princeton: Princeton University Press, 1988), 7, 38, 62; Dmitry Shvidkovsky, *Russian Architecture and the West*, tr. Antony Wood (New Haven: Yale University Press, 2007), 225; Kozlova, *Liudi driakhlye*, 62.

that large cities bred immorality and unhealthy extremes of wealth and poverty, and sucked the vitality from the countryside.[38]

Catherine wasted little time in tackling the reconstruction of her empire's major cities. Within months after coming to power she established a commission to oversee urban planning for St Petersburg and Moscow. Its responsibility expanded rapidly to include the drafting of new plans for all of Russia's towns, reflecting what John T. Alexander calls her desire "to remold Russia's cities and towns in the Europeanized image of St. Petersburg—planned, prosperous, beautiful, fireproof, orderly, clean, and tranquil."[39] One leader of this commission was Ivan Betskoi, who was also the architect of her early plans for educational reform. "Betskoi's philosophy," as the historian Wladimir Berelowitch puts it, "came down to a few rules: arteries that were broad and straight, vast squares, 'convenient locations' for public buildings . . . The new environment was going to promote discipline, unlike the medieval city, which, far from being an embodiment of the 'celestial city' as tradition would have it, had instead become synonymous with filth, disease, fire, superstition, laziness, and rebellion."[40]

The efforts to reconstruct Moscow were stepped up after the plague of 1771. Large textile manufactories, where masses of serf laborers were packed together under filthy conditions, had been the outbreak's epicenter, and Catherine demanded (to no avail) that all manufactories be removed from the city. Of the 11,825 wooden buildings in Moscow at the start of the plague, 4,172 were gone by 1775, mostly burned as an anti-plague measure during the epidemic or destroyed in the huge conflagrations that swept Moscow in May and July 1773.[41] The resulting need to rebuild entire neighborhoods, combined with the breathing room that the regime had once both the Russo-Ottoman War and the Pugachev revolt ended in 1774, prompted a shift to more vigorous urban planning.

The result was the general plan of 1775, an ambitious blueprint for a future neoclassical Moscow designed (apparently) by the distinguished trio of architects Ivan Blank, Matvei Kazakov, and Vasilii Bazhenov. The White City, designated as the future downtown along with Kitai-Gorod, was zoned for reconstruction with harmonious neoclassical building ensembles. The standard building materials were to be masonry in the White City, wood and masonry in the Earthen City, and wood in the areas beyond. Along the boundary separating the White City from the Kremlin and Kitai-Gorod, the existing wooden houses and ramparts were to make way for a chain of imposing plazas. Boulevards—that is, elegant, tree-lined promenades modeled after the boulevards of Paris—

[38] Alexander, "Petersburg and Moscow," 148–9.

[39] John T. Alexander, *Catherine the Great: Life and Legend* (New York: Oxford University Press, 1989), 79.

[40] Berelowitch and Medvedkova, *Histoire de Saint-Pétersbourg*, 218.

[41] John T. Alexander, "Catherine II, Bubonic Plague, and the Problem of Industry in Moscow," *American Historical Review*, 79/3 (June 1974), 637–71, here: 637–43.

and neoclassical plazas were to replace the walls separating the White City from the Earthen City, and new commercial plazas were to arise in Zamoskvorech'e. Implementation was halting and the plan underwent numerous revisions, but Moscow's redevelopment proceeded broadly along the lines sketched out in 1775, and its general principles were retained when Moscow was rebuilt after its destruction in 1812 during the occupation by Napoleon.[42]

THE IMPERIAL SOCIAL PROJECT

The year 1775 marked a turning point in the reconstruction of Moscow's social order as well. Following a period of searching and experimentation, Catherine issued a series of legislative acts creating the framework for urban governance and the imperial social project down to the era of the Great Reforms. She and many of her compatriots accepted Montesquieu's notion that Russia needed an urban "third estate" if it was to escape its curse of despotism and poverty.[43] To create this third estate, she tried two approaches: educating a "new race of men," and remaking the system of social estates.

"New men" (or "new people") is an image that the Enlightenment adopted from the ancient world. A "new race of men" is an element of the restored golden age of justice and happiness prophesied in Virgil's fourth eclogue, and in the New Testament, one who accepts Christ becomes a "new person."[44] Enlightenment thinkers revived this expression to describe how people who absorbed enlightened values could beget a lineage, or "race," steeped in reason and justice. The Baron d'Holbach wrote in 1770 that a rationalist education free of religious mumbo jumbo would engender a "new race of men," and in 1782 Hector St John Crèvecoeur applied the same phrase to the newly independent Americans because they had "left behind all ancient prejudices and manners."[45]

These ideas resonated in Russia as well. In a memorandum that Catherine endorsed and that was published in 1766, her adviser Betskoi wrote that to "overcome the superstition of centuries," Russia had "to create, by means of education, a new race [*novuiu porodu*], so to speak, or new fathers and mothers,"

---

[42] Albert J. Schmidt, *The Architecture and Planning of Classical Moscow: A Cultural History* (Philadelphia: American Philosophical Society, 1989), 42–5, 59.

[43] A. Kamenskii, *"Pod seniiu Ekateriny…": Vtoraia polovina XVIII veka* (St Petersburg: Lenizdat, 1992), 166–9; Madariaga, *Russia in the Age of Catherine the Great*, 153–4; David M. Griffiths, "Eighteenth-Century Perceptions of Backwardness: Projects for the Creation of a Third Estate in Catherinean Russia," *Canadian-American Slavic Studies*, 13/4 (Winter 1979), 452–72.

[44] Proskurina, *Mify imperii*, 60; Victoria Frede, *Doubt, Atheism, and the Nineteenth-Century Russian Intelligentsia* (Madison: University of Wisconsin Press, 2011), 158.

[45] Baron d'Holbach D. M., *Essai sur les préjugés, ou, De l'influence des opinions sur les mœurs & sur le bonheur des hommes* (London: no pub., 1770), 59; Hector St. John Crèvecoeur, *Letters from an American Farmer* (London, 1782; repr. New York: Fox, Duffield, 1904), 54–5.

who would transmit enlightened ways "from generation to generation through the centuries to come." "The root of all good and evil," he declared, "is education." He argued that Peter the Great's policies had not changed the consciousness of either nobles or commoners, "which is why Russia has not so far been able to produce people of the condition that elsewhere is called the third or middle rank." The solution was to educate young people in an environment where they were cut off from the harmful influences of society. Boarding schools for boys and for girls, and the foundling homes that Catherine opened in St Petersburg and Moscow, were to be incubators of the new "race."[46]

Betskoi's schools and foundling homes never produced enough graduates or provided a sufficiently transformative education to meet the utopian hopes initially vested in them. Hence, Catherine adopted a second strategy: reforming the system of estates and local administration. Beyond educating "new people" in isolation from society, she sought to reshape the social mainstream itself.

In 1767, to give Russia the secure legal foundation that a non-despotic monarchy required according to Montesquieu, Catherine summoned delegates from across the country to the Moscow Kremlin to the so-called Legislative Commission. Their charge was to draft a new law code, Russia's first since 1649. Of the 564 delegates, 28 were appointed by the government, including one from the Holy Synod to represent the clergy, but in a democratic experiment unparalleled in pre-Reform Russian history, the rest were elected by constituencies of nobles, urban dwellers, and state peasants.[47] To guide them in their deliberations, Catherine wrote the *Instruction to the Commission for the Composition of a New Code of Laws*, known by its abridged Russian title as the *Nakaz* (Instruction). It was drafted by Catherine herself and vetted by her top advisers. The importance that she attached to it is evident from its repeated publication and widespread international distribution. Ten Russian editions appeared during her lifetime, and the foreign translations that appeared by 1771 included one edition in England, three in francophone Switzerland, two each in Italy and the Netherlands, and five in Germany and Russia's German-dominated Baltic Provinces.[48] Drawing its ideas primarily from Montesquieu, Beccaria, and the German cameralists, the *Nakaz* laid out foundational principles of an enlightened polity, illustrated with examples from classical and modern European experience. Two chapters are particularly important for understanding her thinking about urban matters: "Of Towns," which was adapted from the

---

[46] Ivan Betskoi, "General'noe uchrezhdenie o vospitanii oboego pola iunoshestva," in I. A. Solovkov, ed., *Antologiia pedagogicheskoi mysli Rossii XVIII v.* (Moscow: Pedagogika, 1985), 150; J. L. Black, *Citizens for the Fatherland: Education, Educators, and Pedagogical Ideals in Eighteenth Century Russia* (Boulder, Colo.: East European Quarterly, 1979), 78–81.

[47] François-Xavier Coquin, *La Grande Commission législative (1767–1768). Les cahiers de doléances urbains* (Paris: Nauwelaerts, 1972), 21–2, 28.

[48] William E. Butler, "The Nakaz of Catherine the Great," *American Book Collector*, 6/5 (1966), 18–21.

German cameralist J. H. G. von Justi, and "Of the Middling Sort of People," a chapter that is Catherine's own original work.[49]

Legally, there was no such thing in Russia as a unified urban community, because the towns were fragmented into discrete spaces and estates. Catherine rejected this tradition. A town, she declared in the chapter "Of Towns," should be a single entity under "one common Law" (art. 393). The privileges of municipal citizenship should be enjoyed by all "burghers" (*meshchane*, a term that can also be rendered as "townspeople"), meaning "those who are Interested in the Welfare of the Town, possessing House and Property in it, and . . . [who] are obliged to pay certain Taxes" (art. 394). "Burghers" were here conceived as a community of taxpayers and property owners, regardless of estate; they evidently included merchants, nobles, and the clergy, the groups that owned most urban real estate. The chapter "Of the Middling Sort of People," on the other hand, equates "burghers" specifically with "the middling sort" (arts. 377–8). Nobles and peasants were excluded, but otherwise the middling sort comprised all non-serfs "employed in Arts, Sciences, Navigation, Trade and Manufactures," as well as graduates of church or secular schools and children of government officials (arts. 379–82).[50] If we map this list onto the estate system, the middling sort seems to include the following groups: government clerks; "personal nobles," that is, minor officials whose service rank gave noble status only to them personally, not their offspring; merchants, tradespeople, and educated professionals; and, judging by the reference to church schools, the clergy.

The experience of the elections to the Legislative Commission poured cold water on Catherine's hopes of fostering urban communities that transcended estate divisions. Town dwellers who owned a house could theoretically vote no matter what their estate, but in practice, merchants dominated the elections. The 58 delegates from the towns of Moscow Province (1 per town) included 1 nobleman, 1 artisan, 7 officials, and 49 merchants. Merchants participated in 57 of the 58 elections; in 28, they made up the entire electorate. Officials, the next most active group, took part in only 26 of the 58 elections. Nobles participated in 9, clergy in 8, artisans in 7, and peasants in 5.[51]

The voters in each town provided their delegate with a written "instruction." Those from the towns of Moscow Province, far from embracing Catherine's idea of multi-estate communities, pleaded instead for special privileges for the merchant estate. The instructions were generally compiled from petitions that the towns had sent to the government in the past and thus reiterated long-standing requests:[52] for freedom from unpaid state-service obligations (maintaining city

---

[49] Paul Dukes, ed., *Russia under Catherine the Great*, 2 vols. (Newtonville, Mass.: Oriental Research Partners, 1977), 2:19, 21.

[50] Dukes, ed., *Russia under Catherine the Great*, 2:92–3.

[51] Coquin, *La Grande Commission législative*, 29–32, 51, 54.

[52] Wallace Daniel, "The Merchants' View of the Social Order in Russia as Revealed in the Town *Nakazy* from Moskovskaia *Guberniia* to Catherine's Legislative Commission," *Canadian-American Slavic Studies*, 11/4 (Winter 1977), 503–22, esp. 509.

streets, quartering soldiers, serving as night watchmen, and the like); the right to own serfs; protection from economic competition by peasants; the right to be subject only to courts and administrative bodies controlled by merchants; and protection against insults to their personal honor.[53] The nobles had been freed from compulsory state service in 1762, and now the merchants wanted the same. In effect, as the historian François-Xavier Coquin puts it, they sought a privileged status within urban society comparable to what the nobility enjoyed in the countryside.[54] Almost none asked for reforms that reflected Enlightenment urban ideals and would have served a wider public interest, such as the creation of schools or improvements in sanitation.[55]

The exceptions that proved the rule were the strongholds of the nobility and the bureaucracy, Moscow and St Petersburg. Here, it was the nobles who monopolized the elections. Participation in Moscow was slight—only 878 of 10,000–12,000 householders cast a vote—and it was the only city in Moscow Province to elect a noble as its delegate. The instructions from the electors in the two metropolitan cities were adapted from those for the delegates from agencies of the government, so it is no surprise that, unlike the provincial towns, they asked for the kinds of urban improvements that were dear to Catherine.[56]

Echoing Catherine's own views, the instruction from Moscow complained that the metropolis fell short of enlightened European standards. It was malodorous, polluted, blighted by uncontrolled sprawl, and cluttered with wooden firetraps. It lacked stately buildings and vital institutions such as schools, hospitals, a lunatic asylum, a workhouse, and pharmacies. The citizens had to perform unpaid state services that ought to be the job of salaried officials, merchants faced unfair competition from other estates, and a drunken rabble roamed the streets. The solution: properly enforce the laws of the estate system because this was the basis for "well-established order in all states," and introduce building codes "on the model of other European cities," factory regulations "on the model of other states," a workhouse to discipline the poor "on the model of other lands," and improved law courts "on the basis of [those in] European cities."[57]

The Legislative Commission proved unable to transcend parochial interests and did not produce the hoped-for new legal code. Chastened by this experience, Catherine henceforth favored a more top-down approach to lawmaking. Still, the consultation with her subjects had not been in vain, for she took their grievances to heart. In her subsequent urban reforms, she preserved the estate system,

---

[53] Coquin, *La Grande Commission législative*, 96–154.
[54] Coquin, *La Grande Commission législative*, 174, 182.
[55] Coquin, *La Grande Commission législative*, 168–70.
[56] Schmidt, *Sozialkontrolle in Moskau*, 177–8; Madariaga, *Russia in the Age of Catherine the Great*, 141–4; Coquin, *La Grande Commission législative*, 46, 54, 63.
[57] "Nakaz ot zhitelei goroda Moskvy," *Sbornik Imperatorskago Russkago Istoricheskago Obshchestva*, 93 (1894), 119–35.

abolished various unpopular taxes and labor services, and accorded valuable privileges to the elite of the merchantry—all requests that had been put forward in the towns' instructions to the Legislative Commission.[58] Her *Nakaz*, meanwhile, became a touchstone of Russian legal and political thought. It was regularly cited until the mid-nineteenth century in Russian laws, government decrees, and judicial rulings; during the reign of Alexander I (1801–25), it was cited in at least forty-one court cases.[59]

CATHERINE'S REFORMS OF URBAN SOCIETY

Catherine's urban reforms were a response to the existing institutional arrangements in Russian towns, which were in turn based on an older system that had been partially reorganized by Peter the Great.

Before Catherine, the inhabitants of Russian towns formed discrete groups that did not constitute a unified civic body. Clergymen were subject to church authority; soldiers, to military authority; nobles, migrant peasant laborers, and others were likewise separate. The commercial and manufacturing population formed a community called the *posad* (the same term that also designated a town's business district). Its members were jointly liable for the soul tax, which was calculated on the basis of the number of males registered as inhabitants of the community, and for the labor services that the community owed to the crown. In the seventeenth century, the *posad* was divided into three "classes" (*stat'i*) based on wealth and thus ability to contribute to the *posad's* tax obligations. The richer classes carried more of the tax burden but also exercised disproportionate power in the community. Laws issued by Peter the Great in 1721 and 1724 instructed each *posad* to establish a magistracy (*magistrat*) that had jurisdiction over the *posad's* members and was given a broad mandate to promote trade and manufacturing, establish schools, succor the poor, and discipline petty criminals. Peter also replaced the *posad's* wealth-based classes with occupational categories. The highest group, which was supposed to dominate the magistracy, was the first guild (*gil'diia*). It included bankers, wealthy merchants, doctors, apothecaries, skippers of merchant ships, gold and silver craftsmen, icon painters, and artists. The artisans and petty traders formed the second guild. The remaining *posad* members, hired laborers, were the "base people" (*podlye liudi*). The first guild represented a conceptual innovation because it departed from the traditional wealth-based system, instead bringing together groups that provided commercial or cultural leadership in the community. The creation of the first guild gave

---

[58] Coquin, *La Grande Commission législative*, 184–9.

[59] Dukes, *Russia under Catherine the Great*, 2:22–4; Dixon, *Catherine the Great*, 325; Simon Dixon, "The Posthumous Reputation of Catherine II in Russia, 1797–1837," *Slavonic and East European Review*, 77/4 (October 1999), 646–79, here: 671–4.

expression to Peter's desire to transform Russia's poorly educated, change-averse merchantry into a literate, economically dynamic, civically engaged European burgher class. It also anticipated Catherine's proposals for a "middling sort" or "third estate." Another European-inspired innovation was the establishment of artisan guilds (*tsekhi*).[60]

Peter's reforms exhibited a variety of shortcomings that arose from the difficulty of grafting foreign-inspired institutions onto existing Russian realities. The shift from classes to guilds was in practice old wine in new bottles. The old system remained legally in force in many towns. In places where the new guilds were in fact established, they were often identical to the old classes, a fact highlighted by the redesignation of the "base people" as the "third guild" by analogy with the "third class."[61]

A further problem was that while the new system represented an attempt to organize the towns according to a comprehensive scheme of social categories, in practice it touched only a small share of the inhabitants. At the second revision (census of male inhabitants), conducted in 1743–7, Moscow's *posad*—by far the largest in Russia—consisted of 13,458 males.[62] Assuming an equal number of females, this meant that a city of several hundred thousand inhabitants had only 27,000 *posad* members. (Most of the rest were presumably serfs or other rural migrants.) Moscow's exceptionally large population and complex economy should have offered more promising conditions than anywhere else in Russia for a dynamic burgher class, yet in practice its *posad* was made up mostly of laborers and petty traders: in the 1760s, only 8.9 percent were in the first guild, compared with 46.7 percent in the second, and 44.4 in the third.[63]

Russians' lack of enthusiasm for joining the *posad* was due in part to the ambiguousness of the function for which it was created. It was meant to stimulate the kind of urban vitality that corporate organizations fostered in the West, but the government refused to grant it the commercial monopolies and political powers that made membership in its Western prototypes attractive. Instead, it pressed the *posad* into service as an instrument of fiscal coercion against its own members. For instance, it had to act as the government's agent in collecting taxes and selecting men for lifelong military conscription. Belonging to the *posad* thus entailed more burdens than privileges. The artisan guilds faced the same problems, and since membership was not compulsory, few artisans joined: the second revision registered only 117 men in Moscow who belonged to artisan guilds.[64]

This was the system, then, that Catherine set out to change. She pursued multiple goals that were in tension with each other: maintain a static social order

[60] Hittle, *The Service City*, 82–90; A. A. Kizevetter, *Posadskaia obshchina v Rossii XVIII st.* (Moscow: Universitetskaia tipografiia, 1903), 127–8.
[61] Kizevetter, *Posadskaia obshchina*, 128–9.
[62] Kizevetter, *Posadskaia obshchina*, 121.
[63] Kizevetter, *Posadskaia obshchina*, 158.
[64] Hittle, *The Service City*, 126–9; Kizevetter, *Posadskaia obshchina*, 165.

by preserving the distinction among estates; create a unified municipal citizenry through multi-estate institutions; and increase urban dynamism by facilitating mobility between estates.[65] Her key legislative acts were the guild reform of 17 March 1775,[66] the provincial reform of 7 November 1775,[67] the Police Code of 8 April 1782,[68] the Charter to the Towns of 21 April 1785,[69] and the Code for Public Schools of 5 August 1786.[70] These reforms, which were refined but not fundamentally altered by her successors, formed the basis for Russian municipal governance until 1870.

Compared with the Petrine system, the one built by Catherine and her successors sought to elevate the "middling sort" higher above the masses. The guild reform and the Charter to the Towns broke up the unity of the *posad*. The rank-and-file members, henceforth called "townspeople" (*meshchane*), remained collectively liable for their tax and service obligations, and their community continued as before to have the power to discipline them with floggings, forced labor, or even banishment to Siberia. However, a privileged but non-hereditary elite was freed from these communal controls and obligations. If a townsman (or other eligible individual) declared that he owned the legally prescribed amount of capital, and paid a fee calculated on the basis of that capital, he could join one of three merchant guilds. The first guild required the largest amount of capital and gave the right to conduct commerce and manufacturing on the largest scale; membership in the second and third guilds was correspondingly cheaper and offered more restricted privileges. Merchants of all three guilds were exempted from the soul tax, conscription, and state-service obligations, and membership in the first and second guilds in addition offered exemption from corporal punishment—no small matter in a polity where the police had extensive power to inflict floggings on the citizenry. Inability to pay the annual guild fee, however, resulted in demotion back to the rank of townsman. The Charter to the Towns also established a further elite category, "eminent citizens" (*imenitye grazhdane*), which comprised exceptionally rich businessmen as well as people in other fields whom the regime wished to recognize—architects, painters, sculptors, scholars, university graduates, and distinguished former holders of local public offices.

The same template was applied to other estates that formed part of the "middling sort." In the bureaucracy, if clerks earned promotion to rank 14, the

---

[65] Hugh D. Hudson, "Urban Estate Engineering in Eighteenth-Century Russia: Catherine the Great and the Elusive *Meshchanstvo*," *Canadian-American Slavic Studies*, 18/4 (Winter 1984), 393–410.

[66] PSZ (First Series), vol. 20, no. 14,275, art. 47.

[67] Dukes, *Russia under Catherine the Great*, 1:140–57.

[68] PSZ (First Series), vol. 21, no. 15,379.

[69] David Griffiths and George E. Munro, eds. and tr., *Catherine II's Charters of 1785 to the Nobility and the Towns* (Bakersfield, Calif.: Charles Schlacks, 1991).

[70] PSZ (First Series), vol. 22, no. 16,421.

bottom rung on the Table of Ranks, they became personal nobles. (Rank 8 conferred hereditary ennoblement.) Personal nobles did not have power or status equal to hereditary nobles. They could not own serfs; their names were entered into the registers of urban inhabitants, not those of the nobility; they were in practice marginalized from the provincial noble associations that were the nobility's principal form of corporate organization; and, of course, their status was not hereditary. On the other hand, they were not subject to the soul tax or communal controls, and from 1785 on they had legal immunity from corporal punishment and conscription. Thus they had privileges broadly similar to merchants. (In a publicly visible sign of this similarity, officials in ranks 14 to 9 and merchants of the first two guilds were allowed to hitch two horses to their carriages, whereas hereditary nobles without state-service ranks and third-guild merchants had to make do with only one.[71]) The parish clergy, too, evolved in this direction. Over the course of the eighteenth century, it became an entirely endogamous estate. Catherine exempted it in the 1760s from conscription, taxes, and state services, and by the early nineteenth century, priests (though not sacristans) had received the same rights as personal nobles.[72]

These reforms had the effect of dividing urban dwellers into several broad juridical categories. At the top was an elite of hereditary nobles. Below them were the middling sort, who were divided into a privileged elite (priests, merchants, eminent citizens, personal nobles) and a much larger lower tier (sacristans, townspeople, artisans, clerks) who formed the pool from which the elite was recruited. Farther down were the state peasants and serfs who lived in the city on temporary work permits and formed the bulk of the laboring class. At the bottom, finally, were paupers and other undesirables, whom the regime subjected to harassment and repression. Using estate-based police records that unfortunately map only imperfectly onto the categories outlined here, it seems that in the last years of Catherine's reign, the nobles plus the elite of the middling sort (merchants and clergy) were 13.8 percent of Moscow's population. Another 15.3 percent formed the lower tier of the middling sort: townspeople, artisans, clerks, and the catchall category of *raznochintsy* ("people of various ranks"). Another 4 percent were soldiers; 1.3 percent were foreigners; and all the rest—65.7 percent—were serfs or state peasants.[73]

Except for paupers, all these groups were supposed to have a connection to the community of urban citizens. The core of that community was the middling sort, but the others were supposed to be integrated as well. The nobles were connected politically because if they owned urban real estate, they had voting rights (see

[71] PSZ (First Series), vol. 20, no. 14,290 (3 April 1775), art. 5–6.
[72] Boris Mironov, *Sotsial'naia istoriia Rossii perioda Imperii (XVIII—nachalo XX veka): Genezis lichnosti, demokraticheskoi sem'i, grazhdanskogo obshchestva i pravovogo gosudarstva*, 2 vols. (St Petersburg: Dmitrii Bulanin, 1999), 1:86, 100–2.
[73] Statistics for 1789–93, cited in Gastev, *Materialy*, 264.

below). As for the lower classes, their connection with the civic community was supposed to operate through culture and education. One of the aims of Catherine's urban reforms was to raise the standard of culture and gentility. For example, the Charter to the Towns prescribed—with a pedantic didacticism typical of Catherine's legislation—that at their official meetings, artisans were to "observe decorum . . . both in words and in actions": no "deliberately drenching someone, or spitting, or jostling, or showing up drunk, or habitually dressing inappropriately, or such like."[74] The laboring classes, too, were supposed to be acculturated into the community of enlightened citizens. In their case, the mechanism was the school system that Catherine proposed to create.

Catherine's school reform of 1786 was the first attempt in Russian history to create a broad-based system of primary schools. The law called for the establishment of locally funded *narodnye* ("national," i.e. public and secular) schools in towns across Russia. The capital of each province (*guberniia*) was to have a school offering a five-year education, and in every district (*uezd*) of a province there was to be a two-year school. The schools were to be free of charge and open to all estates and both sexes. Teachers were to use the newest pedagogical methods, treat the children with kindness, and not administer corporal punishment. The primer required for use in the schools discouraged any notions of social mobility—"We should never wish for something that is unsuited to our occupation," it read[75]—but it also taught genteel manners appropriate to the middling sort more broadly: don't shuffle when you walk, sit straight, make eye contact, keep your elbows off the table, cover your mouth when yawning, don't bite your nails, wear clean linens.[76] In practice, the schools attracted mainly the lower classes. When the schools first opened in Moscow in 1786, they enrolled a total of 105 children, including 60 who were serfs or peasants, 12 soldiers' children, 10 nobles, 8 from the clergy, and 7 from merchant or townspeople's families.[77] Catherine wrote that over the long term, thanks to this reform, "ignorance will disappear" and "morals will be improved."[78] As will be discussed in Chapter 5, shortages of students, teachers, and money greatly impeded the growth of the schools, and their design was significantly modified in the early nineteenth century. Nonetheless, they formed the beginning of a Russian public-education system that has endured ever since.

Catherine's reforms also restructured the system of provincial and municipal government. The plague revolt and the Pugachev rebellion had shown that the

---

[74] Griffiths and Munro, *Catherine II's Charters*, 49.

[75] "Book on the Duties of Man and the Citizen," in Black, *Citizens for the Fatherland*, 213.

[76] Black, *Citizens for the Fatherland*, 231–4.

[77] L. M. Artamonova, *Obshchestvo, vlast' i prosveshchenie v russkoi provintsii XVIII–nachala XIX vv. (Iugo-vostochnye gubernii Evropeiskoi Rossii)* (Samara: Izdatel'stvo Samarskogo nauchnogo tsentra RAN, 2001), 64–82, 96; Max J. Okenfuss, "Education and Empire: School Reform in Enlightened Russia," *Jahrbücher für Geschichte Osteuropas*, 27/1 (1979), 41–68.

[78] Artamonova, *Obshchestvo, vlast' i prosveshchenie*, 87.

imperial government's presence on the ground was thin, as was its ability to mobilize the resources of local society. The provincial reform of 1775 and the police code of 1782 sought to build a denser network of local officials, a more efficient chain of command, and closer cooperation between imperial officials and local inhabitants. Moscow Province was shrunk to a manageable size and placed under the authority of a governor-general. The province was endowed with a reformed administration and judiciary, both of which included elected noble and urban representatives. A provincial Board of Public Welfare (*Prikaz obshchestvennogo prizreniia*) was created to establish and manage schools, orphanages, hospitals, almshouses, lunatic asylums, workhouses, and the like, to be funded in large part through private philanthropy. In Moscow and other cities, a Police Board (*uprava blagochiniia*) was in charge of most administrative functions: not only law enforcement, but a vast array of matters pertaining to the regulation of commerce and public health, the maintenance of roads and bridges, and myriad other aspects of administration and public order. It was headed by an appointed chief of police (*oberpolitseimeister*), who was assisted by two appointed councilors and two councilors elected by the citizenry. For the purposes of police administration, Moscow was divided into districts (*chasti*) and wards (*kvartaly*), and a continuous chain of command extended from the ward upward to the district, then to the chief of police, the governor-general, and finally the empress.[79]

Catherine wanted to stimulate participation in government by society rather than have to rely on coercive measures by the bureaucracy and compulsory state service reluctantly provided by urban residents. Once the Charter to the Towns had laid down the principle that a town was a unified community, and had created corporate bodies such as the merchant guilds, the next step was to draw these groups more deeply into the management of local affairs.[80]

These ideas lay behind the system of urban self-government that the Charter to the Towns established. In keeping with the ideas expressed in Catherine's *Nakaz*, the charter conceived of a town as a civic community composed of multiple estates. The largest political institution it created, the Town Corporation (*gradskoe obshchestvo*), was composed of all residents who were over 25 and met certain wealth requirements; how severely these wealth requirements limited access to voting rights is disputed.[81] The Town Corporation met only once every

---

[79] Madariaga, *Russia in the Age of Catherine the Great*, 281–6, 292–4; Janet M. Hartley, "Philanthropy in the Reign of Catherine the Great: Aims and Realities," in Roger Bartlett and Janet M. Hartley, eds., *Russia in the Age of the Enlightenment: Essays for Isabel de Madariaga* (New York: St Martin's Press, 1990), 167–202.

[80] Hittle, *The Service City*, 222–4; Robert E. Jones, "Jacob Sievers, Enlightened Reform and the Development of a 'Third Estate' in Russia," *Russian Review*, 36/4 (October 1977), 424–37; David Griffiths, "Of Estates, Charters and Constitutions," in Griffiths and Munro, *Catherine II's Charters*, xxvi.

[81] Hittle, *The Service City*, 224; Janet Hartley, "Town Government in Saint Petersburg Guberniya after the Charter to the Towns of 1785," *Slavonic and East European Review*, 62/1

three years and elected various local officials, including the town chief (*gorodskoi golova*), the judges of the Oral Court (a summary court for minor civil cases), and the two councilors who sat on the Police Board. Local citizens in addition voted by estate to elect the Common Council (*obshchaia duma*), which was made up of the town chief plus one representative elected every three years by each of the following six categories of inhabitants: (1) each of the three merchant guilds; (2) each of the artisan guilds, whose number varied but could be quite large; (3) the eminent citizens; (4) the merchants or tradespeople who were citizens of other towns or countries; (5) the townspeople; and (6) the people of any estate—in practice, mainly nobles and clergy—who owned land or buildings in the city. Since the Common Council met only once every three years, it elected a Six-Man Council (*shestiglasnaia duma*), made up of the town chief and one representative from each of the aforementioned six categories of inhabitants, to handle the town's ongoing affairs.

The powers and functions of these institutions were limited. Under the Charter to the Towns, their only revenues came from local business activities (e.g. running a mill or selling fishing rights), fines on local citizens, and a 1 or 2 percent share of the income from locally collected customs duties or the state liquor monopoly. The municipality of St Petersburg, one of Russia's richest cities, had annual revenues of only 36,000 rubles in 1797; by comparison, just one of the diamond rings that Prince Grigorii Potemkin left behind when he died in 1791 was valued at 20,000 rubles.[82] The only expenditures that municipalities were allowed were salaries for their officials, construction and upkeep of public buildings, and contributions to the institutions maintained by the Board of Public Welfare. Under the Charter to the Towns, their only tasks were promoting economic development, settling minor disputes among the inhabitants, and raising money for the Board of Public Welfare.

An in-depth discussion of municipal institutions in pre-Reform Moscow is not within the scope of this book, but certain basic points should be noted. Urban self-government continued to rest on a narrow social base of merchants, townspeople, and artisans, and exercised little real control over local affairs. Much of the city population consisted of peasants who competed economically with local traders and manufacturers but were not under municipal jurisdiction. The clergy and (especially) the nobility dominated local society but showed no interest in participating in municipal governance. Law enforcement, the judiciary, much of the provision of public welfare, and most forms of government regulation were under the imperial bureaucracy, and provincial governors were in

(January 1984), 61–84, here: 71; George Munro, "The Charter to the Towns Reconsidered: The St. Petersburg Connection," *Canadian-American Slavic Studies*, 23/1 (Spring 1989), 17–35, here: 27, 29–30.

    82 Hittle, *The Service City*, 232; Dixon, *Catherine the Great*, 304–5.

the habit of treating elected officials like subordinates in a chain of command.[83] Not surprisingly, the urban citizenry showed little interest in the institutions that Catherine created, although their level of participation is disputed. The older scholarship represents them as apathetic and hemmed in by institutions that stifled true self-government, whereas more recent historians have found signs of healthy civic initiative.[84] In any case, the sheer complexity of the legislation made it difficult to implement. The broad range of social groups to which the law assigned a political role simply did not exist in many towns, and the law's attempt to micromanage the work of local officials ignored the reality that they often based their decisions on personal relationships, local custom, and informal rules of thumb, not written statutes. The legislation therefore provides only a highly imperfect sense of how local government in Russia actually operated.

CONCLUSION

From the vantage point of Catherine II, her advisers, and much of the Russian elite, Moscow epitomized the urban backwardness that retarded Russia's progress toward becoming an enlightened European state. Solving this wider problem required turning Moscow into an enlightened metropolis like St Petersburg, with a middling sort and a Europeanized urban landscape. In 1775, as soon as Pugachev was dead and the war with the Ottomans concluded, the court began issuing legislation to redirect the social and spatial development of Moscow and other towns. These acts created a legal and institutional framework that remained fundamentally unchanged until the Great Reforms.

How the resulting transformation was experienced by the inhabitants, and what impression it made in Russia and abroad, will be the subject of the remainder of this book.

---

[83] Madariaga, *Russia in the Age of Catherine the Great*, 303–4.

[84] For the view that foregrounds public apathy, see, for example: Hittle, *The Service City*, 5–9, 231; Daniel Brower, "Urbanization and Autocracy: Russian Urban Development in the First Half of the Nineteenth Century," *Russian Review*, 42/4 (October 1983), 377–402, esp. 394–401. For the view that the civic dynamism of Russian towns has been underestimated, see, for example: Boris Mironov, "Bureaucratic or Self-Government: The Early Nineteenth Century Russian City," *Slavic Review*, 52/2 (Summer 1993), 233–55; Mironov, *Sotsial'naia istoriia Rossii*, 1:496, 499; Hartley, "Town Government in Saint Petersburg Guberniya," 84; Munro, "The Charter to the Towns Reconsidered," 32.

2

Space and Time in the Enlightened Metropolis

In 1767, five years into Catherine II's reign, the architect Vasilii Bazhenov drafted plans to demolish the Kremlin. In its place was to arise a vast palace, the largest neoclassical complex in Europe. With a façade 30 to 40 meters high and 1,200 meters long, it would dwarf Versailles. On one side, grand staircases and terraces would descend from the palace to the river. On the other, Moscow's main streets would converge on a mammoth plaza where the people would congregate on holidays. Only the ancient cathedrals would remain to recall the Kremlin of the tsars of Muscovy. What Moscow would gain instead was a pendant to the palace complex in St Petersburg that formed the heart of Catherine's Europeanized empire.[1]

After extensive preparatory work, Bazhenov's plan was shelved for reasons that remain unclear, but Catherine's willingness to embrace his plan in the first place bespeaks her belief that the city's urban space required fundamental reconstruction. Moscow in the middle of the eighteenth century was mostly a jumble of log buildings and vacant lots along winding, unpaved lanes that were barely passable after a heavy rain. Periodically—for example, in 1737 and 1748—huge fires devastated the city.[2] The streets were pitch dark at night, refuse rotted where it fell, and there was little clean water. What the inhabitants saw, heard, and smelled—the urban sensory environment that has drawn so much scholarly interest in recent decades[3]—was typical of early modern Europe, but Moscow's low-density development pattern gave the city a rural quality as well.

The present chapter will explore Moscow's urban space under Catherine and her successors. The focus will be on four inescapable aspects of the physical environment that shaped the lives of the inhabitants: the city's quasi-rural geography; its smell; its water supply; and the nighttime darkness, with its attendant challenges to public safety and law enforcement. Each formed an obstacle to Moscow's transformation into an enlightened metropolis. How this urban environment was experienced and perceived by contemporaries, and how

---

[1] Schmidt, *The Architecture and Planning of Classical Moscow*, 37–40; Shvidkovsky, *Russian Architecture*, 242–4; Dixon, *Catherine the Great*, 212–13.

[2] Gulianitskii, *Moskva i slozhivshiesia russkie goroda*, 36, 50.

[3] See, for example: Alexander Cowan and Jill Steward, eds., *The City and the Senses: Urban Culture since 1500* (Aldershot: Ashgate, 2007).

the government responded to the problems that arose from it, are the subject of this chapter.

URBAN SPACE AND THE BUILT ENVIRONMENT

Moscow's urban space presented a distinctive set of challenges. In much of Europe, where city walls historically constricted urban expansion and wood construction was hampered by fire codes and the effects of deforestation, towns were compact, with narrow streets and tightly packed masonry buildings. In Moscow, these limiting factors were absent, so the city was characterized on the contrary, much like a Russian village, by wooden buildings and low-density sprawl. Some Westerners inferred from this pattern of urbanization that Moscow was essentially Asiatic, not European, and accordingly gave an exotic flavor to their accounts of Moscow through fantastical comparisons with Beijing, Baghdad, Isfahan, or Constantinople.[4] In their attempt to Europeanize Moscow, the Russian elites therefore faced the dual problem of managing the city's rustic spatiality and expunging the Orientalist stigma.

These aspects of Moscow's urban space were apparent even to the casual traveler, particularly the foreigners who wrote most of the surviving descriptions of eighteenth-century Moscow. The vista that greeted new arrivals approaching the city moved Engelbert Wichelhausen, a German physician who lived in Russia from 1786 to 1793, to a rare expression of wonderment:

Even if you have seen Paris, London, and many of the greatest cities of Europe, your imagination still has no scale to conceive of the impression created by the panorama of this gigantic city . . . This mass of buildings, whose expanse fades into the horizon, creates such a bizarre effect that you think you are seeing a magical scene from the fairy world.[5]

As they drew closer to the city, travelers reached the customs wall. It had been erected under the empresses Anna and Elizabeth, and was retained even after 1754, when the abolition of customs duties on intra-Russian trade made its original function obsolete, because it formed a perimeter around the city that gave definition to Moscow's otherwise fluid boundaries and permitted police controls of those who entered and left. To enter, one had to pass a checkpoint at

---

[4] This particular list of exotic locales appears in the recollections of Louise Fusil, Georges Le Cointe de Laveau, Charles-Joseph de Ligne, Elisabeth-Louise Vigée-Lebrun, Charles de Saint-Julien, de Staël, and Francisco de Miranda: L. Fusil, *L'incendie de Moscou, La petite orpheline de Wilna, Passage de la Bérésina, et Retraite de Napoléon jusqu'à Wilna* (2nd edn., Paris: Pillet, 1817), 83–4; G. Le Cointe de Laveau, *Guide du voyageur à Moscou* (Moscow: Auguste Semen, 1824), 59–60; Claude de Grève, ed., *Le voyage en Russie. Anthologie des voyageurs français aux XVIIIe et XIXe siècles* (Paris: Robert Laffont, 1990), 394, 396, 401, 425; Francisco de Miranda, *Diario de Moscú y San Petersburgo* (Caracas: Biblioteca Ayacucho, 1993), 13.

[5] Engelbert Wichelhausen, *Züge zu einem Gemählde von Moskwa* (Berlin: Johann Daniel Sander, 1803), 5–6.

the city gates, which Catherine's government in the 1780s had adorned (as Wichelhausen noted approvingly) with "two guard houses (*zastavy*) built in a noble style and handsome obelisks with gilded eagles, which, like some of the gates of Paris, at once give the arriving stranger an advantageous idea of the city."[6] (These obelisks can be seen in the background in Illustration 7.1.)

The wall, obelisks, and gilded eagles signaled the elites' resolve to make Moscow into a great European metropolis, but this attempt was undercut by the neighborhoods immediately adjacent: the formerly autonomous suburbs, which resembled nothing so much as peasant villages.[7] Much of the city's surface outside the center was farms, woods, and undeveloped river banks, or else industry, coaching inns, or vast aristocratic estates. Catherine and her successors also established army barracks there, as well as hospitals, cemeteries, slaughterhouses, and other insalubrious institutions.[8] The area drew peasant migrants and the poor, but also fugitive serfs, army deserters, traveling coachmen, and other peripatetic or rootless groups. The outer neighborhoods of Moscow formed a semi-deserted urban frontier where poverty and marginality were concentrated next to aristocratic wealth and large institutions. Moscow was not unique in this regard, for once other European cities expanded past their medieval walls, they too incorporated areas that remained quasi-rural. For example, when the customs wall around Paris was completed in the 1780s, writes the historian Daniel Roche, "the newly defined perimeter enclosed a zone that was vast and often without buildings, occupied by fields and vineyards, a territory that was undeveloped and transitional, difficult to control, conducive to fraud and, in the eyes of the police, to crime."[9]

What made Moscow seem unusual to Westerners was the fact that even its built-up areas had neither the medieval nor the Baroque layout that were the hallmark of European urbanism. St Petersburg was no more densely populated, but its buildings were larger and arrayed along geometrically designed streets, suggesting that a true city was coming into being.[10] In Moscow, by contrast, the winding streets and smallish, irregularly designed wooden houses created a village atmosphere, and even grand and impressive buildings did not seem to lend structure and coherence to their surroundings.[11] In 1775, the French naval officer Daniel Lescallier observed that

[Moscow's] greatest length, from southwest to northeast, is around ten *verst* [10.6 kilometers], and its breadth, six to seven [6.36–7.42 kilometers], an extension that is immense

---

[6] Wichelhausen, *Züge zu einem Gemählde von Moskwa*, 23.

[7] See the painting by Francesco Camporesi, in Natal'ia Skorniakova, *Staraia Moskva: Graviury i litografii XVI–XIX vekov iz sobraniia Gosudarstvennogo Istoricheskogo Muzeia* (Moscow: Galart, 1996), 107.

[8] Alexander, *Bubonic Plague*, 273–4.

[9] Roche, *Le peuple de Paris*, 27.

[10] Berelowitch and Medvedkova, *Histoire de Saint-Pétersbourg*, 172; for a systematic comparison of the two cities, see pp. 178–80.

[11] Roche, *Le peuple de Paris*, 46.

and surpasses that of Paris or London; but all this space offers only a shapeless mass of wooden huts, poorly constructed brick or wooden palaces, ruins, gardens, cultivated land, ponds, pastures, and abandoned areas, with a prodigious number of churches.[12]

A dozen years later, in 1787, the Venezuelan Francisco de Miranda had a similar impression: "It is a city of very great extension. I have not, however, been able to obtain a map; but what does that matter, when in the middle there are empty areas that many times make one wonder whether one is in the city or in the country?"[13] In 1793, the Bohemian naturalist Joachim von Sternberg found it difficult at first to be sure

whether [I had] strayed into a large village or a city. Over long distances, the lanes consist of low, half-rotted wooden buildings. But one also drives through large areas where the buildings are all built of stone and at great cost: there, this place acquires the appearance of immeasurable wealth. Never have I seen penury and excess in such close proximity.[14]

These accounts were informed, no doubt, by literary conventions. Jean-Jacques Rousseau's story of his arrival in Paris taught readers to expect cities to appear seductive when seen from afar but filthy and squalid at close range.[15] Moscow, too, had long been described in these terms. For instance, Adam Olearius, in his widely read travelogue of 1647, had written that Moscow "shines like Jerusalem from without but is like Bethlehem within."[16] Still, when visitors described Moscow as vast and underpopulated, they were not merely repeating literary clichés. Moscow's 7,267 hectares (72.67 square kilometers) made it more than twice the size of Paris at the end of the *ancien régime*,[17] but compared with Paris it felt empty. The official police statistics recorded a population of 161,181 in 1776 and 216,935 in 1805, compared with 600,000 to 700,000 in prerevolutionary Paris.[18]

The statistics on population and housing density convey some of the differences between the two cities. Moscow's historic core consisted of the Kremlin, the adjacent Kitai-Gorod, and, forming a semicircle around both, the White

---

[12] Quoted in de Grève, *Le voyage en Russie*, 388.

[13] Miranda, *Diario*, 65–6.

[14] J. Graf von Sternberg, *Reise von Moskau über Sofia nach Königsberg mit einer kurzen Beschreibung von Moskau nebst meteorologischen und mineralogischen Beobachtungen* (Berlin: no pub., 1793), 4.

[15] Jean-Jacques Rousseau, *The Confessions* (Ware: Wordsworth, 1996), 154; Roche, *Le peuple de Paris*, 18–19.

[16] *The Travels of Olearius in Seventeenth-Century Russia*, ed. and tr. Samuel H. Baron (Stanford, Calif.: Stanford University Press, 1967), 113.

[17] The data on Moscow's surface area are based on *Statisticheskii atlas goroda Moskvy: Ploshchad' Moskvy, naselenie i zaniatiia* (Moscow: Moskovskaia Gorodskaia Tipografiia, 1887), col. 6; the same number is given in *Statisticheskii vremennik Rossiiskoi Imperii*, vol. 1 (1866), 115. By contrast, *Istoriia Moskvy s drevneishikh vremen do nashikh dnei*, 3 vols. (Moscow: Mosgorarkhiv, 1997), 1:287, arrives at a total near 10,000 hectares. Paris's surface in the late eighteenth century was 3,400 hectares; Roche, *Le peuple de Paris*, 23.

[18] *Istoriia Moskvy s drevneishikh vremen*, 1:283; Roche, *Le peuple de Paris*, 31. On working with pre-Reform Russian urban demographic data, see Mironov, *Russkii gorod*, 85–93.

City. Here, in the city center between the river and today's Boulevard Ring, were concentrated Moscow's government, commerce, and much of the aristocracy. Covering about 10 percent of the city's surface, this area in the 1820s had 83 inhabitants per hectare. Farther out lay the Earthen City, between today's Boulevard Ring and the Garden Ring, also about 10 percent of the city's surface, with a density of 76 per hectare. All around the Earthen City, on the north side of the river, lay the sprawling suburbs that took up 61 percent of Moscow's territory but where only 22 people lived per hectare. Finally, the area south of the river, Zamoskvorech'e, had 19 percent of Moscow's surface and 25 inhabitants per hectare.[19] By comparison, in eighteenth-century Paris, the outskirts averaged 25 to 100 per hectare, and the central districts ranged from 500 per hectare (similar to the City of London in 1801) to 1,300 (comparable to the most overcrowded parts of Manhattan's Lower East Side at the turn of the twentieth century). Not surprisingly, expansion in eighteenth- and nineteenth-century Paris was concentrated on the periphery; Moscow, by contrast, saw infill development in the city center.[20]

Housing density and construction materials followed the same pattern. In Paris, the citywide average in 1789 was 7.35 houses per hectare. In Moscow, the White City in 1782 had only 1.60 homesteads[21] per hectare, a figure that rose to 2.25 in the less aristocratic Earthen City (where houses were smaller) before dropping to 0.99 in the suburbs and 1.14 in Zamoskvorech'e. In Paris and London by 1789, wooden houses had been rare for over a century. In Moscow by contrast, 52 percent of the houses in the White City in 1782 were built of wood, as were 87 percent in both the Earthen City and Zamoskvorech'e, and 94 percent in the suburbs.[22]

Just how rural Moscow looked to Westerners is apparent in the French painter Auguste Cadolle's drawing from the 1820s of the area just outside the White City where the Iauza flows into the Moscow River. From the artist's vantage point about a mile east of Red Square, near the present-day location of the Foreign Literature Library, the foreground consists of a broad meadow, dotted with trees, littered with boulders and logs, and criss-crossed by dirt paths. Only in the distance do we see the low houses and tall church spires of more densely settled neighborhoods.[23]

---

[19] The population figures are based on Le Cointe, *Guide*, table facing p. 86.

[20] Roche, *Le peuple de Paris*, 48, 137, 154–5; Jean-Luc Pinol, *Le monde des villes au XIXe siècle* (Paris: Hachette, 1991), 141–2.

[21] *Dvory*, units composed of a house and its associated sheds and outbuildings.

[22] V. G. Ruban, *Opisanie imperatorskago stolichnago goroda Moskvy* (St Petersburg: pri Artilleriiskom i Inzhenernom Shliakhetnom Kadetskom Korpuse, 1782); Roche, *Le peuple de Paris*, 31, 48, 138–9; Le Cointe, *Guide*, 86; Fernand Braudel, *The Structures of Everyday Life: The Limits of the Possible*, Civilization and Capitalism 15th–18th Century, vol. 1, tr. Siân Reynolds (New York: Harper & Row, 1985), 268; Emily Cockayne, *Hubbub: Filth, Noise & Stench in England, 1600–1770* (New Haven: Yale University Press, 2007), 131.

[23] Skorniakova, *Staraia Moskva*, 203.

Moscow's rurality had advantages, as foreigners sometimes conceded, especially when considered in conjunction with the climate. The winter cold, widely regarded as conducive to good health, suppressed both disease and the stench of sewage, trash, and polluted waterways. The snow cover, and the use of sleighs instead of carriages, eliminated the noisy clatter of hooves and wheels, and facilitated provisioning the city with wholesome frozen foods. The easy availability of firewood eliminated the need for the foul-smelling coal fires that filled the air (and blanketed the streets, interiors, and even food) of London and other cities with soot.[24] As for the persistence of wood construction, many Russians considered log houses to be warmer and drier than masonry buildings, and the low cost of lumber as a building material may have shielded Moscow from the housing shortage afflicting many Western cities.[25]

Moscow's rural quality and cold winters seemed to exercise a beneficent influence on its social structure as well. The streets appeared less crowded than in Paris or London, a welcome sight in an age when Western elites increasingly feared the urban "mob,"[26] and Moscow exhibited lower levels of conspicuous poverty.[27] European Russia before the mid-nineteenth century had no shortage of arable land, and since villages managed their land in common and periodically redistributed it, no large class of landless peasants emerged. Moreover, it was difficult for peasants to leave their villages because they were bound by the system of communal liability for taxes and military conscription, and half of them were enserfed in addition. As a result, although Moscow teemed with migrant workers, the influx of paupers was limited, the more so as the government conducted periodic sweeps to expel beggars and vagrants from the city. The homeless in any case faced long odds in the cold climate, which also discouraged displaying one's physical ailments to elicit alms.

Sexual vice was also less visible. Foreign men marveled at the casual immodesty with which Russian women stripped naked to use the steam baths,[28] but there was a consensus that prostitution was less conspicuous than in the West. When Paul I ordered a crackdown in 1800, Moscow police found only sixty-nine women to arrest.[29] Owing perhaps to the climate, the sex trade in Moscow and

---

[24] Cockayne, *Hubbub*, 93, 146, 152.

[25] Heinrich Storch, *Gemaehlde von St. Petersburg*, 2 vols. (Riga: Hartknoch, n.d. [1794]), 1:33–4; Lees and Lees, *Cities and the Making of Modern Europe*, 59–60.

[26] On this topic, see Robert Shoemaker, *The London Mob: Violence and Disorder in Eighteenth-Century England* (London: Hambledon Continuum, 2004), passim.

[27] Le Cointe, *Guide*, 305; Wichelhausen, *Züge zu einem Gemählde von Moskwa*, 291–2.

[28] On this topic, see A. G. Cross, "The Russian *Banya* in the Descriptions of Foreign Travellers and in the Depictions of Foreign and Russian Artists," *Oxford Slavonic Papers*, New Series, vol. 24 (1991), 34–59.

[29] N. I. Solov'ev, "Presledovanie prostitutok v tsarstvovanie Imperatora Pavla I-go," *RS*, 165 (January–March 1916), 363–4. According to another source, the number arrested was 139: Gastev, *Materialy*, 293. On the seeming paucity of streetwalkers, see Friedrich Raupach, *Reise von St. Petersburg nach dem Gesundbrunnen zu Lipezk am Don: Nebst einem Beitrage zur Charakteristik der Russen* (Breslau: Wilhelm Gottlieb Korn, 1809), 207; Georg Reinbeck, *Flüchtige Bemerkungen*

St Petersburg operated more out of taverns and brothels than openly in the streets.[30] Francisco de Miranda's diary includes repeated entries about sending his servant to procure prostitutes, but he does not mention streetwalkers.[31]

In general, the low density of population and housing served to alleviate all sorts of urban ills. While not a utopian "green country Towne" as envisioned by William Penn, Moscow apparently did not assault the senses or present a spectacle of human degradation to quite the same degree as large cities in Western Europe.

The goal of Catherine and her successors was to make Moscow more "urban" in a European sense. As we have seen, many foreigners were skeptical about the results, but to judge by the memoirs of the Siberian Bishop Nikodim (Nikodim Kazantsev, 1803–74), provincial Russians were impressed. Kazantsev was the son of a cleric from a village near Moscow, and saw the metropolis for the first time in 1818 when he was an impressionable 15-year-old on his way to the seminary with his mother. By that time, Catherine was long dead, but the reforms she had launched had transformed the urban landscape. Looking back a quarter-century later, Kazantsev recalled that

Until then I had known only two towns, Ruza and Zvenigorod. Next to Moscow, those are villages. We enter through the Tver' Gate; I am amazed: the streets are paved with stone, something I had not seen before, and I dare not walk on them. The houses are all of stone, and huge; they seemed to me as though each was a palace.

Accustomed to the softness of country paths, the two walkers' legs soon hurt from the cobblestone, but Kazantsev nonetheless talked his mother into going immediately to the Kremlin. "I was continually in a state of inexpressible exuberance and could not believe my eyes: so amazed was I by Moscow's magnificence. Here I particularly recall one incident: on Tverskaia [Street], across from the Razumovskii house, I saw a brawl between chimney-sweeps and watchmen. Those villainous watchmen! How inhumanely they beat the chimney-sweep."[32] Catherine's tools of imperial pedagogy and social control—the paved streets, grand buildings, and omnipresent police—thus made a deep impression on people who had never seen such things.

One way to gain a sense of Moscow's transformation is to follow Kazantsev's path. He entered Moscow through the Tver' Gate, located at the site of today's Belorussian Railroad Station. This was one of the checkpoints in the customs

auf einer Reise von St. Petersburg über Moskwa, Grodno, Warschau, Breslau nach Deutschland im Jahre 1805, 2 vols. (Leipzig: Wilhelm Rein, 1806), 2:134.

[30] Miranda, *Diario*, 45; L. Khaliutin, "Moskovskii syshchik Iakovlev: Vospominaniia," *Sovremennik*, 75 (May 1859), 79–94, here: 85–6; Alexander M. Martin, "Sewage and the City: Filth, Smell, and Representations of Urban Life in Moscow, 1770–1880," *Russian Review*, 67/2 (April 2008), 243–74, esp. 256–7.

[31] Miranda, *Diario*, 16, 36, 86, 103, 104, 105, 139, 159, 211, 213.

[32] Nikodim Kazantsev, "Zhizn' arkhimandrita Nikodima Kazantseva," part 3: *Bogoslovskii vestnik*, no. 3 (March 1910), 404–27, here: 404–5.

wall where the police verified travelers' identities. These checkpoints existed until 1852, when the railroads rendered them obsolete and police control of travelers' identity was abolished.[33] Once inside the city, Kazantsev would have encountered few additional obstacles to movement. As will be described below, the nighttime police barriers in the streets had disappeared under Catherine, and she also initiated the process of razing the old fortifications inside the city. Moscow's master plan of 1775 called for the wall of the White City to be replaced with the Boulevard Ring, work on which began in earnest under Paul I and was completed under Nicholas I.[34] In substituting a tree-lined public promenade for a militarily useless rampart that obstructed the circulation of people and fresh air, Moscow followed the same model as the boulevards of Paris and, later, the Ringstrasse of Vienna in the 1860s.[35] The outer ring of fortifications, the Earthen Wall, was demolished in 1816–30 to make way for the Garden Ring.[36] Only the Kitai-Gorod Wall remained, to be razed at last in the 1930s.

Other aspects of Moscow's reconstruction were the stuccoed masonry buildings and cobblestone streets that impressed Kazantsev. Cobblestone was common across the Western world. It had drawbacks, as Kazantsev noted when he complained of his sore legs, but it was better than the alternative: dirt roads that were drenched in animal waste and were continually churned up by man, beast, and vehicles. It was also believed that cobblestone protected public health by blocking harmful vapors that emanated from the soil. Making the city clean, safe, and beautiful was likewise the aim of efforts to remove slaughterhouses, tanneries, and other polluting or malodorous industries from the city center.

Unifying and beautifying the city and creating public spaces (squares, boulevards), while demarcating the city clearly from the countryside and subjecting new arrivals to strict controls: these policies originated in the mid-eighteenth century, were systematized by Catherine II, and continued unabated until the Great Reforms.

SMELL, HYGIENE, AND WATER

Most descriptions of Moscow prior to the mid-nineteenth century focus on what people observed visually, but in fact the first indication that one was approaching the city seems to have been the smell. New arrivals suffered a veritable olfactory assault. One who recorded his experiences was Julius Klaproth (1783–1835), an

[33] P. B. Sytin, *Iz istorii moskovskikh ulits (Ocherki)* (3rd edn., Moscow: Moskovskii rabochii, 1958), 528–9; D. Blagovo, *Rasskazy babushki: Iz vospominanii piati pokolenii, zapisannye i sobrannye ee vnukom D. Blagovo* (Leningrad: Nauka, 1989), 6.

[34] Gulianitskii, *Moskva i slozhivshiesia russkie goroda*, 81, 159.

[35] Delattre, *Les douze heures noires*, 155; Carl E. Schorske, *Fin-de-Siècle Vienna: Politics and Culture* (New York: Vintage, 1981), 27–33.

[36] Sytin, *Iz istorii moskovskikh ulits*, 334.

Orientalist scholar from Berlin and seasoned globetrotter. He had joined the Academy of Sciences in St Petersburg in 1804, participated in a mission to China, and upon his return in 1807 was sent to the Caucasus. In his account of the latter expedition, which was written after he had left Russia in disgust and was published in German, French, and English editions, Klaproth writes:

When after a slow and cautious journey we were yet several wersts from the gates of Moskwa, I perceived a strong and extremely disagreeable smell, which, as I was assured, proceeded from the city, and grew more intolerable the nearer we approached to it. In the streets, most of which are unpaved, the mud was nearly up to the axle, and it was with difficulty that with our weary horses we reached the so-called Polish inn.

He did little sightseeing in Moscow, he added, because of "the endless filth and the stench in the streets."[37]

Moscow's olfactory impact on Russians could be similarly strong. As noted earlier, how the city looked and felt made a deep impression in 1818 on the village cleric's son Nikodim Kazantsev, who was 15 years old at the time and headed for the seminary. A rare account of how it *smelled* (albeit written in the 1870s, when such sensibilities were far keener) is provided by another participant in the imperial social project, Kazantsev's contemporary Mikhail Nazimov (1806–78), a nobleman and provincial official's son. Nazimov was 17 years old when he first arrived in Moscow in the summer of 1824 to enroll in the university:

We were still only approaching [Moscow] when I already noticed the stench in the air, which was especially unpleasant and oppressive after seven days' traveling on the open country road. From the direction of the Rogozhskaia Gate, Moscow offers no particular vista to hold the traveler's attentive gaze, and in addition it was almost night when we reached the gate. Driving along Rogozhskaia Street and beyond, I thought I would suffocate from all the foul vapors in the streets and lanes, and looked forward anxiously to spending the night more agreeably somewhere in a closed room. Our carter took us to a place he knew, known at the time as the Ukrainian Inn, in the narrowest lane between Nikol'ka and Il'inka Streets [in Kitai-Gorod]. They gave us a room for 25 kopeks a day. They brought in our unassuming luggage and showed us our beds and the other accouterments, and all of this was filthy and unclean, and the pestilential air seemed unbearable, the more so because of the noise and chatter in the hallways and the courtyard. I didn't sleep at all that night, and learned by experience what it means to be homesick.[38]

---

[37] Julius von Klaproth, *Travels in the Caucasus and Georgia, Performed in the Years 1807 and 1808 by Command of the Russian Government*, tr. F. Shoberl (London: Henry Colburn, 1814), 54; *Russkii Biograficheskii Slovar': Izdanie Imperatorskago Russkago Istoricheskago Obshchestva*, 25 vols. (St Petersburg, 1896–1918; repr. edn. New York: Kraus Reprint, 1962), 8:727–9; *Allgemeine Deutsche Biographie*, ed. Historische Commission bei der Königl. Akademie der Wissenschaften, 56 vols. (Leipzig: Duncker & Humblot, 1875–1912), 16:51–60.

[38] M. Nazimov, "V provintsii i v Moskve s 1812 po 1828 god: Iz vospominanii starozhila," *Russkii Vestnik*, 124 (July 1876), 74–161, quotation on 127–8; N. Liubimov, "Mikhail Leont'evich Nazimov," in *Rech' i otchet, chitannye v torzhestvennom sobranii Imperatorskago Moskovskago universiteta 12-go ianvaria 1879 goda* (Moscow: V Universitetskoi Tipografii, 1879), 279–87.

None of this was peculiar to Moscow. At the epicenter of Western refinement, Versailles, an observer in 1764 reported that "The unpleasant odors in the park, gardens, even the château, make one's gorge rise. The communicating passages, courtyards, buildings in the wings, corridors, are full of urine and feces." "Livestock defecated in the great gallery" of Versailles, notes the historian Alain Corbin, and "the stench reached even the king's chamber."[39] Malodorous filth was a universal feature of life in the eighteenth century, and Moscow was less bad than many Western cities. In Moscow, thanks to the dispersed housing pattern, there was a greater likelihood of the sun drying up refuse and air currents dispersing odors, and the detached houses with private courtyards made it possible to install privies and bury rubbish. Less density translated into less awful hygienic conditions.

Still, the nastiness was everywhere. The root cause was common to all pre-modern towns: the colossal amounts of waste generated by animals, households, and industry. Rodents—particularly numerous because of Moscow's wooden buildings and grain warehouses, but unrecognized at the time as carriers of disease—as well as cats and dogs were everywhere.[40] The strongest smell came from horses, of which there were an estimated 50,000 in Moscow in the late eighteenth century.[41] A horse typically produces about 8,278 kilograms of raw sewage per year,[42] of which some, but by no means all, was collected as fertilizer.[43] (In 1813 in the town of Tambov, a Moscow aristocrat was appalled that dung was simply left in the streets, which caused a terrible stench.[44]) As for rubbish and slops from households and industries, including such malodorous ones as tanners and tallow-chandlers, Moscow had no public provision for trash collection or wastewater drainage. Instead, householders dumped their waste into pits dug on their property; a grate at the bottom caught the solid materials while the liquids seeped into the soil.[45]

Another challenge was human waste. How this was disposed of in private homes is described by the physician Heinrich Ludwig von Attenhofer in his medical topography of St Petersburg in 1817:

---

[39] Corbin, *The Foul and the Fragrant*, 27.

[40] Lapin, *Peterburg: Zapakhi i zvuki*, 61–2, 216; Alexander, *Bubonic Plague*, 67–9.

[41] Wichelhausen, *Züge zu einem Gemählde von Moskwa*, 364.

[42] Eileen Fabian Wheeler, *Horse Stable and Riding Arena Design* (Ames, Ia.: Blackwell, 2006), 91.

[43] Lapin, *Peterburg: Zapakhi i zvuki*, 155; Vladimir Dal', "The Petersburg Yardkeeper," in Nikolai Nekrasov, ed., *Petersburg: The Physiology of a City*, tr. and ed. Thomas Gaiton Marullo (Evanston, Ill.: Northwestern University Press, 2009), 61; A. Roger Ekirch, *At Day's Close: Night in Times Past* (New York: W. W. Norton, 2005), 160, 166.

[44] "Griboedovskaia Moskva v pis'makh M. A. Volkovoi k V. I. Lanskoi 1812–1818 gg," part 1: *VE*, kniga 8 (August 1874), 572–666, here: 642.

[45] M. A. Tikhomirov, "Otchet sanitarnago vracha Prechistenskoi chasti," *IMGD* (1 August 1878), 44–55, esp. 44–5; V. Shervinskii, "Otchet sanitarnago vracha Sushchevskoi chasti," *IMGD* (27 January 1879), 6–34, esp. 14.

The privies of very many houses are merely a box, nailed together from decaying boards, from which the stinking tube leads to manure beds that are rarely dug deep enough into the ground. Not only do these boards soon begin to rot and threaten at any moment to collapse, but the mephitic air that develops in the adjoining areas, which at times are bedrooms and kitchens, is certainly neither appetizing nor healthful, especially when a thaw sets in.

Some houses had their privy in the courtyard, Attenhofer explained, and people who used them risked catching a cold. In other houses, especially wooden ones, the privies were so close to the main house that their stench spread through the interior rooms. Lastly, some had no privy at all: the residents simply added their waste to the dung heap or dumped it in the courtyard, and "it is surely only thanks to the climate that this highest degree of human uncleanness does not more often bring about calamitous diseases."[46]

Sewage was supposed to be hauled by private contractors to dumps outside the city. The best-case scenario was reflected in a contract from 1815 with cesspool cleaners who serviced the houses of Moscow's governor-general, the civil governor, and the police chief, as well as barracks, prisons, and other institutions: twice a year, the cesspools were to be drained completely, but otherwise they were only to be kept from overflowing.[47]

As in other countries, the infrastructural problem was compounded by indifference. The enormous palace that Bazhenov planned to build in the Kremlin was a marvel of neoclassical design, but when Catherine reviewed the plans, she was dismayed to find that they made no provision for privies.[48] Where privies existed, the cesspools were rarely drained. Much waste was simply abandoned in the mostly unpaved streets and courtyards, where it mixed with soil, rain water, and assorted rubbish to form the mud and dust for which Moscow was notorious. Many people were in Moscow only temporarily and had no access to sanitary facilities. Accounts from St Petersburg in the 1790s speak of migrant workers sleeping in the open in the summer,[49] and reports from Moscow in the 1870s indicate that in many coaching inns, the coachmen spent the night either in their vehicles or crammed into small huts and with no access to a privy.[50] Remains of slaughtered animals and noxious wastes from manufacturers were disposed of in similarly unceremonious manner.

---

[46] Heinrich Ludwig von Attenhofer, *Medizinische Topographie der Haupt- und Residenzstadt St. Petersburg* (Zurich: Orell, Füssli, 1817), 18.

[47] TsIAM f. 105, op. 4, d. 423, ll. 2–3 ob. In London and Paris, human waste was recycled as agricultural fertilizer: Cockayne, *Hubbub*, 93, 184, 200; Donald Reid, *Paris Sewers and Sewermen: Realities and Representations* (Cambridge, Mass.: Harvard University Press, 1991), 11.

[48] Dixon, *Catherine the Great*, 212.

[49] Storch, *Gemaehlde von St. Petersburg*, 2:366.

[50] Shervinskii, "Otchet," 19; K. N. Nikitin, "Otchet sanitarnago vracha Meshchanskoi chasti," *IMGD* (15 September 1878), 10–31, here: 22.

The problem was partly seasonal. It was eased in the winter when everything froze, but then returned with a vengeance when the sun warmed up what had accumulated in the snow. Thus, a visiting Russian general wrote sarcastically in 1727: "It is only two days since the thaw started, but because of the cleanliness here, which you know about, the air is now so balsamic and there is such a mist that one can't even go out of the cabin."[51]

The same merciful cold that neutralized the stench outside also drove people indoors. There, overcrowding—John T. Alexander estimates the average density at more than seven people per room on the eve of the plague of 1771[52]—as well as lack of sanitation, the proximity of animals, and a preference for warmth over ventilation, created grim conditions. A vivid account is provided by Dr Wichelhausen in the medical topography of Moscow that he wrote after several years practicing medicine there toward the end of Catherine's reign. Sometimes, he was called by nobles to attend to their serf domestics. These people, he writes, were typically housed in a simple log building, a mere 24 to 28 feet in length and width and 9 to 10 feet in height. (The length of a foot was defined variously in different countries; if Wichelhausen was using the English foot, which was also used in Russia, the measurements are 7.87 to 9.18 meters for height and 2.95 to 3.28 meters for width.) The servants' huts were usually blackened by smoke, and almost devoid of ventilation.

In the middle of such a room one sometimes finds a hole in the ground into which liquid refuse is poured. In one corner there is always a large stove in which bread is baked and meals are cooked. Near the stove is a wooden scaffolding (*lezhanka*) that is intended for sleeping and where the wash is put to dry as well. If you imagine such a room, where the greatest lack of cleanliness prevails and a horde of 15 to 20 serfs—men, women, and children, all intermingled—are encamped: then you have to wonder how these unfortunates can stand it, since clean air is one of the most urgent necessities of the biological economy. I was sometimes asked by nobles to attend to dangerously ill patients in such a room. When I would enter, I thought I was going to suffocate from the heat and foul air. There would be an almost unbearable smell if meals had recently been prepared with hempseed oil and garlic or if bread had just been baked. The sick often lay on the stove or the scaffolding, and I had to climb up a small ladder to reach them. In the winter, they generally wore a dirty sheepskin coat and lay with their head on their gown (*kaftan*). When I wanted to feel their pulse, and they opened their sheepskin, a vapor always rose from their skin that smelled of garlic.

Wichelhausen was shocked: even horses, he thought, were treated better than this.[53] The conditions he described were little different from those in the crowded cities of nineteenth-century Britain. The average of Wichelhausen's estimates is 390 cubic feet of air per person. By comparison, in mid-Victorian

[51] *Istoriia Moskvy s drevneishikh vremen*, 1:285.
[52] Alexander, *Bubonic Plague*, 77.
[53] Wichelhausen, *Züge zu einem Gemählde von Moskwa*, 322–4.

Britain, the urban poor often had 100 to 200 cubic feet, and the law required at least 300 cubic feet in workhouses and 600 in army barracks. None of these levels appeared wholesome to British doctors; in their view, a person needed at least 1,000 cubic feet of air.[54]

The stench of the big city was rarely problematized in Russia before the era of the Great Reforms, but a related issue, the shortage of clean drinking water, was already raised in the Moscow instruction to the Legislative Commission of 1767.[55] "Among Moscow's inhabitants, very few—only the well-to-do and the rich—could enjoy clean, healthful water," an article in the journal *Messenger of Europe* (*Vestnik Evropy*) recalled in 1804, when it briefly looked as though the problem might be solved. Clean water had to be carted from distant springs and was expensive: the article's author, although he had only "a small family and very few servants," paid over 60 rubles a year. Those who could not afford these prices depended instead on rivers, streams, stagnant ponds, and wells, and hence "consumed water that was either hard and foul-tasting, or stale and turbid, or rotten and harmful."[56] The alternative to drinking water, the article might well have added, was alcohol, which sustained the crown's liquor-tax revenues but also contributed to the widespread drunkenness that threatened public order, harmed family budgets, and undercut the government's efforts to improve Russia's international image.

To remedy this situation, Catherine initiated an ambitious plan in 1779 for an aqueduct that would supply the city's 160,000 or so inhabitants with 330,000 *vedro* per day from the springs at Mytishchi. One *vedro* ("bucket") is 12.3 liters, so the anticipated per capita average was 25 liters a day. After a quarter-century of delays and cost overruns, it was completed in 1804. It was a difficult engineering project, because the aqueduct, which was built of brick and 24 kilometers long, had to maintain a steady downward slope across hilly terrain. The critical point was the Sokol'niki woods in northeast Moscow, where the aqueduct had to be buried underground: the wooden grillage supporting the pipes rotted and settled in the soft, sandy soil, the pipes cracked and sprang leaks, and groundwater seeped in. The outcome was that the aqueduct ended up transporting only poor-quality groundwater from Sokol'niki, as became apparent when a cave-in in Sokol'niki blocked the aqueduct in 1823 but 40,000 *vedro* a day kept coming out anyway. After extensive reconstruction of the aqueduct, Moscow by 1835 was receiving 200,000 *vedro*, not even two-thirds of Catherine's target, and for a

---

[54] Charles A. Cameron, *A Manual of Hygiene, Public and Private, and Compendium of Sanitary Laws* (Dublin: Hodges, Foster; London: Bailliere, Tindall, & Cox; 1874), 106, 108, 113. I thank Christopher Hamlin for drawing my attention to the British laws against overcrowding.

[55] "Nakaz ot zhitelei goroda Moskvy," 122; V. Androssov, *Statisticheskaia zapiska o Moskve* (Moscow: V tipografii Semena Selivanovskago, 1832), 3–5; Robert Lyall, *The Character of the Russians and a Detailed History of Moscow* (London: T. Cadell; Edinburgh: W. Blackwood; 1823), 47; Raupach, *Reise*, 88; Wichelhausen, *Züge zu einem Gemählde von Moskwa*, 69–76.

[56] "Mytishchinskoi vodovod (Prislannaia stat'ia)," *VE*, 23 (December 1804), 213–29, here: 226–7.

population that had doubled since her time. This water was piped to public reservoirs, whence it was delivered across the city by commercial water carriers.

Viewed in international perspective, the story of the Moscow aqueduct suggests that urban modernization in Russia lost momentum in the first half of the nineteenth century. In Catherine's time, an aqueduct to supply 25 liters of water a day per inhabitant was a forward-looking project. In Paris, the average at the beginning of the nineteenth century was a mere 8 liters. Given the uncertainty of the statistics on population size and water usage (e.g. how much was used for domestic versus industrial purposes), these figures should be treated with caution, but they indicate that Moscow was not backward by European standards. In the next half-century, however, Moscow fell behind. England led the way in the 1810s with the development of municipal water-supply systems. In Paris, the average daily supply rose to 100 liters by the 1830s, and when New York's Croton Aqueduct opened in 1842, it provided a daily supply in excess of 400 liters per inhabitant. In Germany, the first citywide water-supply systems began operating in Hamburg (1848) and Berlin (1853). In Moscow, meanwhile, the old aqueduct once more deteriorated so badly that by the winter of 1847–8, it was back down to 100,000 *vedro* (1.23 million liters)—less than one-third of Catherine's target, and equivalent to less than 4 liters a day per inhabitant. After failed attempts to pump water from the Moscow River, the city council in 1870 began discussing the need for a completely new aqueduct, but work got under way only in 1890. The extent of the unmet need is apparent from the fact that the goal, for a city now approaching a million inhabitants, was 3.5 million *vedro* per day, or 43 million liters.[57]

Over a period of decades, the water problem developed damaging consequences for the imperial social project. In Catherine's time, the health implications of clean water were poorly understood. Her government subscribed to the accepted theory that airborne miasmas were key sources of disease. Officials therefore strove to eliminate foul smells emanating from slaughterhouses, stagnant ponds, and the like. They also tore down ramparts and widened streets to promote air circulation, and laid pavement to block ground emanations. Water, on the other hand, was held by medical theory to be harmful, so efforts to promote hygiene tended to discourage bathing.[58]

---

[57] Ann F. La Berge, *Mission and Method: The Early Nineteenth-Century French Public Health Movement* (Cambridge: Cambridge University Press, 1992), 190–1; George J. Lankevich, *New York: A Short History* (New York: New York University Press, 1998), 82; I. F. Rerberg, *Moskovskii vodoprovod: Istoricheskii ocherk ustroistva i razvitiia vodosnabzheniia g. Moskvy. Opisanie novago vodoprovoda* (Moscow: Tipo-litografiia A. P. Khailova, 1892), 4–27; *Zhurnaly zasedanii kommissii po vodosnabzheniiu goroda Moskvy* (St Petersburg: Tipografiia brat. Panteleevykh, 1882), 4–6; Pinol, *Le monde des villes*, 101–2; Philipp Steuer, *Die Wasserversorgung der Städte und Ortschaften: Ihre wirtschaftliche Entwicklung und Analyse* (Berlin: Franz Siemenroth, 1912), 18–19.

[58] See, for example, the advice on bathing and clean linens offered in "Ob odezhde," *Moskovskii Kur'er*, chast' 2 (1805), 201–4.

Europe in the nineteenth century experienced a revolutionary change in attitudes, as cleanliness and water consumption came to be seen both as necessary to good health and as signs of cultural progress. British per-capita soap consumption almost doubled from 1841 to 1861,[59] and a British journal wrote in 1866 that "The quantity of water [that man] employs is the test of his civilisation. The community that uses five gallons of water per head per diem is less civilised than that which uses ten gallons, and so on."[60] Middle-class urban reformers in Britain gave top priority to sanitation, especially the construction of water mains and sewers, thereby suggesting that the misery of the slums was not caused by poverty and overcrowding but by the workers' own lack of hygiene.[61] In France, the liberal bourgeoisie used the notion of cleanliness both to discredit conservatives (Jules Michelet derided the Middle Ages, which conservatives idealized, as "a thousand years without a bath"[62]) and to rationalize its own fear and hostility toward the working class. Dirtiness also loomed large in Orientalist and colonialist rhetoric: Germans invoked this trope to assert their superiority over the peoples of Eastern Europe, and Russians did likewise when their army occupied the Danubian Principalities.[63]

In a variety of ways, the revolution in sensibilities about water and cleanliness contributed to the progress-oriented, nationalist, middle-class culture developing in nineteenth-century Europe. Water and cleanliness were consequently important barometers of Russia's civilizational progress. In 1830, writing in German for a foreign audience, the German-Russian academician Georg Engelhardt boasted that the "the biggest water closet in the world," an odor-free marvel of engineering, could be found at the fair grounds in Nizhnii Novgorod.[64] On the other hand, Faddei Bulgarin, a journalist otherwise unstinting in his praise for Russia's accomplishments, complained in 1843 that Russian restaurants were below European standards because they gave the same napkin to several customers in a row, something Bulgarin found disgusting.[65] If Russia was to be respected by

---

[59] Francis Barrymore Smith, *The People's Health, 1830–1910* (New York: Holmes & Meier, 1979), 219.

[60] Review of J. F. Bateman, *On the Supply of Water to London from the Sources of the River Severn*, in *Journal of Social Science*, 1/4 (1866), 230–1, here: 230.

[61] See, on this topic: Christopher Hamlin, *Public Health and Social Justice in the Age of Chadwick: Britain, 1800–1854* (Cambridge: Cambridge University Press, 1998).

[62] This famous quotation is from Jules Michelet, *La sorcière* (Paris: E. Dentu, 1862), 110.

[63] Corbin, *The Foul and the Fragrant*; see also Constance Classen, "The Odor of the Other: Olfactory Symbolism and Cultural Categories," *Ethos*, 20/2 (June 1992), 133–66; Vejas Gabriel Liulevicius, *The German Myth of the East: 1800 to the Present* (Oxford: Oxford University Press, 2009), 44; Victor Taki, "Russia on the Danube: Imperial Expansion and Political Reform in Moldavia and Wallachia, 1812–1834," PhD diss., Central European University, Budapest, 2007, 84.

[64] "Bemerkungen auf einer Reise von St. Petersburg nach dem Ural, im Sommer 1830," in Georg Engelhardt, *Russische Miscellen zur genauern Kenntniss Russlands und seiner Bewohner*, 4 vols. (St Petersburg: bei der Kaiserlichen Akademie der Wissenschaften, 1828–32), 4:165.

[65] Faddei Bulgarin, *Peterburgskie ocherki F. V. Bulgarina*, ed. Al'bin Konechnyi (St Petersburg: Petropolis, 2010), 164.

Europeans and inhabited by people who were European, it had to embrace a rising standard of cleanliness. The failure of the regime to build an adequate water-supply infrastructure in Moscow was therefore a hindrance to the success of the imperial social project.[66]

MOSCOW NIGHTS

Another area of dramatic change in everyday sensory experience was the daily cycle of light and dark. Urban modernity would be unrecognizable without what the sociologist Murray Melbin calls the city's "expansion into the dark hours."[67] The historian Joachim Schlör argues that in nineteenth-century Europe, darkness, by temporarily weakening social controls, created the "possibility of widening one's own horizons, of transgressing boundaries," which in turn promoted the "internal urbanization" of the individual.[68] This transgressiveness also had a sinister side that was embodied memorably by the figure of Jack the Ripper. The urban night of the nineteenth century gave rise to images that are an indelible part of the modern social imaginary—brightly lit boulevards and cabarets, vice and crime, and policemen patrolling their beat.

Prior to the nineteenth century, European cities and towns lived under what the French historian Simone Delattre calls a "nocturnal old regime," a premodern nighttime order that persisted until the nineteenth century. Night was fraught with perils both real and imagined. Medicine warned that it brought on toxic miasmas, and of course it heightened the risk of fires and accidents. In the West in the early modern period, religious and social tensions aggravated long-standing fears of demons, witches, and robbers, causing nighttime to appear even more threatening than in the Middle Ages. As the historian A. Roger Ekirch puts it, "the early modern nightscape [was] a forbidding place plagued by pestilential vapors, diabolical spirits, natural calamity, and human depravity, the four horsemen of the nocturnal apocalypse. Of these were the darkest nightmares composed."[69]

Faced with these threats, early modern townspeople battened down the hatches. Referring to France, Simone Delattre writes that "The urban night of the past, hostile to any pursuit of individual fulfillment, was announced by the ceremony of the community's twofold closing against the indistinct perils that besieged it at nightfall: closing the city walls against threats from without; closing the streets, across which chains were extended by the inhabitants, against

---

[66] On the topic of water supplies, see Alison K. Smith, "Public Works in an Autocratic State: Water Supplies in an Imperial Russian Town," *Environment and History*, 11 (2005), 319–42.

[67] Murray Melbin, "Night as Frontier," *American Sociological Review*, 43 (February 1978), 3–22, here: 3.

[68] Schlör, *Nights in the Big City*, 16, 241, 287, quotation on 241.

[69] Ekirch, *At Day's Close*, 20, 56.

disturbances from within."[70] Not only the public routines of society, but also the inner lives of individuals were molded by the "nocturnal old regime." Artificial light allowed the rich to stay up into the night and then sleep until morning. By contrast, argues Ekirch, darkness made common people in early modern Europe more likely to go to sleep early but then experience an interval of quiet wakefulness after midnight that encouraged prayer, conversation, intimacy, or reflecting on one's dreams.[71]

Similar conditions prevailed in mid-eighteenth-century Moscow. There was almost no street lighting, and clouds frequently blotted out the moon and stars. Most houses were dimly lit with rush-lights (*luchiny*) or at best tallow candles, and only a faint glow escaped through their small windows. The dark forced officials from their offices and merchants from their shops, which fire-safety laws forbade them to heat or light,[72] so that in the evening, a journalist noted in 1830, it was "empty, dark and silent as in a tomb" in the shopping district of Kitai-Gorod, the heart of Moscow's retail trade.[73] Nighttime reduced the bastions of state and aristocracy to scattered islands of illumination. Lanterns often lit the carriages of the wealthy, and in upscale neighborhoods light shone through glass windows that could, by the end of the century, be made over three meters high for the staggering price of 200–300 rubles—the yearly salary of a junior official.[74] An isolated few used light to dramatize their wealth, like the owners of the Pashkov mansion (see Illustration 2.1), whose magnificent wrought-iron fence near the Kremlin was crowned by huge lanterns that were "illuminated every night [and] exhibit a scene at once majestic and enchanting," according to a book that the Russian writer Pavel Svin'in published in the United States in 1813.[75] Illuminations and fireworks on festive occasions displayed wealth and power by briefly dispelling the darkness.[76] Candles were also lit in front of roadside shrines: according to the early nineteenth-century German traveler Georg Reinbeck, "In the suburbs, every ten steps you take, you come across images of saints that are erected in front of a little wooden chapel, where wax candles burn within and donations are made in boxes that are placed alongside."[77] Artificial light was thus associated with government, aristocracy, and religion, but only inside upper-class

[70] Delattre, *Les douze heures noires*, 23.

[71] Ekirch, *At Day's Close*, 300–23.

[72] Wichelhausen, *Züge zu einem Gemählde von Moskwa*, 33; Abbé Jean-François Georgel, in de Grève, *Le voyage en Russie*, 220; Lyall, *The Character of the Russians*, 279; I. Slonov, *Iz zhizni torgovoi Moskvy (Polveka nazad)* (Moscow: Tipografiia Russkago T-va Pechatnago i Izdatel'skago Dela, 1914), 166.

[73] XLXXLXXX, "Moskovskie riady," *Moskovskii Vestnik*, vol. 1 (1830), 207–18, here: 209.

[74] L. V. Tydman, *Izba. Dom. Dvorets. Zhiloi inter'er Rossii s 1700 po 1840-e gody* (Moscow: Progress-Traditsiia, 2000), 174; Lyall, *The Character of the Russians*, 74.

[75] [Svin'in], *Sketches of Moscow and St. Petersburg*, 31.

[76] On fireworks, see for example: Wortman, *Scenarios of Power*, 1:104–6, 118–22; Berelowitch and Medvedkova, *Histoire de Saint-Pétersbourg*, 136.

[77] Reinbeck, *Flüchtige Bemerkungen*, 2:127.

Illus. 2.1. "View of Mokhovaia Street and Mr Pashkov's House in Moscow." Etching from the early 1800s by Gabriel Ludwig Lory, after a painting from 1795 by Gérard de la Barthe. Courtesy of The New York Public Library. <http://digitalgallery.nypl.org/nypl-digital/id?1215576>.

homes was there continuous illumination; elsewhere, indoors and out, there were only islands of dim light to help orient people in the dark.

Like its European counterparts, the Russian government had little power over the streets after nightfall. Lacking a professional police, Moscow authorities made use instead of local residents and roving military patrols. When Catherine II ascended the throne, each of Moscow's then-fourteen police districts was assigned only three police officers and two scribes, while keeping watch in the streets was left to 2,274 men (as of 1780) who were conscripted to stand guard at nighttime barriers that choked off movement through the city.[78] Like watchmen elsewhere in Europe, they were often underage, elderly, or infirm. Many were serfs of local householders and found it easy to go home when the weather was

---

[78] Schmidt, *Sozialkontrolle in Moskau*, 343–9; Ivan Zabelin, *Opyty izucheniia russkikh drevnostei i istorii: Izsledovaniia, opisaniia i kriticheskiia stat'i*, 2 vols. (Moscow: Tipografiia Gracheva i Ko., 1872–3), 2:356.

inclement, so absenteeism was high.[79] Early modern townspeople everywhere were afraid of criminal gangs and considered it louche to skulk in the shadows or to hide one's face or the clothes that identified one's rank. Accordingly, like their equally unpopular colleagues abroad, Moscow watchmen were under orders to detain people moving in groups or without a lantern, and their penchant for harassing the public often exceeded their zeal for rooting out crime.[80]

The shortcomings of this approach to law enforcement are suggested by the wide popularity of Matvei Komarov's book from 1779 about the robber Van'ka Kain, a picaresque tale based on the true story of a mid-century kingpin of the Moscow underworld. Drawing on folk memories and a first-person narrative attributed to Kain himself, Komarov captures the popular memory of the brutality, corruption, and ineffectiveness of mid-century policing, the fluid boundaries between police and criminals, and the extent to which Muscovites preferred to entrust their security to private watchmen or enforcers rather than the police.[81]

Night created a parallel world that stood in tension with the imperial social project. One response to the dark, perhaps the most common, was to retreat into the security of one's home and social network. For some, this meant continuing the workday. Government clerks often took work home with them, and women kept busy with weaving or spinning. People also gathered in dimly lit rooms to share gossip, songs, tales, or prayers. The gardener's son Ivan Slonov (b. 1851) recalled that during his boyhood in Kolomna near Moscow, "On long winter evenings we would all gather at home, in one room that was lit with a tallow candle (we did not have a lamp). Father would read Psalms and Akathists aloud, and we would all sing in chorus."[82] Such pastimes strengthened the bonds of folk culture and communal solidarity, but not the Westernized culture and formalized social hierarchies that the regime wished to promote.

Another possibility was to go out in the evening, preferably to the light, shelter, and raucous company of the tavern. (As in other large European cities, taverns could legally stay open until near midnight.[83]) Even among the privileged strata, this was a site of male rebellion against the tightly regimented order that upheld civility during the day.[84] In the nineteenth century, when things grew

[79] G. Esipov, "Van'ka Kain," *Osmnadtsatyi vek*, 3 (1869), 280–335, esp. 291–3; Ekirch, *At Day's Close*, 81; Cockayne, *Hubbub*, 108–9.

[80] Delattre, *Les douze heures noires*, 22–5; Schmidt, *Sozialkontrolle in Moskau*, 346, 348–51; Ekirch, *At Day's Close*, 67, 80–2.

[81] Matvei Komarov, *Istoriia moshennika Van'ki Kaina; Milord Georg*, ed. V. D. Rak (St Petersburg: Zhurnal "Neva," Letnii Sad, 2000).

[82] Slonov, *Iz zhizni*, 16.

[83] The mandated closing time was 11:00 p.m. until the end of 1821, when it was changed to midnight: *Polozhenie o dokhodakh i raskhodakh Moskovskoi stolitsy i ob uplate dolgov, na tamoshnei dume lezhashchikh, Vysochaishe konfirmovannoe v 13 den' Aprelia 1823 goda* (Moscow: V Tipografii Semena Selivanovskago), 174. On other cities, see Schlör, *Nights in the Big City*, 101–4, 111.

[84] Iurii Lotman gives a similar explanation for the popularity of high-stakes gambling among noblemen: "Kartochnaia igra," in Iu. M. Lotman, *Besedy o russkoi kul'ture: Byt i traditsii russkogo dvorianstva (XVIII–nachalo XIX veka)* (St Petersburg: Iskusstvo-SPB, 1994), 143.

more sedate, the taverns of the old days became the stuff of legend.[85] For example, the provincial official Gavriil Dobrynin in 1808–10 recalled a group of his colleagues from the 1770s. It had been their specialty, he wrote, to make petitioners buy them cheap champagne by the caseful. During the ensuing drinking bouts, "using a corkscrew was forbidden; instead, they made a show of their skill at breaking a bottle's neck on the edge or leg of the table; if one did not break cleanly, or if a bottle cracked below the neck, they would throw it out the window with the wine still in it."[86] Grigorii Vinskii similarly recalled in 1813 that as an unemployed military officer in St Petersburg in the 1770s, he had spent his evenings in taverns drinking and gambling; in earlier times, he had also frequented prostitutes.[87]

Going to the tavern was all the more appealing as Moscow's latitude and weather were surely conducive to seasonal affective disorder, especially among the many who could not afford bright interior lighting. The opening lines of a short story from 1862 capture this feeling: "A morose autumn evening stared gloomily through the lone window of my gloomy lair. I didn't light my one-ruble economy lamp, because it's much easier in the dark to curse the darkness of my life." To boost his spirits, the down-and-out narrator repairs to the tavern.[88]

Men who suffered oppressive social control during the day—especially young, single men, including students, apprentices, soldiers, and domestics—took advantage of the night to assert a hell-raising machismo. In the 1790s, the village sacristan's son Aleksandr Voskresenskii (b. 1778) roomed with apprentice choristers at the Pokrovskii monastery on the southeastern edge of Moscow while attending the seminary. As he later recalled, in barely translatable rhyming and alliterative prose, "the Pokrovskii choristers are the most outstanding drinkers . . . They spend all their time with idleness and drunkenness, and often also with brawling . . . Every evening until midnight there is noise, din, and all manner of disgrace: some bawl, some tell lies, some drink."[89] Ivan Slonov in the 1860s worked for an employer who enforced a curfew on his shop assistants by locking the gate every evening. Thus confined, they would pass the time in card games that often descended into fisticuffs, after which the winners climbed over the fence and spent their winnings at a tavern "where they would booze until morning."[90]

---

[85] See, for example, Bulgarin, *Peterburgskie ocherki*, 150–65; Mikhail Tret'iakov, "Imperatorskii Moskovskii universitet v vospominaniiakh Mikhaila Prokhorovicha Tret'iakova, 1798–1830," part 1: *RS*, vol. 75 (July 1892), 105–31, here: 124.

[86] Gavriil Dobrynin, *Istinnoe povestvovanie ili Zhizn' Gavriila Dobrynina, (pozhivshago 72 g. 2 m. 20 dnei) im samim pisannaia v Mogileve i v Vitebske. 1752–1823* (St Petersburg: Pechatnia V. I. Golovina, 1872), 194.

[87] G. S. Vinskii, *Moe vremia* (St Petersburg: OGNI, n.d.), 57–8. On the working-class tavern culture of the late imperial period, see Laura L. Phillips, *Bolsheviks and the Bottle: Drink and Worker Culture in St. Petersburg, 1900–1929* (DeKalb, Ill.: Northern Illinois University Press, 2000).

[88] "Krym," in A. Levitov, *Moskovskiia nory i trushchoby* (2nd edn., St Petersburg: Izdanie V. E. Genkelia, 1869), 241.

[89] A. Voskresenskii, "Umstvennyi vzor na protekshiia leta moei zhizni ot kolybeli do groba (1778–1825 g.)," part 2: *Dushepoleznoe chtenie*, no. 11 (1894), 367–84, here: 374–5.

[90] Slonov, *Iz zhizni*, 77–8.

A major attraction of the tavern was the availability of prostitutes, as the following police records from 1803 suggest. The 25-year-old soldier's wife Tat'iana Timofeeva was arrested one night in January and admitted that she "went every day to the Tsar'grad alehouse, whence she would be taken by soldiers to their barracks or by noble servants to their houses to engage in lewdness."[91] The townswoman Fedos'ia Ivanova confessed that "on the 5th of May past, she was in an alehouse by the Arbat Gate, whence she was taken at dusk...by the house serf Iakov...who brought her to the coach-house at his master's home to engage in lewdness with him, and that is where she spent the night."[92] When the 50-year-old soldier's wife Aleksandra Petrova emerged from a tavern, she was approached in broad daylight by a young artisan who correctly guessed that he could buy her sexual services for 25 kopeks plus drinks.[93] In Russia, men with courtly manners were likely to be nobles, many of whom could find sexual satisfaction (and hoped to avoid venereal disease) with female serfs instead of going to prostitutes.[94] This may account for the impression of Heinrich Storch, in his book about St Petersburg from the 1790s, that there was something especially coarse about prostitution in Russia. Storch usually tried to cast Russia in a favorable light, but he felt that prostitutes in the taverns of St Petersburg were treated by their customers with a crudeness that would be unusual in Paris or Berlin.[95]

Nighttime thus unleashed a raunchy, misogynistic masculinity that subverted the imperial social project. To promote greater civility, the authorities encouraged men to socialize with women in a genteel, orderly atmosphere. Peter the Great had ordered nobles to hold polite "assemblies" in which men and women mingled. The civilizing role of femininity was likewise a premise of the "scenario of power" of both Empress Elizabeth and Catherine II,[96] and Catherine promoted education for girls because she believed in the power of mothers and wives to mold an enlightened society.

The civilizing impact that polite socializing with women could have on men is suggested by the case of Ivan Lapin (1799–1859), a townsman from the small town of Opochka near the Livonian border. In the diary that he kept as a young bachelor, Lapin records what he did after closing time at his store. Sometimes he would join his male friends to quaff alcohol and boisterously roam the streets. He preferred, however, to pass the evening in the company of young women,

---

[91] TsIAM f. 105, op. 3, d. 88, l. 2 ob.
[92] TsIAM f. 105, op. 3, d. 634, l. 2.
[93] TsIAM f. 105, op. 3, d. 100, l. 3 ob.
[94] Raupach, *Reise*, 205–6; Reinbeck, *Flüchtige Bemerkungen*, 2:134; Andrei Zorin, "Pokhod v bordel' v Moskve v ianvare 1800 goda (Shiller, gonoreia, i pervorodnyi grekh v emotsional'nom mire russkogo dvorianina)," *Novoe Literaturnoe Obozrenie*, no. 92 (2008) <http://www.nlobooks. ru/rus/magazines/nlo/196/1070/1083/> accessed 8 December 2008.
[95] Storch, *Gemaehlde von St. Petersburg*, 2:321. The claim that prostitution in Russia was morally coarser than in in the West also appears in Attenhofer, *Medizinische Topographie*, 97.
[96] Wortman, *Scenarios of Power*, 1:56, 86.

especially his beloved Anna. Then he would play the flute, Anna would share novels from her library, and together they would dance the quadrille and the écossaise or sit in her grandfather's garden and lose themselves in soulful conversation and passionate kisses.[97]

Moscow's "nocturnal old regime" obstructed the development of such a culture of genteel sociability, as the following example suggests. In 1756, Elizabeth's government took a step to advance the diffusion of elite culture by launching the semiweekly *Moscow Gazette* (*Moskovskiia Vedomosti*). In one of its first issues (Friday, 31 May 1756), the *Gazette* carried the following advertisement: "In the German Suburb, in the house of Madame General Litskina, there will be weekly Wednesday concerts, beginning on the 5th of June at six o'clock in the evening; every person will be charged one ruble per ticket." Here was the imperial social project in action: a newspaper that any literate person could read advertised the elite's sponsorship of the arts; anyone who could afford the fee was promised admission; and the evening hour suited officials, merchants, and others who worked for a living.

In practice, only a wealthy few could easily take advantage of such opportunities. Like many entertainments that the aristocracy opened to the public, this one was located far from the city center, and by 6 p.m. it was dark, at least during the cold months when Moscow's social season was at its liveliest. (On the shortest day of the year, the sun set at 3:23 p.m.[98]) Traveling to such events by carriage was unpleasant enough, given the bumpy streets and the character of Moscow law enforcement. A Briton who visited in 1737 reported that "I was stopped a short time by a party of dragoons, who patrol through the city in the night-time, notwithstanding there are many thousand citizens who keep watch, like our watchmen of London, to prevent robberies, thefts, and incendiaries. After a short examination, the dragoons looked into the coach with a lanthorn [lantern], and let me pass."[99]

Going out was especially onerous for people of genteel status but limited means. Walking the streets after dark meant slipping and sliding on the ice or wading through the snow, or when temperatures went above freezing, feeling one's way along muddy thoroughfares littered with dung and refuse, and always at risk of being splattered by passing carriages. Dogs were usually chained up by day but let loose at night. In a novel from 1861, a man is warned in a provincial town that "It's eleven o'clock and the dogs are being let out all over; if Your Honor stays much longer they'll tear your coattails off and perhaps even get at your legs."[100] After such a trek, one was unlikely to arrive looking, smelling, or

---

[97] I. I. Lapin, "Dnevnik," in Semenova, *Kupecheskie dnevniki i memuary*, 92–130.

[98] Wichelhausen, *Züge zu einem Gemählde von Moskwa*, 129.

[99] John Cook, *Voyages and Travels through the Russian Empire, Tartary, and Part of the Kingdom of Persia*, 2 vols. (Edinburgh: Printed for the Author, 1770), 1:124–5.

[100] Nadezhda Khvoshchinskaia, *The Boarding-School Girl*, tr. Karen Rosneck (Evanston, Ill.: Northwestern University Press, 2000), 26.

feeling particularly respectable, especially compared with one's social superiors who came by sleigh or carriage, and one's soiled or rain-soaked clothes would be difficult to clean and expensive to replace.

In addition to humiliation before one's betters, there was the risk of encounters with one's inferiors. Like other *anciens régimes*, Russia's social order was a finely calibrated system of ranks in which clothing and body language conveyed status and were supposed to command deference. In dark and deserted streets, however, the unwary might cross paths with commoners who were drunk or aggressive. For example, the protagonist of Gogol's short story "The Overcoat," Akakii Akakievich, is a petty St Petersburg official whose pride and joy is the new coat on which he has spent his meager savings. It so elevates his status in the eyes of his colleagues that the normally reclusive Akakii Akakievich, who previously spent his evenings at home doing work from the office, is invited to a party. Tragedy strikes on his walk home: he is mugged and robbed of his coat, and his fruitless effort to recover it ends in his death.

Public concern about these conditions is apparent from the fact that in the Moscow instruction for the 1767 Legislative Commission, the very first request was "that to provide all who live in this city with the desired safety and peace, orders be given to establish a trustworthy watch in place of the current [system of nighttime] barriers."[101] The government and its supporters understood that the "nocturnal old regime" obstructed their goals. Their response was to light the streets and reform the police.[102]

One responsibility of the Police Board, as the new city police established in 1782 was called, was to light the streets at night. The number of hempseed-oil street lights in Moscow grew rapidly under Catherine, from a mere 600 in 1766 to 3,500 by 1782.[103] A new push under Paul I doubled the number to around 7,000 by 1801. In the aftermath of the Napoleonic occupation of 1812, the number dropped to 5,200 by the early 1820s, but rose again to around 8,000 by 1850. Under rules from 1823, the lights were to be lit from September through April, for seven to eleven hours per night depending on the month; as a result, a whiff of hempseed in the streets became a sign that summer was ending. By 1849, the lamps were lit in August as well, but still only on moonless nights, and for fewer hours than the darkness lasted.[104] Throughout the period, the only technical innovation was the increasing use of *réverbères* (lamps equipped with reflectors of polished metal) from the 1800s on.[105] The lights were distributed very unevenly among Moscow's districts. In 1826,

---

[101] "Nakaz ot zhitelei goroda Moskvy," 120.

[102] On the organization and structure of the local police, see LeDonne, *Absolutism and Ruling Class*, 127–51.

[103] Zabelin, *Opyty*, 2:357.

[104] *Polozhenie o dokhodakh i raskhodakh Moskovskoi stolitsy*, 132; Lapin, *Peterburg: Zapakhi i zvuki*, 38; N. M. Bychkov, "Istoricheskii ocherk osveshcheniia goroda Moskvy," *IMGD*, vypusk 1 (October 1895), otdel 2, pp. 1–52, here: 6.

[105] Gastev, *Materialy*, 252; Delattre, *Les douze heures noires*, 84.

Tverskaia District in the city center had 852 lanterns, and five other districts in mostly central locations had between 322 and 478. On the other hand, seven districts located on the outskirts of the city had fewer than 150 lanterns each.[106]

Aside from their practical uses, the street lights were a barometer of the regime's effort to make Moscow into a European metropolis. In the 1820s to 1840s, the months and hours when the lamps were lit were roughly the same in Moscow as in Berlin.[107] Paris, for Russians the ultimate model of a great European city, had introduced the first street lights under Louis XIV but replaced tallow candles with the more luminous oil-burning *réverbères* only in the 1760s—not long before Moscow. However, after the Napoleonic Wars, Moscow began to fall behind. Whereas it became a commonplace in Paris to deride the *réverbères* as dim and obsolete, especially in comparison with lighting by coal gas,[108] in Moscow they remained a symbol of national success: as one Russian wrote with pride in the early 1820s, "The total of the street lights in Moscow is 5,010; in Paris, the count is over 4,777. There the entire city is illumined within forty minutes, but in Moscow, within a half-hour."[109] London had a thousand oil lamps in the 1730s, giving it a head start that was not insuperable.[110] By 1823, however, with nearly 40,000 gas lamps, the British capital had left Moscow in the dust.[111]

Catherine II established a system of illumination that underwent little change until the Great Reforms. Using oil lamps, like drawing water from wells and disposing of sewage in cesspits, made sense in Moscow's low-density environment because it obviated the need for an expensive infrastructure of gas, water, or sewer pipes. However, the light that the oil lamps provided was increasingly seen as inadequate. Already in the 1840s, when censorship prevented overt criticisms, the secret police reported that the educated public ridiculed the government's boasts about its street lights.[112] By the 1860s, the dim light and the familiar scent of hempseed seemed embarrassingly backward in comparison with the kerosene that finally replaced it in 1865 and whose very smell was associated with progress. Also during the 1860s to 1880s, half of the city's street lights—particularly in the central districts—switched to gas, which burned more brightly, although its light was cold and greenish-white, unlike the dimmer but warmer reddish-yellow tones of the oil and kerosene lights that continued to predominate in the outskirts.[113] Looking back in 1878, city officials were merciless: "In times past,

---

[106] Le Cointe, *Guide*, table facing p. 86.

[107] Schlör, *Nights in the Big City*, 60.

[108] Delattre, *Les douze heures noires*, 83–6.

[109] A. F. Malinovskii, *Obozrenie Moskvy* (Moscow: Moskovskii rabochii, 1992), 114.

[110] Cockayne, *Hubbub*, 223.

[111] Ekirch, *At Day's Close*, 331.

[112] "Doneseniia agentov o dukhe v Moskve v 1848 godu," *Minuvshie Gody*, 5–6 (May–June 1908), 344–9, here: 347.

[113] Lapin, *Peterburg: Zapakhi i zvuki*, 38; Bychkov, "Istoricheskii ocherk osveshcheniia," 16, 30, 34–5.

when Moscow was illumined with old-fashioned lamps and hempseed oil served as fuel, the poverty of the light was in complete harmony with the scantiness of the time during which these modest night lights were lit."[114]

For her time, Catherine's street lights had represented a profound innovation: the attempt by the state to tame the night so that respectable citizens could experience culture and sociability. The other purpose was to render life on the streets transparent and hence controllable for the authorities. Both aims—aiding the citizenry and strengthening state power—were also furthered by the reform of the police.

An important job of the new Police Board was to maintain a permanent police force that remained on duty even during the daytime—those very watchmen whose brutality shocked Nikodim Kazantsev on his walk through Moscow. Like the lighting of the streets, this had been proclaimed as a goal under Peter I and his successors, but little had been done prior to Catherine's accession. Her police reform drew extensively on the model of the police of Paris, whose experience was also studied by her Habsburg counterpart Maria Theresa.[115] Paris was divided into 20 *quartiers* in which public tranquility was maintained by troopers who were posted at guardhouses or else conducted foot or horse patrols.[116] Each *quartier* was under the command of one or several *commissaires*, who in turn answered to the city's lieutenant-general of police and who were tasked with a vast range of functions, among them resolving disputes, enforcing order, uphold-ing public cleanliness and morals, and regulating, registering, and licensing all manner of people and activities.[117]

Catherine adopted a similar model. In keeping with her overall approach of dividing the empire into smaller, more easily controlled units, her police code of 1782 divided Moscow into twenty districts (*chasti*), made up in turn of eighty-eight wards (*kvartaly*). Scattered throughout were guardhouses manned by teams of three watchmen who, like their Parisian colleagues or the watchmen of eighteenth-century London,[118] watched over their neighborhood and reported to the "district house" (*chastnyi dom*, the district's police station). Like their counterparts in Paris, Moscow's watchmen were assigned broad responsibilities that included strict control over the lower classes in the interest of both the state

---

[114] A. Petunnikov, "Po povodu osvetitel'nago kalendaria na 1878 god," *IMGD*, vypusk 1 (15 January 1878), 35–45, here: 35.

[115] According to Isabel de Madariaga, the document both empresses studied is the one later published as Jean-Baptiste-Charles Le Maire, "La Police de Paris en 1770: Mémoire inédit composé par ordre de G. de Sartine sur la demande de Marie-Thérèse," *Mémoires de la Société de l'histoire de Paris et de l'Île de France*, 5 (1878), 1–131; Madariaga, *Russia in the Age of Catherine the Great*, 293.

[116] Le Maire, "La Police de Paris," 67–8.

[117] Steven L. Kaplan, "Note sur les commissaires de police de Paris au XVIIIe siècle," *Revue d'histoire moderne et contemporaine*, 28/4 (1981), 669–86, here: 678.

[118] Tim Hitchcock, *Down and Out in Eighteenth-Century London* (London: Hambledon, 2004), 152–7.

and the upper classes; thus, nobles who wanted their serfs to be imprisoned or flogged could have the punishment carried out by the police.

This reform initiated a limited professionalization of the police, but it was a slow process. Police commanders always had military forces at their disposal as backup, but otherwise the total complement of 1,056 watchmen, 600 staff for the district houses, and 1,500 firemen continued initially to be drawn from conscripted local residents. An edict of 1802 instructed authorities to hire paid volunteers, but this was stymied by lack of funds. Finally in 1803–4, following a model pioneered in St Petersburg, soldiers deemed unfit for front-line service were shifted to police and fire duty.[119] This system survived largely unchanged until the Great Reforms.

As with its street lighting, Moscow was brought up to Western standards but then lagged. Law enforcement in Europe was traditionally left to watchmen and soldiers, but in 1829, London broke new ground by creating a force of trained, professional policemen. Similar reforms took place in Berlin in 1848 and Paris in 1854.[120] Moscow did not change at the same pace. From 1823 to 1863, while the city's population doubled in size, the lower ranks of the police remained unchanged at about 1,600 men. Most continued to have little police training and were not physically vigorous (otherwise they would still have been on active military duty), and they continued to wield archaic halberds until 1856, after Nicholas I's death, when these were at last replaced with sabers. Their officers did not even receive a pay raise between 1823 and 1861.[121]

Even the number 1,600 overstated their strength, as the governor-general laid out in a report in 1863. He started by subtracting the 312 infantrymen assigned to the police. (His reason for doing this is unclear, since they had the same duties as policemen.[122]) A further 273 men did desk work or served as messengers, and usually the police were short 25 men and another 25 were sick, so only 965 were actually based at guardhouses and available for patrol duty. Usually, some of these men were busy escorting prisoners or providing security at public events, and of the three men per guardhouse, at any given time one was off duty and another had to be on call at the guardhouse. That left one man per guardhouse, in other words, 300 or so for the entire city, to walk the beat and keep order in the streets.[123]

[119] Gastev, *Materialy*, 242–56.

[120] Andreas Roth, *Kriminalitätsbekämpfung in deutschen Großstädten, 1850–1914: Ein Beitrag zur Geschichte des strafrechtlichen Ermittlungsverfahrens* (Berlin: Erich Schmidt, 1997), 121–2; Delattre, *Les douze heures noires*, 276–92, 307.

[121] M. P. Shchepkin, "Istoricheskaia zapiska o raskhodakh goroda Moskvy po soderzhaniiu politseiskikh uchrezhdenii v 1823–1879 gg.," *IMGD*, vypusk 2 (1880), cols. 5–72, esp. 5–20; A. V. Borisov et al., *Politsiia i militsiia Rossii: Stranitsy istorii* (Moscow: Nauka, 1995), 75–80; "Vysochaishiia poveleniia po delam obshchago upravleniia," *ZhMVD*, chast' 20, otdel 1 (October 1856), 87–9.

[122] Shchepkin, "Istoricheskaia zapiska o raskhodakh," 32.

[123] Shchepkin, "Istoricheskaia zapiska o raskhodakh," 21–3.

By the time the system was overhauled in the 1870s, the old-time watchmen—gruff, ignorant, often somnolescent—had become fixed in intelligentsia lore as figures of ridicule. The social status of the police was low: so low that in Tolstoi's *War and Peace*, the aristocrat Pierre Bezukhov's idea of youthful high jinks in St Petersburg is to tie a neighborhood police captain to a bear and throw both into a canal, for which Pierre receives no punishment beyond an order to remove himself to Moscow.[124] Higher-ranking police officers were recalled as brutal and corrupt, and criminal investigators acquired notoriety for their sleazy methods and shady ties to the criminal world.[125] As one author complained at the dawn of the Great Reforms, policemen were generally soldiers who had been conscripted in the first place because they were convicts or vagrants or because their communities wanted to be rid of them. "Obviously," he wrote, men like these would willingly "sell all justice for a glass of vodka or a ten-kopek piece."[126] The Moscow police of the eighteenth century gave the Russian language a colloquialism that was still in use more than a century later. In memory of Nikolai Arkharov, Moscow's chief of police from 1775 to 1782, "Arkharovite" came to mean (according to Dal's dictionary) "police detective.//Dissolute person; hell-raiser [*otchaiannaia golova*]; ragamuffin."[127] As Mikhail Pyliaev noted in 1891 in his popular history of Moscow, "among the people, the name of Arkharovite serves as a synonym of rogue."[128]

Catherine's police, street lights, and pavements all outlived their time. None were suited for the modern traffic and nighttime commerce, sociability, and entertainment that were modeled by large Western cities. Only a localized sense of order emanated from the solitary watchmen who stood by their guardhouses, armed with halberds like their early modern counterparts in the West, and called out "Who goes?" when they heard footsteps in the night. Likewise, the *réverbères* produced only islands of light, not a continuous illumination. They appear prominently in government statistics and in paintings of daytime urban scenes, suggesting that Russia's elites appreciated them as symbols of modernity, but they showed little interest in their actual effect. Russian literature in the eighteenth century (with the signal exception of Komarov's *Van'ka Kain*) rarely depicted the city at night, and the same was true of the visual arts. In two large volumes of images of eighteenth- and nineteenth-century Moscow, not a single picture shows the city after dark with the street lights lit.[129] The volume *Pushkin's*

[124] Leo Tolstoy, *War and Peace*, tr. Louise and Aylmer Maude (New York: Simon and Schuster, 1942), 37–8, 54.

[125] See, for example: Khaliutin, "Moskovskii syshchik Iakovlev."

[126] Nikolai Orlov, "Sledstvennaia chast' v gradskikh politsiiakh," *Russkii Vestnik*, 20 (1859), "Sovremennaia letopis'," 328–36, here: 334.

[127] Vladimir Dal', *Tolkovyi slovar' zhivogo velikorusskogo iazyka*, 4 vols. (1903–9; repr. Moscow: Progress, Univers, 1994), vol. 1, col. 63.

[128] M. I. Pyliaev, *Staraia Moskva: Rasskazy iz byloi zhizni pervoprestol'noi stolitsy* (Moscow: Svarog, 1995), 330.

[129] Skorniakova, *Staraia Moskva*; Gulianitskii, *Moskva i slozhivshiesia russkie goroda*.

St. Peterburg reproduces so many early nineteenth-century images that the historian Richard Stites calls it "a kind of visual database" for the imperial capital, yet only a single image shows street lights that are lit: the 1830s canvas *Neva Embankment Near the Academy of the Arts (Night)*, attributed to G. G. Chernetsov, in which three street lights emit a dim glow that draws attention to their location but does little to illumine their surroundings.[130] Even when kerosene lighting was introduced in Moscow in the 1860s, the light it produced fell short of the reformers' hopes. Out-of-the-way streets were equipped with lights whose brightness was only two to four candlepower, with intervals between them of up to 60 sazhens (126.81 meters); the city council wanted nine-candlepower lamps on both sides of the street every 10 to 25 sazhens (21.33 to 53.34 meters).[131]

Regarding the pavement of Moscow's streets, the arc of public perceptions also went from admiration to disappointment. Streets continued to be paved with cobblestone, which Ivan Slonov in the early twentieth century called "an Egyptian plague for Muscovites."[132] More modern cities increasingly used asphalt. When 11-year-old Aleksandr Benois (the future painter) visited Warsaw in 1881, he was amazed at how quiet the traffic was on the asphalted streets; after his return home to St Petersburg, the city struck him as noisy, dusty, and depressing.[133]

All of this was outliving its usefulness in the middle decades of the nineteenth century, just as Russian literature and journalism were coming into their own. As a result, the urban infrastructure of pre-Reform Moscow acquired a retrospective reputation as backward and stagnant. It would be a mistake to think that this made Moscow un-European. Londoners, Parisians, and Berliners were equally disdainful about oil lamps and night-watchmen,[134] and Rome was no different from Moscow in retaining the name of its eighteenth-century police (*sbirri*) as a colloquial term of abuse.[135] Conversely, as the urban night became more modern, some in both Russia and the West grew nostalgic for the 1820s and 1830s, when nighttime streets were still quiet, dim, and conducive to introspective reverie. The writer Apollon Grigor'ev (1822–64), for instance, recalled that

Often, when I came home at night [to Zamoskvorech'e] from Sokol'niki, always choosing the longest route, for I loved wandering around Moscow at night, I . . . would stop in front of the old house at the corner of the lane, the first place my grandfather stayed in

[130] Stites, *Serfdom, Society, and the Arts*, 366; A. M. Gordin, *Pushkinskii Peterburg/Pushkin's St. Petersburg* (St Petersburg: Khudozhnik RSFSR, 1991), plate 144.
[131] Bychkov, "Istoricheskii ocherk osveshcheniia," 8, 34–5.
[132] Slonov, *Iz zhizni*, 48.
[133] Lapin, *Peterburg: Zapakhi i zvuki*, 52.
[134] Schlör, *Nights in the Big City*, 59, 73, 79–80, 83.
[135] Susan Vandiver Nicassio, *Imperial City: Rome under Napoleon* (Chicago: University of Chicago Press, 2005), 142.

Moscow . . . and . . . wait for a half hour to see if my old grandfather might appear to me and resolve the multitude of questions that troubled my soul.[136]

Life was never the same again after street lights, pavement, and the dismantling of the nighttime barriers enabled Muscovites to move about at night with a modicum of safety and comfort. Like their contemporaries in large Western cities, Muscovites discovered opportunities for a new freedom and a deeper individuality. I am not aware of any narrative that documents what Catherine II's efforts to push back the "nocturnal old regime" meant to her people. Most likely, nocturnal mobility was a factor that helped them begin to reflect on their lives in the first place. They could expand their horizons by visiting sites of culture and sociability, but they could also just amble in the street, unburdened by their daily business, unmarked by strangers, alone with their thoughts, and free, for a few hours, from the rigid controls of the day.[137] A sense of what such freedom meant to a later generation that took it for granted is offered by Nikolai Vishniakov (b. 1844), whose memoirs describe the stifling narrowness of the pre-Reform merchant life that he experienced in Moscow as a child. In one passage, he imagines what his own father experienced as a young man when Paul I came to power and newly restrictive police controls were temporarily imposed:

Petia saw with his own eyes how Moscow became virtually lifeless by night, how gates were closed toward evening and locked with sturdy bolts, how barriers were erected in the streets to block the passage of peaceful inhabitants. There was no staying out late or getting lost in conversation with acquaintances. At the appointed hour you had to rush home and sit as though under siege. No one knew why this was necessary. But that lack of knowledge is precisely what was terrible.

Vishniakov associated these controls with Paul's persecution of dissidents, but he also argued that such experiences were the reason for the typical Russian commoner's civic passivity and cowering timidity before authority.[138]

CONCLUSION

The arc of the transformation of Moscow extended over roughly a century. Inspired by the Enlightenment and appalled by Moscow's realities, Catherine II launched sweeping reforms to make the city clean, elegant, and safe, and to

---

[136] Apollon Grigor'ev, *Vospominaniia*, ed. B. F. Egorov (Moscow: Nauka, 1988), 14; Schlör, *Nights in the Big City*, 43. On Grigor'ev's contribution to the transformation of Moscow's literary image, see Robert Whittaker, "'My Literary and Moral Wanderings': Apollon Grigor'ev and the Changing Cultural Topography of Moscow," *Slavic Review*, 42/3 (Fall 1983), 390–407.

[137] Schlör, *Nights in the Big City*, 274.

[138] N. Vishniakov, *Svedeniia o kupecheskom rode Vishniakovykh*, 3 vols. (Moscow: Tipografiia G. Lissnera i A Geshelia [vols. 2–3: G. Lissnera i D. Sobko], 1903–11), 1:34–5.

give the middling sort the freedom to circulate after dark and share in the experience of genteel sociability and culture.

Compared with Western cities, these measures were neither particularly belated nor especially ineffective. However, Catherine's successors failed to reconceive them in light of the dawning industrial age. Urban policy stagnated just as the imperial social project was giving rise to a public that thought critically about urban issues. As a result, while substantively successful, Catherine's policies backfired politically by the 1860s and 1870s because educated Muscovites were growing convinced once more that their city was archaic and benighted, and that the government's urban policies were largely to blame.

Those frustrations, however, did not set in until the mid-nineteenth century. For several decades after she initiated them, as we will see in the next two chapters, Catherine's urban policies helped persuade educated Russians that Moscow was indeed becoming an enlightened metropolis.

3

Envisioning the Enlightened Metropolis

Images of Moscow under Catherine II

It was critical to the regime's goals that Moscow's reconstruction as an enlightened metropolis take place not only in physical reality but also in the imagination. As advertisers might say, the city needed to be rebranded. Making Moscow into a great European city was likely to build support for the current monarch among the Russian elites, which was no small consideration in a country where every successful ruler between 1741 and 1825 came to power through a palace coup. Furthermore, if the wider population could be taught to understand and embrace the ideological vision underlying the regime's urban policies, the regime's base of support would strengthen and a repetition of disasters like the plague revolt would become less likely. Finally, international respect for Russia would increase if Westerners could be made to see Moscow as part of the same urban civilization as Paris, London, or Vienna.

This chapter will argue that the leading role in constructing the city's new image was played by cartographers, graphic artists, statisticians, and historians. The common denominator of their work was its triumphalist visuality. The culture of the eighteenth-century Russian elites was highly visual, favoring forms of expression such as clothing, architecture, gardening, urban planning, and the staging of fireworks and court ceremonies.[1] The regime privileged visuality over other forms of cognition because visuality seemed especially well suited for expressing the enlightened rationality of the imperial order. This principle guided the representation of Moscow as well. Maps, paintings, statistical tables, and histories of buildings and monuments made it possible to "see" Moscow as an enlightened metropolis.

THE RUSSIAN ENLIGHTENMENT

The celebratory tone of eighteenth-century representations of Moscow reflects a distinctive feature of Russian Enlightenment culture: its persistent reluctance to

---

[1] This argument is developed in Levitt, *The Visual Dominant*, passim.

engage critically with the concrete everyday problems of the country's social and political order.

In part this was a function of the lack of distance between Russian thinkers and the imperial regime. The Russian Enlightenment was the work of a narrow elite of officials and intellectuals, who were often the same individuals. They were drawn from a diversity of social and national backgrounds, but, as Elise Wirtschafter argues, this did not "produce a corresponding cultural or ideological pluralism." Instead, "When compared with the educated classes of the nineteenth century, those of the eighteenth articulated a uniform brand of Enlightenment thought barely distinguishable from that of the court."[2] Three individuals who will receive particular attention in this chapter are the historian Gerhard Friedrich Müller, the statistician Vasilii Ruban, and the painter Fedor Alekseev. They were typical representatives of the imperial polity that Russia became in the eighteenth century. They came from the social and ethnic margins: the first was a German immigrant, the second a Ukrainian, the third a soldier's son. They lived mostly in St Petersburg and spent formative years at imperial academic institutions. They were culturally European and participated in the colonialist appropriation of Russia's frontier regions. Powerful bonds of education, life experience, and self-interest connected people like these to the imperial regime and its vision for transforming the country.

Censorship was another factor that helped maintain the ideological consensus of the Russian Enlightenment. Writers and artists faced considerable informal pressure to conform. The educated class was small, and one's government-service career, financial prospects, and general social standing were dependent on the support of one's family and patronage network, so making waves with controversial opinions was risky. The government also kept an eye on what appeared in print. From 1763 on, imported books could be sold only with the approval of Moscow University or the Academy of Sciences. There was initially no censorship of domestic publications, but the government and the Orthodox Church controlled the institutions that owned the printing presses (such as the Holy Synod or Moscow University), and when private presses were legalized in 1783, it was with the proviso that manuscripts be vetted by the police. Censorship was lax and haphazard until the outbreak of the French Revolution. After that, the government enforced its control much more aggressively. Thus, Catherine sent Aleksandr Radishchev, the author of the anti-serfdom polemic *A Journey from St Petersburg to Moscow*, into Siberian exile in 1790, and imprisoned the Moscow Freemason and publisher Nikolai Novikov in 1792.[3]

---

[2] Elise Kimerling Wirtschafter, "The Groups Between: *Raznochintsy*, Intelligentsia, Professionals," in Dominic Lieven, ed., *The Cambridge History of Imperial Russia*, vol. 2: *Imperial Russia, 1689–1917* (Cambridge: Cambridge University Press, 2006), 254.

[3] Madariaga, *Russia in the Age of Catherine the Great*, 334–5, 537; Marker, *Publishing, Printing*, 105–8, 212–32; Gabriela Lehmann-Carli et al., "Zensur in Rußland: Von der zweiten Hälfte des

Russian Enlightenment thinkers mostly focused their energies on a moral critique of the individual person, not on systemic analyses of Russia's social or political order. When they discussed such topics at all, it was often to promote projects that were future-oriented, propagandistic, and remote from the everyday reality that most Russians actually experienced. One example is Catherine's *Nakaz*, which was widely disseminated domestically and abroad. Its portrayal of Russia's government was largely aspirational. For instance, it stated that the monarchy was limited by fundamental laws, when in fact no such laws existed.[4] The foundling homes that Catherine established in St Petersburg and Moscow are another example. To publicize the Russian government's concern for the poor, officials regular showed these institutions to foreign tourists. A typical reaction was that of Thomas Malthus, who visited the St Petersburg Foundling Home in 1799 and praised its "extraordinary degree of neatness, cleanliness, and sweetness." This was a mere façade: what visitors were not told was that most of the foundlings died.[5]

The regime's favorite demonstration projects were far from the Russian heartland, in places where the construction of the new imperial order was not hampered by structures inherited from the past. For much of the eighteenth century, the quintessential showpiece was St Petersburg, built in an underpopulated northwestern frontier region near the Baltic that Peter the Great had annexed from Sweden. Catherine II tried to shift the orientation of Russia's imperial expansion southward to "New Russia," the sparsely settled steppe north of the Black Sea that her armies conquered from the Ottomans. In 1787, she took Emperor Joseph II of Austria and other influential Westerners on a lengthy tour of the area, traveling down the Dnepr and on to Crimea. A high point was the groundbreaking for Ekaterinoslav ("Catherine's Glory"), a new city that was meant to embody Catherine's thrust to the south much as St Petersburg had embodied Peter's march to the west.[6] Catherine's wider plan, the "Greek Project," entailed conquering the Ottoman Empire and replacing it with a revived Byzantine Empire under Romanov rule. To create a justification for these ambitions, her propagandists used imagery from classical civilization to create a symbolic association between Russia, the newly annexed Black Sea coast,

18. bis zu Beginn des 19. Jahrhunderts," in Erich Donnert, ed., *Europa in der Frühen Neuzeit: Festschrift für Günter Mühlpfordt,* 7 vols. (Cologne: Böhlau, 1997–2008), 6:739–73.

[4] V. M. Zhivov, "Gosudarstvennyi mif v epokhu Prosveshcheniia i ego razrushenie v Rossii kontsa XVIII veka," in Koshelev, *Iz istorii russkoi kul'tury,* 4:668.

[5] Malthus was suspicious, and kept asking questions until he discovered that the mortality was "prodigious." Given the admirable conditions in the Foundling Home, though, he did not blame the Russians, instead concluding that institutionalized foundling care was inherently doomed to failure. Thomas Robert Malthus, *An Essay on the Principle of Population,* 2 vols. (Washington City: Roger Chew Weightman, 1809), 1:359–69, quotations on 361, 364–5. I thank Christopher Hamlin for drawing my attention to Malthus's comments on Russia.

[6] A. M. Panchenko, "'Potemkinskie derevni' kak kul'turnyi mif," in Koshelev, *Iz istorii russkoi kul'tury,* 4:694–5.

and ancient Greece. Sites in the conquered areas were given Greek names (e.g. Crimea became "Tauris"); Catherine's second grandson, who was to rule the future empire, was given the symbolic name Constantine; and to greet Catherine and her company on their visit to the region, which according to classical legend was the homeland of the Amazons, Catherine's viceroy Grigorii Potemkin deployed armed female "Amazons" outfitted in turbans with white ostrich feathers.[7]

The fact that the government's justification of its imperial ambitions was built to such a large extent on symbolism from classical antiquity, as opposed to fact-based arguments about the progress of Russian society, illustrates a paradox of eighteenth-century culture. The Russian monarchy from Peter the Great onward sought to create a "well-ordered police state" that used statistics, maps, and other data to guide state policy.[8] The larger framework for imagining state and society, however, was provided by a mystical belief that monarchs were demiurges of history who had the power to restore the world to a lost state of harmony, justice, and plenty. Empirical data were less useful for evoking this coming golden age than was a poetic idiom from classical mythology. Accordingly, poets in the 1760s and 1770s celebrated Catherine by likening her to Minerva, Augustus Caesar, the Carthaginian Queen Dido from the *Aeneid*, an Amazon, and Astrea, the messianic virgin whose coming, in Virgil's fourth eclogue, heralds the birth of a "new race of men" and a new golden age.[9]

In the years around 1780, a cultural shift occurred. The turbulence of the period from 1768 to 1774—the Russo-Turkish War, the Moscow plague, the First Partition of Poland, and the Pugachev revolt—had subsided, and Catherine's attention was focused on reforms to strengthen the bonds uniting Russian society. From 1775 to 1786 she issued her most important legislation to reshape the social order in the Russian heartland: the reform of provincial and municipal government, the creation of local police administrations, the charters to the nobles and the towns, and the creation of a system of public schools. Building a bond between state and society entailed a new cultural nationalism; thus, Catherine in 1783 established the Russian Academy, dedicated to perfecting the Russian literary language. In this context, cultural symbolism drawn from the classical world played a diminishing role, although Catherine's southern journey in 1787 showed that it had not lost its usefulness. Instead, poets took to exalting her reign by celebrating Russia as a land of joy and prosperity where the courtly virtues of gallantry, generosity, and wit prevailed. The cultural idiom was no longer classical, but modern; the tone grew more nationalistic; and the

---

[7] Panchenko, "'Potemkinskie derevni' kak kul'turnyi mif," in Koshelev, *Iz istorii russkoi kul'tury*, 4:689; Zorin, *Kormia dvuglavogo orla*, 31–64.

[8] Raeff, *The Well-Ordered Police State*, 133–4, 158.

[9] Proskurina, *Mify imperii*, 12, 46, 48, 59; Zhivov, "Gosudarstvennyi mif v epokhu Prosveshcheniia," in Koshelev, *Iz istorii russkoi kul'tury*, vol. 4, passim.

vocabulary of myth and allegory gave way to a cautious engagement with everyday realities.[10]

Nonetheless, in the absence of a clear sense of what constituted Russia's distinctive national features, writers and artists remained focused on supposedly universal themes that were inspired by Western models. Playwrights sought to depict a timeless human condition, not the specific circumstances of life in Russia.[11] Architects dotted the country with white-columned, pastel buildings that celebrated a universal ideal of beauty and could as easily have stood in Europe or America. Gardeners from the 1760s on abandoned the geometric designs associated with "French" gardens for the "English" style that mimicked an idealized natural scenery, but the landscapes that the English gardens imitated—and the grottoes, temple ruins, classical statues, and other installations that adorned them—were Western, not Russian.[12]

CARTOGRAPHY

Some of the earliest contributions to Moscow's new image as an enlightened metropolis were made by cartographers. Their work formed part of a wider transformation in the way educated Russians thought about space. The monarchs of pre-Petrine Muscovy had conceived of themselves as ruling over populations rather than territories, and made no comprehensive effort to map their lands, mark their borders, compile information about provinces, or otherwise build a systematic corpus of geographic knowledge. This changed after Peter the Great. The cameralist approach to governance assumed that a primary goal of the state was to maximize the utility of the country's resources. Hence it became important to develop detailed, accurate maps and descriptions of territories and their inhabitants, to serve as tools of government policy and provide visible proof of the state's power and sophistication.[13]

The accumulation of geographic data not only assisted in the construction of a more effective state administration; it also helped to crystallize a sense of national and imperial identity. Over the course of the eighteenth century, the work of geographers and cartographers increasingly molded how educated Russians and Europeans imagined the Russian Empire. Largely at the initiative of the

[10] Proskurina, *Mify imperii*, ch.6.
[11] Elise Kimerling Wirtschafter, *The Play of Ideas in Russian Enlightenment Theater* (DeKalb, Ill.: Northern Illinois University Press, 2003), 35.
[12] Ananieva, *Russisch Grün*, 183–99.
[13] James C. Scott, *Seeing Like A State: How Certain Schemes to Improve the Human Condition Have Failed* (New Haven: Yale University Press, 1998), passim; Mack Walker, *German Home Towns: Community, State, and General Estate, 1648–1871* (Ithaca, NY: Cornell University Press, 1971; repr. 1998), 145–51, 168–71; Raeff, *The Well-Ordered Police State*, 158; Keith Tribe, "Cameralism and the Science of Government," *Journal of Modern History*, 56/2 (June 1984), 263–84.

scholar-statesman Vasilii Tatishchev (1686–1750), Russian geographers relocated Europe's eastern limit from the Don (where it had traditionally been placed) to the Urals and hardened the distinction between the empire's Russian core and its historically non-Russian periphery. One consequence was to shift Moscow, which had previously straddled the boundary of Europe and Asia, into a position squarely within Europe and at the center of historic Russia. Moscow's place in the Russian imaginary as both a European city and the metropolis of the Russian heartland was shaped in no small measure by the changes in geographic thinking that developed in conjunction with the Petrine reforms.[14]

How maps represented Moscow reflected these new approaches. Prior to Peter the Great, there were no accurate, reliable maps of the city. Pre-Petrine mapmakers were government officials who had no specialized training in cartography, and the maps they drew were colorful works of art that lacked consistent scale or orientation.[15] Some of them reached the West and became the basis for maps of Moscow that were printed in Europe in the sixteenth and seventeenth centuries. These Western maps had a consistent orientation, but otherwise, similar to those made by Russians, they drew the city from a bird's-eye perspective as a mass of individual houses and churches, with a scale that was distorted to make the Kremlin and Kitai-Gorod occupy a disproportionately large area of the city.[16] When the first and only map of Moscow ever printed in pre-Petrine Russia was published in 1663, it had these features as well (see Illustration 3.1).

This changed in the eighteenth century, when, in Russia as in Europe, scientifically precise maps that only professional geodesists could draw became an important part of government administration and propaganda.[17] The new maps functioned much like the statistics that officials increasingly collected: they affirmed officialdom's claim to a monopoly of objective knowledge and raised the prospect that such methods could be refined to yield an ever more precise understanding of the world. Similar to the administrative categories that underlay statistics, the maps homogenized and standardized space, and identified administrative constructs—for example, precisely drawn provincial and district boundaries, or the hierarchy of provincial capitals, district capitals, and villages—as the key elements of human geography. Statistics were compiled not just to reflect existing reality but to guide future policymaking; similarly, maps showed projected developments alongside the actual realities on the ground. On maps as

[14] Willard Sunderland, "Imperial Space: Territorial Thought and Practice in the Eighteenth Century," in Jane Burbank, Mark von Hagen, and Anatolyi Remnev, eds., *Russian Empire: Space, People, Power, 1700–1930* (Bloomington, Ind.: Indiana University Press, 2007), 33–66; Martin Aust, "Vermessen und Abbilden des russländischen Raumes nach der kulturellen Revolution Peters des Großen," in Lars Behrisch, ed., *Vermessen, Zählen, Berechnen: Die politische Ordnung des Raums im 18. Jahrhundert* (Frankfurt: Campus, 2006), 27–44.

[15] Valerie A. Kivelson, *Cartographies of Tsardom: The Land and its Meanings in Seventeenth-Century Russia* (Ithaca, NY: Cornell University Press, 2006), 3, 11.

[16] Skorniakova, *Staraia Moskva*, 18, 22–5.

[17] Lindsey Hughes, *Russia in the Age of Peter the Great* (New Haven: Yale University Press, 1998), 311–12.

Illus. 3.1. The frontispiece to the 1663 Moscow Bible. Courtesy of Bridwell Library Special Collections, Perkins School of Theology, Southern Methodist University.

in statistics, symmetry and generalizing abstraction replaced idiosyncrasy and specificity. The little houses and onion domes that dotted Muscovite maps created an image of an Orthodox land composed of many individualized features. By contrast, later maps showed Moscow as an amalgam of geometrically drawn streets and neighborhoods, framed by allegories symbolizing the Westernizing ideology of the regime.[18] These changes began under Peter the Great and intensified in the decades that followed.

A comparison of the first two printed maps of Moscow is instructive. The first map was part of the elaborate frontispiece of the 1663 Moscow Bible, which remained in widespread use in the eighteenth century because it was the only complete Bible printed in Russia between Ivan Fedorov's Bible of 1575 and the so-called Elizabeth Bible of 1751. The second map was the so-called Michurin map of 1739, commissioned by Empress Anna and compiled under the supervision of the Dutch-trained architect Ivan Michurin.

The 1663 map places Moscow in a context of monarchy and religion, with an image of God at the top of the page, symbols of the tsar in the middle, and the map of Moscow at the bottom, all flanked by biblical scenes.

The Michurin map could hardly be more different (see Illustration 3.2). In keeping with Muscovite cartographic tradition, the 1663 map faces east; the Michurin map, like modern European maps, faces north. While the 1663 map occupies only about one-ninth of the frontispiece, clearly subordinating the city to God and the tsar, the Michurin map takes up the whole sheet. It also contains no religious symbolism. Instead, its blank spaces are taken up by emblems of science (a large compass rose and an explanation of the map's scale) and an allegory from pagan mythology: the Moscow River, represented as a barebreasted maternal goddess surrounded by lush vegetation in an Arcadian setting.

Moscow's space is proportioned dissimilarly on the two maps. The 1663 map focuses on the Kremlin and Kitai-Gorod, the areas of the city that were most closely associated with the monarchy and the church. By contrast, the adjacent White City, Earthen City, and Zamoskvorech'e are compressed, and the outer suburbs are not included at all. The importance of the center is further heightened by the churches and little houses that fill the space of the Kremlin and Kitai-Gorod, whereas for the adjacent White City the map shows only the outline of the streets. (The Earthen City and Zamoskvorech'e are, like the center, filled with individual houses.)

The Michurin map takes a completely different tack, privileging the periphery over the center and emphasizing macro-level geometry, not symbolically important sites or buildings. Its geometric orderliness is all the greater because the map includes projected future construction alongside existing features of the city. It includes all the suburbs as far as the customs wall and shows the city in geodetically correct proportions, so the Kremlin and Kitai-Gorod appear very small. In the

---

[18] On reading maps in general, see J. B. Harley, "Deconstructing the Map," *Cartographica*, 26/2 (Summer 1989), 1–20.

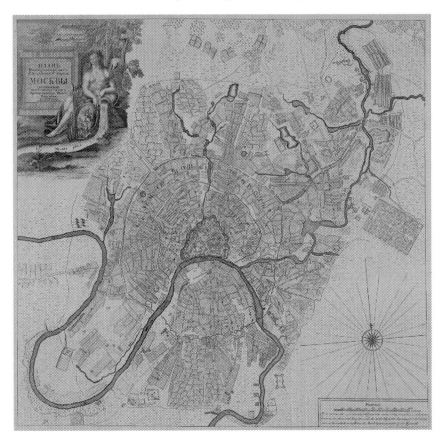

Illus. 3.2. "Plan of the Imperial Metropolitan City of Moscow, Drawn under the Supervision of the Architect Ivan Michurin in 1739." Etching combined with line engraving from 1741 by Georg Johann Unverzagt. Courtesy of The National Library of Israel, Eran Laor Cartographic Collection, Shapell Family Digitization Project and The Hebrew University of Jerusalem, Department of Geography—Historic Cities Research Project.

absence of images of buildings, the viewer's eye is drawn to the layout of the streets. The Kremlin and Kitai-Gorod remain important because of their central location, but they appear as an irregular triangle containing a maze of buildings and streets that is counterbalanced by the geometric regularity of the vast palace-and-gardens complex of Letnii Annengof (Anna's Summer Court) in the northwestern suburbs, which appears larger than the Kremlin and Kitai-Gorod combined.[19]

---

[19] Gulianitskii, *Moskva i slozhivshiesia russkie goroda*, 36–8; Skorniakova, *Staraia Moskva*, 100–1; Simon Franklin, "Printing Moscow: Significances of the Frontispiece to the 1663 Bible," in Simon Dixon, ed., *Personality and Place in Russian Culture: Essays in Memory of Lindsey Hughes* (London: Modern Humanities Research Association, 2010), 73–95.

The maps that followed over the course of the eighteenth century were recognizably heirs of the Michurin map, except that they lacked the river goddess and were instead adorned with the imperial double eagle. The Gorikhvostov map of 1767 improved on Michurin by using a larger scale and showing the boundaries of properties inside the Earthen Wall. Then came the map of 1775 that laid out plans for future urban development, followed in rapid succession by others in 1789, 1790, 1797, 1800, 1805, and 1810.[20]

Compared with their pre-Petrine forerunners, these maps achieved a far higher degree of cartographic accuracy, and they served to promote the regime's image of the city by showing it as subdivided into police districts, not parishes or historically constituted neighborhoods. Unlike maps in Muscovy (and some in the early modern West), which were guarded as official secrets, these were engraved, printed, and sold, thereby disseminating the regime's preferred image of Russia to audiences at home and abroad.[21] Catherine also initiated a program to map Russia's provinces, and Western authors noted after her death that "The numerous collections of geographical maps which Russia has of late years produced, are famous abroad, not less for their intrinsic worth, as they are mostly formed on new discoveries, than for their beauty and neatness."[22]

The newly available maps were only one part of a broader body of geographic data assembled by the authorities and disseminated in society. Once Moscow was mapped, subdivided into districts and wards, and staffed with an expanded bureaucracy, and once the houses within each district were numbered, compiling a directory became a simple matter. The first appeared in 1793, its very title revealing its indebtedness to the record-keeping categories created by the state's fiscal and police apparatus: *Directory of Moscow, Showing in Alphabetical Order the Names of the Owners of All Houses in This Metropolis; For Each House, in Which District of the City, Which Ward, Under Which Number, in Which Parish, on Which Main Street, Or in Which Lane It is Located; Supplemented With an Illuminated Map of Moscow Divided into Districts. With Permission From the Authorities.*[23]

---

[20] Gulianitskii, *Moskva i slozhivshiesia russkie goroda*, 63–7, 73–6, 90–1; Skorniakova, *Staraia Moskva*, 146; Schmidt, *The Architecture and Planning of Classical Moscow*, 49, 50, 55.

[21] Skorniakova, *Staraia Moskva*, 147; Kivelson, *Cartographies of Tsardom*, 25–8.

[22] [Jean-Henri Castéra and William Tooke], *The Life of Catharine II, Empress of Russia*, 3 vols. (4th edn., London: A. Strahan [vol. 1], H. Baldwin [vol. 2], T. N. Longman and O. Rees [vol. 3], 1800), 3:422; the book is discussed in Anthony Cross, *By the Banks of the Neva: Chapters from the Lives of the British in Eighteenth-Century Russia* (Cambridge: Cambridge University Press, 1997), 112.

[23] *Ukazatel' Moskvy, pokazyvaiushchii po azbuchnomu poriadku imena vladel'tsev vsekh domov sei stolitsy; kazhdoi dom v kotoroi chasti goroda, v kotorom kvartale, pod kakim nomerom, gde v prikhode, na kakoi glavnoi ulitse, ili v kakom pereulke nakhoditsia; s prilozheniem illiuminovannago plana Moskvy, na chasti razdelennoi. S dozvoleniia nachal'stva,* cited in A. D. Chertkov, ed., *Vseobshchaia biblioteka Rossii ili Katalog knig dlia izucheniia nashego otechestva vo vsekh otnosheniiakh i podrobnostiakh* (2nd edn., Moscow: V tipografii Lazarevskago Instituta vostochnykh iazykov, 1863), cols. 130–1.

How the state's approach to urban geography affected Muscovites' sense of place in the era of Catherine II is not easy to tell, but there are certain clues.[24] One is the way locations were described in Moscow's only newspaper, the twice-weekly *Moscow Gazette*. Mostly the *Gazette* carried news from St Petersburg or abroad, usually under the dateline of a particular European or (more rarely) colonial city, thereby helping readers situate themselves mentally in a wider international context. In addition to news, the *Gazette* carried classified advertisements relating to locations within Moscow. Taking one issue at random—Saturday, 28 March 1780, five years before the numbering of houses was introduced[25]—we note the following pattern. Advertisers who were evidently familiar to readers and had well-known downtown locations could refer simply to their street or the nearest landmark, like the book sellers "at the Resurrection Town-House [*podvor'e*] on Il'inka [Street]," "on Kuznetskii Most," and "by the Resurrection Gates." Other places were apparently harder to find and could be described with a mix of traditional toponyms and local lore. For example, a gunsmith indicated that he could be found "on Pokrovka [Street], in the parish of the Transfiguration of the Lord on the Clay Pits, in the house of Brigadier Prince Iakov Aleksandrovich Golitsyn, formerly the Izmailov house." A number of advertisers, however, found it convenient to rely at least in part on the police districts shown on the new city maps, even if these had to be supplemented with more traditional sorts of information. An ensign's house was "across the Moscow River, in the 11th district, on Iakimanskaia Street"; a second lieutenant of the guards owned a house "in the 9th district, in the parish of Peter and Paul in New Basmannaia"; and a merchant was trying to sell a house located "in the 13th district, in the parish of Great Martyr Irina, going from the city toward the village of Pokrovskoe and passing Gavrilov Lane, third house on the right."[26] By the early nineteenth century, it was standard in official documentation to identify a house by district and house number. In common usage, though, older reference points prevailed, and an author noted as late as 1846 that "in Moscow they indicate addresses by parish and lane, whereas in Petersburg, it is by [the nearest] bridge."[27]

HISTORY AND STATISTICS

In creating the new image of Moscow, the mapmakers were joined by historians and statisticians, above all Gerhard Friedrich Müller and Vasilii Ruban. Their

---

[24] See also Roche, *Le peuple de Paris*, 312.
[25] Houses were numbered from 1785 on; Alexander, *Bubonic Plague*, 63.
[26] *MV* (28 March 1780), 175–6.
[27] A. L., "Pis'ma iz Peterburga v Moskvu (Prodolzhenie)," *Zvezdochka, zhurnal dlia detei starshago vozrasta*, 6 (1847), 370–86, quotation on 375.

writings about Moscow resembled the new cartography in using quasi-visual forms of representation, aspiring to scientific objectivity, and emphasizing the power of the regime to mold urban society.

Müller and Ruban were characteristic figures of the milieu in which Russian Enlightenment culture took shape. They were at once intellectuals and state officials. They were men of undistinguished background who were steeped in European culture and parlayed professional expertise and ideological loyalty to the regime into social advancement. They were also ethnic outsiders who embraced the Russian nationality, and their worldview was formed in imperial peripheries where the role of the state in shaping society, indeed creating it virtually *ex nihilo*, was especially evident—St Petersburg, Siberia, and Ukraine. These factors combined to make them dedicated supporters of the regime's civilizing enterprise.

Müller (1705–83) belonged to the cohort of German immigrants who helped establish academic scholarship in Russia in the wake of the Petrine reforms.[28] He came from a school director's family in Westphalia and arrived in St Petersburg in 1725 to teach Latin, history, and geography at the newly established Academy of Sciences. He had just turned 20, but immigrants could go far if they were talented, driven, and tough. By the early 1730s, he was an academician, professor of history, and publisher of the first journal that disseminated (in German) information about Russian history to foreign audiences. In 1733, tensions in the academy drove Müller, a notoriously short-tempered and difficult man, out of St Petersburg. He spent the next ten years criss-crossing Siberia as part of Vitus Bering's second Kamchatka expedition, and wrote extensively on history, geography, ethnography, archaeology, and linguistics. He then returned to St Petersburg. Russian nationalism and Germanophobia had by then become widespread at the academy, and Müller's colleagues, especially his archrival Mikhail Lomonosov, were sharply critical of his occasional negative observations about aspects of Russian history. The greatest scandal of his career occurred in 1749, when Müller proposed a public lecture on the origins of medieval Rus'. He intended a scholarly exposition of historical sources, but was blindsided when Lomonosov accused him (falsely) of inflating the role of Scandinavians in Rus' history and thereby insulting Slavic Russia's national dignity.[29]

---

[28] On Müller, see J. L. Black, *G.-F. Müller and the Imperial Russian Academy* (Kingston: McGill-Queen's University Press, 1986); Peter Hoffmann, *Gerhard Friedrich Müller (1705–1783): Historiker, Geograph, Archivar im Dienste Russlands* (Frankfurt: Peter Lang, 2005); S. S. Ilizarov, "Akademik Miller—grazhdanin i istorik Moskvy," in S. S. Ilizarov, ed., *Moskva v opisaniiakh XVIII veka* (Moscow: Ianus-K, 1997), 45–60; A. B. Kamenskii, "Akademik G.-F. Miller i russkaia istoricheskaia nauka XVIII veka," *Istoriia SSSR*, no. 1 (January 1989), 144–59; also the biographical introduction to S. S. Ilizarov, ed., *Akademik G. F. Miller—pervyi issledovatel' Moskvy i Moskovskoi provintsii* (Moscow: Ianus, 1996).

[29] Peter Hoffmann, "Michail Vasil'evič Lomonosov, Gerhard Friedrich Müller und die 'Normannentheorie': Eine historiographiegeschichtliche Studie," in Donnert, *Europa in der Frühen Neuzeit*, 7:827–36.

Müller knew and admired the much younger Catherine II and shared her imperial vision. Both of them were Germans who embraced their adopted Russian homeland. Catherine wanted to extend the imperial culture deeper into Russian society and promote an enlightened image for Russia abroad. Müller thought along the same lines, as was apparent from his work in Siberia and (later) in Moscow, his correspondence with intellectuals across Russia and abroad, and his popularizing scholarship and extensive activity as an educator.[30] Catherine appointed him in 1764 to a commission tasked with developing proposals for a system of public education, and in 1765 she made him head of the newly established Moscow Foundling Home, one of the institutions through which she and Betskoi planned to foster the "new race of men."[31] In 1767, she named him to the Legislative Commission that she hoped would draft a new legal code to implement her ideas. Müller worked to bolster Russia's image by publishing articles (in Russia and abroad) that rebutted foreign writings that he thought misrepresented Russia, and when French publishers approached the Russian government in 1771 about articles on Russia for the revised edition of Diderot and d'Alembert's *Encyclopédie*, the Academy of Sciences entrusted the task to Müller. (The articles were written but ultimately not published.)

Müller accepted his new post at the Moscow Foundling Home both to get away from the intrigues and personal enmities at the Academy of Sciences and because he viewed Moscow as the ideal location for his historical research.[32] In 1766, he obtained a transfer from the Foundling Home to become head of the College of Foreign Affairs' Moscow archive, the repository for documents relating to pre-Petrine Russia's foreign relations. In this position, which he retained until the end of his life, he became Russia's "first professional historian-archivist, the organizer of the first Russian historical archive and the founder of the first Russian archivists' school."[33] He was intolerant of self-congratulatory patriotism, and thought historians should impart moral and political lessons and be antiquarians who collected and published documentary materials.[34]

The story of Vasilii (in Ukrainian, Vasyl) Ruban was different, yet in its own way no less typical of the people who built Russian Enlightenment culture.[35]

---

[30] Galina Smagina, "Gerhard Friedrich Müller als Pädagoge," in Donnert, *Europa in der Frühen Neuzeit*, 7:837–46; Gudrun Bucher, "Auf verschlungenen Pfaden: Die Aufnahme von Gerhard Friedrich Müllers Schriften in Europa," in Dittmar Dahlmann, ed., *Die Kenntnis Rußlands im deutschsprachigen Raum im 18. Jahrhundert: Wissenschaft und Publizistik über das Russische Reich* (Göttingen: Bonn University Press, V&R unipress, 2006), 111–23.

[31] Hoffmann, *Gerhard Friedrich Müller*, 150–4.

[32] Hoffmann, *Gerhard Friedrich Müller*, 138.

[33] Ilizarov, "Akademik Miller," in Ilizarov, *Moskva v opisaniiakh XVIII veka*, 52.

[34] Black, *G.-F. Müller*, 114–15, 130.

[35] On Ruban, see: Iu. N. Aleksandrov, *Prilozhenie k faksimil'nomu izdaniiu Opisanie Moskvy* (Moscow: Kniga, 1989), 85–97; "V. G. Ruban," in N. S. Tikhonravov, *Sochineniia*, 3 vols. in 4 (Moscow: Izdanie M. i S. Sabashnikovykh, 1898), vol. 3, pt. 1, 163–81; B. L. Modzalevskii, "Vasilii Grigor'evich Ruban," *RS*, 28/8 (August 1897), 393–415; David Saunders, *The Ukrainian Impact on Russian Culture, 1750–1850* (Edmonton: Canadian Institute of Ukrainian Studies, 1985), 119–26.

Like Müller, Ruban (1742–95) was a social and ethnic outsider. He was born to a Ukrainian family (possibly of Cossack ancestry) in Belgorod, a fortress town built to fend off raids across the steppe by Crimean Tatars. As a boy he attended the Kiev Ecclesiastical Academy, whose ties to Counter-Reformation Poland had made it one of Russia's first conduits for cultural contact with Europe. He thus grew up in a frontier culture molded by the encounter of Russians, Cossacks, Poles, and Tatars. Around 1754 he transferred to the Moscow Ecclesiastical Academy, and thence to one of the gymnasia of Moscow University. Since he is not listed among the students of the nobles' gymnasium, his social status must have qualified him only for the gymnasium for *raznochintsy* ("people of various ranks"). Trained in languages, he returned to Ukraine as a translator before finding a position in St Petersburg. In 1774 he became secretary to Potemkin, the architect of Catherine's policy of imperial expansion in his home region; Ruban retained this position for eighteen years.

Ruban had literary ambitions. He dabbled in journalism and translated Western and classical authors. In his lifetime, a later scholar noted sardonically, "Ruban was known primarily as a panegyric poet who glorified the mighty of this world [who were] his patrons."[36] A partial bibliography of his writings includes five odes to Potemkin and four to Catherine II, whose grandees he likened to classical heroes: for instance, he discerned a new Cato in her Procurator-General Viazemskii, and a new Pompey in Field Marshal Rumiantsev. A typical if undistinguished writer in the neoclassical style, Ruban declared that he composed verse so that posterity "might learn in what years the Russian land | Purified its reason and its morals | And ascended to the status of greatness and glory."[37]

He was a hack in poetry and journalism—in his book *The Ukrainian Impact on Russian Culture*, David Saunders discusses him in a chapter titled "Ukrainians on Grub Street"—but he found a niche with almanacs and reference books that appealed to the Enlightenment belief that an objective picture of the world could be constructed from the factual data that were increasingly compiled by scientists and bureaucrats. His roots in a land adjoining Turkey and Poland (both of whose languages he spoke), his broad if eclectic interests, his bureaucratic career under Potemkin, the context of Russian expansion and the partitions of Poland—these circumstances are reflected in his Ukrainian patriotism and his preference for publishing about Ukrainian history and geography, always from a perspective that was Orthodox, Russophile, and anti-Polish. In 1779, he ventured farther afield by publishing the first Russian-language guide to St Petersburg.[38] This he followed in 1782 with a book on Moscow.[39]

---

[36] Modzalevskii, "Vasilii Grigor'evich Ruban," 412.

[37] Quoted in Tikhonravov, "V. G. Ruban," in Tikhonravov, *Sochineniia*, vol. 3, pt. 1, 171.

[38] Ruban's book on St Petersburg was a revised version of an unpublished text by another author, Andrei Bogdanov, 1751–2; Emily D. Johnson, *How St. Petersburg Learned to Study Itself: The Russian Idea of Kraevedenie* (University Park, Pa.: Pennsylvania State University Press, 2006), 20–2.

[39] Ruban, *Opisanie.*

Müller and Ruban differed in their approach to writing about Moscow. Müller in 1773 contributed an article on Moscow to Russia's first geographic dictionary, the impressively titled *Geographic Lexicon of the Russian State, or Dictionary Describing in Alphabetical Order the Rivers, Lakes, Seas, Mountains, Cities, Fortresses, Prominent Monasteries, Stockades, Tribute-Collection Outposts, Mines, and Other Noteworthy Sites of the Vast Russian Empire*.[40] Müller's text, twelve dense pages long, focuses on geographic detail ("Moscow . . . lies 734 *verst* [783 kilometers] from St. Petersburg") and on specific sites that the reader was encouraged to visualize and that had historical and cultural significance, particularly churches, monasteries, and buildings associated with past tsars. In the section on the Kremlin, for example, we learn that the word *Kreml'* is derived from the Tatar for fortress, that Tsar Boris Godunov had the "Ivan the Great" bell tower erected in 1600, and that Catherine II was planning "a new magnificent palace" for the Kremlin. Elsewhere Müller describes at length the beneficence represented by the Moscow Foundling Home and various government hospitals, and briefly praises recent infrastructure improvements. ("The streets are being put in order; few are unpaved, and all large streets are lined with street lights."[41]) Moscow appears in Müller's text as a place where the enlightened ideals and policies of the monarchy blended with the traditions of the Orthodox Church and Muscovite tsars.

Absent is almost any reference to the *people* of Moscow. "The people" was no alien topic to Müller. He spoke excellent Russian, and few knew the country as he did. He had traveled vast distances on his decade-long Siberian odyssey, and had written extensively on Siberian ethnography; the very word *ethnography* originated as a calque of a term, *Völker-Beschreibung*, that Müller coined in his writings on Siberia.[42] He must have become keenly aware of the complexities of urban society in Moscow as head of the Foundling Home. He had lived in St Petersburg for three decades and in Moscow for eight years by the time his article appeared in 1773, just two years after the plague revolt had demonstrated the class hatreds and failure of "enlightened" governance in Moscow. He found the plague so memorable that he later made a point of collecting documents relating to it, and his article briefly mentions the lynching of the archbishop during the plague revolt.

---

[40] Fedor Polunin, *Geograficheskii leksikon Rossiiskago gosudarstva, ili Slovar', opisuiushchii po azbuchnomu poriadku reki, ozera, moria, gory, goroda, kreposti, znatnye monastyri, ostrogi, iasashnyia zimovyia, rudnyia zavody, i prochiia dostopamiatnyia mesta obshirnoi Rossiiskoi Imperii*, ed. and introd. Gerard Friderik Miller (Moscow: Pri Imperatorskom Moskovskom Universitete, 1773).

[41] Ilizarov, *Moskva v opisaniiakh XVIII veka*, 69.

[42] Han F. Vermeulen, "Von der Völker-Beschreibung zur Völkerkunde: Ethnologische Ansichten Gerhard Friedrich Müllers und August Ludwig Schlözers," in Donnert, *Europa in der Frühen Neuzeit*, 7:784.

If Müller did not discuss the people of Moscow in his article, he had his reasons. For one thing, he worked within intellectual traditions that privileged a top-down perspective and left little space for the people as autonomous historical actors. One such tradition was Enlightenment historical writing, which focused on great men, not the common people or impersonal social processes.[43] Another was the European tradition of travel guidebooks, which favored narratives of great historical events, descriptions of monuments and churches, and lists of streets and prominent buildings.[44] A third tradition that shaped Müller's work was the collecting of numerical data by cameralist bureaucracies; these data were meant to catalogue the resources available to the state, not investigate the dynamics of social development.[45]

Another factor that must have deterred Müller from engaging sensitive issues was his vulnerable personal status. He obtained a government-service rank—the all-important marker of social status—only when he was appointed to the Foundling Home when he was already 59 years old, and as an immigrant, he had cause to avoid offending the prickly patriotism of the Russians. It is therefore no surprise that, to quote his colleague and rival August Ludwig Schlözer, "In honoring Russia, which had greatly neglected him to that time, he was a warm patriot, and with regard to the faults of the government of the time, which no one knew better than he, he was extremely restrained."[46]

Müller's silence did not mean indifference, as is apparent from an article that he wrote on the Pugachev revolt. The subject was utterly taboo in Russia, but Müller could be candid because the article appeared abroad, anonymously, and when he was already dead. The article praised the "mild and calm reign" of "the empress [Catherine], for whom the well-being and love of her subjects is the first fundamental law of government." The rebellion, he wrote, reflected the irrationality of the populace—the Cossacks with their "natural inconstancy and wildness," and "the mob [which is] a friend of innovation and change." He grimly described rebel atrocities and conceded that "all Moscow desired his [Pugachev's] arrival, and was prepared on his first approach to take his side. Of course this applies only to the mob, but the latter is exceedingly numerous there."[47] Müller

---

[43] Cynthia Hyla Whittaker, "The Idea of Autocracy among Eighteenth-Century Russian Historians," in Sanders, *Historiography of Imperial Russia*; on eighteenth-century Russian historiography, see also Erich Donnert, "Von Tatiščev bis Schlözer: Zur Geschichtsschreibung in Russland im 18. Jahrhundert," in Donnert, *Europa in der Frühen Neuzeit*, 7:763–80.

[44] Laurent Turcot, *Le promeneur à Paris au XVIIIe siècle* (n.p.: Gallimard, 2007), 277–84.

[45] Susan Smith-Peter, "Defining the Russian People: Konstantin Arsen'ev and Russian Statistics before 1861," *History of Science*, 45/1 (March 2007), 47–64, esp. 48.

[46] A. L. Schlözer, *August Ludwig Schlözers öffentliches und Privatleben: Erstes Fragment* (Göttingen: im Vandenhoeck- und Ruprechtschen Verlage, 1802), 29.

[47] "Zuverläßige Nachrichten von dem Aufrührer Jemeljan Pugatschew, und der von demselben angestifteten Empörung," in Anton Friedrich Büsching, ed., *Magazin für die neue Historie und Geographie*, no. 18 (1784), 3–70, quotations on 18, 6, 17, 47. On Müller's authorship of this article, see Kamenskii, "Akademik G.-F. Miller," 154.

thus shared the outlook of Catherine II: he believed in the autocracy's civilizing mission but had deep misgivings about the character of the people.

The coolly optimistic tone of Müller's article on Moscow, the top-down perspective, the elision of "the people"—these were conscious authorial choices. A similar effect was achieved by Ruban in his *Description of the Imperial Metropolitan City of Moscow* (*Opisanie imperatorskago stolichnago goroda Moskvy*, 1782). Müller assisted him with advice,[48] but their methodologies could hardly have been more different. Ruban's book, 159 pages long, consisted entirely of facts and numbers that were culled from government records and were presented without commentary. Neatly arranged in lists and statistical tables, Ruban's data gave readers the same visual sense of the state's rationality and control as did the maps of the same period. Müller's article had divided the city into its historic sections (Kremlin, Kitai-Gorod, White City, Earthen City, suburbs) and was all narrative, although he did add a few statistics in later unpublished revisions.[49] Ruban, by contrast, based his approach on the city's police districts and was all lists and numbers. Going district by district, he listed streets, lanes, and public buildings, as well as the number of churches, houses belonging to people of various estates, and businesses of different types. The remainder of the book provided aggregate data of the same sort for the entire city.

Ruban's approach was rooted in the tradition of statistical topography. This was a form of social analysis that came to Russia from Western Europe, especially the German states. It arose from two sources. One was statistics as we understand the term today: numerical data about society and the economy, which were collected in growing quantities by governments and private individuals in the eighteenth century, especially in Prussia.[50] The other source was *Statistik*, an academic field designed to provide governments with useful knowledge about their own and other states, often in narrative, non-quantitative form. Statistical topography was the combination of *Statistik* with numerical data. "Of German origin," writes one historian, "a direct offshoot of [cameralism], these numerical descriptions of the physical environment, history, political structure, economic activities and social organisation of administratively delimited areas encapsulated at one and the same time the educated public's thirst for easily acquired knowledge, the trader's need for practical information and the scientifically oriented administrator's search for classified and hence comparable empirical data."[51]

Statistical approaches were new in Russia. Müller's colleague August Ludwig Schlözer recalled that as late as 1763, when he spoke about the hemp trade with merchants in St Petersburg and cited Russian export figures, he was warned against divulging state secrets. Schlözer also reported that when a few years earlier, a British

---

[48] Black, *G.-F. Müller*, 186–7.
[49] Ilizarov, *Moskva v opisaniiakh XVIII veka*, 299.
[50] Ian Hacking, *The Taming of Chance* (Cambridge: Cambridge University Press, 1990), 18–20.
[51] Stuart Woolf, *Napoleon's Integration of Europe* (London: Routledge, 1991), 4.

traveler had asked in the Academy of Sciences' bookstore for Russian books on the country's judiciary, commerce, and finances, "the factor answered, '*Gospodi pomilui* (Lord have mercy), who would print such things!' and crossed himself." In Schlözer's view, it was Catherine's encouragement of the press that made possible

"the beginning of Russian statistics"—yes, the very beginning; that, literally and without presumption, is the truth. Only now did I myself begin to undertake the study of the Russian state . . . And the Russian too began only in the following years to study his vast fatherland in public, that is, to write and print about it. Let a future writer tabulate how much [literature] of this sort appeared in Russia itself before the year 1765, and compare that with the quite unexpected volume of great and small works—most of them as yet unknown to foreigners—on statistical subjects of all sorts, to which the great empress's liberal way of thinking, proclaimed by her in 1764, gave life between 1770 and 1790.[52]

Subsequent statistical topographies built on the example set by Müller and Ruban. They produced varying combinations of Müller's historical approach with Ruban's focus on administrative statistics, and in addition provided information on the city's commerce. The surveyor Faddei Okhtenskii (b.1730s, d. 1781 or later), a priest's son and former student of Müller, produced a manuscript description of Moscow in 1775. Müller's archival assistant Lev Maksimovich (1754–before 1816), also a priest's son, included a lengthy entry on Moscow in the six-volume *New and Complete Geographic Dictionary of the Russian State* (*Novyi i polnyi geograficheskii slovar' Rossiiskago gosudarstva*) that he published in 1788–9. Maksimovich's collaborator Afanasii Shchekatov (*c.*1753–1814), of whose biography almost nothing is known, published a seven-volume *Geographic Dictionary of the Russian State* (*Slovar' geograficheskii Rossiiskago gosudarstva*) in 1801–9. Aleksei Malinovskii (1762–1840), another priest's son, wrote an unfinished description of Moscow in the 1820s; Malinovskii worked at Müller's archive from 1778 to 1840—almost his entire life—and was its director from 1814 on.[53]

These men were at once products and supporters of the imperial social project. Müller served them as a model of scholarly research and writing, and his archive was a source of historical information. They were also connected with the circle of Nikolai Novikov, Moscow's most influential Freemason, publisher, journalist, philanthropist, and educator. Müller and the other authors of statistical topographies do not appear to have been members of masonic lodges, but Müller provided archival materials to assist Novikov in his historical research, and Maksimovich and Malinovskii served as translators for journals that Novikov published and that specialized in religious, philosophical, and morally edifying texts by European authors.[54] Novikov's diverse activities were directed toward

[52] Schlözer, *August Ludwig Schlözer's öffentliches und Privatleben*, 130–1.

[53] For biographies of these authors and the texts of their writings on Moscow, see Ilizarov, *Moskva v opisaniiakh XVIII veka.*

[54] Hoffmann, *Gerhard Friedrich Müller*, 172; A. I. Serkov, *Russkoe masonstvo 1731–2000: Entsiklopedicheskii slovar'* (Moscow: ROSSPEN, 2001), 512, 514.

the construction of a civil society in which Russians of diverse backgrounds embraced the Christian faith, moral and spiritual self-improvement, and a commitment to serving the wider public good.[55] The authors of the statistical topographies were receptive to such ideas. Their own roots were in the clergy, an estate that was deeply attached to Russian traditions and resentful of the nobility for its cultural cosmopolitanism and claims to social supremacy, but whose more educated members were cautiously open to Enlightenment ideas.[56] These attitudes informed the content of the statistical topographies: they expressed pride in Russia's dynastic and ecclesiastical history and in the regime's modernizing urban policies, but were silent about the aristocracy and elided any comparisons between Moscow and other European cities.

The historical approach that was first introduced by Müller appealed to the patriotism of readers because it suggested that their country's progress grew organically out of its own national traditions. On the other hand, it did little to bring the character of the people into focus. Moscow was depicted as a microcosm of Russia, but what it meant to be Russian was left vague. The emphasis on church and dynasty suggested that Russians were the community of Orthodox subjects of the tsar, but writers did not ask whether being Russian also meant sharing a particular ethnic ancestry, national character, or way of life, or whether Muscovites were in any way different from other Russians. The anonymous author of the *Historical and Topographical Description of the City of Moscow* (*Istoricheskoe i topograficheskoe opisanie goroda Moskvy*, 1787), most likely Müller's assistant Maksimovich,[57] wrote merely that "As for the mores and customs of the inhabitants, to describe them one would have to describe the mores and customs of all the regions of the vast Russian Empire, for a very great multitude from each of them have their residence here out of the most varied motivations." Maksimovich reproduced this passage almost verbatim in his geographic dictionary of 1788–9, and Shchekatov did so again in 1805.[58]

The use of government statistical data had implications for the way the city was represented. Local officials collected data to monitor compliance with the laws on urban planning and the estate system. Like the maps that showed both actual and

[55] Douglas Smith, *Working the Rough Stone: Freemasonry and Society in Eighteenth-Century Russia* (DeKalb, Ill.: Northern Illinois University Press, 1999), 7, 24, 37–52; on Novikov, see Raffaella Faggionato, *A Rosicrucian Utopia in Eighteenth-Century Russia: The Masonic Circle of N. I. Novikov*, tr. Michael Boyd and Brunello Lotti (Dordrecht: Springer, 2005), and Gabriela Lehmann-Carli, "Kulturelle Übersetzung westlicher Konzepte und nachpetrinische Identitätsentwürfe bis zur Mitte des 19. Jahrhunderts," in Gabriela Lehmann-Carli, Yvonne Drohsin, and Ulrike Klitsche-Sowitzki, eds., *Russland zwischen Ost und West? Gratwanderungen nationaler Identität* (Berlin: Frank & Timme, 2011), 13–80, esp. 35–49.

[56] Elise Kimerling Wirtschafter, "Religion and Enlightenment in Eighteenth-Century Russia: Father Platon at the Court of Catherine II," in Dixon, *Personality and Place in Russian Culture*, 180–4.

[57] Ilizarov, *Moskva v opisaniiakh XVIII veka*, 173.

[58] Ilizarov, *Moskva v opisaniiakh XVIII veka*, 177, 244, 271.

projected elements of the urban space, the social and spatial categories that officials used served two distinct functions. Some categories described present realities, but others were instruments of future-oriented social engineering. For example, the estate of merchants was established in 1775 to help foster an as yet non-existent middling sort. Likewise, when a thoroughfare was designated as either a "street" or a "lane" (*ulitsa, pereulok*), the point was to identify which zoning law applied to its future development.[59] Hence, when a statistical topography reported that Moscow had 25 "main" streets, 61 "middling" streets, and 672 lanes, these were city-planning designations, and only secondarily descriptive categories.[60]

Using such data as tools of social analysis could produce a distorted view of reality. For example, Ruban in 1782 used records on property ownership to determine the city's social composition. He found that Moscow contained 8,778 homesteads. Of these, 60 percent belonged to nobles, clergy, or merchants; the rest belonged to "people of various ranks"—an umbrella category for people who were not legally registered in an estate or otherwise did not fit neatly into the authorities' scheme of estates.[61] The author of an anonymous text from 1785 went farther and tried to count inhabitants. Like Ruban, he broke them down into nobles, clergy, and merchants, to which he added the categories of towns-people, coachmen, Tatars, and possessional serfs (i.e. peasants obligated by law to work in a particular factory). With the odd precision of administrative statistics, he counted 25 male Tatars, 1,063 female dependents of the parish clergy, and so on. But all of these added up to only 28,703 people; another 156,217—presumably peasants and serfs—were unspecified "people of various ranks."[62]

The estate-based approach to demographic analysis was further refined in the 1805 article on Moscow in the geographic dictionary by Shchekatov, which used a much larger number of categories. Ever finer distinctions were made among the groups that Catherine had intended as components of the middling sort. Shche-katov provided data on the elite group of "eminent citizens" (27 individuals), and then—in descending order of prestige and privilege—the three merchant guilds, manufacturers, townspeople, and artisans, followed by clergy, government clerks, "people of various ranks" (only 2 percent of the total), soldiers, and the staff and students of various state institutions. At the bottom, however, were 57,695 peasants and 58,871 house serfs, almost 54 percent of the total population of 216,953, who were differentiated only by whether they were legally Moscow residents.[63] The picture of society was more nuanced than in earlier studies, but the basic approach was unchanged. Like his predecessors, Shchekatov ignored the difficulties encountered by a rudimentary bureaucracy in counting a highly

[59] On the regulation of the width of streets and lanes, see Schmidt, *The Architecture and Planning of Classical Moscow*, 23.
[60] Ilizarov, *Moskva v opisaniiakh XVIII veka*, 159.
[61] Ruban, *Opisanie*, 52; Wirtschafter, *Structures of Society*, esp. ch.3.
[62] Ilizarov, *Moskva v opisaniiakh XVIII veka*, 159–60.
[63] Ilizarov, *Moskva v opisaniiakh XVIII veka*, 280–1.

mobile population; he made subtle distinctions among legally privileged groups but hardly any among the bulk of the population; and he used the state's administrative and fiscal categories as a proxy for sociological ones.

The reliance on official data skewed the representation not only of spaces and populations, but also of institutions. Rather than describe how the state dealt with particular issues, authors sometimes simply reproduced the official organizational table (*shtat*) of relevant state institutions. The *shtat* that appears most comprehensively in the statistical topographies is that of the university. The anonymous text from 1785 reports that Moscow University had 1 director, 4 professors, 25 teachers, 61 university students, 553 gymnasium students, 14 other officials, and 51 clerical employees and soldiers; this was followed by only a brief summary list of subjects that were taught. The unstated implication was that if an institution was so organized, it must also be functioning successfully. Maksimovich reproduced the same information, albeit with updated numbers.[64]

When the numbers were not a source of pride, authors sometimes limited themselves to praising an institution's mission. A case in point is the Moscow Foundling Home. The regime boasted of the enlightened philanthropy that the Foundling Home represented, but in reality it was an unmitigated disaster. From 1764 to 1797, over 80 percent of the foundlings died before reaching their majority. Of the 1,089 children admitted in 1767, a particularly grim moment, 1,074 died before the year was out.[65] As former director of the Foundling Home, Müller must have known these facts, yet he wrote cheerfully in his encyclopedia article of 1773 that "here are received infants of unfortunate birth, of both sexes, who previously faced a terrible fate and mortal peril. They are supported at state expense [*soderzhatsia s udovol'stviem*], are raised to be virtuous, and are taught various trades and arts as befits their station and intelligence."[66] Maksimovich and Shchekatov later repeated these claims in their geographic encyclopedias.[67]

Historians and statisticians in the eighteenth century constructed an image of Moscow that expressed the aspirations of the regime, not the realities that actually existed. The same was true in the graphic arts.

THE GRAPHIC ARTS

Various imperatives shaped the images of Russia that artists produced in the second half of the eighteenth century. Following the rules of European academic art, they believed that the artist should not depict the physical world naturalistically, but rather idealize it according to a Western aesthetic sensibility that was

---

[64] Ilizarov, *Moskva v opisaniiakh XVIII veka*, 166, 183, 240.
[65] Ransel, *Mothers of Misery*, 45, 48.
[66] Ilizarov, *Moskva v opisaniiakh XVIII veka*, 66–7.
[67] Ilizarov, *Moskva v opisaniiakh XVIII veka*, 184, 241, 274.

held to be universal.[68] At the same time, they also wanted to show what made Russia different from other countries. Lastly, in keeping with the ideals of neoclassicism, they wanted to represent Russia as a land of harmony and contentment, while minimizing any elements of ugliness or dissonance.

These goals were sometimes in conflict. In his study of Russian landscape art, Christopher Ely argues that Russian painters had difficulty seeing beauty in their country's natural landscape because their aesthetic sense was molded by the scenery of Italy. One reason for this was the training provided by the Imperial Academy of the Arts, which taught students to paint scenes that were characteristic of the Mediterranean but not of Russia. For example, the academy recommended in 1793 that landscape paintings include features such as the following: "on a hot summer day beneath the setting sun shepherds, leading their flock to the city, and others, stopping by a stream in the fields to rest." Some painters, such as Fedor Matveev and Semen Shchedrin, achieved success with these techniques, but as Ely notes, "Most often their paintings of Russian locations portrayed the royal family's landscaped parks in the vicinity of Petersburg, which were, of course, already modeled on contemporary European neoclassical forms. Logically (and tautologically) enough, both of these painters eventually went to the original source of the image they had been taught to reproduce—the Italian countryside."[69] Not until the 1830s and 1840s did Russian artists develop an approach to painting their country's landscape that went beyond attempts to reproduce West European models.[70]

A coherent, believable visual image of Russia's inhabitants proved similarly elusive. Under Catherine II, the Academy of Sciences dispatched scholarly expeditions to produce descriptions and pictures of the empire's diverse peoples. One of Catherine's aims, according to the historian Elena Vishlenkova, was to build a sense of unity among her subjects by promoting a shared understanding of their country's ethnic composition. The images of Russia's peoples that the artists on these expeditions produced were widely disseminated in Russia and the West, but the ethnographic artists faced the same conundrum that baffled the landscape painters: how to create a visual idiom to show that Russia was vast and diverse yet also unified and coherent, and that it was civilized and beautiful yet different from Western Europe. Part of the problem was that well into the nineteenth century, there was no consensus about what it meant to be "Russian." Was this, as Catherine herself preferred, a sociopolitical category that included all who were "enlightened" and loyal to the empire? Or was it an ethnic category determined by ancestry, language, and custom?

The ethnographic artists, most of whom were foreigners, were torn between these competing ways of conceptualizing nationality. The German Christoph

[68] Vishlenkova, *Vizual'noe narodovedenie imperii*, 37–42
[69] Ely, *This Meager Nature*, 41.
[70] Ely, *This Meager Nature*, 87–9.

Melchior Roth, working from images drawn by artists who had accompanied various expeditions, made engravings of individual figures in supposedly typical costumes and poses ("a merchant from Kaluga," "a maiden from Valdai," "a Tatar from Kazan'," and so on), suggesting that Russia's inhabitants were a mosaic of subgroups that lacked unifying national characteristics. The Frenchman Jean-Baptiste Le Prince, on the other hand, drew not only individuals but also genre scenes, thereby drawing attention to shared customs that created a unified Russian national identity among otherwise dissimilar groups. The Englishman John Augustus Atkinson took yet another approach: he divided Russia's inhabitants into two broad groups based on their level of civilization—sedentary peoples were categorized as "Russians," while nomadic ones, even the Cossacks, were "Tatars."[71]

Developing a visual image for Russia's two metropolitan cities was similarly a gradual process. Three sets of themes—architecture, monarchy, and genre scenes—predominated in images of Moscow in the eighteenth century. Artists depicted the city's architectural grandeur, first with bird's-eye panoramas and later in the century with perspective views of streets and buildings. They also celebrated the monarchy and the church by showing palaces, cathedrals, court ceremonies, triumphal arches, fireworks, and monasteries. Albums of such engravings were published in Russian and in Western languages to commemorate the coronation of monarchs from Empress Anna (r. 1730–40) onward. Catherine II's coronation was the first to highlight the importance of popular (as opposed to elite) acclamation for the new empress, and perhaps for this reason, her album broke new ground by including genre scenes.[72] (For examples of images from Catherine's coronation album, see Illustrations 0.1 and 1.1.)

Syntheses of these elements began to appear at the end of the century. Among foreign artists, the most significant were the Italian Francesco Camporesi, who made a series of engravings of Moscow in 1789, and the Frenchman Gérard de la Barthe, who produced a set of oil paintings in 1794–8. Both men's works were repeatedly published abroad as engravings and circulated in Russia as well. They drew attention to the same tensions and contradictions that one finds in written accounts by Europeans. Stately neoclassical architecture and upper-class people in Western attire testified to Moscow's European quality, but all around were reminders of the city's otherness: empty, undeveloped spaces around many buildings; a profusion of onion-domed churches; and a common people whose exotic character was apparent from their folk dress, their games, and their lack of civilized inhibitions—for example, men and women bathing naked in public in each other's presence.[73]

---

[71] Vishlenkova, *Vizual'noe narodovedenie imperii*, 52, 68–87.
[72] Skorniakova, *Staraia Moskva*, 17–20, 49–51, 79–81, 290, 293; Wortman, *Scenarios of Power*, 1:91, 114.
[73] Skorniakova, *Staraia Moskva*, 103–13, 120–43, 291–2.

Illus. 3.3. "Moscow. Lubianka Square. View Toward the Vladimir Gates." Painting from the 1800s by Fedor Alekseev. © All-Russian A. S. Pushkin Museum, St Petersburg.

More congruent with the notion of Moscow as an enlightened metropolis were the canvases that Fedor Alekseev and his assistants painted in 1800–2, a few years after Catherine's death. Alekseev had made his career in St Petersburg and was a pioneer in Russian cityscape painting. Previous artists had depicted St Petersburg either gazing from a distance upon vast geometric architectural ensembles, or offering intimate views of picturesque scenes from the vantage point of a street-level observer. A synthesis of the two, combining architectural grandeur with a sentimentalist interest in the life of the people, appeared for the first time in 1793 in paintings of St Petersburg by Alekseev and the Swede Benjamin Patersson.[74]

Alekseev's paintings of Moscow followed the same method. An example is his view from the Lubianka toward the Vladimir Gates of the Kitai-Gorod Wall (seen in the background) and the Kremlin (see Illustrations 3.3, 3.4).

[74] Grigory Kaganov, *Images of Space: St. Petersburg in the Visual and Verbal Arts*, tr. Sidney Monas (Stanford, Calif.: Stanford University Press, 1997), 38–41.

Illus. 3.4. "Moscow. Lubianka Square. View Toward the Vladimir Gates." (Detail.)

Like Alekseev's other Moscow canvases, this one shows the city center, thereby avoiding the unsightly vacant spaces we see in Camporesi and de la Barthe. Churches with onion domes and ancient fortifications dominate the scene. In keeping with the aesthetic of sentimentalism and the pre-Romantic fascination with the Middle Ages, they appear weathered and timeworn, giving them a historic air at once charming and majestic.[75] A closer look reveals that the street is populated with human figures, solitary or in small clusters, who exude an air of unhurried dignity. They form a cross-section of society, but all are tall and slender, fitting a specifically noble ideal of physical beauty. Many are men in the latest European clothes—military men in the French-style, tight-fitting green uniforms introduced by Alexander I, and civilians in brown dress coats with the new round hats that Paul I had banned because he associated them with revolutionary France. The other figures wear timeless, colorful Russian attire. The middling sort, though clearly distinguished from each other, form a harmonious unity: in the center (see Illustration 3.4), an officer chats with a European-clad civilian and a bearded merchant in Russian garb, while at a door in the wall on the left, another Westernized civilian exchanges polite bows with a black-robed cleric. "Enlightened" urban policy is likewise in evidence: the street is paved; in the left foreground, a lamplighter replenishes the oil in a street light; in the background, troops are on parade and a watchman stands guard in front of his guardhouse.

Alekseev (1753–1824) deserves closer attention because his biography and his *œuvre* make him a classic representative of the imperial social project. He climbed the social ladder to become a nobleman, an academician, and a well-paid artist

---

[75] Alessandra Tosi, *Waiting for Pushkin: Russian Fiction in the Reign of Alexander I (1801–1825)* (Amsterdam: Rodopi, 2006), 326–7.

whose paintings were acquired by the court, the aristocracy, and foreign collectors, but he began life at the very lowest rung of the social strata connected with the imperial culture. His father, a retired soldier, was a watchman at the Academy of Sciences in St Petersburg. Young Fedor attended a garrison school for soldiers' sons, and was then enrolled in 1764 for nine years in the boarding school of the Academy of the Arts. Ivan Betskoi was the academy's president, and Alekseev, as a child of lowly background who could be given an education in a tightly controlled boarding school, was the perfect raw material for the "new race of men" that Betskoi and Catherine envisioned in the 1760s as the regime's future social base. His background was not unusual for the academy: as Richard Stites notes, its "original nucleus of students [was drawn] from the Moscow University gymnasium and Petersburg soldiers' sons" and "amplified by children from the foundling homes."[76] In Russia as elsewhere in Europe, monarchical institutions were tools for domestic social pedagogy and international propaganda. The Academy of the Arts, too, was shown off to visitors. When Francisco de Miranda visited St Petersburg in 1787, his itinerary included a tour of the academy, and he noted in his diary that "the building is beautiful, of the most handsome architecture," and "[the students'] lodgings, beds, tables, food, kitchen, infirmary, etc., are all very clean and quite tidy." This mattered because, as he added sardonically, "cleanliness is a virtue that needs to be taught to this nation."[77]

In 1773, after completing the course at the academy, Alekseev left for Venice, where he studied under Giuseppe Moretti, a disciple of the celebrated Canaletto (Giovanni Antonio Canal, 1697–1768).[78] It was a heady time to be a Russian in Venice. Venice was at the center of Russian diplomacy when Russia backed the Greek revolt against the Ottomans in the Russo-Turkish War of 1768–74, and Russia made great efforts to persuade public opinion in Venice and elsewhere in Italy of the enlightened character of Catherine's regime. The receptiveness of educated Italians, many of whom were frustrated by conditions in their own states, is suggested by the fact that three separate Italian versions of Catherine's *Nakaz* appeared in 1769.[79] For Alekseev, the years in Venice must have deepened a sense of Russia as a widely admired model of enlightened governance and a rising Mediterranean power.

After he returned in 1777 to St Petersburg, he worked as a set designer for the Imperial Theaters Directorate and painted copies of Canaletto's views of Venice. In 1794, after another stay abroad, he was sent by Catherine to paint the sites that she had visited in 1787 during her trip with Emperor Joseph II. Painting theater sets and copying Canaletto was good preparation for this new assignment. Catherine's trip to the south had been a public-relations exercise to give Russia

---

[76] Stites, *Serfdom, Society, and the Arts*, 284–5, 296.
[77] Miranda, *Diario*, 98–9.
[78] *Russkii Biograficheskii Slovar'*, 2:15–17.
[79] Venturi, *The End of the Old Regime*, 55–72, 80–1.

a new, quasi-Mediterranean image, and Alekseev was supposed to provide pictorial evidence that the Black Sea coast was a sun-kissed paradise that would replace frigid St Petersburg as the site of Russia's imperial destiny.[80]

It was his work in St Petersburg in the 1790s that made him, as one scholar describes him, "the founder of the cityscape genre in Russia."[81] Recognizing his source of inspiration, contemporaries dubbed him "the Russian Canaletto." The art historian Grigorii Kaganov, commenting on his paintings of St Petersburg, observes that "Alekseev's Neva was filled with the greenish water of the Adriatic lagoon and coated with a fine Canalettian dazzle," and that he visually narrowed the Neva to suggest spatial dimensions reminiscent of Venice.[82] Even the weather looked Italian, for he suffused his views of both St Petersburg and Moscow with a warm Mediterranean sun, not the muted grays that more often form the palette of these chilly, cloudy northern cities. We saw earlier that Russian landscape artists in Alekseev's time, many of whom were trained (like Alekseev) at the Academy of the Arts in St Petersburg and in Italy, tended to paint either Italian landscapes or Russian gardens that were landscaped to look Italian. The same pattern is apparent in Alekseev, who was likewise immersed in Italian influences. He was trained in Venice and developed his technique in the "Northern Venice," St Petersburg, whose Baroque or Palladian palazzos were in large part designed by the Italian architects Francesco Bartolomeo Rastrelli and Giacomo Quarenghi. After his return from Italy, he painted sets for the imperial theater, where Italian singers and musicians regularly staged spectacular performances of Italian operas.[83] He also copied the canvases of Canaletto, who frequently painted for British patrons who wanted souvenirs of their grand tour;[84] Alekseev thus drew inspiration from an image of Venice that was itself idealized for the benefit of foreign tourists and that harmonized with Catherine's vision of Russia as a future southern empire.

By following Canaletto, Alekseev was opting for one particular interpretation of the urban space and its people while rejecting alternative interpretations. We can only speculate how his Russian scenes might have appeared had he adopted a different model, but it is instructive to consider the differences between Canaletto and other artists when they painted the same urban sites in other countries. For example, the historian Tim Hitchcock compares paintings of one location, Charing Cross in London, by Canaletto, William Hogarth, and Thomas Rowlandson. In Canaletto's painting ("London: Northumberland House," 1752),

---

[80] Panchenko, "'Potemkinskie derevni' kak kul'turnyi mif," in Koshelev, *Iz istorii russkoi kul'tury*, 4:685–700; Zorin, *Kormia dvuglavogo orla*, 33–9, 97–122; Sunderland, *Taming the Wild Field*, 70–3; *Russkii Biograficheskii Slovar'*, 2:15–17.

[81] Skorniakova, *Staraia Moskva*, 287.

[82] Kaganov, *Images of Space*, 43–4.

[83] See Marina Ritzarev (Rytsareva) and Anna Porfirieva, "The Italian Diaspora in Eighteenth-Century Russia," in Reinhard Strohm, ed., *The Eighteenth-Century Diaspora of Italian Music and Musicians* (Turnhout: Brepols, 2001), 211–53.

[84] Michael O'Toole, *The Language of Displayed Art* (London: Leicester University Press, 1994), 234.

the impression created of this most vibrant and occasionally disorderly of urban spaces is of one that is somehow empty of life . . . [W]hat he chose to record was a clean and modern city, peopled by clean and modern individuals. The figures he includes seem to exist on the cityscape rather than in it. They wander and promenade, they chat and flirt, they stare fixedly from the canvas, but seem oddly purposeless.[85]

This is an "urban idyll" that faithfully renders the site's architecture but "obscures the life that existed between the buildings." By contrast, Hogarth's satirical view of the same location ("The Night," from the series "The Four Times of the Day," 1738) focuses on the poor and the outcast and "cram[s] ever more people" into a picture "full of disorder and distress"—a scene of mayhem in which a coach is overturned, a pistol is fired, and a chamber pot is emptied onto the head of a passer-by. In Rowlandson's painting ("The Pillory," 1808), finally, "the architecture and the crowds seem more in balance," and "London is full of people and disorder but lacks the sense of social crisis so much to the fore in Hogarth's vision."[86]

In Western Europe, Canaletto's serene vistas—architectural grandeur plus a dash of local color—competed with a tradition of genre art that foregrounded the urban lower classes. Sketches of the distinctive costumes and trades of urban folk had been a staple of European art since the Renaissance. In 1687, Marcellus Laroon published the much-imitated *Cryes of the City of London Drawne after Life*, a collection of engravings that showed a motley variety of people from the lower classes (hawkers, beggars, street entertainers, prostitutes, and so on) in the garb and pose specific to their status and occupation. The book was such a success that it was repeatedly republished until 1821.[87] In France, an analogous series that achieved wide success was Edmé Bouchardon's *Studies Taken among the Common People, or the Cries of Paris* (*Etudes prises dans le bas peuple ou Les Cris de Paris*, 1737–46). Images like those by Bouchardon not only appeared as bound volumes but were sold as individual pictures and reproduced as porcelain figurines and on cups and bowls, thus achieving a wide circulation. Eighteenth-century Russian art lacked a comparable multiplicity of traditions of viewing the urban space. The German artist Augustin Dahlstein published *Russian Costumes and Public Criers in St Petersburg* (*Russische Trachten und Ausrufer in St. Petersburg*) in Kassel in 1750, and a few other Western artists working in Russia under Catherine II drew similar themes, but for the most part, urban genre art remained little developed until after the Napoleonic Wars.[88]

---

[85] Hitchcock, *Down and Out in Eighteenth-Century London*, 14.

[86] Hitchcock, *Down and Out in Eighteenth-Century London*, 13–18.

[87] Sean Shesgreen, ed., *The Criers and Hawkers of London: Engravings and Drawings by Marcellus Laroon* (Stanford, Calif.: Stanford University Press, 1990), esp. 1–49.

[88] Stites, *Serfdom, Society, and the Arts*, 366–72; Elena V. Barkhatova, "Visual Russia: Catherine II's Russia through the Eyes of Foreign Graphic Artists," in Cynthia Hyla Whittaker, ed., *Russia Engages the World, 1453–1825* (Cambridge, Mass.: Harvard University Press, 2003), 72–89.

Alekseev had studied in Venice and honed his technique in St Petersburg and on the Black Sea coast, two recently conquered spaces where the imperial regime was free to mold the social and spatial environment. Under Catherine II, however, the cultivation of Russian nationality acquired importance at court and in Russian high culture, and this heightened the importance of Moscow as the metropolis of the Russian heartland. Foreigners, to whose opinion the Russian elites were keenly sensitive, were inclined to describe Moscow as a benighted place, much as Catherine herself did. Alekseev, whom Paul I sent on a mission to paint historic and picturesque sites of the Russian interior, countered such derogatory narratives by projecting an image of order and harmony under a clement sky in imitation of Canaletto. He mostly interpreted Moscow as a place where the imperial social project blended harmoniously with an idealized if timeworn old Russia. In his painting of the Lubianka, the buildings evoke Orthodox piety and the glories of the Muscovite tsardom. The people who inhabit this idyllic cityscape reflect the ideals of the imperial social project. Neither clustered in unsettling crowds nor personalized as distinct individuals, they form a kaleidoscope of small figures or groups whose attire situates them within the dualistic categories devised by the regime: military versus civilian, clerical versus lay, Westernized versus Russian. Alekseev's other Moscow canvases are similar: venerable buildings convey a sense of history; dignified figures in Western or Russian garb suggest a harmonious, hierarchical social order; and the improvement of the urban environment is signified by street lights, police guardhouses, and paved thoroughfares.[89]

It was possible, though, to detect hints of poverty, disorder, and injustice in Alekseev's painting of the Lubianka. In the shadows at the right-hand edge of the canvas, a lower-class man urinates against a wall (a "ribald, mischievous and deflating" motif familiar from Canaletto and Hogarth[90]) and a woman sits on the ground with her baby, begging for alms. Alekseev repeats these motifs—urinating and begging—in at least one other Moscow painting.[91] It was perhaps reassuring that potentially rebellious lower-class males are largely absent from the canvas, which is dominated by Westernized upper-class males and by female commoners in lovely national costumes. Alekseev here draws on the Enlightenment's dichotomous view of nature versus civilization, and perhaps also Russian culture's symbolic association of St Petersburg with masculinity and Moscow with femininity,[92] to suggest an identification of Westernization, nobility, and masculinity as active

[89] See the reproductions in Gulianitskii, *Moskva i slozhivshiesia russkie goroda*, 39, 40, 41, 46–7, 51, 96, 97, 100, 102, 103, 116, 121, 123.

[90] Robert L. S. Cowley, *Marriage A-La-Mode: A Re-View of Hogarth's Narrative Art* (Manchester: Manchester University Press, 1983), 164; Filippo Pedrocco, *Visions of Venice: Paintings of the 18th Century*, tr. Susan Scott (London: Tauris Parke, 2002), 79.

[91] "Moskvoretskaia ulitsa v Moskve," reproduced in Gulianitskii, *Moskva i slozhivshiesia russkie goroda*, 100.

[92] Ian K. Lilly, "Female Sexuality in the Pre-Revolutionary 'Moscow Text' of Russian Literature," in Ian K. Lilly, ed., *Moscow and Petersburg: The City in Russian Culture* (Nottingham: Astra Press, 2002), 31–47.

principles linked with civilization, whereas their opposites—Muscovite tradition, peasantry, femininity—were passive and linked with nature.[93] He thus invites the upper-class male viewer to see idealized lower-class females as integral to an idyllic cityscape, much as a pretty shepherdess might be placed strategically in a landscape to enhance the sensual appeal of the pastoral painting and poetry of the same era.[94]

Alekseev's canvas may have reminded some people of Moscow's potential for social conflict. Viewers familiar with "Poor Liza" ("Bednaia Liza"), Nikolai Karamzin's bestselling short story from 1792 about a poor country girl ruined by a Moscow rake, might identify the pretty women in national costume on the canvas as potential victims of upper-class exploitation. Moreover, by depicting a Moscow where enlightenment (in the form of street lights and people in Western attire) was visually dwarfed by buildings redolent of religion and pre-Petrine tradition, the painting could evoke thoughts of the plague revolt of 1771. The revolt had begun less than a kilometer away from the site of Alekseev's picture, when soldiers tried to enforce disease-control measures against worshippers gathered by a miraculous icon. The response had been an outburst of popular rage at a regime that trampled the people's faith in the name of science. Religion and enlightenment, government and the people—these had been bitter antagonists, not elements of a harmonious whole.[95]

CONCLUSION

For most of the eighteenth century, the image of Moscow in Russian elite culture—in maps, statistics, histories, and the graphic arts—reflected the propaganda needs of the regime, the sensibilities of the Russian Enlightenment, and the desire to apply Western representational techniques and aesthetic standards to a Russian context. The resulting image of the city was static, idealized, and flat, giving little sense of the human reality behind the statistics, how the lives of Muscovites were affected by their city's physical space, or how its history affected their consciousness.

This visual celebration of the regime's accomplishments was dismissed as deceptive and lifeless when the underlying paradigm of Russian culture shifted in the first half of the nineteenth century. Artists and thinkers changed their focus from celebrating the enlightened imperial order to exploring the depths of the human soul; mystery and irrationality, not clarity and order, took center stage,

---

[93] On the sentimentalist association of femininity with naturalness, see Tosi, *Waiting for Pushkin*, 211.

[94] Ely, *This Meager Nature*, 42–3.

[95] Alexander, *Bubonic Plague*, passim; Andreas Renner, "Wissenschaftstransfer ins Zarenreich des 18. Jahrhunderts: Bemerkungen zum Forschungsstand am Beispiel der Medizingeschichte," *Jahrbücher für Geschichte Osteuropas*, 53/1 (2005), 64–85, esp. 71, 81, 84.

and visuality was displaced by the word—prose, poetry, drama—as the preferred tool for apprehending reality.[96] In Chapter 2, we saw that the urban infrastructure of Catherine II's Moscow seemed impressive to contemporaries but not to posterity in the nineteenth century. The same was true of the city's representation by the artists and intellectuals of the Catherinean era.

---

[96] Levitt, *The Visual Dominant*, 6, 264.

4

Barbarism, Civility, Luxury

Writing about Moscow in the 1790s–1820s

Beginning in the last years of Catherine II's reign, writers created a richly textured picture of urban Russia. They trained their gaze for the first time on the everyday experience of urban life, and constructed images of Russian cities, especially Moscow and St Petersburg, that achieved lasting influence in Russia and abroad.

The authors discussed in this chapter worked in genres ranging from fiction and moral commentary to economic and social analysis. Some wrote for Russian audiences; others, for readers in the West. Some, like Nikolai Karamzin or the political economist Heinrich Storch, were giants in their fields. Others are known today only to specialists. Taken together, they mark a historical turning point, for they broached questions that increasingly shaped the cultural image of Moscow and all of Russia: was Moscow fundamentally a European city? Or was it part of Asia, and if yes, what were the implications? Did it have a special "Russian" essence, and was this an atavism or on the contrary an admirable sign of national authenticity? Were urban luxuries a boon to enlightenment or a source of moral corruption?

Western authors had a critical part in constructing Moscow's new image, for they shaped how Russia was perceived abroad and modeled ways of thinking that helped set the intellectual agenda in Russia itself. This chapter will begin with a discussion of Western writers, and then examine works by Russians—principally Karamzin, Sergei Glinka, Aleksei Malinovskii, and Konstantin Batiushkov—that illustrate the penetration into Russian culture of new ways of imagining the metropolis.

WESTERN APPROACHES TO WRITING ABOUT CITIES

The European public's curiosity about Russia increased all through the eighteenth century, particularly in the era of Catherine II. In *Eighteenth Century Collections Online*, a database of over 180,000 mostly English-language publications from the eighteenth century, the word *Russia* occurs in 1,629 items published in the six decades from 1700 to 1759. Then the curve rises steeply: 980 items in the 1760s; 1,332 in the 1770s; 1,997 in the 1780s; and 3,455 in the 1790s.[1]

This surge of interest arose in part from Russia's growing importance in European affairs. Thanks to Catherine's conquests along the Black Sea and in Poland, Russia became a neighbor of the German states and sent fleets to the Mediterranean. Its trade grew by leaps and bounds: the number of ships calling annually at Kronstadt, the island port of St Petersburg, grew from a mere 75 in 1720, to 338 in 1760, and to 1,267 by 1797.[2] Another factor was the growing attention of the West's intellectual elites, whom Catherine assiduously cultivated, to events on the continent's peripheries. Enlightenment thinking about cultural geography was built on a binary contrast between the enlightened West and the Orient; Russia was an object of fascination because it was thought to be where the two met.[3] In addition, the upheavals of the 1760s and 1770s along the edges of the European world—including Russian-backed rebellions in Corsica (1768–9) and Greece (1770), the anti-Russian uprising of the Bar Confederation in Poland (1768–72), the Pugachev revolt (1773–4), and the American Revolution (1776–83)—led Enlightenment thinkers to see the peripheries of the West, and Russia in particular, as laboratories for political and social change.[4] Russia became a blank screen onto which the *philosophes* projected their ideological visions and fantasies. Voltaire praised Peter the Great and Catherine II for dragging Russia and the lands it conquered from the night of barbarism toward European enlightenment, while Jean-Jacques Rousseau condemned their policy of Westernizing Russia and partitioning Poland as an assault on the unique national soul of both peoples.[5] The turmoil of the Napoleonic Wars injected further urgency into the Western discussion about Russia because Europeans wanted to understand the rising power that was Napoleon's principal continental rival.

Russia was written about by geographers, *philosophes*, and travelers. Of these, the first two generally described it from afar, and the third often lacked elementary cultural knowledge. For example, Casanova visited Russia at the beginning of Catherine II's reign. When he wrote his memoirs in the 1790s, he ridiculed Rousseau—"the ignorant great man!"—for thinking that the Russian language was a bastardized form of Greek, but his own information was no better.

---

[1] *Eighteenth Century Collections Online* <http://gdc.gale.com/products/eighteenth-century-collections-online/> accessed 26 April 2012. The exact number of items that the database finds for each decade can vary from one search to the next.

[2] Jones, "Getting the Goods to St. Petersburg," 414.

[3] Wolff, *Inventing Eastern Europe*, 6–7.

[4] This is the central argument of Venturi, *The End of the Old Regime*.

[5] Wolff, *Inventing Eastern Europe*, 197–9, 236–42.

According to Casanova, Russian was "a purely Tatar dialect" and "a more or less primordial idiom, born in the depths of the Orient."[6]

A more knowledgeable literature in Western languages, especially in German, began to appear around the time when Casanova was working on his memoirs. This literature drew on new approaches to social analysis that were forerunners of the urban sociology and realist fiction of the nineteenth century. One such approach was medical topography, that is, the study of local-scale environmental conditions, both natural (climate, water quality, drainage) and man-made (diet, housing, urban design). Neo-Hippocratic medicine taught that these factors were of decisive importance for public health, and cameralist governments therefore wanted to regulate them.[7]

A second new approach was inspired by the teachings of Adam Smith. In the area of socioeconomic analysis, cameralist officials mostly limited themselves to studying the fiscal activities of the state. Smith's ideas, on the other hand, encouraged research about society itself. For example, cameralists tabulated how many people belonged de jure to various estates that were defined by their fiscal obligations, whereas Smithians asked about the system of social classes that existed de facto and how they structured people's social and economic interactions.[8]

A third new approach was ethnography, which in turn grew out of two separate traditions. In Germany, Scotland, the Czech lands, and other countries where national identities were weak or contested, Romantic intellectuals studied folklore to recover the ancient spiritual essence of the nation, which they believed had been diluted or suppressed by the ruling classes and the state but survived intact among the peasantry. The other tradition of ethnography, which emerged specifically in Germany, aimed on the contrary to strengthen the power of the state by collecting information about popular customs that would help it administer its subjects more efficiently.[9]

---

[6] Casanova, *Mémoires*, 9:293, 301.

[7] Thomas Broman, "Rethinking Professionalization: Theory, Practice, and Professional Ideology in Eighteenth-Century German Medicine," *Journal of Modern History*, 67/4 (December 1995), 835–72; George Rosen, *A History of Public Health*, expanded edn., ed. Elizabeth Fee and Edward T. Morman (1958; repr. Baltimore: Johns Hopkins University Press, 1993), 152–6; Roche, *Le peuple de Paris*, 65–7; Pinol, *Le monde des villes*, 46–7; Conevery Bolton Valencius, "Histories of Medical Geography," in Nicolaas Rupke, ed., *Medical Geography in Historical Perspective* (London: Wellcome Trust Centre for the History of Medicine at UCL, 2000), 12–13; Michael A. Osborne, "The Geographical Imperative in Nineteenth-Century French Medicine," in Rupke, ed., *Medical Geography*, 32–4.

[8] On Adam Smith's influence in Germany, see Klaus Epstein, *The Genesis of German Conservatism* (Princeton: Princeton University Press, 1966), 179–81.

[9] Uli Linke, "Folklore, Anthropology, and the Government of Social Life," *Comparative Studies in Society and History*, 32 (January 1990), 117–48; see also: Anne Godlewska, "Traditions, Crisis, and New Paradigms in the Rise of the Modern French Discipline of Geography 1760–1850," *Annals of the Association of American Geographers*, 79 (June 1989), 192–213.

Narrative techniques for depicting urban life were changing as well. The pioneering figure in this area was the Frenchman Louis-Sébastien Mercier, the author of *The Tableau of Paris* (*Tableau de Paris,* 1781–8). (The title is sometimes also rendered in English as *Panorama of Paris.*) Mercier abandoned the bird's-eye perspective and compositional neatness that was typical of the statistical topographies, with their orderly inventories of streets, buildings, social groups, and institutions. Instead, he tried to capture the sprawling complexity of Paris by writing over a thousand vignettes that examined the metropolis at eye level and addressed every imaginable topic. For example, one of his volumes contained the following topics (among many others): drunkards; abandoned children; bourgeois tableware; the order of the Brothers of Charity; a dialogue between a duke and a count; cold weather; used-book sellers; clocks; and spiritualists.[10] According to Jeremy D. Popkin, Mercier was "the spiritual ancestor of nineteenth-century campaigners for urban improvement," "the inventor of a new kind of urban journalism, known in France as the *feuilleton,*" a forerunner of Balzac, and the original *flâneur* who roamed the city in search of new impressions.[11] Like the statistical topographers, he aimed for a comprehensive, objective representation of the city, but instead of adopting a static, top-down perspective, he tried to paint a "picture" (*tableau*) of the city's ever-changing flux.[12] As we will see, Mercier served as a direct source for Karamzin's *Letters of a Russian Traveler* (*Pis'ma russkogo puteshestvennika*). In the longer term, through his influence on Balzac and the French physiological literature of the 1830s, he also helped shape the realist literature about Moscow that emerged in the 1840s and that will be discussed in Chapter 8.

The first authors who described Russian cities using Mercier's approach were Germans. Reflecting the peculiarities of eighteenth-century German culture, their works generally lacked the element of sociopolitical criticism that one finds in Mercier. In Germany, unlike Great Britain and France, the Enlightenment was in large part the work of academics and officials, two groups that saw themselves as allies of the state in bringing enlightenment to the people. Their ideal was an orderly society in which moral, rational, fundamentally conservative citizens lived in harmony under a law-based government.[13] As the German writer Johann Pezzl put it,

---

[10] [Louis-Sébastien Mercier], *Tableau de Paris, nouvelle édition corrigée et augmentée,* 12 vols. (Amsterdam: no pub., 1782–8), vol. 12.

[11] Louis-Sébastien Mercier, *Panorama of Paris: Selections from* Tableau de Paris *by Louis-Sébastien Mercier,* ed. Jeremy D. Popkin, tr. Helen Simpson (University Park, Pa.: Pennsylvania State University Press, 1999), 1, 14, 17.

[12] Jörn Steigerwald, *Die fantastische Bildlichkeit der Stadt: Zur Begründung der literarischen Fantastik im Werk E. T. A. Hoffmanns* (Würzburg: Königshausen & Neumann, 2001), 64–7; see also Turcot, *Le promeneur à Paris,* 359–410.

[13] Epstein, *The Genesis of German Conservatism,* 32–4, 52–8.

An enlightened man is one whose moral sense is properly developed; who knows how to find satisfaction in the calling where chance or the laws have placed him; who acts righteously out of reasoned calculation; who has habituated himself to a love of work, reverence for the laws, openness to instruction, love of order in his domestic and public affairs, dietary moderation, and concern for his health; ... who knows and exercises the duties of citizen, friend, husband, and father; ... who never immoderately attacks the religion publicly established by the state, and who, if he has acquired beliefs that are different, is discreet in honoring those beliefs.[14]

This passage is taken from Pezzl's *Sketch of Vienna* (*Skizze von Wien*, 1786–90), a book that inspired numerous imitations elsewhere in the German lands. Pezzl was an ardent anticlerical but also a loyal servant of the Habsburgs, first as secretary to Prince Kaunitz, the empire's leading statesman, and later as a counter-intelligence operative. He had read Mercier and was well versed in French travel literature, some of which he published in German translation.[15] Contemporary reviewers recognized his *Sketch of Vienna* as inspired by Mercier and accordingly translated its title into French as *Tableau de Vienne*,[16] but Pezzl lacked Mercier's socially critical edge. Instead, typical of the German Enlightenment, he was more interested in the way individuals internalized enlightened values. This outlook, which was shared by other German Enlightenment writers, affected how the *tableau* as a literary genre evolved as it traveled eastward from France.

It is no accident that the new approaches to writing about cities, from medical topographies to the urban *tableau*, were introduced to Russia primarily by Germans. Germans were far more numerous in Russia than other Westerners. In Moscow, the police in 1811 counted 275,477 inhabitants, of whom 3,214 were foreigners. By far the largest contingent was formed by Germans, who numbered 1,349. The French, at 668, were a distant second.[17] In more cosmopolitan St Petersburg, the numbers were much larger and the proportions even more lopsided. In 1817, the police counted 285,500 inhabitants. Of these, 35,687 were foreigners, including 23,612 Germans, and in second place, 4,000 French.[18] Even these numbers understate the German presence because they do not seem to include the ethnic Germans from Russia's Baltic provinces.

---

[14] Johann Pezzl, *Skizze von Wien: Ein Kultur- und Sittenbild aus der josefinischen Zeit*, ed. Gustav Gugitz and Anton Schlossar (Graz: Leykam, 1923), 382.

[15] Pezzl, *Skizze von Wien*, v–xvi, 47; Balázs Trencsényi and Michal Kopček, *Discourses of Collective Identity in Central and Southeast Europe (1770–1945): Texts and Commentaries*, 4 vols. in 3 (Budapest: Central European University Press, 2006–10), 1:81–3; Franz A. J. Szabo, "Changing Perspectives on the 'Revolutionary Emperor': Joseph II Biographies since 1790," *Journal of Modern History*, 83/1 (March 2011), 111–38, esp. 118–19.

[16] Review of Johann Pezzl, *Skizze von Wien*, in *L'esprit des journaux, françois et étrangers* (December 1791), 421.

[17] P. I. Shchukin, ed., *Bumagi, otnosiashchiesia do Otechestvennoi voiny 1812 goda*, 10 vols. (Moscow: T-vo Tip. A. I. Mamontova, Tvo Tip. A. I. Mamontova, 1897–1908), 4:226, 228.

[18] Attenhofer, *Medizinische Topographie*, 85–6.

Members of the German diaspora were in a favorable position to serve as analysts of Russian society. Many lived in Russia for long periods, achieved a high level of acculturation, and were active in medicine, scholarship, administration, or other fields that taught habits of precise observation and offered a first-hand view of Russian life. They rarely raised fundamental objections to Russia's hierarchical sociopolitical order, although some were dismayed at the persistence of serfdom. Everyday life in Russia was of great interest to them because, similar to Pezzl, they measured a society's degree of enlightenment by the mores of the inhabitants. Writings by German-language authors reached audiences in the German lands and (through translations) in Russia and across Europe. At once insiders and outsiders in Russia, they were able to serve as cultural intermediaries with the West.

Some of the German authors made their careers in the service of the Russian state. The most influential, and the man most responsible for introducing the urban *tableau* to Russia, was Heinrich Storch (1766–1835), a political economist from Riga. Storch had studied at the universities of Jena and Heidelberg and become a devoted follower of Adam Smith. After his return to Russia in 1787, he taught at the Noble Cadet Corps in St Petersburg, wrote on Russian history and statistics, and became Catherine II's personal secretary for literature. He later became a member of the Academy of Sciences and one of the imperial court's favorite educators. From 1799 to 1819, he tutored the sons and daughters of the imperial family in history, law, statistics, and political economy.[19]

In 1794, Storch published *The Tableau of St Petersburg* (*Gemaehlde von St. Petersburg*), a book whose title was a clear reference to Mercier. (*Gemälde* was the standard rendering of the French word *tableau* in German book titles.) One of his main sources was the recent historical and statistical survey of St Petersburg by Johann Gottlieb Georgi (1729–1802), a German-born naturalist and ethnographer who belonged to the Russian Academy of Sciences.[20] Georgi's book, the first of its kind about St Petersburg, exemplifies the link between German, Western, and Russian writing about cities. It was modeled after a book on Berlin by the Prussian enlightener Friedrich Nicolai and became an important influence on later Russian writings about St Petersburg. It appeared in German in 1790, in French in 1793, and in Russian in 1794.[21]

Storch's book described St Petersburg, but its analysis was equally applicable to Moscow. The gist was that under the aegis of a wise monarchy and thanks to the development of lawful order and enlightened mores, Russia's metropolitan

---

[19] *Russkii Biograficheskii Slovar'*, 23:428–30.

[20] Johann Gottlieb Georgi, *Versuch einer Beschreibung der Rußisch Kayserlichen Residenzstadt St. Petersburg und der Merkwürdigkeiten der Gegend* (St Petersburg: Müller, 1790).

[21] Johnson, *How St. Petersburg Learned to Study Itself*, 22–5; Dittmar Dahlmann, "Stadtgeschichtschreibung in bürgerlicher Absicht: Friedrich Nicolai und Johann Gottlieb Georgi und ihre Beschreibungen der Haupt- und Residenzstädte Berlin und St. Petersburg," in Donnert, *Europa in der Frühen Neuzeit*, 7:535–44.

middle and upper classes were on a path of gradual but steady progress.[22] Storch acknowledged that there were dark sides to Russian life, but a favorable bias inhered in the very structure of his book because it sidestepped the aspects of Russia that were most often criticized in the West: the autocratic system of government, rural serfdom, and what Europeans considered to be the civilizational backwardness of the peasantry. *The Tableau of St Petersburg* was not translated into Russian,[23] but it and other works by Storch appeared in French and English editions.[24]

In Great Britain and France, Storch was criticized as an apologist for the Russian regime. The Russophobic French writer Frédéric Masson, who had lived in Russia himself, attacked *The Tableau of St Petersburg* as "flattering paintings" meant to please Catherine II.[25] An otherwise laudatory review in the *Edinburgh Review* observed that what Storch considered a paradox—that government-service ranks carried greater weight in Russia than did noble birth— was a logical byproduct of despotism, and a review in the *Critical Review* stated outright that Russia's government was a "despotism," and that "the people are slaves, and the great body of subjects in this vast empire are immersed in sloth, ignorance, and superstition." However, Storch's arguments were persuasive enough to convince the *Edinburgh Review* that in St Petersburg, even "traders and artizans" were experiencing "an universal refinement of manners, and much polished urbanity."[26]

---

[22] Roderick E. McGrew, "Dilemmas of Development: Baron Heinrich Friedrich Storch (1766–1835) on the Growth of Imperial Russia," *Jahrbücher für Geschichte Osteuropas*, 24/1 (1976), 31–71. On Storch, see also: Esther Kingston-Mann, "In the Light and Shadow of the West: The Impact of Western Economics in Pre-Emancipation Russia," *Comparative Studies in Society and History*, 33/1 (January 1991), 86–105, esp. 93–4; Susan P. McCaffray, "Confronting Serfdom in the Age of Revolution: Projects for Serf Reform in the Time of Alexander I," *Russian Review*, 64/1 (January 2005), 1–21, esp. 12–13.

[23] P. N. Petrov, *Istoriia Sankt-Peterburga, s osnovaniia goroda, do vvedeniia vybornago gorodskago upravleniia, po uchrezhdeniiam o guberniiakh, 1703–1782* (St Petersburg: Tipografiia Glazunova, 1884), 11.

[24] *The Picture of Petersburg: From the German of Henry Storch* (London, 1801; repr. Adamant, 2002); *Tableau historique et statistique de l'empire de Russie à la fin du dix-huitième siècle, par M. Henri Storch*, 2 vols. (Basel, 1801). On the impact of Storch and J. G. Richter on British views of Russia, see A. G. Cross, "Der deutsche Beitrag zur britischen Rußlandkunde im 18. Jahrhundert," in Helmut Graßhoff, ed., *Literaturbeziehungen im 18. Jahrhundert: Studien und Quellen zur deutsch-russischen und russisch-westeuropäischen Kommunikation* (Berlin: Akademie-Verlag, 1986), 277–81.

[25] Charles François Philibert Masson, *Mémoires secrets sur la Russie, et particulièrement sur la fin du règne de Catherine II et le commencement de celui de Paul I*, 3 vols. (Paris: Charles Pougens, 1800), 1:107–8; see also: Chrétien Müller, *Tableau de Pétersbourg, ou Lettres sur la Russie, écrites en 1810, 1811 et 1812* (Paris: Treuttel et Wurtz; Mainz: Florien Kupferberg; 1814), x; Damaze de Raymond, *Tableau historique, géographique, militaire et moral de l'Empire de Russie*, 2 vols. (Paris: Le Normant, 1812), 1:xi. For a similarly critical analysis by a modern scholar, see Esther Kingston-Mann, *In Search of the True West: Culture, Economics, and Problems of Russian Development* (Princeton: Princeton University Press, 1999), 62–4.

[26] Review of Henry Storch, *The Picture of Petersburg*, in *Edinburgh Review*, no. 2 (January 1803), 305–7, quotation on 307; Review of Henry Storck, *An Historico-Statistic Picture of the Russian Empire*, in *Appendix to the Twenty-Fourth Volume of the New Arrangement of the Critical Review* (December 1798), 481–7, quotation on 481.

Another influential scholar and official was Storch's slightly younger compatriot from Riga, Georg Engelhardt (Egor Antonovich Engel'gardt, 1775–1862). He was the author of a four-volume *Russian Miscellany* (*Russische Miscellen*, 1828–32) that chronicled the spread of refined manners among merchant wives, the rising quality of small-town restaurants, and other signs of enlightenment among middling Russians. Like Storch, Engelhardt was an influential educator. He was appointed in 1811 to head the St Petersburg Pedagogical Institute, which soon after became St Petersburg University, and from 1816 until 1823 he was director of Russia's most prestigious boys' boarding school, the Lyceum of Tsarskoe Selo.[27]

Other foreign-language authors belonged to the diaspora of educated expatriates who came to Russia in search of employment. Johann Gottfried Richter (1763–1829) came to Moscow in 1787 as a private tutor after dropping out of divinity studies at the University of Leipzig, and stayed until 1804.[28] In 1800 he published *Moscow: A Sketch* (*Moskwa: Eine Skizze*), a highly favorable depiction of upper-class Russian life. In the years that followed, he produced three volumes entitled *Russian Miscellany* (*Russische Miszellen*, 1803–4). The country's detractors presented Russians as a historically uncivilized people resistant to enlightenment. Richter's *Miscellany* countered these claims with sympathetic accounts of popular customs, translations of folktales, and travelogues. Richter showed the progress of enlightenment through translations of Russian literature, cheery reports about liberalized censorship and manumitted serfs, and reports on the growth of philanthropy, publishing, and education. "Hail *Russia*, which has *citizens* like these!" he exclaimed in a passage about the charity of Moscow aristocrats. "Hail the *noble emperor*, who by his example and by the spirit of his government is the cause of *such actions!*"[29]

Less is known about the Frenchman Georges-Étienne Le Cointe de Laveau (1783–?), who in 1824 published *A Traveler's Guide to Moscow* (*Guide du voyageur à Moscou*), a highly laudatory historical, statistical, and institutional survey of Moscow. Le Cointe was secretary to the Imperial Society of Naturalists in Moscow and editor of the *Northern Bulletin: A Scientific and Literary Journal* (*Bulletin du Nord: Journal scientifique et littéraire*). He moved back to France in the 1830s.[30]

[27] *Russkii Biograficheskii Slovar'*, 24:253–7.

[28] On Richter, see: Ernst Eichler et al., eds., *Slawistik in Deutschland von den Anfängen bis 1945: Ein biographisches Lexikon* (Bautzen: Domowina, 1993), 321–3; Heike Joost, "Das Moskaubild Johann Gottfried Richters," in Mechthild Keller, ed., *Russen und Rußland aus deutscher Sicht—19. Jahrhundert: Von der Jahrhundertwende bis zur Reichsgründung (1800–1871)* (Munich: Wilhelm Fink, 1992).

[29] "Zwey Beyspiele von außerordentlicher Wohlthätigkeit des Grafen *Scheremetiew* und des Bergraths *Demidow*," in Johann Richter, ed., *Russische Miszellen*, 3 vols. (Leipzig: Hartknoch, 1803–4), 2/4 (1803), 90.

[30] Review of Johannes Gistl, *Die jetzt lebenden Entomologen, Kerffreunde und Kerfsammler Europa's und der übrigen Continente*, and of G. Silbermann, *Énumération des entomologistes vivans*, in

The uncritical, at times sycophantic tone of Richter and Le Cointe does not lessen their importance as cultural intermediaries. Richter's *Moscow: A Sketch* appeared in Russian, French, and English editions, and Le Cointe's *A Traveler's Guide to Moscow* was translated into Russian.[31] Both men were active as literary translators at a time when Russian literature was little known in the West. Richter introduced Western readers to Karamzin, Russia's foremost writer of the turn of the nineteenth century.[32] Le Cointe was among the first French translators of Pushkin,[33] and his son, Henri-Hippolyte Delaveau, later published French translations of Aleksandr Herzen's *My Life and Thoughts* and Ivan Turgenev's *A Hunter's Sketches*.[34]

Travelogues, in which Moscow figured prominently, were also significant in spreading knowledge and promoting debate about Russia. German travelogues of the Enlightenment were a form of ethnographic literature and aimed to provide comprehensive descriptions of lands and peoples.[35] In that sense they resembled the medical topographies and the writings of Storch and Engelhardt. Two writers who lived in Russia for long periods were Georg Reinbeck (1766–1849) and Johann Friedrich Raupach (1775–1819). Both were clergymen's sons from Prussia who came to St Petersburg as tutors to aristocratic families. Reinbeck lived in St Petersburg from 1792 until ill health prompted his return to Germany in 1805. He then published a scathing travelogue, *Cursory Remarks on a Journey from St Petersburg via Moscow, Grodno, Warsaw, and Breslau to Germany in the Year 1805* (*Flüchtige Bemerkungen auf einer Reise von St. Petersburg über Moskwa, Grodno, Warschau, Breslau nach Deutschland im Jahre 1805*). Reinbeck's book depicted Russia as a corrupt, backward, oppressive society. An unhappy German immigrant to Russia later wrote that this had been his only warning that the country was not what "the panegyrists of Russia" claimed it was.[36] The book prompted Goethe to have lengthy conversations with

Bulletin de la Société Impériale des Naturalistes de Moscou, no. 8 (1837), 137–63, here: 152; for his date of birth, see "GeneaNet," <http://gw4.geneanet.org/index.php3?b=pierfit&lang=fr;p=georges+etienne;n=lecointe+de+laveau> accessed 13 February 2009.

[31] *Moskva, nachertanie* (St Petersburg, 1801), cited in: Vasilii Sopikov, ed., *Opyt rossiiskoi bibliografii, ili polnyi slovar' sochinenii i perevodov, napechatannykh na Slavenskom i Rossiiskom iazykakh, ot nachala zavedeniia tipografii, do 1813 goda*, 5 vols. in 4 (St Petersburg: V Tipografii Imperatorskago Teatra, 1813–21), 3:398. The (abridged) French version is *Description historique et topographique de Moskow, ou Détails sur les mœurs et usages des habitans de cette grande ville* (Paris: Pillet, 1812). On the English translation, see Cross, "Der deutsche Beitrag," in Graßhoff, *Literaturbeziehungen im 18. Jahrhundert*, 278.

[32] Cross, "Der deutsche Beitrag," 281; A. G. Cross, *N. M. Karamzin: A Study of his Literary Career (1783–1803)* (Carbondale, Ill.: Southern Illinois University Press; London: Feffer & Simon; 1971), 93–5.

[33] A list of the Pushkin poems translated by Le Cointe appears in Alexandre Pouchkine, *Œuvres poétiques*, ed. Efim Etkind, 2 vols. (Lausanne: L'Âge d'homme, 1993), 2:431.

[34] Glyn Turton, *Turgenev and the Context of English Literature, 1850–1900* (London: Routledge, 1992), 17.

[35] Linke, "Folklore, Anthropology, and the Government of Social Life," 127–8.

[36] Müller, *Tableau de Pétersbourg*, vii.

Reinbeck about Russia,[37] and it was translated into Dutch, English, French, and Italian.[38]

Raupach, who lived in St Petersburg from 1797 to 1807, published a far more sympathetic travelogue in 1809: *Journey from St Petersburg to the Mineral Spring at Lipetsk on the Don, Together With a Note on the Character of the Russians* (*Reise von St. Petersburg nach dem Gesundbrunnen zu Lipezk am Don: Nebst einem Beitrage zur Charakteristik der Russen*). This was evidently a response to Reinbeck and was also published (in excerpts) in Russian translation.[39] One of Germany's most widely circulated literary periodicals pronounced Raupach's book derivative and unpersuasive, declared that what it described was already familiar from Storch and Reinbeck, and accused Raupach of defending serfdom.[40] The reviewer seems to have taken for granted that German readers knew Storch and Reinbeck, were curious about the Russians' national character and degree of enlightenment, and viewed serfdom as evil and retrograde. Raupach confirmed the latter in his rebuttal when he vehemently denied being an apologist for serfdom.[41]

Aside from the *tableau* and the travelogue, a third approach to describing urban Russia was medical topography. Two such studies were published, in 1803 and 1823, by doctors who had practiced in Moscow: the German Engelbert Wichelhausen (1760–1814) and the Scotsman Robert Lyall (1790–1831).[42] Compared with Richter, Raupach, or Reinbeck, the two physicians provided far greater detail about the everyday life of various strata of Moscow society.

Wichelhausen's book argued that Russian serfdom was a disgrace, but that otherwise Moscow was a European and enlightened city.[43] His motivation for

---

[37] John Hennig, *Goethes Europakunde: Goethes Kenntnisse des nichtdeutschsprachigen Europas: Ausgewählte Aufsätze* (Amsterdam: Rodopi, 1987), 306.

[38] G. Reinbeck, *Travels from St. Petersburgh through Moscow, Grodno, Warsaw, Breslaw, &c., to Germany, in the Year 1805: In a Series of Letters* (London: R. Phillips, 1807); a French edition is cited in Conrad Malte-Brun, *Précis de la géographie universelle, ou description de toutes les parties du monde sur un plan nouveau*, 8 vols. (Paris: F. Buisson, 1812–29), 6:586; translations into Dutch (1807–8) and Italian (1816) are cited in Karol Józef Teofil Estreicher, *Bibliografia Polska*, vol. 4 (1878; New York: Johnson Reprint, 1964–78), 38. On Reinbeck, see *Allgemeine Deutsche Biographie*.

[39] F. Raupakh, "Puteshestvie po Evropeiskoi Rossii iz Sankt-Peterburga na teplye vody v Lipetske letom 1804 goda," *Zhurnal noveishikh puteshestvii*, chast' 2, no. 3 (1810), 55–72; chast' 3, no. 5 (1810), 110–27; chast' 3, no. 6 (1810), 239–46; chast' 7, nos. 7–8 (1810), 41–53.

[40] Review of Dr. R(aupach) [*sic*], *Reise von St. Petersburg nach dem Gesundbrunnen zu Lipezk am Don*, in *Allgemeine Literatur-Zeitung*, no. 356 (24 December 1810), cols. 937–44; no. 357 (25 December 1810), cols. 945–51; no. 358 (26 December 1810), cols. 953–7. On Raupach, see Raupach, *Reise*, v–xi; *Allgemeine Deutsche Biographie*, 27:430–4; *Russkii Biograficheskii Slovar'*, 15:499–501; "Nekrolog," *Allgemeine Literatur-Zeitung*, no. 245 (October 1819), cols. 253–6.

[41] Dr. Raupach, "Antikritik," *Allgemeine Literatur-Zeitung*, no. 93 (3 April 1811), cols. 737–40.

[42] Willi Gorzny, ed., *Deutscher biographischer Index*, 4 vols. (Munich: K. G. Saur, 1986), 4:2199; *Dictionary of National Biography*, 63 vols. (London: Smith, Elder, 1885–1900), 34:304–5.

[43] Martin Dinges, "L'image de Moscou entre la description standardisée des Lumières et la recherche de la singularité russe. La topographie médicale (1803) de Engelbrecht Wichelhausen," *Cahiers du monde russe*, 44/1 (2003), 35–56; Martin Dinges, "Kann man medizinische Aufklärung

writing was the lack of medical topographies of Russian cities, which, he said, had allowed "French travel writers" to spread unfounded negative images of Russia.[44] This statement of intent notwithstanding, reviewers do not seem to have read his book as either anti-French or pro-Russian. A favorable but rather superficial review appeared in France and was reprinted in Britain.[45] In Germany and Russia, on the other hand, the book came under attack for depicting Russia in a negative light. Wichelhausen was criticized by two German reviewers who said they had lived in Moscow for many years. They took issue with factual inaccuracies and mistranslations of Russian terms that they treated as evidence of his general ignorance, but their central criticism was that he exaggerated the evils of serfdom.[46] A reviewer for the Moscow journal *Messenger of Europe*, perhaps constrained by censorship, sidestepped the issue of serfdom. Instead, he heaped scorn on Wichelhausen for being an ignorant foreigner, and then attacked his claim that the cold climate had a stunting effect on Russians' minds and bodies.[47] This climatic theory had been propounded by Montesquieu in the 1740s and was rebutted in 1770 in a pamphlet by Catherine II herself.[48] It stung because it implied that Russians were incapable of what the literary Sentimentalists who edited the *Messenger of Europe* considered the prerequisite for true enlightenment: the capacity for moral and aesthetic sensitivity.[49]

Robert Lyall was a generation younger than Wichelhausen, came of age in the ideologically more polarized era of the Napoleonic Wars, and hailed from a country where suspicion of Russia's illiberal order ran deeper than in Germany. His book dwells far more than Wichelhausen's on the oppressiveness of the regime and the benighted mores of all levels of Russian society. He professed to admire Alexander I's reformist inclinations, but was sharply critical of the pro-serfdom outlook of the nobility and Alexander's support for authoritarian

---

importieren? Kulturelle Probleme im Umfeld deutscher Ärzte in Rußland in der zweiten Hälfte des 18. Jahrhunderts," in Mathias Beer and Dittmar Dahlmann, eds., *Migration nach Ost- und Südosteuropa vom 18. bis zum Beginn des 19. Jahrhunderts: Ursachen—Formen—Verlauf—Ergebnis* (Stuttgart: Jan Thorbecke, 1999), 229–32.

[44] Wichelhausen, *Züge zu einem Gemählde von Moskwa*, vii–x.

[45] L . . . n, review of Engelbert Wichelhausen, *Züge zu einem Gemählde von Moskwa*, in *Magasin encyclopédique, ou Journal des sciences, des lettres et des arts*, no. 21 (1804), 129–33; this review was reprinted without attribution in *L'esprit des journaux français et étrangers, par une société de gens de lettres*, vol. 6 (February 1805), 84–9, and reappeared, in translation and slightly modified, on pp. 263–4 of "Modern Discoveries, and Improvements in Arts, Sciences, and Literature," *Universal Magazine*, 4/22 (September 1805), 252–65.

[46] Anonymous reviews of Wichelhausen, *Züge zu einem Gemählde von Moskwa*, published in *Allgemeine Literatur-Zeitung*, no. 54 (21 February 1804), cols. 429–32, and in *Neue Leipziger Literaturzeitung*, no. 72 (14 December 1803), cols. 1055–8.

[47] "Smes'" (review of Engelbert Wichelhausen, *Züge zu einem Gemählde von Moskwa*), *VE*, no. 22 (30 November 1804), 138–40.

[48] Marcus C. Levitt, "An Antidote to Nervous Juice: Catherine the Great's Debate with Chappe d'Auteroche over Russian Culture," *Eighteenth-Century Studies*, 32/1 (1998), 49–63.

[49] Maarten Fraanje, "La sensibilité au pays du froid. Les Lumières et le sentimentalisme russe," *Revue des études slaves*, 74/4 (2002–3), 659–68, here: 660.

regimes in post-Napoleonic Europe.[50] The *Messenger of Europe*, not surprisingly, declared him ignorant and biased.[51] British reviewers, too, were struck by the hostile tone of his remarks—"His pen revels in the nastiness of the Russians," wrote one[52]—but some of them allowed that his criticisms might be valid.[53]

WESTERN IMPRESSIONS OF MOSCOW

Certain themes run through the foreign-language literature. Did Moscow's rural qualities make it more or less enlightened than other cities? Moscow sometimes had the crowds and bustle of a large city, yet the level of public safety was remarkable: what did this reveal about the system of government and the social order? How developed were the city's infrastructure and the opportunities for genteel sociability? Lastly, was Moscow developing an enlightened middle-class culture? Authors gave divergent answers to these questions.

Westerners were uniformly struck by the rural appearance of Moscow and most other Russian towns. Moscow's city gates reminded Wichelhausen of Paris,[54] but after that the arriving traveler entered suburbs where, as Lyall put it, one "might suppose himself as distant from Moscow as from London."[55] What this signified for Russia's place in the community of nations was a matter for debate. For many Western thinkers, Russia and Eastern Europe were a frontier zone where European enlightenment ended and the Orient began.[56] This seems to be the framework that Reinbeck adopted when he claimed that Russian towns, in contrast to German ones, were benighted places marked by backwardness and oppression:

As everything in Silesia and Saxony carries the stamp of superior culture, so the absence of civilization is ubiquitous in the provinces of Russia. Russian towns, with few exceptions, are filthy, gloomy holes . . . For the man whose expectations are higher than what he has in common with an animal, dwelling in those same [towns] is entirely unbearable, for he finds no diversion at all that could satisfy him.

---

[50] Lyall, *The Character of the Russians*, preface, 9.

[51] Review of Lyall, *The Character of the Russians*, in *VE*, no. 17 (September 1824), 74–6.

[52] Anonymous reviews of Lyall, *The Character of the Russians*, in *Eclectic Review*, vol. 24 (December 1825), 532–50 (quotation on 541), and in *Quarterly Review*, 31/61 (April 1824), 146–66.

[53] Anonymous reviews of Lyall, *The Character of the Russians*, in *The European Magazine, and London Review*, vol. 85 (January 1824), 50–3; in *The Literary Magnet of the Belles Lettres, Science, and the Fine Arts*, vol. 1 (1824), 70–1; and in *The Atheneum; or, Spirit of the English Magazines*, 1/3 (1 May 1824), 124.

[54] Wichelhausen, *Züge zu einem Gemählde von Moskwa*, 23; Lyall, *The Character of the Russians*, 381.

[55] Lyall, *The Character of the Russians*, 381.

[56] Wolff, *Inventing Eastern Europe*, 12–13.

German towns hummed with the cheerful bustle of a free people, he wrote; Russian ones felt deserted, their sparse inhabitants burdened by the invisible chains of serfdom.[57]

Raupach turned Reinbeck's argument on its head by invoking the Sentimentalist idealization of the countryside and the neo-Hippocratic medical critique of densely built-up medieval towns. Moscow's suburbs, he conceded, were unsightly and underpopulated, but at least people breathed a "balsamic country air."[58] Reinbeck claimed that Russian urban life was marred by the cruelty of serfdom; Raupach fired back that German towns were disfigured by war and violence. Unlike German towns, he wrote, Russian ones "do not lie concealed behind bomb-proof walls that keep out all fresh air, nor have they narrow, filthy alleys with towering houses that barely admit the sun's lovely light even at high noon." Russia, he suggested, was a bucolic garden kingdom, free from the medieval barbarism of the West. Gardens—wild nature domesticated by man—were one of Catherine II's preferred metaphors for a society ruled by an enlightened monarch.[59] Raupach evoked similar associations when he wrote that "Little groves, waterways, romantically sited monasteries, [and] charming country homes are what heralds [a Russian town's] proximity, not an avenue of gallows, execution sites, and [breaking] wheels with their ornaments [i.e. human remains]. You needn't fear this repulsive, outrageous sight anywhere in Russia, for here no capital punishment is customary."[60]

Johann Richter, in his *Russian Miscellany*, developed a similar argument about the Russian people's closeness to nature. Muscovites moved with ease through their city's busy traffic, he wrote, because they were endowed with an agility of mind and body that was remarkable by German standards. The reason was that they were of peasant stock and uncorrupted by urban civilization. Only in the past seventy to eighty years had Russians encountered "the many refinements in ways of living that Paris and London have created and disseminated and through which weakness, sickliness, and deterioration of the human race have befallen most countries of Europe." Most Russians even now rejected these innovations, and the majority continued to grow up without formal schooling. Hence their understanding of the world around them was not impeded by artificial habits of abstract thought: "Nature (in Rousseau's sense), the affairs of life, social intercourse, travel, observation, and experience have given these people a perhaps greater measure of practical reason than what we usually achieve after many years of education at school."[61]

---

[57] Reinbeck, *Flüchtige Bemerkungen*, 2:316–17.

[58] Raupach, *Reise*, 68–9, 89.

[59] Andreas Schönle, *The Ruler in the Garden: Politics and Landscape Design in Imperial Russia* (Oxford: Peter Lang, 2007), 44–8, 68, 72.

[60] Raupach, *Reise*, 53–4.

[61] "Briefe über Rußland, von einem in Moskwa lebenden Deutschen, an einen seiner Freunde in Leipzig," in Richter, *Russische Miszellen*, 2/5 (1803), quotation on 68; no. 6 (1803), 63–73, quotation on 72–3.

Aside from civilization/barbarism and city/nature, a further binary in Western writings was Europe versus Asia. Moscow is on a longitude just west of the Don, which until the mid-eighteenth century was considered the boundary of Asia. In the European mind, to be Asiatic was to be mired in a way of life that was unchanging and alien to enlightenment. Asia's supposed archaism made it possible for Orientalist narratives to include allusions to the classical world as well.[62] French writers in particular used Orientalist imagery to convey Russia's essential foreignness. For Louise Fusil (1771–1848), a French actress who lived in Moscow, the city evoked exotic images ranging from "the plains of Arcadia" to "the gardens of Semiramis" and on to "how one might imagine Beijing or Isfahan"; similar to other foreigners, she concluded that "Europe and Asia often find themselves united there."[63] Other authors used Orientalist language to describe specific cultural practices. For example, the physicians Wichelhausen and Lyall describe as "Asiatic" the Russian custom of building detached wooden houses surrounded by gardens and courtyards.

Writers who wanted to stress Russia's Europeanness eschewed such imagery. The juxtaposition of buildings of different eras and styles was taken by Raupach and Engelhardt as proof that Moscow was (as Engelhardt put it) "a city that has *evolved* over centuries,"[64] much like other European cities. Fusil and Le Cointe characterized the same sight with Orientalist language and described it with the French word *bizarre*, which the 1798 Dictionary of the French Academy defined as meaning "fantastical, extravagant, capricious."[65] The detached houses that Wichelhausen and Lyall called Asiatic were described by Engelhardt as *hôtels*, the term used for the townhouses of the upper classes in France.[66] Asianness was not always understood pejoratively, however. Fusil and Le Cointe found Moscow's "bizarre" architecture beautiful,[67] and Wichelhausen and Lyall argued from a medical point of view that detached wooden houses benefited public health by promoting ventilation and not blocking the sun.[68]

For all that its outskirts seemed rural, Moscow was also a restless and variegated place that resembled large cities elsewhere in Europe. Authors tried to convey this. A Russian visitor from St Petersburg reported with awe that day and

---

[62] Tosi, *Waiting for Pushkin*, 114.

[63] Fusil, *L'incendie*, 83–4.

[64] "Bemerkungen auf einer Reise," in Engelhardt, *Russische Miscellen*, 4:106; Raupach, *Reise*, 67.

[65] Le Cointe, *Guide*, 59–60; Fusil, *L'incendie*, 83–4; *Dictionnaire de l'Académie française* (5th edn., 1798), available on *The ARTFL Project: Department of Romance Languages and Literatures, University of Chicago* <http://artfl-project.uchicago.edu/node/17> accessed 11 December 2011.

[66] "Bemerkungen auf einer Reise," in Engelhardt, *Russische Miscellen*, 4:110; Wichelhausen, *Züge zu einem Gemählde von Moskwa*, 45–6; Lyall, *The Character of the Russians*, 34–5.

[67] [G. Le Cointe de Laveau], *Moscou avant et après l'incendie, ou Notice concernant la description de cette capitale et des mœurs de ses habitans, par deux témoins oculaires* (2nd edn., Paris: Gide Fils, 1818), 3; Fusil, *L'incendie*, 83–4.

[68] Wichelhausen, *Züge zu einem Gemählde von Moskwa*, 45–6; Lyall, *The Character of the Russians*, 34–5.

night, the roads to Moscow were packed with carts, often two or three abreast, as far out as 50 to 60 kilometers from the city.[69] Reinbeck evoked this spectacle with particular vividness. Approach Moscow in the summer, he wrote, and "you see the road before and behind you covered with thousands of transports that carry necessities to the monstrous maw . . . Each transport consists of a cart with two wheels, packed high with heavy loads, and hitched to a big, strong horse that, for all its exertion, can advance only step by step." When the city filled with people on market days, the chaos was overwhelming, he wrote in a critique of the city that echoed Rousseau or Mercier:

the loud crying of the hawkers; the singing of the *izvoshchiks* [coachmen]; the shouting inside and in front of the countless *kabaks* [taverns]; the fiddling and piping and organ-grinding on the dance floors; the rattling of the carriages; the pealing of the thousands of bells, of which every single belfry has several, often twenty; interspersed with the drums and music of the considerable garrison.—In the first weeks one is utterly numb.[70]

In a similar vein, Storch reported that "the throng of humanity was indescribable" at the coronation of Alexander I in 1801, which drew over 100,000 visitors to Moscow. However, his emphasis as always was on the beneficent role of the state: "This extraordinary confluence of the people necessitated the strictest measures to maintain order." Police and soldiers were deployed to keep the masses far from the coronation site in the Kremlin, and the day passed without incident.[71]

As Storch's remarks suggest, an enlightened city was one where the level of public safety was high. On this point, observers were unanimous in their praise. Even the acerbic Reinbeck found that "security [is] admirable" in Moscow.[72] One explanation focused on the police. Wichelhausen paid tribute to the alacrity with which the watchmen responded to disturbances, and Richter praised the police's success at crowd control.[73] Le Cointe, writing from a top-down perspective similar to the eighteenth-century statistical topographies, described in detail the formal structure of the Moscow police—watchmen, police stations, cavalry patrols—with the implication that an institution so impressively organized must be correspondingly effective.[74]

---

[69] "Perepiska: Otdykh v Moskve izdatelia Otechestvennykh Zapisok na puti v Astrakhan' i Sibir'," *OZ*, 18/52 (August 1824), 251–63, here: 253.

[70] Reinbeck, *Flüchtige Bemerkungen*, 1:186, 206–7.

[71] "Zur Krönungsgeschichte Alexanders I: Bruchstücke aus Briefen eines Reisenden im Gefolge des Hofes, an einen seiner Freunde in St. Petersburg," in Heinrich Storch, ed., *Rußland unter Alexander dem Ersten*, 9 vols. (St Petersburg: Hartknoch, 1804–8), 1:85. On Alexander's coronation, see also Wortman, *Scenarios of Power*, 1:197.

[72] Reinbeck, *Flüchtige Bemerkungen*, 1:209.

[73] Wichelhausen, *Züge zu einem Gemählde von Moskwa*, 63–4; "Die Feyer der Osterwoche in Moskwa," in Richter, *Russische Miszellen*, 1/1 (1803), 162.

[74] Le Cointe, *Moscou*, 58–9; Le Cointe, *Guide*, 196–7.

The credit for the high level of public safety was often given to the population rather than the police. It seemed that the populace remained close to its rural roots and hence did not constitute a dangerous urban mob that required aggressive policing. Storch observed that there was little crime in St Petersburg, even at night and in remote neighborhoods. This, he wrote, was "less the work of the well-organized, vigilant police than the effect of the benign character of the people": common Petersburgers were averse to crime because they were reared in wholesome rural environments where serfdom prevailed, and were easily cowed even by isolated members of the higher classes.[75] Other writers went farther in downplaying the role of the police. In Reinbeck's view, the police were powerless to enforce lawful authority against people of high social status, and the policemen themselves were "coarse, ignorant, ill-bred people, and not capable of earning respect for themselves."[76] Engelhardt, too, was hardly awestruck. The public visibility of the police was limited, he wrote. In an entire week in Moscow, he saw only three officers (as opposed to lower ranks) of the police in the streets. He remarked that the watchmen were "poor wretches" who passed their lives in "sad monotony." At least, he added with gentle irony, the "humane city authorities" allowed some of them to plant "a little tree, a berry bush, [or] a few heads of cabbage" next to their uncomfortable little guardhouses.[77]

In other ways as well, the efforts to upgrade Moscow's infrastructure left Europeans unimpressed. Streets remained dusty or muddy, paved surfaces were few and of poor quality, there were few gutters to drain liquid waste, and the lack of sidewalks exposed pedestrians to danger from speeding vehicles.[78] Wichelhausen found the street lighting in the early 1790s "very mediocre: it consists only of lanterns that stand quite far apart, and in remote areas they are often not even lit, or else they soon go out." He praised the police for doing a better job than its counterpart "in enlightened Berlin" in keeping the river free from pollution, and he anticipated improvements once the embankments were lined with stone and the new aqueduct was completed, but he also complained that the Neglinnaia, a small tributary of the Moscow River that flowed through downtown, was little more than a stinking marsh.[79] Thirty years later, Lyall saw little change for the better. Like Wichelhausen, he decried the insalubrious marshes and ponds in low-lying neighborhoods, and he observed "numerous manufactories" on the banks of the river upstream from the city; this was "a circumstance which

---

[75] Wichelhausen, *Züge zu einem Gemählde von Moskwa*, 63–4; Storch, *Gemaehlde*, 1:167–8, 207–8, quotation on 167.

[76] Reinbeck, *Flüchtige Bemerkungen*, 2:112–24, quotation on 122.

[77] "Bemerkungen auf einer Reise," in Engelhardt, *Russische Miscellen*, 4:117–18, quotations on 117.

[78] Lyall, *The Character of the Russians*, 36, 51–2; Reinbeck, *Flüchtige Bemerkungen*, 1:200–1; Wichelhausen, *Züge zu einem Gemählde von Moskwa*, 59–60.

[79] Wichelhausen, *Züge zu einem Gemählde von Moskwa*, 61, 68–9, 72, quotations on 61, 68.

astonishes us, in a country where the police is so attentive to the health of the inhabitants."[80]

An enlightened city required not only attention to health and safety, but also public promenades where citizens could learn the habits of genteel sociability. According to Le Cointe,

In populous cities, public gardens should be considered not only under the aspect of pleasantness but also under that of their influence on the morals of the inhabitants. Indeed, the need to appear if not richly, then at least decently dressed; a restraint that increases along with one's social intercourse; and a certain habit of [showing] regards and considerations that are reciprocated and that one becomes accustomed to extending to persons whom one sees but does not know—[all this] must exercise a salutary influence on the mass of the population.[81]

Moscow had few such promenades, but the trend lines pointed in the right direction. This was particularly true after the 1812 war, when the city's reconstruction included the development of several large squares as well as the Kremlin Garden (the present-day Alexander Garden). The Kremlin Garden was inaugurated on Alexander I's nameday in August 1821. Nobles and merchants were admitted to the festivities, while the common people, said to be over 100,000 strong, watched through the fence. The evening opened with a splendid illumination and a band concert, and wrapped up long after midnight with a procession of carriages around the Kremlin. Throughout, wrote one newspaper, "thanks to the activity and watchfulness of the Police, order and decorum were perfectly maintained." The celebration of monarchism, nighttime lighting and entertainment, and the mingling of nobles and merchants while the people stood by as spectators, all under the watchful eye of the police—all the key elements of imperial urban policy were present on this occasion.[82]

Such promenades were scarce, however. Le Cointe cited only two in the city center: the Kremlin Garden and the Boulevard, both of which were too new by the 1820s for their trees to offer much shade.[83] Lyall similarly reported that Moscow "has few remarkable squares. Besides the Kremle and the *boulevards*, few situations where a pedestrian can enjoy himself."[84] The development of promenades was hampered by distance, transportation, weather, and habit. It was a commonplace that because of Moscow's size—Le Cointe pointed out that the hour at the city's eastern edge was in advance of its western edge by

---

[80] Wichelhausen, *Züge zu einem Gemählde von Moskwa*, 93–9; Lyall, *The Character of the Russians*, 35, quotation on 38.

[81] Le Cointe, *Guide*, 407.

[82] Pav. Ivanov, "Otkrytie Kremlevskago sada v den' tezoimenitstva Gosudaria Imperatora," *OZ*, 7/17 (September 1821), 375–8, quotation on 377–8. For a similar description of public festivities that were segregated by estate, see "Nekotoryia podrobnosti o Moskovskom gulian'e pod Novinskom," *OZ*, 10/26 (June 1822), 450–3.

[83] Le Cointe, *Guide*, 407, 410.

[84] Lyall, *The Character of the Russians*, 36.

44 seconds[85]—and poor pavement, people were more likely than in other countries to travel by vehicle. For much of the year, inclement weather confined people indoors, and when it was sunny and warm, access to vehicles encouraged the affluent to repair to the country. Storch observed the same pattern in St Petersburg: the city "has several of these [promenades], some of them very attractive, but in comparison with the promenades of other large cities they are very little frequented."[86]

Indoor sites for genteel *public* sociability—as opposed to the private balls, serf theaters, and so on of the aristocracy—were likewise in short supply. The police reported in 1811 that Moscow had only one theater, two clubs, and fourteen coffee houses.[87] Reinbeck grumbled that there was nowhere to go in the evening except the theater, "a [socially] very mixed Burgher Club full of tobacco smoke, and a very pretentious so-called English Club in sumptuous rooms full of glittering stars[88] and gold-covered gaming tables." However, he noted more cheerfully, one could also go to the suburban "Vauxhall" on Sunday evenings in the summer. The crowds there were substantial and included Russian nobles as well as foreigners. "For a silver ruble"—the price of two or three cheap books or an inexpensive bottle of wine[89]—"one is offered a small theatrical or singing performance, afterwards an illumination with colored lights, then a firework that comes out nicely enough, and finally a ball. Can one ask for more for one silver ruble?"[90] Raupach, putting a favorable spin on the situation, claimed that the hospitality of the Russian upper classes was such that "public opportunities for entertainment are missed very little here." He also pointed out that owing to its sheer size, Moscow would require an extraordinary number of sites of public sociability to serve the entire city.[91]

Non-Russian writers took a keen interest in the imperial social project. Was Russia, they wondered, developing a middle-class culture along lines familiar in the West? Engelhardt answered in the affirmative, noting for example that the trade in second-hand books and household furnishings facilitated the diffusion of genteel culture from the metropolitan elites to provincial commoners.[92] Le Cointe found the opposite. He wrote that the Moscow Lombard (pawnshop), unlike its Parisian equivalent, did not accept household goods as pledges because they lacked resale value. "In Moscow," he explained, "the classes remain distinct even in their clothes and their furnishings, and since what suits one [class] is not

---

[85] Le Cointe, *Guide*, 59.
[86] Storch, *Gemaehlde*, 2:297.
[87] Shchukin, *Bumagi*, 4:230–1.
[88] "Glittering stars" may be a reference to the decorations worn by important government officials.
[89] Prices cited in *MV* (25 June 1800), 165; *MV* (4 July 1800), 1270.
[90] Reinbeck, *Flüchtige Bemerkungen*, 1:214, 218–19.
[91] Raupach, *Reise*, 91–2, quotation on 91.
[92] "Bemerkungen auf einer Reise," in Engelhardt, *Russische Miscellen*, 4:174–5.

acceptable to the other, moveable objects are not subject to the common estimation that allows them to be appraised in other capitals."[93] According to Raupach, the very nature of Russia's social order prevented the spread of middle-class values. While not explicitly embracing the widespread Western view that autocracy and serfdom made Russian society despotic, he found that "Russians remain far from having the sense of respect for human dignity and human worth, the sense of duty, honor, and shame, that would characterize a fully cultivated nation." This produced "the spirit of groveling and haughtiness that extends through all classes" and that undermined public sociability, as he observed in connection with the subordination of women among the affluent classes: "This is the main cause, I believe, of the distinct *penchant of the Russian for domesticity*. At home he feels at ease; here he is the lord who commands, whereas in most external relationships he feels constrained and oppressed."[94]

The authors discussed in the preceding pages viewed themselves as Europe's Russia experts. They were acknowledged as such in the West, where translations and book reviews allowed them to reach audiences across national borders. In their books, they cited and argued with one another, giving unity and coherence to the discourse they constructed. The questions they raised—about Moscow's place between civilization and nature, its relation to Europe and Asia, its prospects for an enlightened middle-class culture—helped to shape how Russia was imagined in nineteenth-century Europe.

In Russia itself at the time, their works rarely reached a broad readership. However, leading intellectuals and the elites at court paid close attention to what was written abroad about their country. Some of these authors also held positions that gave them personal influence in Russia's government and intellectual life. For example, Reinbeck tutored Nicholas I's future education minister Sergei Uvarov,[95] and Storch, the future Nicholas I himself. Storch also did much to develop political economy and statistics in Russia as a member of the Academy of Sciences. Well into the first half of the nineteeth century, medical topographies about Russia were published mainly in German or Latin; these had a formative influence on Russian medical thought.[96] The influence of these authors reached the wider Russian public a generation later, in the 1830s. Storch's *Tableau of St Petersburg* served as a model for one of the first Russian-language urban *tableaux*, Aleksandr Bashutskii's *Panorama of St Petersburg* (*Panorama Sanktpeterburga*, 1834).[97] The first major medical topography of St Petersburg that was not translated from a foreign original likewise appeared in 1834.[98]

---

[93] Le Cointe, *Guide*, 299.

[94] Raupach, *Reise*, 184, 208.

[95] Erik Amburger, *Beiträge zur Geschichte der deutsch-russischen kulturellen Beziehungen* (Gießen: Wilhelm Schmitz, 1961), 166.

[96] A. P. Markovin, *Razvitie meditsinskoi geografii v Rossii* (St Petersburg: Nauka, 1993), 50.

[97] See Chapter 8.

[98] [S. F. Gaevskii], "Mediko-topograficheskiia svedeniia o S.P.burge. 1833," *ZhMVD*, chast' 11, no. 2 (February 1834), 153–98, no. 3 (March 1834), 285–364.

Among the Russian literati of their own time, the influence of these Western-ers is harder to detect. The Westerners anticipated the concerns of nineteenth-century realist fiction and social science, whereas their Russian contemporaries were cultural critics preoccupied with questions inherited from the eighteenth century. The Russian discussions therefore differed in important ways from those among authors from the West.

KARAMZIN AND SENTIMENTALISM

No Russian who wrote about Moscow in the years around 1800 could rival the stature of Nikolai Karamzin (1766–1826), Russia's most popular writer of that period and the first Russian to be widely translated in the West. Karamzin shared Catherine's hopes for the imperial social project and for Moscow's transform-ation into an enlightened metropolis. Like Catherine, he wanted Russia to be an enlightened European country. To achieve this destiny, he thought, Russia needed a national literature, which in turn presupposed a suitable literary language and a Europeanized reading public imbued with a strong sense of Russian nationality. This was the overarching project that gave coherence to his multifaceted cultural enterprises. Through the example set by his writings, he single-handedly reformed the Russian literary language. His *Letters of a Russian Traveler* gave many readers their first introduction to urban life in the West. His Sentimentalist fiction and journalism, especially the short story "Poor Liza," were groundbreaking attempts to construct a literary image of Moscow. Lastly, his *History of the Russian State* (*Istoriia gosudarstva rossiiskago*, 1818–24) transformed Russian readers' sense of their country's history.

Karamzin was close ideologically, and sometimes personally, to the Germans who wrote about Russia's progress toward enlightenment. Richter translated his works into German; once Karamzin had proofread and corrected them, these translations became "originals" that were then retranslated into other lan-guages.[99] "My authorial ego is in [Richter's] debt for many pleasures," Karamzin wrote in 1803, because "his translations have made me famous in Germany, England, and France."[100] After he moved from Moscow to St Petersburg in 1816, he became personally acquainted with Engelhardt and Storch.[101] He and Storch had long been providing favorable publicity for each other's writings in their journals and miscellanies.[102] Karamzin was intellectually drawn to history

[99] Cross, *N. M. Karamzin*, 93–5.
[100] Letter of 24 December 1803 to M. N. Murav'ev, in A. Starchevskii, *Nikolai Mikhailovich Karamzin* (St Petersburg: Tipografiia Karla Kraiia, 1849),186.
[101] Ia. Grot and P. Pekarskii, eds., *Pis'ma N. M. Karamzina k I. I. Dmitrievu* (St Petersburg: v tipografii Imperatorskoi Akademii Nauk, 1866), endnotes, p. 99.
[102] "Istoricheskoe opisanie Rossiiskoi torgovli, sochinennoe A. Shtorkhom," *VE*, chast' 5 (September 1802), 55–6; "Allgemeine Maßregeln zur Beförderung der Volksaufklärung," in

while Storch gravitated to economics, but they agreed that Russia's progress required the spread of enlightenment, not constitutional reforms or the emancipation of the peasants. This outlook became a hallmark of Russian conservatism. As Roderick McGrew puts it, "Karamzin provides a critical insight into the historical perceptions which shaped Russian conservatism" while "Storch frames conservatism's political economy."[103]

Ideological sympathies notwithstanding, Karamzin and his Russian contemporaries had a different agenda than did the Westerners. For various reasons, Russian writers showed little sustained interest in urban social issues before the reign of Nicholas I (r. 1825–55). Few Russian authors or readers were trained in statistics, medicine, or other disciplines that encouraged rigorous social observation, or had experience of other countries against which Russia could be measured. Literary conventions also played a role. Lowbrow literature in the eighteenth century included picaresque novels whose plots were set in a specific social context, but since many were adapted from foreign originals, they give little insight into Russian conditions. Among the intellectual and social elites, meanwhile, the predominant literary tendency was neoclassicism, which valued narrative prose far below poetry and drama and did not encourage the realistic exploration of concrete social contexts.[104]

Prose gained higher status in the 1790s thanks to the influence of Sentimentalism, whose leading proponent was Karamzin. Sentimentalists were interested in the sensitive individual's moral and aesthetic response to natural beauty and the sight of human goodness or suffering. Unlike neoclassicism, this paradigm valorized prose narratives and called attention to physical and social environments, but these mainly served to provide a context for the expression of the narrator's private feelings. Since those feelings were supposed to be gentle or melancholy, the environment had to be conducive to serene contemplation— preferably a pastoral idyll, but not the noisy urban crowd, let alone rural poverty and oppression.[105]

Storch, *Rußland unter Alexander dem Ersten*, 1/1 (1804), 137; "Miscellen," in Storch, *Rußland unter Alexander dem Ersten*, 3/7 (1804), 169; "Übersicht der russischen Literatur während des fünfjährigen Zeitraums von 1801 bis 1805," in Storch, *Rußland unter Alexander dem Ersten*, 9/ 26–7 (1808), 225.

[103] McGrew, "Dilemmas of Development," 40 (see also 42 n. 33); Richard Pipes, "Karamzin's Conception of the Monarchy," in Hugh McLean, Martin E. Malia, and George Fisher, eds., *Russian Thought and Politics*, Harvard Slavic Studies, vol. 4 (Cambridge, Mass.: Harvard University Press, 1957), 24–58, esp. 36–7; A. G. Cross, "N. M. Karamzin's 'Messenger of Europe' (*Vestnik Yevropy*), 1802–3," *Forum for Modern Language Studies*, 5/1 (January 1969), 1–25, esp. 19.

[104] Tosi, *Waiting for Pushkin*, 104–10.

[105] Tosi, *Waiting for Pushkin*, 193–210; Gitta Hammarberg, *From the Idyll to the Novel: Karamzin's Sentimentalist Prose* (Cambridge: Cambridge University Press, 1991), 46; Jean Breuillard, "Introduction" to "Le Sentimentalisme russe," special issue of *Revue des études slaves*, 74/4 (2002–3), 653–7.

The tendency of Sentimentalism to paint a gauzy, sanitized picture of reality was heightened by the growing importance of aristocratic salons as sites where literature was read and discussed. Writers adjusted to the etiquette of the salon, particularly what they supposed were the taste and sensitivities of aristocratic women. They tried to keep their prose light, elegant, and free of archaisms and academic pedantry, and steered clear of depicting base emotions, ugly social phenomena, or "masculine" topics such as politics or economics.[106] Sentimentalists considered it all the more important to show consideration for female readers because this proved, in their view, that gender relations in Russia—and by extension, the entire social and political system—were not despotic in the Asiatic manner, as some Westerners alleged, but were governed by enlightened norms of civility and delicate sentiment.[107]

In Karamzin's thinking, the conventions of Sentimentalism dovetailed with a broader vision that he shared with Catherine II: the belief that the meaning of reality derived not from reality itself but from men's imagination. If Russia was to become an enlightened European state, Catherine believed, it first had to be one in people's minds. Karamzin thought likewise. He believed, as Andreas Schönle puts it, that "Individuals and societies alike can freely construct, fashion, and model themselves." Storch and the other authors discussed earlier assumed that reality was primordial and words only approximated it. With Karamzin it was the reverse. "To him," Schönle writes, "the only existing order of being is that brought about by the word. Only what is written truly exists."[108] In *Letters of a Russian Traveler*, a visit to the Swiss village of Clarens was meaningful to Karamzin because it was the setting for Rousseau's novel *La nouvelle Héloïse*.[109] Similarly, the pond near the Simonov Monastery in Moscow became a pilgrimage site for readers of Karamzin because it was here that the fictional heroine of "Poor Liza" drowned herself. Art not only described reality; it created reality.

Karamzin's understanding of literature was connected with his views on Russian culture, which likewise resembled Catherine's. To be an enlightened nation, Russians had to integrate European values into a national culture that was authentically their own. One of his main contributions to this goal was his reconstruction of literary Russian, which was of fundamental importance to the future development of the Russian language. Karamzin's idiom was modeled on the oral speech of Russia's most Westernized stratum, the metropolitan

[106] Tosi, *Waiting for Pushkin*, 50–4, 211; Hammarberg, *From the Idyll to the Novel*, 93–101.

[107] Fraanje, "La sensibilité au pays du froid," 662; Yuri Slezkine, "Naturalists Versus Nations: Eighteenth-Century Russian Scholars Confront Ethnic Diversity," *Representations*, no. 47 (Summer 1994), 170–95, here: 182.

[108] Andreas Schönle, *Authenticity and Fiction in the Russian Literary Journey, 1790–1840* (Cambridge, Mass.: Harvard University Press, 2000), 45, 71.

[109] Schönle, *Authenticity and Fiction*, 50; Andrew Kahn, "Karamzin's Discourses of Enlightenment," in Nikolai Karamzin, *Letters of a Russian Traveller: A Translation and Study*, ed. Andrew Kahn, Studies on Voltaire and the Eighteenth Century 2003:04 (Oxford: Voltaire Foundation, 2003), 491–2.

nobility, particularly the ladies of the aristocracy. He purged it of "bookish" elements, especially the bureaucratese of government clerks and the clergy's Church Slavonic, that were unsuited to oral conversation and were specific to subcultures that were non-noble and male. He aimed to create a unified culture for the educated classes, but his approach discriminated against social climbers—usually men—from the non-noble strata because it devalued the cultural capital of those who had learned how to write in government offices, church schools, or private lessons from local clergymen.[110]

Under Alexander I, Karamzin moved away from fiction toward journalism and history. Particularly relevant to his thinking about Moscow are articles he wrote for the *Messenger of Europe*, which he founded in 1802 and edited until he was named imperial court historian in 1804. The *Messenger* was an instant hit. By the second issue, the print run had to be raised from 600 to 1,200, a figure unrivaled in Russian journalism. Karamzin was then at the height of his fame but becoming more conservative. The wars against France made him into a nationalist who favored disentangling Russia from the political affairs of Europe, and he was disturbed by the attack on the nobility that he saw in the French Revolution, in the tyranny of Paul I, and in the attempts by Alexander I to reform serfdom and strengthen the bureaucracy. In response he embraced a Burkean conservatism, defending the nobility's privileged status and condemning reforms that were inspired by Enlightenment theories instead of the organic traditions of the nation. Whereas he had earlier seen literary and cultural criticism as an essential role of journalism, he now believed that journalists should foster pride in Russia's accomplishments. Still, he did not back away from his core belief that Russia's progress depended on the spread of enlightened mores, and that this process had to originate among the educated nobility.[111]

Life in the big city is the subject of two texts from the early 1790s that helped establish Karamzin as Russia's premier Sentimentalist prose writer (*Letters of a Russian Traveler* and "Poor Liza"), and also of several articles that he wrote for the *Messenger of Europe*. I will not attempt a new interpretation of these texts, which are among the most canonical in all Russian literature. My aim, more modestly, is to see what they tell us about how Karamzin imagined life in Moscow.

KARAMZIN AND THE CITY

Karamzin's engagement with the everyday realities of Moscow was constrained by censorship, the conventions of Sentimentalism, and what Iurii Lotman and

---

[110] Iu. M. Lotman and B. A. Uspenskii, "'Pis'ma russkogo puteshestvennika' Karamzina i ikh mesto v razvitii russkoi kul'tury," in N. M. Karamzin, *Pis'ma russkogo puteshestvennika*, ed. Iu. M. Lotman, N. A. Marchenko, and B. A. Uspenskii (Leningrad: Nauka, 1987), 582–601.

[111] On the *Messenger of Europe*, see Cross, "N. M. Karamzin's 'Messenger of Europe'."

Boris Uspenskii call the "underlying utopianism that characterized his ideology"[112]—his persistent desire to show Russians what their country should become, not what it actually was. Another text, however, is available to help us understand how he thought about cities: *Letters of a Russian Traveler*, his partly fictionalized account of his travels through Germany and Switzerland to Paris and London in 1789–90.

Most Russians knew little of the European cities that formed such an important model for their own country. By providing readers with a rich, vivid picture of those cities, Karamzin's *Letters* helped fill that lacuna. Their main Russian antecedent was Denis Fonvizin's epistolary travelogue about Western Europe during the reign of Catherine II, but the two were different in important ways. Fonvizin's narrator is irascible and chauvinistic; Karamzin's is cosmopolitan, at ease wherever he goes, and at all times a gracious ambassador for his nation.[113] Fonvizin's letters circulated only in manuscript form, whereas Karamzin's were published: parts appeared in installments in 1791–5, and the entire text, which Karamzin reworked over the course of the 1790s, appeared in several volumes in 1797 and 1801 and was repeatedly reissued over the next decades. *Letters of a Russian Traveler* was an instant classic and served as the principal model for Russian travelogues until the era of Pushkin.[114]

As a general matter, Karamzin's narrator discerns no antithesis between Russia and Europe. The West is neither a superior civilization nor a source of moral corruption, and its cities do not feel overwhelmingly alien.[115] The traveler finds Central Europe especially congenial. What most arrests his attention there are meetings with famous writers, but he also comments on the cities he visits. In the typical Sentimentalist manner, he responds to the aesthetic appeal of picturesque natural vistas and of medieval castles and other relics of history, but otherwise he judges German and Swiss cities by the same criteria that Westerners applied to Russian cities: Are they prosperous? Are their streets bustling and orderly? Are the buildings impressive, the streets wide, the air clean? How plentiful are opportunities for culture and enlightened sociability—bookshops, coffee houses, public gardens? As a cultivated Russian, the traveler feels neither overawed nor out of place, and freely renders judgment. Thus, Bern receives high marks for its good pavement and drainage, whereas Berlin is rebuked for its bad smells and throngs of prostitutes.[116]

---

[112] Lotman and Uspenskii, "'Pis'ma'," in Karamzin, *Pis'ma russkogo puteshestvennika*, 529.

[113] Sara Dickinson, *Breaking Ground: Travel and National Culture in Russia from Peter I to the Era of Pushkin* (Amsterdam: Rodopi, 2006), 109–10.

[114] On the powerful literary impact of the *Letters*, see Cross, *N. M. Karamzin*, 66, 92–3; Derek Offord, *Journeys to a Graveyard: Perceptions of Europe in Classical Russian Travel Writing* (Dordrecht: Springer, 2005), 73–101; Dickinson, *Breaking Ground*, 105–42; Schönle, *Authenticity and Fiction*, 6; Tosi, *Waiting for Pushkin*, 276.

[115] Kahn, "Karamzin's Discourses of Enlightenment," in Karamzin, *Letters of a Russian Traveller*, 504; Lotman and Uspenskii, "'Pis'ma'," in Karamzin, *Pis'ma russkogo puteshestvennika*, 564.

[116] Karamzin, *Letters of a Russian Traveller*, 56, 73, 158.

The tone changes completely when he reaches Paris and London, the places that most powerfully radiated the urban energy that foreigners missed in Russia. Karamzin's response foreshadows the ambivalence that these cities inspired in Russians in the nineteenth century. Paris and London appear to him as cities of an entirely different order than a Berlin or Frankfurt, and he approaches them with tense anticipation. Paris brims with life and refined culture, but also the kind of disorder that Russia's elites later denied existed in Moscow. Karamzin's description of Paris follows Mercier.[117] He gasps at the extremes of excess and squalor, likens the crowds to a surging ocean, speaks with curiosity to strangers of all conditions, and evokes the sounds, smells, and moods of different moments of the day and night. He roams the city, a *flâneur* in search of impressions. After morning coffee and a newspaper, he spends his day window-shopping and seeing the sights, dines out, takes in a play or opera, and ends the evening at a café or the Palais-Royal.

He is no less entranced by London, but for different reasons. The British metropolis has the wealth and modernity to which Russians aspired, but not the human warmth that Russians later thought distinguished social relations in Moscow. In Paris, the traveler is interested principally in the culture and sociability of the upper classes and the contrasts of urban life. The essence of London, on the other hand, is laissez-faire liberalism. Unlike France, everything here is clean and exudes prosperity. The physical infrastructure is admirable. For example, "there are thousands [of street lights] here, one after another, and wherever you look, there is everywhere a vista of flame, which from a distance looks like an endless fiery thread suspended in the air. I have never seen anything like it."[118] The English impress him with their patriotism, individual freedom, and independence of character, but he is appalled at their callousness to the poor and their calculating self-interestedness, ethnocentrism, and general emotional coldness.[119]

In its account of Paris and London, *Letters of a Russian Traveler* describes the anonymity and restlessness of the big city as conducive to cultural and material progress but also as disruptive of social and moral order. That similar concerns informed Karamzin's thinking about Moscow is suggested by two brief but revealing texts. One, the tale "Poor Liza" (1792), recounts a peasant girl's tragic romance with an aristocratic cad and her eventual suicide. "Poor Liza" was a huge success with readers and remains one of the most studied works in Russian fiction, in part because it became a model for future literary depictions of such themes as female suicide and peasant women in love. The other text, "Notes of an Old Moscow Resident" ("Zapiski starago Moskovskago zhitelia,"

---

[117] Lotman and Uspenskii, "'Pis'ma'," in Karamzin, *Pis'ma russkogo puteshestvennika*, 650.
[118] Karamzin, *Letters of a Russian Traveller*, 383.
[119] Karamzin, *Letters of a Russian Traveller*, 447–52; Lotman and Uspenskii, "'Pis'ma'," in Karamzin, *Pis'ma russkogo puteshestvennika*, 566.

1803), published a decade after "Poor Liza," contains the musings of a nobleman on the increasing enlightenment of Muscovite mores. Both works circulated abroad in a translation by Richter.[120] A comparison of "Poor Liza" and "Notes" shows continuities in Karamzin's thinking but also a shift from a socially critical outlook to a deepening conservatism.

Both texts depict Moscow's social order through a nobleman's encounter with a young peasant woman. The protagonists (Liza and the Old Moscow Resident) are stock characters: the sweet country girl of the pastoralist idyll, and the avuncular nobleman who embodies salt-of-the-earth decency and old-fashioned common sense. The two are of the same generation (born in the 1740s), and both stories are set in the present but look back to the 1760s. ("Poor Liza" is framed as a present-day narrator's recollection of events from the past.) The two texts anticipate the nineteenth-century literary cliché according to which Moscow was a tradition-bound city of nobles and peasants. The middling sort and the modernization of the urban space, issues central to Catherine II's agenda and to the foreign literature about Moscow, are largely absent.

In both texts, Moscow is linked with nature. As we have seen, observers often remarked on Moscow's rustic character. Russian literature in the nineteenth century expanded on this theme by creating a symbolic association between Moscow and nature. The origin of this motif lies in "Poor Liza" and "Notes."[121] In both stories, the nobleman meets the peasant girl when she comes into Moscow to sell lilies of the valley. What nature represents in the two texts, however, could hardly be more dissimilar.

Karamzin's writings from the 1790s generally suggest that contemplating the beauty of nature aids the spread of enlightenment by liberating the imagination, teaching man to know his own heart, and thus freeing him from the moral shackles of society.[122] "Poor Liza" shows this scenario's dark side. The young nobleman is drawn to Liza because she embodies natural beauty and innocence, but after the two violate the norms of society by having an affair, he abandons her and she commits suicide. In this case, the beauty of nature inspires an act of liberation from convention that ends in tragedy, not enlightenment.

In "Notes," there is no such dark side. This time, the flowers sold by the pretty peasant girl symbolize an enlightenment that embraces tradition rather than rebelling against it. Ignoring the chronology of "Poor Liza," the Old Moscow Resident declares that no one sold flowers in the streets as recently as the 1760s. The fact that this has changed, he says, leads "Philosophers"—that is,

---

120 "Die arme Lisa," in *Erzählungen von N. Karamsin*, tr. Johann Richter (Leipzig: Hartknoch, 1800); "Bemerkungen eines alten Bewohners von Moskwa," in Richter, *Russische Miszellen*, 2/5 (1803), 150–63.

121 Ian K. Lilly, "Conviviality in the Prerevolutionary 'Moscow Text' of Russian Culture," *Russian Review*, 63/3 (July 2004), 427–48, here: 431.

122 Schönle, *The Ruler in the Garden*, 232–3, 237.

enlightened people—to "conclude that the inhabitants of Moscow have become enlightened: for to love the flowers of the countryside is to love Nature, and a love for Nature presupposes a delicate taste refined by Art."[123] Philosophy, he continues, at first encourages freethinking but later brings people back to religion. Likewise, civilization separates people from nature but later reunites them with it. As Andreas Schönle puts it in his analysis of Karamzin, "The contemplation of nature is here no longer aligned with the forward movement of progress, but with a return to immemorial values. Progress leads to a restoration of a patriarchal mindset."[124]

Both texts attribute great symbolic meaning to the architectural relics of Moscow's Orthodox past. In "Poor Liza," the golden domes of the city's skyline are a thing of beauty, but the area near the Simonov Monastery where Liza lived and died is given a Gothic quality that harmonizes with the mood of the narrator.[125] The derelict Simonov Monastery itself is portrayed as a spooky place where the wind howls in dark hallways and amid overgrown tombstones, bringing to mind long-ago wars and a joyless monastic asceticism.[126] By contrast, in "Notes of an Old Moscow Resident," history blends seamlessly with modern enlightenment. As readers knew from *Letters of a Russian Traveler*, Karamzin admired the beauty and democratic sociability of public spaces like Berlin's Unter den Linden and the boulevards of Paris. In "Notes," the narrator fantasizes about surpassing this in Moscow. Imagine, he writes, if the section of the Kremlin wall facing the Moscow River were demolished and replaced with a terraced park. People could then gather in peaceable intercourse while contemplating history (the Kremlin cathedrals), enlightenment (the adjacent Moscow Foundling Home), and nature (the river and the scenery beyond), all forming a single artistic composition. "What a picture! What a promenade, worthy of a great nation! Then an inhabitant of Paris or Berlin who sits on the terrace of the Kremlin hill would forget all about his own *boulevard* or his *linden street*."[127]

The Old Resident's imaginary Kremlin promenade brings different classes together in a setting that teaches them to appreciate beauty and civility. Karamzin had described such places—coffee houses, gardens, and the like—with great enthusiasm in *Letters of a Russian Traveler*. In "Poor Liza," tragedy results from the mingling of classes amidst a corrupt urban civilization and an oppressive

---

[123] "Zapiski starago Moskovskago zhitelia," in N. M. Karamzin, *Sochineniia*, 8 vols. (Moscow: V Tipografii S. Selivanovskago, 1803–4), 8:290. (The text originally appeared in *VE*, 10/16 (August 1803)).

[124] Schönle, *The Ruler in the Garden*, 233.

[125] Gitta Hammarberg, "Poor Liza, Poor Èrast, Lucky Narrator," *Slavic and East European Journal*, 31/3 (Autumn 1987), 305–21, here: 308.

[126] "Bednaia Liza," in N. M. Karamzin, *Pis'ma russkogo puteshestvennika; Povesti*, ed. N. N. Akopova, G. P. Makogonenko, and M. V. Ivanov (Moscow: Pravda, 1982), 532.

[127] "Zapiski starago Moskovskago zhitelia," in Karamzin, *Sochineniia*, 8:298; Karamzin, *Letters of a Russian Traveller*, 56, 257–8.

social hierarchy.[128] In "Notes," on the other hand, the narrator is optimistic. As we have seen, Westerners as late as the 1820s found Moscow severely lacking in public promenades, but Karamzin's purpose was to evoke what might become, not what actually was. Thus he depicts the opening of Moscow's new boulevard as proof of Russia's full membership in European civilization:

You can laugh, gentlemen, but I boldly declare that enlightenment alone makes the people of the cities want to promenade, something that would never occur to the rude Asiatics, for example, whereas the wise Greeks were famous for it. Where the citizens love to gather daily in pleasant leisure and with different estates intermingled; where aristocrats are not ashamed to stroll with non-aristocrats, and where neither disturbs the other's enjoyment of a bright summer evening: there, people have reached the happy convergence of the spirit that is the result of a refined civic education. Our ancestors had no promenade in Moscow; even we have only very recently begun to want this pleasure, but now we do love it very much.[129]

In *Letters of a Russian Traveler*, Karamzin writes that on the boulevards of Paris, with their shady trees and clean air, "the worthy craftsman relaxes with his wife and daughter."[130] In "Notes," the Old Resident observes that Muscovites, too, have come to love suburban summer homes and Sunday strolls in the park. From the nobility, the appreciation for clean air and natural beauty spreads downward through society, to the point that "Tailors and shoemakers, with their wives and children, go to pick flowers in the meadows and bring bouquets back to town. You have seen this in foreign lands, but at home we have been seeing it only recently, and it should make us happy."[131]

The equivalence between Moscow and the West extends to the city's hinterland as well. In a text from 1802 that also appeared in a translation by Richter,[132] Karamzin describes a trip along the pilgrimage route to the Trinity-St Sergius Monastery, about 70 kilometers northeast of Moscow. Few journeys could be more evocative of Orthodox Russianness, yet in Karamzin's rendering, it differs little from Western Europe. In *Letters of a Russian Traveler*, he praises the "splendid villages" and "rich vineyards" that make the Rhineland an "earthly paradise." Around Moscow as well, he now writes, the land is improved by human hands. In medieval times, this was an area of "forest gloom and wild solitude," but today it is covered with "cheerful meadows and fields."[133] Abroad,

---

[128] Inna Gorbatov, "*La nouvelle Héloïse* de Jean-Jacques Rousseau et la *Pauvre Liza* de N. M. Karamzine," *Neohelicon*, 30/2 (2003), 227–40, here: 234.

[129] "Zapiski starago moskovskago zhitelia," in Karamzin, *Sochineniia*, 8:295.

[130] Karamzin, *Letters of a Russian Traveller*, 258.

[131] "Zapiski starago moskovskago zhitelia," in Karamzin, *Sochineniia*, 8:293.

[132] "Reise von Moskwa nach dem Kloster Troiza, nebst historischen Erinnerungen," in Richter, *Russische Miszellen*, 1/3 (1803), 57–139.

[133] Karamzin, *Letters of a Russian Traveller*, 119; "Istoricheskiia vospominaniia i zamechaniia na puti k Troitse," in Karamzin, *Sochineniia*, 8:328, 319. (The text originally appeared in *VE*, 4/15 (1802).)

he remarks on medieval and Renaissance buildings. Now he notes that the Kremlin's great Assumption Cathedral was built by architects from Renaissance Italy; "before that, people in Russia had no idea of good architecture."[134] As in Europe, so in Russia, a site gained deeper meaning if he could view it through the lens of European literature. The derelict palace of Empress Elizabeth at Tainin-skoe, he writes, looks like a setting for a Gothic novel by Ann Radcliffe, and the surrounding grounds remind him of the burial site of Rousseau, familiar to readers from the lengthy description in *Letters of a Russian Traveler*. Echoing his own account of England, he describes a prosperous village where the peasants live "in pretty little houses, no worse than the wealthiest peasants in England and other European lands."[135]

Karamzin's hopes for Russia were rooted in memories of Catherine II. He had few illusions about her real accomplishments. In the *Memoir on Ancient and Modern Russia*, a memorandum that he wrote for Alexander I in 1811, he had far more praise for her aspirations than for her actual policies.[136] Even so, he stood by the ideals behind her policies. In 1802, just as Alexander—who came to power promising to govern in accordance with Catherine's principles—embarked on his domestic reforms, Karamzin published a panegyric to her memory. While allegedly a "historical survey of Catherine's achievements," this text, as A. G. Cross notes, "is a fantasy of what might have been."[137] It claims that she transformed a coarse, balkanized society into one united by culture and enlightened urbanity. Landowners had earlier lived in a state of "savage independence on their estates," but she drew them into provincial governance, thereby making them into public-spirited citizens and bringing "the enjoyments of the best European cities" to Russian towns that foreigners had once deemed "empty, desolate."[138] Although "Writers say even now that in Russia there is no *middle estate*," in fact Catherine's reforms unified the commercial, learned, and professional classes into a single corporate estate.[139] Genteel culture trickled down, so "even the mores of people in commerce, through frequent and close intercourse with the more enlightened Nobility, have lost their earlier coarseness; and the wealthy merchant, seeing before him models of a better art of living, has imperceptibly acquired taste and polite affability."[140] Education made young noblewomen into "the delight of society, the treasure of their spouse, and the first teacher of their children," and army cadets were no longer learning "only the art

---

[134] "Istoricheskiia vospominaniia," in Karamzin, *Sochineniia*, 8:331.

[135] "Istoricheskiia vospominaniia," in Karamzin, *Sochineniia*, 8:312–13, 315; Karamzin, *Letters of a Russian Traveller*, 358–63, 380.

[136] Richard Pipes, *Karamzin's Memoir on Ancient and Modern Russia: A Translation and Analysis* (New York: Atheneum, 1966), 133–4.

[137] Cross, *N. M. Karamzin*, 208; see also Dixon, "The Posthumous Reputation of Catherine II," 660.

[138] "Istoricheskoe pokhval'noe slovo Ekaterine II," in Karamzin, *Sochineniia*, 8:111–13.

[139] "Istoricheskoe pokhval'noe slovo Ekaterine II," in Karamzin, *Sochineniia*, 8:126–7.

[140] "Istoricheskoe pokhval'noe slovo Ekaterine II," in Karamzin, *Sochineniia*, 8:115–16.

of killing people."[141] Civility spread down through society and out from the towns, refining and unifying what had been a brutal and fragmented people.

The social compact that Karamzin envisioned, and the initiation of which he attributed to Catherine II, extended deep into the urban population. He praised the beneficent aims of the Moscow Foundling Home and lauded the aqueduct that Catherine had ordered built to supply "fresh, healthful water" to "every poor person" in Moscow.[142] Moscow's trade in newspapers and books, he wrote, now reached classes previously averse to secular reading, including rural nobles and the urban middle classes. "It is true that many nobles, even wealthy ones, do not receive the newspapers; on the other hand, the merchants and townspeople already love to read them. Even poor people subscribe, and even the illiterate want to know 'what they are writing from foreign lands'."[143] The people's desire to learn about current events reflected a healthy civic instinct and deserved to be encouraged, not feared.

Even peasants had a place in this dream of a better Russia. In "Poor Liza," Karamzin had suggested that peasants could suffer harm through contact with the city, but in the *Messenger of Europe* he highlighted the positive. Traditionally, in Russia as elsewhere, nobles assumed that only ignorance, poverty, and compulsion kept the peasants in their lowly station with its back-breaking toil. Karamzin, though a defender of serfdom, argued that a genteel lifestyle would make them more, not less, industrious and loyal. Nobles should promote education in order to make their peasants more like those German, Swiss, and English rustics who were "hard-working but enlightened farmers, living with elegance and good taste, peaceful and contented—the more enlightened they are, the more contented they become."[144]

Karamzin, who shared the ideals of Catherine II and was shocked at the radical turn of the French Revolution, did not believe that Russia could achieve enlightenment by changing its laws or government. As he told Alexander I in his *Memoir on Ancient and Modern Russia*, Russia had been ill served by the despotism of his father, Paul I, and would not benefit by the liberal reforms of the legal and administrative system that were mulled by Alexander himself. The key to bettering society was urban civility, which Karamzin saw as a force for good even when it subverted traditional cultural patterns and class identities; thus, he wrote approvingly in 1803 that peasants near Moscow who made money from the textile trade "have begun to live like lords, with cleanliness, good taste, and even luxury."[145]

---

[141] "Istoricheskoe pokhval'noe slovo Ekaterine II," in Karamzin, *Sochineniia*, 8:135, 141.

[142] "Istoricheskiia vospominaniia," in Karamzin, *Sochineniia*, 8:308.

[143] [N. M. Karamzin], "O knizhnoi torgovle i liubvi ko chteniiu v Rossii," *VE*, 3/9 (May 1802), 57–64, here: 58.

[144] [N. M. Karamzin], "O novom obrazovanii narodnago prosveshcheniia v Rossii," *VE*, 8/5 (March 1803), 49–61, here: 52.

[145] [N. M. Karamzin] M., "Puteshestvie vokrug Moskvy," *VE*, 7/4 (February 1803), 278–89, here: 285.

THE LUXURY DEBATE

Not everyone shared Karamzin's sanguine assessment of urban "luxury" and "good taste." A competing interpretation held that the metropolis fostered unhealthy social extremes as well as corruption and debauchery, especially among the rich, their masses of servants, and the idle poor. Catherine II leaned toward this opinion, and it was a common theme in eighteenth-century picaresque novels and in neoclassical comedies, satiric journals, and other didactic literature.[146] The nobleman Grigorii Vinskii (1752–*c*.1820) wrote around 1813 about one of his first sexual experiences. When he was an adolescent in Ukraine in the 1760s, his teacher (a recent arrival from Moscow) employed "two servant girls, real Muscovites, so my chastity was doomed: it was a bestial pleasure that at once revolted me."[147] Gavriil Dobrynin (1752–1823), a clergyman's son and middling provincial official, likewise thought that the big city corroded the bonds of society. Writing around 1810, he described the material and moral disorder he had seen when he first visited Moscow in 1785:

the intermingling . . . of abundance and poverty, extravagance and miserliness; immense stone houses, and poor wooden huts buried in the ground up to their windows; sacred shrines next to commerce and taverns; good breeding and depravity, enlightenment and ignorance; I saw heirs to fortunes who were poor, haughty, and ignoble. There, from evening till morning, the pillars of the fatherland engage in important trifles called games, and over a game they provoke duels, while from dawn to dusk they sleep.

They say that there are houses in Moscow that are most respectable, that are purportedly all honor, virtue, and enlightenment. Very likely indeed. The same was true in remotest antiquity, when God himself and one of the patriarchs searched the great city of Nineveh for ten righteous men.[148]

Anti-urban critiques like these drew fuel from the long-standing debate in eighteenth-century Europe about "luxury." According to the pro-luxury argument, luxury was a byproduct of the economic growth that undergirded national power, and a modest spread of luxuries among the people was proof of broad-based prosperity, promoted the refinement of morals, and encouraged a spirit of citizenship. Voltaire, Montesquieu, and the *encyclopédistes* shared this opinion, and so did, mostly, Karamzin. The opposing argument harkened back to the moralists of ancient Rome, who thought that luxury had corrupted the Roman Republic by leading the citizens to put their private interests ahead of their public duties and thus cede undue influence to women, slaves, and others incapable of civic virtue.

---

[146] Tosi, *Waiting for Pushkin*, 160, 238.

[147] Vinskii, *Moe vremia*, 21.

[148] Dobrynin, *Istinnoe povestvovanie*, 260. Dobrynin seems to be confusing the story of Jonah in Nineveh with Abraham's attempt to save the people of Sodom.

This classical anti-luxury tradition was given new life in France in the 1740s and 1750s. The French provincial nobility felt its social position threatened from above by the court at Versailles, with its royal mistresses and rich aristocrats and financiers, and from below by upstart commoners who bought their way into the nobility. The argument was made that while honest nobles struggled to make a living the old-fashioned way, through agriculture, their antagonists grew fat from colonial trade, the manufacture of luxury goods, and high finance— pursuits that were unproductive and depended on a corrupt system of privileges awarded by the court. France's military and economic weakness relative to Great Britain added to the anxiety that luxury was sapping the nation's spirit. According to John Shovlin, on whose work this analysis is based, French thinking on this issue was shaped by the dialectical tension between an anti-urban discourse that attacked the court aristocracy and represented farming and the provincial nobility as alone capable of regenerating the nation, and an opposing discourse that endorsed commerce and the spread of luxuries. During the French Revolution, the anti-aristocratic argument—the attack on leisure and conspicu- ous consumption—was turned against nobles in general, and even against non- noble capitalists.[149]

Not all of these ideas were relevant to Russia. A key element of the French luxury critique was the claim that a nexus of aristocrats, court financiers, despotic kings, and royal mistresses was causing the nation's power to decline. Russians, on the other hand, did not consider their eighteenth-century rulers (except Paul I) to have been despots. They also had no equivalent of France's powerful bankers and tax farmers, and Russia was clearly not a declining power. However, the snobbery and opulent lifestyle of the metropolitan aristocracy were similar in both countries, as were the resentments of provincial gentry and struggling literati, and Russian writers drew on French books to help make sense of their world. Despite the differences between the two countries, the French luxury critique therefore resonated in Russia.[150]

The subversive implications of the luxury critique are apparent from the fact that Radishchev (whom Catherine II called "a rabble-rouser, worse than Pug- achev"[151]) could use it in his book *A Journey from St Petersburg to Moscow* to attack the whole system of serfdom and noble privilege. At one point, he contrasts the superb oral health of virtuous peasant girls with the rotting teeth and foul breath of the metropolitan aristocracy, which he blames on the

---

[149] John Shovlin, *The Political Economy of Virtue: Luxury, Patriotism, and the Origins of the French Revolution* (Ithaca, NY: Cornell University Press, 2006); John Shovlin, "The Cultural Politics of Luxury in Eighteenth-Century France," *French Historical Studies*, 23/4 (Fall 2000), 578–606; Daniel Roche, *La culture des apparences. Une histoire du vêtement (XVIIe–XVIIIe siècle)* (Paris: Arthème Fayard, 1989), 438–9, 486–9.

[150] Simon Dixon, *The Modernisation of Russia, 1676–1825* (Cambridge: Cambridge University Press, 1999), 204.

[151] Quoted in Alexander, *Catherine the Great*, 283.

unbridled sexual promiscuity of aristocratic women and their husbands.[152] Elsewhere, he warns a peasant woman against letting her man work in the city:

"Don't let him, gentle Aniutushka, don't let him; he goes to his doom. There he will learn to drink, to become wasteful and spoiled, to stop loving agriculture, and above all he will stop loving you, too." "Oh, milord! Don't frighten me," Aniuta said, almost in tears. "It will be worse, Aniuta, should he work in a noble house: the example of the city infects the higher servants, the lower [servants] are infected by the higher ones, and through them the evil of depravity spreads to the villages. Imitation is a veritable plague. What people see, they do."[153]

The luxury debate provides a helpful framework for interpreting the discussions about Moscow. An aspect that is particularly relevant for understanding how the urban community was imagined is the question of sites of public sociability. Karamzin saw much civilizing value in such sites but was ambivalent about their social effects. In a passage in *Letters of a Russian Traveler* that seems to be modeled on Mercier's *Tableau of Paris*, Karamzin writes of the shops, cafés, and gardens of the Palais-Royal. Mercier calls the Palais-Royal "the capital of Paris." "This enchanted place," Mercier writes, "is a small luxurious city enclosed in a great one; it is the temple of voluptuousness, where the glittering vices have banished any specter of modesty." A young man of wealth would be seduced into wanting to stay forever, and become trapped, according to Mercier, like "[the legendary crusader] Rinaldo in this palace of [the lovesick Saracen sorceress] Armida."[154] Karamzin, too, was drawn to the Palais-Royal's bustling vitality yet disturbed by its falseness and moral disorder. "The treasures of the world shone in numerous shops," he writes, offering "all that luxury could invent to embellish life!" Its arcades were

illuminated by bright multicoloured lights that blind the sight. Imagine the concourses of people who crowd into these galleries and walk around only in order to look at one another! Here you see the coffee houses (the first ones in Paris), which are also packed with people; here they read newspapers and journals aloud, make noise and quarrel, make speeches, etc.

"Nymphs of joy"—prostitutes—approach him, "promising an abundance of pleasures." Cacophonous noise and blinding light, politics and consumerism in the hands of the masses, the seduction of commerce and commercialized seduction—it is all, he concludes ambiguously, "an enchantment" akin to "Calypso's island, Armida's fortress."[155]

---

[152] Aleksandr Radishchev, "Puteshestvie iz Peterburga v Moskvu," in *O povrezhdenii nravov v Rossii kniazia M. Shcherbatova i puteshestvie A. Radishcheva: Faksimil'noe izdanie* (Moscow: Nauka, 1985), 210.

[153] Radishchev, "Puteshestvie iz Peterburga v Moskvu," 216.

[154] [Mercier], *Tableau de Paris*, 9:132–3.

[155] Karamzin, *Letters of a Russian Traveller*, 251.

The same treacherous siren song could be heard in Moscow, as we learn from the *Moscow Spectator* (*Moskovskii Zritel'*), a journal edited by the Sentimentalist writer Petr Shalikov (1767–1852). One Sunday evening, Shalikov writes in 1806, his attention was drawn to the "brilliant lighting and thunderous music" emanating from a restaurant that held Sunday "balls" in its "large round hall," which it advertised with bills posted on mirrors inside the establishment. Bright lights, music, mirrors, large ballrooms, and elaborate after-dark entertainments were associated with upper-class life, but when he entered and surveyed the scene, all he saw was a crowd of "man-servants and clerks" waiting for Gypsy women to dance for them. Looking around the room, he saw "nymphs of joy to whom foppish valets were declaring their tender feelings," and "priestesses of Venus who quickly drew everyone's glances, carefully scrutinizing them for the immodesty from which they expected their reward." On his way out, he read a bill advertising the ball. "'*The most esteemed Public* is informed' etc.—Now, think about the arrogance of those words: *the most esteemed Public*!... What an idea!... Of course, for *that* place, the Public I have described really is *most esteemed*."[156]

Shalikov's outrage betrayed his fear that the diffusion of upper-class mores might boomerang by degrading the enlightened public that Karamzin and others sought to foster. "The public" (*publika*) was a concept that arose in Russia in the late eighteenth century. According to the playwright Aleksandr Sumarokov (1717–77), it applied to "people of knowledge and taste," that is, people of any condition whose manners and aesthetic sense were guided by the exacting canons of neoclassicism. Most emphatically *not* part of the public, according to Sumarokov, were ignorant Moscow "clerks" and "man-servants" who behaved in the theater as though buying a ticket gave them license to annoy other spectators by talking loudly and crunching nuts.[157] In this view, which Shalikov shared, the true public had to be shielded from contamination by vulgar upstarts who mimicked the public's external forms but made a mockery of its cultural ideals. This explains Shalikov's alarm at prostitutes posing as lovers, valets masquerading as gentlemen, and a rabble that pretended to be "the public."

Shalikov's concerns were echoed by Sergei Glinka (1776–1847), the editor of the nationalistic Moscow journal *Russian Messenger* (*Ruskoi Vestnik*). In 1811, Glinka published an excerpt from a book, apparently by the writer and government official Aleksei Golitsyn,[158] denouncing luxury. The French Revolution, Golitsyn argued, had been caused by a breakdown of traditional morals that began in the nobility and spread to other classes. A similar process was now under way in Moscow and St Petersburg. For example, instead of going to alehouses to

---

[156] "Smes'," *Moskovskii Zritel'*, chast' 4 (December 1806), 74–5; ellipses in original.

[157] Sumarokov is quoted in A. Nikitenko, "Rech' o kritike, proiznesennaia v torzhestvennom sobranii Imperatorskago Sankpeterburgskago Universiteta, marta 25-go dnia 1842 goda," *OZ*, vol. 24 (1842), otdel 5 "Kritika," 1–42, here: 28–9.

[158] N. N. Golitsyn, *Materialy dlia polnoi rodoslovnoi rospisi kniazei Golitsynykh* (Kiev: Tipografiia E. Ia. Fedorova, 1880), 26–7, 147.

drink, the people increasingly adopted the nobility's taste for more refined establishments:

In the new-style restaurants I have seen merchants, artisans, servants of the nobility, and all manner of indecent women; mostly they are not drinking but passing the time with billiards and very strange conversations. The luxury that has spread among all social classes, the taste for entertainments, [and] the impossibility of appearing in these places without appropriate attire, have caused this class of the people to become every day more indifferent to the means of earning money; and how many families of these artisans have no bread, because their fathers spend the fruits of their labors on tea, Don wine, and the Gypsy women who fill almost all these restaurants.

Compounding the damage, Golitsyn continued, was the easy availability of novels that taught the people "to reason and theorize falsely about everything." Migrant peasants were exposed to these influences and carried the rot back to the country. Their villages might seem wealthy, but in fact "luxury [is] inappropriate to rural inhabitants." In an implicit criticism of Karamzin, Golitsyn rejected any comparison with prosperous villages in Austria, Holland, or Switzerland. True peasant well-being, he declared, manifested itself "not in masonry-built houses, tea, [or] the foreign wines that are found in the homes of trading peasants, but in everyday abundance, perennial happiness, ignorance of urban customs, and the truest devotion to the faith."[159]

Glinka viewed Moscow's eateries and watering holes as sources of corruption, not refinement. Like Karamzin, he viewed drink as the bane of lower-class life. Describing villages near Moscow, Karamzin wrote of "lovely peasant women with berries, flowers, [and] herbs for the pharmacies" who came to trade in Moscow but whose shiftless husbands then spent the money on alcohol, "that dreadful vice" that caused "not only poverty and illness but even crime." Karamzin argued that the lure of the bottle could be neutralized if hard work—and, evidently, enhanced respect for women—created prosperity and genteel manners.[160] Glinka was skeptical. One of his articles opened with the observation that "In Moscow, restaurants, so-called hotels, and alehouses are multiplying by the hour." Glinka associated alehouses with the violence and drunkenness of Moscow's seventeenth-century *strel'tsy* revolts, the 1771 plague revolt, and the Terror in France. While alehouses were intended by law for the meaner sort, the designations "restaurant" (*traktir*) and "hotel" (*gerberg*) were reserved to establishments of a better class. To Glinka, however, they were all

---

[159] [S. N. Glinka], "Vypiska iz Ruskoi knigi, nazvannoi: Sobranie otryvkov, vziatykh iz nravstvennykh i politicheskikh Pisatelei, i izdannoi G . . . 1811," *RV*, chast' 6 (June 1811), 73–86, quotations on 79–80, 82, 83.

[160] "Istoricheskiia vospominaniia i zamechaniia," in Karamzin, *Sochineniia*, 8:315–16, quotations on 316.

equally "refuges of idleness, violence, and drunkenness," and those who worked there were labor not available for "agriculture, the arts, trades, and crafts!"[161]

Glinka's thinking was rooted in a critique of luxury similar to the classical critique advanced in eighteenth-century France.[162] As a cadet in St Petersburg in 1785–95, he had been immersed in the Roman classics and the French Enlightenment, most of all Rousseau. He retained a reverence for classical republican virtue, a sentimental humanitarianism, and what the scholar Liubov' Kiseleva calls "a foundational tendency of the eighteenth century": a determination to overlook unsavory realities and imagine the world as it should be.[163]

A sensitive, quixotic soul, Glinka was shocked to discover, upon leaving the cloistered cadet corps, that Russia's social order had little in common with his ideals. He rebelled by refusing the serf estate he inherited,[164] resigning his military commission, and turning his back on high society. In 1808, he dedicated himself to the renewal of the Russian spirit by launching the *Russian Messenger*, the very title of which was a challenge to the cosmopolitan agenda of Karamzin's *Messenger of Europe*. Glinka wanted to teach Russians to see themselves as a great family bound by love, duty, and respect for the unique role of each estate, not as selfish classes and atomized individuals guided by the atheistic materialism of the *philosophes*.[165]

To encourage a sense of national pride, Glinka claimed that Russia's eighteenth-century monarchs had neither Westernized the country nor oppressed the common people. He applauded Catherine II for the same social and urban policies that were praised by other Enlightenment thinkers—her *Nakaz*, the foundling homes, the schools to foster "new people," the Moscow aqueduct, the opening of primary schools—but he claimed in addition that she had opposed the aristocracy's addiction to foreign luxuries and wanted to free the serfs. In Glinka's version of history, Catherine revered Moscow for its attachment to ancient customs, and her reforms built on Russian traditions that reached deep into pre-Petrine times; the fact that the wisest foreign writers applauded her ideas was merely testament to their universality.[166] Glinka knew that this was fantasy. Privately, he wrote that

[161] [S. N. Glinka], "Zamechanie o Moskve," *RV*, chast' 1 (February 1808), 159–61, quotations on 159; Georgi, *Versuch einer Beschreibung*, 341–4.

[162] I discuss Glinka's views on the social order in "The Family Model of Society and Russian National Identity in Sergei N. Glinka's *Russian Messenger* (1808–1812)," *Slavic Review*, 57/1 (Spring 1998), 28–49.

[163] Liubov' Kiseleva, "S. N. Glinka i kadetskii korpus (iz istorii 'sentimental'nogo vospitaniia' v Rossii)," *Uchenye zapiski Tartuskogo gosudarstvennogo universiteta*, vypusk 604 (1982), 48–63, quotation on 57.

[164] S. N. Glinka, *Zapiski Sergeia Nikolaevicha Glinki* (St Petersburg: Russkaia Starina, 1895), 177.

[165] Liubov' Kiseleva, "Sistema vzgliadov S. N. Glinki (1807–1812 gg.)," *Uchenye zapiski Tartuskogo gosudarstvennogo universiteta*, vypusk 513 (1981), 52–72.

[166] [S. N. Glinka], "Napominanie o Ekaterine Vtoroi," *RV*, chast' 2 (April 1808), 3–45.

Catherine was an inept legislator and that both she and Peter had failed in their attempts to reform the country.[167] Yet in print he tirelessly claimed the opposite, for what mattered was inspirational effect, not historical accuracy.

These dreams and disappointments shaped Glinka's thinking about public institutions and spaces. The purpose that he envisioned for them was not Karamzin's Enlightenment project of cultural cosmopolitanism, elitist sociability, and individual critical inquiry, but a Rousseauian utopia of organic social harmony rooted in reverence for ancestral traditions. He depicted Red Square as a site of masculine civic virtue rather like the Roman forum, where men of all ages and stations gathered in pre-Petrine times to debate public affairs and pay homage to patriots.[168] Red Square's antipode was Kuznetskii Most (Blacksmiths' Bridge), a nearby street lined with high-end foreign shops and associated with female vice: rich ladies went there to indulge their vanity with overpriced fashion goods, and the women who worked there were said to be sexually loose.

Kuznetskii Most was the epicenter of "fashion" and "luxury," Glinka's terms for the twin roots of Russia's troubles. Glinka believed that emulating foreign countries, especially France, sapped the upper classes' loyalty to their own nation. The passion for imported luxuries led them to bankrupt themselves and their serfs, undermined religion, alienated Westernized Russians from their compatriots, and generally undermined personal, familial, and civic virtue. The pedigree of these ideas was European—Glinka bolstered his arguments with citations to Voltaire, Rousseau, Fénelon, Schiller, Madame de Genlis, and Mercier, among others—but the central argument was that the cosmopolitan consumer culture of the elites was a threat to Russia's integrity.[169]

Glinka was not blind to the civilizing effects of socioeconomic modernization. Rather, as his criticism of Kuznetskii Most suggests, he was disturbed by the connection between elite Westernization, the importation of foreign goods, and the mutual estrangement of Russia's social classes. He favored manufacturing and consumerism when they involved non-elite groups and promised to bring Russians together. For instance, he advocated an expansion of provincial manufacturing as a way to bring prosperity to provincial towns and thus "make society more pleasant, morals gentler, and the necessities of life easier to obtain." It would also (here he agreed with Karamzin) discourage alcoholism among the peasants. Lastly, he thought that the opening of manufactories was usually accompanied by the establishment of primary schools, which promoted the spread of literacy and thus disseminated "an enlightenment that will soften the harshness of morals and bring man closer to man."[170]

[167] Liubov' Kiseleva, "Zhurnal 'Zritel' i dve kontseptsii patriotizma v russkoi literature 1800-kh gg.," *Uchenye zapiski Tartuskogo gosudarstvennogo universiteta*, vypusk 645 (1985), 3–20, esp. 18.

[168] [S. N. Glinka], "Vzor na Moskvu," *RV*, chast' 1 (January 1808), 23–35, esp. 24–5.

[169] [S. N. Glinka], "Kuznetskoi Most, ili vladychestvo mody i roskoshi," *RV*, chast' 3 (September 1808), 331–60.

[170] [S. N. Glinka], "O pol'ze v Rossii remesl, khudozhestv, iskusstv," *RV*, chast' 1 (March 1808), 300–15, here: 307, 310, quotations on 301, 309.

Glinka's distinction between good and bad public spaces and consumer habits was connected with his wider view of Moscow's place in Russian life. Like Karamzin, he wanted the historical memories associated with the city to provide his nation with a useable past. Karamzin thought history could help give Russians a sense of rootedness so they could build a future that was more cosmopolitan. Glinka, on the other hand, treated the Russian past as he had been taught as a cadet to treat ancient Rome: as a timeless, ahistorical ideal that united patriots in service to the nation.[171] For Karamzin, Moscow as a present-day metropolis was beneficial to Russia's progress because it fostered an enlightened public of men and women who were united by art, commerce, and genteel sociability. Glinka, by contrast, valued the metropolis when it encouraged austere, manly virtues and civic mobilization.

The works of Karamzin and Glinka suggest that the early nineteenth century was a time of flux in Russian thinking about the big city. Both authors remained within an eighteenth-century framework inasmuch as they eschewed social or ethnographic realism and offered a moral critique of the elites by depicting an obviously idealized social order. At the same time, like their contemporaries who wrote in Western languages, and anticipating Russian authors of the 1830s, they were interested in the dynamics of urban class relations and explored the city from an individualized, eye-level perspective, not the Olympian vantage point of the state bureaucracy. Karamzin, and to a lesser extent Glinka, were among the most widely read Russian authors of their day. Two texts that remained unpublished at the time (although they may have circulated in manuscript form), by Karamzin's friends Aleksei Malinovskii and Konstantin Batiushkov, show even more clearly the transitional character of this moment in Russian thinking, and how eighteenth-century thought patterns persisted alongside emerging nineteenth-century ways of imagining the city.[172]

MALINOVSKII AND BATIUSHKOV

Malinovskii and Batiushkov were highly dissimilar figures. Malinovskii (1762–1840) was a contemporary of Karamzin and grew up under Catherine II; Batiushkov (1787–1855), a quarter-century younger, came of age in the Napoleonic era. Batiushkov was of old noble stock, whereas Malinovskii was a priest's son and suffered humiliation in his service career because he could not

---

171 Glinka, *Zapiski*, 63; Kiseleva, "Zhurnal 'Zritel'' i dve kontseptsii patriotizma," 14–17.

172 Batiushkov's "Progulka po Moskve" was first published in 1869, and Malinovskii's *Obozrenie Moskvy* in 1992 (K. N. Batiushkov, *Sochineniia*, 2 vols. (Moscow: "Khudozhestvennaia Literatura," 1989), 1:468; Malinovskii, *Obozrenie Moskvy*, 228). All citations to "Progulka po Moskve" will refer to Batiushkov, *Sochineniia* (1989), vol. 1.

adequately document the noble ancestry that he claimed. Batiushkov was a poet and spent lengthy periods in the St Petersburg bureaucracy and the army, whereas Malinovskii was a scholar and lifelong Muscovite: educated at Moscow University, he was recruited in 1780 by Gerhard Friedrich Müller for the College of Foreign Affairs archive, where he worked for sixty years and became extraordinarily knowledgeable about the history of Moscow. In 1814 he became the director of the archive, which was a major Moscow institution partly because working there gave young aristocrats an attractive alternative to the army. Malinovskii thus became a mentor to young men who went on to renown as literati or statesmen. The four Turgenev and the two Bulgakov brothers, Dmitrii Bludov, and Filipp Vigel' were among the first cohort of "archive youths" in the early years of the century, followed by the two Kireevskii brothers, Dmitrii Sverbeev, and others in the 1820s and 1830s.[173]

No less different than their biographies were the ways Malinovskii and Batiushkov wrote about Moscow. Malinovskii's unfinished *Description of Moscow* (*Opisanie Moskvy*) stood in Müller's tradition. Begun after the defeat of Napoleon and completed by the late 1820s, when Malinovskii was well into his sixties, it crowned a lifetime of painstaking scholarship. Malinovskii's survey of Moscow begins with the Kremlin, then moves outward to Kitai-Gorod, and then to the White City. That was all he was able to finish. Within each area, he proceeds from church to church, palace to palace, dwelling at length on the history and architecture of each. The Kremlin is given as much space as Kitai-Gorod and the White City combined, for Malinovskii's Moscow is primarily an architectural monument to tsars, clerics, and aristocrats of the sixteenth to eighteenth centuries.

Only occasionally do the people make an appearance and give a hint of Malinovskii's thinking about Russian society and its history. For all his love of the pre-Petrine past, he equates Westernization with progress, even though he resents the foreign domination of Russia's commerce and schools and is outraged at the devastation wrought by Napoleon in 1812. He digresses to recall the popular irrationality and violence of the plague revolt, and briefly remarks on the life that fills some of the urban spaces he describes: markets where illegal goods are traded, or the elegant promenade at the Kremlin Gardens. Government efforts to improve the city are given their due: paved thoroughfares, street lights, the police (grudgingly), and—with evident enthusiasm—the fire department. At bottom, though, Malinovskii's Moscow is a city of buildings and memories, not living people.[174]

Batiushkov's "Stroll around Moscow" ("Progulka po Moskve"), an essay composed in 1811, could hardly have been more different. The poet was 24 years old when he recorded these impressions. Whereas Malinovskii's text

---

[173] Malinovskii, *Obozrenie Moskvy*, 184–93.
[174] Malinovskii, *Obozrenie Moskvy*, 86, 87, 113–16, 124, 132, 154, 156.

breathes a reverential Moscow patriotism, Batiushkov writes as a haughty tourist from St Petersburg. Confident of his own cultural superiority, he observes the locals with ironic condescension. Malinovskii aims to write an exhaustive scholarly *Description of Moscow* by focusing on historic buildings. Batiushkov opts for the more informal genre of a letter to a friend, and flippantly announces that "a description of Moscow" is for him "a completely impossible thing," for two reasons: he lacks "information about history etc. etc.," so the many historical monuments remain "mute" to him; and he is too lazy.[175] Like Malinovskii, he begins in the Kremlin, but it is the mood of piety and antiquity that interests him, not the actual history that the buildings represent, and he soon leaves for places where there is more bustle and movement. Like Mercier and Karamzin (in *Letters of a Russian Traveler*), two authors he read and admired,[176] he adopts the pose of the *flâneur*. His aim is to sample the colorful variety of urban life. "And so, as I go along, wandering from house to house, promenade to promenade, dinner to dinner, I will jot down a few observations about the city and the mores of the inhabitants, without respecting sequence nor order, and you will find them a pleasure to read."[177]

Where Malinovskii's Moscow is a city of harmonious monuments, Batiushkov's is a living cacophony. "Here, luxury and destitution, abundance and extreme poverty, piety and unbelief, the firmness of our grandfathers' time and incredible flightiness, are like hostile elements in eternal conflict and form that wondrous, shapeless, gigantic *whole* that we know by the collective name of *Moscow*."[178] To explore these jarring contrasts, he takes the reader on a tour of sites where urban life pulsates with particular intensity: the elegant shops of Kuznetskii Most, the bazaar of Kitai-Gorod, and the promenade of Tverskoi Boulevard. Everywhere he foregrounds restlessness and diversity. The traders and customers of Kuznetskii Most are a microcosm of the nations of Europe. Kitai-Gorod, while utterly different, is no less diverse. "Here we see the Greek, the Tatar, the Turk...; there the dry Frenchman..., yonder the grave Persian, there the coachman..., here the poor peasant..." On the boulevard, it is the variety of upper-class types that draws his attention. "Good manners and fashion demand sacrifices: at the first hour of the morning, the dandy and the coquette and the old gossip and the fat tax-farmer all race to Tverskoi Boulevard from the far ends of Moscow."[179]

---

[175] Batiushkov, "Progulka po Moskve," 287.
[176] On Batiushkov and Mercier, see: K. N. Batiushkov, *Sochineniia*, 3 vols. (St Petersburg: Tipografiia (byvshaia) Kotomina, 1885–7), 2:454–5; on Karamzin, see *Russkii Biograficheskii Slovar'*, 2:581.
[177] Batiushkov, "Progulka po Moskve," 288.
[178] Batiushkov, "Progulka po Moskve," 294.
[179] Batiushkov, "Progulka po Moskve," 291–2.

While particularly drawn to sites where classes and cultures mingle, he does not rhapsodize, as Karamzin might have, about the diffusion of civility. Instead, he finds that for all its claims to sophistication, Moscow is really just "a big provincial town." On Kuznetskii Most, people he thought at first were English, French, or Germans turn out to be Russian provincials affecting foreign airs, and in the bookshops, pulp fiction and mind-numbing mystical tracts are treated with reverence because they are in French. The booksellers of Kitai-Gorod "deal in books as they do in fish, pelts, vegetables, and so on . . . the book mongers buy their learned merchandise, that is, translations and [original] works, by weight, and continually tell the poor authors: it's not about quality, but quantity! Not the style, but the number of pages!"[180] As for Moscow's aristocrats, they combine ancestral coarseness with modern pretentiousness. Enter their mansions, and you meet "the master in his sheepskin, the mistress in her cape [*salop*]; to the right, the parish priest, the parish schoolmaster, and the jester, and to the left, a horde of children, an old sorceress, the [French] madame, and the tutor from Germany."[181] Karamzin, Glinka, and Malinovskii subordinate the living reality to an organizing concept such as Russia's historical inheritance or its progress toward enlightenment. Batiushkov's focus, on the contrary, is on the disorderliness inherent to urban society. As a result, he offers a sociological concreteness that the others lack, and is alive to the opacity and ambiguities of urban social processes.

What distinguishes Moscow, in his view, is not so much a unique essence as the diversity of its constituent parts, for it is a meeting ground of Russia, Europe, and the Orient. The non-European and lower-class Russian elements—whose world he does not investigate further—are lumped together as an Orientalized other, as when he declares that the sprawling markets of Kitai-Gorod are "quite the Eastern bazaar."[182] It is among the higher classes that the meaning of Russianness is negotiated. Like Karamzin, Batiushkov operates with the notion of progress toward enlightenment. To illustrate this idea, he describes the mansion of "an old Muscovite, a pious prince." The courtyard is strewn with rubbish, the servants are drunk and ragged, the rooms lack curtains and cushions, and guests are served cabbage soup and kvas. The adjacent house, by contrast, is small but genteel. The valet is courteous, the décor exquisite, and "the company as well is entirely the opposite of that which we saw in the house next door. Here is the abode of affability, decorum, and civility."[183] Batiushkov stresses Moscow's shocking contrast of wealth and poverty, virtue and vice. These were staples of European urban literature, and themes that Karamzin associated with Paris and London. In *Letters of a Russian Traveler*, Karamzin claimed that the English

[180] Batiushkov, "Progulka po Moskve," 294, 291.
[181] Batiushkov, "Progulka po Moskve," 295.
[182] Batiushkov, "Progulka po Moskve," 291.
[183] Batiushkov, "Progulka po Moskve," 295.

upper classes were pathologically splenetic, bored, and eccentric. Batiushkov says the same about Muscovites: their febrile quest for novelty arises from a boredom induced by idleness, and "London itself is poorer than Moscow in the area of moral caricatures."[184] He thus makes explicit what Karamzin only implied: that Moscow was European not only in its potential for enlightenment but also in its urban ills.

CONCLUSION

A persistent feature of eighteenth-century European culture was the preference for representing life as it should be, not as it was. This tendency was heightened in the Russian case because the elites analyzed their country using foreign interpretive categories and with an eye to proving that Russia, too, was an enlightened European state. Hence the eighteenth-century representations of Moscow feel idealized, derivative, and disconnected from reality.

The last decade of the century witnessed a profound change. Western, most often German, authors reassessed urban Russia in light of the latest European approaches. The result was a body of writing that described Moscow and St Petersburg with unprecedented social concreteness and allowed Russia to be incorporated into wider European discourses about national specificity and urban modernization.

A vigorous literature on urban themes developed in Russia as well, but before the 1820s and 1830s, the new approaches from the West were not fully embraced. Russian writers shared the interest of their Western contemporaries in sociological and ethnographic themes, but while the Europeans adopted the aspiration to objectivity and factual accuracy that became a hallmark of nineteenth-century science, the Russians—most prominently Karamzin and Glinka—remained in the eighteenth-century tradition of depicting the ideal for which they wanted society to strive, not reality with its warts and ambiguities.

The writers, artists, cartographers, historians, and statisticians of the eighteenth and early nineteenth century have a threefold relevance to the imperial social project. Their work had a lasting impact on how Russian cities were imagined in Russia and abroad. They also created a body of evidence that gives historians unprecedented insight into urban conditions. Lastly, it was to them that Moscow's increasingly literate middling sort looked for guidance as they tried to articulate their own thoughts about life in the city in memoirs, diaries, and letters. Thanks to these developments, the experience of middling Muscovites comes into clearer focus by the turn of the nineteenth century. It is to the everyday realities of their world that we now turn.

---

[184] Karamzin, *Letters of a Russian Traveller*, 451–2; Batiushkov, "Progulka po Moskve," 294–5, quotation on 295.

5

Government, Aristocracy, and the Middling Sort

The imperial social project unfolded principally along the contact zone between the aristocracy and the middling sort (lesser nobles, clergy, and merchants). Thanks to their wealth and social power, the aristocrats not only modeled European culture but drew the middling sort into participating in it, for instance by hosting cultural events, opening their manors to the public, and providing employment. Yet the scale of the aristocracy's magnificence also had the effect of making everyone else feel small and inferior. As a result, compared with smaller towns, the middling sort in Moscow had more cultural opportunities but harbored deeper resentments and a weaker sense of civic identity.[1]

The present chapter will explore the encounter between the aristocracy, the middling sort, and the state in Moscow in the decades before and after 1800. Four questions will structure the chapter. First, how the social hierarchy worked: the institutions, legal rights, and everyday forms of power and influence that determined a group's social status. Next, the material underpinnings of this hierarchy: how incomes, wealth, and access to comforts and conveniences shaped the lives of the aristocracy and the middling sort. Third, the means by which the aristocrats maintained their dominant position, especially their ostentatious display of wealth and authority and their alternation between graciousness and snobbery. The final question will be how the pre-Reform school system, with its bifurcation between all-estate schools and estate-specific schools, helped to shape the lives of Moscow's middle social strata.

The source base for this chapter includes both quantitative data and narrative sources. Personal narratives can help us understand how large-scale social dynamics, which the statistics show in the aggregate, operated in the lived experience of individuals. Many of the narratives date from the mid- to late nineteenth century, when improved education had expanded the pool of authors and there was a vigorous public debate about which aspects of the pre-Reform system Russia should preserve or discard. These texts were written when pre-Reform Russia was fading into the past; this is their strength and their weakness.

---

[1] Kupriianov, *Gorodskaia kul'tura*, 394–5, 476.

Authors sought to convey the alterity of the past through a finely textured reading of how people had formerly thought and behaved, but what especially arrested their attention were the retrograde features of the old order that became the focus of debate during the Great Reforms. Authors differed in their overall assessment—some were nostalgic for a past they thought had been simple and innocent, while others denounced its coarseness and brutality—but to all it appeared, in retrospect, as archaic and alien.

An influential template for reading the old order was supplied by literary works that created easily recognizable stereotypes of social groups. Thanks to Aleksandr Griboedov's *Woe from Wit* (*Gore ot uma*, 1823), a satirical play about Moscow aristocrats, the phrase "Griboedov's Moscow" (*Griboedovskaia Moskva*) became a shorthand for the aristocracy of the early nineteenth century. The benighted Moscow merchants portrayed in Aleksandr Ostrovskii's plays were so memorable that the memoirist Ivan Slonov could describe his former employer simply as "a prototype for Dikoi from Ostrovskii's *The Storm*." Nikolai Pomialovskii's *Seminary Sketches* (*Ocherki bursy*, 1862–3) were so widely known that the memoirist Pavel Bogatyrev called his own teachers, who were ex-seminarians, "a coarse, intellectually backward lot, right out of Pomialovskii's *Seminary*."[2]

Seeing the past through the lens of canonical literary works, often satirical ones to boot, lent a certain homogeneity to pre-Reform Russia's image in the later memoir literature and heightened its grotesque features. The memoirs are an invaluable historical source, but they are literary constructs of their era, not a direct window into the earlier time.

THE ARISTOCRACY AND THE MIDDLING SORT

Law, lifestyle, and culture created the fault lines that determined pre-Reform Moscow's social structure. By law, some Muscovites were enserfed while the rest were free; among those who were free, a few estates (nobles, merchants, clergy) were further privileged by being legally exempt from conscription, the soul tax, and corporal punishment. Cutting across the legal division among estates, the growth of a consumer society promoted a three-way split in lifestyle between the masses, the middle, and the rich. Finally, education and sociability created a third split, this one based on participation in the imperial culture. The cumulative result was a division of the population into three unequal segments. At the top was a tiny subset of the nobility, the aristocracy. Beneath them, the middling sort: most of the 13.8 percent who, at the end of Catherine II's reign, belonged to

---

[2] P. I. Bogatyrev, "Moskovskaia starina," in Iu. N. Aleksandrov, ed., *Moskovskaia starina: Vospominaniia moskvichei proshlogo stoletiia* (Moscow: Pravda, 1989), 130; Slonov, *Iz zhizni*, 77.

the estates of nobles, clerics, or merchants, plus the more prosperous among the 15.3 percent who were townspeople, guild artisans, government clerks (*kantse-liarskie sluzhiteli*), or miscellaneous groups that defied easy categorization (*raznochintsy*, "people of various ranks"). At the bottom was everyone else, the lower classes.

Muscovites were divided into estates as shown in Table 5.1. These data are based on lists of residents kept by the police, so they likely undercount people, mostly of the lower classes, who failed to register because they were in Moscow illegally (i.e. without passports) or only for a short time.[3]

The population changed less over time than these numbers suggest. The nobles, clergy, and merchants consistently represented around 5 percent, 2 percent, and 5 to 7 percent, respectively, of the overall population. The largest shift was due to laws from the 1820s and 1830s that made it easier for peasants and manumitted serfs to enroll in the urban estates.[4] This led to an increase in the number of townspeople and artisans relative to peasants and house serfs, but the four estates' combined weight changed little: they represented 70.9 percent of

Table 5.1. Population of Moscow by estate and sex, 1789–1839

	1789–93			1835–39		
	Total	Percent of total population	Male–female ratio	Total	Percent of total population	Male–female ratio
Nobles	8,600	4.9	1.3:1	15,700	4.7	1.2:1
Clergy	3,600	2.1	1.4:1	8,200	2.4	1.6:1
Merchants	11,900	6.8	1.5:1	17,800	5.3	1.2:1
Townspeople & artisans	9,100	5.2	1.9:1	75,300	22.5	1.6:1
Soldiers & their families	7,000	4.0	2.9:1	33,700	10.1	2.0:1
Clerks & *raznochintsy*	17,600	10.1	1.7:1	27,700	8.3	2.0:1
Peasants	53,700	30.7	2.6:1	84,500	25.2	1.8:1
House serfs	61,300	35.0	1.6:1	67,000	20.0	1.3:1
Foreigners	2,200	1.3	2.1:1	4,800	1.4	1.7:1
Total	175,000	100.0	1.9:1	335,000	100.0	1.6:1

Source: Gastev, *Materialy*, 264.

Note: The totals are those calculated by Gastev. In the figures for 1835–9, the males add up to 300 fewer than Gastev's total. The percentages for 1835–9 are based on the totals indicated by Gastev.

[3] P. Semenov, "Predislovie," *Statisticheskii vremennik Rossiiskoi Imperii*, vol. 1 (1866), i–xxxvi, here: xviii.

[4] Hildermeier, *Bürgertum und Stadt*, 234–45, 365.

the total in 1789–93, and 67.7 percent in 1835–9. Also, the Napoleonic Wars brought an influx of soldiers. In all of Russia, 1,616,199 men were conscripted into the army between 1796 and 1815. Their wives and children likewise became members of the soldiers' estate.[5] In Moscow, soldiers and their families went from 4 percent of the inhabitants in 1789–93 to 13.9 percent in 1816, before dropping back to 10.1 percent in the 1830s.[6] Because so many Muscovites were migrants, who tended to be men, the population as a whole skewed male. The discrepancy was greatest among the estates with the most transients or men who were too poor to marry, such as soldiers, peasants, clerks, and townspeople.

The nobility, the most privileged estate of the empire, formed a steep pyramid of status and wealth. At its apex stood the aristocrats, whom Russians called *znat'* or *svet* or *vel'mozhi*, the narrow circle of elite families that was immortalized by Griboedov and later by Tolstoi's *War and Peace* and popular histories of Moscow.[7] Thanks to their voluminous legacy of letters, diaries, and memoirs, they can seem intimately familiar to modern readers and frequently dominate our view of the city. To this day, imperial Moscow is sometimes imagined as populated mainly by these few people, with all the other inhabitants reduced to a shadowy, undifferentiated mass.

This upper crust was vanishingly thin. In 1775, there were in Moscow only 48 wives or unmarried daughters of men in the top five ranks, that is, generals and their civilian equivalents.[8] Individual aristocrats were so recognizable that plays achieved notoriety by lampooning specific people,[9] and the *Moscow Gazette's* rubric for recent arrivals routinely included entries such as this one from 6 September 1783: "On September 1st, His Excellency Major-General Ivan Ivanovich Golokhvastov arrived from his suburban estate; also, two *shtab*-officers [officials in ranks 8 through 6, who were automatically hereditary nobles], and 469 persons of various conditions." The data on serf ownership tell the same story. In all of Russia as of 1858, a mere 2.8 percent of all hereditary nobles owned over 500 "souls" (male serfs) each, including an elite few who owned many thousands. These 2.8 percent owned 43.8 percent of all the serfs. By contrast, 33.8 percent of hereditary nobles owned twenty or fewer "souls," and

[5] Janet M. Hartley, *Russia, 1762–1825: Military Power, the State, and the People* (Westport, Conn.: Praeger, 2008), 26.

[6] Hildermeier, *Bürgertum und Stadt*, 365. Hildermeier gives slightly higher figures—11.4 and 13.7 percent, respectively, for 1829 and 1842 (*Bürgertum und Stadt*, 365).

[7] Examples of such popular histories include Pyliaev, *Staraia Moskva*, and N. Matveev, *Moskva i zhizn' v nei nakanune nashestviia 1812 g.* (Moscow: Duma, 2008).

[8] "Vedomost' o nakhodiashchikhsia v Moskve pervykh piati klassov zhenska pola personakh v 1775 godu," *RS*, 8 (July–December 1873), 94–7.

[9] A. L. Grishunin, "Griboedovskaia Moskva," in N. D. Bludilina et al., eds., *Moskva v russkoi i mirovoi literature: Sbornik statei* (Moscow: Nasledie, 2000), 70, 86–7; Alexander M. Martin, *Romantics, Reformers, Reactionaries: Russian Conservative Thought and Politics in the Reign of Alexander I* (DeKalb, Ill.: Northern Illinois University Press, 1997), 71–2.

another 21.3 percent owned none at all. Together, these last two groups were over half the hereditary nobility but owned only 3.2 percent of all the serfs.[10]

The aristocracy's ascendancy over the middling sort was tremendous, especially in the early nineteenth century. One wellspring of this supremacy was political and social power. Aristocrats had ties to the imperial court, held key governmental posts in Moscow, surrounded themselves with retinues of favor-seekers, and exercised patronage through charity to the poor and generosity to fellow nobles. Another source of social dominance was the magnificent yet intimidating spectacle of their lifestyle, made possible by huge incomes from serf estates. Affluent merchants were often frugal, hard-working, and culturally traditionalistic; in the nineteenth century, many were also Old Believers. By contrast, aristocrats were expected to engage in conspicuous consumption, patronize the arts, and live a life of refined leisure (at least if they resided in Moscow, which offered fewer career opportunities than St Petersburg). They also cultivated their eccentricities—poodles, for example: in 1800, Count Kirill Razumovskii placed a notice in the *Moscow Gazette* offering 10 rubles for the return of his lost poodle,[11] and the entire city police was alerted in 1812 or 1813 to search for the poodle of Prince Petr Drutskoi-Sokolinskii, this time for a finder's fee of 50 rubles. To put these sums into perspective, the purchase price for a serf maid at the time was 80–100 rubles.[12]

The aristocracy's lavish hospitality and cultural patronage facilitated the spread of the Westernized imperial culture. Ivan Tolchenov, a merchant from Dmitrov near Moscow, recorded in his diary that while on a trip to St Petersburg in 1776 he watched an English tightrope walker named Sanders perform at a theater in an aristocratic home.[13] He could have done this in Moscow as well. The *Moscow Gazette* of 19 February 1773 announced that "The famed English-man Mr Sander [*sic*] will display his new art, never before seen here." Sanders, according to the *Gazette,* had presented his show at royal courts across Europe, and now "he will display it here to eminent [*znatnym*] personages, the nobility, the merchantry, and all the public at the house of Count Roman Larionovich Vorontsov, every week on Tuesdays, Thursdays, and Saturdays." On the next page, readers learned from another notice that daily in the house of General Aleksei Spiridov "an Italian company will present various tricks" for an admission price of 1 ruble or 50 kopeks. In addition to hosting visiting performers, aristocrats organized private theaters that were staffed with serf actors or noble amateurs. Thirty-one such theaters are known to have existed at various times in eighteenth-century Moscow.[14]

---

[10] Mironov, *Sotsial'naia istoriia Rossii*, 1:88 (figures excluding Finland and Poland).
[11] *MV* (3 March 1800), 465.
[12] Shchukin, *Bumagi*, 3:206; Raupach, *Reise*, 250.
[13] Ransel, *A Russian Merchant's Tale*, 65.
[14] Wirtschafter, *The Play of Ideas*, 20–1.

Refined entertaining was likewise dominated by the aristocracy. For the provincial nobles who migrated every winter from their country estates to the metropolis, the marquee events of the season were the Tuesday night balls and concerts at the Noble Assembly. The display of wealth and refinement at these gatherings awed Ivan Vtorov (1772–1844), a young noble visiting Moscow in 1801. To see "as many as four thousand people assembled in one building," he later recalled, "dressed in the finest clothing, especially the ladies and young women bedecked with diamonds and pearls, was a magnificent spectacle, the likes of which I had never enjoyed before." The men were equally resplendent, all "in uniform, with swords and buckled shoes and powdered hair." His principal worry, Vtorov wrote, was "the poor state of my finances amidst the society splendor."[15] The aristocracy also extended its hospitality to a broader public that included non-nobles. Recalling her youth in Moscow under Catherine II, the aristocrat Elizaveta Ian'kova (1768–1861) told her grandson that "[the Eropkins] would keep an open table, meaning that every day all who wished could come to lunch so long as they were properly dressed and behaved appropriately at the table. No matter how many people were at their table, there was always enough food for everybody. The great lords of that time certainly knew how to live!"[16]

All of this hospitality and cultural patronage by aristocrats, both in the metropolis and on their suburban estates, sucked the air out of commercial or citizen-sponsored alternatives in and around Moscow. At the beginning of the nineteenth century, Moscow had only one single theater that was not private, and foreign visitors noted an astounding lack of public entertainments for such a large city. They also found the hotels in the city scarce, dirty, and overpriced, and complained that there were hardly any hotels at all along the route between Moscow and St Petersburg, Russia's most important highway.[17] Measured by the sponsorship of theaters, libraries, and schools by local citizens, the towns around Moscow lagged behind those in much more remote places, such as Western Siberia, where there was no competition from aristocrats.[18]

The middling sort were composed principally of lesser nobles, clergy, and merchants. These groups were broadly similar in their personal rights and their sources of influence over the common people, but there were significant differences in their social composition and internal dynamics. A distinctive feature of the middling sort was the fluidity of many people's estate status. The government

[15] Ivan Alekseevich Vtorov, "Moskva i Kazan' v nachale XIX veka," *RS*, 70 (April 1891), 1–22, here: 3, 4, 8. See also: P. Vistengof, *Ocherki Moskovskoi zhizni* (Moscow: V tipografii S. Selivanovskago, 1842), 156–8; "Dopotopnaia ili dopozharnaia Moskva," in P. A. Viazemskii, *Polnoe sobranie sochinenii kniazia P. A. Viazemskago*, 12 vols. (St Petersburg: Tipografiia M. M. Stasiulevicha, 1878–96), 7:80–116, esp. 84.
[16] Blagovo, *Rasskazy babushki*, 31.
[17] Reinbeck, *Flüchtige Bemerkungen*, 1:189–90, 213–14; Raupach, *Reise*, 9, 91.
[18] Kupriianov, *Gorodskaia kul'tura*, 471.

generally wanted to bind people on a hereditary basis to their estates, but it also used the prospect of an improved estate status as an incentive for individuals to excel in business, various professions, or service to the state or the church. This improved status did not, however, automatically become hereditary. The result was that the middling sort included many people who lacked clear moorings in the estate system and to whom officials referred simply as *raznochintsy*, "of various ranks."[19]

Legally, belonging to the middling sort meant being exempt from certain oppressive and humiliating obligations. Under the system created by Peter the Great, each of the lower estates (serfs, state peasants, townspeople, and so on) in a given locality formed a community that was collectively liable for the soul tax and conscription. Each community had to provide, annually, a fixed overall soul-tax payment and a set number of men for lifelong military service. (In 1793, military service was reduced to twenty-five years.) The community decided collectively whose son or husband was to be sent to the army and how the tax bill was allocated among the various households. Communities had extensive power to impose punishments on recalcitrant members, and to prevent taxpayer flight, no one was allowed to leave the community without its permission. The middle estates, however, were exempt from the soul tax and military service. Their members thus not only escaped the dread prospect of conscription but also enjoyed a degree of personal freedom from the tyranny of their neighbors.[20]

Belonging to the middle estates also brought the possibility of exemption from corporal punishment. After Empress Elizabeth abolished the death penalty in 1754, people convicted of serious crimes were usually flogged and branded and had their nostrils slit, all before the greatest possible number of spectators. Then, if they were still alive, they were deported to remote parts of the empire. Beginning with Catherine II, as Abby Schrader argues, the regime used selective exemption from flogging and disfigurement to separate the genteel classes, those deemed capable of reason and honor, from the rabble who supposedly understood only pain. Whether an estate was exempt became a barometer of its ability to lobby the government and of the official esteem in which it was held. Catherine's charters to the nobles and the towns of 1785 exempted the nobles and the elite of the merchantry (the first and second guild, but not the third). This was extended in 1796 to the upper tier of the clergy (priests and deacons, but not sacristans). Alexander I broadened it further to include monks and the wives and children of those whose exemption was only individual, not hereditary, that is, personal nobles and the upper tier of clerics and merchants.[21]

---

[19] Wirtschafter, *Structures of Society*, 53, 60–2, 74.

[20] Wirtschafter, *Russia's Age of Serfdom*, 22–5.

[21] Abby M. Schrader, *Languages of the Lash: Corporal Punishment and Identity in Imperial Russia* (DeKalb, Ill.: Northern Illinois University Press, 2002), 12, 23. These exemptions were rescinded by Paul I in 1796 but restored by Alexander I in 1801; Schrader, *Languages of the Lash*, 23.

The middle estates thus enjoyed personal freedom as well as the respect for their dignity implied by the exemption from corporal punishment. What distinguished them (except those who were hereditary nobles) from the aristocracy is that these rights were not hereditary, and because they could not legally own serfs, they could acquire neither the vast sources of wealth nor the power over other people that were the prerogative of aristocrats.

The influence of Moscow's middling sort radiated far beyond the metropolis itself. Moscow was at the center of bureaucratic, ecclesiastical, and mercantile networks that held much of the empire together. For example, Alexander I gave Moscow University authority over all public education throughout a ten-province area of central Russia,[22] and the Moscow departments of the Senate provided administrative oversight, and heard judicial appeals, for all the provinces from Moscow to the Black and Caspian seas, and in criminal cases, for the Caucasus and Siberia in addition.[23] Equivalent institutions of the Orthodox Church (the Moscow Ecclesiastical Academy in nearby Sergiev Posad, and the Moscow Office of the Holy Synod) made Moscow a major center of religious education and administration, and the Moscow metropolitan was one of Russia's most senior Orthodox hierarchs. As for the reach of Moscow's merchantry, the geographer Maksimovich noted in 1788 that "Moscow's trade is so extensive that it embraces nearly the greater part of Russia's entire trade, and the [goods] that individually are the glory of the Russian Empire's other towns—in Moscow, they are accumulated and multiplied beyond what the eye can see and beyond count."[24]

If the nobility was a pyramid with the aristocracy as its pinnacle, its capacious base consisted of personal nobles: civil servants of non-noble birth who held ranks 14 through 9, the bottom tier of Peter the Great's Table of Ranks. In the unlikely event that they worked their way up to rank 8, their noble status became hereditary. (In 1845, the threshold for hereditary nobility was raised to rank 5.) They came from diverse backgrounds, enjoyed a modest prosperity, and could rise through skill and effort. They could not own serfs. Their sons often became clerks in their fathers' offices, hoping to reach rank 14 and thus become personal nobles in their turn. They were 44 percent of the entire Russian nobility in 1795, and 31.1 percent in 1858. In Moscow their share was likely higher because there were so many jobs for low-level officials. Thus, around 1850, 84.4 percent of

22 PSZ (First Series), vol. 34, no. 27,106 (24 October 1817), art. 34.
23 *Svod Zakonov Rossiiskoi Imperii, poveleniem Gosudaria Imperatora Nikolaia Pavlovicha sostavlennyi*, 15 vols. (St Petersburg: V Tipografii Vtorago Otdeleniia Sobstvennoi Ego Imperatorskago Velichestva Kantseliarii, 1842), chast' 1, "Svod uchrezhdenii gosudarstvennykh," kniga 3, razdel 1, art. 39, 40, 45, 46, 50.
24 Ilizarov, *Moskva v opisaniiakh XVIII veka*, 244.

Moscow officials owned no serfs, compared with only 45.3 percent of all nobles (personal and hereditary) across Russia.[25]

Compared with the nobility, the clergy was more homogeneous. It was divided into the parish clergy (priests, deacons, and sacristans), who were married, and the celibate monastic clergy. Bishops were recruited from the monastic clergy. In the eighteenth century, the clergy acquired increasingly caste-like features. New entrants were sons of clergymen, attended schools for sons of the clergy, and married clergymen's daughters. The law considered the clergy less a hereditary estate than a service class. To remain a member, one had to hold an actual appointment, so *popovichi* (sons of clergymen) who failed to secure a position in a parish or monastery had to find a social niche elsewhere. An attractive option was joining the state service, where the demand for literate men increased greatly after the nobility was released from obligatory state service in 1762 and Catherine expanded the provincial bureaucracy in 1775. According to Walter Pintner, 25.7 percent of Moscow officials around 1850 were *popovichi*— only slightly fewer than sons of nobles (29.8 percent) and of junior military officers and personal nobles (32.9 percent). The state also used *popovichi* to fill the growing need for school teachers, university professors, and physicians. *Popovichi* who did not find employment could be drafted into the army or demoted to the status of state peasants or townspeople.[26]

The merchant estate, created by Catherine II in 1775, was divided into three guilds. Merchants declared the total value of their capital, and that figure determined the guild in which they were enrolled. According to the 1785 Charter to the Towns, the third guild was supposed to be made up of local shopkeepers, the second was to conduct inter-regional trade, and the first guild, large-scale domestic and foreign trade. The first and second guild together made up only 17.8 percent of Moscow's total merchantry in 1786 and only 12.6 percent in 1823. The government did not ask for proof that a merchant actually had the capital that he declared; since the annual guild fee was a fixed percentage of one's declared capital, exaggerating one's capital was self-defeating. A merchant unable to pay the annual guild fee was demoted to the status of townsman.[27]

Unlike clerics, merchants rarely entered the bureaucracy. In Walter Pintner's sample, only 1.3 percent of Moscow officials around 1850 had merchant fathers.

[25] Mironov, *Sotsial'naia istoriia Rossii*, 1:88 (statistics excluding Poland and Finland); Walter M. Pintner, "The Social Characteristics of the Early Nineteenth-Century Russian Bureaucracy," *Slavic Review*, 29/3 (September 1970), 429–43, here: 434.

[26] Gregory L. Freeze, *The Russian Levites: Parish Clergy in the Eighteenth Century* (Cambridge, Mass.: Harvard University Press, 1977), 18, 34–41; Pintner, "The Social Characteristics," 435–6; Hartley, *Russia, 1762–1825*, 28.

[27] [I. Ia. Rudchenko], *Istoricheskii ocherk oblozheniia torgovli i promyslov v Rossii* (St Petersburg: Tipografiia V. Kirshbauma, 1893), 94, 99; Hildermeier, *Bürgertum und Stadt*, 169; Hittle, *The Service City*, 218.

Instead, they stood atop a separate social ladder that reached down to the townspeople and artisans, and out into the peasantry. Until the 1830s, when new laws made it easier for outsiders to register as townspeople, government policy sought to stem the migration of peasants into the cities by imposing restrictions and steep costs for joining an urban estate. This kept out most peasants except the affluent. Those peasants who did enter the urban estates often went straight to the top by registering as merchants, and became townspeople or guild artisans only if business troubles forced them out of the merchantry. In Moscow Province, according to the 1808 revision (census of males), there were 1,824 merchants who were former state peasants, but only 336 townsmen and guild artisans who were former state peasants. Between 1795 and 1811, 4,318 men joined the Moscow city merchantry; 49.6 percent of these had previously been serfs or state peasants, compared with only 18.7 percent who had been townsmen or guild artisans. During those same years, 6,977 men left the merchantry; almost all—94.7 percent—became Moscow townsmen.[28]

Moscow's power to attract upwardly mobile peasants was exceptional. In 1808, former state peasants made up 12.4 percent of the merchants in Moscow Province, compared with only 3.1 percent in St Petersburg Province, and fewer still in the provinces around Moscow—2.3 percent in Tula, 1.4 in Vladimir, 1.3 in Riazan', 0.6 in Kaluga, 0.4 in Tver'.[29] This continual influx of peasants (including many Old Believers) impeded the assimilation of the Moscow merchantry as a whole into a Europeanized urban culture, delayed the consolidation of a metropolitan merchant patriciate, and made it harder for the merchants to assert themselves in a city ruled by aristocrats.

Nobles, clergy, and merchants had varied sources of influence over the groups below them in the social hierarchy. They had enormous economic clout: they provided jobs for laborers and domestics; their spending kept shops and tradesmen in business; they were moneylenders in a city with few financial institutions; and they owned most of the housing in which the others lived.[30] Another source of influence was institutional. Merchants dominated the elected municipal government, state officials could decide whether to grant or withhold the licenses that people required for all manner of activities, and priests determined whether a marriage was valid, what name a child was given, and whether someone had complied with the legal obligation to attend confession.

If all else failed, social power rested on brute force. Merchants were quick to violence against recalcitrant assistants, as were bishops against clerical

---

[28] Hildermeier, *Bürgertum und Stadt*, 93–100; see also O. E. Nilova, *Moskovskoe kupechestvo kontsa XVIII–pervoi chetverti XIX veka: Sotsial'nye aspekty mirovospriiatiia i samosoznaniia* (Moscow: Institut rossiiskoi istorii RAN, 2002), 66–7.

[29] Hildermeier, *Bürgertum und Stadt*, 99.

[30] Ruban, *Opisanie*, 159; Androssov, *Statisticheskaia zapiska*, 31–50.

subordinates.[31] The police routinely inflicted brutal, humiliating punishment on lower-class people who broke laws or were merely slow to follow instructions,[32] and nobles and merchants caned their serfs or employees or had the police do it for them.[33]

All of these powers were the more impressive for being enacted with a theatricality characteristic of early modern European regimes in general. The men who represented state and church wore specialized attire, had arcane titles, and drew their power from the written word (bureaucratic and religious texts) in an otherwise largely illiterate society. Their spaces were distinctive and imposing, whether incense-filled, gold-domed churches or neoclassical office buildings. On special occasions, they demonstrated their performative powers in truly spectacular ways. Midnight at Easter was one of the greatest of these occasions. In St Petersburg, Russia's military and naval capital, the resurrection of Jesus Christ was proclaimed by the thunderous fire of cannons from the Peter-Paul Fortress. In Moscow, a bell weighing 4,000 poods—65.5 metric tons—atop the highest tower in the Kremlin would begin to peal majestically into the night, to be answered within seconds by hundreds of churches whose combined ringing drowned out all other sounds, even the celebratory artillery salvoes.[34]

Compared with the nobles and clergy, the performative role of wealthy merchants was less scripted but nonetheless imposing. The men of the merchantry—heavy, bearded, dignified, dressed in plain Russian garb—were tight-fisted in business but generous to churches and the poor. Their demonstratively corpulent wives, with their cosmetically blackened teeth, rouged faces, and magnificent folk dress, lived lives of piety and leisure. To most Muscovites, who were culturally conservative and unsure of their next meal, wealthy merchants embodied earthly success as surely as the officials and priests represented the tsar and God.

The middling sort were important intermediaries in society. They were clients of the aristocracy, whether as guests at their parties, subordinates in government offices, or merchants dependent on their patronage. At the same time, they were themselves authorities and role models to the lower classes. An important

---

[31] Dobrynin, *Istinnoe povestvovanie*, 31, 47; A. Ia. Butkovskaia, "Razskazy Babushki," *Istoricheskii Vestnik* (December 1884), 594–631, here: 595; Dmitrii Rostislavov, *Provincial Russia in the Age of Enlightenment: The Memoir of a Priest's Son*, tr. Alexander M. Martin (DeKalb, Ill.: Northern Illinois University Press, 2002), 8–9; Slonov, *Iz zhizni*, 66; Vishniakov, *Svedeniia*, 2:84.

[32] N. V. Davydov, "Moskva: Piatidesiatye i shestidesiatye gody XIX veka," in Aleksandrov, *Moskovskaia Starina*, 52; Bogatyrev, "Moskovskaia starina," in Aleksandrov, *Moskovskaia Starina*, 128, 137; D. A. Pokrovskii, "Kulachnye boi," in Aleksandrov, *Moskovskaia Starina*, 177–8; E. I. Kozlinina, "Doreformennyi politseiskii sud," in Aleksandrov, *Moskovskaia Starina*, 182, 185; Vtorov, "Moskva i Kazan'," 17.

[33] Heinrich von Reimers, *St. Petersburg am Ende seines ersten Jahrhunderts: Mit Rückblicken auf Entstehung und Wachstum dieser Residenz unter den verschiedenen Regierungen während dieses Zeitraums*, 2 vols. (St Petersburg: F. Dienemann, 1805), 1:331; Grigor'ev, *Vospominaniia*, 18; Davydov, "Moskva," in Aleksandrov, *Moskovskaia Starina*, 29–30; Vishniakov, *Svedeniia*, 2:84.

[34] Lapin, *Peterburg: Zapakhi i zvuki*, 105–7; Malinovskii, *Obozrenie Moskvy*, 42–3.

dimension of this role as intermediaries was their position in the hierarchy of money and material wealth.

THE HIERARCHY OF WEALTH

The consumer economy of early modern Europe was long dominated by aristocrats who used ostentatious consumption to demonstrate their status. In northwestern Europe, this slowly changed from the seventeenth century on. Commoners increasingly produced for the market to earn cash for consumer goods. Urban laborers acquired the means to buy individual items—a watch here, a kerchief there—but for the middle classes, the entire material environment grew more comfortable and fashion-oriented. Glass windows and mirrors became common, china replaced wood or pewter, interior lighting improved, and clothing and furniture gained in elegance and convenience.[35] This broadbased consumer culture was fundamental to the formation of modern urban civilization. In the years around 1800, similar developments were under way in Moscow, but before examining them, we should consider the financial realities that underlay them.

The aristocratic lifestyle, in its heyday in the late eighteenth and early nineteenth century, cost tens of thousands of rubles a year. In *War and Peace*, Count Nikolai Rostov loses 43,000 rubles in one card game, and Count Pierre Bezukhov has an annual income of a half-million rubles.[36] Tolstoi drew characters like these from life. Count Nikolai Sheremetev, one of the grandest of Moscow's grandees, had an income of 632,200 rubles in 1798, but even that was not enough to pay for his expenses, so he had to borrow almost 60,000 more to cover the shortfall.[37] Farther down the scale, Mariia Volkova in 1813 described two newlyweds with a more conventional aristocratic income: "Bibikov has 10,000 a year, and Sophie has five; hence, the total is 15,000; with an income like that, you can live quite decently in Moscow, indeed anywhere except Petersburg."[38]

Among middling Muscovites, incomes were more often in the hundreds or low thousands of rubles. As of 1804, a professor at Moscow University earned 2,000 rubles a year. This salary is worth a closer look because it was supposed to attract academics from abroad, especially Germany, and German writers accordingly took an interest in the living standard that it made possible. Johann Richter, Karamzin's Russophile translator, argued that this salary was adequate for "a man of middling condition who lives on a decent footing." A hypothetical budget, he

[35] On this topic, see de Vries, *The Industrious Revolution*, 57, 72, 126–41.
[36] Tolstoy, *War and Peace*, 362–7, 409.
[37] Jerome Blum, *Lord and Peasant in Russia from the Ninth to the Nineteenth Century* (Princeton: Princeton University Press, 1961), 379.
[38] "Griboedovskaia Moskva," part 2: *VE*, kniga 9 (September 1874), 115–68, here: 150–1.

wrote, might include 530 rubles for rent, heat, and light; 360 for a servant, a cook, and a maid; and 400 for a carriage and two horses. Add in food, alcohol, coffee, tea, and 200 rubles for sundries, and the total came to 2,009 rubles. Friedrich Raupach concurred that on 2,000 rubles, "a family that is not too large can live decently" in Moscow. Georg Reinbeck disagreed, and wrote that professors had to supplement their income by working as private tutors because their base salary of 2,000 rubles would "barely suffice for a bachelor."[39]

Service to the crown, which formed the main source of employment for nobles, usually paid far less than a professor's salary. Of the 250 civil-service positions (excluding clerks and other subaltern personnel) budgeted for the administration of Moscow Province and its ten districts in 1796, only the governor and three others drew annual salaries in excess of 600 rubles. In the army, infantry officers below the rank of colonel earned under 700 rubles.[40] These salaries did not represent officials' entire income. Russia, Susanne Schattenberg argues, was a "gift-giving society" where relationships were routinely cemented with favors. Officials accepted bonuses from their chiefs and bribes from the public, and many also worked on the side or received free housing or cash for rent, firewood, and candles.[41] Quantifying all this is difficult, but it seems likely that even with bribes and bonuses, few reached the 2,000 rubles of a professor.

Employment for nobles was available in private households as well. The *Moscow Gazette* carried frequent advertisements for estate managers, household stewards, tutors, and so forth. In many cases, the job seekers were retired officials who continued to identify themselves by their rank. One advertisement from 1800 promised 150 rubles a year plus board and clothing (and, presumably, housing) for a clerk. Nearer the upper end of the pay scale, an estate manager could earn 1,000 a year.[42] On the eve of the 1812 war, a private tutor in one Moscow aristocratic household was paid "lodgings, board, candles, all his upkeep, and 700 rubles a year."[43]

The parish clergy, too, had a variety of sources and levels of income. The best-paid clergy were those attached to the Kremlin cathedrals: under rules from 1764, archpriests received salaries of 300 to 600 rubles a year, and priests, 150 to

---

[39] Richter, *Russische Miscellen*, 2/5, pp. 211–14; Raupach, *Reise*, 90; Reinbeck, *Flüchtige Bemerkungen*, 1:299.

[40] *Rossiiskaia Imperiia razdelennaia v gubernii v 1796 i 1797 godakh: Prezhde byvshie staty gubernskie, koi nyne peremeneny. 1796 do 1797* (no pub., n.d.); Storch, *Rußland unter Alexander I*, 3:92 (army pay scale introduced in April 1802).

[41] Schattenberg, *Die korrupte Provinz?*, 48–50, 119–20.

[42] *MV* (1 September 1800), 1565; Aleksandr Nikitenko, *Up from Serfdom: My Childhood and Youth in Russia, 1804–1824*, tr. Helen Saltz Jacobson (New Haven: Yale University Press, 2001), 54.

[43] "Iz pisem Aleksandra Iakovlevicha Bulgakova k bratu ego Konstantinu Iakovlevichu," part 2: *RA*, 2/5 (1900), 5–36, here: 24.

200 rubles.[44] Most parish clergy made do with much less. Some of their income came from fees for performing baptisms, weddings, funerals, and other rites. On important holidays they would tour their parishioners' homes and sing hymns, again for a fee. Rural clerics also had farms and in addition received food from their parishioners. In the case of one rural priest in the 1770s whose finances are documented, annual cash income averaged about 40 rubles. In Moscow at that time, fees for specific rites were five to ten times higher than in the country, suggesting an income of several hundred for a priest; a sacristan could expect one-third or one-half that amount.[45] By the era of Nicholas I, a rural priest might earn between 50 and 400 rubles. If incomes in Moscow remained five to ten times higher, they would have been in the hundreds or low thousands.[46]

Merchants' incomes are difficult to estimate, but the cost of guild membership provides some indication. In 1785, the minimum annual fee for the third guild was set at 10 rubles. The following year, 82.2 percent of Moscow merchants were in the third guild. Presumably they found 10 rubles affordable, but not the 50 rubles required for the second guild, despite the incentive of receiving exemption from corporal punishment through membership in the second guild. In 1810, after inflation and multiple fee increases due to the government's financial woes in the Napoleonic Wars, the fees were 140 rubles for the third guild and 350 for the second. The next year, 88.1 percent of merchants in Moscow were in the third guild, suggesting that 350 rubles was too high for most.[47]

The most common way to improve one's income was to become a rentier. Hereditary nobles could acquire landed estates, but that required a large upfront investment. The *Moscow Gazette* in 1800 ran advertisements for several estates on which each male "soul" reportedly produced about 10 to 30 rubles income per year. The price for these estates was about 150 to 400 rubles per soul. For example, one estate with 378 male and 398 female serfs reportedly generated 4,000 rubles of revenue a year. It was advertised for 68,040 rubles, discounted to 65,500 if the buyer paid the entire sum at once.[48] Assuming an income of 10 to 30 rubles per soul, the 33.8 percent of hereditary nobles who owned twenty or fewer souls could have collected no more than 200 to 600 rubles a year. On other hand, the top 2.8 percent, those with more—sometimes many more—than 500 souls, could count on incomes that started at 5,000 to 15,000 rubles.

One could also become a rentier by buying urban rental property. Rents in Moscow varied greatly. One sacristan rented out a small room for 30 rubles a

[44] Freeze, *The Russian Levites*, 121.

[45] V. I. Semevskii, "Sel'skii sviashchennik vo vtoroi polovine XVIII veka," *RS*, 19 (May–August 1877), 501–38; Freeze, *The Russian Levites*, 166.

[46] F. F. Ismailov, *Vzgliad na sobstvennuiu proshedshuiu zhizn' Ismailova* (Moscow: V Universitetskoi Tipografii, 1860), 84–5.

[47] Hildermeier, *Bürgertum und Stadt*, 100, 127, 169.

[48] *MV* (3 March 1800), 455, 458–60; *MV* (17 March 1800), 571–2, 575, 577; Blum, *Lord and Peasant*, 367–8, 470.

year, whereas a mansion with twenty rooms, a stable, and a carriage house cost around 2,000.[49] In 1812, one police scribe earned only 120 rubles at his job but owned an 8,000-ruble house that yielded 100 rubles annual income,[50] and three clergymen rented out all or part of their homes, worth 2,500 to 5,000 rubles each, for 150 to 500 rubles a year.[51]

People could also earn money by lending out their savings. Mar'ia Voronina, the orphan daughter of a minor official, inherited 5,900 rubles that had been loaned to individuals. During the year 1815, she earned 332.50 rubles on 1,500 rubles' worth of these loans, an interest rate of 22.2 percent.[52] Similarly, the junior official's widow Nastas'ia Ivanova supported herself, her young daughter, and her elderly mother with the interest from 4,000 rubles in loans.[53]

The broad economic homogeneity of middling Muscovites was reflected in the value of their possessions, which can be gleaned from petitions for assistance that the inhabitants filed after the city burned during the Napoleonic occupation of 1812. (For more on the petitions, see below, pages 211–14.) Based on a sample of 2,000 petitions, Table 5.2 summarizes the value of the movable personal property (i.e. excluding houses and commercial merchandise) reported lost by households of different estates.[54] The table shows the range of losses

Table 5.2. Value (in rubles) of movable personal property lost in the 1812 occupation of Moscow

Estate	Poorest 20%	Middle 20%	Wealthiest 20%	Wealthiest 5%	N =
Nobles	50–800	1,865–3,760	9,335–500,000	42,000–500,000	295 (95%)
Merchants	50–1,800	3,575–6,000	10,148–102,000	20,405–102,000	195 (38%)
Townspeople	4–470	830–1,576	3,100–20,823	6,878–20,823	478 (77%)
Guild artisans	70–387	550–945	2,835–14,781	5,290–14,781	117 (96%)
Clerks	64–200	480–1,154	2,095–8,395	4,826–8,395	55 (96%)
Soldiers	46–200	300–415	700–4,623	1,500–4,623	197 (100%)
All estates combined	4–400	800–1,940	4,622–500,000	14,841–500,000	1,448 (73%)

Note: the total of 1,448 petitioners includes members of other estates not included in this table.

[49] Tret'iakov, "Imperatorskii Moskovskii universitet" (part 1), 124; Raupach, *Reise*, 89–90.
[50] Shchukin, *Bumagi*, 2:206.
[51] Shchukin, *Bumagi*, 2:142–4, 159–60.
[52] Shchukin, *Bumagi*, 4:257–9.
[53] Shchukin, *Bumagi*, 3:149, 5:185–6.
[54] These 2,000 are apparently a random sample of the entire body of petitions from Moscow in 1813. They represent the full content (petitions 12,701–14,700) of one of the ten volumes in which the responsible government commission summarized the petitions it received. TsIAM f. 20, op. 2, d. 2380.

reported by the richest, middle, and poorest segment of each estate. N is the number of petitions that include data on lost movable possessions and the percentage of the total for each estate that these petitions represent. (The remainder did not include information on the value of lost possessions.) The table is based on 1,448 petitions that include such data, representing 73 percent of the total sample of 2,000 petitions.

Three caveats are in order. First, the data on the merchants are problematic because only 38 percent indicated the value of their lost personal possessions. The rest provided no estimates, reported only lost merchandise, or conflated merchandise with personal possessions. Since it is unclear how systematically they differentiated between possessions and merchandise, the table may give an inflated impression of merchant wealth. Second, the wealthiest nobles typically owned houses or estates outside Moscow, so their overall wealth was greater than suggested here. Third, the clergy are not represented because they took part in a separate program for providing assistance to war victims.

Not surprisingly, wealth tracked the overall status hierarchy. Nobles were the richest estate; townspeople, artisans, and clerks formed the middle; and the soldiers' estate (in most cases, wives and daughters of soldiers) brought up the rear. At the top of the scale, the discrepancies were dramatic. Nobles topped out at a half-million rubles, compared with just over 20,000 for the townspeople and under 5,000 for the soldiers' estate. However, aside from aristocrats and impoverished military families, the remainder exhibited a degree of homogeneity. All estates combined, the wealthiest 40 percent were those whose losses exceeded 1,940 rubles. This group included 58 percent of the nobles, 35 percent of the townspeople, 26 percent of the artisans, and 24 percent of the clerks. Poorer nobles (and, most likely, merchants) were thus economically similar to successful townspeople, artisans, and clerks.

POSSESSIONS AND SOCIAL STATUS

Money, and the access to material goods that it enabled, played a dual role in the life of middling Muscovites. It made possible a more comfortable and genteel home life, and it allowed people to go out in respectable dress and gain admittance to upper-class public spaces.

The lower boundary of respectable dress was contested. In 1828, a provincial alehouse operator petitioned the government to declare that no form of lower-class dress was to be considered respectable. Why? Because by law, patrons of restaurants and coffee houses had to look respectable (*prilichno* or *pristoino*) whereas customers of alehouses did not, so granting the request would have diminished the customer base of the restaurants and coffee houses that competed with the petitioner's alehouse. After an inter-ministerial review, the government ruled that in this case, urban lower class clothing was to be deemed respectable but peasant dress was not.[55]

Even people who looked indisputably urban and wore Western attire exposed themselves to ridicule and humiliation if their clothes suggested poverty or lack of refinement. An alumnus of the St Petersburg naval cadet corps in the Napoleonic era later recalled one of his teachers in these terms:

he rarely shaved . . . He wore a long-skirted frock coat that he did not have cleaned, and that was worn through at the elbows and had torn cuffs. Through the holes in his boots you could see his dirty puttees, sometimes even his bare toes. Like Gogol's Petrushka [the buffoonish valet in *Dead Souls*], he carried his own odor with him, and when he spoke, the sense of smell of those near him was unpleasantly tickled by a stream of air saturated with the stink of cheap vodka or onions.[56]

Fear of such mockery caused some people to shun the elite's culture altogether. For instance, a townsman from Tver' said in 1861 that he stayed away from the local library in part because he felt uncomfortable around "gentlemen" readers with their "shiny buttons" and "fashionable frock coats."[57] This was a problem elsewhere in Europe, too. In Belfast in the 1850s, Protestant clergy took to preaching outdoors because, according to one minister, the poor were "ashamed to enter any church in [their] threadbare garments."[58]

Some of the petitions that Muscovites filed after the 1812 war include inventories of possessions that give an indication of the extent to which their owners valued a refined appearance or personal comfort. One petitioner, Semen Nikitin, was an illiterate townsman. Nikitin worked in a merchant's shop and lived with his wife and young daughter in a sacristan's house. Their household's total value was a modest 731.80 rubles. Nikitin's wardrobe (several fur coats and hats, two gowns, a silk sash, and several shirts) was typical for a Russian commoner, as was that of his wife. The Nikitins also owned a mirror and a samovar (to heat water for tea), which suggests that they valued appearances and good manners. In merchant homes that had mirrors on the wall, according to Georg Engelhardt, the women were generally more fashion-conscious, and less stiff and reserved, than was usual in the conservative merchant milieu, and the *popovich* Dmitrii Rostislavov describes tea as an expensive but more genteel alternative to drinking alcohol.[59]

---

[55] Kupriianov, *Gorodskaia kul'tura*, 316–18.

[56] L. Khaliutin, "Vospitanie v kadetskom korpuse za polveka nazad," *Sovremennik*, 71 (October 1858), 630–54, here: 650.

[57] Kupriianov, *Gorodskaia kul'tura*, 113.

[58] Janice Holmes, "The Role of Open-Air Preaching in the Belfast Riots of 1857," *Proceedings of the Royal Irish Academy*, 102C, no. 3 (2002), 47–66, here: 58.

[59] TsIAM f. 20, op. 2, d. 2213, ll. 79–80 ob; Engelhardt, *Russische Miscellen*, 3:176–9; Rostislavov, *Provincial Russia*, 86.

A more comfortable life was possible when a household's value reached the low to mid-thousands, as in the case of the elderly navy captain Ivan Alekseev.[60] By 1812 he had retired and lived in Moscow with his wife and three house serfs. He had married late, but by now he had two grown daughters whose husbands were in state service. Alekseev owned a modest four-room house in down-market Meshchanskaia District, which he shared with lodgers who paid 170 rubles a year in rent. He also received a pension of 500 rubles a year, owned a 1,000-ruble savings bond, and apparently had at least 750 in cash. When the French occupied Moscow, he reported, he lost around 2,235 rubles' worth of money and possessions.

The detailed household inventory submitted by Alekseev suggests conventional piety and concern about appearances. The first items listed are five icons, several gold or silver crosses, religious books (but no secular ones), and a silver lamp to illumine the icons. In his will, he left 200 rubles to two churches, "that they may pray for me, my wife, and my other kin," and 100 to his confessor "as a small token of my sincere regard for him, and I beseech him to keep my sinful soul in his prayers." The four fur coats that he and his wife had owned were worth 520 rubles. This was not especially expensive—perhaps they were old and worn—but it represents one-fourth of the total value of their household, which testifies both to Moscow's climate and to fur's significance as a symbol of affluence. The inventory includes no dresses for Mrs Alekseeva, but for the captain himself it lists various items that allowed him to maintain a respectable appearance: a frock-coat and trousers, silk vests (waistcoats), and a pocket watch. On the other hand, the Alekseevs apparently did not own a large set of linens for comfort and hygiene. The inventory lists only 62 rubles' worth of linens and 17 rubles' worth of caps and stockings. To put those sums into context, the petition of the townsman Semen Kaftannikov gives his wife's twelve chemises and six pairs of stockings a value of 90 rubles.[61]

The same primacy of appearances over comfort is evident in the Alekseevs' other possessions. Linen tablecloths and napkins, mahogany tables and chairs, a wall clock, fine tableware—all of this allowed the Alekseevs to receive guests in the proper manner. On the other hand, the inventory lists no bed frame or bedding. These were costly and bulky items, unlikely to be overlooked when composing the inventory and difficult to rescue from the Alekseevs' burning house during the French occupation. Since they shared their four rooms with their renters and servants, perhaps there was no separate bedroom, only improvised sleeping arrangements. The value of their possessions placed the Alekseevs in the second-wealthiest fifth of the petitioners, yet their household was spartan and geared mainly to upholding appearances.

---

[60] TsIAM f. 20, op. 2, d. 28, ll. 53–61ob.
[61] Shchukin, *Bumagi*, 6:24. On the importance attached to changing one's linens, see "Ob odezhde," 201–4.

Similar possessions could be found among the wealthiest townspeople, as we learn from the petition of Semen Kaftannikov. With his wife and their ward, a young orphan named Lugovskii, he rented lodgings in the house of a widowed noblewoman for 180 rubles a year. The Kaftannikovs owned 4,590 rubles' worth of possessions, and young Lugovskii, another 3,000. Both inventories begin by listing their icons, which represent 15 percent of the entire household's value and highlight their owners' piety. As in the Alekseev household, the four mahogany tables and place settings for twelve (silver spoons, forks, and knives, tea cups, plates, napkins, chairs) suggest aspirations to refinement in dining and hospitality. Mrs Kaftannikova must have looked stylish in her 700-ruble fur coat, five dresses of imported taffeta, calico, and chintz, and two muslin skirts, as did her husband in his fur coat, tailcoat, and pantaloons. A washstand and towel, mirrors, and handkerchiefs show that appearances were valued, while the wall clock hints at a modern, abstract sense of time. Mrs Kaftannikova's twelve chemises suggest a concern about cleanliness and personal modesty. The Kaftannikovs were old-fashioned in storing their possessions in trunks, which were traditionally associated with the peripatetic existence of the poor, but young Lugovskii already owned a chest of drawers: a bulky, expensive piece of furniture that permitted the orderly arranging of possessions and implied a more settled life of relative plenty.[62] The Kaftannikov–Lugovskii household thus displayed characteristic features of middle-class culture and values.[63]

How people like the Alekseevs or Kaftannikovs may have lived—that is, how one kept up appearances on a modest budget—is illustrated by the writer Aleksei Galakhov's account of his aunt in the 1820s. She was "a very kind but utterly uneducated woman" who was fiercely proud of her noble ancestry. She did not work for a living, instead spending her time with social calls. Her only income was from her twenty male peasant "souls" and rent from her wooden house in Zamoskvorech'e, an area largely inhabited by merchants. She had so little money that she was often forced, humiliatingly, to pay visits on foot. There was no question of going to the balls downtown at the Noble Assembly, as it "was not open to people from that mix of nobles and commoners with whom my aunt socialized; that would have required considerable expenses for clothing and carriages." Instead, she hosted parties at her home. A few musicians were hired, food was kept to a minimum, dim and smelly tallow candles provided the lighting, and everyone danced merrily into the wee hours. When the party finally broke up, young Galakhov, who was a university student at the time, would walk five kilometers to go home because he could not afford a cab.[64]

When Galakhov wrote his reminiscences in the 1870s, tallow candles and the inability to afford a carriage sufficed to evoke an entire milieu. This cliché already

---

[62] Shchukin, *Bumagi*, 6:23–6; Roche, *Le peuple de Paris*, 200–5.
[63] Roche, *La culture des apparences*, 110–13.
[64] A. D. Galakhov, *Zapiski cheloveka* (Moscow: Novoe Literaturnoe Obozrenie, 1999), 103–6.

existed in the 1840s, when the feuilletonist Mikhail Zagoskin described the social contrasts among the ladies of Moscow: on the one hand, "the luxurious flower of Moscow's beauties," who could be found in "our aristocratic drawing rooms" amidst "magnificent decoration and illumination"; on the other, "some Zamovorech'e noblewoman whose house is lighted with one-ruble Quinquet [oil] lamps and tallow candles."[65]

Transport and lighting were conspicuous markers dividing the rich from those in straitened circumstances (see Illustration 5.1). A good suit, dress, or fur coat was a durable item that required only a one-time purchase, but horses and candles required ongoing expenditures beyond the abilities of many in the middling sort; the annual cost of keeping two horses in Moscow was estimated in 1809 at 300 rubles.[66]

The problem of transportation was rooted in urban sprawl and the competitive consumerism of the aristocracy. Many aristocrats, rather than live in townhouses, preferred manors on the edge of the city. This made vehicular transport indispensable, and the social dynamics operating within the aristocracy inflated its cost. Since the law regulated who was entitled to drive with how many horses,

Illus. 5.1. "Dandy in a Droshky." Lithograph from the 1820s by Aleksander Orłowski. © 2012, State Russian Museum, St Petersburg. A droshky was a light carriage used for traveling within a city; this scene is set in St Petersburg.

⁶⁵ M. N. Zagoskin, *Sochineniia*, 7 vols. (St Petersburg: V. I. Shtein, 1889), 5:116.
⁶⁶ Raupach, *Reise*, 89.

large teams became important status symbols. As Reinbeck observed in 1806, officials in rank 8 (army majors and their civilian counterparts) and higher "are permitted to drive with four horses, so this is in fact done by everyone who can at all afford it, as well as by those who cannot."[67]

For the middling sort, lack of transportation posed a serious obstacle to participation in upper-class culture. Suburban manors were important sites of entertainment and sociability. For instance, Prince Shakhovskoi's park at Nes-kuchnoe in the 1820s offered concerts and fireworks on Sundays in the sum-mer.[68] However, distance made such places difficult to reach without a vehicle. Thus, in its description of the Slobodskoi Palace in the outlying German Suburb, a guidebook from 1826 reported that on most days "very few stroll here, because the garden is too remote from the middle of the city."[69] Cab fares were moderate, but traveling long distances was expensive. In a fictional story by Zagoskin from the 1840s, when cab drivers are approached about a 16-kilometer round trip across Moscow, the bidding starts at 10 rubles before going down to three and a half.[70] Ivan Vtorov, the nobleman who visited Moscow in 1801, lamented that "merely crossing the long distances of this vast city causes me considerable expenditures."[71] Suburban estates lost some of their importance after 1812, as the aristocracy's wealth declined and public promenades were developed in the city center. Still, as late as 1870 a German visitor remarked that due to the preference for suburban living, "the very streets where high society lives are neither paved nor equipped with sidewalks, and are covered in winter with knee-deep snow and in spring and fall with as much mud, and a cultivated person can only frequent the better circles of Moscow society if he has a carriage at his disposal. This makes life in Moscow very expensive."[72]

Bright lights, like horse-drawn carriages, signified high status. At the Noble Assembly, Vtorov wrote admiringly, "the hall, magnificent and extremely vast, was lit with a multitude of chandeliers and colored lights in little glasses."[73] Such lighting enhanced people's appearance. As the writer Pavel Vistengof noted in the 1840s, "at a daytime ball [at the Noble Assembly] there are many whom you won't recognize if you have met them only in the evening. Often you will find that the girl whose facial complexion seemed so attractive by the flattering light of

---

[67] Reinbeck, *Flüchtige Bemerkungen*, 1:204–5; Georgi, *Versuch einer Beschreibung*, 365; Storch, *Rußland unter Alexander I*, 1:80.

[68] Aleksandr Kuznetsov, *Almanakh na 1826 dlia priezzhaiushchikh v Moskvu i dlia samikh zhitelei sei stolitsy, ili Noveishii ukazatel' Moskvy* (Moscow: V Tipografii Avgusta Semena, 1826), 53.

[69] Kuznetsov, *Almanakh*, 50.

[70] Zagoskin, *Sochineniia*, 5:236. According to another source from the 1840s, renting a cab for a day cost from 5 to 15 paper rubles, depending on the type of vehicle; Vistengof, *Ocherki*, 176.

[71] Vtorov, "Moskva i Kazan'," 8.

[72] Prinz Kraft zu Hohenlohe-Ingelfingen, *Aus meinem Leben: Aufzeichnungen*, 4 vols. (Berlin: Ernst Siegfried Mittler, 1897–1907), 4:542.

[73] Vtorov, "Moskva i Kazan'," 4.

the chandeliers and ballroom candles looks excessively pale and sallow."[74] Light also stood for power and freedom. Aleksandr Herzen recalled that his uncle, a former ambassador, "had spent his whole life in a world illumined by lamps, the world of government and diplomacy and of the court and service." Elsewhere, Herzen contrasts the oppression that a house serf experiences from his master with the dignity he enjoys when he eats out at a restaurant, where "he is a free man, he is a lord, the table is set for him, lamps are lit . . . [and where] he gives orders and is obeyed."[75]

Light created class distinctions in shopping, too. In the labyrinthine bazaar at Red Square, safety rules forbade fires of any kind, so the shops could not be heated. On dark autumn days they had to close by three o'clock because there was no light.[76] By contrast, the elegant foreign stores on nearby Kuznetskii Most remained open late into the evening.[77] The connection between light and status was noted by Aleksei Golitsyn, who wrote a critique of the spread of luxury that Glinka reprinted in the *Russian Messenger*:

> in all the streets [of St Petersburg and Moscow] we have restaurants in which the music and lighting make you think they are the houses of great lords . . . All who habitually frequent these magnificently lighted restaurants disdain the swings and other amusements that Russian merchants used to enjoy twenty years ago; now these are left to the lowest tier of the populace.[78]

Artificial light was expensive. Poor people made do with rush-lights, long strips of dried wood that were attached to metal holders and lit at one end. They generated fumes and soot, and often little light.[79] More expensive were tallow candles. Made from animal fat, they were smoky and dim, smelled rancid, and required continuous trimming of the wick. The best were wax candles, which were prized for their clear flame and pleasant smell.[80] Wax candles were expensive. In Moscow, officials in government housing were allocated two candles a day for each room, each weighing about 0.12 Russian pounds (49 grams).[81] In 1800, wax candles were advertised for 56 kopeks a pound. At that price, the daily cost of two wax candles to light one room was over 13 kopeks. By comparison, Moscow's prestigious Alexander School fed each of its students lunch plus dinner for only 16–19 kopeks a day.[82]

---

[74] Vistengof, *Ocherki*, 68–9.

[75] A. I. Gertsen, *Sobranie sochinenii v vos'mi tomakh*, 8 vols. (Moscow: Pravda, 1975), 4:26, 35.

[76] Slonov, *Iz zhizni*, 166.

[77] [I. G. Gur'ianov], *Moskva, ili Istoricheskii putevoditel' po znamenitoi stolitse Gosudarstva Rossiiskago*, 4 vols. (Moscow: V Tipografii S. Selivanovskago, 1827–31), 3:160; see also XLXXLXXX, "Moskovskie riady," 209.

[78] [Glinka], "Vypiska iz Ruskoi knigi," 77–8.

[79] Rostislavov, *Provincial Russia*, 26; Engelhardt, *Russische Miscellen*, 3:202.

[80] Ekirch, *At Day's Close*, 104–6.

[81] *Polozhenie o dokhodakh i raskhodakh Moskovskoi stolitsy*, 48–9.

[82] *MV* (18 January 1800), 116; OPI GIM f. 14, op. 1, d. 4243, ll. 49–67 (menus for the Alexander School, apparently either 1813 or 1819). A Russian pound was 0.409 kg.

Wax candles were a luxury few could afford. The St Petersburg merchant's son Nikolai Leikin recalled from his childhood in the 1840s that his parents prominently displayed their wax candles and carefully cleaned them before holidays, but never actually lit them, instead using tallow candles for light.[83] Likewise in the 1840s, a short story by Dmitrii Grigorovich depicts a St Petersburg official whose wife marks a festive occasion by illumining their home "with lighted tallow candle ends" that she had "painstakingly saved."[84]

The state and the aristocracy took advantage of light's social connotations to awe the people with illuminations and fireworks. Looking back on the coronation of Nicholas I, Mikhail Nazimov wrote that for three nights, the Kremlin walls, towers, and gardens "were bathed in beautiful illumination from top to bottom; all the streets and houses shimmered like a river of fire, with enormous banners and monograms with lights of various colors."[85] In the space of a single paragraph about Moscow aristocrats under Catherine II and Alexander I, the merchant Nikolai Kotov writes that Count Sheremetev gave "a gorgeous firework" every Sunday, to which "all respectable people were admitted"; Count Orlov "magnificently illuminated his gardens and had fireworks," to which "respectable merchants were admitted"; and at the wedding of Grand Duke Constantine, "in the winter there were fireworks and a powder wheel on the river, while at Count Orlov's there were transparent pictures and a powder wheel, and the entire city was illuminated."[86] The village cleric's son Nikodim Kazantsev wrote that when he was a baby (around 1803), the noblewoman who owned his village decided, "in the Catherinean spirit," to arrange a fireworks display. "My mother wanted very much to see these wonders," he writes, so she left her husband to look after little Nikodim. Father, however, "wanted to see this same illumination himself," so he left the house once the baby was asleep. When both parents returned later that evening, they found the baby crying furiously.[87]

GRANDEUR AND SNOBBERY

The spectacle of aristocratic grandeur inspired wonder, even admiration, and opportunities to participate were recalled with gratitude. As an adolescent, the

[83] Nikolai Leikin, "Moi vospominaniia," in Al'bin Konechnyi, ed., *Peterburgskoe kupechestvo v XIX veke* (St Petersburg: Giperion, 2003), 128.

[84] Dmitrii Grigorovich, "The Lottery Ball," in Nekrasov, *Petersburg*, 265.

[85] Nazimov, "V provintsii i v Moskve," 155.

[86] Nauchno-Issledovatelskii Otdel Rukopisei Rossiiskoi Gosudarstvennoi Biblioteki f. 54, ch. 8, l. 38, "Zapiski Nikolaia Fedorovicha Kotova." On the opulent hospitality of the Sheremetevs at their estate at Kuskovo, see also Douglas Smith, *The Pearl: A True Tale of Forbidden Love in Catherine the Great's Russia* (New Haven: Yale University Press, 2008), 43, 121–2.

[87] Kazantsev, "Zhizn'," part 1: *Bogoslovskii Vestnik*, 1 (January 1910), 59–77, here: 61–2.

clergyman Filip Ismailov (1794–1863) was a tutor in an aristocratic home. "I was like family," he later wrote. "I often dined there, spent evenings, learned to play Boston whist, and discovered the theater; in the summer I would go for rides with the children and their mother, and visit [the aristocratic estates of] Kuzminki, Liublino, Kuskovo, Ostankino, and other suburban places beloved of the Moscow public."[88] On one visit to Kuskovo, "I happened to meet some prince, no longer a young man, who taught me how to meet girls"; the episode seemed significant enough that decades later, Ismailov included it in his memoirs.[89] Any encounter with aristocrats made a deep impression. Knowing this, caterers who planned merchant weddings were in the habit of hiring a "wedding general" (*svadebnyi general*) to pronounce a toast. The fee that the general received varied according to his rank.[90]

Ismailov's experience illustrates the aristocracy's power to influence the cultural horizons of the middling sort. Such encounters occurred less often than they might have, however, because of the aristocracy's heavy reliance on the services of serfs and foreigners rather than free Russians of the middle estates. This pattern was especially conspicuous in the decades before the Napoleonic invasion in 1812, but in attenuated form it persisted throughout the pre-Reform era.

Affluent landowners spent the warm months on their estates, and when they came to Moscow in the fall, they tried to replicate their country life in the city. Many brought their own food supplies.[91] They also brought their household staffs: governesses, physicians, clerks, maids, coachmen, hairdressers, musicians, and other specialized attendants, many of them serfs, thereby reducing the need to hire such people on site.[92] These dynamics were not unique to Russia. In colonial British America, writes the historian Gordon Wood, "not only did the great planters' reliance on the labor of their own slaves prevent the growth of large middling groups of white artisans in the South, but their patronage and hence dominance of the communities beyond their plantations was correspondingly reduced."[93]

The serf domestics of the aristocracy had an ambiguous effect on the diffusion of upper-class culture. By the logic of Karamzin and other advocates of "luxury," they were potential ambassadors of civilization. For example, Dr Wichelhausen wrote that if living in the city accustomed them to "cleanliness, order, diverse activities, better victuals, better lodgings, and other conveniences of life," they

[88] Ismailov, *Vzgliad*, 48.

[89] Ismailov, *Vzgliad*, 150–1.

[90] [Il'ia Selivanov] S—v, "Vospominaniia o Moskovskom kommercheskom uchilishche," *Russkii Vestnik*, 36 (November–December 1861), 719–54, here: 722; A. F. Koni, "Kupecheskaia svad'ba," in Aleksandrov, *Moskovskaia Starina*, 313; I. A. Belousov, "Ushedshaia Moskva," in Aleksandrov, *Moskovskaia Starina*, 378.

[91] F. F. Vigel', *Zapiski*, 2 vols., ed. S. Ia. Shtraikh (Moscow: Artel' pisatelei KRUG, 1928) 1:162; Blagovo, *Rasskazy babushki*, 81.

[92] Blagovo, *Rasskazy babushki*, 43; [Svin'in], *Sketches of Moscow and St. Petersburg*, 32.

[93] Gordon S. Wood, *The Radicalism of the American Revolution* (New York: Vintage, 1993), 115.

might carry these habits back to their villages and "soften the morals" of the other peasants.[94] Undoubtedly, this did in fact occur. For example, Vasilii Sapozhnikov was sent to Moscow under Nicholas I to learn a manual trade, and then returned to teach on his master's rural estate. To the peasant pupils at his village school, he was the height of urbanity: he was elegant with his mustache and sideburns, and he taught them an aria from an opera. Even the rituals of courtesy and deference that he required made an impression. One of the local serfs later recalled looking up to his cousins when he was little, because they already went to the village school and "took off their hats before the teacher and generally before older people, while I rarely even wore a hat."[95]

Within urban society, on the other hand, serfdom inhibited the spread of elite culture. The prevalence of serf musicians, cooks, and so on diminished those professions' social prestige and reduced the job opportunities for people from other estates. In addition, because serfdom allowed nobles to provide entertainment and hospitality to each other on a private basis, they could avoid hotels, public theaters, and other venues where they had no control over who was admitted. This retarded the growth of those institutions and reduced the nobility's interaction with other estates.[96]

A further factor limiting the aristocracy's contact with middling Russians, as Glinka and other critics of "luxury" noted, was the prestige of foreigners and imported goods. A demonstrative association with foreign people and things, Richard Wortman argues, allowed the monarchs and elites to distance themselves symbolically from the rest of society and legitimize their power,[97] but it also weakened their everyday social influence. The aristocracy's defenders claimed that its lifestyle created jobs for skilled Russian workers,[98] but critics argued that serfdom and the reliance on foreigners and imports stunted the bonds connecting the elites with the people.[99] Here lay another similarity with colonial America. According to Gordon Wood, "[American] aristocrats tended to import from abroad many of their accouterments—from carriages to furniture; and to the extent that they did, they weakened their influence among artisans and workmen where they lived."[100] Foreign observers noticed this in Russia as well. A Briton

---

[94] Wichelhausen, *Züge zu einem Gemählde von Moskwa*, 320–1.

[95] [L. M. Korkhov] L. Checherskii, "Shkol'nyia vospominaniia krest'ianina," *VE* (August 1870), 503–40, esp. 514–18, quotation on 504.

[96] Stites, *Serfdom, Society, and the Arts*, 149–50; *Istoriia Moskvy s drevneishikh vremen*, 1:286; Blagovo, *Rasskazy babushki*, 152, 154.

[97] Wortman, *Scenarios of Power*, 1:6–7, 86.

[98] [V. L'vov] M. Zh., "Zhizn' v Moskve v 1845," *Moskvitianin*, chast' 1, no. 1 (1846), 269–76, here: 275–6. "M. Zh." is identified as Vladimir L'vov's pseudonym in N. G. Okhotin and G. Iu. Sternin, *Nashi, spisannye s natury russkimi: Prilozhenie k faksimil'nomu izdaniiu* (Moscow: Kniga, 1986), 78.

[99] See, for example: [Pavel Svin'in] P. S., "Ivan Alekseevich Grebenshchikov, Moskovskii kupets-izobretatel'," *OZ*, 7/16 (August 1821), 153–72; 7/17 (September 1821), 243–61; [Pavel Svin'in] P. S., "Pis'mo chetvertoe v Moskvu, o Mekhanike Soboleve," *OZ*, 10/26 (June 1822), 379–409.

[100] Wood, *The Radicalism of the American Revolution*, 115.

who visited St Petersburg in the late 1760s observed that the nobles "are ridiculously shewy" and "profuse in every thing: this has a very bad effect; for their revenues, a part of which ought to be expended upon their estates in improvements, and finding employment for their neighbouring poor, are all squandered in the luxury of the capital, giving employment to Englishmen, Frenchmen, and Dutchmen, instead of their own countrymen."[101] Kuznetskii Most, where Moscow's fashion trade was concentrated, was known for its French shops. In aristocratic households, foreigners held many of the better positions, for example as tutors and governesses. In 1800, a notice in the *Moscow Gazette* announced the upcoming departure of Prince Vasilii Dolgorukoi, his family, and their party: an abbé Brad from France, a Miss Envard from England, and—a pair about whom one would love to know more—"Ivan Mener, a Moor [*Arap*] born in North America, and his wife, Magdalina Sokolovskaia, born in Poland." Traveling with them were five serfs, presumably Russians, whom the notice did not bother to name.[102]

Serfdom was part of a wider culture in which aristocrats drew a sharp line between themselves and the middling sort by surrounding themselves with hordes of underlings. Most striking was the large number of house serfs, many of whom seemed to have no purpose but to provide an impressive entourage for their master. The statistician Konstantin Arsen'ev summed up the consensus when he wrote in 1818 that Russians kept "five or six times more servants than the same houses in the other nations of Europe."[103] The memory of this phenomenon entered intelligentsia lore as proof of the extravagance of the Moscow aristocracy in the early nineteenth century. For example, in the 1870s, the former Decembrist Dmitrii Zavalishin recalled one house that was

something of a charitable institution. Here lived, in retirement and with a pension, deserving house serfs, elderly butlers, aged wet-nurses; some even had separate little rooms, and on certain days, some were even given a carriage, especially the old women, so they could visit faraway monasteries.[104]

Russian aristocrats resembled their counterparts elsewhere in early modern Europe in using servants to demonstrate their social status. For maximum effect, servants should be conspicuous, tall, and male. The law required that their livery

[101] Joseph Marshall, *Travels through Holland, Flanders, Germany, Denmark, Sweden, Lapland, Russia, the Ukraine, and Poland, in the Years 1768, 1769, and 1770*, 3 vols. (London: Printed for J. Almon, 1772–3), 3:141.

[102] *MV* (16 May 1800), 988.

[103] K. I. Arsen'ev, *Nachertanie statistiki Rossiiskago gosudarstva*, 2 vols. (St Petersburg: V Tipografii Imperatorskago Vospitatel'nago Doma, 1818–19), 1:104. See also, for example: Marchioness of Londonderry and H. M. Hyde, eds., *The Russian Journals of Martha and Catherine Wilmot* (London: Macmillan, 1934), 56; Storch, *Gemaehlde*, 2:398–9; Lyall, *The Character of the Russians*, xlix.

[104] Dmitrii Zavalishin, "Tysiacha vosem'sot dvenadtsatyi god: Iz vospominanii sovremennika," *MV* (29 March 1884).

reflect their master's rank; hence, lavish outfits for one's servants were an important status symbol.[105]

Such ostentation was one of the most remarked-upon features of aristocratic households and was denounced by contemporaries (including Catherine II) and later memoirists as retrograde and wasteful. The point of the criticism was that extravagant display satisfied neither the demand for efficiency associated with laissez-faire economics nor the ideal of domesticity of the emerging bourgeoisie. From the eighteenth century onward, it was common in bourgeois European households to employ a few female domestics to serve the employer's convenience and comfort, but in the interest of discretion they were dressed in austere colors and kept out of sight. People with bourgeois expectations were appalled at the garish display and lack of basic comforts or privacy that they encountered in Moscow. The Scottish physician Robert Lyall, who worked for Moscow aristocrats in the years after 1815, was shocked that at dinner, "tens, and even twenties" of servants stood behind the guests and warmed their plates under their armpits. Walking through the house after dark, Lyall complained, one continually risked tripping over servants sleeping on the floor. Yet the same masters who kept these armies of servants usually had no proper bedrooms for themselves, for these "form a luxury which the Russian knows nothing of, except what he has learned in foreign countries, heard of from travellers, or read of in books."[106]

The sense of social superiority of the aristocracy, and more generally of people socialized among the hereditary nobility, was reinforced by a pattern of estate-specific body language. Nobles were taught to project confidence, discipline, and authority. Their young people acquired "posture and grace" through lessons in dancing, riding, and, in the case of the men, fencing.[107] Noble girls at elite "institutes" (boarding schools) learned graceful manners and rituals of politeness, such as what one alumna called the "the deep, institute-style curtsey."[108] Service as army officers gave males an erect soldierly bearing, and from the prestige of their uniforms they drew a self-confidence that civilians could only envy. Young noble ladies, the radical writer Dmitrii Pisarev (1840–68) observed, found a man in uniform irresistible,[109] and enterprising Moscow University students found that when they altered their student uniforms to look like those of army officers, sentries saluted them and the police admitted them to all public promenades.[110]

[105] Roche, *Le peuple de Paris*, 94; Angela Rustemeyer, *Dienstboten in Petersburg und Moskau, 1861–1917: Hintergrund, Alltag, soziale Rolle* (Stuttgart: F. Steiner, 1996), 11–13, 59.

[106] Lyall, *The Character of the Russians*, xlix, lv, lvi; see also Blagovo, *Rasskazy babushki*, 23.

[107] B. N. Chicherin, *Moskva sorokovykh godov* (Moscow: Izdatel'stvo Moskovskogo universiteta, 1997), 29.

[108] F. P. Leont'eva, "Zapiski F. P. Leont'evoi (1811, 1812 i 1813 gody)," part 3: *Russkii Vestnik*, 169/2 (February 1884), 670–721, here: 674.

[109] Frede, *Doubt*, 262–3.

[110] Nazimov, "V provintsii i v Moskve," 152.

Popovichi who attended seminaries internalized the opposite attitudes: humility, denial of the flesh, and distrust of the opposite sex. Rostislavov, a *popovich* and graduate of the St Petersburg Ecclesiastical Academy, thought this put them at a deep social disadvantage vis-à-vis nobles. His fellow students at the academy in the 1820s, he wrote, were taught a graceless demeanor likely to repel any cultivated outsider. "Surely it is clear," he wrote, "that students who are sullen, who lower their gaze or look up from under their brows, who are shy, awkward, clumsy, and don't know how to bow properly, are unlikely to make a good impression on lay visitors."[111] The antipathy between nobles and *popovichi* was strong and mutual. Male nobles under Alexander I, one hereditary noblewoman recalled, avoided working in the civil service because "no one wanted to have to associate with office clerks, whose origin was mostly in the clerical estate or else among townspeople or manumitted serfs."[112] As for the *popovichi*, Laurie Manchester argues that they equated their own lack of refinement with saintliness and closeness to the people, and despised the nobles for lacking morals, loving all things foreign, and oppressing the peasants.[113]

The dress and body language of merchants were likewise apt to be viewed with disdain by nobles. At Nicholas I's coronation in Moscow in 1826, a delegation of merchants was presented to the tsar. These were accomplished men, leaders of their community, and their traditional Russian dress and stiff demeanor were meant to convey dignity and gravitas. Yet that is not how they appeared to the noble memoirist Mikhail Dmitriev: "With great humility and pomp, the merchants walked in single file, like geese, and they all wore boots that squeaked, so that in addition to smelling of leather, their procession sounded like the quacking of a duck; most likely, there was never before a smell or music like this in the palace."[114] This disdain did not extend to the appearance of women. Male folk dress was culturally coded as lower-class, but female costume was regarded—by Catherine II and Nicholas I, among others—as beautiful and symbolizing Russian nationality. Noble women were therefore explicitly required, from Catherine II's reign onward, to wear a form of folk dress for public functions at the imperial court. By contrast, if their menfolk sported beards or donned elements of peasant attire, they risked harassment by the police.[115]

---

[111] D. I. Rostislavov, "Peterburgskaia dukhovnaia akademiia pri grafe Protasove, 1836–1855 gg.," *VE*, 18/7 (July 1883), 121–87, quotation on 135.

[112] Leont'eva, "Zapiski," part 2: *Russkii Vestnik*, 168/12 (December 1883), 878–902, here: 887.

[113] Laurie Manchester, *Holy Fathers, Secular Sons: Clergy, Intelligentsia, and the Modern Self in Revolutionary Russia* (DeKalb, Ill.: Northern Illinois University Press, 2008), 51–8.

[114] M. A. Dmitriev, *Glavy iz vospominanii moei zhizni* (Moscow: Novoe Literaturnoe Obozrenie, 1998), 249. On the disdain that the nobility and the intelligentsia harbored toward the merchantry, see Aleksandra A. Levandovskaia and Andrei A. Levandovskii, "The 'Dark Kingdom': The Merchant Entrepreneur and his Literary Images," *Russian Studies in History*, 47/1 (Summer 2008), 72–95.

[115] Kupriianov, *Gorodskaia kul'tura*, 318–21, 352–4.

Illus. 5.2. "The Arrival of a Governess in a Merchant's House." Painting from 1866 by Vasilii Perov. © The State Tretyakov Gallery, Moscow.

Vasilii Perov captures some of the social nuances of body language in "The Arrival of a Governess in a Merchant's House" (see Illustration 5.2). The painting shows the awkward encounter between merchants on their way up the social ladder and nobles on their way down. Governesses were often boarding-school graduates who, whatever their estate origin, were taught to behave like nobles. Here, the young governess presenting her letter of introduction is svelte and demure as befits a lady. Her new employer has aspirations to gentility, as is apparent from the elegant furnishings, the clothing of his son and daughter, and the fact that he is hiring a governess. However, his domineering posture, his boots, his family's corpulence, and the bearded ancestor on the wall—all of these betray his roots in the conservative, patriarchal world of the merchantry.

SCHOOLS AND EDUCATION

The lives of middling Muscovites bore the imprint of their city's economy and social structure as well as of the subcultures of particular estates. More and more, they were shaped also by its school system, as the centrality of the school experience in mid-century memoirs attests. To understand the mental world of Moscow's middling sort, it is important to understand what it meant to go to school in the pre-Reform era.

When Catherine II became empress, education for Russians of any estate was mostly provided by local clergy or chance tutors, or by church schools. In Moscow, the principal educational institution until the mid-eighteenth century was the Slavonic-Greek-Latin Academy. It had enrollments of 200 to 280 students in the 1740s and 1750s, in large part sons of the clergy.[116] Even many nobles received an education that was at best unsystematic. Grigorii Vinskii (1752–c.1820), a young Ukrainian noble and later a guards officer in St Petersburg, received a good education by the standards of his time. First he attended a local church school, then his family hired two Polish tutors, then he attended a church school in Chernigov for a year and the Kiev ecclesiastical academy for five years, and finally he attended a private boarding school to learn French.[117]

Memoirs written in the nineteenth century create the impression that the nobles of the eighteenth were an unrefined lot, not unlike commoners. To the extent that this was true, it may have had something to do with their school experience. Aside from the aristocracy, the education of many nobles seems to have had a socially leveling effect because they experienced treatment usually meted out only to commoners. Vinskii had this to say about his church school: "how and what [the sacristan] taught me, I do not remember; but that he caned me often and painfully, especially on Saturdays, that I do remember. This stupid, barbaric custom was observed in almost all parish schools because of the nice little income it brought the sacristan." On Saturdays, the sacristan caned everyone he deemed deserving, with those whose families had not paid enough receiving the blows on their naked buttocks instead of their clothes.[118] Gavriil Derzhavin (1743–1816), who went on to be a high-ranking official and one of Russia's leading poets, was an officer's son and grew up on the steppe frontier in Orenburg. Together with the sons and daughters of "the best nobles in Orenburg," he attended a school run by an exiled German. "In addition to his depraved morals," Derzhavin wrote in his memoirs, "this teacher was cruel: the punishments he inflicted on his students were utterly excruciating, even indecent, and it would be repellent to describe them here."[119]

[116] S. V. Eshevskii, *Sochineniia po russkoi istorii*, ed. K. N. Bestuzhev-Riumin (Moscow: Izdanie M. i S. Sabashnikovykh, 1900), 159.
[117] Vinskii, *Moe vremia*, 6–9, 11–14.
[118] Vinskii, *Moe vremia*, 8.
[119] G. R. Derzhavin, *Zapiski 1743–1812* (Moscow: Mysl', 2000), 10.

Catherine II wished to change these conditions. She wanted schools to promote both intellectual knowledge and improved moral sensibilities among an expanding body of enlightened citizens. Her school reform of 1786 attempted to create a network of two- and five-year primary schools in Russian towns that were public, all-estate, co-educational, and secular. Alexander I built on this with his own reform of 1804, which established a hierarchy of parish (primary) schools, district (middle) schools, gymnasia (secondary schools), and universities. Nicholas I maintained this system but restricted the non-noble estates' access to secondary education.[120]

The all-estate public schools continually expanded during the pre-Reform period, but their growth was slow. In 1799, in all of Moscow Province, out of a total population of 1,139,000, the schools enrolled only 1,981 children. At the five-year school in the city of Moscow, almost half (48 percent) of the children in 1800 were peasants or house serfs.[121] The schools were hobbled by inadequate funding, a shortage of teachers, and the stubborn particularism of the estates: nobles preferred private tutors, the clergy maintained their own school system, and few merchants were attracted to schools if the education they provided was neither religious nor vocational.

The other track along which education developed was the creation of a large number of estate-specific schools. The preparatory school of Moscow University, established under Elizabeth, was divided from the beginning into separate gymnasia for nobles and commoners. In 1779, the university established an additional boarding school for noble boys.[122] Two girls' boarding schools were established in Moscow under the patronage of the imperial family: the Catherine Institute (in 1802) for hereditary nobles, and the Alexander School (1805) for daughters of personal nobles, merchants, clerics, and certain professions (physicians, artists, teachers). There also existed numerous small, privately run boarding schools that enrolled mostly nobles. Sons and daughters of deceased officials in ranks 14 through 6 were eligible for the Minors' Division, established in 1842. Lastly, because military cadet schools were popular among noble families, one was established in Moscow in 1824.[123]

[120] James T. Flynn, *The University Reform of Tsar Alexander I, 1802–1835* (Washington, DC: Catholic University of America Press, 1988), 20–1, 176; Mikhail Polievktov, *Nikolai I: Biografiia i obzor tsarstvovaniia* (Moscow: Izd-vo M. i S. Sabashnikovykh, 1918), 237, 243.

[121] Artamonova, *Obshchestvo, vlast' i prosveshchenie*, 237, 307; Storch, *Statistische Übersicht*, 38.

[122] N. V. Khristoforova, *Rossiiskie gimnazii XVIII—XX vekov: Na materiale g. Moskvy* (Moscow: Greko-latinskii kabinet Iu. A. Shichalina, 2001), 11, 13; P. I. Strakhov, *Kratkaia istoriia akademicheskoi gimnazii, byvshei pri Imperatorskom Moskovskom universitete* (1855; repr. Moscow: Izdatel'stvo Moskovskogo universiteta, 2000), 58–9.

[123] *Istoricheskaia zapiska o Moskovskikh uchilishchakh ordena sv. Ekateriny i Aleksandrovskom* (Moscow: Tipografiia i Litografiia I. N. Kushnera, 1875), 19, 159; "Kratkii obzor zavedenii: Maloletniago Otdeleniia, Fel'dsherskoi Shkoly i Bogadel'ni Vospitatel'nago Doma," *Moskvitianin*, chast' 4, otdel 5 (1849), 17–22, esp. 18; [A. Korsakov] K—v, "Moskovskii kadetskii korpus, 1824–1828," *Drevniaia i novaia Rossiia*, 17 (May–August 1880), 287–304; *Istoriia Moskvy s drevneishikh vremen*, 2:152.

The Orthodox Church operated a system of education for sons of the clergy. After an extensive reform in 1808–14, it included parish (primary) schools, district (middle) schools, seminaries (equivalent to gymnasia), and ecclesiastical academies (post-secondary). Russia's first school for daughters of the clergy opened in 1843 in Tsarskoe Selo near St Petersburg. A similar institution was established in Moscow only in 1865.[124]

For the merchantry, a Commercial School was established in 1772. It failed to attract many students from merchant families and was relocated to St Petersburg. Another attempt was made with the founding of a new Moscow Commercial School in 1804, followed in 1806 by the Practical Commercial Academy, but these too never attracted more than a small minority of the merchantry. A Townspeople's School was added in 1835 and soon after began admitting girls.[125]

In 1840, according to the annual report of the city's chief of police, schools in Moscow enrolled 11,404 students. Their distribution across different types of educational institutions is shown in Table 5.3.

Table 5.3. Schools in Moscow, 1840

	Number of schools	Students			
		Male	Female	Total	Percentage of total
Public institutions:					
University	1	930		930	
Gymnasia	4	829		829	
District (middle) schools	3	231		231	
Primary schools	13	629		629	
Subtotal		*2,619*		*2,619*	22.96%
Military:					
Cadet schools	3	794		794	
School for soldiers' sons	1	1,048		1,048	
Subtotal		*1,842*		*1,842*	16.15%
Orthodox Church:					
Seminary	1	606		606	
Monastery (primary and middle) schools	3	841		841	
Subtotal		*1,447*		*1,447*	12.68%

[124] O. D. Popova, ed., *Eparkhialki: Vospominaniia vospitannits zhenskikh eparkhial'nykh uchilishch* (Moscow: Novoe Literaturnoe Obozrenie, 2011), 6; I. K. Kondrat'ev, *Sedaia starina Moskvy: Istoricheskii obzor i polnyi ukazatel' eia dostopamiatnostei* (Moscow: Izdanie knigoprodavtsa I. A Morozova, 1893), 604.

[125] Ransel, *A Russian Merchant's Tale,* 9–10, 226; Kupriianov, *Gorodskaia kul'tura,* 38; Nilova, *Moskovskoe kupechestvo,* 89–95; *Istoriia Moskvy s drevneishikh vremen,* 2:159.

Upper-class boarding schools:				
Private (boys)	4	180		180	
Private (girls)	12		561	561	
Catherine Institute and Alexander School	2		437	437	
Schools for orphans of nobles or officials	3	350	606	956	
Subtotal		*530*	*1,604*	*2,134*	18.71%
Schools for merchants and townspeople	5	714		714	6.26%
Professional schools:					
Medico-Surgical Academy	1	422		422	
Other professional schools	8	568	74	642	
Subtotal		*990*	*74*	*1,064*	9.33%
Schools of the Foundling Home	3	285	133	418	3.66%
Other schools:					
Primary schools of the Moscow Charitable Society	6		197	197	
Moscow Workhouse	1		113	113	
Protestant and Catholic schools	8	395	132	527	
Other schools	4	329		329	
Subtotal		*724*	*442*	*1,166*	10.22%
Total	86	9,151	2,253	11,404	100%

Source: "Otchet moskovskago ober-politsmeistera, za 1840 god," *ZhMVD*, chast' 41, no. 7 (July 1841), 1–161, esp. 27–31.

Note: The total number of schools was actually 85. Here it is 86 because the Aleksandrinskii Sirotskii Institut is counted twice: the males appear under "cadet schools," and the females, under "schools for orphans of nobles and officials." The latter category also includes the Institut Ober-Ofitserskikh Sirot and the Cherniaevskoe Uchilishche. The category "Gymnasia" includes the Dvorianskii Institut.

Source: P. Nikolaev, *Istoricheskii ocherk maloletniago otdeleniia Moskovskago Nikolaevskago Sirotskago Instituta (za 50 let ego sushchestvovaniia) 1842–1892 g.* (Moscow: Tipografiia E. G. Potapova, 1892), 7, 68; V. Troitskii, *Istoricheskii ocherk soveta Imperatorskago Chelovekoliubivago Obshchestva i podvedomstvennykh emu blagotvoritel'nykh uchrezhdenii* (St Petersburg: no pub., 1898), 209.

As this table shows, the largest contingent of students were in the public education system (22.96 percent), followed by upper-class boarding schools (18.71 percent) and the schools of the army (16.15 percent) and the Orthodox Church (12.68 percent). The upper-class boarding schools are actually in first place if we redefine the category to include the cadet schools. Education for girls was available mainly in boarding schools, charitable institutions, and Protestant (usually German) religious schools. The education system was better developed at the secondary than the primary level, which tended to deepen the divide between the middling sort who were connected to the imperial social project and the masses who were not.

Judging by the subject's prominence in the memoir literature, the pre-Reform schools had a profound impact on the lives of the middling sort. The experience of attending school helped to homogenize them, as people became literate, studied broadly similar subjects, and experienced the discipline, work rhythms, and patterns of social interaction characteristic of a school. However, perhaps because the very fact of education was increasingly taken for granted, what stands out in the narrative sources is how deeply people's school experience varied depending on their sex and social background.

The pronounced gender gap in education contributed to the cultural separation of the different estates. In 1840, only 2,253 students in Moscow (19.75 percent of the total) were girls. Of these, 71.11 percent attended boarding schools intended mainly or exclusively for daughters of nobles or officials. The nobility was the only estate in which the experience of socialization through formal schooling was widely shared by both sexes.

The gender gap in formal schooling had consequences even for Russians who were home-schooled, because the men and women who were available as private tutors came from different backgrounds and carried dissimilar cultural baggage. The archetypal unemployed educated male was a *popovich* who had attended a seminary. His female counterpart was an *institutka* (boarding-school graduate) from the petty nobility or other middle estates. Worlds separated the educations that the two received.

Aleksandr Voskresenskii (b. 1778), the son of a rural sacristan, exemplifies what Laurie Manchester describes as the mentality of seminary-educated *popovichi* throughout the nineteenth century.[126] To support himself while at the *bursa* (the generic term for the Orthodox Church's educational institutions) in Moscow, he worked as a tutor in the household of a noble, a merchant, and a priest. In his memoirs, he recalls his poverty-stricken childhood as a virtuous rustic idyll and casts a hard, moralistic gaze on life in the metropolis. He does not dwell on the cruel punishments and demand for rote memorization for which the *bursa* became notorious in the nineteenth century, but one senses that they informed how he approached his own teaching. His pupils, as he describes them, were all lazy and disobedient, and needed the threat of the rod to make them behave.[127] How people like Voskresenskii appeared to nobles is illustrated by the recollections of the nobleman Apollon Grigor'ev about the seminary graduate who was his tutor. Grigor'ev remembered his tutor as having "downcast eyes," and when Grigor'ev's father teased him, he "coughed a little as seminarians do, blushed, and stammered something in response." Later "he blushed horribly

---

[126] Manchester, *Holy Fathers, Secular Sons*, esp. chs 4–5.
[127] Voskresenskii, "Umstvennyi vzor," part 1: *Dushepoleznoe chtenie*, no. 10 (1894), 203–11, here: 205–5; part 2, 373, 376–7, 380.

when he saw my younger nanny." The only teaching method he knew was the rote learning typical of the *bursa*.[128]

The experience of the merchant's son Il'ia Selivanov, who was educated by *institutki*, was quite different. Girls' boarding schools had no more tolerance for rebels than did the *bursa*, but they cultivated rigidly ladylike manners that allowed teachers to assert their authority with an icy glare instead of the cane. Whereas seminarians were stereotyped as coarse and awkward, the cliché about *institutki* was that they were childlike, emotionally overwrought, and inclined to make older schoolmates, members of the imperial family, or anyone else who struck their fancy into objects of sentimental "adoration" (*obozhanie*). Hence the behavior of the *institutki* who helped raise Il'ia Selivanov: they rarely used corporal punishment, and while they were strict with the girls, boys who knew their lessons were "often rewarded with ardent kisses."[129]

Education formed a dissimilar outlook in other ways as well. In the government's view, the ideal city was clean and airy, and correspondingly government buildings were supposed to maximize ventilation and natural light.[130] Churches, with their dim lighting and smell of incense, aimed to create a more other-worldly atmosphere. These differences were reflected in the schools. The Catherine Institute (for hereditary noble girls) installed water closets in 1829, a mere three years after they were first installed in the imperial palace at Tsarskoe Selo. The Alexander School (for girls from the other middle estates) followed suit in 1832.[131] The merchant-turned-singer Pavel Bogatyrev (1851–1908), who was otherwise not shy about describing the filth of pre-Reform Moscow, recalled admiringly that at the Townspeople's School "all the rooms were spacious, with a mass of air and light; especially clean were the bedrooms."[132] The ecclesiastical schools, on the other hand, were notorious for their squalor. Rostislavov writes that at the Riazan' seminary, which he attended in the 1820s, it was common for seminarians to walk on the classroom tables. When they sat down to lunch, they "saw before them on the table not only a layer of fresh mud, but sometimes also what was called 'gold' that was tracked in from the seminary latrines, which were maintained in the most revolting filthiness and where, as they say, one often could not take a step without soiling one's feet."[133] Others told similar stories of

---

[128] Grigor'ev, *Vospominaniia*, 24, 32–3.

[129] Selivanov, "Vospominaniia," 720; A. F. Belousov, "Institutki," in V. M. Bokova and L. G. Sakharova, eds., *Institutki: Vospominaniia vospitannits institutov blagorodnykh devits* (Moscow: Novoe Literaturnoe Obozrenie, 2001), 5–32.

[130] See, for example, Betskoi's views on the importance of ventilation: Solovkov, *Antologiia pedagogicheskoi mysli*, 177, 194.

[131] *Istoricheskaia zapiska o Moskovskikh uchilishchakh*, 144, 205; Igor' Zimin, "Nochnoi sosud s pozolotoiu: Povsednevnaia zhizn' imperatorskikh dvortsov: kanalizatsiia," *Sankt-Peterburgskie Vedomosti* (28 September 2007), *Daidzhest Peterburgskoi pressy* <http://base.pl.spb.ru/FullText/spbiblio/digest_spb/SPb_v070928_3.pdf> accessed 30 April 2009.

[132] Bogatyrev, "Moskovskaia starina," in Aleksandrov, *Moskovskaia Starina*, 130.

[133] D. I. Rostislavov, "Zapiski D. I. Rostislavova," *RS*, 77 (February 1893), 448–80, here: 477–8.

the state of the Orthodox seminaries. *Popovichi* regarded living in such conditions as something akin to martyrdom that elevated them above the pampered children of the nobility.[134]

The schools of the various estates differed in their connections to the culture of the West. *Institutki* and cadets learned French, the language of the aristocracy. Seminarians learned Latin because their curriculum was influenced by Western scholasticism.[135] Merchants seem to have been more likely to study the languages of Russia's major trading partners: German, Dutch, or English. Some merchants sent their sons to Protestant church schools, both to learn skills useful in the business world and, as the merchant sons Leikin and Vishniakov recalled, because their fathers admired "how employees were treated" and the general "superiority of the educated West European ways" that they observed among Western merchants.[136]

In schools of all types, children accustomed to the warm informality of home had to adjust to a new life of material austerity, rigid routines, authoritarian teachers, and sometimes—especially at the *bursa*—violence. Everywhere, senior students lorded it over junior ones, and teachers and administrators who had difficulty policing large numbers of students delegated power to student prefects and teaching assistants. Schools varied only in the harshness with which students asserted their authority over each other. Not surprisingly, families sent their children with a sense of trepidation. Ivan Kurganskii (1795–1858), a leading merchant from Riazan', sent his son to a prestigious school so he could become a civil servant. In the notes that he jotted down from time to time, Kurganskii was generally spare about his own feelings, but the day in 1852 when his son first left for school forms a stark exception. A few hours after seeing him off, "I dreamed that they caned him for a long time in class, with the pus flowing as thick as a finger and looking like bouillon."[137] School unnerved noble parents as well. Sofiia Khvoshchinskaia (1828–65), an alumna of the Catherine Institute, recalled that nobles from the provinces "are terrified by everything about the institute. The doorman is pompous, the rooms are too tidy, and the class matron seems to be looking askance. And there are some fathers who are intimidated by their daughters."[138]

---

134 Manchester, *Holy Fathers, Secular Sons*, 134–7.

135 Donald Treadgold, "Russian Orthodoxy and Society," and Robert L. Nichols, "Orthodoxy and Russia's Enlightenment," in Robert L. Nichols and Theofanis George Stavrou, eds., *Russian Orthodoxy under the Old Regime* (Minneapolis: University of Minnesota Press, 1978), 26–7, 77–9.

136 Leikin, "Moi vospominaniia," in Konechnyi, *Peterburgskoe kupechestvo*, 161; Vishniakov, *Svedeniia*, 2:95; see also Butkovskaia, "Razskazy Babushki," 595–6, and A. W. Fechner, *Chronik der evangelischen Gemeinden in Moskau*, 2 vols. (Moscow: J. Deubner, 1876), 2:410–43.

137 I. A. Kurganskii, "Pamiatnye zapiski [1818–1858 gg.]," in Semenova, *Kupecheskie dnevniki i memuary*, 142.

138 Sofia Khvoshchinskaia, "Reminiscences of Institute Life," in Toby W. Clyman and Judith Vowles, eds., *Russia through Women's Eyes: Autobiographies from Tsarist Russia* (New Haven: Yale

Schools reinforced the divisions both within and among estates. In the parish clergy, priests wielded oppressive authority over deacons or sacristans; in retaliation, according to Rostislavov, the sons of priests were exposed to violent bullying at the *bursa* from the sons of deacons and sacristans.[139] Speaking for *institutki* from the petty nobility, Khvoshchinskaia recalled new arrivals from elite families: "we'll probably dislike them. They'll start by putting on airs and sitting together with their aristocratic noses in the air." Another *institutka* complained that spoiled aristocratic underachievers avoided expulsion only because of their family connections.[140] Group identities were also heightened by rivalries with other schools. The girls of the all-noble Catherine Institute cultivated a snobbish disdain for their less elite counterparts at the nearby Alexander School.[141] Education at a noble boys' school instilled contempt for the sons of priests.[142] The church schools, by making asceticism one of their central values, reinforced the clergy's disdain for the corpulence and love of money of the merchantry.[143] Boys also engaged in fights to assert their estate identity and prove their manhood. In downtown Moscow, church-school students brawled with the students and staff of the Surveyors' School; in one such incident, windows were shattered, carriages were stoned, and finally the police had to intervene.[144] Elsewhere, fights broke out between townspeople's boys and boys from church schools, public schools, and schools for soldiers' sons.[145]

Schools that brought diverse estates together made a deep impression that is reflected in the memoirs. For people from the bottom of society, the encounter with their "betters" could be a transformative experience that justified the hopes vested in the imperial social project. Aleksandr Nikitenko (b. 1804), the son of a highly educated serf, attended the district school in Voronezh. This was a rare time, he later recalled, when his mind counted for more than his status as a serf. "The students," he wrote, "came from all kinds of families"—noble and common, wealthy and poor, free and serf—but "Despite such variation in social class, the children at the school fraternized freely, and among them there were no

University Press, 1996), 87; see also A. N. Engel'gardt, "Ocherki institutskoi zhizni bylogo vremeni," in Bokova and Sakharova, *Institutki*, 210.

[139] Rostislavov, *Provincial Russia*, 155–7.

[140] Khvoshchinskaia, "Reminiscences," in Clyman and Vowles, *Russia through Women's Eyes*, 85; A. V. Sterligova, "Vospominaniia," in Bokova and Sakharova, *Institutki*, 93.

[141] Engel'gardt, "Ocherki," in Bokova and Sakharova, *Institutki*, 205; Galakhov, *Zapiski cheloveka*, 132.

[142] Grigor'ev, *Vospominaniia*, 23.

[143] See, for example: Rostislavov, *Provincial Russia*, 177–80; [V. I. Marenin] Prot. V. M-n, *Shkol'nyia i semeinyia vospominaniia (Ocherk dukhovnoi shkoly i byta dukhovenstva v polovine proshlago stoletiia)*, vol. 1 (St Petersburg: Tipografiia Glazunova, 1911), 101–4.

[144] Ismailov, *Vzgliad*, 28.

[145] Nikitenko, *Up from Serfdom*, 86; Rostislavov, *Provincial Russia*, 154; Slonov, *Iz zhizni*, 33; Marenin, *Vospominaniia*, 92–3.

pretensions or jealousy. What did confer status was academic excellence," as well as skill at fistfights or ball games.[146]

Nobles were sometimes appalled at the experience of going to school with the lower classes. Aleksei Galakhov (b. 1807) and Mikhail Nazimov (b. 1806) were Nikitenko's contemporaries and attended similar district schools in the provinces. What they found most memorable at their schools was the anarchy that they witnessed. As Galakhov put it, in terms similar to those also used by Nazimov:

> The estate diversity of my classmates was apparent in both their clothes and their haircut ... This whole motley company, truth to tell, was not especially well-behaved. Until the teacher arrived, the classroom groaned with noise, ruckus, and fighting. Unprintable words flew from all sides ... My and my brother's position amidst these scenes is hard to conceive. Raised at home to be respectably restrained, and experienced in neither wrestling nor fistfighting, we were amazed, stunned, at what went on in front of us.

At least, he added, they were spared the usual brutal punishments, both because they behaved well and because "the teachers acted differently toward us as the only students from the noble estate." Similar tensions, he wrote, existed at Moscow University, where many of the students retained the coarse manners of the gymnasia or seminaries where they had received their education.[147] The nobleman Dmitrii Sverbeev (b. 1799) took a more tolerant view. University students, he wrote, consisted of two groups. They were either *gimnazisty* and *seminaristy* who were old enough to shave, or *aristokraty* like himself who were not: "the former really studied, while we only played around and goofed off."[148]

Mid-century memoirs about the pre-Reform education system often stressed its negative aspects, but their criticisms were tempered by a sense that great civilizational strides had since been made. Even those who defended the old ways shared this view. Ismailov, who was an apologist for the pre-Reform church schools, wrote that "There was much that was dark, but at the time, Russia itself was dark. Coarseness, foolishness, and vulgarity prevailed in everything."[149] According to another veteran of the pre-Reform seminary, "seeing nothing better, we told ourselves that this was how it had to be."[150] Impressions of the cadet schools were similar. Both the Decembrist Dmitrii Zavalishin and the staunch monarchist A. Ia. Butkovskaia agreed that noble cadets under Paul and

[146] Nikitenko, *Up from Serfdom*, 87.

[147] Galakhov, *Zapiski cheloveka*, 53, 54, 55, 74, quotations on 53–5; Nazimov, "V provintsii i v Moskve," 101, 129, 137.

[148] D. N. Sverbeev, "Iz vospominanii," in Iu. N. Emel'ianov, ed., *Moskovskii universitet v vospominaniiakh sovremennikov* (Moscow: Sovremennik, 1989), 65.

[149] Ismailov, *Vzgliad*, 100.

[150] P. S. A., *Iz vospominanii o vladimirskikh dukhovnykh (prikhodskom i uezdnom) uchilishchakh i seminarii 1818–1832 godov* (Vladimir: Pechatnia A. A. Aleksandrovskago, 1875), 20.

Alexander I had been a coarse bunch, but subsequently, Butkovskaia thought, "education made morals gentler."[151]

CONCLUSION

In the first half of the nineteenth century, the middling sort became progressively more modern and unified in their culture and life experience, with rising economic prosperity and legal protections, access to education and print culture, and more refined standards of behavior. However, having internalized the genteel sensibilities that the regime wished to instill, they also grew more sensitive to the flaws of the regime itself. The successes of the imperial social project thus did not have the effect of creating a strong base of support for the regime.

Nikolai Vishniakov's family chronicle from the turn of the twentieth century illustrates this phenomenon. Vishniakov came from a Moscow merchant family. His father was born in 1781, his mother around 1808, and Vishniakov himself in 1844, so his narrative draws on memories that stretched back to Catherine II. Vishniakov despised the old Moscow merchantry, which he considered coarse, narrow-minded, and insular. Only his mother brought light into this gloom, because she "retained in her mental outlook the spirit of the age of Karamzin." By immersing herself in Russian literature, he thought, she had reached a higher level of sensitivity and humaneness. Vishniakov gave the imperial state and Karamzin's beloved nobility no credit for this progress. Instead, he blamed the regime's brutality and corruption for sustaining society's moral backwardness.[152]

The middling sort also remained deeply divided by the estate subcultures that they had developed. These subcultures engendered memories and resentments that outlasted the tsarist regime, as can be seen in Dmitrii Ushakov's dictionary from the 1930s. Ushakov provides these figurative meanings for terms derived from the social world of the prerevolutionary middle estates. *Institutskii*: "naively enthusiastic, affected." *Seminarskii*: "coarse, ill-bred." *Meshchanin* (townsman): "person with petty, limited, proprietary interests and narrow intellectual and social horizons."[153]

In the summer of 1812, roughly the halfway point from Catherine's accession to the dawn of the Great Reforms, such disillusionment, or at least its public articulation, still lay in the future. Karamzin, Glinka, and Storch were at the height of their powers. The pre-Reform education system was still being constructed. Vishniakov's mother was a mere child, as were most of the memoirists

---

[151] Dmitrii Zavalishin, "Vospominaniia o morskom kadetskom korpuse s 1816 po 1822 god," *Russkii Vestnik,* 105 (June 1873), 623–55, esp. 626–9; Butkovskaia, "Razskazy Babushki," 610, 626.

[152] Vishniakov, *Svedeniia,* 2:30–5, 93–4; 3:18–19, quotation on 2:52.

[153] D. N. Ushakov, ed., *Tolkovyi slovar' russkogo iazyka,* 4 vols. in 3 (Cambridge, Mass.: Slavica Publishers, 1974) <http://enc-dic.com/ushakov/> accessed 30 June 2011.

who later analyzed the imperial social project. The imperial elites continued to be haunted by the specter of Pugachev and the plague revolt, for Moscow remained highly combustible—physically, with its masses of wooden buildings, and socially, with its restive serfs and marginalized Old Believers, its vast gulf between aristocrats and the middling sort, and its feeble state institutions.

Then came Napoleon.

6

The 1812 War

Titular Councilor Vasilii Popov was a typical product of the imperial social project. His surname suggests that he was a *popovich* who had parlayed his education into a civil-service career and personal-noble status. (His rank was just one grade shy of the level that conferred hereditary nobility.) After losing his eyesight, he retired to a life of genteel squalor, renting a room from a townsman in a modest neighborhood and employing a peasant widow as his maid. Blind, poor, aging, alone, he was vulnerable and dependent.

Monday, 2 September 1812, was a fateful day for Popov. On that day, Napoleon's army entered Moscow, where it remained until 10 October. It was also a moment of truth for the imperial social project.[1] Would the government stand by its subjects in their hour of need? Absent direct compulsion, would the lower classes honor the privileges of their betters? Would European invaders recognize Westernized Russians as deserving of civilized consideration? In other words, the social contract underlying the imperial social project—would it hold?

It did not. As Popov wrote bitterly to Governor-General Fedor Rostopchin, he had not been overly worried about Napoleon's eastward march, for "it had pleased Your Excellency to assure the inhabitants of Moscow that they need not be afraid, that the French would not be permitted to enter" the city. When the French arrived anyway, Popov's maid stole his money, and his landlady, most of his other valuables. He begged to be guided out of his burning neighborhood, so his landlord took him to a park and abandoned him to be robbed by enemy soldiers. He pleaded with passers-by to help him. Instead, three young men took away most of his threadbare clothes and the icons he was clutching, beat him mercilessly, and left him in a nearby village where he wandered helplessly, begging in vain for the peasants to take him in. Finally, he spent the night alone outside a villager's door. The next morning, a kindly old woman invited him in, but enemy soldiers later savagely beat him when they found that he had nothing worth stealing. Eventually, a peasant led him back into Moscow, where he found refuge in an almshouse.[2]

---

[1] I borrow the concept of a "moment of truth" from Teodor Shanin, *Russia, 1905–07: Revolution as a Moment of Truth* (Houndsmills: Macmillan, 1986).

[2] "Proshenie tituliarnago sovetnika Vasiliia Popova grafu F. V. Rastopchinu, 10 noiabria 1812 goda," in Shchukin, *Bumagi*, 1:121–2.

Count Rostopchin, the tsar's top man in Moscow, had his reasons for betraying the trust of people like Popov. A foreign invasion, he reasoned, might trigger a meltdown of Russia's social order. Nothing was therefore as important as beating back the invader. When Napoleon crushed the Prussian army in 1806, the Berlin authorities posted bills that read: "The king has lost a battle. Now the first duty of the citizenry is to remain calm." This appeal for civic passivity, which outraged German nationalists, summed up a civilizational accomplishment of the eighteenth century: the ability to fight wars without disrupting the orderly flow of civilian life.[3] Had Rostopchin thought that Russia could afford this attitude, he could have allowed Moscow to pass intact under French control, or at least attempted an orderly evacuation. Instead, his chief goal was to prevent popular unrest and deny Napoleon winter quarters. Hence he tried to delay any mass evacuation of the city, and ordered the city to be burned once the Russians abandoned it.[4] Napoleon's army in turn, its hopes for victory fading and convinced that Russians were barbarians, vented its fury and disappointment by sacking the city. The zest with which lower-class Russians joined in the looting completed the misery of middling Muscovites who felt abandoned and betrayed by their leaders, their fellow Europeans, and their compatriots.

We can reconstruct these experiences with some accuracy because the war, reflecting the spread of secular literary culture, was the first event in Moscow's history to generate significant numbers of autobiographic texts by the middling sort, including resident foreigners. (By comparison, hardly any emerged from the 1771 plague.) These appeared in print over the course of the entire nineteenth century. The events in wartime Moscow are central to some texts and peripheral in others. Depending on which texts are counted, most—at least three dozen individuals, including perhaps a half-dozen women—were nobles, officials, or people active in the arts or professions. Slightly over a dozen were clerics, all of them male save a few nuns tasked with writing official reports. There were also a half-dozen or fewer texts by males of other backgrounds. In the era of the Great Reforms, educated Russians grew increasingly anxious to know how the world appeared to the common people. Reflecting these concerns, the author Ekaterina Novosil'tseva (1820–85), writing under the pseudonym T. Tolycheva, collected at least thirty-one oral accounts of the war, mostly by non-nobles from Moscow, between 1864 and 1884. Unfortunately for historians, she published these as seamless first-person narratives, with no indication of her own role as interviewer and editor. They exhibit a common narrative structure and pacifistic sensibility,

---

[3] David A. Bell, *The First Total War: Napoleon's Europe and the Birth of Warfare as We Know It* (Boston: Houghton Mifflin, 2007), 44–51.

[4] The evidence that Rostopchin gave orders to burn the city is discussed in A. A. Smirnov, "Pozhar Moskvy," in V. M. Bezotosnyi et al., *Otechestvennaia voina 1812 goda: Entsiklopediia* (Moscow: ROSSPEN, 2004), 482–3, and V. A. Presnov, "Rostopchin (Rastopchin) Fedor Vasil'evich," in Bezotosnyi, *Otechestvennaia voina 1812 goda,* 624.

Illus. 6.1. "Moscow, 24 September." Sketch from 1812 by Christian Wilhelm Faber du Faur. Courtesy of The New York Public Library. <http://digitalgallery.nypl.org/nypldigital/id?1224930>. The original accompanying text reads: "Here and there groups of unfortunate inhabitants could be seen wandering in the grim labyrinth, hoping to discover some part of their home that had escaped destruction or to dig up some miserable food in order to prolong their unhappy existence. Our troops were everywhere, hoping to discover some trophy and, like children, satisfy their greed with some bauble, only to discard it as soon as they came across some other novelty." *With Napoleon in Russia: The Illustrated Memoirs of Faber du Faur, 1812,* ed. and tr. Jonathan North (London: Greenhill Books; Mechanicsburg, Pa.: Stackpole Books; 2001), text opposite plate no. 60.

but are also markedly individual in the stories they tell and, sometimes, the language they use.[5]

---

[5] On the history of this memoir literature (including an exhaustive bibliography), see: A. G. Tartakovskii, *1812 god i russkaia memuaristika: Opyt istochnikovedcheskogo izucheniia* (Moscow: Nauka, 1980). On Tolycheva's oral histories, see also Alfred Rambaud, "La Grande Armée à Moscou d'après les témoignages moscovites," *Revue des deux mondes,* vol. 106 (1873), 194–228; and N. V. Ostreikovskaia, "Memuarnye zapisi Tolychevoi kak dokumental'nyi istochnik," *Vestnik Cheliabinskogo Gosudarstvennogo Universiteta,* no. 39 (177) (2009), *Filologiia, Iskusstvovedenie* (vypusk 38), 122–4 <http://www.lib.csu.ru/vch/177/024.pdf> accessed 27 April 2011.

The present chapter will begin by examining the elites' anxieties about social instability in the event of a French invasion. Then we will explore the chaos that engulfed Muscovites as the war unfolded, and how these events were remembered over the course of the nineteenth century. From 1789 to 1848 and beyond, Europe was shaken by revolutionary upheavals. Moscow lay far from these events geographically but not psychologically. Cacophonous propaganda, anticlerical violence, conflict between city and country and between rich and poor, paranoia about saboteurs, the collapse of a civilized urban life, executions by firing squad—all of these entered Muscovites' daily reality and became part of their collective consciousness. (See Illustration 6.1.)

RUSSIA'S ELITES AND THE WAR

The imperial social project was part of an attempt by the Russian regime to improve the country's domestic stability and international power. Adopting a similar approach but taking it much farther, the French after 1789 constructed a formidable state that rested on the support of a moneyed elite and a broad middle class. This allowed Napoleon to raise sufficient revenue and troops to reduce even major states like Prussia and Austria to the status of French satellites.

Were Russia to suffer the same fate, the potential consequences for its political and social order were grave. The nobles' sense of collective identity was founded on their role as military servitors of an absolute monarch and as rulers over the enserfed peasantry. Hence they were dismayed at Alexander I's abolitionist and constitutionalist sympathies and his defeat by Napoleon in the war of 1805–7. The ensuing Peace of Tilsit in 1807 forced Russia to join the Continental System (the French-led trade embargo against Great Britain) and thereby undermined the lucrative British trade that enriched noble landowners and merchants alike. Expressing an opinion that was widespread among the governing elite, General Levin Bennigsen believed (as paraphrased by the historian Dominic Lieven) that "if Napoleon was allowed to strangle Russia's foreign trade then the economy would no longer be able to sustain Russia's armed forces or the European culture of its elites. The country would revert to its pre-Petrine, semi-Asiatic condition."[6] Not surprisingly, rumors abounded that Alexander would fall victim to a coup, as had his father (Paul I) and grandfather (Peter III) before him.

Worse than the Continental System was the possibility of a full-scale French invasion of Russia. Napoleon, as the heir of the French Revolution, might rouse the Russian serfs to rebellion. Such an appeal to revolt would be especially redoubtable if a successful invasion revealed that the tsar was powerless to defend

---

[6] Dominic Lieven, *Russia against Napoleon: The Battle for Europe, 1807 to 1814* (London: Allen Lane, 2009), 64.

his people and that the tyranny of the serf owners and bureaucrats rested on feet of clay. A foreign invasion might also trigger a xenophobic popular backlash that would strike at the Westernized Russian elites. The experience of the Time of Troubles in 1598–1613 and the revolutions of 1905–21 suggests that had authority disintegrated, horrific mayhem might have ensued, to be followed, once the dust settled, by a new regime even harsher than the old. The collapse of Russia's social order would have been calamitous for all.

Alexander I tried to improve Russia's defenses by adopting domestic policies similar to Napoleon's, but this was at best a long-term solution.[7] It was also fraught with political risk. One reason was the threat it posed to powerful class interests. After Tilsit, Alexander entrusted broad powers to the *popovich* Mikhail Speranskii, his liberal adviser. Speranskii sought to strengthen the Russian state domestically by instituting higher educational requirements for bureaucrats, a tax on noble landowners, and a code of civil laws inspired by the Napoleonic Code. The nobles retaliated by attacking him as an enemy of the nobility and traitor to the nation; this perception, so they claimed, was shared by the lower classes as well.[8] Alexander's other chief aide was War Minister Aleksei Arakcheev, who sought to modernize the army but was disliked as a brutal martinet.[9] Both Speranskii and Arakcheev, who were in many ways opposites, found that their efforts to strengthen the state met with wide noble opposition.

Speranskii's reforms also faced an antagonistic zeitgeist. Russian elite culture took a nationalistic turn as it worked out the implications of the Enlightenment and responded to French imperialism. Literati increasingly identified "Russian" values—monarchism, Orthodoxy, refusal to ape foreign ways—as attributes of the model citizen. This did not imply a social reorientation of the imperial social project, for it was the middling sort, not the Westernized aristocracy or the unfree peasantry, that were imagined as archetypally "Russian." However, the imperial social project required a new rhetoric that could justify it as arising from the nation and its history, not as a top-down effort to acculturate Russians into European civilization.

Moscow was an important center of opposition to Speranskii, for its aristocrats and literati fancied themselves spokesmen of authentic national values. One prominent critic was Karamzin, who worried that the Petrine reforms had weakened Russians' esteem for their own heritage and thereby sapped their civic solidarity. The nation required a civil society with a restored sense of nationality, he argued, but these goals were in jeopardy owing to the pressures of war and

---

[7] On Napoleon as a role model for Alexander, see Wortman, *Scenarios of Power*, 1:206, 210, 216.

[8] Marc Raeff, *Michael Speransky, Statesman of Imperial Russia, 1772–1839* (2nd edn., The Hague: Martinus Nijhoff, 1969), 64–5, 68–9, 104; "Iz pisem Aleksandra Iakovlevicha Bulgakova" (part 2), 19; Dmitrii Zavalishin, "Tysiacha vosem'sot dvenadtsatyi god (Iz vospominanii sovremennika)," *MV* (8 March 1884); [A. Bestuzhev-Riumin], "Kratkoe opisanie proisshestviiam v stolitse Moskve v 1812 godu," *ChOIDR*, 29/2 (April–June 1859), "Smes'," 65–92, here: 72.

[9] Lieven, *Russia against Napoleon*, 102–5.

reforms that imitated the institutions of foreign countries. In the *Memoir on Ancient and Modern Russia*, which Karamzin submitted to Alexander I in 1811, he criticized recent or projected reforms that included a university system on the German model, a civil code inspired by that of Napoleon, and the emancipation of a serf population that was unprepared for the responsibilities of citizenship.[10]

Whereas Karamzin stressed the fragility of civil society, it was the fraying bonds farther down the social hierarchy that worried Ivan Lopukhin (1756–1816). Lopukhin was a leading Moscow Freemason, and, like Karamzin and Glinka, a believer in the universal brotherhood of man. However, his long service in the criminal-justice system (first as judge, then as senator) left him with few illusions about the reality of Russian social relations. During the 1805–7 war, when he was sent to inspect troops levied for the wartime militia, he warned the tsar that mobilization was not creating national unity. Moscow's poorer merchants, he reported, were shedding "tears of despair" at the financial demands they faced, and people in and around Moscow resented what they considered their unfair share of the militia levies. The people mistakenly took the creation of the militia as evidence that the enemy was already deep inside Russia, and they neither understood nor believed the official claim that militia service, unlike conscription into the army, was only for the duration of the war and did not free a man from serfdom. Lopukhin fretted that agents of Napoleon would be able to "seduce the common people." He also distrusted the "sham enlightenment, founded on unbelief," of the nobles and literati, and he feared that abusive behavior by militia officials would trigger unrest among the peasantry.[11]

With war appearing increasingly likely, Alexander yielded to the growing political pressure and dismissed Speranskii from his post as state secretary on 17 March 1812. Karamzin was considered as a possible successor before the post was given instead to Admiral Aleksandr Shishkov, another emblematic figure of the emerging Russian nationalism.[12] On 29 May 1812, Alexander appointed as governor-general of Moscow another nationalistic grumbler, this one a man who particularly irritated him: Count Fedor Rostopchin.[13]

Rostopchin (1763–1826), an admirer and erstwhile adviser of Paul I, was a hard man with a keen mind, caustic wit, and skeptical view of humanity. He

---

[10] Pipes, *Karamzin's Memoir*, 158, 166, 184.

[11] I. V. Lopukhin, *Zapiski senatora I. V. Lopukhina* (1859; repr. edn., Moscow: Nauka, 1990), 170–87, quotations on 170, 177, 178.

[12] Ia. K. Grot, "Ocherk deiatel'nosti i lichnosti Karamzina," cited in A. S. Shishkov, *Zapiski, mneniia i perepiska*, 2 vols. (Berlin: B. Behr's Buchhandlung, 1870), 1:123; see also the chapter "Dva kandidata na rol' gosudarstvennogo ideologa? De Mestr i Karamzin," in M. I. Degtiareva, *Zhozef de Mestr i ego russkie "sobesedniki": Opyt filosofskoi biografii i intellektual'nye sviazi v Rossii* (Perm': Aster, 2007), 192–223.

[13] N. K. Shil'der, *Imperator Aleksandr I: Ego zhizn' i tsarstvovanie*, 4 vols. (St Petersburg: A. S. Suvorin, 1897–8), 3:67. On Rostopchin, see Martin, *Romantics, Reformers, Reactionaries*, chs. 3–5; a well-researched but apologetic study is A. O. Meshcheriakova, *F. V. Rostopchin: U osnovaniia konservatizma i natsionalizma v Rossii* (Voronezh: Izdatel'skii dom "Kitezh," 2007).

shared the cosmopolitan culture and increasing nationalism of Karamzin, to whom he was related by marriage, but not his faith in the perfectibility of society.[14] As an habitué of the St Petersburg court and (after Paul's overthrow) the salons of Moscow, he thought he knew what aristocrats were: weak-willed, self-important windbags. The rest of the year he lived on his country estate near Moscow,[15] where he observed his serfs and concluded that the common people were tough, coarse, and volatile. What he did *not* discern was any sign that an enlightened urban culture could build a broad, stable social base for the regime.

Rostopchin doubted that Moscow's state institutions created genuine social cohesion. The police, he wrote, were "depraved men and scoundrels, underpaid, despised."[16] The workhouse, designed for rehabilitation through labor? It only taught petty offenders to become hardened criminals; better, he wrote to Alexander I, to draft them into the army.[17] The lunatic asylum? As governor-general, so he later recalled with glee, he sent rumormongers there "for treatment, that is, they were daily given cold showers, and on Saturdays they were made to swallow medication."[18]

He likewise had little respect for public venues of culture and sociability. For example, he considered the masonic lodges to be seditious conspiracies, in cahoots with Napoleon.[19] The shops of Kuznetskii Most spread decadence and subversion. Restaurants, he agreed with Glinka and Shalikov, "are schools for debauchery. They offer music, billiards, Gypsies, buffets, and girls, and there is drink, gambling, and disease for everyone from peasants to officers."[20]

Order rested on serfdom and on the bonds of family. The greatest families, those of the aristocracy, formed the glue that held society together. Rostopchin later wrote that

---

[14] *Matériaux en grande partie inédits pour la biographie future du Comte Théodore Rastaptchine rassemblés par son fils* (Brussels: M.-J. Poot, 1864), 315; Viktor Zhivov, "Chuvstvitel'nyi natsionalizm: Karamzin, Rostopchin, natsional'nyi suverenitet i poiski natsional'noi identichnosti," *Novoe Literaturnoe Obozrenie*, no. 91 (2008), 114–40.

[15] Lydie Rostoptchine, *Les Rostoptchine* (n.p.: Balland, 1984), 28.

[16] F. V. Rostopchin, "Tysiacha vosem'sot dvenadtsatyi god v Zapiskakh grafa F. V. Rostopchina," *RS*, 64 (December 1889), 643–725, here: 665.

[17] Letter to anonymous, 10 September 1810, in "Novo-naidennyia bumagi grafa F. V. Rostopchina," *RA*, kniga 3, vypusk 1 (1881), 215–27, here: 219. In the summer of 1812, he repeated this proposal and obtained the tsar's consent: N. Dubrovin, ed., *Otechestvennaia voina v pis'makh sovremennikov (1812–1815 gg.)* (St Petersburg: Tipografiia Imperatorskoi Akademii Nauk, 1882), 13, 32.

[18] Rostopchin, "Tysiacha vosem'sot dvenadtsatyi god," 689. According to Michel Foucault, cold showers, long in use as remedies for mental illness, were employed by psychiatrists from the 1790s on as a disciplinary measure to punish unruly mental patients. Rostopchin's use of psychiatry for social control thus has a distinctly modern quality. Michel Foucault, *Madness and Civilization: A History of Insanity in the Age of Reason*, tr. Richard Howard (New York: Vintage Books, 1988), 266–7.

[19] "Zapiska o Martinistakh, predstavlennaia v 1811 godu grafom Rostopchinym velikoi kniagine Ekaterine Pavlovne," *RA*, 13/3 (1875), 75–81.

[20] "Novo-naidennyia bumagi," 217.

The wars fought in Italy and Germany [in 1799–1807] disrupted ancient habits and introduced new customs. Hospitality—one of the Russian virtues—began to disappear, under the pretext of economy but in fact as a consequence of selfishness. Restaurants and hotels multiplied, and their number grew along with the increasing difficulty of coming to dinner uninvited or of staying with relatives or friends . . . What also disappeared was the grand style of living that they [the aristocracy] had preserved since the beginning of Catherine's reign.[21]

Moscow, he wrote in 1810, was a powder keg:

Day and night, [the lower classes] now mingle ceaselessly in restaurants with people whose outlook, ideas, and talk inspire an impertinence that did not previously exist among the people. At the first commotion, crowds of people will appear, with leaders ready for action who will be driven by their own motivations and perhaps also by promises from others. It will start with the robbing and killing of foreigners (at whom the people are angry); next will be the revolt of the nobility's servants, the death of their lords, and the sacking of Moscow.

The police were feeble, Rostopchin continued, and the lower classes had shown their volatility in the plague revolt. The costly wars, the corruption of the officials, the crisis of the economy,

and most of all the example of the French Revolution and the terror that grips everyone at the successes and boundless prospects of Napoleon, produce dejection among the loyal, indifference among fools, and in the rest, freethinking . . . The gang of the Martinists [i.e. Freemasons]—who have their members in high places, their preachers in society, and their confederates everywhere—is working secretly toward its goal, and by destroying authority is preparing to establish its own power.[22]

Rostopchin disputed the rationality of popular opinion, but because he was alive to its power, he took up political pamphleteering. His strategy was to appeal to the presumed xenophobia and anti-intellectualism of the middling sort, thereby showing that the imperial social project could be detached from its roots in the Enlightenment. In his tracts, he posed as a country squire who was all folksy colloquialisms, nationalistic belligerence, good Russian common sense, and populist disdain for Frenchified aristocratic fops. At a time when few Russian journals achieved circulations over 1,000, the pamphlet that made him famous—*Thoughts Aloud on the Staircase of Honor* (*Mysli vslukh na krasnom kryl'tse*, 1807)—apparently sold 7,000 copies and was widely read among non-nobles.[23]

---

21 Rostopchin, "Tysiacha vosem'sot dvenadtsatyi god," 661–2.
22 "Novo-naidennyia bumagi," 220–1.
23 B. N. Bochkarev, "Konservatory i natsionalisty v Rossii v nachale XIX v.," in A. K. Dzhivelegov, S. P. Mel'gunov, and V. I. Picheta, eds., *Otechestvennaia voina i russkoe obshchestvo*, 7 vols. (Moscow: Izdanie T-va I. D. Sytina, 1911–12), 2:206; "Rostopchin, Graf Fedor Vasil'evich," in D. N. Bantysh-Kamenskii, ed., *Slovar' dostopamiatnykh liudei russkoi zemli*, 3 vols. (St Petersburg: Tipografiia Karla Kraiia, 1847), 3:106–75, here: 122.

On 12 June 1812 (or 24 June, by the Gregorian calendar used in the West), Napoleon's *Grande Armée* crossed the Russian border, and the war was on. Rostopchin swiftly launched an aggressive propaganda campaign. No later than 22 June, he began issuing almost daily news bulletins that were printed in the official *Moscow Gazette* or Glinka's *Russian Messenger*, distributed as leaflets to private homes, or read by town criers.[24] This was an innovative attempt to disseminate information and influence opinion. There were precedents, such as the announcements and edicts that were read by police criers or by priests in church. Another model is suggested by the fact that people called his bulletins *afishi*, like the bills announcing new theater performances that were distributed to private homes.[25] Some of Rostopchin's bulletins reproduced messages from the government, the bishop of Moscow, military headquarters, and other authorities, but twenty-three are known to have been written or at least edited by Rostopchin himself.[26] Most were terse news communiqués, but eight were appeals to the lower classes, written in his trademark folksy style and calling for resistance to the enemy and loyalty to the authorities.[27]

On 19 July, five weeks into the war, Rostopchin summoned Glinka. Aleksandr Bulgakov, Rostopchin's aide, probably echoed his chief's views when he described Glinka and his brothers condescendingly as "a race of honest people" who were "rabid patriots."[28] As Glinka told the story twenty-four years later, Rostopchin informed him that "in the holy name of the sovereign emperor I untie your tongue for all that is of use to the fatherland." He also offered Glinka a subsidy of 300,000 rubles—a princely figure, considering that five years later, Glinka had to beg the government for 5,000 rubles that he said would suffice to have his writings printed.[29]

Unlike Rostopchin, Glinka welcomed the disruption of the status quo that war was likely to produce. This was due to his peculiar way of experiencing and imagining the city. Rostopchin, to judge by his writings, was interested in Moscow street life only when he needed to project power. Like the French elites of the *ancien régime*, Moscow aristocrats preferred to travel by carriage, the better to signal their wealth and status and avoid the grime, crowds, and unpredictability of the streets. Rostopchin, too, moved about in the comfort and isolation of his carriage. As governor-general, he thought that showing up in widely separated places within a short interval of time enhanced his effectiveness by

[24] For a reference to a leaflet being read in public, see: [T. Tolycheva], "Razskazy ochevidtsev o dvenadtsatom gode: V Rozhdestvenskom monastyre," *MV* (25 March 1872).

[25] Aleksandr Popov, "Moskva v 1812 godu," part 2: *RA* 2/8 (1875), 369–402, here: 389.

[26] P. A. Kartavov, ed., *Rostopchinskie afishi* (St Petersburg: Kommercheskaia Tipo-Litografiia M. Vilenchika, 1904), iv.

[27] Kartavov, *Rostopchinskie afishi*, 13, 44, 51, 52, 58, 60, 64, 75.

[28] "Iz pisem Aleksandra Iakovlevicha Bulgakova," part 4: *RA*, 2/7 (1900), 294–329, here: 297.

[29] S. N. Glinka, *Zapiski o 1812 gode* (St Petersburg: V tipografii Imperatorskoi Rossiiskoi Akademii, 1836), 28; "Pros'ba S. N. Glinki o vydache emu posobiia na izdanie ego sochinenii," *RS*, 107 (September 1901), 480.

awing the people and allowing him to take stock of conditions in the city.[30] Glinka, on the other hand, walked. Every morning, according to his memoirs, he would leave his home, in a plebeian area in Novinskaia District, on strolls that brought him "close to the people; I lived with the people in the streets, the squares, the markets; everywhere within Moscow and the surroundings of Moscow." As a result, he claimed, the people knew him and accepted him as their leader.[31]

If Rostopchin thought like a French aristocrat of the *ancien régime*, Glinka's models were the critics of the *ancien régime*: Rousseau, who hiked in the countryside to commune with nature, and Mercier, who roamed the streets of Paris to experience the bustle of the city.[32] Glinka was more Rousseau than Mercier inasmuch as what drew him out the door was not the ever-shifting kaleidoscope of the metropolis but the timeless Russian essence that he, like Tolstoi in *War and Peace*, thought Moscow embodied.[33] Anticipating *War and Peace*, he felt that leaders like Rostopchin did not understand this essence because they were isolated from the people. Their statistical studies, Glinka argued, failed to penetrate the people's soul, and they erred when they ridiculed the people for mangling foreign words or when they misread their anti-Napoleonic resistance as sedition or xenophobic hate. He also felt personally insulted that Rostopchin alternately tried to buy his services as a propagandist and sent the police after him as though his loyalty were under suspicion.[34] Glinka, by his own estimation, could bond with the people because he had forsworn the privileges of his class. As he describes it in his various memoirs, he had repudiated the lifestyle of the country squire and the hierarchies of wealth and service—he had married for love (not money or status), refused to own serfs, declined a career in government service, and refused to spend Rostopchin's subsidies for the *Russian Messenger*.

Glinka saw the war as a providential mystery in which Napoleon, a great genius corrupted by power and hubris, confronted a "Russian spirit" whose governing principles were love and humility.[35] If the war revealed to Russians the "Russian spirit" that united them, there was hope that they might at last transcend their bitter class antagonisms. Glinka had glimpsed this possibility as a militia officer during the 1805–7 war, and it motivated his subsequent campaign, in the *Russian Messenger*, to promote martial pride and hostility to the French-oriented culture of the aristocracy.

From 11 to 19 July 1812, Alexander I visited Moscow. On the morning of the 11th, a large crowd formed to welcome the tsar. "I followed after them," Glinka wrote later, "out of a desire to listen to the people's opinion and add another

---

[30] Turcot, *Le promeneur à Paris*, 34–6; Rostopchin, "Tysiacha vosem'sot dvenadtsatyi god," 656.

[31] Glinka, *Zapiski o 1812 gode*, 9, 26, 42, quotation on 42.

[32] Turcot, *Le promeneur à Paris*, 100–2, 393–6, 405.

[33] On *War and Peace*, see Maiorova, *From the Shadow of Empire*, 144, 151–2.

[34] Glinka, *Zapiski o 1812 gode*, ix, 10, 15, 21, 33–4, 42.

[35] Martin, *Romantics, Reformers, Reactionaries*, 135–6.

article for the *Russian Messenger*." When the people recognized him and asked him to lead them, "I cried: *Hurrah! Forward!* And thousands of voices repeated: *Hurrah! Forward.*" This bond with the people gave him prophetic powers, so that at the tsar's subsequent meeting with the Moscow nobility at the Slobodskoi Palace, Glinka could foretell that Moscow would fall and thereby seal Napoleon's doom.[36]

Rostopchin's retrospective account of the tsar's visit, and of his meeting with separate assemblies of nobles and merchants, was rather different. Rostopchin recalled with satisfaction that he had deployed police to intimidate nobles whom he thought likely to ask critical questions, and he was bemused at the pathos with which the merchants received the tsar's appeal for sacrifice: "It was, in its own way, a unique spectacle, for the Russian expressed his feelings freely, and forgetting that he was a slave, he rose in anger at being threatened with chains that a foreigner was preparing."[37]

Unlike Glinka, Rostopchin saw Muscovites as a volatile mob whose xenophobia he had to both stoke and control. He made a public spectacle of herding dozens of allegedly disloyal foreign residents onto a barge for deportation from the city.[38] He also leveled groundless accusations of treason at the Freemason Fedor Kliucharev, who was the director of the Moscow Post Office and hence an important figure in Russia's system of censorship and domestic intelligence-gathering.[39] His weapon against Kliucharev was a young merchant's son named Vereshchagin, who was found in possession of Napoleonic propaganda from foreign newspapers that the post office was supposed to intercept. Rostopchin arbitrarily expelled Kliucharev from Moscow, denounced Vereshchagin in one of his published bulletins, and asked the tsar to sentence him to death and then, just before the execution, commute the sentence to hard labor. The tsar refused, but as the French entered the city on 2 September, Rostopchin's last act before leaving was to declare Vereshchagin a traitor and hand him over to a frenzied mob.[40] He had earlier tried to have the disgraced Speranskii sent to Moscow; according to a study by Andrei Zorin, the dramatic lynching of Vereshchagin had in fact been intended for the "traitor" Speranskii.[41]

As the divergent views of Karamzin, Lopukhin, Rostopchin, and Glinka attest, Moscow's elites disagreed whether the war was a threat to Russia's social harmony or on the contrary an opportunity to forge a new national solidarity. The experience of the people of Moscow in 1812 would put these theories to the test.

---

[36] Glinka, *Zapiski o 1812 gode*, 7, 18–19, quotations on 7, 9.

[37] Rostopchin, "Tysiacha vosem'sot dvenadtsatyi god," 673–4, quotation on 674.

[38] Popov, "Moskva v 1812 godu," part 4: *RA*, 4/10 (1875), 129–97, here: 131–3.

[39] Popov, "Moskva v 1812 godu" (part 2), 383.

[40] Martin, *Romantics, Reformers, Reactionaries*, 129–30; Dubrovin, *Otechestvennaia voina v pis'makh sovremennikov*, 90, 111.

[41] Zorin, *Kormia dvuglavogo orla*, 230–7; "F. V. Rostopchin," in A. Kizevetter, *Istoricheskie otkliki* (Moscow: Izdatel'stvo K. F. Nekrasova, 1915), 25–186, here: 184.

THINGS FALL APART

On the eve of the war, Muscovites with ties to the government were aware of the brewing crisis with France,[42] but for most others the invasion came as a surprise. Some recalled that they knew nothing of international affairs.[43] Many falsely expected British or other foreign troops to come to the rescue, and initially some even mistook Napoleon's troops for allies of the Russians.[44] As the French marched eastward across Russia, lack of knowledge aggravated the widespread panic throughout the war zone and intensified the mass exodus of the population. According to the officer's wife Anna Zolotukhina, Russians heard that the French "were pillaging and burning, and destroying the shrines of God." The fear was contagious: "None of us knew what to do . . . our kin were preparing to leave; many neighbors had already left." The scorched-earth tactics of the Russian side were an additional factor. "Everywhere there were many marauders," Zolotukhina noted. "The Cossacks . . . were frightening people that the French were near and ordered villages to be burned, while they themselves looted."[45] The fall of Smolensk on 6 August provided a grim preview of what later occurred in Moscow: the population fled and a firestorm incinerated the city, including, as in Moscow a month later, thousands of wounded left behind by the Russian army.[46]

The refugees spread the panic eastward.[47] Beginning in mid-August, Rostopchin ordered the evacuation of government offices from Moscow,[48] but his public stance remained confident. On 13 August, his aide Bulgakov wrote in a letter that the fall of Smolensk was causing panic in Moscow, with the result that

[42] See, for example: "Iz pisem Aleksandra Iakovlevicha Bulgakova," part 1: *RA*, 1/4 (1900), 493–518, here: 495, 500, 506; part 4, 12–13, 16; [Bestuzhev-Riumin], "Kratkoe opisanie," 66.

[43] See, for example: Leont'eva, "Zapiski" (part 2), 878–9.

[44] A. G. Khomutova, "Vospominaniia A. G. Khomutovoi o Moskve v 1812 godu," *RA*, vol. 3 (1891), 309–28, here: 323; "Razskaz ieromonakha Chudova monastyria, ottsa Pavla (v miru Petr Grigor'evich Borovskii)," in [T. Tolycheva], "Razskazy ochevidtsev o dvenadtsatom gode," *Russkii Vestnik*, vol. 102 (November 1872) [henceforth cited as: Tolycheva, "Razskazy ochevidtsev" (1872)], 266–304, here: 281; "Razskaz nabilkinskoi bogadelenki, Anny Andreevny Sozonovoi, byvshei krepostnoi Vasil'ia Titovicha Lepekhina," in Tolycheva, "Razskazy ochevidtsev" (1872), 286; A. Lebedev, "Iz razskazov rodnykh o 1812 gode (Izvlechenie iz semeinykh zapisok)," in Shchukin, *Bumagi*, 3:260; "Moskovskii Novodevichii monastyr' v 1812 godu: Razskaz ochevidtsa—shtatnago sluzhitelia Semena Klimycha," *RA* (1864), cols. 843–58, here: 845; T. Tolycheva, "Razskaz Leontiia Petrovicha Lepeshkina," *MV* (8 January 1880); [T. Tolycheva], "Razskazy ochevidtsev o dvenadtsatom gode: V Zubove," *MV* (7 February 1872).

[45] A. I. Zolotukhina, "Dvenadtsatyi god v zapiskakh Anny Il'inishny Zolotukhinoi (1812 g.)," *RS*, vol. 64 (October–December 1889), 257–88, here: 260, 262, 264; see also 274. On the destruction of villages by the retreating Russian army, see E. V. Tarle, *1812 god: Izbrannye proizvedeniia* (Moscow: Pressa, 1994), 129; Anatolii Shakhanov, ed., "Moskovskaia politsiia v 1812 g.: Raport ober-politsmeistera P. I. Ivashkina na imia glavnokomanduiushchego v Moskve A. P. Tormasova," *Istoricheskii Arkhiv*, no. 3 (2003), 162–5, here: 162.

[46] Tarle, *1812 god*, 120.

[47] Le Cointe, *Moscou avant et après l'incendie*, 130; Kazantsev, "Zhizn'" (part 1), 70.

[48] Meshcheriakova, *F. V. Rostopchin*, 187; F. Biuler, "Moskovskii Arkhiv Kollegii Inostrannykh Del," *RA*, 4/11 (1875), 289–96, here: 291.

"the wenches, male and female, have been running away and losing their heads; everyone is leaving." As for himself, Bulgakov declared that "I swear that Bonaparte won't see Moscow," but he added that he was moving his own family to safety, just in case.[49] In a similar vein, Rostopchin, in a bulletin a few days before the battle of Borodino, denounced the effeminate rich: "I am actually glad that noble ladies and merchant wives are leaving Moscow so they can feel safe. [This will mean] less panic, less gossip; but one cannot praise their husbands, brothers, and kinsmen" who were also leaving. He went on to tout the strength of the army, and if that should fail, "Then I say: now, Militia of Moscow! Let us go, too! And let us march forth, a hundred thousand stout fighters, taking with us the [wonderworking icon of the] Iverskaia Mother of God and 150 cannon, and let all of us together put an end to this business."[50]

On Monday, 26 August, the armies clashed in the titanic but inconclusive battle at Borodino. Even in Moscow, 115 kilometers away, people heard the thunderous roar of the more than 1,200 cannon.[51] Four days later, on Friday, 30 August, Rostopchin's bulletin reported General Kutuzov's assurances "that he will defend Moscow to the last drop of blood; and he is prepared, if need be, to fight in the streets. As for you, brothers, don't worry that the government offices are closed; there is still business to take care of, and we will settle accounts with the villains on our own." That day or the next, he called on the people to take up arms: "I will be with you, and together we will destroy the villains."[52]

But Kutuzov kept retreating, and no last-ditch defense was mounted. Instead, one eyewitness recalled, "Moscow soon grew empty." The affluent snapped up the remaining horses, leaving the rest to flee with pushcarts.[53] Travel permits issued by the police suggest the variety and vagueness of people's destinations. "To the town of Vladimir and wherever she [the bearer] will require." "To the town of Riazhsk and elsewhere." "To Kolomna and beyond." "To Kostroma Province and wherever necessary." "To various towns." "To Russian towns."[54]

Anarchy engulfed the city. Later that fall, the director of the Foundling Home, Ivan Tutolmin, reported:

On 31 August, Saturday, the suburban house of the Foundling Home . . . was looted by advance forces of our Cossacks.

On 1 September, Sunday, after entering Moscow, our forces smashed the alehouses; the common people burst into them, hauled away the liquor in buckets and jugs, and got

[49] "Iz pisem Aleksandra Iakovlevicha Bulgakova" (part 2), 32.

[50] Kartavov, *Rostopchinskie afishi*, 51.

[51] [T. Tolycheva], "Razskazy ochevidtsev o dvenadtsatom gode: V Strastnom monastyre," *MV* (14 February 1872); Lieven, *Russia against Napoleon*, 194, 203.

[52] Kartavov, *Rostopchinskie afishi*, 58, 60.

[53] [K. Bauer] K. B . . . r, "Vospominanie o dvenadtsatom gode v Moskve," *Atenei*, no. 2 (1858), 119–34, here: 119.

[54] OPI GIM f. 160, ed. khr. 193, ll. 27–27 ob.

drunk. All the government offices, and most of the well-to-do inhabitants, had left the city a few days earlier.[55]

A cleric who left in the early hours of Monday, 2 September, recalled that

it seemed that the entire city was in constant movement, while the glow from the direction of Mozhaisk [near Borodino] so illumined half the sky that it was light in the streets. . . . All the carriages hastening to leave made it so noisy in the streets that it was impossible to understand what anyone said. There was hardly any room to move, and everyone was trying to push ahead of the others.[56]

Later that day, after the murder of Vereshchagin, Rostopchin joined the army in abandoning the city, followed by most of the remaining inhabitants. Napoleon's *Grande Armée* was close on their heels. As late as that morning, reported an army officer passing through Moscow, it was not clear that the French were about to enter the city.[57] A noblewoman wrote later that autumn that "we were assured by the government that there was no danger," but as the French entered the city, friends urged her to leave. "We went only in what we were wearing; in utter despair we took leave of our home and all our possessions, which stayed behind to be looted by our enemies; we were completely dazed, and all we heard was the military police coming to the gate and shouting, hurry, they are already in the city."[58]

Poorer Muscovites felt little sympathy for the plight of their betters. In one of the first published accounts of the occupation, a merchant in 1813 wrote that "all rushed to find shelter from those [French] monsters, but the poor were forced to stay and breathe the same air with them. I did not escape that misfortune."[59] Later testimonies were even blunter. According to one priest's son, "The people grew agitated and said that the nobles were saving their own skins while surrendering them [the people] and the metropolis itself to Napoleon."[60] A townsman

---

[55] "Moskovskii Vospitatel'nyi Dom v 1812 godu," *RA*, vol. 3 (1900), 457–75, here: 462.

[56] [Archimandrite Lavrentii], "Zapiski ochevidtsa o sokhranenii dragotsennostei Nikolaevskago Perervinskago monastyria, i o dostopamiatnykh sobytiiakh v sei obiteli v 1812 godu," *Maiak*, vol. 2, kniga 4 (1842), section "Zamechatel'," 53–67, here: 57–8.

[57] A. P. Kapitonov, ed., "Moskva v 1812 g. (Raport starshego ad'iutanta N. Ia. Butkovskogo)," *Rossiiskii Arkhiv*, 2–3 (1992), 68–72, here: 71.

[58] Tat'iana A. Iakovleva to Ol'ga Petrovna, 12 November 1812, in "Gore moskovskikh zhitelei v 1812 g. (sovremennyia pis'ma)," *RS*, 154 (April–June 1913), 61–5, here: 61–2. Other nobles who voiced similar complaints about being misled by Rostopchin's propaganda include: Petr Volkonskii, "U frantsuzov v Moskovskom plenu 1812 goda," *RA*, no. 11 (1905), 351–9, esp. 352; S. A. Vsevolozhskii, quoted in "Imprimerie Impériale de la Grande Armée," in T. Tolycheva, *Razskazy ochevidtsev o dvenadtsatom gode* (2nd edn., Moscow: Tipografiia G. Lissnera i D. Sobko, 1912), 20; [Bestuzhev-Riumin], "Kratkoe opisanie," 78, 83; "Otryvok iz rukopisi 'Istoriia moei zhizni' otstavnago general-maiora Sergeia Ivanovicha Mosolova," in Shchukin, *Bumagi*, 8:336; Mikhail Evreinov, "Pamiat' o 1812 gode," *RA*, 1/1 (1874), cols. 95–110, here: 100.

[59] [Petr Zhdanov], *Pamiatnik Frantsuzam, ili Prikliucheniia Moskovskago Zhitelia P . . . Zh . . .* (St Petersburg: Tipografiia I. Baikova, 1813), 4.

[60] [T. Tolycheva], "Razskazy ochevidtsev o dvenadtsatom gode: Na Mokhovoi," *MV* (1 March 1872). For a similar view, see Adam Glushkovskii, "Moskva v 1812 godu: Iz zapisok Adama Glushkovskogo," *Krasnyi Arkhiv*, vol. 4 (1937), 121–59, here: 140; report from anon. to Rostopchin,

recalled that because the people had sympathy for women who left the city, male nobles sometimes fled in female disguise, bandaging their sideburns to simulate a toothache.[61] A crippled young nun from a merchant family told of being left behind while "our rich miladies"—nuns of more aristocratic background—headed to safety.[62]

Rostopchin, who had not known that Kutuzov planned to abandon Moscow, became the scapegoat. When the wife of a deacon told her husband that according to the sacristan's wife, the French were already in the city, the husband laughed: "Look at you, he said, foolish woman, you believe the sacristan's wife but you won't believe the governor-general. Look, here's the count's leaflet, I've already read it to you." When moments later he glimpsed a French cavalryman, "he got up, took Rostopchin's leaflet, and tore it to shreds."[63] These last four accounts—the priest's son, the townsman, the crippled nun, and the deacon's wife, all of them from Tolycheva's oral histories—date from the reign of Alexander II, reflecting the longevity of memories formed by the war. Later still, when Nicholas II was tsar, a deacon's son born shortly after the war recounted what he had heard from his parents. After Borodino,

people who were prudent and affluent began leaving the city; people who were not affluent were forced either to stay in Moscow and throw themselves on the mercy of fate, or else run in despair wherever their legs took them. My father, being among the latter, tarried to leave, for he lacked accurate information about the enemy's approach and trusted Rostopchin's promises not to let Napoleon into Moscow—promises that confused everyone."[64]

A catastrophic fire broke out as soon as the French occupied the city. It raged for several days and could be seen from 200 kilometers away.[65] Multiple causes contributed to the disaster. Rostopchin, who had spoken of burning Moscow rather than surrendering it, ordered all fire-fighting equipment removed and instructed the police to set fire to the city. Fires were also set by retreating troops

20 September 1812, in "Novyia podlinnyia cherty iz istorii otechestvenoi voiny 1812 goda," *RA* (1864), cols. 786–842, here: 792.

[61] "Razskaz meshchanina Petra Kondrat'eva," in [Tolycheva], "Razskazy ochevidtsev" (1872), 275–6.

[62] Tolycheva, "V Rozhdestvenskom monastyre."

[63] [T. Tolycheva], "Razskazy ochevidtsev o dvenadtsatom gode: V prikhode Petra i Pavla na Iakimanke i na Orlovom lugu," *MV* (4 March 1872).

[64] N. I. T—v, "O 1812 gode (Vospominaniia iz razskazov sovremennikov i ochevidtsev)," in Shchukin, *Bumagi*, 4:331–46, here: 333. For similar criticisms of Rostopchin's propaganda, see also: [Ioann Mashkov], "1812-i god. Sozhzhenie Moskvy. Pokazaniia ochevidtsa (Protoiereia Kazanskago na Krasnoi ploshchadi sobora)," *RA*, 3/12 (1909), 455–63, esp. 460; [Tolycheva], "V Rozhdestvenskom monastyre"; "Razskaz meshchanina Petra Kondrat'eva," in [Tolycheva], "Razskazy ochevidtsev" (1872), 275; G. N. Kol'chugin, "Zapiska G. N. Kol'chugina," *RA*, 3/9 (1879), 45–62, here: 46; Vishniakov, *Svedeniia*, 2:39.

[65] A. Sverbeev, "Vospominaniia o moskovskikh pozharakh 1812 goda," *VE*, 7-i god, no. 11 (November 1872), 303–20, here: 303.

and departing inhabitants, and they were further spread by Kutuzov's order to burn supply depots, by the campfires of the French, and by the dry, windy weather that broke only on 7 September, when rain and diminishing wind finally helped extinguish the conflagration.[66]

When it was all over, most of the city was reduced to cinders, including nearly the entire downtown. The fire was ferocious. A Napoleonic officer noted in his diary that "The earth's burning, the sky's on fire, we're drowning in a sea of flame."[67] The inhabitants were stunned. "The conflagration flowed in all directions, like a sea of fire," a terrified eyewitness recalled a half-century later.[68] Like the firestorms of World War II, it compounded the terror of heat, smoke, and flame with the power of air currents that sucked oxygen into the conflagration. As one Muscovite reported, "a storm of such strength developed that it would knock a man off his feet."[69] Another wrote, a few months after the events, that "Night fell—the wind intensified—and how could it be otherwise—when the ubiquitous flames disrupted the equilibrium of the atmosphere?"[70] "The fire devoured buildings," recalled a third, "and generated a strong wind; the bursts of fire dancing over the buildings were a horrible and terrifying spectacle to behold."[71] Survivors tried to convey the horror through almost magical-realist details. It was "so bright that at night, one could easily count small coins." The intense heat melted glass and metal, and caused water in wells and buckets to boil and flocks of pigeons to fall from the sky. In a village 30 kilometers away, it rained singed paper.[72] A merchant's daughter was haunted by the memory of her merchant landlady. Urged to leave the burning house, the old lady dressed as though for her own funeral, lit the lamps in front of her icons, and announced calmly that "I've lived my life in this house, and I won't leave it alive." The smoke, she was sure, would suffocate her before the flames could burn her alive.[73]

---

[66] Smirnov, "Pozhar Moskvy," in Bezotosnyi, *Otechestvennaia voina 1812 goda*, 482–3.

[67] Cesare de Laugier, *La Grande Armée* (Paris, 1910), quoted in Paul Britten Austin, *1812: Napoleon in Moscow* (London: Greenhill; Mechanicsburg, Pa.: Stackpole; 1995), 47.

[68] Tolycheva, "V prikhode Petra i Pavla."

[69] "Zapiski moskovskogo zhitelia, zhivushchego v Zapasnom dvortse, o proisshestviiakh v avguste do noiabria 1812 g.," in A. G. Tartakovskii, ed., *1812 god v vospominaniiakh sovremennikov* (Moscow: Nauka, 1995), 51.

[70] [Zhdanov], *Pamiatnik frantsuzam*, 17.

[71] "Moskva v 1812 godu: Opisanie moego prebyvaniia v Moskve vo vremia Frantsuzov, s 1-go po 21-e Sentiabria 1812 goda," *RA*, no. 8 (1896), 521–40, here: 525.

[72] "Vospominaniia starozhila o 1812 gode v strannopriimnom dome grafa Sheremeteva v Moskve," *MV* (29 March 1859); Tolycheva, "V Zubove"; Anton Wilhelm Nordhof, *Die Geschichte der Zerstörung Moskaus im Jahre 1812*, ed. Claus Scharf and Jürgen Kessel (Munich: Haraldt Boldt Verlag im R. Oldenbourg Verlag, 2000), 180; [Mashkov], "1812-i god," 457; Glushkovskii, "Moskva v 1812 godu," 153; Voskresenskii, "Umstvennyi vzor," part 3: *Dushepoleznoe chtenie*, no. 12 (1894), 590–600, here: 593.

[73] [T. Tolycheva], "Razskazy ochevidtsev o dvenadtsatom gode: Razskaz kupchikhi Anny Grigor'evny Kruglovoi, Sheremetevskoi bogadelenkoi," *MV* (13 March 1872).

THE GREAT FEAR

Most Muscovites fled. Landowners and their servants repaired to their estates, many clergymen had kin in other communities, and other people relied on the kindness of strangers. All came into contact with peasants and provincial folk. Like other Europeans displaced by the Napoleonic Wars, they often found hospitality and solidarity, but also fear and animosity.

At the outbreak of the French Revolution in 1789, rural France was haunted by the Great Fear, when villagers imagined that vagrants and bandits were attacking the peasantry at the secret behest of the aristocracy. In 1812, Russian peasants similarly conflated Napoleon's army, Westernized Russians, and resident foreigners into a single frightening menace to their villages.[74] Away from the larger towns and contact with foreigners, people had only the vaguest idea of what to expect from Napoleon. Some hoped that he would bring freedom. On one estate near Moscow, a former house serf later recalled, the peasants announced that "we're with Bonaparte" and sacked the manor house, but they changed their minds after French troops looted their village.[75] More typical seems to have been the recollection of a village priest's son then studying in a small town near Moscow: "They say there was fear in Moscow before the French came, but in the district towns and the villages, I think, the fear was even greater. What stories the common people told each other! Listen to enough of those tales, and you couldn't sleep at night."[76]

These terrors compounded the peasants' perennial distrust toward nobles, foreigners, and other outsiders. Nobles and officials worried that agents of Napoleon might incite the people to revolt,[77] but the people had their own suspicions. Hostility toward foreigners was intense and often violent.[78] Russian nobles who were overheard speaking French risked being attacked as spies, as did even Russian clerics coming from Moscow.[79] Peasants were outraged at the

[74] This comparison is suggested by the editors of Nordhof, *Die Geschichte der Zerstörung Moskaus*, 255.

[75] T. Tolycheva, "Razskaz o dvenadtsatom gode Glafiry Klimovny Rozhnovoi, zhivushchei v Pokrovskoi bogadel'ne," *MV* (6 February 1884); see also Tolycheva, "V Strastnom monastyre."

[76] "Razkashchik rannii sviashchennik tserkvi Filippa mitropolita na 3-i Meshchanskoi, Fedor Ivanovich Levitskii," in [Tolycheva], "Razskazy ochevidtsev" (1872), 300.

[77] OPI GIM f. 160, ed. khr. 193, ll. 18–18 ob, letter from Rostopchin to the Zvenigorod marshall of the nobility, 20 July 1812; Leont'eva, "Zapiski" (part 2), 884. Some feared that French POWs might incite peasants to revolt: "Sto let nazad: Pis'ma I. P. Odentalia k A. Ia. Bulgakovu o peterburgskikh novostiakh i slukhakh," *RS*, vol. 151 (July–September 1912), 135–44, here: 144. See also the emphatic relief expressed when the people remained calm: "Griboedovskaia Moskva" (part 1), 588.

[78] Leont'eva, "Zapiski" (part 3), 700; M. I. Makaruev, "Zapiski M. I. Makarueva," in *1812 god v vospominaniiakh, perepiske i rasskazakh sovremennikov* (Moscow: Voennoe izdatel'stvo, 2001), 39; Nordhof, *Die Geschichte der Zerstörung Moskaus*, 118, 135, 143.

[79] "Griboedovskaia Moskva" (part 1), 592, 615; Leont'eva, "Zapiski" (part 3), 706–7; Karolina Pavlova, "Moi vospominaniia," *RA*, 4/10 (1875), 222–40, here: 222; Ismailov, *Vzgliad*, 63; Voskresenskii, "Umstvennyi vzor" (part 3) 597.

cowardice of the upper classes. One noble family fleeing Moscow was stopped by militiamen who insisted that the coachman and the manservant stay behind and fight.[80] A former house serf recalled, a half-century or more after the war, that "the people grumbled very much about the lords, saying they had surrendered Moscow, that they had frittered it away." The same accusations were leveled at the clergy. As late as 1898, A. Lebedev, grandson of a Moscow priest, remembered being told that "the peasants came at [grandfather's family] with bear-spears and threatened to slaughter them all for having 'frittered Moscow away'. They all had to buy their way out with money." When another priest attempted to leave his village with his family, the peasants protested that if he went and they died fighting, they would be left without last rites.[81]

Such resentments rationalized looting. After the French finally withdrew from Moscow, peasants descended on the city—"like locusts," as Lebedev put it in 1898[82]—to take whatever the enemy had left behind. Many eyewitnesses reported such looting. One priest recalled in the 1830s that "They were merciless in pillaging Moscow and proffered all sorts of insults against the inhabitants of Moscow, calling them runaways and traitors, and declared resolutely that whatever the enemy had left behind in Moscow belonged to them." Another priest, a child at the time of the war, heard that his father had returned to find his house still standing, but then "five or so peasants came running to him. 'Where are you going?' they shouted. 'Home,' he answered, 'I am the master of this house.' 'There are no masters here,' one of them screamed."[83] A German physician wrote of a horde of peasants whose leader, a saber-wielding priest, told them that it was no crime to loot the houses of foreigners because they were all traitors. Peasant greed was said to take grisly forms. Nikodim Kazantsev, the sacristan's son, recalled that lethal diseases broke out in his village. The cause, he heard, was that "some stupid peasant" had gone to the nearby Borodino battlefield, and unable to strip the boots from a corpse because the legs were frozen, had hacked off the legs and taken them home to thaw out.[84]

[80] "Razskaz meshchanina Petra Kondrat'eva," in [Tolycheva], "Razskazy ochevitsev" (1872), 276. See also: "Griboedovskaia Moskva" (part 1), 607; Glushkovskii, "Moskva v 1812 godu," 156.

[81] "Razskaz nabilkinskoi bogadelenki, Anny Andreevny Sozonovoi," in [Tolycheva], "Razskazy ochevidtsev" (1872), 291; Lebedev, "Iz razskazov rodnykh," in Shchukin, *Bumagi*, 3:257; "Razskaz popad'i Mar'i Stepanovny Nikol'skoi," in [Tolycheva], "Razskazy ochevidtsev" (1872), 292. The Russian expression rendered here as "frittered away" is *propili na chaiu*.

[82] Lebedev, "Iz razskazov rodnykh," in Shchukin, *Bumagi*, 3:259.

[83] [V. I. Lebedev], "Kratkoe opisanie proizshestvii, byvshikh pri Pokhval'skoi, chto v Bashmakove, tserkvi v 1812 godu," *Chteniia v Obshchestve liubitelei dukhovnago prosveshcheniia*, god 36 (March 1914), 54–76, here: 71; "Razskaz Nikolaia Dmitrievicha Lavrova, sviashchennika tserkvi Spiridoniia, chto na Spiridonovke," in Tolycheva, *Razskazy ochevidtsev* (1912), 110.

[84] Nordhof, *Die Geschichte der Zerstörung Moskaus*, 234; Kazantsev, "Zhizn'" (part 1), 77.

The population that remained in Moscow was socially more homogeneous than before the war. Based on police investigations conducted in 1813, when anyone who had stayed behind was considered a possible traitor, the historian Andrei Tartakovskii extrapolates that 6,238 people, just over 2 percent of the pre-war population of 275,000, were still in the city after the first week or so of the occupation. Since most peasants and many nobles (including most of the wealthy ones) had left, the occupation was witnessed mainly by the groups at the center of the imperial social project. On the basis of data from nine of the city's twenty police districts, Tartakovskii calculates that the clergy and the merchants, who together were only 8.7 percent of the pre-war population, represented 23.1 percent of those who stayed. The two estates most closely related to the merchants—the townspeople and guild artisans—were 9.0 percent before, but 22.5 during, the occupation. The share of nobles diminished slightly, from 7.1 to 6.3 percent, and the peasants dropped from 60.2 to 27.0 percent.[85]

Social tensions had not disappeared. One manifestation was widespread drunkenness, as crowds invaded abandoned taverns. The wealth that was left behind was another flashpoint, and eyewitnesses recalled Russians and Napoleonic soldiers looting side by side.[86]

A further manifestation of class conflict was the popular hostility against anyone who looked foreign. Unlike the aristocracy, the middle strata had no protective retinue of servants, so they were dependent for their safety on the goodwill of the people and the watchfulness of the police. In 1812, their sense of security collapsed. One nobleman, a boarding-school student stranded in the city, felt that "there was more to fear from Russian peasants than from the French." One day he saw

a crowd of peasants coming my way, and as they are walking, each has an iron over his shoulder . . . One says to the other, 'Hey, look, isn't that a Frenchman?' I come up to a church and start to pray, so the other answers him: 'No, he's from here, he's one of ours,' and so the prayer saved me.

Another time, "a sick Frenchman is walking along, a couple of peasants come toward him, and he goes up to them and says: 'Gentlemen, where is the hospital?' One of the peasants glances at him, mutters, 'How long do we have to put up with this!', hits him over the head with an iron bar, and that was that."[87] In Russian propaganda, popular violence against collaborators or isolated enemy

---

[85] A. G. Tartakovskii, "Naselenie Moskvy v period frantsuzskoi okkupatsii," *Istoricheskie Zapiski*, 93 (1973), 356–79.

[86] "Razskaz odnogo iz byvshikh krepostnykh g. Soimonova, starichka Vasiliia Ermolaevicha," in Tolycheva, *Razskazy ochevidtsev* (1912), 68; [Bauer], "Vospominanie," 120; OPI GIM f. 402, d. 239, l. 18 ob, J. A. Rosenstrauch, "Geschichtliche Ereignisse in Moskau *im Jahre 1812*, zur Zeit der Anwesenheit des Feindes in dieser Stadt."

[87] G. Ia. Kozlovskii, "Moskva v 1812 godu zaniataia frantsuzami: Vospominanie ochevidtsa," *RS*, vol. 65 (January–March 1890), 105–14, here: 113. See also: F. Bekker, "Vospominaniia Bekkera o razzorenii i pozhare Moskvy v 1812 g.," *RS*, vol. 38 (April–June 1883), 507–24, here: 514.

soldiers was denied or else portrayed as heroic or humorous,[88] but eyewitnesses of all social backgrounds found the memory of it chilling.

Two threats that Muscovites faced were the fire and their fellow Russians. The third was the Napoleonic army.

NAPOLEON'S ARMY IN MOSCOW

The *Grande Armée* was around 100,000 strong when it reached Moscow.[89] It exuded martial splendor as it marched into the city, but soon its discipline collapsed. Although Russians knew from experience the property disputes, drunken quarrels, and sexual tensions that accompanied the billeting of soldiers among a civilian population, nothing prepared them for what they faced in 1812.

Napoleon's forces had a mixed record in dealing with foreign populations. Inadequate supplies often forced them to live off the land, to the detriment of the population. In general, they showed regard for enemy officers and upper-class civilians, and tried to maintain decorum in foreign cities. On the other hand, they were merciless toward people they considered bandits or benighted savages, as in the Vendée or Spain.[90] In Russia in 1812, they advanced too swiftly for their supplies to keep up, yet the low population density made it impossible to live off the land, the more so as the peasants fled before the oncoming army. Napoleon's men suffered increasing deprivation as they marched through poor, sparsely settled lands where the villages lay abandoned and burned. Exhausted from their marathon campaign, especially after the horror of Borodino, they looked forward to recuperating in Moscow and enjoying the comforts of a civilized city. When they discovered that the Russians had abandoned the city and apparently set fire to it, their hopes were dashed and their image of Russians as savages was confirmed.

The French occupation gave Muscovites a taste of the turmoil that accompanied the European urban revolutions of the long nineteenth century.[91] This was not at all what Napoleon had intended. Napoleon frequently introduced domestic reforms on the French model in countries that he conquered, but in Russia his goal was more limited: to defeat the Russians near the border and

---

[88] See, for example, the excerpts from 1812–13 from the journal *Syn Otechestva* in "Dvenadtsatyi god: Sovremennye razskazy, pis'ma, anekdoty, stikhotvoreniia," *RA* (1876) part 1: 2/7, 302–20, here: 302, 308–10, 314, 316; part 2: 2/8, 387–409, here: 406, 407; Stephen M. Norris, "Images of 1812: Ivan Terebenev and the Russian Wartime *Lubok*," *National Identities*, 7/1 (March 2005), 1–21; Vishlenkova, *Vizual'noe narodovedenie imperii*, 197–8.

[89] Count Philippe-Paul de Ségur, *Napoleon's Russian Campaign*, tr. J. David Townsend (Alexandria, Va.: Time-Life, 1958), 94.

[90] Alan Forrest, *Napoleon's Men: The Soldiers of the Revolution and Empire* (London: Hambledon Continuum, 2006), 122–31.

[91] On this topic, see also: Alexander M. Martin, "The Response of the Population of Moscow to the Napoleonic Occupation of 1812," in Eric Lohr and Marshall Poe, eds., *The Military and Society in Russia, 1450–1917* (Leiden: Brill, 2002), 469–90.

thereby impose his will on Alexander I. Only the Russian army's unexpected retreat drew him into the country's interior, and he voluntarily forfeited a powerful weapon by not proclaiming the abolition of serfdom.[92]

As the French drew near and the Russian population fled, public order in Moscow collapsed. The army began looting as soon as it entered Moscow. Napoleon was concerned about the resulting breakdown of discipline but did not try to stop the looting; instead, he merely ordered his various corps to take turns.[93] Memoirists on both sides described the looting as a "carnival" or "playing Harlequin," implying an archaic but temporary overturning of the social order.[94] Soldiers whose gear was in tatters donned whatever they could find, which shocked Russians accustomed to strict laws linking dress to social status. Some soldiers put on priestly vestments. A merchant saw a cavalryman amuse himself by replacing his helmet with a woman's tiara. Later, when the French were leaving Moscow, he watched them on Red Square: "By now they were past dressing up for fun in tiaras; instead, they bundled themselves in all sorts of clothes. This one wore a woman's hat or bonnet, that one had a towel wrapped around his ears while his lips were blue from cold, and another had nothing on one foot and a boot on the other."[95] Russians too joined in the reversal of roles. A French officer noted the incongruous sight of prostitutes wearing stolen aristocratic finery as they consorted with soldiers, a spectacle that reduced elderly Russians to tears.[96]

Other forms of social authority were attacked as well; none more, perhaps, than religion. Jacobin anticlericalism ran deep in the French armies. In the Vendée and in Spain, they blamed the horrors of guerrilla warfare on the bloodlust of primitive peasants led by obscurantist priests.[97] This anticlericalism resurfaced in Russia. It manifested itself in a systematic desecration of churches that was described by most Russian eyewitness accounts as well as some French ones.[98] The soldiers tore the precious ornaments from icons and vandalized the

[92] Janet M. Hartley, "Russia in 1812, Part I: The French Presence in the *Gubernii* of Smolensk and Mogilev," *Jahrbücher für Geschichte Osteuropas*, 38/2 (1990), 178–98, esp. 178–82.

[93] Ségur, *Napoleon's Russian Campaign*, 115.

[94] "Dvenadtsatyi god: Sovremennye razskazy, pis'ma, anekdoty, stikhotvoreniia" (part 2), 391; Albrecht von Muraldt, *Beresina* (Bern, 1942), quoted in Austin, *1812: Napoleon in Moscow*, 49; Louis-Florimond Fantin des Odoards, *Journal du général Fantin des Odoards, étapes d'un officier de la Grande Armée, 1800–1830* (Paris: Plon, 1895), 337.

[95] "Razskaz Apollona Dmitrievicha Sysoeva, iz kupecheskago zvaniia," in Tolycheva, "Razskazy ochevidtsev" (1872), 273.

[96] L.-J. Vionnet de Maringoné, *Souvenirs d'un ex-Commandant des Grenadiers de la Vieille Garde* (Paris: Edmond Dubois, 1899), 43.

[97] Forrest, *Napoleon's Men*, 93, 127–8; Michael Broers, *Europe under Napoleon* (London: Arnold, 1996), 37, 164.

[98] "Opisanie dostopamiatnykh proisshestvii v moskovskikh monastyriakh vo vremia nashestviia nepriiatelei v 1812 godu," *ChOIDR*, 27/4 (October–December 1858), "Materialy otechestvennyia," 33–50, passim; P...F..., "Nekotorye zamechaniia, uchinennye so vstupleniia v Moskvu frantsuzskikh voisk (i do vybegu ikh iz onoi)," in Tartakovskii, *1812 god v vospominaniiakh*

icons themselves. They paraded in clerical robes and, so it was reported, held drunken parties and even fornicated in churches. According to Russian clerics, the soldiers were discriminating in their anticlericalism, treating monks worse than seminarians,[99] but stopped at nothing to make clergymen reveal the whereabouts of hidden church valuables.[100] Many churches were turned into barracks, stables, and slaughterhouses. This was due not only to anticlericalism but also to practical considerations. Napoleon's troops carried no tents, so their only choice at night was to sleep in the open or find shelter in a building; in Moscow, the residential buildings were mostly wooden and perished in the fire, but the masonry-built churches survived.[101]

In addition to the assault on property and religion, Muscovites witnessed a wholesale reversal of the urban improvements of the previous half-century. One example is the street lights. Urban revolutions in the West were often accompanied by an assault on street lights. In the French Revolution, they were used as makeshift gallows: as the sans-culotte anthem *Ça ira* put it, "Les aristocrates à la lanterne!" In the revolutions of 1830 and 1848, crowds in Paris smashed them because they were tools of police surveillance.[102] Similarly, in Moscow in 1812, thousands of street lights were destroyed or disabled.[103] This undermined authority of any sort. A Russian account noted with satisfaction that the darkness facilitated ambushes of enemy soldiers,[104] but it also contributed to higher crime levels after Russian authority was restored. Napoleon's men used lamp posts to hang suspected arsonists. In some cases, the victims had already been shot by firing squads; these, too, were new to Muscovites, though not to residents of Rome, Madrid, and other cities occupied by Napoleon.[105]

sovremennikov, 29; Eugène Labaume, *Relation circonstanciée de la campagne de Russie* (Paris, 1814), quoted in Austin, *1812: Napoleon in Moscow*, 54.

[99] [Lavrentii], "Zapiski ochevidtsa," 67; "Opisanie dostopamiatnykh proisshestvii v moskovskikh monastyriakh," 44–5.

[100] "Kopiia s vypiski iz pis'ma chinovnika moskovskago pochtamta, Andreia Karfachevskago, 6 noiabria 1812 goda," in Shchukin, *Bumagi*, 5:166.

[101] G. de Faber du Faur, *Campagne de Russie 1812 d'après le journal illustré d'un témoin oculaire* (Paris: Ernest Flamarion, n.d.), 207.

[102] Wolfgang Schivelbusch, "The Policing of Street Lighting," in Alice Kaplan and Kristin Ross, eds., *Everyday Life*, Yale French Studies 73 (New Haven: Yale University Press, 1987), 61–74, here: 65–70.

[103] There were only 5,010 street lights in the early 1820s, compared with nearly 7,000 in 1801: Bychkov, "Istoricheskii ocherk osveshcheniia," 5; Malinovskii, *Obozrenie Moskvy*, 114.

[104] "Dvenadtsatyi god: Sovremennye razskazy" (part 2), 392.

[105] "Pervye dni v sozhzhennoi Moskve: Sentiabr' i oktiabr' 1812-go goda (Pis'mo kn. A. A. Shakhovskago, 1836 g., k A. I. Mikhailovskomu-Danilevskomu)," *RS*, vol. 64 (October–December 1889), 31–55, here: 53; Glushkovskii, "Moskva v 1812 godu," 154; Nordhof, *Die Geschichte der Zerstörung Moskaus*, 182; "Zapiski S. A. Maslova," in *1812 god v vospominaniiakh, perepiske i rasskazakh sovremennikov*, 11; T. Tolycheva, "Razskaz o dvenadtsatom gode bogadel'nika Nabilkinskago zavedeniia Pavla Fedorovicha Gerasimova," *MV* (7 July 1882); François-Joseph d'Ysarn-Villefort, *Relation du séjour des Français à Moscou et de l'incendie de cette ville en 1812 par un habitant de Moscou*, ed. A. Gadaruel (Brussels: Fr.-J. Olivier, 1871), 30–1;

Moscow's sensory environment suffered similar devastation. Some of this was collateral damage from the general collapse of order. Since Catherine II's time, the authorities had sought to eliminate the odor of rotting flesh by removing cemeteries and slaughterhouses and ordering the prompt disposal of dead animals. The war undid this progress. In September and October 1812, Moscow was littered with thousands of corpses and animal carcasses that decomposed in the unseasonably warm weather. The resulting stench was suffocating; one Russian reported that 15 kilometers from Moscow "it is already hard to breathe."[106]

In other ways, the assault on the senses seemed deliberate. Accustomed by their government's propaganda to equate cleanliness with civilization, educated Russians were shocked when the occupying army turned churches into stables and slaughterhouses. The ballet master Adam Glushkovskii, a man who by profession was sensitive to disharmonies of sights and sounds, recalled this scene in the Petrovskii monastery: "hanging from the arms of the chandelier and the walls of the church were carcasses of oxen and hogs, and the floor was covered with the blood of slaughtered sheep and calves; French soldiers of various nationalities, with blood-stained hands, used hatchets to cleave the meat and then hung it on scales and distributed it to soldiers and officials."[107]

Another symptom of the breakdown of order was the sanitary degradation of the city. In Russia as elsewhere in Europe, the elites invoked the common people's physical dirtiness as proof of their civilizational backwardness; it was an attitude that British critics denounced as "the old-school slang of 'Swinish multitude,' 'vulgar herd,' 'unwashed mob,' &c."[108] The poor resented such attitudes. In a feuilleton from the 1840s, a peasant working as a concierge in St Petersburg is required by his master to sweep the courtyard and the street. This causes "matters of cleanliness" to become "hateful and wearisome" to him, and to assert his independence, he keeps his own private quarters dirty and smelly.[109] A more defiant response was to embrace dirtiness as a form of protest. The Russian "nihilists" of the 1860s cultivated an appearance that was intentionally slovenly, and during the Russian Revolution of 1917–21, the people turned abandoned upper-class mansions in St Petersburg into public toilets.[110] In 1812 as well, defecation was perceived by the Russian elites as a weapon in a broader assault on order and propriety. Accounts by nobles report that enemy soldiers

Nicassio, *Imperial City*, 23, 53; Owen Connelly, *Napoleon's Satellite Kingdoms* (New York: Free Press; London: Collier-Macmillan; 1965), 97.

[106] "Griboedovskaia Moskva" (part 1), 613.
[107] Glushkovskii, "Moskva v 1812 godu," 154.
[108] "Morality of the Working Classes," *Chartist Circular*, no. 6 (2 November 1839), 22; see also Cockayne, *Hubbub*, 48–9, 232–3.
[109] Dal', "The Petersburg Yardkeeper," in Nekrasov, *Petersburg*, 63.
[110] Lapin, *Peterburg: Zapakhi i zvuki*, 225.

defecated in churches and threw icons into latrines.[111] Nobles wrote that in
upper-class homes, Napoleon's men broke what they could not steal—furniture
was smashed, mirrors shattered, books ripped apart—and defecated in the
refined interiors. Even officers used ballrooms, libraries, and the like as latrines.[112] According to the aristocrat Mariia Volkova,

If you wish to form an idea about that most educated of nations, who call us barbarians,
take note of the fact that in all the houses where French generals and senior officers lived,
their bedrooms also served as larders, stables, and something even worse. At the Valuevs',
in this respect, they fixed up the house in such a way that you can't breathe, and
everything has to be demolished, and yet those swine lived in there.[113]

If excrement represented the enemy's lack of true civilization, it was also symbolic of his inglorious defeat: when Russian civilians overpowered stray soldiers,
they often dumped the bodies—some of them still alive—into latrines.[114]

Russians' encounter with the enemy was not without complexity, particularly
when they developed a personal rapport with individual soldiers. The *Grande
Armée* offered an object lesson in the diversity of European peoples. Napoleon's
invasion force of 611,000 included around 200,000 men from the territory of
pre-1789 France and another 100,000 or so from the Dutch, Belgian, German,
Swiss, and Italian lands later annexed by France. The remainder comprised
around 130,000 Germans from the Confederation of the Rhine, 90,000 Poles
and Lithuanians, 50,000 Prussians and Austrians, 27,000 Italians, and 9,000
Swiss.[115] Russian memoirists showed varying degrees of awareness of this
diversity. There was agreement that the greatest hostility toward Russians was
displayed by Napoleon's Polish troops; some Russians acknowledged that this
was a response to atrocities committed by the Russians when they suppressed the
Polish uprising of 1794.[116] Unlike the Poles, soldiers from France proper were
recalled (in keeping with conventional Russian stereotypes) as relatively friendly
and benign.[117] Napoleon's German allies were perceived by Russians as a
multitude of smaller contingents (Bavarians, Saxons, and so on), not a single
large nationality; perhaps for this reason, they are rarely mentioned. Other

[111] "Griboedovskaia Moskva" (part 1), 601; "Otryvok iz chernovago pis'ma neizvestnago litsa,"
in Shchukin, *Bumagi*, 3:262; "Kopiia s vypiski iz pis'ma chinovnika moskovskago pochtamta,
Andreia Karfachevskago, 6 noiabria 1812 goda," in Shchukin, *Bumagi*, 5:166.
[112] "Pervye dni v sozhzhennoi Moskve," 49, 52; "Iz pisem Aleksandra Iakovlevicha Bulgakova"
(part 2), 35.
[113] "Griboedovskaia Moskva" (part 1), 615–16.
[114] Volkonskii, "U frantsuzov v Moskovskom plenu," 352; Ysarn, *Relation*, 47.
[115] Forrest, *Napoleon's Men*, 18–19.
[116] See, for example: "Moskva v 1812 godu: Opisanie moego prebyvaniia," 525.
[117] Tolycheva, "Na Mokhovoi"; Tolycheva, "Razskaz kupchikhi Anny Grigor'evny Kruglovoi";
T—v, "O 1812 gode," in Shchukin, *Bumagi*, 4:339; Tolycheva, "V Zubove."

nationalities are mentioned only occasionally, often with the implication that they themselves felt oppressed by Napoleon.[118]

The ability of Muscovites to identify and engage the diverse nationalities of Napoleon's army was due in part to the language skills that many possessed. Many nobles, of course, spoke French, but so did some serf domestics of noble households and Russians who worked for foreign-owned businesses.[119] Clergymen found that the languages taught at seminaries, especially Latin, sometimes allowed them to speak with enemy officers.[120] One memoirist even explained that a certain priest could *not* understand the enemy because he was "rural and uneducated."[121] Thanks in part to such communication, enemy commanders sometimes took Muscovites under their wing—granting requests for safe-conducts, posting sentries at Russians' houses, and protecting Russians in whose homes they lodged.[122]

The occupation exposed Muscovites to grim experiences of a sort associated elsewhere with revolutionary upheavals. Over the coming decades, as eyewitnesses relived the events in their minds, and those who had not been there heard the stories at the dinner table or by the fireside, the memories of 1812 helped shape Muscovites' view of the world in the nineteenth century.

THE POPULAR MEMORY OF THE WAR

N. I. T—v, a Moscow deacon's son born in 1819, recalled near the turn of the twentieth century that when he was a boy, "everywhere, in homes and in the streets, there was talk of nothing but the year '12, and whenever people met, once they had exchanged greetings, the conversation shifted at once to the hated French."[123] As the steady stream of memoirs through the century shows, the war was a collective experience that echoed across generations. It was mostly a civilian experience. Army and militia service fell mainly on the peasantry,[124] so there were few demobilized veterans in post-war Moscow. The main exceptions were nobles who had served as officers, soldiers who were reassigned to the police,

---

[118] See, for example: [Bauer], "Vospominanie," 128.

[119] Tolycheva, "Na Mokhovoi"; "Razskaz nabilkinskoi bogadelenki, Anny Andreevny Sozonovoi," in [Tolycheva], "Razskazy ochevidtsev" (1872), 288.

[120] I. S. Bozhanov, "Tetrad' sviashchennika moskovskago Uspenskago sobora I. S. Bozhanova," in Shchukin, *Bumagi*, 4:57; Tolycheva, "V prikhode Petra i Pavla"; Tolycheva, "V Rozhdestvenskom monastyre"; "Zaniatie frantsuzami Devich'iago monastyria," in Tolycheva, *Razskazy ochevidtsev* (1912), 8; T—v, "O 1812 gode," in Shchukin, *Bumagi*, 4:336, 342; "Moskovskie monastyri vo vremia nashestviia frantsuzov," *RA* (1869), cols. 1387–99, here: col. 1393; Laugier, *La Grande Armée*, quoted in Austin, *1812: Napoleon in Moscow*, 100.

[121] "Moskva v 1812 godu: Opisanie moego prebyvaniia," 533.

[122] See, for example: [Bauer], "Vospominanie," 123; Kozlovskii, "Moskva v 1812 godu," 109.

[123] T—v, "O 1812 gode," in Shchukin, *Bumagi*, 4:332.

[124] Hartley, *Russia, 1762–1825*, 26–8.

and some peasant migrants. Few middling Muscovites knew the horror of combat or the power of army solidarities, told stories of marching across foreign lands and making history, or faced the loneliness of the returning veteran.

History provided no ready template for interpreting what had happened. Moscow and its hinterland had not been invaded by a hostile army since the Time of Troubles 200 years before, so there was no collective memory of war. In one of his bulletins, Rostopchin equated Napoleon with Charles XII of Sweden, whose army Peter the Great had crushed at Poltava in Ukraine,[125] and literati drew analogies with the Polish invasion during the Time of Troubles,[126] but the eyewitness accounts do not make these comparisons. Sometimes they report that people called the French *basurman*, "infidel," a term usually reserved for Muslims. Perhaps this reflected memories of past Tatar invasions, of which the last to reach Moscow was in 1571. However, the authors of these accounts do not attribute the use of *basurman* to themselves or their peers, only to uneducated lower-class people.

Some saw the war through the lens of past Russian rebellions. In 1670–1 and 1773–4, Stepan Razin and Emel'ian Pugachev had led vast uprisings of Cossacks and peasants from the borderlands against the imperial government and the towns. Letters published in a newspaper in 1813 compared Napoleon to Pugachev, and Maxim Gorky quotes his grandfather, a provincial merchant born in the early nineteenth century, as likening Napoleon to Razin and Pugachev in wanting "no lords or civil servants but simply a world without classes" (something the grandfather considered "nonsense").[127] The frequent mentions of rural hostility to urban people and of the general breakdown of order support the impression that peasant revolts and banditry served as a model for thinking about what happened in 1812.

Did revolutions in Europe provide a framework for making sense of the war? If what is meant is a corpus of explicitly political ideas, then the answer seems to be no. Unlike the elites, middling Muscovites rarely used the idiom of bellicose nationalism or denounced godless philosophy, masonic conspiracies, and the like. The parallel between 1812 and a revolution makes more sense, however, if we shift our focus from ideological rhetoric to everyday experience. When Russians tried to convey what had happened in 1812, they reported details or episodes similar to those in foreign texts about urban revolutions. For example, Russians recalled the confusion sown by Rostopchin's bulletins, and Russian propaganda praised the combativeness of peasant women against enemy troops.[128] Similarly,

---

[125] Kartavov, *Rostopchinskiia afishi*, 13.

[126] Zorin, *Kormia dvuglavogo orla*, ch. 5.

[127] "Frantsuzskoe nashestvie: Pis'ma iz Moskvy v Nizhnii Novgorod v 1813 godu," *RA*, 3/10 (1876), 129–54, here: 132, 136. This text first appeared in *Syn Otechestva* and may have been written by I. M. Murav'ev-Apostol; *RA*, 3/10 (1876), 154. Maxim Gorky, *My Childhood*, tr. Ronald Wilks (London: Penguin, 1966), 86.

[128] "Dvenadtsatyi god: Sovremennye razskazy, pis'ma, anekdoty, stikhotvoreniia" (part 1), 315–16; Pavlova, "Moi vospominaniia," 228.

the Austrian journalist Sigmund Engländer noted that Parisians in 1848 wcrc struck by the cacophony of political posters and the allegedly maniacal aggressiveness of female insurgents.[129] Engländer had participated in the 1848 revolutions in Vienna and Paris, so he was well situated to know how urban revolutions appeared to the middle classes; Walter Benjamin, another keen student of urban culture, excerpted these passages from Engländer for his own research on nineteenth-century Paris because he, too, thought they captured something about the cultural memory of 1848. To describe the disintegration of order and decorum in Moscow when the city was evacuated in 1812, a former house serf recalled around 1870 that lower-class people had lain face-down on the pavement to lap up puddles of spilled alcohol. A similar scene, set in Paris in 1789, occurs in Charles Dickens's *A Tale of Two Cities* (1859). Dickens's treatment of the French Revolution built on Thomas Carlyle's interpretation of the original French sources, so Dickens was in effect reworking stories already in circulation.[130]

Proving causal links between stories that circulated in different countries is no easy matter, but there are grounds for thinking that such links existed. For one thing, Russians had become sufficiently similar to other Europeans in their thinking about urban life that they responded in similar ways to its collapse. Another connection is that European culture formed a network in which Russians participated. The tsar's manifestos and Rostopchin's bulletins were written by people of cosmopolitan culture. Likewise, Russian artists who produced wartime caricatures were in dialogue with their counterparts abroad. Certain British images of Napoleon's Russian campaign by George Cruikshank are nearly identical in theme and composition to Russian ones by Ivan Terebenev and Andrei Martynov, and warlike lower-class women appear both in French caricatures of 1789 and in Russian images of 1812. Mass-produced at low prices, these caricatures helped teach Russians to see current events much as other Europeans did.[131]

Foreign ideas also filtered into Russia through French memoirs about 1812. (Tolstoi, for example, used them in his research for *War and Peace* in the 1860s.) One such idea was the fear of bestial proletarian masses rising up from the slums to destroy bourgeois civilization. In the eighteenth century, elites across Europe generally shared the attitude that Andrei Bolotov expressed when he called the participants in the Moscow plague revolt a "stupid, unreasoning, and gullible

[129] Walter Benjamin, *The Arcades Project*, tr. Howard Eiland and Kevin McLaughlin (Cambridge, Mass.: Belknap, 1999), 177, 702. The book cited by Benjamin is Sigmund Engländer, *Geschichte der französischen Arbeiter-Associationen* (Hamburg, 1864).

[130] "Razskaz odnogo iz byvshikh krepostnykh g. Soimonova, starichka Vasiliia Ermolaevicha," in Tolycheva, *Razskazy ochevidtsev* (1912), 68 (this particular narrative was first published in 1872); Charles Dickens, *A Tale of Two Cities* (London: Cathay, 1983), 23 (I thank Julia Douthwaite for drawing my attention to this passage); Alev Baysal, "Carlyle's Influence upon *A Tale of Two Cities* (1859)," *The Victorian Web: Literature, History, & Culture in the Age of Victoria* <http://www.victorianweb.org/authors/dickens/2cities/baysal1.html> accessed 3 July 2011.

[131] Vishlenkova, *Vizual'noe narodovedenie imperii*, 166, 178–81, 196–7.

mob."[132] From the 1790s on, however, the French middle and upper classes grew afraid of the poor, and their earlier disdain turned to hatred and dehumanization. These attitudes may have colored their accounts of the occupation of Moscow. The French were appalled at the burning of Moscow, both because it destroyed their hopes of victory and because of its sheer barbarism. One officer called the convicts whom Rostopchin had supposedly unleashed to set the city ablaze "the scum of that barbarous nation."[133] Another called them "wild animals."[134] A sergeant found them "horrible and disgusting," "sinister," "ignoble," and "dirty."[135] To General de Ségur, they were "wild-looking women and men in rags with hideous faces wandering about in the flames, completing an awful image of hell. These wretched creatures, drunk with wine and the success of their crimes, no longer attempted to conceal themselves, but raced in triumph through the blazing streets." When caught, such people were summarily executed.[136]

Similar anxieties stirred in the Russian imaginary in the nineteenth century. Fire was a familiar scourge of Russian towns, but increasingly it aroused fears of treason and revolt. In May 1862, at a tense time between the abolition of serfdom (1861) and the uprising in Poland (1863), mysterious fires destroyed large commercial areas of St Petersburg. Word spread among the merchants, so the merchant's son Nikolai Leikin later recalled, that Poles (according to another version, radical students) had firebombed the markets, drunken mobs were ransacking the alehouses, and artillery was firing on rebels in the streets.[137] The talk of anarchy and revolution colored how people remembered 1812. For example, one former house serf around 1870 described a drunken riot she had witnessed during the war as "a republic."[138]

In addition to exposing the fragility of the social order, the 1812 war showed that urban civilization was capable of massive regression. Muscovites long remembered the eerie silence and the cold, dark, and insecurity that followed the occupation and the fire. F. Bekker recalled that on the eve of the *Grande Armée's* entry, the church bells failed to call the faithful to vespers. According to the priest Voskresenskii, the stillness during the occupation was punctuated only

[132] Bolotov, *Zhizn' i prikliucheniia*, 3:20.

[133] [Michel Combe], *Mémoires du colonel Combe sur les campagnes de Russie 1812, de Saxe 1813, de France 1814 et 1815* (Paris: Plon, 1896), 108. The Russian authorities sent convicts to set fire to selected locations in Moscow; Smirnov, "Pozhar Moskvy," in Bezotosnyi, *Otechestvennaia voina 1812 goda*, 482.

[134] Léon-G. Pélissier, ed., *Lettres inédites du baron Guillaume Peyrousse écrites à son frère André pendant les campagnes de L'Empire de 1809 à 1814* (Paris: Perrin, 1894), 92.

[135] Adrien Bourgogne, *Mémoires du Sergent Bourgogne*, ed. Gilles Lapouge (n.p.: Arléa, 1992), 19, 21, 43.

[136] Ségur, *Napoleon's Russian Campaign*, 107–8; [Combe], *Mémoires*, 111.

[137] Leikin, "Moi vospominaniia," in Konechnyi, ed., *Peterburgskoe kupechestvo*, 222–3; Abbott Gleason, *Young Russia: The Genesis of Russian Radicalism in the 1860s* (New York: Viking Press, 1980), 166–70.

[138] "Razskaz nabilkinskoi bogadelenki, Anny Andreevny Sozonovoi," in [Tolycheva], "Razskazy ochevidtsev" (1872), 291.

by the cawing of birds and the "unusual barking and howling of the dogs." K. Bauer, a boy at the time, remembered that his family's three "very fierce" dogs spent the occupation mostly cowering under the house.[139] It was also cold. The winter that turned Napoleon's retreat to disaster also struck Moscow, where people huddled in the surviving houses, wrapped in blankets, while the snow blew in through the broken doors and windows.[140] Boarded-up windows blocked the light, ruined neighborhoods lay abandoned, street lights were broken, and few carriages (which commonly carried lanterns) circulated in the streets, so the long, overcast autumn and winter nights were even gloomier than before. Dmitrii Zavalishin later recalled that in large areas "there was no glimmer from even the smallest flame" and it was dangerous to go out after dark. The sense of insecurity, especially at night but also by day, was also noted by the German physician Anton Wilhelm Nordhof, who blamed the many uprooted peasants from the devastated countryside who survived as squatters in burned-out houses.[141]

People responded in dissimilar ways to this collapse of urban civilization. Many found it deeply disturbing. According to the noblewoman Anna Khomutova, "wandering among the snow-covered ruins, we did not hear the rumble of carriages, or for that matter, any noise at all: it was the silence of a burial vault. In the evenings, all of a sudden, a pistol shot would ring out; whether it was a chance occurrence or a crime, no one knew."[142] To others, the experience was weirdly liberating. Bauer recalled that

As for me personally, I felt very happy. Although already ten years old, I did not really grasp either the overall situation or my own, and freed from my studies and from supervision, I abandoned myself completely to the joys of freedom, roaming with Pavlushka and the other neighborhood boys in vacant lots, gardens, and kitchen-gardens—at the time, there were almost no fences: the French, when they were looting, had made shortcuts for themselves by knocking them down wherever they stood in the way.[143]

All who were there carried lasting memories of the emptiness and desolation. Bekker, a physician and son of German immigrants, was 8 years old in 1812. He wrote in 1870 that his dreams still often carried him back to the ruined streets and houses where he and his friends had played Cossacks and Frenchmen. As he was writing these lines, the ongoing German siege of Paris in the Franco-Prussian

---

[139] Bekker, "Vospominaniia," 510; Voskresenskii, "Umstvennyi vzor" (part 3), 590; [Bauer], "Vospominanie," 125.

[140] Nordhof, *Die Geschichte der Zerstörung Moskaus*, 233. See also Bekker, "Vospominaniia," 520.

[141] Dmitrii Zavalishin, "Tysiacha vosem'sot dvenadtsatyi god (Iz vospominanii sovremennika)," *MV* (25 March 1884); Nordhof, *Die Geschichte der Zerstörung Moskaus*, 106, 276.

[142] Khomutova, "Vospominaniia," 327.

[143] Bauer, "Vospominanie," 129.

War gave him grim satisfaction: "let the French find out how it is to be put on a diet, as we were in Moscow in 1812."[144]

THE GOVERNMENT'S RESPONSE

The scale of the disaster in Moscow was staggering. No European city of comparable size had suffered war-related damage of this magnitude in centuries. Over two-thirds of the residential structures were in ruins. Peasants conscripted by the police reportedly collected the decomposing remains of 11,955 humans and 12,360 horses.[145] An eyewitness recalled that "for several weeks, the police were burning them by the banks of the river and sweeping the ashes into the water."[146] It was a Dantesque spectacle that people could not get out of their heads for decades. A merchant boy who saw it refused to eat meat for a month,[147] and as late as 1898, a priest's grandson recalled that "a horribly suffocating, stinking smoke spread throughout the whole city, and when Grandfather passed by Pskov Hill [near Red Square] and watched as this auto-da-fé was going on below, it nearly choked him. He actually fell and started to cough, and the cough never left him until his very death."[148]

Disposing of dead bodies was simple compared to dealing with the social and economic damage. The fire had destroyed immense wealth, and looting redistributed much of what remained. Nobles and merchants naturally suffered the greatest losses, but the damage to more modest households—the loss, say, of a craftsman's tools or a young woman's bridal trousseau—was perhaps even more devastating. "Everything has been looted," Rostopchin reported to St Petersburg: "First by the enemy; after he left, by the Cossacks who entered the city; and finally, by peasants from the surrounding villages."[149]

Some hoped that this bonfire of the vanities might heal Russian society by curing the nobles of the craving for luxuries that caused them to extort every last kopek from their serfs.[150] In his memoirs, Glinka wistfully described such hopes as "utopian,"[151] but at the time he was positively giddy. At a victory party with Glinka and his brothers, Bulgakov reported, "Glasses were raised to the glory of Russia and the nation. They brought in a peasant from the street and

[144] Bekker, "Vospominaniia," 519, 506.

[145] N. A. Troitskii, *1812: Velikii god Rossii* (Moscow: Mysl', 1988), 193; A. A. Smirnov, "Moskva," in Bezotosnyi, *Otechestvennaia voina 1812 goda*, 478.

[146] Tolycheva, "Na Mokhovoi."

[147] "Razskaz Apollona Dmitrievicha Sysoeva," in [Tolycheva], "Razskazy ochevidtsev" (1872), 274.

[148] Lebedev, "Iz razskazov rodnykh o 1812 gode," in Shchukin, *Bumagi*, 3:259.

[149] OPI GIM f. 160, op. 1, d. 202, l. 14 ob, Rostopchin to Viazmitinov, 27 October 1812.

[150] See, for example: "Otechestvennaia voina (Pis'mo P. Kikina k materi)," *RS*, vol. 54 (April–June 1887), 738.

[151] Glinka, *Zapiski o 1812 gode*, 91–2.

kissed his boots and hands; in a word, there was a patriotic enthusiasm that I can't even describe."[152]

More widespread than boot-kissing was hostility toward the peasants. They too had suffered grievously, but Muscovites had visions of villages grown fat at the city's expense. Some of this resulted from wartime bartering—refugees from Moscow sometimes traded their valuables for food[153]—but much had also been pilfered. Fedor Tol', a former Moscow police chief, wrote in November 1812 that he had "lost everything"; the French had looted less than had peasants, domestics, "and other scum," and the villages were now filled with stolen furniture and other goods.[154] Similarly, the aristocrat Mariia Volkova remarked in a letter that no one had ever seen such prosperity and expensive houses in the villages around Moscow: "You won't believe it until you see it for yourself."[155] Even two decades later, Prince A. Shakhovskoi expressed grim satisfaction that peasants who might otherwise have continued looting were instead put to the nauseating job of removing dead bodies; the police thereby "saved Moscow from infection, her inhabitants from peasant looting, and the peasants from sinning."[156]

The government's top priority was neither class revenge nor the recovery of stolen goods, but the prevention of further unrest. Hardened by war and equipped with weapons from Napoleon's disintegrating army, some peasants and poorer urban folk were armed and dangerous. Immediately after retaking Moscow, the authorities announced a weapons buy-back program, but the results over the next half-year were disappointing. Peasants told officials that they meant to keep the weapons so they could defend themselves in case the enemy returned. Alexander I was sufficiently concerned that he sent orders, which applied to the city of Moscow as well,[157] to step up the buy-back efforts and suppress the second-hand trade in weapons. Officials, he wrote, should raise the prices they paid and tell the peasants that the army needed the weapons to fight against the French (which was true[158]) but the governors should also understand "that in the normal course of affairs, peasants should not be keeping arms in their homes."[159]

[152] "Iz pisem Aleksandra Iakovlevicha Bulgakova" (part 4), 298.

[153] Glushkovskii, "Moskva v 1812 godu," 144.

[154] "Moskva v 1812 godu," *RS*, vol. 8 (July–December 1873), 992–4, here: 994; see also "Griboedovskaia Moskva" (part 1), 643.

[155] "Griboedovskaia Moskva" (part 2), 118.

[156] "Pervye dni v sozhzhennoi Moskve," 47.

[157] OPI GIM f. 160, ed. khr. 197, ll. 19–20, "Uvedomlenie ot General-Maiora Ilovaiskogo 4-go" (Moscow, 12 October 1812); OPI GIM f. 160, op. 1, d. 198, ll. 11–11 ob, A. I. Gorchakov to S. K. Viazmitinov, 24 April 1814; Shchukin, *Bumagi*, 3:158, 164.

[158] Lieven, *Russia against Napoleon*, 234.

[159] OPI GIM f. 160, op. 1, d. 198, ll. 10–10 ob, Alexander I to S. K. Viazmitinov, Bautzen, 29 April 1813. See also: S. N. Khomchenko, "Sbor oruzhiia u naseleniia po okonchanii voiny 1812 goda," in A. V. Gorbunov, ed., *Otechestvennaia voina 1812 goda: Istochniki, pamiatniki, problemy—Materialy XII Vserossiiskoi nauchnoi konferentsii, Borodino, 6–8 sentiabria 2004 g.* (Moscow: Poligraf servis, 2005), 240–60.

The antagonisms created by the war ran through Moscow society as well. Property disputes proliferated, with charges that neighbor had stolen from neighbor, and servants, from their masters, and that networks existed to ship stolen goods to the provinces.[160] Old Believers were reported to have accepted French authority and helped loot Orthodox churches,[161] and people who had served in the French administration were arrested for treason.[162] Rostopchin ordered the police to compile a list of every individual who had remained in the city during the occupation so that suspicions of collaboration or looting could be investigated.[163]

As in its dealings with the peasants, the government's response was ultimately pragmatic, aiming to alleviate tensions while letting bygones be bygones. A crucial issue was the mass of stolen goods that filled the surviving houses and local markets and placed Rostopchin in an awkward position. Identifying the rightful owners was an impossible task for his policemen, the more so as they were themselves accused of embezzling stolen property,[164] yet uncertainty about ownership rights deterred potential buyers and impeded the revival of commerce.[165] To remedy this situation, Rostopchin announced in March 1813 that by order of Alexander I, all private property looted during the occupation henceforth belonged to whoever had possession of it.[166] A day later, Rostopchin wrote an irate letter to Glinka's *Russian Messenger*, denying accusations that his propaganda had caused people to delay leaving the city and thereby caused the enormous property losses in the first place. In 1814, Alexander announced an amnesty for most offenses committed during the invasion, and criminal investigations related to looting were generally dropped.[167]

Instead of pursuing lower-class looters to recover the property of the affluent, the authorities decided to offer compensation instead. To provide immediate relief, the police were instructed on 25 November 1812 to pay a fixed per diem to any individual whom Rostopchin certified as needy.[168] Then, on 5 May 1813, the government issued an invitation to residents of Moscow (city and province)

[160] Shchukin, *Bumagi*, 2:79–82, 3:44–56, 4:1–49 (esp. 35), 4:144–51, 9:85–91.
[161] Report from anon. to Rostopchin, 18 September 1812, in "Novyia podlinnyia cherty," col. 786; Sverbeev, "Vospominaniia," 310; A. Panktratov, "Staroobriadtsy i Napoleon," *RS*, vol. 157 (January–March 1914), 39–51; Aleksandr Popov, "Frantsuzy v Moskve v 1812 godu," part 3: *RA*, 1/4 (1876), 440–63, here: 456–7.
[162] Shchukin, *Bumagi*, 2:20.
[163] Tartakovskii, "Naselenie Moskvy," 360–1.
[164] For examples of such charges, see: "Griboedovskaia Moskva" (part 1), 619, 635, 641; (part 2), 117, 141; Nordhof, *Die Geschichte der Zerstörung Moskaus*, 240, 246, 253–4, 263–4.
[165] Makaruev, "Zapiski," in *1812 god v vospominaniiakh, perepiske i rasskazakh sovremennikov*, 40.
[166] Rostopchin to Police Chief Ivashkin, 28 March 1813, in Shchukin, *Bumagi*, 2:214.
[167] Letter of 29 March 1813, in "Pis'mo grafa F. V. Rostopchina k izdateliu Russkago Vestnika S. N. Glinke," *RA*, 3/12 (1876), 430–2; Shishkov, *Zapiski, mneniia*, 1:307; Shchukin, *Bumagi*, 3:55, 4:49, 151, 257, 5:131.
[168] OPI GIM f. 160, op. 1, d. 203, l. 17; Shchukin, *Bumagi*, 1:125–6, 3:206.

to submit petitions for financial assistance (see above, pages 153–4). Aid was geared primarily to the middle strata, especially homeowners and business people.[169]

The public response was impressive. It appears that a total of 18,133 petitions were submitted.[170] They came mostly from the urban middle strata, broadly defined, of the city of Moscow. In a sample register of 2,000 petitions that the commission reviewed, I found 310 personal or hereditary nobles (15.50 percent of the total); 510 merchants (25.50 percent); 622 townspeople (31.10 percent); 197 (9.85 percent) who were soldiers or non-commissioned officers and their wives or daughters (women known as *soldatki*); 122 guild artisans (6.10 percent); 57 petty state employees (2.85 percent); and 182 who belonged to other categories (9.10 percent).[171] (Few clergymen participated, because the clergy received aid through a separate program administered by the Holy Synod.[172]) This sample is probably representative of the total corpus of petitions, because the petitions were reviewed in the random order in which they were received.[173]

Participation in the aid program seems to have been widespread among the middling sort. Of the petitioners in my sample, 78.20 percent were nobles, merchants, townspeople, or guild artisans. Extrapolating from this percentage suggests that those estates accounted for 14,180 of the total of 18,133 petitions. Many petitions represented entire families, so the number of individuals was much larger. As of 1 March 1813, according to the police, 27,631 people who belonged to these four estates lived in the devastated city.[174] By July, when most of the petitions were submitted, the population was larger, but even so, the

[169] PSZ (First Series), vol. 32, no. 25,378; TsIAM f. 20, op. 2, d. 2243, ll. 92–6 ob, report to Alexander I from the Komissiia o razsmotrenii proshenii razzorennykh obyvatelei Moskovskoi Gubernii i Stolitsy, 5 November 1813. Documents related to the aid program can also be found in Shchukin, *Bumagi*, 2:153–6, 6:74–6, 81–8.

[170] This number is cited in what seem to be the only works of scholarship dealing with the petitions: E. G. Boldina, "O deiatel'nosti Komissii dlia rassmotreniia proshenii obyvatelei Moskovskoi stolitsy i gubernii, poterpevshikh razorenie ot nashestviia nepriiatel'skogo," in E. G. Boldina, A. S. Kiselev, L. N. Seliverstova, eds., *Moskva v 1812 godu: Materialy nauchnoi konferentsii, posviashchennoi 180-letiiu Otechestvennoi voiny 1812 goda* (Moscow: Mosgorarkhiv, 1997), 47; E. G. Boldina, "Komissiia dlia rassmotreniia proshenii obyvatelei Moskovskoi stolitsy i gubernii, poterpevshikh razorenie ot nashestviia nepriiatel'skogo," in Bezotosnyi, *Otechestvennaia voina 1812 goda*, 358. I discuss the petitions in Alexander M. Martin, "Precarious Existences: Middling Households in Moscow and the Fire of 1812," in Marsha Siefert, ed., *Extending the Borders of Russian History: Essays in Honor of Alfred J. Rieber* (Budapest: Central European University Press, 2003), 67–82, and Alexander M. Martin, "Down and Out in 1812: The Impact of the Napoleonic Invasion on Moscow's Middling Strata," in Roger Bartlett et al., eds., *Eighteenth-Century Russia: Society, Culture, Economy. Papers From the VII International Conference of the Study Group on Eighteenth-Century Russia, Wittenberg 2004* (Münster: LIT-Verlag, 2007), 429–41.

[171] TsIAM f. 20, op. 2, d. 2380, the commission's journal that summarizes petitions no. 12,701–14,700.

[172] TsIAM f. 20, op. 2, d. 2243, ll. 40–40 ob, Bishop Avgustin to N. N. Golovin, 8 July 1813.

[173] TsIAM f. 20, op. 2, d. 2243, ll. 92 ob.

[174] The March 1813 population figures are in OPI GIM f. 160, op. 1, d. 202, l. 86.

14,180 petitioners must have represented a large portion of the members of those estates who were then in Moscow.

Most of the aid took the form of ten-year, interest-free loans. Because recipients had to provide loan guarantees, the process of disbursing the aid was slow.[175] Table 6.1 illustrates this problem, using data for the year 1815.[176] By March 1818, of the 16,020,176 rubles allocated for loans, 13,385,546 had been disbursed; of the 500,000 for direct grants, 459,052 had been disbursed.[177]

The main beneficiaries were nobles and merchants, and their number was small. Between September 1816 and November 1817, 262 Moscow townspeople received from 100 to 1,000 rubles, with a median award of 500 rubles. During the same period, 201 Moscow nobles were given 100 to 5,000 rubles, with a median of 1,000.[178] Aid was reaching so few people that when Alexander I visited Moscow for two weeks in the summer of 1816, he received another 12,000 petitions. To review these, he established a second aid commission, whose purpose was to make smaller grants to the many poorer war victims not assisted the first time around. By 1819, when this second commission wrapped up its work, it had received 20,959 petitions, and awarded a total of 1,391,280 rubles to 15,335 petitioners. Based on incomplete data, it appears that the average award was 136 rubles for nobles, 67 for merchants, 61 for clergy, 50 for townspeople and guild artisans, and 33 for others.[179]

According to the commission that reviewed the first round of petitions in 1813, the possessions and merchandise lost by residents of the city of Moscow totaled 165,045,840.93 rubles, in addition to 84,741,547.995 in immovable property.[180] By comparison, the Russian government's total tax receipts for 1805 had been only 147 million rubles.[181] Next to such colossal losses, the sums disbursed in aid were a drop in the bucket. Hardly any memoirs mention the aid program, suggesting that its impact was limited. There was also grumbling about the process. In a novel from 1831, Faddei Bulgarin, usually an unapologetic

---

[175] TsIAM f. 20, op. 2, d. 2432, ll. 16–17, A. P. Tormasov (?) to N. I. Saltykov, 10 January 1816.

[176] TsIAM f. 20, op. 2, d. 2432, ll. 1 ob-2, "Vedomost' o summe vydannoi iz vysochaishe uchrezhdennoi Kommissii dlia vspomozheniia obyvateliam Moskovskoi Stolitsy i Gubernii, s 19 genvaria 1815go po 1 genvaria sego 1816 goda i skol'ko za tem ostaetsia v nevydache."

[177] TsIAM f. 20, op. 2, d. 2432, ll. 531–9 ob, V. Arsen'ev to A. P. Tormasov, 27 March 1818. For a slightly different set of numbers, see Boldina, "Komissiia dlia rassmotreniia proshenii," in Bezotosnyi, *Otechestvennaia voina 1812 goda*, 358.

[178] TsIAM f. 20, op. 2, d. 2384, ll. 1 ob-111.

[179] P. Ivanov, *Opisanie Gosudarstvennago Arkhiva starykh del* (Moscow: V Tipografii S. Selivanovskago, 1850), 117; A. A. Kostin, "I. I. Dmitriev—predsedatel' Komissii pod predsedatel'stvom Ivana Dmitrieva (1816–1819)," in A. A. Kostin and N. D. Kochetkova, eds., *Ivan Ivanovich Dmitriev (1760–1837): Zhizn', tvorchestvo, krug obshcheniia*, Chteniia Otdela russkoi literatury XVIII veka, vypusk 6 (St Petersburg, 2011), 92–108, here: 101–2.

[180] TsIAM f. 20, op. 2, d. 2432, l. 454 ob, "Vedomost' o ponesennykh poteriakh ot nepriiatel'skago nashestviia obyvateliami Moskovskoi Stolitsy i uezdov, uchinennaia v vysochaishe uchrezhdennoi v Moskve kommissii dlia vspomozheniia razzorennym," 20 July 1817.

[181] K. V. Sivkov, "Finansy Rossii pered voinoi 1812 goda," in Dzhivelegov et al., *Otechestvennaia voina i russkoe obshchestvo*, 2:261.

Table 6.1. Government loans to war victims in Moscow

Recipients (City of Moscow only)	Funds allocated		Funds disbursed during 1815		Funds remaining 3 January 1816	
	Individuals	Total sum (rubles)	Individuals	Total sum (rubles)	Individuals	Total sum (rubles)
Nobles*	1,227	4,201,553	444	1,860,950	783	2,340,603
Merchants	2,163	9,316,700	209	1,345,850	1,954	7,970,850
Townspeople	788	948,750	40	113,000	748	835,750
Guild artisans	94	131,900	1	1,000	93	130,900
City merchant corporation**	1	100,000	1	100,000		
Total for the City and Province of Moscow***	5,852 (100%)	16,020,176 (100%)	2,108 (36.0%)	4,356,278 (27.1%)	3,744 (63.9%)	11,663,898 (72.8%)

* Includes nobles throughout Moscow Province.
** Gradskoe kupecheskoe obshchestvo.
*** Includes data from other districts of Moscow Province not included in this table.

cheerleader for the regime, claimed that government aid had unfairly benefited those who had connections on the aid commission.[182] In fairness, the scale of the calamity would have overwhelmed any relief effort, and the need to distribute vast monies quickly based on little documentation was bound to produce abuses. The fact that aid was received by more than 20,000 households, many of them poorer members of the middling sort, showed the government's goodwill and helped people through the hardships of the immediate post-war years.

THE MEANING OF THE WAR

Whatever else the aid program hoped to accomplish, it was not an invitation to reflect on the meaning of the war. Anyone studying the petitions to discover a popular understanding of the war will be disappointed. All that most petitioners provided, usually in the flat bureaucratese of the clerks who drafted such documents, was a sketchy (though at times heart-rending) outline of their personal travails. For example, the widow Sof'ia Bolgarova wrote: "I had my residence in the 4th Ward of Presnenskaia District in the house of the Moscow Townswoman Anna Elagina together with my father the retired collegiate councilor Iakov Alekseevich Maksimov and my mother Elisaveta Vasil'evna and during the enemy's invasion of Moscow my parents burned and both their and my possessions burned and were looted." Her father's death meant the end of his 300 ruble annual pension, so Bolgarova and her two young sons no longer had any source of income.[183] Since the government accepted claims only for damage caused by enemy troops,[184] no one explicitly mentioned looting by Russians. At most, like Bolgarova, they might use the passive voice, or else, like one petitioner, write vaguely that their possessions were "looted by unknown persons."[185]

On 30 August 1814, with the Russians in Paris and the conflict safely over, Alexander I dismissed Rostopchin. He had become widely disliked. He had his defenders, who argued that he had prevented disorders that might have spread across the country,[186] and he himself later claimed to have been "the principal tool of Napoleon's destruction . . . for if there had been a revolt in Moscow, where would the nobility have gotten to, and what would have been the

---

[182] [Faddei Bulgarin], *Ivan Vyzhigin i ego prodolzhenie Petr Ivanovich Vyzhigin* (Moscow: Zakharov, 2002), 468–9, 500. On the corruption in the commission, see also Nordhof, *Die Geschichte der Zerstörung Moskaus*, 263.

[183] TsIAM f. 20, op. 2, d. 2214, ll. 133–33 ob.

[184] TsIAM f. 20, op. 2, d. 2432, l. 452 ob., V. Arsen'ev to A. P. Tormasov, 20 July 1817.

[185] Shchukin, *Bumagi*, 6:30.

[186] "Griboedovskaia Moskva" (part 1), 572–666, here: 607. See also: "Iz pisem Aleksandra Iakovlevicha Bulgakova" (part 4), 300; Glushkovskii, "Moskva v 1812 godu," 144–5; "Vospominanie o 1812 gode," in Viazemskii, *Polnoe sobranie sochinenii*, 7:193–4, 209–13.

consequences?" The fire, he argued, had doomed Napoleon, although he added angrily that "with us everyone talks, but no one wants to reason; all they do is moan about their houses."[187] Rostopchin became the object of widespread criticism among nobles and intellectuals because he seemed to think that the imperial social project was a luxury that Russia could afford only in good times, whereas in a crisis, survival depended on the same elemental forces—harsh weather, vast distances, urban fires, popular xenophobia—that had long kept the country on the margins of European civilization. He had conspicuously made no effort to protect the material wealth that undergirded Muscovites' aspirations to gentility, and it speaks volumes about his public image that he was widely thought to have given the orders that led to the disastrous fire.[188] His propaganda and brutal use of power raised troubling questions about the government's commitment to rational public discourse and the rule of law. At least some literate commoners bridled at the way he talked down to them. A merchant memoirist from Rostov, for example, wrote that Rostopchin's leaflets "exasperated everyone by the rustic, folk-tale style with which he tried to approach the mindset of the common people. These clumsy fabrications of his aroused disdain, and for some reason the common people harbored the greatest hatred for him."[189] Removing him was an important step for the government in advancing an interpretation of the war that was compatible with a resumption of the imperial social project.

The government had its own vision of the war, in which little significance accrued to the military operations of 1812. Tsar Alexander, like his father (Paul I) and brother (Nicholas I), saw the army's discipline and top-down hierarchy as a model for the wider social order, but he had no love for the bottom-up civic mobilization implicit in the idea of a nation in arms.[190] In 1812 his ineffective conduct of the war had helped lead the French all the way to Moscow, whence only a massive national mobilization plus the harshness of nature and geography had dislodged them. These were not memories Alexander was keen to perpetuate. In nineteenth-century Berlin, London, and Paris, streets and squares were named after battles and generals of the Napoleonic Wars, but in Moscow, little was done. The new *manège* was built for a smallish victory parade in 1817, and a few monuments had appeared by the early 1840s—a triumphal

---

[187] Letter of 3/15 October 1815 to one of his estate managers, in "Novyia podlinnyia cherty," 834–5.

[188] Rostopchin later denied having ordered the fire; F. V. Rostopchin, *La vérité sur l'incendie de Moscou* (Paris: Ponthieu, 1823). On his orders to set the fire, see Smirnov, "Pozhar Moskvy," in Bezotosnyi, *Otechestvennaia voina 1812 goda*, 482–3.

[189] Makaruev, "Zapiski," in *1812 god v vospominaniiakh, perepiske i rasskazakh sovremennikov*, 36. For criticisms by nobles of the leaflets' demagogic style, see "Vospominanie o 1812 gode," 194, and "Kharakteristicheskiia zametki i vospominaniia o grafe Rostopchine," in Viazemskii, *Polnoe sobranie sochinenii*, 7:504–5; [Bestuzhev-Riumin], "Kratkoe opisanie," 77.

[190] Wortman, *Scenarios of Power*, 1:222.

arch at the edge of the city, captured French artillery in the Kremlin, and in the
Kremlin Garden, a grotto built of remains of houses destroyed in 1812—but
otherwise, even thirty years after the war, no street, square, or city gate was
named after anything from the Napoleonic Wars.[191] In a recent survey of
commemorative sites, all the Moscow street names that recall 1812 date from
the twentieth century.[192]

The government after 1812 found three other ways to use the war to revitalize
the imperial social project in Moscow. The need to rebuild most of the city after
the fire seemed a perfect opportunity at last to complete Moscow's transformation along neoclassical lines. In July 1813, Alexander I approved an ambitious
plan by the architect V. I. Geste to straighten the radial avenues that converged on
the city center as well as many secondary downtown streets, and build imposing
squares (or expand existing ones) where the radial avenues intersected the customs
wall and the boundaries of the White City (the Boulevard Ring) and the Earthen
City. This plan was abandoned later in 1813 when the government's Commission for Construction in Moscow objected that it ignored Moscow's uneven
topography, the rights of local property owners, and the need to give priority to
rebuilding the city's housing stock. A less ambitious plan, more closely adapted
to existing conditions, but one that—like Geste's—built on Catherine's plan of
1775, was adopted in 1817 and guided the city's development until the middle
of the nineteenth century.[193] Impressive improvements were the outcome. The
polluted River Neglinnaia was shifted underground, making way for the Kremlin
Garden and Theater Square. Red Square was enlarged and embellished when the
weed-infested Kremlin moat was filled in and the clutter of market stalls was
removed. Lastly, the tree-lined Boulevard Ring was completed.[194] With these
majestic public spaces, the Russian monarchy, like other monarchies in turbulent
post-Napoleonic Europe, signaled its continued commitment to an urban
environment that was grand, beautiful, and orderly.[195]

Beyond the renewed commitment to the neoclassical reconstruction of
Moscow, a second way of making sense of the war drew on memories of the
Time of Troubles. A project in the works since 1807 was a monument to the
merchant Minin and Prince Pozharskii, the leaders of the movement that
ended the Time of Troubles by driving the Poles from Moscow in 1612–13
and bringing the Romanov dynasty to power.[196] Karamzin was a leading

---

[191] K. Nistrem, *Moskovskii adress-kalendar', dlia zhitelei Moskvy, sostavlen po offitsial'nym
dokumentam i svedeniiam*, 4 vols. (Moscow: V tipografii S. Selivanovskago, 1842), vol. 1;
L. V. Zaichenko, *Moskva v Otechestvennoi voine 1812 goda* (Moscow: Moskvovedenie, 2006),
216–23, 256–9.

[192] Zaichenko, *Moskva v Otechestvennoi voine 1812 goda*, 259–80.

[193] Gulianitskii, *Moskva i slozhivshiesia russkie goroda*, 130–4.

[194] Schmidt, *The Architecture and Planning of Classical Moscow*, 65, 143–53, 169–71.

[195] Lees and Lees, *Cities and the Making of Modern Europe*, 101–2.

[196] On the statue's genesis, see Zorin, *Kormia dvuglavogo orla*, 159–61.

organizer of the drive to create the monument, which was dedicated on Red Square on 20 February 1818 while Alexander I was in Moscow. That same year, Karamzin published the first eight volumes of his *History of the Russian State*, which reached a broad readership and identified autocracy and pre-Petrine tradition as foundations of Russian national identity. The associations of the Time of Troubles came to include national unity, dynastic loyalty, reverence for Moscow as Russia's spiritual core, and hostility to Western ideological and military aggression. By the 1830s, writes Andrei Zorin, the events of 1612–13 in effect had been "canonized as the mythological origins of Russian statehood."[197]

Lastly, aided by Filaret (Drozdov), the archbishop and then metropolitan of Moscow from 1821 to 1867, Alexander I offered a religious interpretation of the war. For the remainder of the nineteenth century, the annual Christmas liturgy in Orthodox churches was followed by a prayer, written by Filaret, to thank God for delivering Russia from "the invasion of the Gauls and the twenty nations."[198] In Moscow itself, a grand cathedral of Christ the Savior was to be erected in thanks for Russia's victory; after multiple false starts, the plans were approved in 1832, and construction was finally completed in 1883.[199]

This religious interpretation of the war—that God, not the people or the generals, had saved Russia in 1812—was part of a wider effort to rejuvenate the imperial social project by shifting its ideological basis from Enlightenment rationalism to an ecumenical, Protestant-inspired Christianity. A framework to remake international relations along these lines was created in 1815, when Orthodox Russia joined with Protestant Prussia and Catholic Austria to form the Holy Alliance.[200] The Russian Bible Society, an offshoot of the British and Foreign Bible Society, was established in 1813 to disseminate vernacular Bibles at affordable prices, and in 1817, the Holy Synod and the government departments for education and for non-Orthodox faiths were amalgamated in a single Ministry of Spiritual Affairs and Popular Enlightenment that was charged with making religion the basis of Russian life. By the end of Alexander's reign, much of this was abandoned. The effort to transform European politics through the Holy Alliance was recognized as a failure, and domestic political pressures led to the disbanding of the Ministry of Spiritual Affairs and Popular Enlightenment and of the Russian Bible Society. What survived were bodies such as the Prison Reform Society and the Imperial Philanthropic Society; these organizations were closely connected to the imperial court, and like their counterparts elsewhere

[197] Zorin, *Kormia dvuglavogo orla*, 161.
[198] I. E. Andreevskii, ed., *Entsiklopedicheskii slovar'*, 43 vols. (St Petersburg: Brokgauz-Efron, 1890–1907), 26:942.
[199] Gulianitskii, *Moskva i slozhivshiesia russkie goroda*, 176; Russkii Biograficheskii Slovar', 21:90.
[200] Wortman, *Scenarios of Power*, 1:229–34.

in post-Napoleonic Europe, they combined religion, charity, education, and coercion in an effort to make society more cohesive.[201]

CONCLUSION

Over the long term, the war weakened the liberal, cosmopolitan, rationalist impulse at the heart of the imperial social project. To the government, the war demonstrated that society was brittle but could be held together through repression and appeals to nationalism. As for middling Muscovites, they learned that Europe was their enemy and other Russians considered them expendable. The memory of the social order's violent destruction lasted through the century, and the war highlighted fissures—country versus city, natives versus foreigners, commoners versus elites—that returned with a vengeance in the late imperial period.

In the medium term, however, the disaster may have stabilized the regime by convincing Muscovites that to emulate foreign revolutions was to invite a repetition of 1812. Nationalist Russians interpreted the Polish uprisings of 1830–1 and 1863 not as a political protest against tsarism but as foreign attacks on Russia that were analogous to 1812.[202] During the European revolutions of 1848, the secret police reported rumors in Moscow that the French intended to force other countries to abolish serfdom and that in Poland, which had already rebelled against Russian rule in 1831, people were circulating French leaflets (including a constitution for Poland) and murdering Russian soldiers. The police also reported in 1848 that Muscovites worried about the Polish students in their midst and the "many" policemen who were Poles or baptized Jews.[203] In 1812, the tsar's manifesto after the outbreak of the war had warned that "with cunning in his heart and flattery on his lips, [Napoleon] brings to [Russia] eternal chains and fetters."[204] Echoing this language, an Old Believer from Moscow who witnessed the events of 1848 in Vienna, especially the promulgation of religious freedom, wrote home about the "dreadful prospect of a worldwide constitution, which is a dagger dipped in [the] honey [of freedom] . . . If you hear 'constitution', be afraid, as of a bloodthirsty murderer who comes to you disguised as a peacemaker."[205] Soon after, in the Crimean War, which the poet

---

[201] Lees and Lees, *Cities and the Making of Modern Europe*, 105–11; Martin, *Romantics, Reformers, Reactionaries*, ch. 7.

[202] Maiorova, *From the Shadow of Empire*, 107, 139–41.

[203] "Doneseniia agentov o dukhe v Moskve v 1848 godu," 344–9; "Moskovskaia zhizn' vesnoi 1848 goda (Pis'ma moskovskago ober-politsmeistera Luzhina nachal'niku III otdeleniia grafu A. F. Orlovu)," *Minuvshie Gody*, no. 11 (November 1908), 47–9.

[204] Shishkov, *Zapiski, mneniia*, 1:426.

[205] "Otzyv russkago staroobriadtsa o venskoi revoliutsii 1848 goda: Pis'mo iz Avstrii v Moskvu na Rogozhskoe kladbishche, ot nastoiatelia belokrinskago monastyria Pavla Velikodvorskago," *RA*, 2/5 (1875), 112–14, here: 114.

F. I. Tiutchev described as "a resumption of 1812,"[206] Russia was invaded by a coalition that included Napoleon's nephew Napoleon III, and once more rumors spread among the serfs that the French emperor demanded their liberty as a precondition for peace.[207]

The war thus left an ambiguous legacy, stabilizing the regime for several decades but undermining the social order over the longer term.

---

[206] Tartakovskii, *1812 god i russkaia memuaristika*, 230.
[207] P. A. Kropotkin, *Zapiski revoliutsionera* (Moscow: Moskovskii rabochii, 1988), 153.

7

Common Folk in Nicholaevan Moscow

"I am seeing Moscow for the first time since the fire," Count Nikolai Rumiantsev confided to Count Arakcheev in June 1817. The devastation was shocking, but "what gives me pause is that the fire of this conflagration has consumed her spirit as well. In her second edition, Moscow will be something new; her earlier majesty, power, and ascendancy over us all will not come back."[1] Looking back in 1865, Prince Petr Viazemskii concurred that Moscow after 1812 had "become provincial."[2] What he meant was that the aristocracy had gone into a gradual decline. Its hegemony and extravagance did indeed wane after the war. As the aged Elizaveta Ian'kova lamented in the 1850s, not only did aristocrats no longer display their coats of arms on their vehicles,

But what do they use to draw their carriages? Never mind that it's not teams of four—nowadays, you won't find twenty people in all Moscow who drive with four horses—but they actually drive rented horses...[P]eople drag themselves around town in simple rental carriages in broad daylight without a twinge of conscience, or worse yet, they go about in cabs.[3]

The decline of the aristocracy took place against a backdrop of broader urban change. Moscow continued to grow, fueled by Russia's general population increase as well as by expanding commerce and manufacturing. Its population, according to the police, grew by 98 percent in fifty years, from 175,000 in 1789–93 to 347,000 in 1840.[4] Measured over a somewhat later half-century interval, 1811 to 1863, it grew by 71 percent.[5] However, in the countries that were Russia's models and rivals, urban growth powered ahead even faster, super-charged by deeper rural poverty and more intensive industrialization. From 1800 to 1850, London, Berlin, and Vienna grew 140 percent. Berlin and Vienna

---

[1] N. Dubrovin, ed., *Pis'ma glavneishikh deiatelei v tsarstvovanie imperatora Aleksandra I (1807–1829 gg.)* (Moscow: Gosudarstvennaia publichnaia istoricheskaia biblioteka Rossii, 2006), 196.
[2] "Dopotopnaia ili dopozharnaia Moskva," in Viazemskii, *Polnoe sobranie sochinenii*, 7:88.
[3] Blagovo, *Rasskazy babushki*, 115.
[4] Gastev, *Materialy*, 264; "Otchet moskovskago ober-politsmeistera, za 1840 god," 2.
[5] A. G. Rashin, *Naselenie Rossii za 100 let (1811–1913 gg.): Statisticheskie ocherki* (Moscow: Gosudarstvennoe Statisticheskoe Izdatel'stvo, 1956), 93.

overtook Moscow, and London came to exceed it by a factor of 7.5. Glasgow and Liverpool posted 350 percent growth and drew even with Moscow.[6]

Other indicators likewise suggested that Moscow lacked dynamism. Of the cities just mentioned, only Moscow had no rail connections by 1845, and ten years later, when the major cities of northwestern Europe were knitted together by a unified rail network, Moscow was connected only to St Petersburg. Moscow developed a significant cotton-spinning industry in the 1840s, but in other sectors, the steep tariffs in force from 1822 to 1850 protected manufacturers against foreign competition and obviated the need to adopt industrial production methods.[7] The streets of Moscow in the 1850s were still lit with hempseed oil, not gas, and the city had few primary schools and no modern police. Paris is preserved on daguerreotypes from 1839 on, but no such views seem to exist of Nicholaevan Moscow, any more than it had an equivalent of the innovative glass-and-iron construction of London's 1851 Crystal Palace.

Under Nicholas I, the tectonic plates of social class slowly shifted. A variety of developments caused the nobility to lose some of its former centrality in Moscow society.

Noble landowners did little to modernize their operations and instead met expenses by going into debt. This caused the share of serfs who were mortgaged by their owners to rise from 20 percent of all male serfs in Russia in 1820 to 66 percent in 1859. Owing to the resulting financial pressures, fewer nobles owned real estate in Moscow or came for the annual winter season.[8] The chief beneficiaries of protectionist trade policies and the changing real-estate market were merchants, many of whom came from the peasantry. The peasant element was also increased by laws of the 1820s and 1830s that made it easier for rural migrants to become townspeople or guild artisans.[9] Meanwhile, the education system produced a growing population of literate commoners. In earlier times, many of them would have been integrated into the nobility through service in the bureaucracy, but Nicholas I made that much more difficult when, in 1845, he raised the threshold for personal-noble status from rank 14 to rank 9, and for hereditary ennoblement, from rank 8 to rank 5.[10]

---

[6] Population figures from Rüdiger Hachtmann, "The European Capital Cities in the Revolution of 1848," in Dieter Dowe et al., eds., *Europe in 1848: Revolution and Reform* (New York: Berghahn Books, 2001), 350.

[7] Walter McKenzie Pintner, *Russian Economic Policy under Nicholas I* (Ithaca, NY: Cornell University Press, 1967), 46, 222, 228, 244.

[8] Blum, *Lord and Peasant*, 380; Androssov, *Statisticheskaia zapiska*, 46.

[9] Hildermeier, *Bürgertum und Stadt*, 234–45, 365.

[10] *Polnoe sobranie zakonov Rossiiskoi Imperii: Sobranie Vtoroe*, 55 vols. (St Petersburg: v tipografii II Otdeleniia Sobstvennoi Ego Imperatorskago Velichestva Kantseliarii, 1830–1885), vol. 20, art. 19,086.

The outcome of all this was a fluidity in the social order that bolstered the middle against the extremes. At the bottom of the ladder, fewer Muscovites were serfs or hereditary peasants, while at the top, aristocrats had to rein in their lavish lifestyle and thus had fewer opportunities to be leaders, patrons, and role models to the strata beneath them. In terms of estate membership, Moscow developed a large lower-middle composed of former peasants (many of them quite poor) who had joined the urban estates, and a much smaller upper-middle of people of non-noble birth who were active in business, the professions, the civil service, or other fields.

What this portended for the imperial social project was ambiguous. As aristocratic hospitality and patronage dwindled in importance, a space opened up for restaurants, theaters, and the like that were open to the general public. Also, peasants who joined the urban estates were more likely to sever their ties to the village and assimilate into urban society. The target population for the imperial social project was thus expanded, but this enlarged public had mixed feelings about Europeanization because of its association with the nobility. For example, it was agreed that wearing European dress made one look "noble." For daughters of merchants, this was advantageous because it enhanced their marriage prospects, but if their menfolk donned European attire, they risked being ridiculed by nobles and fellow merchants for trying to look like nobles.[11] Clerics and *popovichi* were likewise hesitant about adopting noble culture because they wished to project an air of austere Orthodox virtue.[12] The emerging culture of Moscow's middling sort was thus a hybrid of European influences and particularistic Russian estate traditions.

The milieu in which these processes unfolded is the subject of the present chapter. We will begin by focusing on a single individual, a provincial craftsman named Dmitrii Volkov, whose private writings illustrate how far down the social hierarchy the emerging middling culture reached. Then, placing Volkov in the larger context of his neighborhood, we will examine how inhabitants of different estates in a typical district on the periphery of Moscow—Sushchevskaia District, where Volkov settled in 1829—dealt with their surroundings, each other, and the state. Finally, widening our focus still farther to embrace the whole metropolis, we will examine how estate membership across the city correlated with culture, demography, and social interaction. What names did people choose for their children? How common was it for different estates to live in the same neighborhood, even under the same roof? How similar were their family and household structures? In short, what did membership in a particular estate mean in everyday life?

---

[11] Kupriianov, *Gorodskaia kul'tura*, 340–1.
[12] This is a central argument of Manchester, *Holy Fathers, Secular Sons*.

THE GOLDSMITH AND HIS NOTEBOOK

At the bottom rung of educated society were people, known by the late nineteenth century as the "worker intelligentsia," who functioned as cultural intermediaries between the Westernized classes and the rest of the population. When Maxim Gorky was a boy in Nizhnii Novgorod in the 1870s, he knew such a man, a metalworker nicknamed "Just the Job" ("Khoroshee Delo"). He cut an odd figure in the tradition-bound merchant milieu. He wore spectacles and read secular books in the "civil" typeface, not the Church Slavonic print that Gorky's family knew from religious texts. In the manner of the intelligentsia, he waxed poetic about the Russian soul when Gorky's grandmother told folktales, and he conducted strange experiments with metals and chemicals. To young Gorky, this was a tantalizing glimpse of a larger world, but others felt so threatened in their cozy provincialism that they derided him as a "wizard" and "freemason" and finally drove him away.[13]

A visitor to Moscow in 1829 might have met a forerunner of "Just the Job," a skilled, peripatetic goldsmith by the name of Dmitrii Volkov. All we know about him comes from a small copybook, 64 pages (32 folios) long. The first 52 pages contain 23 humorous riddles in verse and various secular and religious texts copied from books and dated March 1822. Both sides of the next folio are left blank, and the remaining 10 pages contain records of his employment as a goldsmith in 1819–20, 1823–4, and 1831–2: where and for whom he worked, and dates when he borrowed money or was not at work.[14]

Artisans in skilled crafts commonly began their careers as boys apprenticed to master craftsmen. It was a hard life, and in Russia as in other countries, the exploitation of young apprentices by masters and journeymen was legendary and helped foster a distinctive sense of artisan identity.[15] Whether Volkov underwent such an apprenticeship is unknown, but his education seems to have gone beyond the needs of his trade. He mentions writing letters home, suggesting that he came from a literate family, and his spelling, penmanship, and prose were fluid and competent. Like "Just the Job," he was intrigued by the mysteries of nature and science. He wrote down "secrets" for making phosphorous and obtaining a hernia remedy from strychnine, and referred to medicinal uses of cochineal and goat's-thorn. In February 1824, when Volkov was working in the town of Bui in Kostroma Province, one Ivan Arstov stole his copybook and wrote

---

[13] Gorky, *My Childhood*, 114–31, quotations on 116. Another memorable depiction of this social type is S. Kanatchikov, *A Radical Worker in Tsarist Rusia: The Autobiography of Semën Kanatchikov*, ed. and tr. Reginald E. Zelnik (Stanford, Calif.: Stanford University Press, 1986).

[14] OPI GIM f. 450, d. 835a, "Zapisnaia knizhka zolotaria Dmitriia Stepanovicha Volkova." All the references to Volkov are drawn from this source.

[15] See, for example, Belousov, "Ushedshaia Moskva," in Aleksandrov, *Moskovskaia Starina*, 319–22, 342.

humorously pompous notes in it. Spoofing sentimentalist poetry, Arstov commented on the copybook's content: "Of your writing I saw | the exercise | In my soul there remains only tender emotion" (*Pis'ma Vashego, videl | ia uprazhnenie | V dushe moei! ostalos' tol'ko umilenie*). Whoever this Arstov was, his play with language suggests that he and Volkov shared an education well beyond the religious or narrowly utilitarian literacy that was common in Volkov's social class.

We don't know when Volkov was born or where he came from, but he seems to have plied his trade mostly along the upper Volga, around 300 kilometers north of Moscow. In addition to Bui (population 900), he mentions the provincial capitals of Iaroslavl' (34,900) and Kostroma (14,300) and the small towns of Mologa (4,300) and Kineshma (3,600).[16] The upper Volga was the main shipping corridor for grain bound for St Petersburg, and the area bustled with merchants who had seen the world and could have been role models to Volkov.[17] David Ransel describes one such figure, Ivan Tolchenov, a wealthy grain trader from Dmitrov, a town between Moscow and the Volga. Tolchenov traveled to Moscow and St Petersburg, socialized with nobles, visited aristocratic homes, and developed refined tastes that ran to book collecting, theater, and horticulture. Yet he remained steeped in the ways of the merchantry—running a family business, giving generously to the church, and serving as mayor of his home town.[18] Figures like Tolchenov had the ability to serve as intermediaries between the metropolitan elites and upwardly mobile provincials like Volkov, thereby enabling Volkov, similar to Gorky's "Just the Job," to play the same role farther down the social hierarchy.

Judging by the way he spent his money, Volkov shared the hybrid consumer taste that developed as the culture of the elites filtered into the wider population. His records for 1819–20 and 1823–4 itemize advances on his pay that add up to over half his salary, yet when (as is mostly the case) he lists a corresponding expense, it is never for food, rent, light, or firewood. This suggests that, like most Russian workers, he lived and boarded at his employer's house. If so, his annual pay of 300 rubles, similar to that of a minor official, made possible what was, by small-town standards, a refined lifestyle.

On 5 March 1820, he went on a shopping spree. He bought "a peaked cap [*kartuz*] for 3.75 rubles, [partly illegible—suspenders?] for 3 rubles, strings [for a musical instrument] for 75 kopeks, beer and vodka for 1.40 rubles, a bottle of Don wine [*tsimlianskoe*] for 2.50 rubles, a watch for 5 rubles, tobacco for 60 kopeks." At other times he bought soap, and he spent large sums, 10.80 rubles in

---

[16] Population figures from "Statisticheskiia tablitsy o sostoianii gorodov Rossiiskoi Imperii, velikago kniazhestva Finliandskago i Tsarstva Pol'skago po 1842 god," *ZhMVD*, chast' 1, "Smes'" (February 1843), 286–313, here: 293–5.

[17] Jones, "Getting the Goods to St. Petersburg," 413–33.

[18] Ransel, *A Russian Merchant's Tale*, 65–6, 84–6, 150.

one case, on sugar and tea. His shopping list suggests that he was a bit of a fop. Soap permitted cleanliness. Peaked caps were standard headgear for provincial men of Volkov's social position,[19] but suspenders (braces) were worn mainly by the higher classes and were used to support the newly fashionable pantaloons (long trousers, as opposed to breeches). A watch was a stylish accessory, as was the cravat-stiffener he purchased on another occasion. In some provincial circles, such attire was viewed as an outright provocation. Dmitrii Rostislavov, who attended a provincial church school in Kasimov during those years, recalled that "the most intense hatred of all was reserved [by the poorer *popovichi*] for pantaloons and pantaloonists, i.e., those who wore them . . . Only students who came from a town, and those country boys who had close ties to the landowners, had pantaloons."[20] Volkov's list also suggests that he enjoyed the finer creature comforts: tobacco, grape wine (uncommon among the lower classes), and the expensive pleasure of tea sweetened with sugar.

Volkov was a reader. Provincial Russia had few bookshops or libraries, so when he came across a book that he deemed especially meaningful, he—like many contemporaries—made his own copy. After the riddles, the next text that he copied was *A Genealogy of Russian Tsars and Princes of Rus' Descended from the Patriarch Meshech, Son of Japheth, Grandson of Noah* (*Rodoslovnaia Tsarei rossiiskikh i kniazei ruskikh proishchedshikh ot Praottsa Mosokha, Syna Afetova Vnuka Noeva*). It lists all the rulers from Riurik to Peter the Great in the style of the biblical patriarchs: who begat whom, when and how long they reigned, and which ones were tonsured as monks. Then followed Rostopchin's anti-French pamphlet of 1807, *Thoughts Aloud on the Staircase of Honor.* Finally, three religious texts: a sermon and a panegyric by the seventeenth-century Greek bishop Elias Meniates, whose works circulated in Russian in multiple editions, and a short primer entitled *Brief Instruction on the Proper Way to Stand in God's Church During the Service, Compiled from Books by Ecclesiastical Teachers* (*Pouchenie kratkoe kako podobaet stoiati v tserkvi bozhiei vo vremia sluzhby, sobrannoe iz knig uchitelei tserkovnykh*).

Volkov's sense of both lived and historical time was a hybrid of the traditional and the modern. He owned a watch, which measured time in a modern, abstract way, but he combined the secular calendar preferred by the elites with the church tradition familiar to the common folk. He used the secular calendar to date events related to work or money, and the church calendar for religious holidays. For example, he writes, "Holy Week: Friday 26 and Saturday 27 [March 1820], [I] did not work and went home." He ends his copy of Rostopchin's pamphlet with a flourish: "written by the goldsmith Dmitrei [*sic*] Stepanov Volkov, March 26th, 1822, on Annunciation Day." Likewise, after the primer: "written by the

---

[19] Aleksei Sergeev, *Russkiia poslovitsy i pogovorki v litsakh* (St Petersburg: v Voennoi Tipografii, 1830), 2–3.

[20] Rostislavov, *Provincial Russia*, 159–60.

goldsmith Dmitrei Volkov, March 20th, 1822, on Palm Sunday." In this instance, the dual dates gave him trouble, for in 1822, Annunciation Day and Palm Sunday fell on 25–6 March. The genealogy of rulers that he copied is also a cultural hybrid. The title links Russia's rulers back to Noah, but the text begins only with Riurik, the legendary founder of Rus'. Unlike Muscovite chronicles, this is a secular, not a sacred history, yet it provides little analysis and is a far cry from the Russian Enlightenment histories that, in Cynthia Whittaker's words, "formulated an idea of progress, demonstrated secular causation, and displayed interpretive sweep and didactic intent."[21]

Volkov was devoted to the monarchy but had no affection for the nobles or the system of estates. He never mentions anyone's estate identity, including his own. Instead, he describes himself with evident pride as a goldsmith, that is, a member of a skilled, honorable profession. He was also a loyal monarchist. After catching a glimpse of Alexander I, he noted, attentive to the official titulature, that he had gone to see "His Majesty." The history of rulers that he copied places the dynasty at the center of Russian history. It does this by its very structure as a genealogy of monarchs, but also by its interpretation of the great rupture in Russian dynastic history, the Time of Troubles. After the pious Riurikids (who had reigned since 862) died out, Russia experienced calamity, but peace and order were restored when the nation chose the Riurikids' lawful heirs, the Romanovs, as its new rulers. At the end of the genealogy, Volkov spelled out the name of Peter the Great, "Tsar Petr Alekseevich Romanov," in reverentially ornate letters.

His opinion of the Europeanized nobility may be inferred from the fact that he copied Rostopchin's *Thoughts Aloud*. This text was a rant by a fictional provincial nobleman against France and the French-educated Russian elites. "How will they make a stand for faith, tsar, and country," Rostopchin's narrator asks,

when they haven't been taught the catechism and think Russians are bears? . . . Lord have mercy! All you see are young people dressed and shod in the French way; in their words, deeds, and thoughts, they are French. Their homeland is Kuznetskii Most; their Kingdom of Heaven, Paris. They disrespect their parents, despise their elders, and though they are nothing, they want to be everything.[22]

After 1824, Volkov's notebook goes quiet. The final pages, which itemize expenses for 1831–2, suggest that half his 250-ruble annual pay was going to support his family. During the six months covered in the notebook, he sends 44 rubles "home" and another 20 to an unidentified "wife." If this was *his* wife, the cryptic reference to his married state contrasts strangely with the joyful enthusiasm with which he earlier spelled out his name and trade as "goldsmith Dmitrii

---

[21] Whittaker, *Russian Monarchy*, 121.
[22] F. V. Rostopchin, *Sochineniia Rastopchina (grafa Feodora Vasil'evicha)* (St Petersburg: V Tipografii A. Dmitrieva, 1853), 9, 10.

Stepanych Volkov." The years and life's burdens were apparently taking their toll.

Volkov scattered additional notes wherever there was space, including this one on the inside front cover: "on March 23rd, 1829, in the fourth week of Lent, Saturday, I began working in Moscow for Vasilii Larionych Krylov." One "Krylov Vasilii" appears among the "masters of the gold and silver trades" listed in the 1826 Moscow directory. He lived in the third ward of Sushchevskaia District, in the house of the army officer's wife Natal'ia Vyndomskaia on Tikhvinskii Lane, near today's Novoslobodskaia metro station.[23] In 1830, the clergy of the nearby church of the Tikhvinskaia Mother of God, after which the lane was named, recorded that the townsman Vasilii *Mikhailov* Krylov—perhaps the same man, give or take a mistaken patronymic—and his wife had come to confession.[24]

Volkov's notebook makes no further mention of Moscow, and he had left the city again by 1831. Other sources, however, allow us to reconstruct what he must have seen when he arrived in the metropolis in March 1829.

SUSHCHEVSKAIA DISTRICT

From Volkov's stomping grounds along the upper Volga, the road to Moscow passed through the Butyrki (or Mius) Gate. Just over 700 meters past the gate was Tikhvinskii Lane. The 286 people who came to confession at the Tikhvinskaia church in 1830 included 85 merchants and townspeople, 39 miscellaneous commoners (*raznochintsy*), 87 house serfs, 14 peasants, 11 clergy, and 50 personal or hereditary nobles. They formed a socially mixed milieu in which an artisan from the provinces might feel at home.[25] It was this kind of area that Vasilii Perov depicted in his 1868 painting "The Last Tavern Near the City Gates" (see Illustration 7.1). In the background, the city gate is marked by imposing twin obelisks topped with imperial double eagles, but otherwise the neighborhood is unassuming and melancholy. The only light comes from a few candles in the windows, and the street is deserted except for a dog, two horses, and a girl sitting in a sleigh, forlorn, shivering, and alone.

The upper classes regarded Sushchevskaia District, and the outskirts of Moscow in general, as an underdeveloped backwater. It was a frontier zone within the city, where patches of rustic provincialism abutted gritty commercial areas and pockets of neoclassical grandeur. This was the Moscow that greeted new arrivals from the provinces, and if, like Volkov, they left again after a

---

[23] V. Sokolov, *Ukazatel' zhilishch i zdanii v Moskve, ili Adresnaia kniga* (Moscow: V Tipografii Avgusta Simena, 1826), part 1:313, part 2:244.

[24] TsIAM f. 203, op. 747, d. 1154, "Ispovednye vedomosti tserkvei Nikitskogo soroka," l. 195.

[25] TsIAM f. 203, op. 747, d. 1154, "Ispovednye vedomosti tserkvei Nikitskogo soroka," ll. 199–199 ob.

Illus. 7.1. "The Last Tavern Near the City Gate." Painting from 1868 by Vasilii Perov. © The State Tretyakov Gallery, Moscow.

temporary stay, it would help form their overall impression of the city. The area straddled the fault lines of Moscow society, and much like Volkov himself, the people who lived there were likely to acquire an ambivalent attitude toward the regime, the elites, and their culture.

Sushchevskaia District (see Map 7.1) occupied a hexagonal area of north-central Moscow between the Garden Ring and the customs wall, roughly the area bounded today by the metro stations Belorusskaia, Maiakovskaia, Tsvetnoi Bul'var, Prospekt Mira, Rizhskaia, and Savelovskaia. In 1824, when the city had not yet regained its pre-war population, the police tally of Sushchevskaia's residents was 10,867. The figure rose to 15,100 in 1835–9 and 37,467 in 1871. Thanks to migrants like Volkov, there were three males to every two females, a ratio that changed little over time and matched the citywide average.[26]

---

[26] Le Cointe, *Guide*, table facing p. 86; Gastev, *Materialy*, 265–6; "Tablitsy smertnosti v Moskve za mai mesiats 1878 g.," *IMGD*, vypusk 12 (1 July 1878), 1–35; V. N. Benzengr, "Otchet sanitarnago vracha Arbatskoi chasti," *IMGD*, vypusk 16 (1 September 1878), 13–21, here: 14.

Sushchevskaia resembled other areas on Moscow's outskirts in its poverty and lack of urban infrastructure. Moscow was divided into twenty districts until 1832, and seventeen thereafter. Among these districts, Sushchevskaia in 1824 had the fifth-lowest ratio of churches to inhabitants;[27] in 1831, the fifth-lowest average house prices;[28] in 1835–9, the highest mortality rate;[29] and in 1852, the fourth-largest area of unpaved road surface.[30] In each case, the other districts with comparable records were also on the city's periphery. Nor was there much progress in replacing wood construction with masonry. By 1878, 46.5 percent of buildings (*stroeniia*) in Moscow were made of wood, 34.6 percent were masonry, and 18.8 percent combined both (often a wooden upper story on a masonry base). In Sushchevskaia, the figures were 71.9 percent wood, 12.9 percent masonry, and 15.0 percent mixed.[31]

Like other outlying districts, Sushchevskaia had an uneven development pattern influenced by the suburbs that had been located there in the seventeenth century. Densely populated areas were located along major streets in the south (the old suburb of the artisans for the Kremlin Armory), the southwest (formerly the Tverskaia coachmen's suburb and the Novo-Dmitrovskaia and Sushchevskaia suburbs), and the northeast (the former Meshchanskaia suburb, populated in the seventeenth century by settlers from Belorussia).[32] Elsewhere, sparse settlement permitted noble estates to survive and encouraged the implantation of schools, hospitals, and prisons. The variations within Sushchevskaia were such that when Moscow's ninety-one wards were ranked in 1879 according to their incidence of typhus, one ward in Sushchevskaia was in 8th place (one case per 162.9 inhabitants) while another was in 86th (one case per 810.6 inhabitants).[33]

To understand how this heterogeneity appeared to those who lived there, let us imagine following Volkov on a tour of the neighborhood. If he went out his door and headed west on Tikhvinskii Lane, which was unpaved as late as 1880,[34] he would pass gardens, orchards, and a few homes belonging to a motley assortment of mostly middling estates. The house where his employer lived was registered to three owners: the officer's wife Vyndomskaia, a lumber

---

[27] Here and later, the source for statistical data on Moscow in 1824 is Le Cointe, *Guide*, table facing p. 86.

[28] Androssov, *Statisticheskaia zapiska*, 38–9.

[29] Gastev, *Materialy*, 272–5.

[30] "Po povodu spiska nazamoshchennykh mestnostei goroda Moskvy," *IMGD*, vypusk 5 (1880), 1–28, here: 1.

[31] *IMGD*, vypusk 16 (1878), untitled series of tables following p. 45.

[32] Sytin, *Iz istorii moskovskikh ulits*, 623, 625, 627, 641.

[33] Shervinskii, "Otchet," 27–8.

[34] "Po povodu spiska nazamoshchennykh mestnostei," 16.

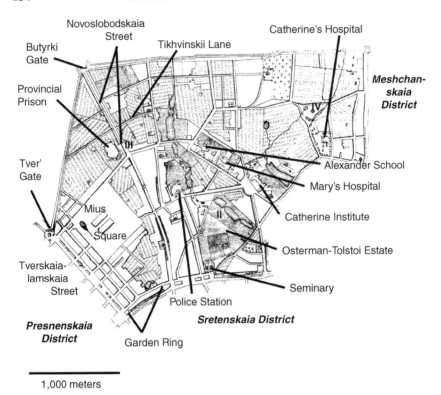

Map 7.1. Map of Sushchevskaia District (Source: A. Khotev, *Atlas stolichnago goroda Moskvy* (Moscow: Tip. Vedomostei Mosk. gor. politsii, 1852–3))

merchant and his family, and a merchant widow who lived from rental income. The other five houses on Tikhvinskii Lane belonged to a countess, a merchant widow, a sacristan, a townsman who worked as a turner, and a minor civil servant.[35] The first intersection he would reach was Novoslobodskaia Street, the area's main thoroughfare. Across the intersection was the Provincial Prison, today Preliminary Detention Center No. 2 (the so-called Butyrki Prison). To the right, a short walk up Novoslobodskaia, past more gardens and a few houses, lay the customs wall and the Butyrki Gate.

---

[35] TsIAM f. 14, op. 7, d. 3488, ll. 6 ob, 20 ob, 27 ob, 31 ob, 50 ob, 52 ob, "Obyvatel'skaia kniga po Sushchevskoi chasti s 1828 po 1831."

We have an impressionistic description of this area, the third ward of Sushchevskaia, by Pavel Bogatyrev. Looking back from the early twentieth century, he wrote that because no major highway entered the city through the Butyrki Gate, the area in the mid-nineteenth century was "quiet" and "deserted." People settled there if they could not afford to live downtown, policemen were posted there for disciplinary infractions, and the only draw for outsiders was cheap liquor. "Anyone who chanced to come to live in Butyrki ended up living there for good: it somehow 'sucked in' the newcomer. This is how the 'native' population there was formed, primarily from Moscow towns-people and artisans."[36]

If Volkov was not in the mood for a bucolic stroll in Butyrki, he could turn at the prison and head southwest toward the Tver' Gate. This was where the highway from St Petersburg entered Moscow and created the bustling corridor of Tverskaia-Iamskaia Street, which formed the boundary between Sushchevs-kaia and Presnenskaia districts. "On the left [Sushchevskaia] side of the street, the houses are wooden and dilapidated," wrote Volkov's contemporary, the St Petersburg journalist Nikolai Grech, in an otherwise gushing account of his visit to Moscow, whereas "on the right [toward Presnenskaia] are new ones of masonry that were built for the Moscow coachmen by the Lord Emperor's generosity."[37] Tverskaia-Iamskaia Street (from *iamshchik*, "coachman") and its side streets, in Sushchevskaia's first ward, were lined with dozens of coaching inns. The 1828–31 police register lists sixty-six of them on the Sushchevskaia side, and according to the 1826 city directory, nine of every ten houses owned by coachmen in Sushchevskaia were on or near Tverskaia-Iamskaia. (A coaching inn provided covered galleries to shelter horses and carriages; the men slept in their vehicles or, in bad weather, in cabins.[38]) Nearby lay the lumber market of Mius Square and the coal, dairy, and produce markets of Ugol'naia and Drov'ianaia squares. According to the 1826 directory, this area had Sushchevskaia's heaviest concentration of houses owned by merchants and townspeople.[39] Thanks to this business district, which probably resembled the bustling neighborhood of St Petersburg shown in Illustration 7.2, Sush-chevskaia in 1824 had the third-highest ratio of shops to inhabitants of any district of the city.

The statistician Vasilii Androssov noted in 1832 that economic dominance in Moscow was passing from the nobility to "the middle estate."[40] Sushchevskaia

[36] Bogatyrev, "Moskovskaia Starina," in Aleksandrov, *Moskovskaia Starina*, 120–2.

[37] "Moskovskiia pis'ma," in Nikolai Grech, *Sochineniia*, 5 vols. (St Petersburg: V tipografii N. Grecha, 1838), 5:99–100.

[38] Nikitin, "Otchet," 21–3.

[39] Sokolov, *Ukazatel' zhilishch i zdanii*, part 1:297–318.

[40] Androssov, *Statisticheskaia zapiska*, 46. Pushkin made a similar observation in 1834 in "A Journey from Moscow to St. Petersburg": Alexander Pushkin, *The Complete Works of Alexander Pushkin*, 15 vols. (Norwich: Milner, 1999–2003), 13:234.

Illus. 7.2. "The Coachmen's Market." Lithograph from 1820 by Aleksander Orłowski. © 2012, State Russian Museum, St Petersburg. This scene is set in St Petersburg.

and other peripheral areas were seeing an influx of poor workers and a steady increase in small-scale entrepreneurship, much of it by women. Noble landholdings, Androssov wrote, were being subdivided "among townswomen, soldiers' wives, and peasant women, who carry on small-scale factory production, and who first acquire the means to build themselves a little house on someone else's property and later become able to buy the property itself as well."[41]

Some of these developments show up in the police register of Sushchevskaia for 1828–31.[42] The 1,853 residents it lists made up 656 households. Of these, 422 were homeowners and 234 were renters. According to the 1826 city directory, Sushchevskaia contained 647 homesteads, so we may surmise that the 422 homeowners included in the register are two-thirds of the total. On the other hand, the police register does not include most renters. The police themselves reported that the area had 10,000 to 15,000 inhabitants, without counting the

41 Androssov, *Statisticheskaia zapiska*, 49.
42 TsIAM f. 14, op. 7, d. 3488, "Obyvatel'skaia kniga po Sushchevskoi chasti."

migrant workers, coachmen, and others who rented temporary lodgings or simply slept in the street, at construction sites, and so on.

The households in the police register provide an economic profile of the area's more settled and prosperous classes. Of the 656 households, 532 reported their livelihood. The largest category was composed of 176 artisans, among whom no single trade predominated. The second-largest, 126 households, engaged in commerce. Since artisans often sold their own wares, the line between the two categories is fluid. Of those engaged in commerce, several traded in the downtown markets around Red Square, but the largest groups dealt in wood and foodstuffs, which were traded at sprawling markets in Sushchevskaia itself. Another 75 provided services. Most of these (66 households) ran coaching inns along Tverskaia-Iamskaia Street; the others were two bathhouse operators, two cabdrivers, two innkeepers, and three barbers. A further 101 households survived on rental income from their house, 39 reported living from their savings, and 15 had various other livelihoods. Perhaps reflecting the female entrepreneurship observed by Androssov, the 335 non-noble homeowners included 85 women, but 54 of these reported living from rental income, while only 17 listed a trade or business; the others provided no information.

Living conditions were harsh, as in most cities in Russia and the West at that time. We lack descriptions from the 1820s or 1830s, but detailed surveys were conducted in the era of the Great Reforms. In 1878, the city government appointed seventeen "sanitary physicians" to investigate health conditions, one for each district of the city.[43] In certain ways, their reports are a product of their time. They express the sentiments of the intelligentsia of the 1870s: a patronizing protectiveness toward the poor; outrage at the government's failure to uplift the people; and a resolve to describe material reality without sentimentality or propagandistic whitewashing. Because the population was larger and denser than in Volkov's time, the problems that the physicians described had grown more severe, but the underlying issues were already present when Volkov was there.[44]

The physician who investigated conditions in Sushchevskaia was a young medical professor, Vasilii Shervinskii (1850–1941), who later gained renown as the founder of endocrinology in Russia.[45] Shervinskii's chief complaint concerned the pollution caused by human and animal waste. Coaching inns, private homes, and even hospitals, he reported, were reluctant to pay to have

---

[43] A. Chertov, *Gorodskaia meditsina v Evropeiskoi Rossii: Sbornik svedenii ob ustroistve vrachebno-sanitarnoi chasti v gorodakh* (Moscow: Pechatnia S. P. Iakovleva, 1903), 102.

[44] Old-timers recalled that the waters and gardens of the early nineteenth century had been far cleaner; Chicherin, *Moskva sorokovykh godov*, 173.

[45] Nikolai Krementsov, "Hormones and the Bolsheviks: From Organotherapy to Experimental Endocrinology, 1918–1929," *Isis*, 99/3 (September 2008), 486–518.

their refuse removed and their cesspits cleaned. Instead, they used the streets, waterways, and parks as sewers. To name but one shocking example, Mary's Hospital allowed its privies to overflow into a pond where people bathed after using the adjacent public bathhouse. Horse dung, of which coaching inns had enormous quantities, was spread across orchards and kitchen gardens as fertilizer, thereby fouling the air in Sushchevskaia's more rustic stretches. Dried dung in the streets mixed with dust and blew around in billowing clouds that forced residents to seal the windows of their "clean rooms," those facing the street and intended for receiving visitors. Matters were even worse toward the rear of people's houses, where the bedrooms were located. These looked out onto the courtyard, which contained a pit for trash and wastewater, and nearby, a privy with a cesspit that was usually allowed to fill up until it threatened to overflow. All of this waste polluted the air and soil, and seeped into the wells where the inhabitants drew their water.[46]

The officially recommended remedy, which consisted of hiring cesspool cleaners to haul one's waste to government-approved dump sites, created its own problems. One doctor wrote about the sewage dump a little over one kilometer south of Zamoskvorech'e. "When it is windy, the stench carries from the city gate up Kaluzhskaia Street. It also spreads almost daily after barrels of waste are carted through the streets; the smell occurs because the barrels are not closed hermetically and through spillage of waste."[47] The sanitary physician for Meshchanskaia District, immediately east of Sushchevskaia, investigated a dump near slaughterhouses just north of the city. He reported that liquid sewage, mixed with rotting animal blood "and so on," formed a "swamp" over a substratum of decomposing animal remains, from which large gassy bubbles rose to the surface and popped with a bang. From this site, a revolting stench wafted back into the city.[48]

Shervinskii and his colleagues found the conditions in stores and artisan shops similarly unsatisfactory. Most employees slept where they worked. Grocery stores were filthy and malodorous.[49] Workshops were insalubrious schools of vice. Seamstresses' shops were staffed with undernourished young girls of 10 to 15 who worked long hours "in very cramped spaces and the most foul air." Laundresses drank all day long and worked in cellars that had "little light, murderous humidity, and air that was stifling beyond belief." In the male trades, the adults were "utterly incorrigible drunkards and the cruelest despots to [the

---

[46] Shervinskii, "Otchet," passim.

[47] K. Kh. Inoevs, "Sanitarnyi otchet po 4 i 5 kvartalam Serpukhovskoi chasti," *IMGD*, vypusk 17 (15 September 1878), 42–5, here: 45.

[48] Nikitin, "Otchet," 28–9; V. K. Papandopulo, "Otchet sanitarnago vracha Presnenskoi chasti," *IMGD*, vypusk 17 (15 September 1878), 31–5, here: 34; Inoevs, "Sanitarnyi otchet," 45.

[49] Nikitin, "Otchet," 26–7.

boys who are] their assistants."[50] In metallurgical shops, "On top of the over-crowding, humidity, and filth, there is also the fine metal dust and the charcoal fumes from the forge."[51] Shoemakers' shops were particularly dangerous: "The boys apprenticed here mostly find themselves in dreadful hygienic circumstances," leading to "anemia, scrofula, and consumption."[52] Shops making fashionable apparel were by far the best places to work. The gold, silver, and jewelry trade, in which Volkov worked, ranked near the top or at least in the middle of the hierarchy of working conditions.[53]

Artisans had a hard life, but at least their craft could provide a steady living. Others had to scrape by on the margins of the economy. In 1845, the government undertook a citywide study of male townsmen. Officials determined that 16,597 of them were registered as businessmen, artisans, coach drivers, or servants, but there was no official record of how the remainder—23,645 men—got by. Some evidently acted as fences for stolen property. Others worked in the gray market, for example buying and reselling goods from peasant traders, ostensibly at a discount but in fact using tricks (say, wetting hay to make it heavier) to make a profit. Still others, so the study concluded, were themselves unable to explain how they made it through the day.[54]

Even lower stood the truly destitute. We learn something of who they were from a commission that studied 5,888 people arrested citywide in 1840 for begging. Owing to the rural distress caused by the bad harvest of 1839, the largest group of paupers, 2,443 individuals (41.5 percent), were peasants or house serfs. Another 1,260 people (21.4 percent) were legally townspeople or artisans, many of whom were in fact elderly manumitted serfs with no means of support. The peasants, house serfs, and artisans (less so the townspeople) were divided evenly between men and women. The third large group, army lower ranks (1,643 individuals, or 27.9 percent), was 78.1 percent female, reflecting the poverty and social isolation of soldiers' wives. Paupers were older than the general population (50.7 percent were over 50) and 59.9 percent were female. The commission noted that 16.2 percent of the men were literate but only 1.7 percent of the women: "Such want of literacy, and of a certain education of the mind that accompanies it, which one notes among the female sex, most likely contributes greatly to the fact that among inveterate paupers one notices far more women than men."[55]

---

[50] Benzengr, "Otchet," 19; Nikitin, "Otchet," 19.

[51] Nikitin, "Otchet," 20. *Ugar*, which I have rendered as "charcoal fumes," can also mean "smelting waste."

[52] I. Zaborovskii, "Sanitarnyi otchet po Basmannoi chasti, za 1879 god," *IMGD*, vypusk 3 (1880), cols. 1–38, quotation on 20.

[53] Nikitin, "Otchet," 20; Zaborovskii, "Sanitarnyi otchet," col. 20; Tikhomirov, "Otchet," 47–8.

[54] "Meshchanskoe soslovie v Moskve (za 1845 god)," *ZhMVD* (January 1847), 71–86.

[55] "Otchet komiteta, vysochaishe uchrezhdennago v Moskve, dlia razbora i prizreniia prosiashchikh milostyniu, za 1840 god," *ZhMVD*, chast' 39 (March 1841), 307–49;

We see something of the anxieties that the poor inspired in the higher classes in an article from the 1850s about crime and poverty in Moscow in the early nineteenth century. The police, the author writes, made

the rounds at night of the repulsive refuges of destitution, debauchery, and crime... These refuges include: a) the repulsively filthy apartments and cellars where people without permanent abode as well as the paupers of the metropolis are allowed only to spend the night; [these paupers] grind out a living by begging for alms with doleful voices outside churches and on the streets, but in the mornings they are the first to gather by the tavern doors and wait for them to open, and in the evening they sing all sorts of audacious songs there with cheerful voices and accompany their orgies with astoundingly foul language; when the taverns' closing time arrives, they have to be expelled by force. All sorts of scoundrels, fugitives in hiding, and criminals often find refuge in such lodgings. b) Houses for the trade in debauchery. c) All public drinking and eating establishments. d) Public bathhouses, and so on.[56]

But let us resume our stroll around Volkov's neighborhood. Aside from rustic Butyrki and the gritty commercial district, Sushchevskaia also had upscale areas. Volkov could head east on Tikhvinskii Lane and make for central Sushchevskaia. Here, amidst spacious gardens and orchards, an archipelago of neoclassical architecture that still impresses visitors today embodied the regime's effort to reshape society through education, health care, and law enforcement.

Three of the major building complexes housed educational institutions. These did not serve the needs of Sushchevskaia itself, which as of 1840 had only two public primary schools that enrolled a paltry 67 boys and no girls. Rather, they drew young people from Moscow and beyond who belonged to the estates targeted by the imperial social project. Moscow's two imperial boarding schools for girls, with a combined enrollment in 1840 of 437 pupils, were located in the middle of Sushchevskaia: the Catherine Institute for hereditary nobles (which today houses the Cultural Center of the Russian Armed Forces), and the Alexander School for daughters of personal nobles and commoners. To the south, facing the Garden Ring, stands a mansion that is now the All-Russian Museum of Decorative Applied and Folk Art. It was damaged in 1812 and was sold in 1834 to the Holy Synod as the new home of the Moscow Ecclesiastical Seminary, which had outgrown its previous space in the Zaikonospasskii monastery in Kitai-Gorod. Once the complex in Sushchevskaia was fully reconstructed, the seminary moved there in 1844; even before, sections of the building that were deemed habitable served as a seminary dormitory. In 1840, the seminary enrolled 606 students.[57]

"Vsepoddanneishii otchet Moskovskago komiteta o prosiashchikh milostyniu, za 1841 god (Izvlechenie)," *ZhMVD*, chast' 43 (March 1842), 221–61, here: 225–7.

[56] Khaliutin, "Moskovskii syshchik Iakovlev," 85–6.

[57] "Otchet moskovskago ober-politsmeistera, za 1840 god," 27–8; *Istoricheskaia zapiska o Moskovskikh uchilishchakh*, 63, 145, 185; N. I. Kedrov, *Moskovskaia dukhovnaia seminariia,*

All three schools were architecturally imposing but presented a rather forbidding appearance to outsiders. An alumna of the Catherine Institute recalled that when she first arrived in 1848, 10 years old, "The carriage brought my father and me to a large, majestic building with a huge courtyard that was enclosed by a cast-iron fence lined with acacias; by the gates, which clanged shut immediately after admitting us, there stood a guardhouse, and a sentry with a rifle paced back and forth."[58]

The two girls' schools carried on the educational philosophy of Catherine II and Betskoi, according to which children should be isolated from the corrupting influences of society. Hence, their pupils were forbidden to leave the school grounds. As *institutki*, they were educated to become enlightened wives, mothers, or governesses to the upper classes, but their schooling ensured that they would not become intermediaries between those classes and the plebeian neighborhood surrounding their schools. On the contrary, they developed a reputation for being sheltered and naive about the wider world. Seminarians had greater contact with the wider community—not by design, but because a shortage of dormitory space forced many to commute from home or from rented lodgings.[59]

Other landmark buildings in Sushchevskaia served as hospitals, which, like the Catherine Institute and the Alexander School, were under the well-publicized patronage of the imperial family. Adjacent to the Alexander School stood Mary's Hospital for the Poor. (Both the school and the hospital today house a medical research center.) A visitor in 1829 might have crossed paths here with 8-year-old Fedor Dostoevskii, whose father was a physician at the hospital and whose literary work later chronicled the hard life of the urban masses. Farther east, past meadows and orchards, lay Catherine's Hospital, also for the poor. The government was proud of these institutions and publicized statistics that documented their work. In 1840, the two hospitals plus the hospital of the Provincial Prison had 569 beds and admitted 4,680 patients; excluding Moscow's two large military hospitals, this represented one-fifth of the city's hospital beds and patients that year.[60] They also provided outpatient services: in 1822, Mary's Hospital provided medications to 35,475 people.[61] The primary purpose of these hospitals was to combat infectious diseases, but they also served a purpose of social pedagogy by bringing European medical science to a population that more often placed its trust in folk healers.[62]

Other prominent buildings belonged to the police. Aside from the guardhouses in the streets, the most conspicuous strongholds of the police were the

---

1814–1889: Kratkii istoricheskii ocherk s prilozheniem spiskov nachal'nikov, nastavnikov i vospitannikov (Moscow: Tipo-litografiia T-va I. N. Kushnerev i Ko., 1889), 75, 91.

[58] Engel'gardt, "Ocherki," in Bokova and Sakharova, *Institutki*, 132.
[59] Kedrov, *Moskovskaia dukhovnaia seminariia*, 75.
[60] "Otchet moskovskago ober-politsmeistera, za 1840 god," 52–61.
[61] Le Cointe, *Guide*, 330.
[62] See, for example: Alexander, *Bubonic Plague*, 54, 93, 278.

Provincial Prison and the Sushchevskaia police station, today the Museum of the Interior Ministry. During 1830, a total of 3,638 prisoners passed through the Provincial Prison; most were charged with minor offenses such as theft or passport violations.[63] In 1819, as part of Alexander I's effort to make ecumenical Christian values the foundation of Russian social relations, British philanthropists and Russian officials established the Prison Reform Society. Its purpose was to bring religion to prison inmates, alleviate their physical sufferings, and make prisons into places of genuine rehabilitation.[64] The Provincial Prison, which the government eagerly showed to visitors, reflected this philosophy. Robert Lyall reported in 1823 that "this prison is built according to the ideas of the distinguished and philanthropic [British prison reformer John] Howard." He added that "the prisoners live remarkably well" and that "the *Smotritel*, or keeper, is very polite." Other visitors under Alexander I came away with similar impressions.[65] Evidently, these conditions did not last. In 1873, a Russian commission on prison reform declared that the Provincial Prison was "the model of all outrages." The commission described it as a hellhole of filthy, moldy, smoky, airless cells, where the guards alternately neglected and brutalized the prisoners. The first step toward improving Russia's prisons should be to close it down.[66]

To the southeast of the Provincial Prison lay the police station. Its most conspicuous feature was a tall observation tower that allowed firemen to keep watch and communicate, using flags or lights, with similar stations across the city. The people who lived there included thirty-four policemen, two *zaplechnye mastera* (wielders of the lash), and eighty-four firemen. In addition to their other functions, these men served pedagogical purposes designed to mold the consciousness of the inhabitants. Thus, the police shamed drunkards of all social stations by making them sweep the streets, and flogged serfs upon the request of their masters. Likewise, the firemen promoted the regime's militaristic aesthetic with the speed of their maneuvers and the smartness of their uniforms, horses, and vehicles.[67]

---

[63] Androssov, *Statisticheskaia zapiska*, 141.

[64] Judith C. Zacek, "A Case Study in Russian Philanthropy: The Prison Reform Movement in the Reign of Alexander I," *Canadian Slavic Studies*, 1/2 (Summer 1967), 196–211; Barry Hollingsworth, "John Venning and Prison Reform in Russia, 1819–1830," *Slavonic and East European Review*, 48/113 (October 1970), 537–56.

[65] Lyall, *The Character of the Russians*, 426, 428. See also: James Holman, *Travels through Russia, Siberia, Poland, Austria, Saxony, Prussia, Hanover, &c. &c. Undertaken during the Years 1822, 1823, and 1824, While Suffering from Total Blindness*, 2 vols. (London: Geo. B. Whittaker, 1825), 1:284; Stephen Grellet, *Memoirs of the Life and Gospel Labours of Stephen Grellet*, ed. Benjamin Seebohm, 2 vols. (3rd edn., London: A. W. Bennett, 1862), 1:379–80; James Sherman, *Memoir of William Allen, F.R.S.* (London: Charles Gilpin; Edinburgh: Adam and Charles Black; Dublin: J. B. Gilpin; 1851), 235–6.

[66] A. F. Koni, *Fedor Petrovich Gaaz: Biograficheskii ocherk* (2nd edn., St Petersburg: Izdanie A. F. Marksa, 1901), 87–8.

[67] S. Gromeka, "Politseiskoe deloproizvodstvo," *Russkii Vestnik*, vol. 16 (1858), 178–94, esp. 182.

Under Nicholas I, medicine and law enforcement became intertwined in ways both coercive and humanitarian. They worked together to tighten social controls, especially over lower-class women. The Moscow police in 1844 established an office to enforce the compulsory hospitalization of people infected with syphilis and to monitor the health of prostitutes, who were sent from all over the city for medical examinations at the Sushchevskaia police station.[68] On the other hand, medicine also helped to humanize the activity of the police. This aspect of the medicine–police nexus was embodied most visibly by the German immigrant Dr Friedrich Joseph Haas (Fedor Petrovich Gaaz, 1780–1853), who lived at Catherine's Hospital in Sushchevskaia and served, from 1829 until his death in 1853, as chief physician for the entire Moscow prison system. Haas worked tirelessly to improve the treatment of imprisoned debtors, convicts, and exiles on their way to Siberia. Charity toward prisoners was a long-standing tradition in Russia, and Haas's efforts won him widespread affection among the common people: 20,000 mourners are reported to have attended his funeral, and as late as the 1890s, the police hospital for the poor that he founded, and the lightened shackles for convicts that he introduced, were popularly known as "Haas's" (*gaazovskii*).[69]

To a neighborhood resident like Volkov, the schools, hospitals, and police buildings of Sushchevskaia embodied an authoritarian social pedagogy. A very different kind of contact with the culture of the elites was available at the Osterman-Tolstoi estate park, adjacent to the seminary, which offered entertainment for anyone with decent manners, proper attire, and a modicum of cash. Renamed "Hermitage," it was opened to the public in 1824. Vistors could see an eagle in a cage and a monkey on a chain, stroll among sculptures of tsars and mythological figures, enjoy boat rides and concerts, and, on imperial holidays, fireworks and illuminations. The only admission requirement was appropriate dress. In the 1830s, following a period of neglect, the park became more commercialized. First it was leased by an Italian who opened a café and hired musicians. Later, it was used for music, fireworks, and freak shows.[70] In 1842, the essayist Pavel Vistengof tried to describe places like this (albeit not the Hermitage in particular). After the elites left town for the summer, "dressmakers, seamstresses, flower girls, merchants, and office clerks" descended on parks and

---

[68] Irina Paert, *Old Believers, Religious Dissent and Gender in Russia, 1760–1850* (Manchester: Manchester University Press, 2003), 209; Laura Engelstein, *The Keys to Happiness: Sex and the Search for Modernity in Fin-de-Siècle Russia* (Ithaca, NY: Cornell University Press, 1992), 86; Shchepkin, "Istoricheskaia zapiska o raskhodakh," 43. The Sushchevskaia police station became the central site for medical examinations of prostitutes at a date prior to 1871; Shchepkin, "Istoricheskaia zapiska o raskhodakh," 45.

[69] Koni, *Fedor Petrovich Gaaz*, 87–8, 162, 168; Hollingsworth, "John Venning and Prison Reform," 554–5; Nistrem, *Moskovskii adress-kalendar'*, 2:312; see also Leitch Ritchie, *Russia and the Russians, or A Journey to St. Petersburg and Moscow through Courland and Livonia* (Philadelphia: E. L. Carey and A. Hart, 1836), 154.

[70] Sytin, *Iz istorii Moskovskikh ulits*, 632–3; N., "Pis'mo iz Moskvy," *Sovremennik*, vol. 52 (July 1855), 191–6; Kondrat'ev, *Sedaia starina Moskvy*, 438–9.

suburban estates for amusements that Vistengof listed with the zest of a carnival barker: "The *Parisian Tivoli*, the *Viennese and Berlin Praters*, and diverse *Elysiums*, which are the site of various amazing *metamorphoses*, magnificent *catastrophes*, *Olympic circuses*, *Spanish pantomimes*, *Labors of Hercules*, *Chinese dances*, *Indian games*, Doctor *Faustus's* journey to *Hell* with his assistant *Pluto*, *Bacchus* riding on a *barrel*, and various unheard-of, picturesque *tableaux* illumined by *Bengal* lights." Bands played, Russian and Gypsy choruses sang, people went for boat rides by the light of fireworks, and throughout, "the gentlemen are very gracious with the ladies."[71] For all his ironic condescension, Vistengof saw evidence that on the outskirts of Moscow, among middling people similar to Volkov, a European urban culture was taking shape.

The copybook of Dmitrii Volkov affords a glimpse of how the world looked to a person near the bottom of the middling sort, and our overview of Sushchevskaia District situates that experience of the city in the spatial context of one neighborhood. Moscow also had larger social dynamics that transcended individual neighborhoods and that shaped Volkov's world.

ESTATES AND NEIGHBORHOODS

Contemporaries divided Moscow into three socially distinct areas. North of the river and inside the Garden Ring lay the city center (the Kremlin, Kitai-Gorod, White City, and Earthen City), where most of the aristocracy, commerce, and officialdom were located. Outside the Garden Ring were socially amorphous suburbs like Sushchevskaia. South of the river was Zamoskvorech'e, home to much of the merchantry. How many people lived in these three areas can be seen in the police statistics in Table 7.1.

To gain a better understanding of the social makeup of these areas, I compiled a database of confessional registers from 1829, the year Volkov arrived in Moscow. Priests drew up these registers annually to record who had come to confession, which was a legal obligation for Orthodox Christians. They list the residents of each house in the parish (including any who failed to come to confession) by name, estate, age, and family relationship.[72] The database contains the complete records for 1829 from four parishes located in the three principal areas of the city: the church of St Nicholas, in central Moscow's Tverskaia District; the church of Venerable Pimen, in suburban Sushchevskaia; and in Zamoskvorech'e, the churches of SS. Kosma and Damian (Piatnitskaia District) and Venerable Maron (Iakimanskaia District). These registers list a total

---

[71] Vistengof, *Ocherki*, 88–9.
[72] For the rules governing these registers, see PSZ (First Series), vol. 10, no. 7,226 (16 April 1737).

Table 7.1. Population of the city center, Zamoskvorech'e, and the suburbs, 1824 and 1871

	1824		1871	
	Inhabitants	Share of total	Inhabitants	Share of total
City center	113,883	46.12%	238,609	39.63%
Zamoskvorech'e	23,362	9.47%	49,163	8.16%
Suburbs	109,400	44.35%	314,217	52.19%
Total	246,645	100%	601,989	100%

Note: Le Cointe, *Guide*, table facing p. 86; "Tablitsy smertnosti v Moskve za mai mesiats 1878 g.," 1–35 (these data were collected in 1871 (see Benzengr, "Otchet," 14)). Only areas north of the river and outside the Garden Ring are counted here as suburbs.

of 2,889 parishioners.[73] To gain further insight into the smaller estates of clergy and nobles, I added the inhabitants of all the houses owned by clergy in another ten parishes (415 individuals of various estates),[74] and the 251 people of various estates who lived or worked at the Imperial Widows' Home.[75] All told, the database includes 3,555 individuals.

Like any document, the registers reflect the concerns of their authors. They cover only registered parishioners, not transients, and the clergymen who faced the burdensome job of compiling a new register every year may have been tempted to save time by copying listings from the previous year without updating them.[76] Unlike the police register of Sushchevskaia residents that we discussed

[73] TsIAM f. 203, op. 747, d. 1130, "Ispovednye vedomosti nikitskogo soroka 1829," ll. 447–61 ob, tserkov' Nikolaia chudotvortsa, chto v Gnezdnikakh (753 parishioners); ll. 508–37, tserkov' Prepodobnogo Pimena, chto v novykh vorotnikakh (1,254 parishioners); TsIAM f. 203, op. 747, d. 1128, "Ispovednye vedomosti tserkvei zamoskvoretskogo soroka [1829]," ll. 236–51 ob, ts. Kosmodamianskaia, chto v nizhnikh sadovnikakh (603 parishioners); ll. 581–89 ob, ts. Prepodobnogo Marona chudotvortsa, chto v starykh panakh (279 parishioners).

[74] TsIAM f. 203, op. 747, d. 1130, Tverskaia District: ts. Aleksiia Mitropolita, chto na Glinishchakh (39 parishioners, ll. 2–3 ob) and ts. Voskreseniia Khristova, chto na Uspenskom vrazhke (21 parishioners, ll. 87–87 ob); Arbatskaia: ts. Blagoveshcheniia presviatoi Bogoroditsy, chto za Tverskimi vorotami (35 parishioners, ll. 14–14a), ts. Vozneseniia Gospodnia, chto na Tsaritsynoi ulitse (53 parishioners, ll. 31–32 ob), ts. Vozneseniia Gospodnia, chto na Bol'shoi Nikitskoi (18 parishioners, ll. 46–46 ob), and ts. Voskreseniia Khristova, chto v Maloi Bronnoi (48 parishioners, ll. 101–2); Presnenskaia: ts. Vasiliia Kesariiskogo, chto v Tverskoi Iamskoi slobode (68 parishioners, ll. 59–60). TsIAM f. 203, op. 747, d. 1128; Iakimanskaia: ts. Nikolaia chudotvortsa, chto v Golutvine (53 parishioners, ll. 1–2) and ts. Bozhiei Materi vsekh skorbiashchikh radosti, chto na Bol'shoi ordynke (45 parishioners, ll. 34–5); Piatnitskaia: ts. Sv. Ioanna Predtechi, chto pod Borom (35 parishioners, ll. 19–19 ob).

[75] TsIAM f. 203, op. 747, d. 1130, l. 397–406, ts. Sviatyia Ravno-Apostol'nyia Marii Magdaliny, chto v Imperatorskom Vdov'em Dome (Presnenskaia District).

[76] The usefulness and reliability of the confessional registers for analyzing the makeup of the urban population is discussed in Mironov, *Russkii gorod*, 7–8. A recent study finds that the registers' reliability varied considerably from one case to another: Daniel H. Kaiser, "The Sacrament of Confession in the Russian Empire: A Contribution to the Source Study of *Ispovednye rospisi*," in

earlier, the confessional registers do not include people's livelihood and street address. On the other hand, they present the advantage that they list many lower-class residents whom the police omitted.

How comprehensively did the confessional registers list the population? As of 1824, Moscow had 263 parish churches.[77] Each compiled an annual confessional register that included a summary table breaking down the parishioners by estate. To test how much of the population was registered in a parish, I examined these tables for 89 of the 91 churches that composed the Zamoskvoretskii and Sretenskii ecclesiastical districts (*soroki*).[78] These 89 churches were spread across ten of the twenty districts into which the police divided the city. (These police districts also had an additional 26 churches that belonged to other *soroki* and are not examined here.) Table 7.2 compares police data covering all the inhabitants and churches in these ten police districts—two in the city center, two in Zamoskvorech'e, and six in the suburbs[79]—with data from the 89 churches.

Table 7.2. Population and parish registration in selected districts, 1824 and 1829

	Police count, 1824*			Confessional registers, 1829**			
	Parish churches	Inhab- itants	Average per church	Parish churches	Parish- ioners	Average per church	Ratio of males to females
City center	42	39,780	947	23	12,782	556	1:1.1
Zamoskvorech'e	34	23,362	687	33	17,964	544	1:1.1
Suburbs	39	65,586	1,682	33	25,955	787	1:1.2

* Le Cointe, *Guide*, table facing p. 86.
** Data from the summary tables in TsIAM f. 203, op. 747, d. 1128 and d. 1132.

Comparing inhabitants per church as counted by the police with the number of registered parishioners, we see that only a minority of Muscovites were registered in a local parish. Vasilii Androssov found that in 1830, out of a total population just over 300,000, only 68,630 males and 70,650 females were registered with local parishes.[80] Those not registered were mainly rural migrants. Most migrants were men, which explains why females formed a majority of registered parishioners even though the overall population (according to the

Brian Boeck, Russell Martin, and Daniel Rowland, eds., *Aporia: Studies in Early Slavic History and Culture in Honor of Donald Ostrowski* (Bloomington, Ind.: Slavica, 2011).

[77] Le Cointe, *Guide*, table facing p. 86.

[78] Of the two remaining churches, one is not identified by name in the register, and the other is located outside the ten police districts covered by this analysis.

[79] City center—Miasnitskaia and Sretenskaia; Zamoskvorech'e—Iakimanskaia and Piatnistkaia; suburbs—Basmannaia, Lefortovskaia, Meshchanskaia, Pokrovskaia, Serpukhovskaia, and Suchchevskaia.

[80] Androssov, *Statisticheskaia zapiska*, 100–1, 116.

police data used by Androssov) was 61 percent male. The unchurched were concentrated in the city center and the suburbs, two areas where manufacturing and large aristocratic households employed migrant laborers. By contrast, Zamoskvorech'e, with its more settled population of traders and minor officials, had a much higher percentage of parish registration.

The database of 2,889 parishioners at four Moscow churches bears out the impression that once we exclude peasants, registered parishioners were representative of the city in terms of their estate composition.[81] Table 7.3 compares those four parishes with the population figures provided by Androssov.

Table 7.3. Estate composition of Moscow and selected parishes, 1829–30

Estate:	Four parishes, 1829			Overall Moscow population, 1830*		
	Total	Including peasants	Excluding peasants	Total	Including peasants	Excluding peasants
Nobles	233	8.06	8.62	22,394	7.38	9.73
Clergy	90	3.11	3.33	4,946	1.63	2.15
Merchants	274	9.48	10.14	16,310	5.38	7.09
Townspeople	776	26.86	28.74	47,287	15.60	20.56
Artisans	112	3.87	4.14	12,461	4.11	5.41
Soldiers	266	9.20	9.85	27,476	9.06	11.94
Peasants	189	6.54	—	73,049	24.10	—
House serfs	743	25.71	27.51	70,920	23.40	30.83
Other	206	7.13	7.62	28,197	9.30	12.26
Total	*2,889*	*100.0*	*100.0*	*303,040*	*100.0*	*100.0*

* Androssov, *Statisticheskaia zapiska*, 52–3 (for the number of merchants, see pp. 57–8); the total given by Androssov, for reasons he does not explain, is 305,631.

Peasants (both serfs and state peasants) made up 24.10 percent of the population but only 6.54 percent of the parishioners. Without them, the composition of the parishes roughly tracks that of the general population, with some discrepancies because these parishes were located disproportionately in Zamoskvorech'e and the suburbs, areas with high concentrations of merchants and townspeople.

The confessional registers thus constitute a useful sample both of Moscow's core urban estates and of its major geographic divisions. Turning now to what they reveal about the world of Muscovites in 1829, we begin with the item most prominently recorded in the registers: the parishioners' names.

---

[81] Here and throughout the chapter, individuals are counted as belonging to the same estate as their head of household.

NAMES AND IDENTITIES

Names, and how they were recorded, were markers of identity. They show how cultural patterns shifted over time and spread from one estate to another.

The significance of a name for one's identity is apparent from Volkov's copybook. He wrote out his name repeatedly and in different forms: Dmitrii Stepanych Volkov; Dmitrei Stepanov Volkov; Dmitrei Stepanov; Dmitrei Volkov. According to Ivan Belousov, who grew up in a Moscow tailor's family in the 1860s and 1870s, apprentices were called only by a nickname, which was derived from their looks, place of origin, or some other characteristic. At the end of their apprenticeship, in an important rite of passage, they bought drinks for everyone in the shop and were henceforth addressed by their name and patronymic.[82] When Volkov wrote his name in its full, formal form, he was affirming his social position as an adult craftsman.

Volkov's experimentation with the form of his patronymic likewise suggests an interest in the linkage between name and status. In everyday interactions, Russians expressed respect by addressing people with their first name and full patronymic (Stepanovich or Stepanych). However, in official documents, this usage was reserved for holders of the top five government ranks, whereas persons of lower status had to be content with the "half patronymic": Stepanov or Stepanov syn (Stepan's son).[83] In his notes in the copybook, Volkov's friend Arstov played with these nuances by addressing him reverentially as "Mr Dmitrii Stepanovich, master of the gold trade," while humbly calling himself "Ivan Stepanov syn Arstov." Using the European form of one's name was especially refined. Arstov made ironic allusion to this, too, when he signed his name in Latin, the international language of scholars, as "Johannes natus, Arstoff vocatus."

Surnames were rare in Volkov's time, and even people who had one did not consistently use it. Since surnames helped locate individuals within extended networks, they were useful to the bureaucracy and to families with a prestigious pedigree or far-flung relations, but they were of little utility in small-scale communities where life required only a given name, perhaps a sobriquet to differentiate people who shared a name, and a patronymic to identify one's parentage. The clergy, who decided how a person appeared in the confessional registers, likewise showed little interest in surnames; what mattered to them were given names, which honored a saint, were assigned at baptism, and were often recorded in their Church Slavonic form. All these tendencies show up in the database of confessional registers.

---

[82] Belousov, "Ushedshaia Moskva," in Aleksandrov, *Moskovskaia Starina*, 320.
[83] L. E. Shepelev, *Chinovnyi mir Rossii, XVIII–nachalo XX v.* (St Petersburg: Iskusstvo-SPb, 1999), 366.

The database includes 2,096 people who were heads of separate households or were listed as living alone.[84] Only 449 of these had a surname that the priest recorded. Their incidence declines rapidly as one descends the estate hierarchy. They include 81.0 percent of the nobles, 51.1 percent of the merchants, 21.2 percent of the townspeople, 11.5 percent of the guild artisans, and just 0.2 percent of the peasants and serfs. Despite being objects of intensive official record-keeping, only 47.1 percent of army non-commissioned officers and enlisted men had surnames noted in the registers. Lastly, a surname was recorded for only 2.7 percent of the clergy, even though all of them used one during their seminary years. The incidence of surnames in the registers thus reflects both their uneven distribution across different estates and the preferences of the clerics who compiled the registers.

In other ways, naming practices were growing more standardized. The rule that the Orthodox should choose a saint's name for their children had gained broad acceptance in the eighteenth century, so pre-Christian Slavic names had largely disappeared. Moreover, confessional registers were required to record the formal form of one's given name—no more nicknames as in earlier times—plus one patronymic and, optionally, a surname.[85] One townswoman's name was recorded in 1711 as "Mavra Mitropolova, daughter of Ivan, wife of Efrem's son Mikhail" (Mavra Ivanova doch' Mikhailovskaia zhena Efremova syna Mitropolova).[86] Had she come back to life in 1829, she would have been listed simply as Mavra Ivanova Mitropolova.

Nineteenth-century literature has bequeathed an image of names as humiliating status markers for the lower classes. To the elites, commoners' surnames could all sound the same, even when they were nothing alike. A nobleman in a play by Ostrovskii tries to recall a merchant's surname, but all he knows is that it is either very common or else derived from the appellation of some kind of food or merchandise: "I forget. Maybe Ivanov, or maybe Perekusikhin; something in between Ivanov and Perekusikhin, I think, Podtovarnikov." Later: "that merchant, Prostokvashin."[87] Given names likewise had class associations. In Aleksandr Levitov's 1863 novella about the tenants of a squalid Moscow flophouse, *Moskovskiia "komnaty snebil'iu"* (roughly, *Moscow's "Furrnushed Room'z"*), the protagonists represent plebeian types, right down to their names: "the Tat'ianas,

---

[84] The point is that these are people who were not listed as someone else's dependents. The figures include the databases for the four parishes, the Widows' Home, and the separate clerical households.

[85] The use of nicknames in official documents had been banned by Peter the Great: PSZ (First Series), vol. 4, no. 1,884 (30 December 1701).

[86] O. N. Trubachev, ed., *Russkaia onomastka i onomastika Rossii: Slovar'* (Moscow: Shkola-Press, 1994), 71.

[87] Quoted in: S. Rassadin, "Svoi liudi, ili russkii obyvatel' (Aleksandr Ostrovskii)," in A. Ostrovskii, *Dramaturgiia* (Moscow: Izdatel'stvo AST—Agentstvo KRPA Olimp, 2002), 9–10. (The play is *Bez viny vinovatye.*)

who rent out rooms...and the Luker'ias, individuals who invariably serve as cooks in the[se] rooms."[88]

Bearing an obscure Byzantine saint's name, of which there were many, suggested that one was either a captive to religious or familial tradition or else socially under the thumb of the parish clergy. In Gogol's tale "The Overcoat," the church calendar at the ill-starred hero's baptism suggests names that ring preposterous and archaic: Mokkii, Sossii, Khozdazat, Trifilii, Dula, Varakhasii, Pavsikakhii, Vakhtisii. Rather than subject her little boy to any of these, the mother reluctantly gives him his father's only marginally less awful name, the vaguely scatological-sounding Akakii. This (fictional) mother was a minor noble and hence had a degree of social authority. People of lesser status were more easily bullied. Looking back in the 1920s on late imperial Moscow, Ivan Belousov recalled a merchant's daughter named Khavron'ia, which sounds like the word for "sow." Her parents had failed to bribe the priest, so he retaliated by giving her a humiliating name.[89] Such conduct by priests was common enough that the church explicitly forbade it.[90]

The evidence from the database suggests that these literary portrayals mix reality with satire. Except for Mokkii, the names cited by Gogol and Belousov never occur in the database. In fact, most of the 2,000 or so names in the church calendar, which include such gems as Gugstsiatazad and Teklagavvaraiat, are not known ever to have been given to anyone in all of Russian history.[91] The database contains one Izot, one Kharlampii, one Filadel'f, and one Makrida, but such names were increasingly rare.

Evidently, parents exercised growing autonomy in choosing names. A comparison of two sets of townsmen—males born before 1780 versus after 1814, with 70 to 80 individuals in each group—illustrates this development. In the grandfathers' generation, one in every three had a name that occurred only once in that cohort. Among the grandsons, it was only one in thirteen. Among male peasants and serfs of those same age groups, the younger cohort was about 50 percent larger than the older, yet the older group had slightly more different names.

Obscure names were less widespread among women simply because there were fewer female saints to choose from. However, evidence for the growing importance of fashion and parental choice can be found by examining the relative popularity of particular names. Consider Duniasha. The flower girl in *Moscow's*

---

[88] "Moskovskiia 'komnaty snebil'iu'," in Levitov, *Moskovskiia nory i trushchoby*, 6.

[89] Belousov, "Ushedshaia Moskva," in Aleksandrov, *Moskovskaia starina*, 375–6.

[90] Alain Blum, Irina Troitskaia, and Alexandre Avdeev, "Prénommer en Russie orthodoxe: Une pratique particulière," in Jean-Pierre Poussou and Isabelle Robin-Romero, eds., *Histoire de la famille, de la démographie et des comportements: En hommage à Jean-Pierre Bardet* (Paris: PUPS, 2007), 341, 343.

[91] V. A. Nikonov, *Imia i obshchestvo* (Moscow: Nauka, Glavnaia redaktsiia vostochnoi literatury, 1974), 143.

"Furrnushed Room'z" is named Duniasha, as are several servants in *War and Peace*. Was this a typical lower-class name? Yes and no. Table 7.4 shows where Avdot'ia, from which the nickname Duniasha is derived, ranked—in first place, third place, and so forth—among names of women of different generations and estates:

Table 7.4. Frequency of the name Avdot'ia

	Age cohort and year of birth			
	50 or older (before 1780)	29–49 (1780–1800)	15–28 (1801–14)	0–14 (1815–29)
Nobles	3	5	6	13
Townswomen	1	1	4	5
Peasants and Serfs	3	1	2	6

Source: databases for the four parishes, the Widows' Home, and the separate clergy households.
Note: N = 279 noblewomen, 482 townswomen, and 485 peasants and serfs. The number of individuals per age cohort, from oldest to youngest: noblewomen—102, 73, 51, 53; townswomen—102, 156, 128, 96; serfs and peasants—69, 166, 184, 66. The category "peasants and serfs" includes manumitted serfs.

Evidently, many commoners answered to Duniasha, but among nobles it was becoming an old woman's name. After having been common throughout society, by the reign of Alexander I Avdot'ia/Duniasha acquired distinctly lower-class connotations. However, after 1815 its popularity among the lower estates waned as well, suggesting a convergence in naming habits among different social strata.

While ever fewer noble girls were named Avdot'ia (or such comparable names as Pelageia or Matrena), more bore the names of current or recent empresses: Ekaterina, Elizaveta, Mariia, or Aleksandra. These names then spread downward through society. Table 7.5 shows what share of all females of several estates bore one of these names. In each of these estates, among girls 14 or younger, there were by 1829 fewer Duniashas than either Aleksandras, Mariias, or Elizavetas. The divergence among parents who christened their children at the turn of the century had disappeared.

Similar trends have been found among peasants in Moscow Province. The "monarchical" names Aleksandr, Nikolai, and Aleksandra, and "urban" names such as Viktor and Antonina, grew steadily more common after the mid-nineteenth century, thanks apparently to the popularity of the "tsar-liberator" Alexander II and to the peasants' closer ties with the city after the end of serfdom. This was a repetition of the developments that we observe in Moscow in 1829.[92]

[92] Blum et al., "Prénommer en Russie orthodoxe," in Poussou and Robin-Romero, eds., *Histoire de la famille, de la démographie et des comportements*, 351–3.

Table 7.5. Frequency of the names Ekaterina, Elizaveta, Mariia, and Aleksandra

	Age cohort and year of birth			
	50 or older (before 1780)	29–49 (1780–1800)	15–28 (1801–14)	14 or younger (1815–29)
Nobles	19.6%	30.1%	37.3%	41.5%
Townswomen	13.7%	19.9%	31.3%	36.5%
Peasants and serfs	8.7%	10.2%	15.2%	37.9%

Source: Database for the four parishes, the Widows' Home, and the separate clergy households.
Note: See note to Table 7.4.

A study by Vladimir Nikonov suggests that distinct naming traditions emerged among peasant, merchant, and noble girls in the late eighteenth century. His evidence for noble names comes from the students of the Smol'nyi Institute, These were all hereditary nobles, hence a narrower stratum than my database's mix of hereditary and personal nobles. Nikonov also notes that the Moscow merchantry, the wealthier kin of the townspeople under discussion here, began in the period between 1801 and 1818 to adopt names similar to those of Smol'nyi students born in the second half of the eighteenth century, and that in general, the Moscow merchantry was closer to the nobility in its naming preferences than were provincial nobles, not to mention the peasants.[93]

The evolution of naming practices suggests that social interactions in a large city caused upper-class cultural patterns to spread through society. What was the spatial environment in which these changes unfolded?

URBAN SPACES

The well-to-do authors who wrote most of the descriptions of pre-Reform Moscow give the impression that the city's space was socially segregated. In their perception, the city center was aristocratic: elegant mansions, cosmopolitan shops, a refined night life—the Moscow one knows from Griboedov's *Woe from Wit* and Tolstoi's *War and Peace*. Zamoskvorech'e was the opposite: the preserve of a hidebound merchantry that preferred shuttered gates and drawn curtains and was immortalized in Ostrovskii's dramas. Lastly, there were the suburbs. Aleksandr Levitov claimed in 1862 that as "America has virgin forests" where no man

[93] Nikonov, *Imia i obshchestvo*, 53–5. The point about the growing association of names with social classes is also made in Daniel H. Kaiser, "Naming Cultures in Early Modern Russia," in Nancy Shields Kollmann et al., eds., Каменъ Краежгъльнъ/*Rhetoric of the Medieval Slavic World: Essays Presented to Edward L. Keenan on his Sixtieth Birthday by his Colleagues and Students*, Harvard Ukrainian Studies 19 (Cambridge, Mass.: Harvard University Press, 1995), 271–91.

had set foot, "Moscow has virgin streets."[94] When authors registered the suburbs at all, it was for their rurality and the blur of lower-status groups that inhabited them.

The database of the four parishes bears out some, but only some, of these clichés. The central parish in Tverskaia District was indeed "aristocratic," but not because of the number of nobles living there. At 8.5 percent, nobles were no more numerous than elsewhere in the city. Rather, it was aristocratic insofar as a few of the nobles were rich aristocrats and much of the population consisted of their servants: 72.8 percent of the parishioners there were house serfs, compared to only 14.2 percent in Sushchevskaia and a mere 1.9 in Zamoskvorech'e. Compared with the city center, the two parishes in Zamoskvorech'e were more diverse, but with 19.3 percent merchants and 39.2 percent townspeople, the commercial element certainly predominated; of the other estates, only the nobles exceeded even 6 percent. The parish in Sushchevskaia was the most heterogeneous of the four: townspeople (30.9 percent) formed the largest group, but the rest was an amorphous mix, with six estates each making up between 5.5 and 15.8 percent of the parishioners.

It would be interesting to know how concentrated certain estates were on particular streets. Here the confessional registers are of little help because they do not include street addresses (although these can sometimes be reconstructed from other sources). They do allow us to zoom in even closer, to the level of the individual house and its inhabitants. Houses diminished in scale as one moved away from the center, with a median of 17 parishioners per house in Tverskaia versus only 9 to 11.5 in the other three parishes. Even where they were small, however, Moscow houses were typically inhabited by multiple households of diverse estates.

Muscovites daily crossed paths in ways that promoted cultural hybridity and social mobility but also a particularistic estate consciousness and traditional forms of authority. We glimpse some of these cross-currents in the letters of Suzanne Voilquin, a Parisian midwife and member of the proto-socialist Saint-Simonian movement who lived in Russia from 1839 to 1846. She lived in St Petersburg, but what she describes could as easily have occurred in Moscow.

Observing the different estates living in her building, Voilquin saw that the lower classes, particularly women, could achieve a degree of personal autonomy but also suffered under the harsh demands of masters, employers, husbands, and the police. For example, a German bootmaker who lived across the hall from Voilquin had hired the serf girl of a poor noblewoman. Eighty percent of the girl's wages were supposed to go toward her manorial dues. When her mistress

---

[94] "Pogibshee, no miloe sozdanie," in Levitov, *Moskovskiia nory i trushchoby*, 195.

came to collect and the girl could not pay up, Voilquin writes in disbelief, she was packed off to the police and given 25 lashes.[95]

Voilquin herself employed a maid named Elena. Elena was born into serfdom and was the teenage lover of her master's son, who helped her learn to read and write. When her father was drafted into the army, she was freed. Her lover abandoned her, and she went to work in the city. Like many *soldatki* (conscripts' wives or daughters), she was not able to establish a stable family life. "Very few maidservants marry," Voilquin explains, "but all are more or less provided with a *brat* (brother). These comforters take the place of the 'cousins' and 'countrymen' who adorn French kitchens." In Elena's case, the boyfriend was "a well-preserved forty-something" clerk whom Voilquin tolerated because "his demeanor is modest, and besides, his uniform is a guarantee of relative probity." On one of the many occasions when Elena's drinking got her into trouble, her boyfriend and his office colleague came to her rescue by composing a letter of apology in stilted, flowery French.[96]

Voilquin eventually dismissed Elena and hired her sister, the gentle Annushka. Back in her native village, Annushka had been married to a brutal drunk named Vasilii, with whom she had three children. Then the children died, Vasilii was drafted, and Annushka became a domestic in Moscow. After a time she learned that Vasilii's unit was coming to Moscow, so she fled to her sister in St Petersburg; painful misadventures ensued when Vasilii turned up there, too.[97]

Nobles and officials, and even clerks like Elena's boyfriend, were *Kulturträger*. They might be poor, but they wore uniforms, shaved, worked in offices, and occasionally knew some French. They had respectable manners and expected deference, the more so when they lived cheek by jowl with the lower orders and were anxious to assert their status. They spread the regime's culture but also sparked friction and resentment.

These fraught interactions are explored in the novella *Savvushka* by Ivan Kokorev (1826–53). The story is set in Sushchevskaia around the time when Volkov was there. The title character is a middle-aged tailor who lives in the same house with a greengrocer, a glovemaker, and a few others. One of the residents is a young official of 22 who holds the lowest rank that confers personal nobility (collegiate registrar, rank 14). One day, Savvushka asks him: "So, Aleksandr Ivanych, what book is it that you deign to read?" The young man answers disdainfully: "Lyric poetry, I mean, verses. Do you understand?" Then he pretentiously declaims a "nebulous poem." Savvushka addresses him respectfully as *vy* ("you") but is answered with a patronizingly informal *ty* ("thou"). Savvushka inquires about the young man's interest in Lizan'ka, a young woman

[95] Suzanne Voilquin, *Mémoires d'une saint-simonienne en Russie (1839–1846)*, ed. Maïté Albistur and Daniel Armogathe (n.p.: Éditions des Femmes, 1977), 175.

[96] Voilquin, *Mémoires*, 131–2, 139, 153–5, quotations on 139.

[97] Voilquin, *Mémoires*, 185–7, 197–203, 212–22.

whose name may have reminded readers of the poor country girl in Karamzin's "Poor Liza." "But you wouldn't actually marry her, right?" Savvushka asks. "What an idea!" comes the incredulous answer: "I'll find myself a proper match, a noble girl. But what is she [Lizan'ka]? A townsman's daughter." Savvushka appeals to Aleksandr Ivanych's conscience and recounts the hardships of his own life, but Aleksandr Ivanych sees his social inferiors as mere playthings and cannot tell the difference between real life and the contrived emotions that he knows from books. "If you wrote all that as a novel, it would be a fascinating story," he remarks, to which Savvushka wearily responds: "What I told you is true and from the heart, yet here you are talking about your books. No, please spare me that."[98]

Savvushka highlights the tension that arose among people of different estates when they lived under the same roof. In Levitov's *Moscow's "Furrnushed Room'z,"* the focus is on the plasticity and opacity of the estate identities themselves. Both authors knew first-hand the poverty and social frustrations described in their fiction. Each led a hand-to-mouth existence in Moscow as a struggling writer. Kokorev was the son of a manumitted serf; Levitov (1835–78), a poor *popovich* from a village in the southern steppe. In Levitov's novella, the protagonist is a young soldier's wife named Tat'iana who left her village to seek a new life in Nicholaevan Moscow. She becomes a cook in a merchant household and discovers the simple yet intoxicating delights of the city: rich, plentiful food, and attentions from men of charm and manners. She grows plump and street-wise. Then she meets a fellow *soldatka* who rents out furnished rooms to down-on-their-luck lodgers "who recommended themselves as unemployed governesses, orphans of a colonel or even a general, or at worst as widows of merchants who went bankrupt but had once belonged to the first guild." Inspired by this example, Tat'iana decides to reinvent herself. She rents a few rooms in a large, gloomy downtown house and posts a misspelled sign advertising "furrnushed room'z." She tells people that her husband is a noble officer who by now has reached high rank. Her lodgers invent similar pedigrees. One of them claims to be a retired army ensign who was once a wealthy landowner. This, he thinks, entitles him to order the artisan boys to bring him liquor and to bully the caretaker who asks him to tone down his drunken nighttime revels. Another lodger is young Praskov'ia Petrovna, recently arrived from the village, who hopes to attract a better class of men by styling herself as the faux-German "Amaliia Gustavovna." In *Moscow's "Furrnushed Room'z,"* estate identities cloak reality as easily as reveal it.[99]

---

[98] I. T. Kokorev, *Ocherki Moskvy sorokovykh godov*, ed. N. S. Ashukin (Moscow: Academia, 1932), 282–3, 289–90.

[99] "Moskovskiia 'komnaty snebil'iu'," in Levitov, *Moskovskiia nory i trushchoby*, quotations on 25, 32.

As in the cases described by Voilquin, Kokorev, and Levitov, most houses in Moscow were home to people of various estates, not counting all the migrants who are absent from the confessional registers but must have lived somewhere. In some houses, nobles lived with house serfs who both belonged to and worked for them. Extreme instances occurred in the downtown parish. In one house, the only registered inhabitants were General Fedor Masolov and eighty-three house serfs. Another, which belonged to Prince Aleksei Shakhovskoi, had eighty-five inhabitants: ten nobles, one student, one peasant, three townspeople, and seventy house serfs.[100] Seven other houses in the parish had between twenty-seven and sixty-nine house serfs each; in all but one, those house serfs formed a clear majority of the inhabitants. In the parish's smaller houses as well, house serfs generally formed the bulk of the inhabitants.

In more modest form, one also encountered this among the service nobility in outlying neighborhoods. For example, the most famous person listed in the parish in Sushchevskaia was Karamzin's heir as editor of the *Messenger of Europe*, the history professor Mikhail Kachenovskii. His rank made him the civilian equivalent of a brigadier, but this Ukrainian-born son of an ethnic Greek townsman was no aristocrat; instead, he had achieved noble status through education and service.[101] The fourteen residents of his house included five nobles (Kachenovskii, his wife, and their three children) and eight house serfs who all belonged to the professor. The remaining resident, a townswoman, was the only person not obviously connected with the family, but she may have been a domestic employee.[102]

Most households were not composed of masters and their serfs. Instead, residents commonly included peasants or house serfs who were not living with their master and were probably wage laborers. For example, a house down the street from Kachenovskii belonged to the family of a deceased aristocrat and had thirteen lodgers: a noble officer's widow; three house serfs who lived apart from their master; a manumitted serf with his wife and son; another manumitted serf; two apparently single townsmen; and three widowed townswomen.[103] A house in an adjacent street had fifty-five inhabitants, more than most suburban houses. They included townspeople, state peasants, peasant and house serfs of at least a dozen different masters, soldiers' wives, artisans, printers, and the landlady herself (a junior official's widow) with her mother, her two children, and her three servants.[104]

How commonly did different estates live in one house without forming part of the same household? The database of the four parishes suggests that the

[100] TsIAM f. 203, op. 747, d. 1130, ll. 450–2, 454–6.
[101] Vl. Kachenovskii, "Mikhail Trofimovich Kachenovskii," *Bibiliograficheskiia zapiski*, 1/4 (April 1892), 259–69, here: 259–60.
[102] TsIAM f. 203, op. 747, d. 1130, ll. 513 ob–514.
[103] TsIAM f. 203, op. 747, d. 1130, ll. 516–516 ob.
[104] TsIAM f. 203, op. 747, d. 1130, ll. 519 ob–520 ob.

townspeople and merchants were more segregated than other estates. In houses where townspeople lived, there was a median of five townspeople per house, and they made up 33.2 percent of the total population of those houses (counting only residents who were registered parishioners). For merchants, the corresponding figures were six per house and 37.6 percent of the total. For the clergy and nobles, the median in the four parishes was only three per house, but while members of the clergy formed 35.0 percent of those houses' residents, for nobles the figure was only 16.1 percent. As for *soldatki* and their children, their median was only one per house, and they formed a mere 9.8 percent of the residents of the houses where they lived.

Table 7.6. Residential segregation of different estates

	Percent who lived in the same house with . . .			
	No other estates	1–2 other estates	3–5 other estates	N =
Nobles	22.7	57.5	19.7	233
Clergy*	15.8	66.7	17.5	297
Merchants	11.3	78.5	10.2	274
Townspeople	30.3	52.8	16.9	776
Artisans	0	53.6	46.4	112
*Soldatki***	7.8	65.2	27.0	115

Source: Database for the four parishes.
* Includes the separate database for clergy households in other parishes.
** Includes wives, widows, and children of soldiers.
N = number of individuals for each estate.

Determining exactly who shared a house with whom is difficult because the evidence is ambiguous. The confessional registers are not always precise about identities and relationships. To what estate did people identified as "servants" belong? Was a "serf" a peasant or a house serf? Were members of subaltern groups lodgers who lived on their own, or live-in employees of higher-status residents of the same house? Fewer ambiguities arise if we isolate the six estates that seem always to be precisely identified: nobles, clergy, merchants, townspeople, artisans, and *soldatki*. In Table 7.6, we see what percentage of members of these six estates shared a house with one or more of the other estates. (Estates other than these six are not counted here.) In general, as the table shows, most Muscovites lived in close proximity to other estates. Even among the most segregated, the townspeople, only 30.3 percent lived in a house with no residents from the other five estates.

One factor that affected an estate's degree of segregation was homeownership. Since merchant status was contingent on paying guild fees, merchants were by definition not poor, allowing many to own their homes. Parish clergy were commonly provided with a house by their parish. Hence, in the four parishes,

83.3 percent of the clergy and 65.7 percent of the merchants owned their home or were members of the homeowner's household. By contrast, many nobles were petty officials who lived on miserly salaries, so the figure for them was only 38.2 percent, and for the townspeople, the merchantry's poorer cousins, it was only 23.3 percent. (Among *soldatki* who lived apart from their husbands, it was a mere 1.1 percent, one single individual.)

There were noteworthy variations among neighborhoods. The parish in Sushchevskaia, where houses were small and cheap, had the highest proportion of people who owned their home or were members of the homeowner's household: 28.2 percent for townspeople, 46.4 for nobles, and 95.6 for merchants. The figures were lower in Zamoskvorech'e, but the lowest occurred in the downtown parish: only 28.1 percent for nobles, and zero for townspeople. The merchants alone enjoyed a high level of homeownership (84.6 percent), perhaps because few other than wealthy merchants lived there at all.

Merchants and clergy typically mingled with other estates when they took in tenants, and many merchants in addition provided housing for their employees. Hence, in the four parishes, merchants and clergy comprised only 12.6 percent of the inhabitants, but their houses accommodated 28.6 percent of the population. By contrast, townspeople and especially *soldatki* encountered other estates as fellow lodgers or else as landlords and/or employers. As for the nobles, some resembled the Kachenovskiis, living in their own home with only their house serfs, but most were too poor and instead rented quarters where they could. In the downtown parish, where nobles owned just over half of the houses, nobles almost always rented from other nobles. In the other parishes, they mostly rented from commoners.

FAMILY

When the parish priests organized their confessional registers by household, they were acknowledging the centrality of households in Muscovites' lives. Households enforced social control, socialized the young, and supported those who could not provide for themselves. Their structure helped to differentiate the estates but also contributed to a more fundamental distinction between the middling and lower classes.

A type of arrangement found particularly among merchants, but also among the clergy, was the extended patriarchal family. Nikolai Vishniakov, who went on to be a harsh critic of what he considered the stifling provincialism of the merchantry, recalled his childhood in a multigenerational merchant family in Zamoskvorech'e in the 1850s: "We led an unsociable life. At home we received only relatives, and we ourselves went to visit only relatives...Among the middling merchantry we had many relatives and acquaintances, but we were intimate with no one ... All our relationships had a ceremonial, formal, almost official character."[105]

An extended family like the Vishniakovs provided an economic safety net, but often at the price of an insular existence under harsh patriarchal authority. At the other extreme, people living on their own had greater autonomy and contact with outsiders but were socially and economically vulnerable. Families were better positioned to realize the consumer aspirations associated with social mobility, for they could deploy the labor of wives, children, and the elderly to bring in additional wages and perform vital domestic chores at no cash expense.[106] The position of people without families was far more precarious.

The confessional registers provide data on the family structure of various estates. It should be noted that they give no information about kinship ties connecting different households. For example, three brothers living with their families in the same building might form a de facto extended family but appear in the register as separate nuclear families. Thus it is possible that the registers understate the prevalence of extended families.[107] With this caveat, Table 7.7 summarizes information about which percentage of different estates lived alone, in nuclear families (head of household plus spouse and/or children), or in extended families (head of household plus dependents other than the nuclear family).

Table 7.7. Household composition among different estates

| | Family structures (percent) | | | |
| | | Families: | | |
	Living alone	Nuclear	Extended	N =
Nobles	15.0	58.4	26.6	233
Clergy*	4.4	63.4	31.7	297
Merchants	5.5	45.3	49.3	274
Townspeople	27.2	54.4	18.4	776
Artisans	21.4	60.7	17.9	112
*Soldatki***	80.4	17.5	2.1	97
House serfs	63.4	33.1	3.5	743

Source: Database for the four parishes.
* Includes the separate database for clergy households in other parishes.
** Includes *soldatki* and their husbands and families (except residents of the Sushchevskaia police station, whom the confessional register lists without indication of their family ties).
N = number of individuals for each estate.

105 Vishniakov, *Svedeniia*, 2:150, 153.
106 On this topic, see de Vries, *The Industrious Revolution*, 86, 111.
107 I thank Alain Blum for drawing my attention to this point.

Family structure followed the same geography as homeownership. The downtown parish, where homeownership was low, had the most nobles, merchants, and townspeople who lived alone—respectively, 23.4, 15.4, and 41.9 percent. The share who lived in extended families was highest in Sushchevskaia (where homeownership was also highest)—respectively, 43.4, 78.0, and 25.6 percent of the three estates. Household size followed this pattern as well. The downtown parish had the smallest families, with a median for all three estates of just one person, while the largest were in Sushchevskaia, with a median of two for nobles and townspeople and four for merchants.

Family structure also reflected the socioeconomic position of different estates. For merchants who ran a family business, like the Vishniakovs, it made sense for adult sons to stay on as their father's assistants and heirs. Such families also had the means to take in widowed daughters or orphaned nephews. The parish clergy likewise lived in families, but the dynamics were not the same as with merchants. The parish typically provided priests, deacons, and sacristans with a house and a stable income. There was no real analogue to a family business, but it was common for elderly clerics to have their own position transferred to a son or son-in-law, who then moved into the same house and supported the retirees. Men had to be married to receive an appointment, so clerics married young. This custom, as well as the prohibition on the remarriage of widowed priests, may help explain why the median age difference between spouses in the database— how much older the husbands were—was only 5 years for clerics, compared with 6 for nobles and 7 for merchants and townspeople. There were few older children in clerical households, because boys left for school and both sexes married young, so the median age of the oldest son was 11, and for the oldest daughter, 10. By contrast, among nobles, merchants, and townspeople, whose sons more rarely went away to school, the corresponding ages ranged from 13 to 14.5 for boys and from 12 to 13 for girls. Even so, the clergy still had more children at home: a median of 3 per household (not counting childless households), compared with 2 for nobles and merchants and only 1 for townspeople.[108]

Nobles were in a harder position than merchants or clerics. Dependent on meager civil-service incomes, many could barely support themselves, let alone a family. Hence, more ended up alone, and fewer lived in extended families. However, they more than any estate were tied institutionally and emotionally to the monarchy, which sometimes substituted for a family by supporting children and the elderly through boarding schools and the Widows' Home. Similarly, the Moscow branch of the Imperial Philanthropic Society provided financial assistance primarily to minor government officials whose rank entitled them to personal-noble status.[109]

---

[108] The preceding paragraph is based on data from the four parishes and the separate clergy households.

[109] Androssov, *Statisticheskaia zapiska*, 136–7.

Merchants, clerics, and nobles thus formed a middle stratum that enjoyed a social safety net provided either by families or by the crown. By contrast, those farther down the ladder either lived as subaltern members in other people's households or else had to fend for themselves. Ivan Slonov's experience was shared by many workers, apprentices, and shop clerks who lived with their employers. Slonov came from a poor family in the town of Kolomna near Moscow. In 1865, the adolescent Slonov's father died and he had to go to work in Moscow for a trader named Zaborov. Decades later, by now a rich businessman, he recalled Zaborov and his sons as "true despots, ignorant and backward people." Zaborov was an old-school merchant. Living in his house in Zamoskvorech'e, Slonov and the twelve other young shop assistants were dressed in what looked like "prison uniforms," and they were beaten, underfed, put to heavy household work, and used in church as the Zaborovs' private choir. "Those were harsh times," Slonov conceded, "and morals and customs were oppressive, so for all his remarkable severity, old man Zaborov"—he was born around 1780—"was nonetheless a man of his time. At the time, among Russian merchants, there were many despots."[110]

Living under the thumb of a Zaborov was hard, but neither did the alternatives have much to recommend them. For instance, *soldatki* who lived in Moscow were typically far from their own or their husbands' families. Like Suzanne Voilquin's maidservant Annushka, or Tat'iana in *Moscow's "Furrnushed Room'z,"* some found an oppressive refuge in domestic service or set up independent businesses. Others lived with their husbands in crowded barracks, while their sons attended schools that trained them to become soldiers. Living with their husbands kept the women off the streets and was encouraged by commanders, who believed that married life civilized the men.[111] For example, the inhabitants of the Sushchevskaia police station included nineteen women, mostly wives of soldiers serving as police- or firemen.[112]

Many *soldatki* lived on their own, had no steady livelihood, and often ended up practicing at least casual prostitution.[113] As with impoverished nobles, the state felt obligated to intervene as paternalistic provider and disciplinarian, but in

---

[110] Slonov, *Iz zhizni*, 73, 75–7, 81.

[111] Pavel Shcherbinin, "Zhizn' russkoi soldatki v XVIII–XIX vekakh," *Voprosy istorii*, no. 1 (2005), 79–92, here: 83–5.

[112] TsIAM f. 203, op. 747, d. 1130, 529 ob-532.

[113] The experience of the *soldatka* has attracted historians' interest for its gendered dimension and as an illustration of social mobility and marginality related to the estate system; see, for example: Elise Kimerling Wirtschafter, "Social Misfits: Veterans and Soldiers' Families in Servile Russia," *Journal of Military History*, 59 (April 1995), 215–36; Beatrice Farnsworth, "The Soldatka: Folklore and Court Record," *Slavic Review*, 49/1 (Spring 1990), 58–73; Shcherbinin, "Zhizn' russkoi soldatki." On *soldatki* as prostitutes later in the century, see Barbara Alpern Engel, "St. Petersburg Prostitutes in the Late Nineteenth Century: A Personal and Social Profile," *Russian Review*, 48/1 (January 1989), 21–44, esp. 26.

much harsher, more punitive form. Androssov found in his 1832 study of
Moscow that

In the records of the Workhouse one finds hundreds of *soldatki* who were sent there by the
commandant for a month's labor after being treated for venereal disease at the Military
Hospital. This triangle—get infected in the city, go to the Hospital, from there to
the Workhouse, then start over with disease, back to the Hospital, and labor in the
Workhouse—is familiar to many of the *soldatki* who live in Moscow.

Paupers with symptoms of sexually transmitted disease constituted the bulk of
the women who were occasionally found frozen to death "in the vast [suburban]
market gardens, or in the poorest remote streets of the city, where they were
driven by debauchery and utter destitution."[114]

As this last passage suggests, neither patriarchal families, paternalistic employers, nor state institutions were capable of integrating everyone into a tight-knit,
controlled community. Many ended up alone. For people from estates that were
permanently settled in the city, this meant poverty. Often those affected were
older women, in many cases serfs whom their masters had manumitted and left
to the mercy of fate. Of the 235 townspeople and artisans in the four parishes
who lived on their own, 138 were female, and half of those (69 individuals) were
45 or older; most were widows. *Soldatki* were in the worst position, with 80.4
percent living alone. Older women from the poorer classes often ended up as
charity cases. In a database of almshouses, comprising 601 individuals with a
median age of 65, women made up 77.2 percent (464 individuals). Only 219 of
these 601 individuals were identified by estate, but within that subset, the lower
orders clearly predominated: *soldatki* were 32.8 percent, and artisans and townspeople, who presumably included impoverished former merchants, another 44.3
percent.[115]

Living alone meant something quite different for house serfs, the group with
the largest share of people living alone.[116] If we compare women who lived
without kin or headed their own household, the median age was 26 for house
serfs versus 44 for *soldatki*. This difference reflects the circumstances that brought
the women to Moscow in the first place. House serfs often came to the city as
girls or young women to work for their master or for a paying employer, and
many later returned to their native villages. *Soldatki*, by contrast, arrived as adults
and had nowhere to go back to. As a result, one-third of female house serfs were

---

114 Androssov, *Statisticheskaia zapiska*, 67, 78. See also: Joseph Bradley, "The Moscow
Workhouse and Urban Welfare Reform in Russia," *Russian Review*, 41/4 (October 1982), 427–44.
115 The almshouse database comprises two elements. First, the two almshouses (*bogadel'ni*)
included in the database on the four parishes. Second, all the almshouse residents recorded in the
confessional registers for the first twenty parishes in the file TsIAM f. 203, op. 747, d. 1128; these
include almshouses in ten parishes plus the House of the Imperial Philanthropic Society. TsIAM f.
203, op. 747, d. 1128, ll. 10, 43, 67 ob–68, 91 ob–96 ob, 145–5 ob, 150, 173–4 ob, 192, 232–2
ob, 245 ob, 338–8 ob; d. 1130, 447 ob. On almshouses, see Kozlova, *Liudi driakhlye*.
116 Based on the same data as the earlier table on family structures (see Table 7.7).

under 22 and only one tenth were 60 or older. For *soldatki*, the figures were none under 22 and one-sixth who were 60 or older. Similar patterns held for males: the median age was 28 for house serfs, 43 for soldiers. Most of the soldiers were veterans who had been reassigned to the police or fire department and leaned toward the older side of middle age: two-thirds were in their forties or fifties.[117] These age structures help to explain why foreign visitors remarked on the alacrity of lower-class Muscovites, many of whom were house serfs, whereas, as Slonov recalled, "a typical thing to see in Moscow" were policemen, outfitted with archaic shakos and halberds, leaning against their guardhouses and taking a nap.[118]

CONCLUSION

A year after Dmitrii Volkov arrived in Moscow, the city was struck by cholera, a cruel and mysterious illness. In the four months from 15 September 1830 to 30 January 1831, it sickened 8,576 Muscovites, killing 4,690 of them. Yet once the initial panic died down, doctors and police cooperated with clergy, merchants, and other leaders of society to ensure that quarantine and sanitary measures proceeded efficiently. When Nicholas I bravely visited the stricken city, his subjects gave him a hero's welcome.[119]

When Moscow in 1771 suffered Europe's last great plague outbreak, chaos erupted, but when Europe's first cholera epidemic arrived in 1830, the system responded well. Moscow also remained quiet during the European revolutionary crises of 1830–1 and 1848–9. State and society were better integrated than in 1771, when the government's quarantine measures were viewed with fear and incomprehension by the population. In 1830, doctors and officials were more numerous and effective, the clergy and merchantry played a more active role in the anti-cholera campaign, and officials showed greater flexibility in responding to the circumstances and sensitivities of the population. As Roderick McGrew puts it, Moscow's leaders during the cholera found "a way to bridge the gap between the authorities and the people."[120]

The material discussed in this chapter suggests, more broadly, that Moscow had resolved some of its eighteenth-century tensions but had not developed the

---

[117] All these figures, for both women and men, include only individuals listed as heads of households or living without kin. "Soldiers" includes enlisted men and non-commissioned officers. These figures represent all the soldiers from the database plus an additional data set composed of all the soldiers mentioned in the confessional registers for the first twenty churches included in TsIAM f. 203, op. 747, d. 1128.

[118] Slonov, *Iz zhizni*, 42.

[119] Roderick E. McGrew, *Russia and the Cholera 1823–1832* (Madison: University of Wisconsin Press, 1965), esp. ch. 4.

[120] McGrew, *Russia and the Cholera*, 81.

conflicts of the contemporary West. Dmitrii Volkov resembled a West European artisan in his intellectual horizons and aspirations to gentility, but unlike many of his Western counterparts he was not politically radicalized. The popularity of particular names shows that the culture of the nobility was spreading to the middle strata, and the role of clerics and merchants as landlords to the masses suggests that they exercised a social leadership role to match their privileged legal status, yet they did not demand a political voice as did the bourgeoisie in Western Europe. Did this mean that Moscow was on a historical trajectory fundamentally different from Western cities? Or did the West's present offer a glimpse of what lay in store for Moscow's future? Under Nicholas I, these questions became the focus of growing debate, as we will see in the next chapter.

8

Complacency and Anxiety

Representations of Moscow under Nicholas I

"Our old lady Moscow is getting herself dressed up, for she expects visitors by rail," wrote Prince Vladimir L'vov in 1846. A rail link to St Petersburg had been under construction since 1843. The feelings this inspired were mixed. According to the literary critic Vissarion Belinskii, Moscow had "become a city of industry, manufacturing, and trade" and stood to profit economically from the railroad, but L'vov wondered whether this benefit would outweigh the harm from closer ties with the outside. At present, the slowness of travel gave visitors time to adjust to "Moscow's semi-European forms," but the prospect of receiving guests at the speed of rail was intimidating, which is why Moscow was being spruced up to make a good impression.[1] Regular passenger traffic between Russia's two metropolitan cities—two trains a day, taking thirty hours to cover the 644 kilometers—opened on 1 November 1851. Another two and a half years, and wires strung along the rails began carrying telegrams. The signals traveled at such incomprehensible speed, one awestruck Russian noted, that they could go from St Petersburg to Kamchatka and back sixteen times in the blink of an eye.[2]

For Moscow and the imperial social project, the reign of Nicholas I (1825–55) was an era of both complacency and anxiety. Complacency, because Moscow was a bastion of tranquility in a Europe that seemed to have lost its moorings. Karamzin had placed Paris and London at the pinnacle of urban civilization, but now those cities appeared as sites of violence and social pathology. Barricades repeatedly went up in the French capital as the country lurched from one revolutionary crisis to the next. Early industrial Britain, meanwhile, descended into depths of mass poverty and degradation without precedent in European urban history. Reading the news from abroad, Russians took comfort in the

---

[1] [V. L'vov] M. Zh., "Zhizn' v Moskve v 1845," 269; V. G. Belinsky, "Petersburg and Moscow," in Nekrasov, *Petersburg*, 28.

[2] P. Krasnov, "Zheleznyia dorogi v Rossi," in F. M. Gol'ms, *Velikie liudi i ikh velikiia proizvedeniia: Razskazy o sooruzheniiakh znamenitykh inzhenerov* (St Petersburg: tipografiia A. Porokhovshchikova, 1897), 261–3; V. Lapshin, "Ob elektro-magnitnykh telegraficheskikh liniiakh v raznykh gosudarstvakh," *Zhurnal Ministerstva Narodnago Prosveshcheniia*, chast' 85, otdel 2 (1855), 247–302, here: 290.

belief that St Petersburg and Moscow had become successful modern cities while remaining free of the restive bourgeoisie, the angry proletarians and paupers, and the general alienation and anomie that corroded the West.

Nonetheless, clouds were gathering on the horizon. With its unreformed regime of autocracy and serfdom, Russia lingered in what the historian Aleksandr Kupriianov calls an "extended late eighteenth century."[3] No real changes were made in the imperial social project inherited from Catherine II. Estate-specific education expanded, but the leap to universal schooling was not attempted. Moscow's civic culture and fiscal resources remained constricted because many inhabitants remained de jure denizens of rural villages and municipal governance remained the preserve of crown bureaucrats and officials elected by the local estates of merchants, townspeople, and artisans.[4] As Prince L'vov's unease about the railroad suggests, thinking people sensed that Moscow might be unprepared for changes that lay ahead.

Belying the slow pace of social change, Russian thinking about urban issues evolved rapidly under Nicholas I. The principal impetus came from new approaches that the British and French devised for analyzing urban society. Starting from the common nineteenth-century premise that taxonomy—the classifying of individual specimens into categories or species—could unlock the deep structures of nature and humanity, British and French writers analyzed urban social systems by studying individual people who were supposedly representative of entire social groups, much as biologists might use individual plants or animals to study entire species. To understand how social systems behaved and evolved, writers drew on a second innovation: statistical social research. Lastly, like biologists who studied the setting in which a species lived, writers paid attention to the city as a physical environment.

The taxonomical impulse was apparent in a literary genre that emerged in France in the 1820s and 1830s: the physiological sketch. This term referred to the study, often in the form of satirical essays accompanied by illustrations, of fictional representatives of social "types." One widely read French anthology included sketches of such figures as the grocer, the aspiring writer, the midwife, the actress's mother, the schoolboy, the chess player, the chimney sweep, and the woman who managed the rental pews in church.[5] Essays on idiosyncratic slices of urban life built on a literary tradition that went back to Mercier's *Tableau of Paris*, but the term *physiology* also points to another context: medicine. Traditionally, physicians had believed that illness was due to an overall imbalance in the human organism, but this approach was challenged after the Napoleonic Wars

---

[3] Kupriianov, *Gorodskaia kul'tura*, 10.

[4] On the political obstacles to expanding municipal fiscal resources in the case of St Petersburg, see W. Bruce Lincoln, *In the Vanguard of Reform: Russia's Enlightened Bureaucrats, 1825–1861* (DeKalb, Ill.: Northern Illinois University Press, 1982), 56–7.

[5] These examples are drawn from *Les français peints par eux-mêmes. Encyclopédie morale du dix-neuvième siècle*, 9 vols. (Paris: Louis Curmer, 1840–2).

by practitioners of "physiological" medicine who treated illness as a malfunction of specific organs or tissues. This entailed a shift from a holistic view of the body to a focus on its parts, and from the unique individuality of each patient to the notion that patients were interchangeable.[6] By analogy with physiological medicine, authors of physiological sketches studied the social body by examining the individual parts—the social types—of which it was composed.

The physiological sketches were usually humorous and sentimental, but discussions of the larger dynamics of urban society, especially its poorer strata, were often pessimistic. British and French statisticians published alarming findings about the incidence of suicide, crime, mental illness, and other social pathologies. Journalists and fiction writers produced frightening evocations of a degraded, menacing urban environment. Nighttime in the slum, with its flickering gas lights, rain-soaked alleys, and seedy taverns, became a literary cliché thanks to the nascent genre of detective fiction. In his blockbuster novel *The Mysteries of Paris* (*Les mystères de Paris*, 1842–4), Eugène Sue promised to lead the reader into neighborhoods "that are horrible and unknown; these impure sewers will crawl with hideous, frightening types, like reptiles in a swamp." These people were "barbarians as much outside civilization as the savage tribes so well depicted by [James Fenimore] Cooper. Only, the barbarians of whom we speak are in our midst... These men have their own customs, their own women, their own language, a mysterious language, full of deathly images, metaphors dripping with blood."[7] This fear of the urban poor was shared by state officials. In France, a book by the Paris police official Honoré-Antoine Frégier in 1840 popularized the label *classes dangereuses* for a broad class of the poor that ranged from prostitutes and the homeless to street criminals, while in Britain, the New Poor Law of 1834 and the sanitary-reform movement led by Edwin Chadwick were built on the premise that the poor required, above all else, control and coercion.[8]

These three approaches—physiological, statistical, and environmental—shaped the debate about urban life in Britain and France and challenged established ways of thinking in Russia. How Russians responded will be the focus of this chapter.

MOSCOW AND OFFICIAL NATIONALITY

In the Russia of Nicholas I, the dark view of urban modernity that was gaining ground in the West met with stiff resistance. According to the regime's official

[6] Hacking, *The Taming of Chance*, 69, 81–3, 133.

[7] Eugène Sue, *Les mystères de Paris*, 4 vols. (Brussels: Meline, Cans, 1844), 1:1–2; Schlör, *Nights in the Big City*, 120–36.

[8] H. A. Frégier, *Des classes dangereuses de la population dans les grandes villes, et des moyens de les rendre meilleures*, 2 vols. (Paris: J.-B. Baillière, 1840); Hamlin, *Public Health and Social Justice*, 27–32.

ideology, known as Official Nationality, Russia was a stable and happy country, and it owed this fortunate condition to the fruits of the imperial social project: wise and effective government, benevolent aristocratic domination, an enlightened middling sort, and a populace content with its place in life. To say that Moscow or St Petersburg shared the pathologies of London or Paris was tantamount to calling Official Nationality a lie and the imperial social project a failure. This was unacceptable to the regime and to influential segments of Russia's expanding class of writers, journalists, and readers.

Sergei Uvarov, Nicholas's minister of education, defined the principles of Official Nationality when he declared in 1832 that Russia was founded on "Orthodoxy, autocracy, nationality." Explicating these ideas, the chief of the Third Section of His Imperial Majesty's Own Chancellery (the secret police), Alexander von Benckendorff, reportedly told an aide that "Russia's past has been admirable; her present is more than magnificent; as for her future, it is beyond all that the boldest imagination can conceive; this, my friend, is the point of view from which Russian history must be conceived and written."[9] There could be no questioning of religion or the political system, nor any discussion of serfdom. Praise of Russia's civilizational achievements was de rigueur, particularly in comparisons with the West.

To ensure the ideological conformity of the press, Nicholas's government required authors to submit their work for pre-publication censorship by Uvarov's Ministry of Education. If the censors failed to block the publication of offensive material, authors and publishers faced the threat of action by Benckendorff's Third Section. In practice, several circumstances conspired to muddy the clarity of the regime's message and prevent its systematic imposition on the press. The meaning of Orthodoxy and autocracy was clear enough, but there was no consensus on "nationality." Did the term embrace all of the tsar's subjects or only ethnic Russians? In the 1820s, the art world debated what constituted "Russian" art: anything by an artist settled in Russia, or only art that expressed a special Russian sensibility?[10] Benckendorff was a German, and two of Official Nationality's most zealous spokesmen, the newspapermen Faddei Bulgarin (Bułharyn) and Osip Senkovskii (Sękowski), were Poles: did they count as "Russians"? Also, who best embodied "nationality": the tradition-bound peasantry, the comparatively more modern and cosmopolitan inhabitants of the cities, or the nobles?

Enforcing censorship rules was in any case no easy matter. Writers introduced forbidden sociopolitical commentary through the back door in the guise of fiction, philosophy, or literary criticism. Moreover, the post of censor was often a part-time job for men who otherwise worked in publishing or academia and were personally close to the authors whose works they censored. Finally, the

---

[9] An early source for this famous quotation is Viktor Frank, *Russisches Christenthum, dargestellt nach russischen Angaben* (Paderborn: Ferdinand Schöningh, 1889), 69.
[10] Vishlenkova, *Vizual'noe narodovedenie imperii*, 287–8.

censors faced an uphill struggle against the demand for novelty and sensationalism in a publishing industry that expanded rapidly despite the government's efforts to restrict the establishment of new periodicals. As a result of all these factors, the enforcement of ideological coherence was unsystematic, alternating between harshness in some cases and laxity in others.[11]

The difficulties facing the censors were proof of the press's dynamism, not its opposition to the regime. The boom in publishing was driven by an expanding readership of merchants, clerics, and minor officials. These strata were the main beneficiaries of the imperial social project, and because they were generally pious, patriotic, and apolitical, they were sympathetic to Official Nationality. They were served by a growing press that was politically loyal and intellectually middlebrow. In the days of Karamzin and Glinka, a journal that achieved a circulation over 1,000 had been considered very successful. By contrast, the St Petersburg *Northern Bee* (*Severnaia Pchela*), a daily edited by Bulgarin and Nikolai Grech, reached 4,000 subscribers in the early 1830s and 10,000 in the 1850s. Senkovskii's monthly *Library for Reading* (*Biblioteka dlia chteniia*) had 7,000 subscribers by the late 1830s.[12] Middlebrow fiction likewise reached growing audiences: Bulgarin's picaresque novel *Ivan Vyzhigin* (1829) sold 6,000 copies and has been called "Russia's first best-seller."[13] These numbers were modest by Western standards. Paris in 1840 had at least twenty-seven dailies with a total circulation over 90,000, and Sue's *Mysteries of Paris* sold 60,000 copies in ten years, in addition to appearing as a newspaper serial.[14] Still, the trend line in Russia was upward, although the democratization of print was neither uncontested nor unlimited. Critics and rival literati depicted Bulgarin, Grech, and Senkovskii as profit-hungry hacks who acted as propagandists for the regime, catered to ignorant readers, and—at least in Bulgarin's case—informed for the secret police.[15] At the same time, the limited circulations achieved by all

[11] Charles A. Ruud, *Fighting Words: Imperial Censorship and the Russian Press, 1804–1906* (Toronto: University of Toronto Press, 2009), 63, 67–82.

[12] A. V. Zapadov, *Istoriia russkoi zhurnalistiki XVIII–XIX vekov* (Moscow: Vysshaia Shkola, 1973), 159–60; Katia Dianina, "The Feuilleton: An Everyday Guide to Public Culture in the Age of the Great Reforms," *Slavonic and East European Journal*, 47/2 (Summer 2003), 187–210, here: 188. See also Nurit Schleifman, "A Russian Daily Newspaper and its Readership: *Severnaia Pchela* 1825–1840," *Cahiers du monde russe et soviétique*, 28/2 (April–June 1987), 127–44.

[13] John Mersereau, Jr., "The Nineteenth Century: Romanticism, 1820–40," in Charles A. Moser, ed., *The Cambridge History of Russian Literature* (rev. edn., Cambridge: Cambridge University Press, 1992), 159.

[14] P. L. Simmonds, "Statistics of Newspapers in Various Countries," *Quarterly Journal of the Statistical Society of London*, 4 (July 1841), 111–36, here: 117; Sara James, "Eugène Sue, G. W. M. Reynolds, and the Representation of the City as 'Mystery'," in Valeria Tinkler-Villani, ed., *Babylon or New Jerusalem? Perceptions of the City in Literature* (Amsterdam: Rodopi, 2005), 247.

[15] T. Shishkova, "O Bulgarine starom i novom: Osnovnye tendentsii sovremennogo bulgarinovedeniia," *Novoe Literaturnoe Obozrenie*, no. 88 (2007) <http://www.nlobooks.ru/rus/magazines/nlo/196/722/740/> accessed 25 November 2009; Sidney Monas, *The Third Section: Police and Society in Russia under Nicholas I* (Cambridge, Mass.: Harvard University Press, 1961), 118–22.

these publications show that most Russians remained beyond the reach of any secular print culture.

Had Moscow not existed, the spokesmen of Official Nationality would have had to invent it, for the city admirably combined Russian tradition and enlightened modernity. It became a cliché that Moscow had a timeless Russianness that transcended social divides.[16] Diverse elements composed this myth: heroic memories of 1812 and the Time of Troubles; the popularity of Karamzin's history of medieval Russia; the fashion for historical novels, launched by Sir Walter Scott and imitated with success by Bulgarin and Mikhail Zagoskin; the vogue for folklore and medieval architecture; even the popularity of "English" gardens with their love of the picturesque and distrust of geometric design—all of this inspired a Romantic respect for Moscow's archaic irregularity and for the reputed reluctance of its inhabitants to embrace "enlightened" values.

At the same time, Moscow continued to be depicted as a model enlightened city. At the outset of Nicholas's reign, an anonymous author—apparently the writer Ivan Gur'ianov—gave expression to this view:

Perhaps no other Power in the world enjoys such internal tranquility as Russia, protected as she is by wise laws... Moscow, a city of such immense size and population, which contains in itself all types of estates without exception, can always serve as a model of the internal good order that reigns in our entire blessed realm.

Thanks to the authorities, this author wrote, "Cleanliness, organization, order, security, quiet, justice, and care for the sick, the disabled, and even those unfortunates who bear the mark of crime—in Moscow all this has been raised to the highest level of perfection."[17]

The work of Mikhail Zagoskin (1789–1852), one of the most popular and prolific Russian writers of the period, illustrates how Moscow could symbolize both tradition and progress. Zagoskin was by birth a provincial nobleman. He began his career in St Petersburg but then moved to Moscow. Perhaps appropriately, since he was director of the theater and the Kremlin Armory, he mainly wrote comedies and historical novels. In the heyday of the physiological sketch, he wrote a multivolume collection of sketches called *Moscow and the Muscovites* (*Moskva i Moskvichi*, 1842–50). They focused on the nobility and its amusing idiosyncrasies, which to him summed up the character of the inhabitants in general. *Moscow and the Muscovites* expressed the pride Zagoskin felt in Moscow

---

[16] See, for example: Sara Dickinson, "Representing Moscow in 1812: Sentimentalist Echoes in Accounts of the Napoleonic Occupation," in Lilly, *Moscow and Petersburg*; Iu. V. Mann, "Moskva v tvorcheskom soznanii Gogolia," in G. S. Knabe, ed., *Moskva i "moskovskii tekst" russkoi kul'tury: Sbornik statei* (Moscow: Rossiiskii Gosudarstvennyi Gumanitarnyi Universitet, 1998), 66–7, 71; A. V. Gulin, "Moskva 1812 goda v romane L. N. Tolstogo 'Voina i mir' (Motivy pravoslavnoi eskhatologii)," in Bludilina, *Moskva v russkoi i mirovoi literature*, 156–69; N. P. Velikanova, "Moskva v knige 'Voina i mir'," in Bludilina, *Moskva v russkoi i mirovoi literature*, 170–84.

[17] [Gur'ianov], *Moskva, ili Istoricheskii putevoditel'*, 1:314–15. Gur'ianov is identified as the likely author in the card catalogue of the Russian National Library.

as a modern European city. He wrote that it had been magnificently rebuilt after the war and boasted some of Europe's finest hotels.[18] Its manufacturing sector was so highly developed that "Moscow, were it not our ancient capital, could with justice be called the Russian Manchester."[19] As for its empty spaces and frequently rural atmosphere—Zagoskin embraced that, too.

That's just what warms my soul! That's precisely what makes Moscow truly representative of all Russia, which does not resemble any Western state just as Moscow does not resemble any European city. A Russian would suffocate in some German town. It's always crowded there, and people shove each other, whereas he loves his native free and easy life, his Russian freedom and open space.[20]

Muscovites thus celebrated both progress and traditionalism. Yet these were also years of growing anxiety. The aristocracy was the linchpin of the Moscow beloved of writers from Karamzin to Tolstoi. It was graceful and hospitable, sophisticated yet tradition-bound, "European" but also "Russian." The 1812 war had destroyed much of its wealth, and its social dominance was challenged by a new class of businessmen, bureaucrats, and market-oriented writers and publishers. It was to these new groups, not the old aristocracy, that the regime increasingly looked for support, the more so as its own bond with the aristocracy was fraying in the aftermath of the Decembrist revolt of 1825.

These changes induced a mood of nostalgia even in people who knew the lost aristocratic Eden only by hearsay. Zagoskin moved to Moscow only in 1820, yet he wrote fondly of the "utterly Asiatic" luxury of the pre-war aristocracy, with its serf theaters and enormous dinners and balls.[21] Belinskii, who arrived in 1829, wrote (less fondly) that stories of the old-time extravagance "sound like excerpts from *The Thousand and One Nights*."[22] In 1865, Prince Petr Viazemskii—who actually had known the old Moscow—likened the war to the biblical Flood when he entitled one of his reminiscences "Moscow before the Deluge, or before the Fire." To Viazemskii, the era of war and revolution before 1815 appeared as a last, exhilarating hurrah of the old aristocratic order.[23] This was a sensibility shared across Europe and expressed most memorably by Talleyrand, the veteran French aristocrat and politician. Speaking in his old age with François Guizot, an advocate of the new bourgeois order, Talleyrand once observed wistfully that unless one had seen the years around 1789, one had no idea how good it could be to be alive.[24]

[18] Zagoskin, *Sochineniia*, 5:137, 420.
[19] Zagoskin, *Sochineniia*, 5:126.
[20] Zagoskin, *Sochineniia*, 5:320.
[21] Zagoskin, *Sochineniia*, 5:70. See also Luba Golburt, "Catherine's Retinue: Old Age, Fashion, and Historicism in the Nineteenth Century," *Slavic Review*, 68/4 (Winter 2009), 782–803.
[22] Belinsky, "Petersburg and Moscow," in Nekrasov, *Petersburg*, 28.
[23] "Dopotopnaia ili dopozharnaia Moskva," in Viazemskii, *Polnoe sobranie sochinenii*, 7:80–116.
[24] François Guizot, *Mémoires pour servir à l'histoire de mon temps*, 8 vols. (Paris: Michel Lévy, 1872), 1:6.

Prince L'vov, who fretted about the railroad, shared this nostalgia. L'vov (1805–56) was an aristocrat of ancient pedigree but little wealth and made a career for himself as a civil servant, educator, and journalist. He thus knew from personal experience how the decline of the old aristocracy changed the city. In "Moscow Chronicle," his regular feature in the journal *The Muscovite* (*Moskvitianin*), he chatted with affection about a Moscow that was aristocratic, tradition-bound, and quintessentially Russian. Two of his columns, both from 1846, capture what became a widely shared image of Moscow before the Great Reforms.

In L'vov's description, Moscow and its people were magnificently, defiantly Russian. He never described the common people with terms like *classes danger-euses* that conveyed anxiety about a modern society in crisis. Instead he preferred words evocative of earlier times—"the Orthodox," "the commoners," or "our peasants." The people's traditionalism endowed them with a naive common sense and shielded them from the disruptive impression that innovations like the railroad could produce. Thus, when a rhinoceros had recently been exhibited in Moscow, "the Orthodox" had gazed in wonder only until someone exclaimed: "Clever folk, those Germans! Look what a monkey they've invented!"[25] As for "educated society," the stratum that most drew L'vov's attention, it combined old-time joie de vivre with a cautious openness to innovation. Like the common people, "society" was conservative. It proudly embraced customs, such as keeping large retinues of idle servants, that Catherine II and Storch had already deemed archaic. "Before the city post was established"—that is, when people still had to go to the post office to pick up their mail—"many claimed that it would not take hold here: 'that's fine', they said, 'for places where they have few domestic servants, but here in Moscow, thank God, in every respectable house we have so many servants that four of every five have nothing to do'." However, society also cautiously embraced progress, flocking to public lectures on science and history and marveling at a demonstration of electric light.[26]

Moscow celebrated its identification with the principles of Orthodoxy, autoc-racy, and nationality in the annual blessing of the waters. L'vov narrated this ritual in sensuous detail. The morning of 6 January 1846 was gloriously cold. Gathered at the Kremlin, the immense throng of the people waited patiently for the religious procession to move out onto the ice of the river. At last it was noon. The solemn hymn to bless the waters was chanted. Artillery fired salvoes in joyous celebration. Bells pealed majestically across the city. Church, state, nation, and city were as one.[27]

---

[25] [L'vov] M. Zh., "Zhizn' v Moskve v 1845," 270.
[26] [L'vov] M. Zh., "Zhizn' v Moskve v Ianvare 1846 goda," *Moskvitianin*, chast' 1, no. 2 (1846), 232–44, here: 234–7, quotation on 234.
[27] [L'vov] M. Zh., "Zhizn' v Moskve v Ianvare 1846 goda," 235.

Moscow's carefree gaiety was marred by poverty, but poverty created an opportunity for the elites to show leadership and compassion and thereby validate the social system as a whole. L'vov paid tribute to the aristocracy's concern for the "little brethren," the poor who lacked food or shelter: how delightful that "tomorrow these [noble ladies'] enchanting eyes will well up with tears of emotion, these hands will reach out to the bed of the sufferer, these lips will speak a word of comfort!" Such unpretentious, hands-on compassion, he wrote, was a national virtue that distinguished Russians from Europeans.[28]

L'vov was more ambivalent about charity provided by large-scale institutions, because their inhabitants formed a parallel social order that existed outside educated society's field of vision. The huge Foundling Home, for instance, was a universe apart. "One cannot help but be amazed," L'vov wrote, "that none of our novelists has yet paid attention to this city within Moscow, where people are born, are educated, serve, marry, [and] die, leaving a good or bad reputation— virtually without leaving the walls of the Foundling Home!"[29] However, it was reassuring to know that such institutions promoted order and rationality among the masses. Another columnist writing in the same "Moscow Chronicle" column as L'vov reported on a charity hospital that was "little known to the reading public, but very familiar to most of the non-reading, common, poor class of the Moscow population," because it treated 8,000 sufferers a year. Thanks to the hospital staff's efforts, "the common working folk have stopped believing in their quacks, [instead] showing greater trust in science and enlightened knowledge, and at the same time they gratefully accept the philanthropy that seeks to aid the poor man amidst the sickness that deprives the unfortunate of the sturdy hands that are the sole source of their wealth."[30]

STATISTICS AND SOCIAL ANALYSIS

When L'vov wrote about Moscow's Russian essence and free-spirited nobility, he was repeating well-worn clichés, but his cautious engagement with pauperism bespoke an interest in urban social questions that was new. This interest was fueled by the growing scale and sophistication of Russian statistical research, which in turn was a response to developments abroad. Russian statistical studies treated Moscow and St Petersburg as models of a successful urbanism for which

---

[28] [L'vov] M. Zh., "Zhizn' v Moskve v 1845," 274. A similar argument is made in E. K., "Poseshchenie etapa dlia ssyl'nykh u Rogozhskoi zastavy v Moskve," *Sovremennik*, vol. 34 (1844), 203–9.

[29] [L'vov] M. Zh., "Zhizn' v Moskve v Ianvare 1846 goda," 239.

[30] Il'ia Muromets, "Bol'nitsa dlia prikhodiashchikh v Moskve," *Moskvitianin*, vol. 3, otdel 5 (1850), 64–8, quotations on 64, 68. The hospital is also described by an unidentified writer in "Kratkii obzor zavedenii," 17–22.

the foils were London and Paris. The tone was generally optimistic, but as Nicholas I's reign wore on, a deepening note of worry crept in.

How and why officials collected statistics reflected their thinking about their own role in society. In the eighteenth century, cameralist officials were mainly concerned about enforcing taxation, conscription, and other laws. To this end, they divided the population into categories and assigned a specific legal status to each. For example, townsmen paid the soul tax, but merchants did not. The purpose of social statistics was to monitor compliance with these laws, not to document social conditions as such.

In the early nineteenth century, cameralism was challenged by Storch and other political economists who wanted economic policy to identify and foster the productive forces within society itself. To this end, they required data that placed the dynamics of society at the center of attention.[31] This need was met by an expanding press and bureaucracy that collected and analyzed factual information of all kinds. In Moscow under Nicholas I, the chief of police started publishing annual statistical reports covering issues that ranged from attendance at festivities to mortality levels and crime rates. City directories appeared that tried to list every homeowner, bureaucrat, and professional. Maps showed neighborhoods in ever more minute detail. For people interested in exploring social questions through data, it was a whole new world.

How to interpret the data remained an open question. One response, widespread among the French and British writers of the 1820s to 1840s who pioneered the study of urban social dysfunction, was statistical fatalism. If a behavior—crime, say, or prostitution—occurred with predictable regularity among a certain population, the participants must be in the grip of a statistical law that left little room for free will.[32] In Prussia, statisticians were more optimistic: they denied that crime rates and the like constituted laws that could actually restrict anyone's freedom of action, for to be a law, a collective behavior had to be enforced by a power of some kind, such as the government or the customs of the people. To understand the forces that were driving their society, Prussians therefore trusted more in history and ethnography than in statistical patterns.[33]

Russians, too, resisted statistical fatalism and viewed ethnography as essential to understanding their own country. An important impetus to ethnographic research came from the Interior Ministry, a stronghold of the reform-minded officials whom W. Bruce Lincoln calls "enlightened bureaucrats."[34] In 1845, the ministry instructed government-sponsored newspapers in the provinces to make

---

[31] For a cogent discussion of Russian statistical thinking, see Smith-Peter, "Defining the Russian People," 47–64.

[32] Hacking, *The Taming of Chance*, 118–20.

[33] Hacking, *The Taming of Chance*, 36–7, 125–32.

[34] Lincoln, *In the Vanguard of Reform*, passim.

local ethnographic research one of their regular features. That same year, ministry officials helped establish the Russian Geographical Society, which soon confronted a schism over what its central mission should be. One faction viewed ethnography as an adjunct to colonialism and wanted to study exotic non-European peoples. The other faction, which ultimately prevailed, wanted to study Russia itself to create the knowledge base for future reforms of Russian society.[35]

One channel by which the public learned about the nexus of statistics, ethnography, and social analysis, particularly concerning urban issues, was the *Journal of the Ministry of Internal Affairs* (*Zhurnal Ministerstva Vnutrennikh Del*). From its founding in 1829 until 1831, its editor was Bulgarin's friend and collaborator Nikolai Grech, but afterwards control fell to the "enlightened bureaucrats" who prepared the ground for the Great Reforms, including Andrei Zablotskii-Desiatovskii, Nikolai Nadezhdin, Konstantin Arsen'ev, and Nikolai Miliutin. In 1835, an unsigned article in the *Journal* outlined a sweeping agenda for social research that combined quantitative and ethnographic approaches under the heading of "statistics." The object of statistics, the author asserted, was nothing less than to "measure the forces of a state." This demanded a holistic view of society, embracing men's mores as well as their actions and integrating quantitative with descriptive methods. The "national [*narodnyi*] character" was best studied in the cities, because there society's "moral forces" evolved "with greater abruptness and speed," and because the urban setting made it easier to gather demographic and economic data.[36] The use of statistics and ethnography in social research thus drew attention to the problems of the cities. Russian thinking on these matters received powerful impulses from the West, as the *Journal*'s editors showed by their extensive coverage of British and French debates about urban affairs.

In 1815, in what the philosopher of science Ian Hacking regards as the founding event of numerical (quantitative) sociology, an article in a British journal triggered a fierce cross-Channel row over who was more suicidal, Parisians or Londoners. The British argued that Parisians were more likely to kill themselves because they had abandoned religion. The French retorted that the effect of the British climate on the spleen induced widespread insanity, leaving Londoners suicidal. Each side resorted to statistics to prove its point, in the

[35] Susan Smith-Peter, *The Russian Provincial Newspaper and its Public, 1788–1864*, The Carl Beck Papers in Russian & East European Studies, no. 1908 (Pittsburgh: Center for Russian and East European Studies, University of Pittsburgh, 2008), 19; Nathaniel Knight, "Science, Empire, and Nationality: Ethnography in the Russian Geographical Society, 1845–1855," in Jane Burbank and David L. Ransel, eds., *Imperial Russia: New Histories for the Empire* (Bloomington, Ind.: Indiana University Press, 1998), 108–41; Lincoln, *In the Vanguard of Reform*, 91–101.
[36] "O vazhnosti statisticheskikh ischislenii (Soobshcheno)," *ZhMVD*, chast' 16/2 (May 1835), 187–97, quotations on 187–9.

process opening up a panoply of issues—not only suicide, irreligion, and insanity, but also crime, pauperism, and more generally the alienation of modern man.

In the aftermath of the European revolutions of 1830, Russia's leaders were anxious to show their country's immunity to the malaise plaguing the West. This concern runs through much of the commentary in the *Journal of the Ministry of Internal Affairs* on Western debates about numerical sociology. For instance, the *Journal* used statistics to show that people were saner in Russia. Only one of every 2,616 Petersburgers was hospitalized in the city's insane asylum, it reported in 1833, compared to one of every 857 Parisians. Moreover, "the nature of the [mental] illness itself" in Paris was such that "as it grows in number, it also intensifies qualitatively": ten of every twenty-seven patients there were deemed incurable, compared with only ten of every seventy-one in St Petersburg.[37]

Other Western ills included urban overcrowding and the menace posed by the *classes dangereuses*. Moscow was lucky to have grown more slowly and become less crowded than London or Paris, the *Journal* wrote in 1832 in its commentary on the annual reports of the police chiefs of Moscow and St Petersburg. Dividing the surface area of Moscow and Paris by the number of inhabitants—which gave skewed results, since Moscow had annexed its suburbs while Paris had not—the author found that Moscow had a generous 240 square meters per inhabitant, whereas Paris had only 38.33. The French capital was afflicted with 50,000 to 60,000 homeless paupers, for whom civil unrest was allegedly an opportunity for personal gain. The figures for London were even more impressive in their grim precision: 114,000 paupers, 30,000 prostitutes, and 118,000 vagrants and thieves. Since the incidence of crime "provides the measure, more or less, of the corruption of morals," it was significant that crime was much lower in Moscow than in "other European capitals."[38] Moscow, the *Journal* reported, had experienced only 278 incidents of theft (*krazha*) in 1832, in which 179,952 rubles' worth of goods were stolen. For St Petersburg, the numbers were 244 thefts and 301,428 rubles. In London, by comparison, the value of what was stolen in 1831 was 2.1 million pounds sterling, or 52.5 million rubles. As London had three times the population of St Petersburg, it followed that it suffered sixty times more theft per capita. London had so many paupers that "it is no surprise that in England, theft has become an industry for a significant portion of the lower class of the people, and it is unlikely that a means will be found to stop it because the galleys and [the Australian penal colony of] Botany Bay represent paradise for the victims of pauperism."[39]

[37] "Zamechaniia o chisle umalishennykh, pol'zovannykh v bol'nitse Vsekh Skorbiashchikh v S. Peterburge 1832 goda," *ZhMVD*, chast' 8, no. 2 (1833), 199–208, here: 203–4.

[38] "Zamechaniia na otchety Ober-Politseimeisterov po obeim Stolitsam," *ZhMVD*, chast' 6, no. 2 (1832), 54–69, here: 63.

[39] "Zamechaniia o chisle krazh, sdelannykh v Moskve, S.P.burge i Londone," *ZhMVD*, chast' 8, no. 3 (1833), 331–4, here: 334.

A decade later, the *Journal* still discerned the same link between poverty, crime, and moral decay. In London, poor women drank and brawled like men and "have nothing female except the name." Female criminality bred juvenile criminality, and the "corruption of women, children, and domestic servants" reflected the decay of English family life. Things had not yet come to a similar pass in France. How, then, to explain France's higher homicide rate? "The reason lies in the difference in character and habits of the two peoples: where the Englishman resorts to his fists, the Frenchman reaches for his knife!"[40]

Like crime and poverty, suicide (which was easier to measure) was much lower in Russia. The *Journal* reported in 1832 that in Moscow there was one suicide per 15,000 inhabitants, versus one per 1,930 in Paris. Citing an analysis by the prefect of Paris, Count de Chabrol, the *Journal* identified the leading causes of suicide in Paris as "illnesses, disappointment with life (*dégoût de la vie*), mental weakness; then poverty, loss of positions [or] offices, disorder in business, love, domestic quarrels; finally debauchery, gambling, the lottery, and so forth." In Moscow, the *Journal* wrote hopefully, "we do not have as yet the kind of destitution that deprives unfortunates of all hope for their lives. Desire remains undeveloped and religious belief undiminished."[41]

The *Journal*'s numbers were so precise, and its arguments so sweeping, because it uncritically used institutional statistics as a proxy for complex social realities. Authors rarely asked, for example, how comprehensively vice and lawlessness were reported to the authorities, or how different countries determined that a social or mental pathology warranted official intervention.

This approach was rejected as overly simplistic only when it contradicted the propaganda of the imperial regime. For example, having noted with concern that mortality was higher in Moscow than in Paris and London, the *Journal* pointed out that many deaths in Moscow involved foundlings who had perhaps been neglected by their parents; whether London or Paris had similar extenuating circumstances was not investigated.[42] When *The Northern Bee* reported on a German study that found fewer people attending school in Russia than elsewhere in Europe, the *Journal* took issue with the study's methodology. It argued, reasonably, that the study counted only Russians attending Ministry of Education schools, not people educated at home or in ecclesiastical, military, or other institutions. In twenty-four pages of detailed analysis, the *Journal* accounted for such alternatives in Russia, but did not inquire whether they existed abroad as well. When the enhanced Russian numbers were compared with the unrevised foreign ones, it turned out that Russia was within the standard range and thus an enlightened country. In any case, the author added, it was hardly a sign of

---

[40] "Sravnitel'naia statistika prestuplenii v Parizhe i v Londone," *ZhMVD*, chast' 2, "Smes'" (1843), 443–57, quotations on 447, 452, 456.

[41] "Zamechaniia na otchety Ober-Politseimeisterov po obeim Stolitsam," 64–5.

[42] "Zamechaniia na otchety Ober-Politseimeisterov po obeim Stolitsam," 61–2.

enlightenment if the poor in other countries—he pointedly mentioned French artisans, who were known for their revolutionary sympathies—could read newspapers that incited them against their government.[43]

The analyses of the Interior Ministry's statisticians provided quantitative support for the picture that Zagoskin and Prince L'vov sketched in their essays. Compared with the vision of squalor and anomie that Russians culled from British and French publications, Moscow appeared as a place of harmony and wholesome values. In London and Paris, community seemed to be steadily eroded by class hatred and materialistic attitudes. Russia, and particularly Moscow, was spared this fate thanks to paternalistic class relations and conservative religious attitudes. This opinion was widely shared in Russia, but it did not preclude critical self-reflection. This is illustrated by the work of Vasilii Androssov (1803–41), the Moscow official who published, under the modest title *A Statistical Note on Moscow* (*Statisticheskaia zapiska o Moskve*, 1832), the first book-length Russian-language study to examine Moscow statistically and ethnographically.[44]

Androssov found much to criticize in Moscow. Mortality was high. Life expectancy was low. The poor suffered from alcoholism and rising levels of out-of-wedlock births, and their indifference to safety precautions caused fatal accidents. Androssov worried about the social effects of the shift toward a capitalist economy that he thought was under way as the "middle estate" displaced the nobility as the city's economic leaders. He found the government's system of collecting statistics by estate useless for studying these developments, so he ignored estate altogether in his book, instead using a classification system of his own devising that divided the population into socioeconomic classes.

Despite these concerns, Androssov argued that Moscow was not staring into the same abyss as Paris or London. Moscow had a remarkably low crime rate, he found.[45] Fewer than half the inhabitants—many of whom were temporary migrants—were registered with a local parish church, but over two-thirds strictly observed the Orthodox rules on fasting, suggesting that conservative values persisted independently of their enforcement by the authorities. Religious traditionalism also explained why Muscovites were seven times less likely than Parisians to kill themselves: "In Paris, Chabrol observes, suicides tend to be family men who take their own lives because of domestic troubles, disputes, illnesses, or destitution; in Moscow by contrast, they are mostly young men who

[43] A. Glagolev, "Sravnitel'noe obozrenie sostoianiia prosveshcheniia v Rossii s sostoianiem onago v prochikh evropeiskikh gosudarstvakh," *ZhMVD*, chast' 16, no. 2 (May 1835), 302–26.

[44] N. G. Okhotin, "Andrósov, Androssov Vasilii Petrovich," in P. A. Nikolaev, ed., *Russkie pisateli 1800–1917: Biograficheskii slovar'*, 5 vols. (Moscow: Sovetskaia Entsiklopediia, 1989–), 1:73–4.

[45] On Russia's low crime rates under Nicholas I in comparison with Western countries, see B. N. Mironov, "Prestupnost' v Rossii v XIX–nachale XX veka," *Otechestvennaia istoriia*, no. 1 (1998), 24–42, esp. 39.

are single or living apart from their families and are drawn to their doom by fast living and debauchery." Muscovites thus suffered from the age-old character flaws that nobles attributed to their peasants and servants—drunkenness, irresponsibility, a constant need for supervision—but not the despair and moral decay of the contemporary West.[46]

The reviews of Androssov's book in the Russian press suggest that many agreed with his analysis. At the Interior Ministry, reform-oriented officials shared his view that Russia needed a better system for gathering data on social issues. The ministry's *Journal* wrote that Androssov's book "has every claim on our enlightened compatriots' attention." It broadly approved of his reading of socioeconomic trends, although it cautioned that his long-term statistical analyses were problematic owing to the paucity of reliable data before 1812. It also argued that he had only anecdotal evidence for some of his generalizations about lower-class pathologies, such as his claim about the people's habitual disregard for safety. The Moscow journal *Telescope* (*Teleskop*) effusively praised Androssov, endorsed his view that the estate system was useless for social analysis, and agreed with his assessment of lower-class pathologies (including the people's indifference to safety). The *Telescope*'s arch-rival, the *Moscow Telegraph* (*Moskovskii telegraf*), criticized Androssov, but only because it thought that he should have given even more attention to Moscow's transformation into "an industrial and commercial city, a city of the middle estate."[47]

The *Journal of the Ministry of Internal Affairs* was not only a vehicle for propaganda but also a forum for critical discussion of Russian urban conditions. For example, after the cholera of 1830–2, the *Journal* published an in-depth study of health conditions in St Petersburg. The author was apparently Semen Gaevskii, the top medical official (*general-shtab-doktor*) of the Interior Ministry. This seems to have been only the second major medical topography of the imperial capital to be published in Russian; the first was a translation of the German book by Ludwig Attenhofer.[48] Gaevskii began with the customary paeans to Russian urban planning:

The spaciousness of the streets in Petersburg and the cleanliness that is observed everywhere is unarguably one of the main causes that help preserve the inhabitants' health. The

---

[46] Androssov, *Statisticheskaia zapiska*, 45–7, 66–7, 69–72, 78–9, 83, 90, 100, 116, 159–60. Mikhail Gastev's work on Moscow likewise provides plentiful statistics, but acknowledges social problems (such as prostitution or substandard housing) mainly in the context of government measures to combat them: Gastev, *Materialy*, e.g., 160–1, 210–11, 293.

[47] Reviews by: anon., in ZhMVD, chast' 6, no. 3 (1832), 70–86, here: 70; N. N., in *Teleskop*, vol. 8, no. 7 (1832), 388–413; anon., in *Moskovskii telegraf*, no. 6 (March 1832), 254–9, here: 258. On the journalistic rivalries in Moscow, see D. P. Bak, "'Teoriia iskusstva' i 'samoe iskusstvo' (Moskovskaia zhurnalistika 1830-kh godov i universitetskaia nauka)," in Knabe, *Moskva i "moskovskii tekst*,*"* esp. 32–7.

[48] Markovin, *Razvitie meditsinskoi geografii v Rossii*, 49–50; *Russkii Biograficheskii Slovar'*, 4:112. The Russian edition of Attenhofer, *Medizinische Topographie*, is Genrikh Liudvig fon-Attengofer, *Mediko-topograficheskoe opisanie Sanktpeterburga Glavnago i stolichnago goroda Rossiiskoi Imperii* (St Petersburg: pri Imperatorskoi Akademii Nauk, 1820).

daily cleaning of the streets and courtyards, [and] the removal of all refuse to sites outside the city assigned by the police, is without any doubt a highly beneficial measure.

Reality, however, subverted the best intentions. Pipes draining wastewater from houses were supposed to be kept separate from privies, yet as Gaevskii observed delicately, "this is perhaps not observed everywhere." When these pipes were cleaned in the summer, their stinking contents were to be carted away, not dumped onto the streets—an admonition that implied that violations occurred. Houses were built to ensure adequate ventilation, but "obviously there is no rule without exceptions." Gaevskii further decried dank, overcrowded basement lodgings where people cooked and baked, dried their laundry, kept domestic fowl, and heated their stoves, all while hardly ever opening the window for fresh air. Unsanitary grocery stores, factories, and workshops were further incubators of disease.[49]

In London and Paris, the misery of the 1820s to 1840s spurred far-reaching urban reforms. In London, law enforcement and public works were unified and professionalized through the creation of the Metropolitan Police (in 1829) and the Metropolitan Board of Works (in 1855). These reforms enabled London to respond to the Great Stink of 1858—when a heat wave caused the water level of the Thames to drop, leaving the city's untreated sewage to bake in the sun—by building a modern sewer system that went into operation in 1864.[50] In Paris, the length of the sewers grew from 96 kilometers in 1840 to 773 kilometers in 1870, and the police was reformed in 1854 along the lines of the London reform of 1829.[51] Paris annexed the adjacent suburbs in 1860, and under the administration of Baron Haussmann, the French capital experienced an extraordinary era of urban renewal between 1853 and 1870.

In Russia, where the "enlightened bureaucrats" gained influence, urban problems also received more attention. In 1839, a committee was established in Moscow to address the problem of pauperism. In 1840, the Third Section investigated the squalid living conditions of laborers in St Petersburg. Urban issues were a particular interest of Lev Perovskii, who became interior minister in 1841 and placed the young "enlightened bureaucrat" Nikolai Miliutin in charge of an office on urban governance and economy. Medical-police committees were created in St Petersburg (1843) and Moscow (1844) to monitor the health of prostitutes and contain the spread of venereal diseases, especially among laborers. In 1846, municipal government in St Petersburg was reformed; this later became the basis for an empire-wide reform of urban government in 1870.[52]

---

[49] [Gaevskii], "Mediko-topograficheskiia svedeniia," *ZhMVD*, chast' 11, no. 2 (February 1834), 163, 167, 176.

[50] David Owen, *The Government of Victorian London, 1855–1889: The Metropolitan Board of Works, the Vestries, and the City Corporation* (Cambridge, Mass.: Belknap, 1982), 23–4, 53–5.

[51] Reid, *Paris Sewers and Sewermen*, 26, 30; Delattre, *Les douze heures noires*, 307.

[52] "Otchet komiteta, vysochaishe uchrezhdennago v Moskve," 332; W. Bruce Lincoln, "N. A. Miliutin and the St. Petersburg Municipal Act of 1846: A Study in Reform under

Under these circumstances, favorable commentary on Western cities grew more common. A few holdouts continued to disagree. One of these was Moscow's police chief Ivan Luzhin, whose boastful claims, the secret police found, made him a figure of public ridicule.[53] In 1847, Luzhin reported in the Interior Ministry's *Journal* that the average inhabitant of Moscow went to the bathhouse at least ten times a year; this proved, according to Luzhin, that "among all European nations, the Russians alone are distinguished by personal cleanliness."[54] By then, however, the *Journal* was increasingly reporting on improvements in the West. In what sounded like oblique criticism of the obsession with appearances that Russian officials carried from the parade ground to every other area of life, the *Journal* noted in 1843 that "the cleanliness and tidiness of cities" was a matter of public health, not just aesthetics, and that in London, Paris, and Berlin, thanks to sewers and running water that removed waste from streets and homes, "the condition of public health has improved remarkably."[55] Reforms of the police and other public services in London and Paris likewise received favorable coverage.[56] The comparison with Russia's metropolitan cities was not explicit, but it was not hard to read between the lines.

Despite these inklings of anxiety, Moscow in the 1820s to 1840s did not become associated in Russian culture with images of poverty and squalor. In Britain, public perceptions of London deteriorated suddenly and drastically during the decade from 1825 to 1835, and the city acquired a lasting association with poverty and filth.[57] No comparable shift occurred in Russia with regard to Moscow. Many Russians shared the regime's belief that state power plus an essentially rustic population meant social harmony, although, reflecting the influence of ethnographic considerations in Russian thinking, the credit went more often to the national character than to the authorities. For example, observers agreed that crime was lower in Moscow than in European cities, but

---

Nicholas I," *Slavic Review*, 33/1 (March 1974), 55–68; Lincoln, *In the Vanguard of Reform*, 109–15; Paert, *Old Believers*, 209; Shchepkin, "Istoricheskaia zapiska o raskhodakh," 49.

[53] "Doneseniia agentov o dukhe v Moskve v 1848 godu," 346–7.

[54] "Moskva v 1846 godu. Izvlechenie is otcheta g. Moskovskago ober-politsiimeistera," *ZhMVD* (November 1847), 254–92, here: 267.

[55] "Sistema ochishcheniia dvorov i ulits posredstvom vodoprovodnykh trub, predprinimaemaia v Berline, po primeru Parizha i Londona," *ZhMVD*, chast' 3, "Smes'" (September 1843), 502–7, quotations on 502–3.

[56] "Sravnenie politseiskago ustroistva v Parizhe i Londone," *ZhMVD*, chast' 9, "Smes'" (January 1845), 161–6; "Sostav i krug deiatel'nosti nyneshnei Londonskoi politsii," *ZhMVD*, chast' 42, no. 5, "Smes'" (May 1853), 317–27; "Preobrazovanie gorodskoi Politsii v Parizhe, po primeru Londonskoi," *ZhMVD*, chast' 8, otdel 4, "Sovremennaia letopis'" (October 1854), 79–83; "Soderzhanie chistoty v Parizhe," *ZhMVD*, chast' 22, otdel 2, "Izsledovaniia i opisaniia" (February 1857), 91–104; "Ustroistvo gospitalei i bogougodnykh zavedenii vo Frantsii," *ZhMVD*, chast' 29, otdel 2, "Izsledovaniia i opisaniia" (April 1858), 155–78.

[57] Donald J. Olson, "Introduction: Victorian London," in Owen, *The Government of Victorian London*, 11.

the reason, they argued, was less the effectiveness of the police than the common Russian's benign temperament and respect for authority.[58]

PHYSIOLOGY AND THE NATURAL SCHOOL

The agenda of the statisticians—to uncover the hidden regularities of urban life and explore their socio-psychological underpinnings—was embraced by a broad variety of Russian writers. For example, Bulgarin wrote in 1836 that in his sketches about life in St Petersburg, the composite characters who synthesized the traits of entire social groups were "true" in the same sense as "*approximate numbers in statistics*," because "[both] the physical and moral worlds are full of exceptions."[59]

From the beginning of the nineteenth century, authors had experimented with realistic depictions of folk customs. Such *bytopisanie* ("writing about everyday life") was widely criticized because it did not depict reality in the idealized form prescribed by eighteenth-century literary convention. A more sophisticated version of *bytopisanie* was the physiological sketch of the 1830s and 1840s, which delved into the psychology of particular urban strata and problematized their relationship to the social order as a whole. The new interest in urban characters and contexts was also fostered by the works of Pushkin and Gogol.[60]

A pioneering figure in the development of the Russian physiological literature was Aleksandr Bashutskii (1803–76). As a young man, from 1826 to 1832, he was an aide-de-camp to the governor-general of St Petersburg. As a result of this experience he was well versed in urban statistics and administration and knew first-hand how the various strata of urban society lived.[61] When he began writing about St Petersburg, he followed two literary models: the analysis of urban social structures in Storch's *Tableau of St Petersburg*, and the depiction of social classes in the French physiological sketches. His literary collaborators likewise straddled the worlds of administration and literature. For his anthology *Our People, Painted from Nature by Russians* (*Nashi, spisannye s natury russkimi*, 1841–2), he recruited the writer Vladimir Dal', and for a time he hoped also to include

---

[58] Engelhardt, *Russische Miscellen*, 4:118; [Nikolai Turgenev] N. Tourgueneff, *La Russie et les Russes*, 3 vols. (Paris: Au comptoir des imprimeurs-unis, 1847), 3:200–1; Aleksandr Bashutskii, *Panorama Sanktpeterburga*, 3 vols. (St Petersburg, V tipografii vdovy Pliushar s synom, 1834), 3:182. Storch had already made this argument in the 1790s (*Gemaehlde*, 1:167–8).

[59] Al'bin Konechnyi, "Bulgarin bytopisatel' i Peterburg v ego ocherkakh," in Bulgarin, *Peterburgskie ocherki*, 14.

[60] Konechnyi, "Bulgarin bytopisatel' i Peterburg v ego ocherkakh," in Bulgarin, *Peterburgskie ocherki*, 10–11; A. G. Tseitlin, *Stanovlenie realizma v russkoi literature (Russkii fiziologicheskii ocherk)* (Moscow: Nauka, 1965), 12–26; Ronald D. LeBlanc, "Teniers, Flemish Art, and the Natural School Debate," *Slavic Review*, 50/3 (Fall 1991), 576–89.

[61] V. N. Shikin and N. G. Okhotin, "Bashutskii Aleksandr Pavlovich," in Nikolaev, *Russkie pisateli 1800–1917*, 1:189–92.

contributions by Vladimir Odoevskii, Vladimir Sollogub, and Ivan Panaev. All of them served in the Interior Ministry or other agencies dominated by "enlightened bureaucrats."[62]

In Bashutskii's opinion, urban Russia was in a deep social crisis that had moral roots. He blamed the crisis on the moral obtuseness of the elites and the cultural and material coarseness of the poor. Only if the elites had a change of heart and devoted themselves to enlightenment and material progress for all was social harmony possible.[63] Similar to Androssov in his *Statistical Note on Moscow*, he thought that urban society could only be understood through the everyday experience of its inhabitants, including those farthest from the centers of wealth and power. This approach highlighted the diversity *within* cities, not the differences *among* them, and thus challenged interpretations that treated Moscow and St Petersburg as monolithic entities embodying opposite principles of Russian culture.

Authors who were less socially critical, for example Zagoskin, Grech, and Bulgarin, held the contrary view. They anthropomorphized Moscow and St Petersburg as cities with unique and opposite personalities. The personality of each city was constituted by the cultural traits of its upper classes; the common people were relegated to the background as a mass distinguished principally by its timeless, undifferentiated Russianness.[64] This approach conveniently elided urban social tensions, but it also bespoke an aesthetic that found the gritty side of urban life unworthy of literary representation.[65] Bashutskii and the others who followed Gogol in exploring the social complexities of urban life were labeled the Natural School by Bulgarin. This was meant as an insulting analogy with artists who painted directly "from nature," without concealing the unseemly sides of reality, and the label stuck.[66]

Bashutskii wrote about St Petersburg, but his interpretive template fit Moscow as well. Two of his books will detain us here. The first, *The Panorama of St Petersburg (Panorama Sanktpeterburga*, 1834), which also appeared in German and French editions,[67] echoes the title as well as some of the themes of Storch's *Tableau of St Petersburg* of 1794.[68] It differs from Storch in its nationalistic tone, and it reflects the influences of the emerging realist literature with its moral

---

[62] Lincoln, *In the Vanguard of Reform*, 50, 69; N. G. Okhotin, "A. P. Bashutskii i ego kniga," in Okhotin and Sternin, *Nashi: Prilozhenie*, 23–4.

[63] Okhotin, "A. P. Bashutskii i ego kniga," in Okhotin and Sternin, *Nashi: Prilozhenie*, 5–8, 13.

[64] See, for example, "Moskovskiia pis'ma," in Grech, *Sochineniia*, 5:87–112.

[65] Kenneth E. Harper, "Criticism of the Natural School in the 1840s," *American Slavic and East European Review*, 15 (October 1956), 400–14.

[66] Tseitlin, *Stanovlenie realizma*, 92–3.

[67] Alexander von Baschuzky, *Panorama von St. Petersburg*, 2 vols., tr. A. von Oldekop (St Petersburg: Eggers und Pelz, 1834–5); Alexandre Bachoutsky, *Panorama de St. Pétersbourg*, 2 vols., tr. Ferry de Pigny (St Petersburg: Pluchart, 1834).

[68] Solomon Volkov writes, without providing a source, that Bashutskii wrote the *Panorama of St Petersburg* as pro-government propaganda at the behest of the police; Solomon Volkov, *St. Petersburg: A Cultural History*, tr. Antonina W. Bouis (New York: Free Press Paperbacks, 1997), 35–6.

judgments on the city and its vivid evocation of the sensory environment. Bashutskii's second work, the anthology *Our People*, was an innovative attempt to explore the everyday world of middling and common Russians through physiological sketches.

The Panorama of St Petersburg is a hybrid of different genres. The first volume, a history of Peter the Great, seeks to give the city a historical depth comparable to Moscow. The second volume is devoted to history, topography, and statistics. The third, finally, is a study of the mores of the inhabitants; it is here that Bashutskii engages with the complexity and opacity of urban life.

Bashutskii shared Androssov's frustration with the estate system as a tool of social analysis, but whereas the alternative classificatory scheme devised by Androssov is socioeconomic (traders, manufacturers, and unskilled laborers), Bashutskii's relies on a combination of wealth, culture, and lifestyle. At the top is "high society" (*bol'shoi svet*). Then comes "the public": middling nobles, scholars, artists, some foreigners, and the most cultured Russian merchants. Farther down is "our *tiers-état* [third estate]," an "amalgamation of people of diverse estates" that grows more numerous as the skilled trades expand and who have in common "a certain degree of education" and "the conveniences of domestic living." At the bottom is "what they call the people [*narod*] or populace [*chern'*]," principally "peasants, a section of the townspeople and *raznochintsy* [people of various ranks], and house serfs." Foreigners make up a separate stratum of their own.[69] Four of these five categories are identical to the four that Storch proposed in his *Tableau of St Petersburg* of 1794.[70] Bashutskii's innovation was to add "our *tiers-état*." By identifying a separate stratum distinguished by access to "education" and "conveniences," and giving it the familiar label of an eighteenth-century European middle class, he placed a novel emphasis on the advances of the imperial social project.

Like Storch, but with more emphasis on the shifting moods and sensory experiences of the city, Bashutskii describes how day and night create temporal niches for various social strata. (Gogol, writing at the same time as Bashutskii, develops a similar theme in "Nevskii Prospekt.") The upper classes rule only at certain hours. At daybreak, laborers fill the streets. "You"—the upper classes— "don't notice them by day: at that time, busy with their work, laboring or relaxing in silence, they belong to the city; but now the city belongs to them; with everyone in the houses asleep, they alone are masters of the earth, air, and sky." Later in the morning, the middle and upper strata begin their day. Bashutskii is attentive to the cacophonous sounds of the city as "the noise and voices rise from *crescendo* to *forte*."[71] By day's close, the bustle dies down again, and eventually the aristocracy's evening entertainments come to an end as well.

[69] Bashutskii, *Panorama Sanktpeterburga*, 3:12–13, 16.
[70] Storch, *Gemaehlde*, vol. 1, ch.12.
[71] Bashutskii, *Panorama Sanktpeterburga*, 3:78, 83.

The wee hours create a mysterious world of silence and ambiguity. The lamp-lighter making his rounds "[looks] in the darkness like some strange specter." In the silent streets, "one only glimpses from time to time, by the light of the lamps, someone's fleeting shadow against a wall." Though spooky and enigmatic, the night is not genuinely frightening. The watchman at his guardhouse can be counted on to startle the unwary with his "pointed, funereally doleful, and unintelligibly contracted *toid'? (kto idet)* [Who goes there?]," while guard dogs bark in the distance and the sound of cavalry patrols and the calls of sentries echo in the empty streets.[72]

Explorations of what went on after the sun went down were a new development in Russian literature. In Paris, Mercier and Restif de la Bretonne had already described in the 1780s how nightfall undercut the daytime order of society.[73] In Russia, where writers had close ties to the state and an orderly urban society was a recent and cherished development, literature preferred to validate, not subvert, the diurnal order. When authors wrote about night, it was mostly to describe how the elites extended their daytime world past nightfall, say, through nocturnal policing or aristocratic festivities. By the 1830s, however, writers came to appreciate the urban night on its own terms, as an eerie counterpoint to the orderly and regimented life of the day. Examples include Evgenii's nightmare of being chased by Peter the Great in Pushkin's *The Bronze Horseman*, or Akakii Akakievich's return as a ghost in Gogol's "The Overcoat." Bashutskii's account of the night is part of this literary development.

Both Storch and Bashutskii seek to present a general overview of the city. Storch writes that he would prefer a high vantage point from which to survey the entire city, but since St Petersburg lacks tall buildings, he takes the reader on a walking tour instead. Thus seeing St Petersburg at ground level, one street after another, draws our attention to the diversity of human types and social interactions that, to Storch, are constitutive of urban society.[74]

Bashutskii, because he sees the city as a moral community, requires a godlike vantage point from which to observe and judge it in its totality. Hence he does what Storch could not: he ascends atop a building so tall that it presents a sweeping vista of all the social, sensory, and moral diversity of the metropolis. He echoes Glinka's critique of luxury when he shows us the downtown, teeming with self-important people in uniform who exude "vanity," "luxury," and "refinement." Unlike Glinka, he then dwells on the contrast with the nearby Haymarket district—filthy and dark, yet noisy and alive with honest toiling folk. Finally, between the two extremes lies the district of the "middling condition," where everything breathes "moderation and tranquility." Here, people work by the light of tallow (not wax) candles; their apartments face the courtyard,

---

[72] Bashutskii, *Panorama Sanktpeterburga*, 3:93–5.
[73] Delattre, *Les douze heures noires*, 33–77.
[74] Storch, *Gemaehlde*, vol. 1, ch.1.

not the street; they have modest shops (*lavki*), not elegant stores (*magaziny*); for them, walking is for getting around, not just for promenading; they rise when the rich are still in bed, turn in when the rich prepare to go out for the night, and have as luxuries only the cast-offs of the aristocracy.[75]

Bashutskii's sentimental idealization of the middle and lower classes was part of a polemic against the West, especially France. Western writings about St Petersburg, he charged, were filled with malicious lies.[76] For example, they claimed that the streets were lifeless and devoid of people. Wrong, he retorted, they only *seemed* empty. Thanks to the native qualities of the Russian peasant and the wisdom of the government, the men who migrated to the city found work while their families stayed at home in the village. Hence St Petersburg was not empty. It merely lacked a *classe dangereuse*, "those hungry, sullen crowds of the people, with their rags, their disorderly noise, their insolence and rowdy behavior." Hence also, the (upper-class) pedestrian ran no risk of being accosted by beggars or having refuse dumped on his head from upper-floor windows, and the populace would never mock you for your dress or throw mud or stones.[77] To make absolutely clear to whom Russia was being contrasted, Bashutskii provided the relevant terms in French. St Petersburg, he wrote, had few "*thieving swindlers (filoux),*" and "no troublemakers, street rakes, or mischievous schoolboys (*gamins*)."[78] Citing the same statistics as Androssov and the *Journal of the Ministry of Internal Affairs*, Bashutskii, too, found that St Petersburg had many fewer lunatics, paupers, crimes, and suicides than London or Paris. Granted, the poor lived in squalor, but they tolerated such discomfort out of the same uncorrupted closeness to nature that made them so patient and peaceful.[79]

Bashutskii pushed farther in the "physiological" direction with *Our People, Painted from Nature by Russians*. Published in 1841–2 in the (unrealized) hope of making money by reaching the middling audience that read authors like Bulgarin, *Our People* contained what one recent scholar calls "the *first* physiological sketches in Russian literature."[80] An important model for Bashutskii was the massive anthology *The French, Painted by Themselves* (*Les français peints par eux-mêmes*, 1840–2), which consisted of 254 sketches spread over eight volumes and was in turn inspired by *Heads of the People, or Portraits of the English* (1838–40). By the time their venture was cut short by censorship hassles and organizational and financial difficulties, Bashutskii, Prince L'vov, Grigorii Kvitka-Osnov'ia-nenko, Vladimir Dal', and two others who remain unidentified were able to publish sketches of a water carrier, a noble spinster, an army officer, undertakers, a serf nanny, a village folk-healer, and a Urals Cossack. All were accompanied by

75 Bashutskii, *Panorama Sanktpeterburga*, 3:138–9.
76 Bashutskii, *Panorama Sanktpeterburga*, 1:vi, 3:3–9.
77 Bashutskii, *Panorama Sanktpeterburga*, 3:13–15, 69, quotation on 15–16.
78 Bashutskii, *Panorama Sanktpeterburga*, 3:183–4.
79 Bashutskii, *Panorama Sanktpeterburga*, 2:80, 89–93; 3:29, 32.
80 Okhotin, "A. P. Bashutskii i ego kniga," in Okhotin and Sternin, *Nashi: Prilozhenie*, 17.

Illus. 8.1. "The Water Carrier." Woodcut by Vasilii Timm, in A. Bashutskii et al., *Nashi, spisannye s natury russkimi* (St Petersburg: Izdanie Ia. A. Isakova, 1841), 1. Courtesy of Syracuse University Library.

engravings depicting the protagonists with maximum documentary realism (see Illustration 8.1). Aside from the folk-healer and the Cossack, the stories take place in St Petersburg or unnamed provincial towns, but the setting is sufficiently unspecific to carry implications for cities anywhere in Russia.

In these sketches, the protagonists are embedded in a micro-level social milieu, but their stories are also a commentary on much larger social dynamics. Bashutskii himself wrote the first sketch in the series. Its central figure is a water carrier, who delivers water with his horse-drawn cart and carries it into people's homes. He is a rural migrant, and throughout he exhibits a goodness and resignation that Bashutskii thought typical of the folk and that contrast with the decadence of the elites. He lives in wretched circumstances, but what most interests Bashutskii is the hierarchy that presses down on him. His customers, with whom the reader is identified, are cold and indifferent. Mostly he deals with their servants; they have their own oppressive hierarchy, but all are equally spoiled by the comforts of the city and think themselves superior to the water carrier. Nor do the authorities look out for him. Disgruntled customers send the police after him, and as he lies dying and his comrades take him to the hospital, he is turned away—come back tomorrow, he is told, when a few patients will be dead and their beds available. Even in his virtuous death he is morally superior to many of his social betters. In a coda to the story, Bashutskii echoes Androssov and the European debates on suicide as he imagines a dialogue about the identity of a different man whose body was fished from the river: "An unhappy lover? A desperate gambler? Insulted in his [career] ambitions? . . . perhaps he squandered government money?"[81]

---

[81] A. Bashutskii, "Vodovoz," in *Nashi, spisannye s natury russkimi* (1841–2; repr. edn. Moscow: Kniga, 1986), 29.

Bashutskii's sentimental tale about the water carrier was an appeal to the hearts of the upper classes, not a frontal assault on the social order. The initial installment of *Our People*, which included "The Water Carrier," was greeted with effusive praise by Bulgarin's *Northern Bee*, a paper that was usually well attuned to the sensibilities of the government. Soon, however, things went sour. The censor who approved *Our People* was a friend of Bashutskii's and had signed off without reading the full text. When the volume became public, Bashutskii was summoned to the Third Section and told by Count Benckendorff himself of Tsar Nicholas's outrage that he had dared to depict the life of the poor in such gloomy terms. His service connections—he was on the staff of the State Council—saved him from further consequences, but the authorities at once instructed Bulgarin to write and publish a story about a water carrier whose life was happier.[82] *Our People* sold fairly well, eventually reaching a respectable 800 subscribers, but after the fourteenth booklet in December 1842, it mysteriously stopped appearing. The most likely explanation seems to be that Bashutskii simply lacked the energy to keep it going, but he also faced ideological headwinds. At least, Bulgarin became increasingly hostile. His *Northern Bee* argued that the French, British, and German physiologies were coarsely naturalistic fare for "maidservants" and "coachmen" who, in those unhappy countries, were literate and insisted on reading about their own kind and in their own vulgar idiom. For Russian authors to imitate such filth, he wrote, was unpatriotic.[83]

Bashutskii's writings opened up a perspective on urban life in which the elites no longer held center stage. He wrote about spaces and contexts that resisted their civilizing efforts: the teeming masses, the stench of crowded cellars, the opacity of night. He questioned whether different classes really lived in harmony and showed that the common folk formed a complex universe of which those at the top knew little. Especially in *Our People*, the usual reductionist binaries— Europe versus Russia, elites versus commoners—yielded to a more nuanced view of urban life. By adapting what in France was a mass-market genre, Bashutskii also reached out, as Bulgarin venomously acknowledged, to a more inclusive readership that might recognize its own world in the stories he published.

PHYSIOLOGIES OF MOSCOW: VISTENGOF AND KOKOREV

In 1845, in his introduction to Nikolai Nekrasov's *Physiology of Petersburg* (*Fiziologiia Peterburga*), Vissarion Belinskii reflected on the state of physiological literature in Russia. After passing in review Gogol, Griboedov, and Bashutskii, he noted that Moscow had recently been the subject of physiologies by Zagoskin

---

[82] Bulgarin's sketch of a happy water carrier is [Faddei Bulgarin] F. B., "Vononos," *Severnaia Pchela* (15 January 1842), 43.

[83] Okhotin, "A. P. Bashutskii i ego kniga," in Okhotin and Sternin, *Nashi: Prilozhenie*, 25–32; Tseitlin, *Stanovlenie realizma*, 82–3, 238, 249.

and Pavel Vistengof. Had he written a few years later, he might have added Ivan Kokorev to the list.[84] It was a cliché, perpetuated among others by Belinskii himself,[85] that Moscow was hospitable, tradition-bound, and dreamy, while St Petersburg was practical, innovative, and all about business. Stereotyped as the modern and "European" half of this pair of opposites, St Petersburg was logically also the preferred setting for early Russian experiments in the literary exploration of city life. The comforting implication was that except for the imperial capital, Russia was largely free of the unsettling social consequences of European urban modernity. When physiological sketches of Moscow began to appear, this distinction crumbled. Viewed from the perspective of everyday people, Moscow turned out to be disturbingly similar to St Petersburg or indeed Paris or London.

Pavel Vistengof (1811–55) and Ivan Kokorev (1826–53) were the writers most responsible for applying the physiological approach to Moscow. Vistengof was a nobleman and minor official who achieved his literary debut with a volume of physiological sketches that appeared in 1842. Kokorev, the author of *Savvushka* (see above, pages 250-1), was the penniless son of a freedman. He published his works in *The Muscovite*, the modest journal—it rarely had more than a few hundred subscribers[86]—that employed him and that also published the essays of Prince L'vov. After Kokorev's untimely death, his essays were reissued as a book in 1858. Like Bashutskii, both Vistengof and Kokorev offered themselves as guides to the "hidden" spatial, temporal, and social niches of the urban world. In their tone and the issues they explored, they differed from Bashutskii and Zagoskin and also from each other. Vistengof was alternately mocking and melodramatic; Kokorev exuded bitter irony. Kokorev's narrator was a streetwise denizen of the slums who took the reader, assumed to be a prissy and disdainful character from the upper classes, on a tour of the misery and degradation of the poor. His preferred subjects were people with fantasies of breaking into the middle strata. Vistengof, on the contrary, was more interested in the glass ceiling blocking upward mobility *out* of the middle strata. Kokorev's writings pushed the boundaries of what the regime permitted; that they passed the censor may have had to do with their nationalistic tone, and perhaps also the influence of *The Muscovite*'s founder, the conservative journalist and professor Mikhail Pogodin.

The similarities and differences between Vistengof, Kokorev, Zagoskin, and Bulgarin can be seen in their analyses of consumerism. Historians have long noted the importance of consumerism—displaying wares, selling them, shopping for them, showing them off after purchase—in the rise of modern urban civilization in Western Europe.[87] An important innovation in the first half of the

---

[84] V. G. Belinsky, "Introduction," in Nekrasov, *Petersburg*, 7–14.
[85] Belinsky, "Petersburg and Moscow," in Nekrasov, *Petersburg*, 52.
[86] Ruud, *Fighting Words*, 96.
[87] The historiography on the origins of the consumer society is vast; for a survey of the recent literature, see Vries, *The Industrious Revolution*, 37–9.

nineteenth century was the opportunity to browse among finished goods in luxuriously appointed shopping arcades and (later) department stores, where goods were sold at fixed prices and the customer was treated with courtesy and respect. In this environment, the act of shopping acquired enhanced social importance, particularly for women. Included among Walter Benjamin's voluminous notes for his *Arcades Project* is the observation that because they were brightly lit and sheltered from the weather, the Parisian arcades of the 1830s and 1840s were popular (like malls today) not only as retail outlets but as promenades. The appeal of shopping and strolling there encouraged respectable women to venture out more into public places, where they frequently crowded out the prostitutes who had previously been the most conspicuous female presence.[88]

Bulgarin yielded to no one in his disdain for the West and its Russian sycophants, yet he was fascinated by the changes emanating from Paris. One of the characters in his popular novel *Ivan Vyzhigin*, published in 1829 but set a few decades earlier, is a woman named Grunia. Grunia, who is all "frivolity and vainglory," becomes a Frenchman's kept woman. Although Bulgarin is critical of her hedonistic enthusiasm for France, he quotes at length from her reflections on life in Paris. "Back home [in Moscow]," she writes, "everything is already dead and deserted by dusk, with only the carriages to remind you that you're not in the woods. Here, on the other hand, it's perpetual life, perpetual movement. There's neither day nor night; only the decor changes, and natural light is replaced by artificial light." After waxing poetic about the elegant stores in Paris, Grunia observes that Russian ladies, who at home "wouldn't take a step on foot unless escorted by two domestics, and who need four horses to cross the street," would go out in Paris on their own. In Russia, women were held down by "Asiatic" customs, but "here, everyone has complete freedom"; even "respectable women" went to restaurants and cafés, and took the stage coach unaccompanied.[89]

Similar developments reached Moscow in the first half of the nineteenth century. Zagoskin, Vistengof, and Kokorev were intrigued by the way the commercial bustle of the city shaped women's experiences in Moscow's highly stratified society. An example described by all three is the annual discount sale of textiles in the Kitai-Gorod bazaar on the Monday after Easter. This was a significant event because in Russia, as elsewhere in Europe, the retail trade in textiles was a leading indicator of the evolution of class and gender relations. Adopting the fashions of one's social superiors was traditionally a way to raise one's social status. In the nineteenth century this became easier because industrial manufacturing lowered the price of textiles. The resulting opportunities for sartorial self-fashioning particularly affected women. By comparison, men's

[88] Benjamin, *The Arcades Project*, 42–3, 52; Christine Ruane, *The Empire's New Clothes: A History of the Russian Fashion Industry, 1700–1917* (New Haven: Yale University Press, 2009), 144–8.
[89] Bulgarin, *Ivan Vyzhigin*, 259–61.

attire was less eye-catching and colorful, and lower-class men were more reluctant than their womenfolk to embrace the clothing of the elites.[90]

The bazaar had earlier been depicted by Glinka as the quintessence of glorious, un-Westernized Russianness. It was the epitome of premodern shopping: a crowded, dark, musty warren of "rows" (*riady*), where hard-sell tactics were the norm and aggressive haggling was expected. Cash was king, blurring social distinctions. An anonymous article from 1830 illustrates this with several fictional examples. The super-rich countess is always behind on her debts, so the shopkeepers refuse her credit, unlike the lowly actress who pays on time. And that portly (that is, unaristocratic) young lady who is paying thousands in cash? She is a former maidservant and owns no assets. Now she is married to an official who earns 250 rubles a year; he must, the nameless author does not add, be engaging in extensive graft to make up the difference.[91]

When Zagoskin describes the Easter sales, he lampoons both the old-fashioned Russian cunning of the merchants and the fantasy of social mobility of shoppers from the lower or middle strata who imagine that clothes make the man (or woman). He initially dwells on the tension between the customers' ladylike appearance and their aggressive throwing of elbows, trading of insults, and fighting over fabric. It is enough to trigger cognitive dissonance in the imagined reader, a lone upper-class male caught in the maelstrom. "But fear not: in this bazaar you will rarely meet a familiar face, and beneath the pretty hat you will very often recognize some housemaid, or the housekeeper of a lady of your acquaintance." The shopkeepers encourage this frenzy to unload surplus merchandise. "After this, how can one not marvel at the mental alacrity and imagination of our traders, or deny that they know their business brilliantly and have fully grasped the character of their [female] Russian customers?"[92]

Vistengof's emphasis is different. In his account, the benign anarchy of the Easter sales—the crowd, the excitement, the haggling—is a game that all classes relish. Other authors described how festive promenades (*gulianiia*), the theater, street musicians, and the first omnibuses created occasions for diverse urban estates to meet and mingle.[93] Vistengof sees something similar at work in the lusty free-for-all that unites women (plus a few men) in a frenzy of consumerism:

You would marvel at the rapture with which they rush out to buy cheap wares—the fashionable Moscow beauty in her stunning carriage and the priest's wife with her huge cap, the prim merchant's wife, the modest seamstress and the young housemaid, the clerk's wife and the cook, the elderly landowner with his family and the young dandy

---

[90] Kupriianov, *Gorodskaia kul'tura*, 341; Ruane, *The Empire's New Clothes*, 118–26.
[91] XLXXLXXX, "Moskovskie riady," 214–16.
[92] Zagoskin, *Sochineniia*, 5:286, 287.
[93] V. G. Belinsky, "The Alexander Theater," in Nekrasov, *Petersburg*, 176–7; Dmitrii Grigorovich, "The Petersburg Organ-Grinders," in Nekrasov, *Petersburg*, 91; M. Kul'chitsky, "The Omnibus," in Nekrasov, *Petersburg*, 209–35.

without any family . . . Yet it is all full of life, color, variety; it is a merry anthill of people, in which there would be no charm at all were it not for the frightening chaos.[94]

Vistengof also praised the more modern type of retail business described by Walter Benjamin. More and more Moscow shops, he noted, boasted handsome signs and displayed their merchandise in enticing ways. The best were still run by foreigners, who outdid their Russian competitors in offering fixed prices, an attractive decor, polite service, and convenient downtown locations like Tverskaia Street and Kuznetskii Most.[95]

Kokorev's take on the Easter sales is darker and tinged with doubt about consumerism's power as an equalizer. He disliked aristocratic consumers, no matter whether they shopped in their own exclusive stores or alongside the common people. Like Glinka forty years earlier, he hated that cold, snobbish retail mecca of the aristocracy, the French shops of Kuznetskii Most, but his affection for the warm, democratic, "Russian" bazaar of "the City" (Kitai-Gorod) likewise did not extend to Frenchified ladies who went there to hunt for bargains.

Poor girls who tried to raise their status by changing their appearance (the class of shoppers ridiculed by Zagoskin) had Kokorev's sympathy, but he thought them victims of a cruel hoax. One of his stories is about Natasha, a hardworking young seamstress who naively goes to Kuznetskii Most to buy herself a kerchief. She feels intimidated by the shop's clientele, but she thinks that surely her rubles are as good as theirs: "I came with my own money, so what should I be ashamed of?" The "garçon," however, refuses to treat her as a customer. Instead, he adopts the usual attitude of sneering malice of Russia's elites and their foreign lackeys. He addresses the sensitive young woman, "whose wealth he could guess at the first glance," with derision, especially when he explains that the high prices are non-negotiable and are denominated in silver rubles, not, as she had believed, in the much cheaper paper rubles. Unwilling to spend all her savings on one kerchief, and humiliated by the salesman, the icy disdain of the other customers, and her own poverty, Natasha retreats: "Frustrated desire and hurt pride cause tears to well up in her pretty eyes. But what can you do, Natasha! Better to go to the City, where they'll both receive you more courteously and charge you less."[96]

Vistengof, too, at times employs dark hues to paint the effect of consumerism, but he displays less sympathy, and his subjects are more often people of lower-middle status who try to rise above their station. Poignant cases include young women who achieve ephemeral success in Moscow's demi-monde: flower girls, seamstresses, and others without a secure place in the estate system, such as "the daughters of the lowliest clerks, widows, wives separated from their husbands, manumitted serfs, townswomen, soldiers' wives, foster daughters, and housemaids with [temporary] work permits." One of Vistengof's stories describes a

94 Vistengof, *Ocherki*, 96–7.   95 Vistengof, *Ocherki*, 130–2.
96 Kokorev, *Ocherki*, 127–8.

young courtesan's fantasies. Her dream is to wear a lined cape called a *salop*. To the upper classes, the *salop* was so passé as to be synonymous with genteel poverty,[97] but to her it is "what that tantalizing rank of collegiate assessor"— which automatically conferred hereditary nobility—"is to the perpetual titular councilor of non-noble birth." Her other pitiful aspirations include employing a maid who has to put up with her whims and call her "your ladyship," adorning her tacky household with little busts of Pushkin and Napoleon (Romantic embodiments of passion, genius, and ambition),[98] and taking dance lessons from "theater extras, pharmacists' apprentices, merchants, and petty civil servants." It all comes crashing down when her charms fade, her boyfriend leaves her, the money dries up, and her life goes into a tailspin. Ultimately, "after some time, she ends up a drunk, all dressed in rags, who does not keep respectable company and whose conduct does not become her station . . . "[99]

The courtesan's male counterpart is the gambler. He too is up at all hours and lives from the character flaws of others. Gamblers fascinated Vistengof. He notes that cards were a staple activity at Moscow's four clubs: the aristocratic English Club, the less exclusive Noble and Merchant clubs, and the German Club, composed of foreigners of all nationalities, especially artisans. A visit to the German Club allows him to evoke the city's opacity and exoticism. The room "was so smoky from tobacco that through the haze, in the dim light of the tallow candles, I could barely make out the human figures with their noses to the table" who were hunched over their cards. Unlike most authors, whose Moscow is inhabited only by Russians and Western expatriates, Vistengof takes seriously the cliché that Moscow was "Asiatic": at the card table are "Germans, Frenchmen, and Russians, Tatars in skullcaps, [and] Turks and Armenians in their national costumes."[100] Elsewhere in Vistengof's book, Gypsies provide a similar blend of exoticism and vice: "amidst the noisy, educated city they lead their own wild, unrestrained life of the steppes." Deceitful traders by day, after dark they provide outlets for a repressed sensuality. Affluent young merchants go to their encampments in the dead of night, drawn by the uninhibited sensuality of their music and dancing, but no matter the money they spend, the Gypsy beauty who seductively displays her charms will always remain beyond their reach.[101]

Vistengof argues that Moscow has multiple lives occupying distinct temporal spaces. While echoing Bashutskii's *Panorama of St Petersburg*, this theme, particularly the account of the city at dawn, is also found more generally in the

---

[97] R. M. Kirsanova, *Kostium v russkoi khudozhestvenoi kul'ture 18–pervoi poloviny 20 vv.: Opyt entsiklopedii* (Moscow: Bol'shaia Rossiiskaia entsiklopediia, 1995), 240–1; see also the essay "Salopnitsa" in Bulgarin, *Peterburgskie ocherki*.

[98] On the image of Napoleon in Russian Romanticism, see Molly W. Wesling, *Napoleon in Russian Cultural Mythology* (New York: Peter Lang, 2001), esp. ch.2.

[99] Vistengof, *Ocherki*, 141–3, 145, 147, 152.

[100] Vistengof, *Ocherki*, 112.

[101] Vistengof, *Ocherki*, 167–70, quotation on 167.

nineteenth-century European literature on cities.[102] Early in the morning, when the upper class "is still fast asleep," sundry working folk begin their labors, while drunks make for the tavern and beggars set out for church to ply their trade. Day and night briefly intersect as these denizens of the daytime begin their routines of work or vice even while the ladies of the demi-monde discreetly conclude theirs ("the girl in the *salop* returns from a night spent away from home"). Between eight o'clock and noon, in a swelling chorus of activity, ever more elite social strata rise from bed and set about their daily rounds. After a late-afternoon lull, the evening belongs to the nobility, who return home past midnight from their theaters, balls, clubs, and dinners. By two in the morning, opposite worlds once more collide, as decadent aristocratic stragglers ("the tired gambler dozing in his comfortable carriage") cross paths with the stinking wagon trains of the cesspool cleaners. Honest labor commences in the early morning, idle privilege prefers the afternoon and evening, and the wee hours cast a modest veil over vice and filth; venturing out at unusual hours entails the risk of encountering an entirely unfamiliar social world.[103] To his intended upper-class readers, Vistengof presents the hours from midnight to mid-morning as a strange and exotic world, quite foreign to the one they thought they knew.

Vistengof's passing reference to the cesspool cleaners is significant because it is so unusual. He and Kokorev agree in depicting a Moscow that is sanitized and odorless. Vistengof, while excruciatingly attuned to the manners and possessions distinguishing the aristocracy from its inferiors, is oblivious to smells. Kokorev emphasizes the sufferings of the poor and sets his stories in tenements and taverns, yet smell is virtually absent. The unwillingness to problematize filth and smell, like the reticence about crime and prostitution, reflects a reluctance to think of the lower classes as utterly "other."[104] Compared with Karamzin or Glinka, the lower-class characters of Bashutskii, Vistengof, and Kokorev are surrounded by a realistic decor and use more realistic language, but that makes them no less worthy and appealing. For example, one of Kokorev's stories is about a junk dealer who goes "to the most remote places" to buy his wares,

into alleys where people live who aren't prissy, who don't know want and sorrow just by hearsay, who aren't ashamed to show their cast-offs... The little boy in his gown of coarse cloth, the barefoot little girl, the old woman dressed half in rags—those are his usual acquaintances; any type of rags, any useless junk—that's their merchandise.

The dealer lives on a muddy street, where "the apartments are cheap and there are little rooms and corners where people can afford to live whose only wealth is their relentless labor." And yet, nowhere does the story describe filth or smell. Instead,

---

102 Schlör, *Nights in the Big City*, 109, 285.
103 Vistengof, *Ocherki*, 8–12.
104 Exceptions to this pattern can be found in Nekrasov, *Petersburg*, particularly the chapters "The Petersburg Corners" and "The Petersburg Yardkeeper."

the focus is on the dignity and humanity of the junk dealer, whose hard work ultimately allows him to become a successful merchant.[105]

The writings of the physiologists suggest various possible explanations for this respectful approach to the urban poor. One is a desire to please the authorities. For example, Vistengof occasionally allows that the populace can be disorderly or resentful. He writes that youths loiter in the streets and harass passers-by (something that Bashutskii denies), and that servants hate wearing livery because it signals their subordinate status and exposes them to the taunts of maidservants and street boys.[106] Elsewhere however, presumably to appease the censors, he aggressively embraces the rhetoric of Official Nationality. Echoing the slogan of "Orthodoxy, autocracy, nationality," he praises the nation's "devotion to Faith, Throne, and Fatherland," which is nowhere more visible than in Moscow, "the heart of Russia."[107] In a book otherwise brimming with mocking irony, he gushes that the "activity and vigilance" of the police in solving crimes is "unbelievable," and that "during the night, the metropolis is luxuriously illumined" down to its smallest alleys, so "those feuilletonists who tell us that you cannot drive in Moscow at night because of the darkness are writing utter falsehoods."[108]

Bashutskii, for his part, grounds his explanation of the benign character of the poor in a contrast with Western Europe. Writing soon after the 1830 revolutions and the cholera, he observes that most Petersburgers are temporary migrants from the countryside who come to work in the city, and asks:

Now tell me, why is it that in the vast and populous metropolis of the North you don't encounter those hungry, sullen crowds . . . ? Is it [as Westerners claim] due to 'the people's bestial unreason and ingrained ignorance', or because they are meek, humble, occupied, well fed, and not made up of idlers, vagrants, and paupers? No one but an utterly depraved layabout could be a pauper in St Petersburg.[109]

Kokorev, whose hard life infused his work with social resentments absent from the writings of Bashutskii and Vistengof, suggests that only his readers' reluctance to face difficult truths restrains his pen. In one story, he describes the various "industries" by which the poor eke out their living. Alluding to Eugène Sue's *The Mysteries of Paris*, with its dark tales of crime and depravity, he assures us that "Thank God, this isn't Paris, and mysteries have never been our custom." On the very next page, however, he remarks cryptically that the poor have another industry, one that "lives and operates in the dark, and hides from good people like a bat; if I weren't afraid of offending your good taste, we would make its acquaintance as well."[110] Moscow, as it turned out, did indeed have its own sinister "mysteries."

---

[105] Kokorev, *Ocherki*, 137–47.   [106] Vistengof, *Ocherki*, 183–5, 194–5.
[107] Vistengof, *Ocherki*, 14.   [108] Vistengof, *Ocherki*, 197, 165–6.
[109] Bashutskii, *Panorama Sanktpeterburga*, 3:16.
[110] Kokorev, *Ocherki*, 65–78, quotations on 76–7.

Even the hint that Moscow shared the urban pathologies of the West was anathema to those who embraced the Nicholaevan brand of Russian exceptionalism. Moscow was different, they declared. Vistengof's gestures of political correctness did not fool his critics, who much preferred Zagoskin's *Moscow and the Muscovites*. In Bulgarin's *Northern Bee*, Vistengof stood accused of recycling outdated, cartoonish clichés about Moscow "with an admixture of Muscovite mores lifted from the Parisian physiologies and the [Parisian] novels of Paul de Kock."[111] Senkovskii's *Library for Reading*, too, condemned him for making Moscow look like "Paris, Naples, Petersburg, and Beijing," and promised that Zagoskin's book would "utterly demolish the *Sketches* of Mr Vistengof" and "exact retribution against anyone who dares to say that Moscow is not Moscow but a city like any other European city."[112] Zagoskin wrote almost only about nobles, but from his premise, that all Russians shared the same character and Moscow was the nation's core, it followed that the nobility was a microcosm of the nation. By contrast, Vistengof hewed more closely to the French physiological model by writing about upstarts and snobs, petty-bourgeois vulgarity and spiritual alienation. In so doing, his critics charged, he was dwelling on unseemly topics and likening Moscow to hotbeds of revolution like Paris and Naples.

Literary observers who were critical of Official Nationality were correspondingly more favorable to what the physiologists were doing. Belinskii had positive words for Bashutskii's attempts to describe the mores of St Petersburg, and he criticized Bulgarin and others who "ignore provocative ideas as well as the striking contradiction between our European appearance and our Asiatic essence." Zagoskin's *Moscow and the Muscovites* was fine, he wrote sardonically, except that "it describes neither Moscow nor Muscovites."[113] An unsigned review in *Fatherland Notes* (*Otechestvennyia Zapiski*), where Belinskii was the book-review editor, likewise ridiculed Zagoskin's portrayal of Moscow. Vistengof's book was more complex, it said, although the relentless tone of mockery—he found nothing praiseworthy in all Moscow, the review claimed, except the police and one ballerina—got in the way of serious social analysis.[114]

CONCLUSION

Many of the social commentators discussed in this chapter belonged to the growing stratum of Russians of non-noble ancestry who had absorbed the elite's

---

[111] Review of P. Vistengof, *Ocherki Moskovskoi zhizni*, in *Severnaia Pchela* (26 April 1843), 358–9.

[112] Review of M. N. Zagoskin, *Moskva i Moskvichi*, and P. Vistengof, *Ocherki Moskovskoi zhizni*, in *Biblioteka dlia chteniia*, 56, otdel 6 (1843), 49–53.

[113] Belinsky, "Introduction," in Nekrasov, *Petersburg*, 5, 7, 13, 14, quotations on 5, 14.

[114] Review of M. N. Zagoskin, *Moskva i Moskvichi*, and P. Vistengof, *Ocherki Moskovskoi zhizni*, in *OZ* 26, otdel 6 (1843), 48–52.

European culture but rejected its ethos of social exclusivity. Both Kokorev's father and his publisher Pogodin were born into serfdom. Androssov came from a merchant family. Belinskii's grandfather was a clergyman, as were the fathers of Konstantin Arsen'ev (a leading Smithian statistician), Nadezhdin (long-time editor of the *Journal of the Ministry of Internal Affairs*), and Aleksandr Ostrovskii (the playwright who was about to transform the literary image of the Moscow merchantry).

The political views of these people covered a wide spectrum, but all wanted their culture to address itself to the realities that they themselves knew from experience. During the reign of Nicholas I, this sentiment fueled a veritable explosion of interest in "Russian" themes in fields ranging from literature, music, and painting to ethnography, history, and cooking recipes.[115] The desire to engage with everyday reality is also what lay behind the new interest in social analysis. Government data-collection generated new knowledge, statistical studies and realist fiction provided models for representing this knowledge, and the quest for the essence of Russianness gave the whole endeavor an overarching purpose.

The new techniques that were developed from the 1820s to the 1840s permitted a quantum leap in the analysis and description of urban life. The picture that resulted was disquieting. It did not show a harmonious hierarchy of estates united by a shared Russian ethos, an image dear to Bulgarin, Zagoskin, and many in the government of Nicholas I. Instead, Moscow turned out to be fluid, opaque, and resistant to external scrutiny and control—similar, ironically, to the urban civilization of West that the imperial social project had been designed to imitate.

---

[115] See, for example: Ely, *This Meager Nature*, 165; Stites, *Serfdom, Society, and the Arts*, 84–7; Smith, *Recipes for Russia*, ch. 3; Knight "Science, Empire, and Nationality," in Burbank and Ransel, eds., *Imperial Russia*, 116–22.

Conclusion

When Nicholas I died on 18 February 1855, the sun was setting on the imperial social project. His grandmother, Catherine II, had believed that education and social engineering could give rise to a "new race of men," loyal sons and daughters of the autocracy who would lead Russia into Europe as an enlightened state with a vibrant urban civilization. One such "new man" was Nikolai Chernyshevskii (1828–89). He was a provincial *popovich* who attended a seminary and a university and became one of Russia's leading journalists. Chernyshevskii was thus a success story of the imperial social project, yet this did not make him a supporter of the regime. Instead, he attacked the regime by turning its own civilizing rhetoric against it. For example, he argued in 1859 that Russia belonged in the same category with Turkey, not the West. "Our cities," he wrote, "have until now remained parodies of cities" because they lacked the urban dynamism of the West, and Russia's agrarian backwardness was evidence that "The Russian people have lived, or rather vegetated or slumbered, in a heavy lethargy that differs little from the mental disposition that prevails among Asiatics."[1]

Chernyshevskii's writings reached so many readers, and were so threatening to the ideology of the regime, that the imperial chief of gendarmes considered him public enemy number one.[2] In prison in 1863, Chernyshevskii wrote *What is to be Done?*, a novel about his vision of the future. In an echo of Catherine II, who had ascended the throne almost exactly a century earlier, he imagined a revolutionary elite of "new men," people of both sexes whose willpower, rationality, and rejection of inherited prejudices would allow them to build a radically transformed Russia. The regime was spooked by the book's popularity and decided never to let him publish anything again. Among those it inspired was Lenin, and *What is to be Done?* helped shape the utopia of the New Soviet Man.[3]

Chernyshevskii embodied the paradoxical outcome of the imperial social project. As the regime had hoped, middling urban Russians had acquired the outlook of modern Europeans while at the same time remaining rooted in the soil of their native culture. However, the timing was unfortunate, because the

---

[1] "Sueverie i pravila logiki," in N. G. Chernyshevskii, *Polnoe sobranie sochinenii*, 10 vols. (St Petersburg: Tipografiia i litografiia V. A. Tikhanova, 1905–6), 4:554, 556.

[2] Franco Venturi, *Roots of Revolution: A History of the Populist and Socialist Movements in Nineteenth Century Russia*, tr. Francis Haskell (New York: Grosset & Dunlap, 1966), 176.

[3] Frede, *Doubt*, 146–7, 158–9; Peter Fritzsche and Jochen Hellbeck, "The New Man in Stalinist Russia and Nazi Germany," in Michael Geyer and Sheila Fitzpatrick, eds., *Beyond Totalitarianism: Stalinism and Nazism Compared* (Cambridge: Cambridge University Press, 2009), 307.

new urban culture emerged just as the structures of Russian society became obsolete in comparison with the West. This had the ironic consequence of channeling much of the intellectual and civic energy that the imperial social project had liberated into criticisms of the failings of the imperial regime itself.

The infrastructure and institutions of Moscow at the death of Nicholas I had changed little since Catherine II's reforms of the 1770s and 1780s. By the time many of Chernyshevskii's readers came of age in the 1860s and 1870s, the problems to which those reforms had been the solution had receded beyond living memory. Instead, the burning issue of the day was how to cope with urban conditions that increasingly resembled early industrial Western Europe. London and Paris, after passing through the purgatory of the 1820s and 1830s, were on the upswing because they had found ways to modernize their infrastructure and reform their institutions. Moscow, on the other hand, remained saddled with urban systems from the late eighteenth century. The city had not made the leap from oil lighting to gas. Public safety still depended on a small corps of aging army veterans, not a modern police force. Moscow had no modern solution to the problems of water provision and waste disposal. Estate-specific schools educated a small minority of the population, but there was no broad system of public schools. The estate system tied migrant laborers to their native villages, thus obstructing their assimilation into the city. The estate system also prevented the leading merchants, clerics, officials, intellectuals, and professionals from coalescing into a unified urban elite. Catherine's legacy had become an obstacle to progress, and to carry on her belief in an enlightened urban civilization meant to oppose the policies of her descendants.

The transformation of Moscow had formed part of a long-term strategy to strengthen the regime's domestic base and enhance its international prestige. The strategy had three main parts: reconstruct Moscow's spaces and institutions; foster estates that could form an enlightened "middling sort"; and persuade public opinion at home and abroad that the regime had succeeded in its historic mission of making Russia an enlightened European state.

This strategy was a response to the European conditions of the eighteenth century. In the first half of the nineteenth century, however, Europe entered a new era. Cities grew at an accelerated pace and underwent a structural metamorphosis. The estate system of the *ancien régime* assigned each person a niche in a compartmentalized social order, but as that system faded away, people in the West increasingly derived their identity from broad social classes. One in particular, the bourgeoisie, united most of the old middling estates, declared itself to be a civil society that spoke for the nation, and challenged the royal courts, aristocracies, and churches for hegemony over government, society, and culture. These changes destabilized the West's political and social systems but also endowed them with great economic dynamism and fearful military strength.

Contemporaries in Russia—some smug, others anxious—watched these developments from the sidelines until the forces of change abruptly arrived in

Russia itself. In the Crimean War of 1853–6, the shattering defeat inflicted by Great Britain and France proved that Russia's social order was too archaic to sustain a leading European power. Nicholas I's death in 1855 removed the most important obstacle to system-wide reform. Under his son Alexander II (r. 1855–81), public opinion engaged in passionate debate about the state of the country, and the Great Reforms of the 1860s and 1870s overhauled the entire social order. Catherine II had already been critical of serfdom, and in reorganizing the urban order, she had tried to counteract the insularity of the estates by creating all-estate institutions and constructing a social hierarchy based on wealth and education. The Great Reforms represented a sweeping effort to remake Russia along these lines. Serfdom was abolished. Military service was extended to all estates. All urban dwellers became subject to a single judiciary. City councils were henceforth elected under a franchise based on wealth, not estate membership. It was a far-reaching attempt to rebuild the urban order on the basis of shared citizenship and a hierarchy of European-type social classes.

In some ways, urban Russia's development since Catherine II had placed the country in a favorable position for a successful entry into European modernity. Russia had developed a culture that synthesized European with native elements and was widely shared by the middle strata. Russians had learned to use the tools of European culture to explore experiences and express sensibilities that were specific to them. Artists painted landscapes that were recognizably Russian, not imitations of West European vistas. Composers brought folk motifs into symphonies and operas. Writers, scholars, and social commentators used European narrative and analytical techniques to engage with the conditions of their society. A distinctive Russian voice took its place in the chorus of Europe, and Russians could embrace European modernity without rejecting their own identity.

The Europeanization of the culture was accompanied by a modernization of mentalities. Russians grew more individualistic, and less inclined to mold their inner life to the dictates of their communities. The change is described in nineteenth-century fiction and autobiographies and has been noted by many historians. Many *popovichi*, Laurie Manchester argues, "were 'modern' in that they were self-reliant agents of their own destiny."[4] Aleksandr Kupriianov finds, in diaries from provincial towns, a new "emotional expressiveness" and concern with "individual, intimate feelings."[5] Boris Mironov writes that Russians came to embrace "the idea of the value of the autonomous and independent personality. Among nobles and *raznochintsy* [here: educated commoners] this occurred in the late eighteenth to early nineteenth century; among various strata of the urban estate, over the course of the nineteenth century; and among the peasants, after the emancipation [in 1861]."[6]

---

[4] Manchester, *Holy Fathers, Secular Sons*, 214.
[5] Kupriianov, *Gorodskaia kul'tura*, 467.
[6] Mironov, *Sotsial'naia istoriia Rossii*, 1:524–5.

This modernization of the mind owed a great deal to the processes described in this book. Public promenades and coffee houses introduced people to a modern sociability that was individualistic and (so long as genteel appearances were maintained) egalitarian. Elegant shop displays, contact with foreigners, and monumental architecture took people beyond the narrowness of provincial horizons. In the anonymous urban crowd, where everyone was a stranger, one was judged on appearances and could shape one's identity by adopting new attire or learning new manners. Books, journals, and the theater taught new ways of imagining the world. Walking home at night from a show or a visit to friends afforded opportunities to be alone with one's thoughts. Observing the kaleidoscopic spectacle of the metropolis, and reading the literature that described it, taught the urban inhabitant to become an individualistic *flâneur*.

Moscow also developed a sense of historical depth. In 1829, Petr Chaadaev had written despairingly that in contrast to Europe, "There are [in Russia] no charming remembrances, no graceful images in the people's memory; our national tradition is devoid of any powerful teaching . . . We live only in the narrowest of presents, without past and without future, in the midst of a flat calm."[7] As the pre-Reform era slipped into history, the sense of existing in a temporal vacuum subsided. The fiftieth anniversary of 1812 prompted an outpouring of writing about what already appeared as a distant age. By the last decades of the century, Russians had a historical memory of Moscow that comprised three layers. The topmost layer, the personally remembered past, reached back to the immediate pre-Reform era. Farther back, known through stories from one's grandparents, was the archaic age before 1812. Finally, there was the time before Catherine II, a layer buried so deep that it was almost in the realm of myth. The book *Old Moscow: Tales from the Past Life of the Former Capital* (*Staraia Moskva: Rasskazy iz byloi zhizni pervoprestol'noi stolitsy*), a popular history from 1891, opens its first chapter with these words: "Moscow under Empress Catherine II still lived according to the traditions of the ancient past."[8] The "old" times thus began with Catherine; what came before was dimly remembered prehistory.

Moscow's transformation helped make Russians into Europeans, but it could not prevent the catastrophic implosion of their political and social system in the early twentieth century. It would be too easy to see this as proof that their Europeanization was incomplete, for the same shocks of World War I that shattered the Russian Empire also destroyed Imperial Germany and Austria-Hungary, and the Bolsheviks soon revived the project of implanting European civilization in Russia. Nonetheless, the collapse of the imperial regime allows us to see more clearly certain essential features of Moscow's modernization between 1762 and 1855.

One important weakness of the imperial social project was that it did not extend to the peasants, who mostly remained illiterate and little affected by modern ways.

---

[7] James M. Edie, James P. Scanlan, and Mary-Barbara Zeldin, eds., *Russian Philosophy*, 3 vols. (Chicago: Quadrangle Books, 1976), 1:110–11.

[8] Pyliaev, *Staraia Moskva*, 1.

Once serfdom was abolished and industrialization started in earnest, peasants began by the millions to stream into the cities; in Moscow by 1902, only 27.6 percent of the population was native to the city.[9] The literate urban society that formed the social base for Russia as a modern European country was swamped by peasants to whom such notions were foreign. Other countries also experienced a version of this phenomenon, but because the cultural divide between city and country in Russia was so pronounced, the impact of what Mironov calls the "peasantization" of its urban society and culture was especially profound.[10]

The prospect that the city could assimilate masses of rural migrants was all the more remote because the urban strata themselves had not coalesced into unified classes of bourgeois and workers, thus offering no coherent urban order for newcomers to join.[11] Russia's experience in this respect was extreme, though not unique. In Germany, artisan guilds survived past the middle of the nineteenth century, creating a divide between artisans and other bourgeois strata that were more at ease in a capitalist economy. In France, too, the lower-middle classes had an ambiguous identity, since their economic interests connected them to the bourgeoisie while their sans-culotte revolutionary tradition created a bond between them and the working classes.[12]

In Russia, the urban strata were divided by estate, wealth, and degree of connection to the culture of the nobility. The clergy was an insular caste that built its identity on a sense of moral superiority over greedy merchants and decadent nobles.[13] The merchants were divided: an abyss yawned between small traders and rich capitalists, and the rich were themselves divided between those who embraced the cosmopolitan culture of the nobility and others (particularly in Moscow) who were tradition-bound, nationalistic Old Believers.[14] The attitudes of the nobility were summed up by Tolstoi. Why, he asked in an early draft of *War and Peace*, had he made "princes, counts, ministers, [and] senators" the heroes of his novel? Because the lives of other classes—he insultingly lumped together "merchants, coachmen, seminarians, convicts, and peasants"—were "tedious" and "monotonous" and animated only by "envy" and "greed." They were as alien to him as animals:

---

[9] Blair Ruble, *Second Metropolis: Pragmatic Pluralism in Gilded Age Chicago, Silver Age Moscow, and Meiji Osaka* (Washington, DC: Woodrow Wilson Center Press, 2001), 77.

[10] Mironov, *Sotsial'naia istoriia Rossii*, 1:341.

[11] Rieber, *Merchants and Entrepreneurs*, xxiv–xxv, 416.

[12] Geoffrey Crossick and Heinz-Gerhard Haupt, eds., *The Petite Bourgeoisie in Europe, 1780–1914: Enterprise, Family and Independence* (London: Routledge, 1995), 33–6, 136–8, 146, 151, 156.

[13] Manchester, *Holy Fathers, Secular Sons*, 52–4, 64.

[14] Kupriianov, *Gorodskaia kul'tura*, 403; Ruble, *Second Metropolis*, 80–7; Christine Ruane, "Caftan to Business Suit: The Semiotics of Russian Merchant Dress," in James L. West and Iurii A. Petrov, eds., *Merchant Moscow: Images of Russia's Vanished Bourgeoisie* (Princeton: Princeton University Press, 1998), 56–8; Galina N. Ulianova, "Old Believers and New Entrepreneurs: Religious Belief and Ritual in Merchant Moscow," in West and Petrov, eds., *Merchant Moscow*, 66–7.

I could never understand what a watchman thinks when he stands by his guardhouse, what a shopkeeper thinks and feels when he hawks suspenders and neckties, what a seminarian thinks when he is led to be caned for the hundredth time, and so on. I don't understand these things just as I don't understand what a cow thinks when it is being milked and what a horse thinks when it hauls a barrel.

As for himself, Tolstoi wrote, "I say boldly that I am an aristocrat," for it meant that "I was raised from childhood . . . to love beauty, represented not only by Homer, Bach, and Raphael, but also by all the small details of life: a love for clean hands, handsome clothes, and fine dining and transport." As an aristocrat, he wrote, he could not imagine finding moral or intellectual qualities in people who picked their noses.[15]

In addition to the exclusion of the peasants and the fragmentation of the middle estates, a third weakness of the imperial system lay in Moscow's institutions. Moscow's reconstruction as an enlightened metropolis was from the start an authoritarian project. Over time, the authoritarian system lost credibility because it did not keep up with the growing demands that were placed on it. In the eighteenth century, in Europe as in Russia, municipal administration was a comparatively simple affair because many important functions were left to private citizens, for example, patrolling and lighting the streets at night, or sweeping and maintaining the pavement. In the nineteenth century, these became functions of the state, and governments were judged by their success at executing them.[16] As Moscow's population grew from 356,511 in the early 1850s to 978,537 in 1897,[17] conditions in the city steadily deteriorated. The poor were packed into overcrowded tenements; the masses of humanity, animals, and industry generated unmanageable filth; and typhus, tuberculosis, and cholera took their cruel toll. Addressing such issues required more effective municipal leadership than Moscow was able to produce. Elected officials had only limited powers, leaving control in the hands of a bureaucracy that treated most civic or labor activism as subversive. The reform of municipal government in 1870 did not fundamentally change this. It imposed a highly restrictive franchise that was further narrowed by a reform in 1892, after which the electorate was limited to 0.6 percent of the inhabitants. This tiny electorate showed little enthusiasm for municipal politics—in 1888 and 1889, only 8 percent of those eligible to vote bothered to cast ballots—and those whom they elected remained subject to extensive interference by imperial officials.[18] It was a system ill suited either to deal aggressively with the city's problems or to build unity among the inhabitants in an era of deepening political and class polarization.

[15] L. N. Tolstoi, *Polnoe sobranie sochinenii*, 90 vols. (Moscow: Gosudarstvennoe izdatel'stvo khudozhestvennoi literatury, 1930–58), 13:238–9.
[16] Konvitz, *The Urban Millennium*, 46.
[17] *Istoriia Moskvy s drevneishikh vremen*, 2:9, 252.
[18] Ruble, *Second Metropolis*, 94–9.

By the early twentieth century, the memory of pre-Reform Moscow inspired both revulsion and nostalgia. It inspired revulsion because it was remembered as a time and place of benighted mores and social relations, when nobles maltreated their serfs, merchant patriarchs oppressed their families, and policemen took bribes and abused the citizenry. Yet as Russia after the Great Reforms lurched from crisis to crisis, there was also nostalgia for the moral clarity, the lack of self-doubt, that seemed in retrospect to have characterized the people of the pre-Reform era.

Mikhail Gershenzon captured this ambivalence in a book published in 1914, just as imperial Russia was about to plunge into the abyss of war and revolution. Gershenzon (1869–1925) was a poor Jew from Moldavia who had risen to become one of Moscow's leading public intellectuals. Such a career would have been unthinkable in the pre-Reform era. Nonetheless, his book on the aristocrats of Moscow in the 1810s and 1820s expresses a degree of affection for their naive sense of entitlement and carefree life of luxury. In his conclusion, he draws an uneasy comparison between the world of his protagonist, M. I. Rimskaia-Korsa-kova, and his own time:

It is on the iniquitous soil of serf labor that this sinful life, this frivolous life that I have described, blossomed in all its glory. Let us not throw stones at Mar'ia Ivanovna: how could she be guilty of what she *did not know*? It is gratifying to think that her age is past. Yet it hardly becomes us to feel superior to her . . . I do not mean to say that our age is just as bad as that age: no, it is immeasurably better . . . but we carry the same poison in our blood, and the signs of poisoning are the same for us as for those people, namely frivolity and heedlessness—only the forms are different: for them, it was balls and picnics and all the 'guileless, childlike depravity' of their way of life, while for us, it is the harmful complexity and sterile refinement of our moods and ideas.[19]

Moscow's reconstruction as an enlightened metropolis has continued down to the present, with paradoxical results. Over the course of the twentieth century, European ways of living and thinking penetrated into every corner of Russian life. Russia at the turn of the twentieth century, and again under the Soviets, built a dynamic economy and a culture that influenced countries around the globe. In this process, however, Moscow has been weighted with a heavier burden of symbolism than it could bear. It was rebuilt by the tsars to show that Russia was part of Europe, but then Russia's modernization stalled, the imperial ideology lost credibility, and the regime collapsed. After 1917, Moscow was transformed into a Soviet metropolis that was supposed to prove the superiority of socialist civilization, and the same cycle was repeated. Since 1991, Moscow has been remade again, this time as a showcase for the new, post-communist Russia. Whether this has broken the cycle remains to be seen.

---

[19] M. O. Gershenzon, *Griboedovskaia Moskva; P. Ia. Chaadaev; Ocherki proshlogo*, ed. V. Iu. Proskurina (Moscow: Moskovskii rabochii, 1989), 105–6.

Archival Sources

Tsentral'nyi Istoricheskii Arkhiv Moskvy (Central Historical Archive of Moscow)
  f. 14 Moskovskie gorodskie obshchaia i shestiglasnaia dumy
  f. 20 Komissiia dlia rassmotreniia proshenii obyvatelei Moskovskoi stolitsy i gubernii, poterpevshikh razorenie ot nashestviia nepriiatelia v 1812 g.
  f. 105 Moskovskaia uprava blagochiniia
  f. 203 Moskovskaia dukhovnaia kontora
Otdel Pis'mennykh Istochnikov Gosudarstvennogo Istoricheskogo Muzeia(Division of Written Sources of the State Hisorical Museum)
  f. 14 Golitsyny
  f. 160 Osobyi komitet po ustroistvu v Moskve Muzeia 1812 goda
  f. 450 E. V. Barsov
Nauchno-Issledovatelskii Otdel Rukopisei Rossiiskoi Gosudarstvennoi Biblioteki (Manuscript Research Division of the Russian State Library)
  f. 54 N. P. Vishniakov

Primary Bibliography

A. L., "Pis'ma iz Peterburga v Moskvu (Prodolzhenie)," *Zvezdochka, zhurnal dlia detei starshago vozrasta*, 6 (1847), 370–86.

Aleksandrov, Iu. N., ed., *Moskovskaia starina: Vospominaniia moskvichei proshlogo stoletiia* (Moscow: Pravda, 1989).

Allgemeine Deutsche Biographie, ed. Historische Commission bei der Königl. Akademie der Wissenschaften, 56 vols. (Leipzig: Duncker & Humblot, 1875–1912).

Andreevskii, I. E., ed., *Entsiklopedicheskii slovar'*, 43 vols. (St Petersburg: Brokgauz-Efron, 1890–1907).

Androssov, V., *Statisticheskaia zapiska o Moskve* (Moscow: V tipografii Semena Selivanovskago, 1832).

Arsen'ev, K. I., *Nachertanie statistiki Rossiiskago gosudarstva*, 2 vols. (St Petersburg: V Tipografii Imperatorskago Vospitatel'nago Doma, 1818–19).

Attenhofer, Heinrich Ludwig von, *Medizinische Topographie der Haupt- und Residenzstadt St. Petersburg* (Zurich: Orell, Füssli, 1817).

Austin, Paul Britten, *1812: Napoleon in Moscow* (London: Greenhill; Mechanicsburg, Pa.: Stackpole; 1995).

Bantysh-Kamenskii, D. N., ed., *Slovar' dostopamiatnykh liudei russkoi zemli*, 3 vols. (St Petersburg: Tipografiia Karla Kraiia, 1847).

Bashutskii, Aleksandr, *Panorama Sanktpeterburga*, 3 vols. (St Petersburg: V tipografii vdovy Pliushar s synom, 1834).

—— et al., *Nashi, spisannye s natury russkimi* (1841–2; repr. edn. Moscow: Kniga, 1986).

Batiushkov, K. N., *Sochineniia*, 3 vols. (St Petersburg: Tipografiia (byvshaia) Kotomina, 1885–7).

—— *Sochineniia*, 2 vols. (Moscow: "Khudozhestvennaia Literatura," 1989).

[Bauer, K.] K. B . . . r, "Vospominanie o dvenadtsatom gode v Moskve," *Atenei*, no. 2 (1858), 119–34.

Bekker, F., "Vospominaniia Bekkera o razzorenii i pozhare Moskvy v 1812 g.," *RS*, vol. 38 (April–June 1883), 507–24.

Benjamin, Walter, *The Arcades Project*, tr. Howard Eiland and Kevin McLaughlin (Cambridge, Mass,: Belknap, 1999).

Benzengr, V. N., "Otchet sanitarnago vracha Arbatskoi chasti," *IMGD*, vypusk 16 (1 September 1878), 13–21.

[Bestuzhev-Riumin, A.], "Kratkoe opisanie proisshestviiam v stolitse Moskve v 1812 godu," *ChOIDR*, 29/2 (April–June 1859), "Smes'," 65–92.

Biuler, F., "Moskovskii Arkhiv Kollegii Inostrannykh Del," *RA*, 4/11 (1875), 289–96.

Blagovo, D., *Rasskazy babushki: Iz vospominanii piati pokolenii, zapisannye i sobrannye ee vnukom D. Blagovo* (Leningrad: Nauka, 1989).

Bokova, V. M. and L. G. Sakharova, eds., *Institutki: Vospominaniia vospitannits institutov blagorodnykh devits* (Moscow: Novoe Literaturnoe Obozrenie, 2001).

Bolotov, A. T., *Zhizn' i prikliucheniia Andreia Bolotova, opisannye samim im dlia svoikh potomkov*, 3 vols. (Moscow: Terra, 1993).

Bourgogne, Adrien, *Mémoires du Sergent Bourgogne*, ed. Gilles Lapouge (n.p.: Arléa, 1992).

[Bulgarin, Faddei] F. B., "Vononos," *Severnaia Pchela* (15 January 1842), 43.

—— *Ivan Vyzhigin i ego prodolzhenie Petr Ivanovich Vyzhigin* (Moscow: Zakharov, 2002).

—— *Peterburgskie ocherki F. V. Bulgarina*, ed. Al'bin Konechnyi (St Petersburg: Petropolis, 2010).

Butkovskaia, A. Ia., "Razskazy Babushki," *Istoricheskii Vestnik* (December 1884), 594–631.

Bychkov, N. M., "Istoricheskii ocherk osveshcheniia goroda Moskvy," *IMGD*, vypusk 1 (October 1895), otdel 2, pp. 1–52.

Cameron, Charles A., *A Manual of Hygiene, Public and Private, and Compendium of Sanitary Laws* (Dublin: Hodges, Foster; London: Bailliere, Tindall, & Cox; 1874).

Casanova de Seingalt, Jacques, *Mémoires*, 10 vols. (Paris: Paulin, 1833–7).

[Castéra, Jean-Henri and William Tooke], *The Life of Catharine II, Empress of Russia*, 3 vols. (4th edn., London: A. Strahan [vol. 1], H. Baldwin and Son [vol. 2], T. N. Longman and O. Rees [vol. 3], 1800).

Chernyshevskii, N. G., *Polnoe sobranie sochinenii*, 10 vols. (St Petersburg: Tipografiia i litografiia V. A. Tikhanova, 1905–6).

Chertkov, A. D., ed., *Vseobshchaia biblioteka Rossii ili Katalog knig dlia izucheniia nashego otechestva vo vsekh otnosheniiakh i podrobnostiakh* (2nd edn., Moscow: V tipografii Lazarevskago Instituta vostochnykh iazykov, 1863).

Chertkov, A., *Gorodskaia meditsina v Evropeiskoi Rossii: Sbornik svedenii ob ustroistve vrachebno-sanitarnoi chasti v gorodakh* (Moscow: Pechatnia S. P. Iakovleva, 1903).

Chicherin, B. N., *Moskva sorokovykh godov* (Moscow: Izdatel'stvo Moskovskogo universiteta, 1997).

Chulkov, Mikhail, Matvei Komarov, and Nikolai Karamzin, *Three Russian Tales of the Eighteenth Century: The Comely Cook, Vanka Kain, and Poor Liza*, tr. David Gasperetti (DeKalb, Ill.: Northern Illinois University Press, 2012).

Clyman, Toby W. and Judith Vowles, eds., *Russia through Women's Eyes: Autobiographies from Tsarist Russia* (New Haven: Yale University Press, 1996).

[Combe, Michel], *Mémoires du colonel Combe sur les campagnes de Russie 1812, de Saxe 1813, de France 1814 et 1815* (Paris: Plon, 1896).

Cook, John, *Voyages and Travels through the Russian Empire, Tartary, and Part of the Kingdom of Persia*, 2 vols. (Edinburgh: Printed for the Author, 1770).

Crèvecoeur, Hector St. John, *Letters from an American Farmer* (London, 1782; repr. New York: Fox, Duffield, 1904).

Dal', Vladimir, *Tolkovyi slovar' zhivogo velikorusskogo iazyka*, 4 vols. (1903–9; repr. Moscow: Progress, Univers, 1994).

Derzhavin, G. R., *Zapiski 1743–1812* (Moscow: Mysl', 2000).

Dickens, Charles, *A Tale of Two Cities* (London: Cathay, 1983).

Dictionary of National Biography, 63 vols. (London: Smith, Elder, 1885–1900).

Dictionnaire de l'Académie française (4th edn., 1762), *The ARTFL Project: Department of Romance Languages and Literatures, University of Chicago* <http://artfl-project.uchicago.edu/node/17>.

Dictionnaire de l'Académie française (5th edn., 1798), *The ARTFL Project: Department of Romance Languages and Literatures, University of Chicago* <http://artfl-project.uchicago.edu/node/17>.

Diderot, Denis, and Jean Le Rond d'Alembert, eds., *Encyclopédie, ou Dictionnaire raisonné des sciences, des arts et des métiers*, 17 vols. (Paris: Briasson, David, Le Breton, Durand, 1751–65).

Dmitriev, M. A., *Glavy iz vospominanii moei zhizni* (Moscow: Novoe Literaturnoe Obozrenie, 1998).

Dobrynin, Gavriil, *Istinnoe povestvovanie ili Zhizn' Gavriila Dobrynina, (pozhivshago 72 g. 2 m. 20 dnei) im samim pisannaia v Mogileve i v Vitebske. 1752–1823* (St Petersburg: Pechatnia V. I. Golovina, 1872).

"Doneseniia agentov o dukhe v Moskve v 1848 godu," *Minuvshie Gody*, 5–6 (May–June 1908), 344–9.

Dubrovin, N., ed., *Otechestvennaia voina v pis'makh sovremennikov (1812–1815 gg.)* (St Petersburg: Tipografiia Imperatorskoi Akademii Nauk, 1882).

—— ed., *Pis'ma glavneishikh deiatelei v tsarstvovanie imperatora Aleksandra I (1807–1829 gg.)* (Moscow: Gosudarstvennaia publichnaia istoricheskaia biblioteka Rossii, 2006).

"Dvenadtsatyi god: Sovremennye razskazy, pis'ma, anekdoty, stikhotvoreniia," *RA*, part 1: 2/7 (1876), 302–20; part 2: no. 8 (1876), 387–409.

Dzhivelegov, A. K., S. P. Mel'gunov, and V. I. Picheta, eds., *Otechestvennaia voina i russkoe obshchestvo*, 7 vols. (Moscow: Izdanie T-va I. D. Sytina, 1911–12).

E. K., "Poseshchenie etapa dlia ssyl'nykh u Rogozhskoi zastavy v Moskve," *Sovremennik*, vol. 34 (1844), 203–9.

Echard, Laurent, *Dictionnaire géographique portatif*, tr. from the 13th edn. of the English original of Laurence Echard, rev. by Monsieur Vaugien (Paris: Didot, 1749).

Edie, James M., James P. Scanlan, and Mary-Barbara Zeldin, eds., *Russian Philosophy*, 3 vols. (Chicago: Quadrangle Books, 1976).

Eighteenth Century Collections Online, <http://gdc.gale.com/products/eighteenth-century-collections-online/>.

Emel'ianov, Iu. N., ed., *Moskovskii universitet v vospominaniiakh sovremennikov* (Moscow: Sovremennik, 1989).

Engelhardt, Georg, *Russische Miscellen zur genauern Kenntniss Russlands und seiner Bewohner*, 4 vols. (St Petersburg: bei der Kaiserlichen Akademie der Wissenschaften, 1828–32).

Eshevskii, S. V., *Sochineniia po russkoi istorii*, ed. K. N. Bestuzhev-Riumin (Moscow: Izdanie M. i S. Sabashnikovykh, 1900).

Esipov, G., "Van'ka Kain," *Osmnadtsatyi vek*, 3 (1869), 280–335.

Estreicher, Karol Józef Teofil, *Bibliografia Polska*, vol. 4 (1878; New York: Johnson Reprint, 1964–78).

Evreinov, Mikhail, "Pamiat' o 1812 gode," *RA*, 1/1 (1874), cols. 95–110.

"Istoricheskoe opisanie Rossiiskoi torgovli, sochinennoe A. Shtorkhom," *VE*, chast' 5 (September 1802), 55–6.

Faber du Faur, G. de, *Campagne de Russie 1812 d'après le journal illustré d'un témoin oculaire* (Paris: Ernest Flamarion, n.d.).

—— *With Napoleon in Russia: The Illustrated Memoirs of Faber du Faur, 1812*, ed. and tr. Jonathan North (London: Greenhill Books; Mechanicsburg, Pa.: Stackpole Books; 2001).

Fantin des Odoards, Louis-Florimond, *Journal du général Fantin des Odoards, étapes d'un officier de la Grande Armée, 1800–1830* (Paris: Plon, 1895).

Fechner, A. W., *Chronik der evangelischen Gemeinden in Moskau*, 2 vols. (Moscow: J. Deubner, 1876).

Frank, Viktor, *Russisches Christenthum, dargestellt nach russischen Angaben* (Paderborn: Ferdinand Schöningh, 1889).

"Frantsuzskoe nashestvie: Pis'ma iz Moskvy v Nizhnii Novgorod v 1813 godu," *RA*, 3/10 (1876), 129–54.

Frégier, H. A., *Des classes dangereuses de la population dans les grandes villes, et des moyens de les rendre meilleures*, 2 vols. (Paris: J.-B. Baillière, 1840).

Fusil, L., *L'incendie de Moscou, La petite orpheline de Wilna, Passage de la Bérésina, et Retraite de Napoléon jusqu'à Wilna* (2nd edn., Paris: Pillet, 1817).

[Gaevskii, S. F.], "Mediko-topograficheskiia svedeniia o S.P.burge. 1833," *ZhMVD*, chast' 11, no. 2 (February 1834), 153–98; no. 3 (March 1834), 285–364.

Galakhov, A. D., *Zapiski cheloveka* (Moscow: Novoe Literaturnoe Obozrenie, 1999).

Gastev, Mikhail S., *Materialy dlia polnoi i sravnitel'noi statistiki Moskvy, chast' pervaia* (Moscow: V Universitetskoi Tipografii, 1841).

Georgi, Johann Gottlieb, *Versuch einer Beschreibung der Rußisch Kayserlichen Residenzstadt St. Petersburg und der Merkwürdigkeiten der Gegend* (St Petersburg: Müller, 1790).

Gershenzon, M. O., *Griboedovskaia Moskva; P. Ia. Chaadaev; Ocherki proshlogo*, ed. V. Iu. Proskurina (Moscow: Moskovskii rabochii, 1989).

Gertsen, A. I., *Sobranie sochinenii v vos'mi tomakh*, 8 vols. (Moscow: Pravda, 1975).

Glagolev, A., "Sravnitel'noe obozrenie sostoianiia prosveshcheniia v Rossii s sostoianiem onago v prochikh evropeiskikh gosudarstvakh," *ZhMVD*, chast' 16, no. 2 (May 1835), 302–26.

[Glinka, S. N.], "Vzor na Moskvu," *RV*, chast' 1 (January 1808), 23–35.

[——], "Zamechanie o Moskve," *RV*, chast' 1 (February 1808), 159–61.

[——], "O pol'ze v Rossii remesl, khudozhestv, iskusstv," *RV*, chast' 1 (March 1808), 300–15.

[——], "Napominanie o Ekaterine Votori," *RV*, chast' 2 (April 1808), 3–45.

[——], "Vypiska iz Ruskoi knigi, nazvannoi: Sobranie otryvkov, vziatykh iz nravstvennykh i politicheskikh Pisatelei, i izdannoi G...1811," *RV*, chast' 6 (June 1811), 73–86.

[——], "Kuznetskoi Most, ili vladychestvo mody i roskoshi," *RV*, chast' 3 (September 1808), 331–60.

—— *Zapiski o 1812 gode* (St Petersburg: V tipografii Imperatorskoi Rossiiskoi Akademii, 1836).

—— *Zapiski Sergeia Nikolaevicha Glinki* (St Petersburg: Russkaia Starina, 1895).

Glushkovskii, Adam, "Moskva v 1812 godu: Iz zapisok Adama Glushkovskogo," *Krasnyi Arkhiv*, vol. 4 (1937), 121–59.

Golitsyn, N. N., *Materialy dlia polnoi rodoslovnoi rospisi kniazei Golitsynykh* (Kiev: Tipografiia E. Ia. Fedorova, 1880).

Gol'ms, F. M., *Velikie liudi i ikh velikiia proizvedeniia: Razskazy o sooruzheniiakh znamenitykh inzhenerov* (St Petersburg: tipografiia A. Porokhovshchikova, 1897).

Gordin, A. M., *Pushkinskii Peterburg/Pushkin's St. Petersburg* (St Petersburg: Khudozhnik RSFSR, 1991).

"Gore moskovskikh zhitelei v 1812 g. (sovremennyia pis'ma)," *RS,* 154 (April–June 1913), 61–5.

Gorky, Maxim, *My Childhood,* tr. Ronald Wilks (London: Penguin, 1966).

Gramsci, Antonio, *The Southern Question,* tr. Pasquale Verdicchio (West Lafayette, Ind.: Bordighera, 1995).

Grech, Nikolai, *Sochineniia,* 5 vols. (St Petersburg: V tipografii N. Grecha, 1838).

Grellet, Stephen, *Memoirs of the Life and Gospel Labours of Stephen Grellet,* ed. Benjamin Seebohm, 2 vols. (3rd edn., London: A. W. Bennett, 1862).

Grève, Claude de, ed., *Le voyage en Russie. Anthologie des voyageurs français aux XVIIIe et XIXe siècles* (Paris: Robert Laffont, 1990).

"Griboedovskaia Moskva v pis'makh M. A. Volkovoi k V. I. Lanskoi 1812–1818 gg.," *VE,* part 1: kniga 8 (August 1874), 572–666; part 2: kniga 9 (September 1874), 115–68; part 3: kniga 10 (Oct. 1874), 542–89; part 4: kniga 12 (December 1874), 637–70; part 5: kniga 1 (January 1875), 219–49; part 6: kniga 3 (March 1875), 230–70; part 7: kniga 8 (August 1875), 660–87.

Griffiths, David, and George E. Munro, eds. and tr, *Catherine II's Charters of 1785 to the Nobility and the Towns* (Bakersfield, Calif.: Charles Schlacks, 1991).

Grigor'ev, Apollon, *Vospominaniia,* ed. B. F. Egorov (Moscow: Nauka, 1988).

Gromeka, S., "Politseiskoe deloproizvodstvo," *Russkii Vestnik,* vol. 16 (1858), 178–94.

Grot, Ia. and P. Pekarskii, eds., *Pis'ma N. M. Karamzina k I. I. Dmitrievu* (St Petersburg: v tipografii Imperatorskoi Akademii Nauk, 1866).

Guizot, François, *Mémoires pour servir à l'histoire de mon temps,* 8 vols. (Paris: Michel Lévy, 1872).

[Gur'ianov I. G.], *Moskva, ili Istoricheskii putevoditel' po znamenitoi stolitse Gosudarstva Rossiiskago,* 4 vols. (Moscow: V Tipografii S. Selivanovskago, 1827–31).

Hohenlohe-Ingelfingen, Prinz Kraft zu, *Aus meinem Leben: Aufzeichnungen,* 4 vols. (Berlin: Ernst Siegfried Mittler, 1897–1907).

Holbach, Baron d', *Essai sur les préjugés, ou, De l'influence des opinions sur les mœurs & sur le bonheur des hommes* (London: no pub., 1770).

Holcomb, William P., *Pennsylvania Boroughs* (Baltimore: N. Murray, 1886).

Holman, James, *Travels through Russia, Siberia, Poland, Austria, Saxony, Prussia, Hanover, &c. &c. Undertaken during the Years 1822, 1823, and 1824, While Suffering from Total Blindness,* 2 vols. (London: Geo. B. Whittaker, 1825).

Ilizarov, S. S., ed., *Akademik G. F. Miller—pervyi issledovatel' Moskvy i Moskovskoi provintsii* (Moscow: Ianus, 1996).

—— ed., *Moskva v opisaniiakh XVIII veka* (Moscow: Ianus-K, 1997).

Inoevs, K. Kh., "Sanitarnyi otchet po 4 i 5 kvartalam Serpukhovskoi chasti," *IMGD,* vypusk 17 (15 September 1878), 42–5.

Ismailov, F. F., *Vzgliad na sobstvennuiu proshedshuiu zhizn' Ismailova* (Moscow: V Universitetskoi Tipografii, 1860).

Istoricheskaia zapiska o Moskovskikh uchilishchakh ordena sv. Ekateriny i Aleksandrovskom (Moscow: Tipografiia i Litografiia I. N. Kushnera, 1875).

Ivanov, P., *Opisanie Gosudarstvennago Arkhiva starykh del* (Moscow: V Tipografii S. Selivanovskago, 1850).

Ivanov, Pav., "Otkrytie Kremlevskago sada v den' tezoimenitstva Gosudaria Imperatora," *OZ*, 7/17 (September 1821), 375–8.

"Iz pisem Aleksandra Iakovlevicha Bulgakova k bratu ego Konstantinu Iakovlevichu," *RA* (1900), part 1: 1/4, 493–518; part 2: 2/5, 5–36; part 3: 2/6, 208–35; part 4: 2/7, 294–329.

Janicki, S., L. Jacquet, and A. Pasqueau, *Improvement of Non-Tidal Rivers: Memoirs*, tr. Wm. E. Merrill (Washington, DC: Government Printing Office, 1881).

Johnson, Samuel, *A Dictionary of the English Language* (3rd edn., Dublin: W. C. Jones, 1768).

Kachenovskii, Vl., "Mikhail Trofimovich Kachenovskii," *Bibiliograficheskiia zapiski*, 1/4 (April 1892), 259–69.

Kanatchikov, S., *A Radical Worker in Tsarist Rusia: The Autobiography of Semën Kanatchikov*, ed. and tr. Reginald E. Zelnik (Stanford, Calif.: Stanford University Press, 1986).

Kapitonov, A. P., ed., "Moskva v 1812 g. (Raport starshego ad'iutanta N. Ia. Butkovskogo)," *Rossiiskii Arkhiv*, 2–3 (1992), 68–72.

[Karamzin, N. M.], "O knizhnoi torgovle i liubvi ko chteniiu v Rossii," *VE*, 3/9 (May 1802), 57–64.

[——], "Puteshestvie vokrug Moskvy," *VE*, 7/4 (February 1803), 278–89.

[——], "O novom obrazovanii narodnago prosveshcheniia v Rossii," *VE*, 8/5 (March 1803), 49–61.

—— *Pis'ma russkogo puteshestvennika; Povesti*, ed. N. N. Akopova, G. P. Makogonenko, and M. V. Ivanov (Moscow: Pravda, 1982).

——, *Pis'ma russkogo puteshestvennika*, ed. Iu. M. Lotman, N. A. Marchenko, and B. A. Uspenskii (Leningrad: Nauka, 1987).

—— *Sochineniia*, 8 vols. (Moscow: V Tipografii S. Selivanovskago, 1803–4).

—— *Letters of a Russian Traveller: A Translation and Study*, ed. Andrew Kahn, Studies on Voltaire and the Eighteenth Century 2003:04 (Oxford: Voltaire Foundation, 2003).

Kartavov, P. A., ed., *Rostopchinskie afishi* (St Petersburg: Kommercheskaia Tipo-Litografiia M. Vilenchika, 1904).

Kazantsev, Nikodim, "Zhizn' Arkhimandrita Nikodima Kazantseva," *Bogoslovskii Vestnik*, part 1: no. 1 (January 1910), 59–77; part 2: no. 2 (February 1910), 291–304; part 3: no. 3 (March 1910), 404–27.

Kedrov, N. I., *Moskovskaia dukhovnaia seminariia, 1814–1889: Kratkii istoricheskii ocherk s prilozheniem spiskov nachal'nikov, nastavnikov i vospitannikov* (Moscow: Tipo-litografiia T-va I. N. Kushnerev i Ko., 1889).

Khaliutin, L., "Vospitanie v kadetskom korpuse za polveka nazad," *Sovremennik*, 71 (October 1858), 630–54.

——"Moskovskii syshchik Iakovlev: Vospominaniia," *Sovremennik*, 75 (May 1859), 79–94.

Khomutova, A. G., "Vospominaniia A. G. Khomutovoi o Moskve v 1812 godu," *RA*, vol. 3 (1891), 309–28.

Khvoshchinskaia, Nadezhda, *The Boarding-School Girl*, tr. Karen Rosneck (Evanston, Ill.: Northwestern University Press, 2000).

Kizevetter, A. A., *Posadskaia obshchina v Rossii XVIII st.* (Moscow: Universitetskaia tipografiia, 1903).

—— *Istoricheskie otkliki* (Moscow: Izdatel'stvo K. F. Nekrasova, 1915).

Klaproth, Julius von, *Travels in the Caucasus and Georgia, Performed in the Years 1807 and 1808 by Command of the Russian Government*, tr. F. Shoberl (London: Henry Colburn, 1814).

Kokorev, I. T., *Ocherki Moskvy sorokovykh godov*, ed. N. S. Ashukin (Moscow: Academia, 1932).

Kol'chugin, G. N., "Zapiska G. N. Kol'chugina," *RA*, 3/9 (1879), 45–62.

Komarov, Matvei, *Istoriia moshennika Van'ki Kaina; Milord Georg*, ed. V. D. Rak (St Petersburg: Zhurnal "Neva," Letnii Sad, 2000).

Kondrat'ev, I. K., *Sedaia starina Moskvy: Istoricheskii obzor i polnyi ukazatel' eia dostopamiatnostei* (Moscow: Izdanie knigoprodavtsa I. A Morozova, 1893).

Konechnyi, Al'bin, ed., *Peterburgskoe kupechestvo v XIX veke* (St Petersburg: Giperion, 2003).

Koni, A. F., *Fedor Petrovich Gaaz: Biograficheskii ocherk* (2nd edn., St Petersburg: Izdanie A. F. Marksa, 1901).

[Korkhov, L. M.] L. Checherskii, "Shkol'nyia vospominaniia krest'ianina," *VE* (August 1870), 503–40.

[Korsakov, A.] K—v, "Moskovskii kadetskii korpus, 1824–1828," *Drevniaia i novaia Rossiia*, 17 (May–August 1880), 287–304.

Kozlovskii, G. Ia., "Moskva v 1812 godu zaniataia frantsuzami: Vospominanie ochevidtsa," *RS*, vol. 65 (January–March 1890), 105–14.

"Kratkii obzor zavedenii: Maloletniago Otdeleniia, Fel'dsherskoi Shkoly i Bogadel'ni Vospitatel'nago Doma," *Moskvitianin*, chast' 4, otdel 5 (1849), 17–22.

Kropotkin, P. A., *Zapiski revoliutsionera* (Moscow: Moskovskii rabochii, 1988).

Kuznetsov, Aleksandr, *Almanakh na 1826 dlia priezzhaiushchikh v Moskvu i dlia samikh zhitelei sei stolitsy, ili Noveishii ukazatel' Moskvy* (Moscow: V Tipografii Avgusta Semena, 1826).

L . . . n, review of Engelbert Wichelhausen, *Züge zu einem Gemählde von Moskwa*, in *Magasin encyclopédique, ou Journal des sciences, des lettres et des arts*, no. 21 (1804), 129–33.

Lapshin, V., "Ob elektro-magnitnykh telegraficheskikh liniiakh v raznykh gosudarstvakh," *Zhurnal Ministerstva Narodnago Prosveshcheniia*, chast' 85, otdel 2 (1855), 247–302.

[Lavrentii, Archimandrite], "Zapiski ochevidtsa o sokhranenii dragotsennostei Nikolaevskago Perervinskago monastyria, i o dostopamiatnykh sobytiiakh v sei obiteli v 1812 godu," *Maiak*, vol. 2, kniga 4 (1842), section "Zamechatel'," 53–67.

[Lebedev, V. I.], "Kratkoe opisanie proizshestvii, byvshikh pri Pokhval'skoi, chto v Bashmakove, tserkvi v 1812 godu," *Chteniia v Obshchestve liubitelei dukhovnago prosveshcheniia*, god 36 (March 1914), 54–76.

[Le Cointe de Laveau, G.], *Moscou avant et après l'incendie, ou Notice concernant la description de cette capitale et des moeurs de ses habitans, par deux témoins oculaires* (2nd edn., Paris: Gide Fils, 1818).

—— *Guide du voyageur à Moscou* (Moscow: Auguste Semen, 1824).

Le Maire, Jean-Baptiste-Charles, "La Police de Paris en 1770: Mémoire inédit composé par ordre de G. de Sartine sur la demande de Marie-Thérèse," *Mémoires de la Société de l'histoire de Paris et de l'Ile de France*, 5 (1878), 1–131.

Leont'eva, F. P., "Zapiski F. P. Leont'evoi (1811, 1812 i 1813 gody)," *Russkii Vestnik*, part 1: 167/10 (October 1883), 815–47; part 2: 168/12 (December 1883), 878–902; part 3: 169/2 (February 1884), 670–721.

Les français peints par eux-mêmes. Encyclopédie morale du dix-neuvième siècle, 9 vols. (Paris: Louis Curmer, 1840–2).

Levitov, A., *Moskovskiia nory i trushchoby* (2nd edn., St Petersburg: Izdanie V. E. Genkelia, 1869).

Liubimov, N., "Mikhail Leont'evich Nazimov," in *Rech' i otchet, chitannye v torzhestvennom sobranii Imperatorskago Moskovskago universiteta 12-go ianvaria 1879 goda* (Moscow: V Universitetskoi Tipografii, 1879), 279–87.

Londonderry, Marchioness of and H. M. Hyde, eds., *The Russian Journals of Martha and Catherine Wilmot* (London: Macmillan, 1934).

Lopukhin, I. V., *Zapiski senatora I. V. Lopukhina* (1859; repr. edn., Moscow: Nauka, 1990).

[L'vov, V.] M. Zh., "Zhizn' v Moskve v Ianvare 1846 goda," *Moskvitianin*, chast' 1, no. 2 (1846), 232–44.

[——] M. Zh., "Zhizn' v Moskve v 1845," *Moskvitianin*, chast' 1, no. 1 (1846), 269–76.

Lyall, Robert, *The Character of the Russians and a Detailed History of Moscow* (London: T. Cadell; Edinburgh: W. Blackwood; 1823).

Malinovskii, A. F., *Obozrenie Moskvy* (Moscow: Moskovskii rabochii, 1992).

Malte-Brun, Conrad, *Précis de la géographie universelle, ou description de toutes les parties du monde sur un plan nouveau*, 8 vols. (Paris: F. Buisson, 1812–29).

Malthus, Thomas Robert, *An Essay on the Principle of Population*, 2 vols. (Washington City: Roger Chew Weightman, 1809).

[Marenin, Vasilii Ivanovich] Prot. V. M-n, *Shkol'nyia i semeinyia vospominaniia (Ocherk dukhovnoi shkoly i byta dukhovenstva v polovine proshlago stolentiia)*, vol. 1 (St Petersburg: Tipografiia Glazunova, 1911).

Marshall, Joseph, *Travels through Holland, Flanders, Germany, Denmark, Sweden, Lapland, Russia, the Ukraine, and Poland, in the Years 1768, 1769, and 1770*, 3 vols. (London: Printed for J. Almon, 1772–3).

[Mashkov, Ioann], "1812-i god. Sozhzhenie Moskvy. Pokazaniia ochevidtsa (Protoiereia Kazanskago na Krasnoi ploshchadi sobora)," *RA*, 3/12 (1909), 455–63.

Masson, Charles François Philibert, *Mémoires secrets sur la Russie, et particulièrement sur la fin du règne de Catherine II et le commencement de celui de Paul I*, 3 vols. (Paris: Charles Pougens, 1800).

Matériaux en grande partie inédits pour la biographie future du Comte Théodore Rastaptchine rassemblés par son fils (Brussels: M.-J. Poot, 1864).

The Memoirs of Catherine the Great, tr. Mark Cruse and Hilde Hoogenboom (New York: Modern Library, 2005).

[Mercier, Louis-Sébastien], *Tableau de Paris, nouvelle édition corrigée et augmentée*, 12 vols. (Amsterdam: no pub., 1782–8).

—— *Panorama of Paris: Selections from* Tableau de Paris *by Louis-Sébastien Mercier*, ed. Jeremy D. Popkin, tr. Helen Simpson (University Park, Pa.: Pennsylvania State University Press, 1999).

"Meshchanskoe soslovie v Moskve (za 1845 god)," *ZhMVD* (January 1847), 71–86.

Michelet, Jules, *La sorcière* (Paris: E. Dentu, 1862).

Miranda, Francisco de, *Diario de Moscú y San Petersburgo* (Caracas: Biblioteca Ayacucho, 1993).

"Modern Discoveries, and Improvements in Arts, Sciences, and Literature," *Universal Magazine*, 4/22 (September 1805), 252–65.

Modzalevskii, B. L., "Vasilii Grigor'evich Ruban," *RS*, 28/8 (August 1897), 393–415.

"Morality of the Working Classes," *Chartist Circular*, no. 6 (2 November 1839).

"Moskovskaia zhizn' vesnoi 1848 goda (Pis'ma moskovskago ober-politsmeistera Luzhina nachal'niku III otdeleniia grafu A. F. Orlovu)," *Minuvshie Gody*, no. 11 (May 1908), 47–9.

"Moskovskie monastyri vo vremia nashestviia frantsuzov," *RA* (1869), cols. 1387–99.

"Moskovskii Novodevichii monastyr' v 1812 godu: Razskaz ochevidtsa—shtatnago sluzhitelia Semena Klimycha," *RA* (1864), cols. 843–58.

"Moskovskii Vospitatel'nyi Dom v 1812 godu," *RA*, vol. 3 (1900), 457–75.

"Moskva v 1846 godu. Izvlechenie iz otcheta g. Moskovskago ober-politsiimeistera," *ZhMVD* (November 1847), 254–92.

"Moskva v 1812 godu," *RS*, vol. 8 (July–December 1873), 992–4.

"Moskva v 1812 godu: Opisanie moego prebyvaniia v Moskve vo vremia Frantsuzov, s 1-go po 21-e Sentiabria 1812 goda," *RA*, no. 8 (1896), 521–40.

Müller, Chrétien, *Tableau de Pétersbourg, ou Lettres sur la Russie, écrites en 1810, 1811 et 1812* (Paris: Treuttel et Wurtz; Mainz: Florien Kupferberg; 1814).

[Müller, Gerhard Friedrich], "Zuverläßige Nachrichten von dem Aufrührer Jemeljan Pugatschew, und der von demselben angestifteten Empörung," in Anton Friedrich Büsching, ed., *Magazin für die neue Historie und Geographie*, no. 18 (1784), 3–70.

Muromets, Il'ia, "Bol'nitsa dlia prikhodiashchikh v Moskve," *Moskvitianin*, vol. 3, otdel 5 (1850), 64–8.

"Mytishchinskoi vodovod (Prislannaia stat'ia)," *VE*, 23 (December 1804), 213–29.

N. N., review of Vasilii Androssov, *Statisticheskaia zapiska o Moskve*, in *Teleskop*, vol. 8, no. 7 (1832), 388–413.

N., "Pis'mo iz Moskvy," *Sovremennik*, vol. 52 (July 1855), 191–6.

"Nakaz ot zhitelei goroda Moskvy," *Sbornik Imperatorskago Russkago Istoricheskago Obshchestva*, 93 (1894), 119–35.

Nazimov, M., "V provintsii i v Moskve s 1812 po 1828 god: Iz vospominanii starozhila," *Russkii Vestnik*, 124 (July 1876), 74–161.

"Nekotoryia podrobnosti o Moskovskom gulian'e pod Novinskom," *OZ*, 10/26 (June 1822), 450–3.

Nekrasov, Nikolai, ed., *Petersburg: The Physiology of a City*, ed. and tr. Thomas Gaiton Marullo (Evanston, Ill.: Northwestern University Press, 2009).

"Nekrolog," *Allgemeine Literatur-Zeitung*, no. 245 (October 1819), cols. 253–6.

Nikitenko, A., "Rech' o kritike, proiznesennaia v torzhestvennom sobranii Imperatorskago Sankpeterburgskago Universiteta, marta 25-go dnia 1842 goda," *OZ*, vol. 24 (1842), otdel 5 "Kritika," 1–42.

—— *Up from Serfdom: My Childhood and Youth in Russia, 1804–1824*, tr. Helen Saltz Jacobson (New Haven: Yale University Press, 2001).

Nikitin, K. N., "Otchet sanitarnago vracha Meshchanskoi chasti," *IMGD* (15 September 1878), 10–31.

Nikolaev, P., *Istoricheskii ocherk maloletniago otdeleniia Moskovskago Nikolaevskago Sirotskago Instituta (za 50 let ego sushchestvovaniia) 1842–1892 g.* (Moscow: Tipografiia E. G. Potapova, 1892).

Nistrem, K., *Moskovskii adress-kalendar', dlia zhitelei Moskvy, sostavlen po offitsial'nym dokumentam i svedeniiam*, 4 vols. (Moscow: V tipografii S. Selivanovskago, 1842).

Nordhof, Anton Wilhelm, *Die Geschichte der Zerstörung Moskaus im Jahre 1812*, ed. Claus Scharf and Jürgen Kessel (Munich: Haraldt Boldt Verlag im R. Oldenbourg Verlag, 2000).

"Novo-naidennyia bumagi grafa F. V. Rostopchina," *RA*, kniga 3, vypusk 1 (1881), 215–27.

"Novyia podlinnyia cherty iz istorii otechestvenoi voiny 1812 goda," *RA* (1864), cols. 786–842.

"Ob odezhde," *Moskovskii Kur'er*, chast' 2 (1805), 201–4.

"Opisanie dostopamiatnykh proisshestvii v moskovskikh monastyriakh vo vremia nashestviia nepriiatelei v 1812 godu," *ChOIDR*, 27/4 (October–December 1858), "Materialy otechestvennyia": 33–50.

O povrezhdenii nravov v Rossii kniazia M. Shcherbatova i puteshestvie A. Radishcheva: Faksimil'noe izdanie (Moscow: Nauka, 1985).

Orlov, Nikolai, "Sledstvennaia chast' v gradskikh politsiiakh," *Russkii Vestnik*, 20 (1859), "Sovremennaia letopis'," 328–36.

"O vazhnosti statisticheskikh ischislenii (Soobshcheno)," *ZhMVD*, chast' 16/2 (May 1835), 187–97.

O vysochaishe utverzhdennom moskovskom blagotvoritel'nom obshchestve 1837 goda i o chastnykh shkolakh onago za 1840 god (Moscow: V tipografii Nikolaia Stepanova, 1841).

Ostrovskiii, A., *Dramaturgiia* (Moscow: Izdatel'stvo AST-Agentstvo KRPA Olimp, 2002).

"Otchet komiteta, vysochaishe uchrezhdennago v Moskve, dlia razbora i prizreniia prosiashchikh milostyniu, za 1840 god," *ZhMVD*, chast' 39 (March 1841), 307–49.

"Otchet moskovskago ober-politsmeistera, za 1840 god," *ZhMVD*, chast' 41, no. 7 (July 1841), 1–161.

"Otechestvennaia voina (Pis'mo P. Kikina k materi)," *RS*, vol. 54 (April–June 1887), 738.

"Otzyv russkago staroobriadtsa o venskoi revoliutsii 1848 goda: Pis'mo iz Avstrii v Moskvu na Rogozhskoe kladbishche, ot nastoiatelia belokrinskago monastyria Pavla Velikodvorskago," *RA*, 2/5 (1875), 112–14.

P. S. A., *Iz vospominanii o vladimirskikh dukhovnykh (prikhodskom i uezdnom) uchilishchakh i seminarii 1818–1832 godov* (Vladimir: Pechatnia A. A. Aleksandrovskago, 1875).

Panktratov, A., "Staroobriadtsy i Napoleon," *RS*, vol. 157 (January–March 1914), 39–51.

Papandopulo, V. K., "Otchet sanitarnago vracha Presnenskoi chasti," *IMGD*, vypusk 17 (15 September 1878), 31–5.

Pavlova, Karolina, "Moi vospominaniia," *RA*, 4/10 (1875), 222–40.

Pélissier, Léon-G., ed., *Lettres inédites du baron Guillaume Peyrousse écrites à son frére André pendant les campagnes de l'Empire de 1809 à 1814* (Paris: Perrin, 1894).

"Perepiska: Otdykh v Moskve izdatelia Otechestvennykh Zapisok na puti v Astrakhan' i Sibir'," *OZ*, 18/52 (August 1824), 251–63.

"Pervye dni v sozhzhennoi Moskve: Sentiabr' i oktiabr' 1812-go goda (Pis'mo kn. A. A. Shakhovskago, 1836 g., k A. I. Mikhailovskomu-Danilevskomu)," *RS*, vol. 64 (October–December 1889), 31–55.

Petrov, P. N., *Istoriia Sankt-Peterburga, s osnovaniia goroda, do vvedeniia vybornago gorodskago upravleniia, po uchrezhdeniiam o guberniiakh, 1703–1782* (St Petersburg: Tipografiia Glazunova, 1884).

Petunnikov, A., "Po povodu osvetitel'nago kalendaria na 1878 god," *IMGD*, vypusk 1 (15 January 1878), 35–45.

Pezzl, Johann, *Skizze von Wien: Ein Kultur- und Sittenbild aus der josefinischen Zeit*, ed. Gustav Gugitz and Anton Schlossar (Graz: Leykam, 1923).

Pipes, Richard, *Karamzin's Memoir on Ancient and Modern Russia: A Translation and Analysis* (New York: Atheneum, 1966).

"Pis'ma Gosudaryni Imperatritsy Ekateriny II-i k kniaziu Mikhailu Nikitichu Volkonskomu," *Osmnadtsatyi vek*, vol. 1 (1868), 52–162.

"Pis'mo grafa F. V. Rostopchina k izdateliu Russkago Vestnika S. N. Glinke," *RA*, 3/12 (1876), 430–2.

Polievktov, Mikhail, *Nikolai I: Biografiia i obzor tsarstvovaniia* (Moscow: Izd-vo M. i S. Sabashnikovykh, 1918).

Polnoe sobranie zakonov Rossiiskoi Imperii: Sobranie Pervoe, 45 vols. (St Petersburg: Pechatano v tipografii II Otdeleniia Sobstvennoi Ego Imperatorskago Velichestva Kantseliarii, 1830).

Polnoe sobranie zakonov Rossiiskoi Imperii: Sobranie Vtoroe, 55 vols. (St Petersburg: v tipografii II Otdeleniia Sobstvennoi Ego Imperatorskago Velichestva Kantseliarii, 1830–1885).

Polozhenie o dokhodakh i raskhodakh Moskovskoi stolitsy i ob uplate dolgov, na tamoshnei dume lezhashchikh, Vysochaishe konfirmovannoe v 13 den' Aprelia 1823 goda (Moscow: V Tipografii Semena Selivanovskago).

Polunin, Fedor, *Geograficheskii leksikon Rossiiskago gosudarstva, ili Slovar', opisuiushchii po azbuchnomu poriadku reki, ozera, moria, gory, goroda, kreposti, znatnye monastyri, ostrogi, iasashnyia zimovyia, rudnyia zavody, i prochiia dostopamiatnyia mesta obshirnoi Rossiiskoi Imperii*, ed. and introd. Gerard Friderik Miller (Moscow: Pri Imperatorskom Moskovskom Universitete, 1773).

Popov, Aleksandr, "Frantsuzy v Moskve v 1812 godu," *RA* (1876), part 1:1/2, 223–47; part 2: 1/3, 316–45; part 3: 1/4, 440–63; part 4: 2/5, 53–80; part 5: 2/6, 161–99; part 6: 2/7, 285–301; part 7: 2/8, 369–87.

—— "Moskva v 1812 godu," *RA* (1875), part 1: 2/7, 269–324; part 2: 2/8, 369–402; part 3: 4/9, 5–46; part 4: 4/10, 129–97; part 5: 4/11, 257–88.

Popova, O. D., ed., *Eparkhialki: Vospominaniia vospitannits zhenskikh eparkhial'nykh uchilishch* (Moscow: Novoe Literaturnoe Obozrenie, 2011).

"Po povodu spiska nazamoshchennykh mestnostei goroda Moskvy," *IMGD*, vypusk 5 (1880), 1–28.

Pouchkine, Alexandre, *Œuvres poétiques*, ed. Efim Etkind, 2 vols. (Lausanne: L'Âge d'homme, 1993).

"Preobrazovanie gorodskoi Politsii v Parizhe, po primeru Londonskoi," *ZhMVD*, chast' 8, otdel 4, "Sovremennaia letopis'" (October 1854), 79–83.

"Pros'ba S. N. Glinki o vydache emu posobiia na izdanie ego sochinenii," *RS*, 107 (September 1901), 480.

Pushkin, Alexander, *The Complete Works of Alexander Pushkin*, 15 vols. (Norwich: Milner, 1999–2003).

Pyliaev, M. I., *Staraia Moskva: Rasskazy iz byloi zhizni pervoprestol'noi stolitsy* (Moscow: Svarog, 1995).

Rambaud, Alfred, "La Grande Armée à Moscou d'après les témoignages moscovites," *Revue des deux mondes*, vol. 106 (1873), 194–228.

Raupach, Friedrich, *Reise von St. Petersburg nach dem Gesundbrunnen zu Lipezk am Don. Nebst einem Beitrage zur Charakteristik der Russen* (Breslau: Wilhelm Gottlieb Korn, 1809).

—— Dr. Raupach, "Antikritik," *Allgemeine Literatur-Zeitung*, no. 93 (3 April 1811), cols. 737–40.

Raymond, Damaze de, *Tableau historique, géographique, militaire et moral de l'Empire de Russie*, 2 vols. (Paris: Le Normant, 1812).

Reimers, Heinrich von, *St. Petersburg am Ende seines ersten Jahrhunderts: Mit Rückblicken auf Entstehung und Wachstum dieser Residenz unter den verschiedenen Regierungen während dieses Zeitraums*, 2 vols. (St Petersburg: F. Dienemann, 1805).

Reinbeck, Georg, *Flüchtige Bemerkungen auf einer Reise von St Petersburg über Moskwa, Grodno, Warschau, Breslau nach Deutschland im Jahre 1805*, 2 vols. (Leipzig: Wilhelm Rein, 1806).

Rerberg, I. F., *Moskovskii vodoprovod: Istoricheskii ocherk ustroistva i razvitiia vodosnabzheniia g. Moskvy. Opisanie novago vodoprovoda* (Moscow: Tipo-litografiia A. P. Khailova, 1892).

Review of Dr. R(aupach) [*sic*], *Reise von St. Petersburg nach dem Gesundbrunnen zu Lipezk am Don*, in *Allgemeine Literatur-Zeitung*, no.356 (24 December 1810), cols. 937–44; no. 357 (25 December 1810), cols. 945–51; no. 358 (26 December 1810), cols. 953–7.

Review of Engelbert Wichelhausen, *Züge zu einem Gemählde von Moskwa Neue Leipziger Literaturzeitung*, no. 72 (14 December 1803), cols. 1055–8.

Review of Engelbert Wichelhausen, *Züge zu einem Gemählde von Moskwa*, in *Allgemeine Literatur-Zeitung*, no. 54 (21 February 1804), cols. 429–32.

Review of Engelbert Wichelhausen, *Züge zu einem Gemählde von Moskwa*, in *L'esprit des journaux français et étrangers, par une société de gens de lettres*, vol. 6 (February 1805), 84–9.

Review of J. F. Bateman, *On the Supply of Water to London from the Sources of the River Severn*, in *Journal of Social Science*, 1/4 (1866), 230–1.

Review of Johann Pezzl, *Skizze von Wien*, in *L'esprit des journaux, françois et étrangers* (December 1791), 421.

Review of Johannes Gistl, *Die jetzt lebenden Entomologen, Kerffreunde und Kerfsammler Europa's und der übrigen Continente*, and G. Silbermann, *Enumération des entomologistes vivans*, in *Bulletin de la Société Impériale des Naturalistes de Moscou*, no. 8 (1837), 137–63.

Review of Henry Storch, *The Picture of Petersburg*, in *Edinburgh Review*, no. 2 (January 1803), 305–7.

Review of Henry Storck, *An Historico-Statistic Picture of the Russian Empire*, in *Appendix to the Twenty-Fourth Volume of the New Arrangement of the Critical Review* (December 1798), 481–7.

Review of M. N. Zagoskin, *Moskva i Moskvichi*, and P. Vistengof, *Ocherki Moskovskoi zhizni*, in *Biblioteka dlia chteniia*, 56, otdel 6 (1843), 49–53.

Review of M. N. Zagoskin, *Moskva i Moskvichi*, and P. Vistengof, *Ocherki Moskovskoi zhizni*, in *OZ.* 26, otdel 6 (1843), 48–52.

Review of P. Vistengof, *Ocherki Moskovskoi zhizni*, in *Severnaia Pchela* (26 April 1843), 358–9.

Review of Robert Lyall, *The Character of the Russians*, in *European Magazine, and London Review*, vol. 85 (January 1824), 50–3.

Review of Robert Lyall, *The Character of the Russians*, in *Quarterly Review*, 31/61 (April 1824), 146–66.

Review of Robert Lyall, *The Character of the Russians*, in *The Atheneum; or, Spirit of the English Magazines*, 1/3 (1 May 1824), 124.

Review of Robert Lyall, *The Character of the Russians*, in *VE*, no. 17 (September 1824), 74–6.

Review of Robert Lyall, *The Character of the Russians*, in the *Literary Magnet of the Belles Lettres, Science, and the Fine Arts*, vol. 1 (1824), 70–1.

Review of Robert Lyall, *The Character of the Russians*, and of James Holman, *Travels through Russia, Siberia, Poland*, in *Eclectic Review*, vol. 24 (December 1825), 532–50.

Review of Vasilii Androssov, *Statisticheskaia zapiska o Moskve*, in *Moskovskii telegraf*, no. 6 (March 1832), 254–9.

Review of Vasilii Androssov, *Statisticheskaia zapiska o Moskve*, *ZhMVD*, chast' 6, no. 3 (1832), 70–86.

[Rudchenko, I. Ia.], *Istoricheskii ocherk oblozheniia torgovli i promyslov v Rossii* (St Petersburg: Tipografiia V. Kirshbauma, 1893).

Richter, Johann, ed., *Russische Miszellen*, 3 vols. (Leipzig: Hartknoch, 1803–4).

Ritchie, Leitch, *Russia and the Russians, or A Journey to St. Petersburg and Moscow through Courland and Livonia* (Philadelphia: E. L. Carey and A. Hart, 1836).

Rossiiskaia Imperiia razdelennaia v gubernii v 1796 i 1797 godakh: Prezhde byvshie staty gubernskie, koi nyne peremeneny. 1796 do 1797 (no pub., n.d.).

Rostislavov, D. I., "Peterburgskaia dukhovnaia akademiia pri grafe Protasove, 1836–1855 gg.," *VE*, 18/7 (July 1883), 121–87.

—— "Zapiski D. I. Rostislavova," *RS*, 77 (February 1893), 448–80.

—— *Provincial Russia in the Age of Enlightenment: The Memoir of a Priest's Son*, tr. Alexander M. Martin (DeKalb, Ill.: Northern Illinois University Press, 2002).

Rostopchin, F. V., *La vérité sur l'incendie de Moscou* (Paris: Ponthieu, 1823).

—— *Sochineniia Rastopchina (grafa Feodora Vasil'evicha)* (St Petersburg: V Tipografii A. Dmitrieva, 1853).

—— "Zapiska o Martinistakh, predstavlennaia v 1811 godu grafom Rostopchinym velikoi kniagine Ekaterine Pavlovne," *RA*, 13/3 (1875), 75–81.

—— "Tysiacha vosem'sot dvenadtsatyi god v Zapiskakh grafa F. V. Rostopchina," *RS*, 64 (December 1889), 643–725.

Rostoptchine, Lydie, *Les Rostoptchine* (n.p.: Balland, 1984).

Rousseau, Jean-Jacques, *The Confessions* (Ware: Wordsworth, 1996).

Ruban, V. G., *Opisanie imperatorskago stolichnago goroda Moskvy* (St Petersburg: pri Artilleriiskom i Inzhenernom Shliakhetnom Kadetskom Korpuse, 1782).

Russkii Biograficheskii Slovar': Izdanie Imperatorskago Russkago Istoricheskago Obshchestva, 25 vols. (St Petersburg, 1896–1918; repr. edn. New York: Kraus Reprint, 1962).

Schlözer, A. L., *August Ludwig Schlözers öffentliches und Privatleben: Erstes Fragment* (Göttingen: im Vandenhoeck- und Ruprechtschen Verlage, 1802).

Ségur, Count Philippe Paul de, *Napoleon's Russian Campaign*, tr. J. David Townsend (Alexandria, Va.: Time-Life, 1958).

[Selivanov, Il'ia] S—v, "Vospominaniia o Moskovskom kommercheskom uchilishche," *Russkii Vestnik*, 36 (November–December 1861), 719–54.

Semenov, P., "Predislovie," *Statisticheskii vremennik Rossiiskoi Imperii*, vol. 1 (1866).

Semenova, A. V., et al., eds., *Kupecheskie dnevniki i memuary kontsa XVIII–pervoi poloviny XIX veka* (Moscow: ROSSPEN, 2007).

Semevskii, V. I., "Sel'skii sviashchennik vo vtoroi polovine XVIII veka," *RS*, 19 (May–August 1877), 501–38.

Sergeev, Aleksei, *Russkiia poslovitsy i pogovorki v litsakh* (St Petersburg: v Voennoi Tipografii, 1830).

[Shafonskii, Afanasii], *Opisanie morovoi iazvy, byvshei v stolichnom gorode Moskve s 1770 po 1772 god* (Moscow: Pri Imperatorskom Universitete, 1775).

Shakhanov, Anatolii, ed., "Moskovskaia politsiia v 1812 g.: Raport ober-politsmeistera P. I. Ivashkina na imia glavnokomanduiushchego v Moskve A. P. Tormasova," *Istoricheskii Arkhiv*, no. 3 (2003), 162–5.

Shchepkin, M. P., "Istoricheskaia zapiska o raskhodakh goroda Moskvy po soderzhaniiu politseiskikh uchrezdenii v 1823–1879 gg.," *IMGD*, vypusk 2 (1880), cols. 5–72.

Shchukin, P. I., ed., *Bumagi, otnosiashchiiasia do Otechestvennoi voiny 1812 goda*, 10 vols. (Moscow: T-vo Tip. A. I. Mamontova, 1897–1908).

Sherman, James, *Memoir of William Allen, F.R.S.* (London: Charles Gilpin; Edinburgh: Adam and Charles Black; Dublin: J. B. Gilpin; 1851).

Shervinskii, V., "Otchet sanitarnago vracha Sushchevskoi chasti," *IMGD* (27 January 1879), 6–34.

Shil'der, N. K., *Imperator Aleksandr I: Ego zhizn' i tsarstvovanie*, 4 vols. (St Petersburg: A. S. Suvorin, 1897–8).

Shishkov, A. S., *Zapiski, mneniia i perepiska*, 2 vols. (Berlin: B. Behr's Buchhandlung, 1870).

Simmonds, P. L., "Statistics of Newspapers in Various Countries," *Quarterly Journal of the Statistical Society of London*, 4 (July 1841), 111–36.

"Sistema ochishcheniia dvorov i ulits posredstvom vodoprovodnykh trub, predprinimaemaia v Berline, po primeru Parizha i Londona," *ZhMVD*, chast' 3, "Smes'" (September 1843), 502–7.

Skorniakova, Natal'ia, *Staraia Moskva: Graviury i litografii XVI–XIX vekov iz sobraniia Gosudarstvennogo Istoricheskogo Muzeia* (Moscow: Galart, 1996).

Slonov, I., *Iz zhizni torgovoi Moskvy (Polveka nazad)* (Moscow: Tipografiia Russkago T-va Pechatnago i Izdatel'skago Dela, 1914).

"Smes'," *Moskovskii Zritel'*, chast' 4 (December 1806), 74–5.

"Smes'" (review of Engelbert Wichelhausen, *Züge zu einem Gemählde von Moskwa*), *VE*, no. 22 (30 November 1804), 138–40.

"Soderzhanie chistoty v Parizhe," *ZhMVD*, chast' 22, otdel 2, "Izsledovaniia i opisaniia" (February 1857), 91–104.

Sokolov, V., *Ukazatel' zhilishch i zdanii v Moskve, ili Adresnaia kniga* (Moscow: V Tipografii Avgusta Simena, 1826).

Solov'ev, N. I., "Presledovanie prostitutok v tsarstvovanie Imperatora Pavla I-go," *RS*, 165 (January–March 1916), 363–4.

Soloviev, Sergei M., *History of Russia, Volume 40: Empress Elizabeth, Politics and Culture, Approach of the Seven Years War, 1748–1756*, ed. and tr. Peter C. Stupples (Gulf Breeze, Fla.: Academic International Press, 2004).

Solovkov, I. A., ed., *Antologiia pedagogicheskoi mysli Rossii XVIII v.* (Moscow: Pedagogika, 1985).

Sopikov, Vasilii, ed., *Opyt rossiiskoi bibliografii, ili polnyi slovar' sochinenii i perevodov, napechatannykh na Slavenskom i Rossiiskom iazykakh, ot nachala zavedeniia tipografii, do 1813 goda*, 5 vols. in 4 (St Petersburg: V Tipografii Imperatorskago Teatra, 1813–21).

"Sostav i krug deiatel'nosti nyneshnei Londonskoi politsii," *ZhMVD*, chast' 42, no. 5, "Smes'" (May 1853), 317–27.

"Sravnenie politseiskago ustroistva v Parizhe i Londone," *ZhMVD*, chast' 9, "Smes'" (January 1845), 161–6.

"Sravnitel'naia statistika prestuplenii v Parizhe i v Londone," *ZhMVD*, chast' 2, "Smes'" (1843), 443–57.

Starchevskii, A., *Nikolai Mikhailovich Karamzin* (St Petersburg: Tipografiia Karla Kraiia, 1849).

Statisticheskii atlas goroda Moskvy: Ploshchad' Moskvy, naselenie i zaniatiia (Moscow: Moskovskaia Gorodskaia Tipografiia, 1887).

"Statisticheskiia tablitsy o sostoianii gorodov Rossiiskoi Imperii, velikago kniazhestva Finliandskago i Tsarstva Pol'skago po 1842 god," *ZhMVD*, chast' 1, "Smes'" (February 1843), 286–313.

Sternberg, J. von, *Reise von Moskau über Sofia nach Königsberg mit einer kurzen Beschreibung von Moskau nebst meteorologischen und mineralogischen Beobachtungen* (Berlin: no pub., 1793).

"Sto let nazad: Pis'ma I. P. Odentalia k A. Ia. Bulgakovu o peterburgskikh novostiakh i slukhakh," *RS*, vol. 151 (July–September 1912), 135–44.

Storch, Heinrich, ed., *Rußland unter Alexander dem Ersten*, 9 vols. (St Petersburg: Hartknoch, 1804–8).

—— *Gemaehlde von St. Petersburg*, 2 vols. (Riga: Hartknoch, n.d. [1794]).

—— *Statistische Übersicht der Statthalterschaften des Russischen Reichs nach ihren merkwürdigsten Kulturverhältnissen* (Riga: Hartknoch, 1795).

Strakhov, P. I., *Kratkaia istoriia akademicheskoi gimnazii, byvshei pri Imperatorskom Moskovskom universitete* (1855; repr. Moscow: Izdatel'stvo Moskovskogo universiteta, 2000).

Studenkin, G. I., "Saltychikha," *RS*, 10 (May–August 1874), 497–546.

Sue, Eugène, *Les mystères de Paris*, 4 vols. (Brussels: Meline, Cans, 1844).

Sverbeev, A., "Vospominaniia o moskovskikh pozharakh 1812 goda," *VE*, 7-i god, 11 (November 1872), 303–20.

[Svin'in, Pavel] Paul Svenin, *Sketches of Moscow and St Petersburg* (Philadelphia: Thomas Dobson, 1813).

[——] P. S., "Ivan Alekseevich Grebenshchikov, Moskovskii kupets-izobretatel'," *OZ*, 7/16 (August 1821), 153–72; 7/17 (September 1821), 243–61.

[——] P. S., "Pis'mo chetvertoe v Moskvu, o Mekhanike Soboleve," *OZ*, 10/26 (June 1822), 379–409.

Svod Zakonov Rossiiskoi Imperii, poveleniem Gosudaria Imperatora Nikolaia Pavlovicha sostavlennyi, 15 vols. (St Petersburg: V Tipografii Vtorago Otdeleniia Sobstvennoi Ego Imperatorskago Velichestva Kantseliarii, 1842).

"Tablitsy smertnosti v Moskve za mai mesiats 1878 g.," *IMGD*, vypusk 12 (1 July 1878), 1–35.

Tartakovskii, A. G., ed., *1812 god v vospominaniiakh sovremennikov* (Moscow: Nauka, 1995).

Tikhomirov, M. A., "Otchet sanitarnago vracha Prechistenskoi chasti," *IMGD* (1 August 1878), 44–55.

Tikhonravov, N. S., *Sochineniia*, 3 vols. in 4 (Moscow: Izdanie M. i S. Sabashnikovykh, 1898).

Tolstoi, L. N., *Polnoe sobranie sochinenii*, 90 vols. (Moscow: Gosudarstvennoe izdatel'stvo khudozhestvennoi literatury, 1930–58).

Tolstoy, Leo, *War and Peace*, tr. Louise and Aylmer Maude (New York: Simon and Schuster, 1942).

[Tolycheva, T.], "Razkazy ochevidtsev o dvenadtsatom gode: V Zubove," *MV* (7 February 1872).

[——], "Razskazy ochevidtsev o dvenadtsatom gode: V Strastnom monastyre," *MV* (14 February 1872).

[——], "Razskazy ochevidtsev o dvenadtsatom gode: Na Mokhovoi," *MV* (1 March 1872).

[——], "Razskazy ochevidtsev o dvenadtsatom gode: V prikhode Petra i Pavla na Iakimanke i na Orlovom lugu," *MV* (4 March 1872).

[——], "Razskazy ochevidtsev o dvenadtsatom gode: Razskaz kupchikhi Anny Grigor'-evny Kruglovoi, Sheremetevskoi bogadelenkoi," *MV* (13 March 1872).

[——], "Razskazy ochevidtsev o dvenadtsatom gode: V Rozhdestvenskom monastyre," *MV* (25 March 1872).

[——], "Razskazy ochevidtsev o dvenadtsatom gode," *Russkii Vestnik*, vol. 102 (November 1872), 266–304.

[——], "Razskaz Leontiia Petrovicha Lepeshkina," *MV* (8 January 1880).

—— "Razskaz o dvenadtsatom gode bogadel'nika Nabilkinskago zavedeniia Pavla Fedorovicha Gerasimova," *MV* (7 July 1882).

—— "Razskaz o dvenadtsatom gode Glafiry Klimovny Rozhnovoi, zhivushchei v Pokrovskoi bogadel'noi," *MV* (6 February 1884).

—— *Razskazy ochevidtsev o dvenadtsatom gode* (2nd edn., Moscow: Tipografiia G. Lissnera i D. Sobko, 1912).

Tourneux, Maurice, *Diderot et Catherine II* (Paris: Calmann Lévy, 1899).

The Travels of Olearius in Seventeenth-Century Russia, ed. and tr. Samuel H. Baron (Stanford, Calif.: Stanford University Press, 1967).

Tret'iakov, Mikhail, "Imperatorskii Moskovskii universitet v vospominaniiakh Mikhaila Prokhorovicha Tret'iakova, 1798–1830," *RS*, vol. 75, part 1: (July 1892), 105–31; part 2: (August 1892), 307–45; part 3: (September 1892), 533–53; part 4: vol. 76 (October 1892), 123–48.

Troitskii, V., *Istoricheskii ocherk soveta Imperatorskago Chelovekoliubivago Obshchestva i podvedomstvennykh emu blagotvoritel'nykh uchrezhdenii* (St Petersburg: no pub., 1898).

[Turgenev, Nikolai] N. Tourgueneff, N., *La Russie et les Russes*, 3 vols. (Paris: Au comptoir des imprimeurs-unis, 1847).

"Uchilishche dlia bednykh detei inostrantsov, nakhodiashchikhsia v S. Peterburge," *OZ*, 14/38 (June 1823), 411–18.

Ushakov, D. N., ed., *Tolkovyi slovar' russkogo iazyka*, 4 vols. in 3 (Cambridge, Mass.: Slavica Publishers, 1974) <http://enc-dic.com/ushakov/>.

"Ustroistvo gospitalei i bogougodnykh zavedenii vo Frantsii," *ZhMVD*, chast' 29, otdel 2, "Izsledovaniia i opisaniia" (April 1858), 155–78.

"Vedomost' o nakhodiashchikhsia v Moskve pervykh piati klassov zhenska pola personakh v 1775 godu," *RS*, 8 (July–December 1873), 94–7.

Viazemskii, P. A., *Polnoe sobranie sochinenii kniazia P. A. Viazemskago*, 12 vols. (St Petersburg: Tipografiia M. M. Stasiulevicha, 1878–96).

Vigel', F. F., *Zapiski*, 2 vols., ed. S. Ia. Shtraikh (Moscow: Artel' pisatelei KRUG, 1928).

Vinskii, G. S., *Moe vremia* (St Petersburg: OGNI, n.d.).

Vionnet de Maringoné, L.-J., *Souvenirs d'un ex-Commandant des Grenadiers de la Vieille Garde* (Paris: Edmond Dubois, 1899).

Vishniakov, N., *Svedeniia o kupecheskom rode Vishniakovykh*, 3 vols. (Moscow: Tipografiia G. Lissnera i A Geshelia [vols. 2–3: G. Lissnera i D. Sobko], 1903–11).

Vistengof, P., *Ocherki Moskovskoi zhizni* (Moscow: V tipografii S. Selivanovskago, 1842).

Voilquin, Suzanne, *Mémoires d'une saint-simonienne en Russie (1839–1846)*, ed. Maïté Albistur and Daniel Armogathe (n.p.: Éditions des Femmes, 1977).

Volkonskii, Petr, "U frantsuzov v Moskovskom plenu 1812 goda," *RA*, no. 11 (1905), 351–9.

Voskresenskii, A., "Umstvennyi vzor na protekshiia leta moei zhizni ot kolybeli do groba (1778–1825 g.)," *Dushepoleznoe chtenie*, part 1: no. 10 (1894), 203–11; part 2: no. 11 (1894), 367–84; part 3: no. 12 (1894), 590–600.

"Vospominaniia starozhila o 1812 gode v strannopriimnom dome grafa Sheremeteva v Moskve," *MV* (29 March 1859).

"Vsepoddanneishii otchet Moskovskago komiteta o prosiashchikh milostyniu, za 1841 god (Izvlechenie)," *ZhMVD*, chast' 43 (March 1842), 221–61.

Vtorov, Ivan Alekseevich, "Moskva i Kazan' v nachale XIX veka," *RS*, 70 (April 1891), 1–22.

"Vysochaishiia poveleniia po delam obshchago upravleniia," *ZhMVD*, chast' 20, otdel 1 (October 1856), 87–9.

Wichelhausen, Engelbert, *Züge zu einem Gemählde von Moskwa* (Berlin: Johann Daniel Sander, 1803).

XLXXLXXX, "Moskovskie riady," *Moskovskii Vestnik*, vol. 1 (1830), 207–18.

Ysarn-Villefort, François-Joseph d', *Relation du séjour des Français à Moscou et de l'incendie de cette ville en 1812 par un habitant de Moscou*, ed. A. Gadaruel (Brussels: Fr.-J. Olivier, 1871).

Zabelin, Ivan, *Opyty izucheniia russkikh drevnostei i istorii: Izsledovaniia, opisaniia i kriticheskiia stat'i*, 2 vols. (Moscow: Tipografiia Gracheva i Ko., 1872–3).

Zaborovskii, I., "Sanitarnyi otchet po Basmannoi chasti, za 1879 god," *IMGD*, vypusk 3 (1880), cols. 1–38.

Zagoskin, M. N., *Sochineniia*, 7 vols. (St Petersburg: V. I. Shtein, 1889).

"Zamechaniia na otchety Ober-Politseimeisterov po obeim Stolitsam," *ZhMVD*, chast' 6, no. 2 (1832), 54–69.

"Zamechaniia o chisle krazh, sdelannykh v Moskve, S.P.burge i Londone," *ZhMVD*, chast' 8, 3 (1833), 331–4.

"Zamechaniia o chisle umalishennykh, pol'zovannykh v bol'nitse Vsekh Skorbiashchikh v S. Peterburge 1832 goda," *ZhMVD*, chast' 8, no. 2 (1833), 199–208.

Zavalishin, Dmitrii, "Vospominaniia o morskom kadetskom korpuse s 1816 po 1822 god," *Russkii Vestnik*, 105 (June 1873), 623–55.

—— "Tysiacha vosem'sot dvenadtsatyi god (Iz vospominanii sovremennika)," *MV* (8 March 1884; 25 March 1884; 29 March 1884).

[Zhdanov, Petr], *Pamiatnik Frantsuzam, ili Prikliucheniia Moskovskago Zhitelia P . . . Zh . . .* (St Petersburg: Tipografiia I. Baikova, 1813).

Zhurnaly zasedanii kommissii po vodosnabzheniiu goroda Moskvy (St Petersburg: Tipografiia brat. Panteleevykh, 1882).

Zolotukhina, A. I., "Dvenadtsatyi god v zapiskakh Anny Il'inishny Zolotukhinoi (1812 g.)," *RS*, vol. 64 (October–December 1889), 257–88.

1812 god v vospominaniiakh, perepiske i rasskazakh sovremennikov (Moscow: Voennoe izdatel'stvo, 2001).

Secondary Bibliography

Aleksandrov, Iu. N., *Prilozhenie k faksimil'nomu izdaniiu Opisanie Moskvy* (Moscow: Kniga, 1989).

Alexander, John T., "Catherine II, Bubonic Plague, and the Problem of Industry in Moscow," *American Historical Review*, 79/3 (June 1974), 637–71.

—— *Bubonic Plague in Early Modern Russia: Public Health and Urban Disaster* (Baltimore: Johns Hopkins University Press, 1980).

—— "Petersburg and Moscow in Early Urban Policy," *Journal of Urban History*, 8/2 (February 1982), 145–69.

—— *Catherine the Great: Life and Legend* (New York: Oxford University Press, 1989).

Amburger, Erik, *Beiträge zur Geschichte der deutsch-russischen kulturellen Beziehungen* (Gießen: Wilhelm Schmitz, 1961).

Ananieva, Anna, *Russisch Grün: Eine Kulturpoetik des Gartens im Russland des langen 18. Jahrhunderts* (Bielefeld: Transcript, 2010).

Artamonova, L. M., *Obshchestvo, vlast' i prosveshchenie v russkoi provintsii XVIII–nachala XIX vv. (Iugo-vostochnye gubernii Evropeiskoi Rossii)* (Samara: Izdatel'stvo Samarskogo nauchnogo tsentra RAN, 2001).

Artem'eva, Tat'iana, *Ot slavnogo proshlogo k svetlomu budushchemu: Filosofiia i utopiia v Rossii epokhi Prosveshcheniia* (St Petersburg: Aleteiia, 2005).

Aust, Martin, "Vermessen und Abbilden des russländischen Raumes nach der kulturellen Revolution Peters des Großen," in Lars Behrisch, ed., *Vermessen, Zählen, Berechnen: Die politische Ordnung des Raums im 18. Jahrhundert* (Frankfurt: Campus, 2006), 27–44.

Baysal, Alev, "Carlyle's Influence upon *A Tale of Two Cities* (1859)," *The Victorian Web: Literature, History, & Culture in the Age of Victoria* <http://www.victorianweb.org/authors/dickens/2cities/baysal1.html>.

Bell, David A., *The First Total War: Napoleon's Europe and the Birth of Warfare as We Know It* (Boston: Houghton Mifflin, 2007).

Berelowitch, Wladimir and Olga Medvedkova, *Histoire de Saint-Pétersbourg* (Paris: Arthème Fayard, 1996).

Bezotosnyi, V. M., et al., *Otechestvennaia voina 1812 goda: Entsiklopediia* (Moscow: ROSSPEN, 2004).

Black, J. L., *Citizens for the Fatherland: Education, Educators, and Pedagogical Ideals in Eighteenth Century Russia* (Boulder, Colo.: East European Quarterly, 1979).

—— *G.-F. Müller and the Imperial Russian Academy* (Kingston: McGill-Queen's University Press, 1986).

Bludilina, N. D., et al., *Moskva v russkoi i mirovoi literature: Sbornik statei* (Moscow: Nasledie, 2000).

Blum, Jerome, *Lord and Peasant in Russia from the Ninth to the Nineteenth Century* (Princeton: Princeton University Press, 1961).

Boeck, Brian, Russell Martin, and Daniel Rowland, eds., *Aporia: Studies in Early Slavic History and Culture in Honor of Donald Ostrowski* (Bloomington, Ind.: Slavica, 2011).

Boldina, E. G., A. S. Kiselev, and L. N. Seliverstova, eds., *Moskva v 1812 godu: Materialy nauchnoi konferentsii, posviashchennoi 180-letiiu Otechestvennoi voiny 1812 goda* (Moscow: Mosgorarkhiv, 1997).

Borisov, A. V., et al., *Politsiia i militsiia Rossii: Stranitsy istorii* (Moscow: Nauka, 1995).

Bradley, Joseph, "The Moscow Workhouse and Urban Welfare Reform in Russia," *Russian Review*, 41/4 (October 1982), 427–44.

Braudel, Fernand, *The Structures of Everyday Life: The Limits of the Possible*, Civilization and Capitalism 15th–18th Century, vol. 1, tr. Siân Reynolds (New York: Harper & Row, 1985).

Breuillard, Jean, "Introduction" to "Le Sentimentalisme russe," special issue of *Revue des études slaves*, 74/4 (2002–3), 653–7.

Broers, Michael, *Europe under Napoleon* (London: Arnold, 1996).

Broman, Thomas, "Rethinking Professionalization: Theory, Practice, and Professional Ideology in Eighteenth-Century German Medicine," *Journal of Modern History*, 67/4 (December 1995), 835–72.

Brower, Daniel, "Urbanization and Autocracy: Russian Urban Development in the First Half of the Nineteenth Century," *Russian Review*, 42/4 (October 1983), 377–402.

Bucher, Gudrun, "Auf verschlungenen Pfaden: Die Aufnahme von Gerhard Friedrich Müllers Schriften in Europa," in Dittmar Dahlmann, ed., *Die Kenntnis Rußlands im deutschsprachigen Raum im 18. Jahrhundert: Wissenschaft und Publizistik über das Russische Reich* (Göttingen: Bonn University Press, V&R unipress, 2006), 111–23.

Burbank, Jane and David L. Ransel, eds., *Imperial Russia: New Histories for the Empire* (Bloomington, Ind.: Indiana University Press, 1998).

—— Mark von Hagen, and Anatolyi Remnev, eds., *Russian Empire: Space, People, Power, 1700–1930* (Bloomington, Ind.: Indiana University Press, 2007).

Burkholder, Mark A. and Lyman L. Johnson, *Colonial Latin America* (3rd edn., New York: Oxford University Press, 1998).

Butler, William E., "The Nakaz of Catherine the Great," *American Book Collector*, 6/5 (1966), 18–21.

Butterwick, Richard, Simon Davies, and Gabriel Sánchez Espinosa, eds., *Peripheries of the Enlightenment*, Studies on Voltaire and the Eighteenth Century 2008:01 (Oxford: Voltaire Foundation, 2008).

Carsten, F. L., *The Ascendancy of France 1648–88*, The New Cambridge Modern History, vol. 5 (Cambridge: Cambridge University Press, 1961).

Classen, Constance, "The Odor of the Other: Olfactory Symbolism and Cultural Categories," *Ethos*, 20/2 (June 1992), 133–66.

Cockayne, Emily, *Hubbub: Filth, Noise & Stench in England, 1600–1770* (New Haven: Yale University Press, 2007).

Connelly, Owen, *Napoleon's Satellite Kingdoms* (New York: Free Press; London: Collier-Macmillan; 1965).

Coquin, François-Xavier, *La Grande Commission législative (1767–1768). Les cahiers de doléances urbains* (Paris: Nauwelaerts, 1972).

Corbin, Alain, *The Foul and the Fragrant: Odor and the French Social Imagination*, tr. Miriam Kochan, Roy Porter, and Christopher Prendergast (Cambridge, Mass.: Harvard University Press, 1986).

Cowan, Alexander and Jill Steward, eds., *The City and the Senses: Urban Culture since 1500* (Aldershot: Ashgate, 2007).

Cowley, Robert L. S., *Marriage A-La-Mode: A Re-View of Hogarth's Narrative Art* (Manchester: Manchester University Press, 1983).

Cross, A. G., "N. M. Karamzin's 'Messenger of Europe' (*Vestnik Yevropy*), 1802–3," *Forum for Modern Language Studies*, 5/1 (January 1969), 1–25.

—— *N. M. Karamzin: A Study of his Literary Career (1783–1803)* (Carbondale, Ill.: Southern Illinois University Press; London: Feffer & Simon; 1971).

—— "Der deutsche Beitrag zur britischen Rußlandkunde im 18. Jahrhundert," in Helmut Graßhoff, ed., *Literaturbeziehungen im 18. Jahrhundert: Studien und Quellen zur deutsch-russischen und russisch-westeuropäischen Kommunikation* (Berlin: Akademie-Verlag, 1986), 277–81.

—— "The Russian *Banya* in the Descriptions of Foreign Travellers and in the Depictions of Foreign and Russian Artists," *Oxford Slavonic Papers*, New Series, vol. 24 (1991), 34–59.

—— *By the Banks of the Neva: Chapters from the Lives of the British in Eighteenth-Century Russia* (Cambridge: Cambridge University Press, 1997).

Crossick, Geoffrey and Heinz-Gerhard Haupt, eds., *The Petite Bourgeoisie in Europe, 1780–1914: Enterprise, Family and Independence* (London: Routledge, 1995).

Daniel, Wallace, "The Merchants' View of the Social Order in Russia as Revealed in the Town *Nakazy* from Moskovskaia *Guberniia* to Catherine's Legislative Commission," *Canadian-American Slavic Studies*, 11/4 (Winter 1977), 503–22.

Degtiareva, M. I., *Zhozef de Mestr i ego russkie "sobesedniki": Opyt filosofskoi biografii i intellektual'nye sviazi v Rossii* (Perm': Aster, 2007).

Delattre, Simone, *Les douze heures noires. La nuit à Paris au XIXe siècle* (Paris: Albin Michel, 2000).

Dianina, Katia, "The Feuilleton: An Everyday Guide to Public Culture in the Age of the Great Reforms," *Slavonic and East European Journal*, 47/2 (Summer 2003), 187–210.

Dickinson, Sara, *Breaking Ground: Travel and National Culture in Russia from Peter I to the Era of Pushkin* (Amsterdam: Rodopi, 2006).

Dinges, Martin, "Kann man medizinische Aufklärung importieren? Kulturelle Probleme im Umfeld deutscher Ärzte in Rußland in der zweiten Hälfte des 18. Jahrhunderts," in Mathias Beer and Dittmar Dahlmann, eds., *Migration nach Ost- und Südosteuropa vom 18. bis zum Beginn des 19. Jahrhunderts: Ursachen—Formen—Verlauf—Ergebnis* (Stuttgart: Jan Thorbecke, 1999), 229–32.

—— "L'image de Moscou entre la description standardisée des Lumières et la recherche de la singularité russe. La topographie médicale (1803) de Engelbrecht Wichelhausen," *Cahiers du monde russe*, 44/1 (2003), 35–56.

Dixon, Simon, *The Modernisation of Russia, 1676–1825* (Cambridge: Cambridge University Press, 1999).

—— "The Posthumous Reputation of Catherine II in Russia, 1797–1837," *Slavonic and East European Review*, 77/4 (October 1999), 646–79.

—— *Catherine the Great* (New York: Ecco, 2009).

—— ed., *Personality and Place in Russian Culture: Essays in Memory of Lindsey Hughes* (London: Modern Humanities Research Association, 2010).

Donnert, Erich, ed., *Europa in der Frühen Neuzeit: Festschrift für Günter Mühlpfordt*, 7 vols. (Cologne: Böhlau, 1997–2008).

Dowe, Dieter, et al., eds., *Europe in 1848: Revolution and Reform* (New York: Berghahn Books, 2001).

Dukes, Paul, ed., *Russia under Catherine the Great*, 2 vols. (Newtonville, Mass.: Oriental Research Partners, 1977).

Eichler, Ernst, et al., eds., *Slawistik in Deutschland von den Anfängen bis 1945: Ein biographisches Lexikon* (Bautzen: Domowina, 1993).

Ekirch, A. Roger, *At Day's Close: Night in Times Past* (New York: W. W. Norton, 2005).

Ely, Christopher, *This Meager Nature: Landscape and National Identity in Imperial Russia* (DeKalb, Ill.: Northern Illinois University Press, 2002).

Engel, Barbara Alpern, "St. Petersburg Prostitutes in the Late Nineteenth Century: A Personal and Social Profile," *Russian Review*, 48/1 (January 1989), 21–44.

Engelstein, Laura, *The Keys to Happiness: Sex and the Search for Modernity in Fin-de-Siècle Russia* (Ithaca, NY: Cornell University Press, 1992).

Epstein, Klaus, *The Genesis of German Conservatism* (Princeton: Princeton University Press, 1966).

Etkind, Alexander, *Internal Colonization: Russia's Imperial Experience* (Cambridge: Polity, 2011).

Faggionato, Raffaella, *A Rosicrucian Utopia in Eighteenth-Century Russia: The Masonic Circle of N. I. Novikov*, tr. Michael Boyd and Brunello Lotti (Dordrecht: Springer, 2005).

Farnsworth, Beatrice, "The Soldatka: Folklore and Court Record," *Slavic Review*, 49/1 (Spring 1990), 58–73.

Flynn, James T., *The University Reform of Tsar Alexander I, 1802–1835* (Washington, DC: Catholic University of America Press, 1988).

Forrest, Alan, *Napoleon's Men: The Soldiers of the Revolution and Empire* (London: Hambledon Continuum, 2006).

Foucault, Michel, *Madness and Civilization: A History of Insanity in the Age of Reason*, tr. Richard Howard (New York: Vintage Books, 1988).

Fraanje, Maarten, "La sensibilité au pays du froid. Les Lumières et le sentimentalisme russe," *Revue des études slaves*, 74/4 (2002–3), 659–68.

Frede, Victoria, *Doubt, Atheism, and the Nineteenth-Century Russian Intelligentsia* (Madison: University of Wisconsin Press, 2011).

Freeze, Gregory L., *The Russian Levites: Parish Clergy in the Eighteenth Century* (Cambridge, Mass.: Harvard University Press, 1977).

—— "The *Soslovie* (Estate) Paradigm and Russian Social History," *American Historical Review*, 91/1 (February 1986), 11–36.

Frierson, Cathy A., *Peasant Icons: Representations of Rural People in Late Nineteenth-Century Russia* (New York: Oxford University Press, 1993).

Gasperetti, David, *The Rise of the Russian Novel: Carnival, Stylization, and Mockery of the West* (DeKalb, Ill.: Northern Illinois University Press, 1998).

"GeneaNet," <http://gw4.geneanet.org/index.php3?b=pierfit&lang=fr;p=georges+etienne; n=lecointe+de+laveau>.

Geyer, Michael and Sheila Fitzpatrick, eds., *Beyond Totalitarianism: Stalinism and Nazism Compared* (Cambridge: Cambridge University Press, 2009).

Gleason, Abbott, *Young Russia: The Genesis of Russian Radicalism in the 1860s* (New York: Viking Press, 1980).

Godlewska, Anne, "Traditions, Crisis, and New Paradigms in the Rise of the Modern French Discipline of Geography 1760–1850," *Annals of the Association of American Geographers*, 79 (June 1989), 192–213.

Golburt, Luba, "Catherine's Retinue: Old Age, Fashion, and Historicism in the Nineteenth Century," *Slavic Review*, 68/4 (Winter 2009), 782–803.

Gorbatov, Inna, "*La nouvelle Héloïse* de Jean-Jacques Rousseau et la *Pauvre Liza* de N. M. Karamzine," *Neohelicon*, 30/2 (2003).

Gorbunov, A. V., ed., *Otechestvennaia voina 1812 goda: Istochniki, pamiatniki, problemy. Materialy XII Vserossiiskoi nauchnoi konferentsii, Borodino, 6–8 sentiabria 2004 g.* (Moscow: Poligraf servis, 2005).

—— ed., *Otechestvennaia voina 1812 goda: Istochniki. Pamiatniki. Problemy. Materialy XV Mezhdunarodnoi nauchnoi konferentsii, 9–11 sentiabria 2008 g.* (Mozhaisk: Gosudarstvennyi Borodininskii voenno-istoricheskii muzei-zapovednik, 2009).

Gorzny, Willi, ed., *Deutscher biographischer Index*, 4 vols. (Munich: K. G. Saur, 1986).

Griffiths, David M., "Eighteenth-Century Perceptions of Backwardness: Projects for the Creation of a Third Estate in Catherinean Russia," *Canadian-American Slavic Studies*, 13/4 (Winter 1979), 452–72.

Grinina, I. R. and S. S. Ilizarov, *Akademik G. F. Miller—pervyi issledovatel' Moskvy i Moskovskoi provintsii* (Moscow: Ianus, 1996).

Gulianitskii, N. F., ed., *Moskva i slozhivshiesia russkie goroda XVIII–pervoi poloviny XIX vekov* (Moscow: Stroiizdat, 1998).

Hacking, Ian, *The Taming of Chance* (Cambridge: Cambridge University Press, 1990).

Hamlin, Christopher, *Public Health and Social Justice in the Age of Chadwick: Britain, 1800–1854* (Cambridge: Cambridge University Press, 1998).

Hammarberg, Gitta, "Poor Liza, Poor Èrast, Lucky Narrator," *Slavic and East European Journal*, 31/3 (Autumn 1987), 305–21.

—— *From the Idyll to the Novel: Karamzin's Sentimentalist Prose* (Cambridge: Cambridge University Press, 1991).

Harley, J. B., "Deconstructing the Map," *Cartographica*, 26/2 (Summer 1989), 1–20.

Harper, Kenneth E., "Criticism of the Natural School in the 1840s," *American Slavic and East European Review*, 15 (October 1956), 400–14.

Hartley, Janet M., "Town Government in Saint Petersburg Guberniya after the Charter to the Towns of 1785," *Slavonic and East European Review*, 62/1 (January 1984), 61–84.

—— "Russia in 1812, Part I: The French Presence in the *Gubernii* of Smolensk and Mogilev," *Jahrbücher für Geschichte Osteuropas*, 38/2 (1990), 178–98.

—— "Philanthropy in the Reign of Catherine the Great: Aims and Realities," in Roger Bartlett and Janet M. Hartley, eds., *Russia in the Age of the Enlightenment: Essays for Isabel de Madariaga* (New York: St Martin's Press, 1990), 167–202.

—— *Russia, 1762–1825: Military Power, the State, and the People* (Westport, Conn.: Praeger, 2008).

Hennig, John, *Goethes Europakunde: Goethes Kenntnisse des nichtdeutschsprachigen Europas: Ausgewählte Aufsätze* (Amsterdam: Rodopi, 1987).

Hildermeier, Manfred, *Bürgertum und Stadt in Rußland 1760–1870: Rechtliche Lage und soziale Struktur* (Cologne: Böhlau, 1986).

Hitchcock, Tim, *Down and Out in Eighteenth-Century London* (London: Hambledon, 2004).

Hittle, J. Michael, *The Service City: State and Townsmen in Russia, 1600–1800* (Cambridge, Mass.: Harvard University Press, 1979).

Hoffmann, Peter, *Gerhard Friedrich Müller (1705–1783): Historiker, Geograph, Archivar im Dienste Russlands* (Frankfurt: Peter Lang, 2005).

Hohenberg, Paul M. and Lynn Hollen Lees, *The Making of Urban Europe, 1000–1950* (Cambridge, Mass.: Harvard University Press, 1985).

Hollingsworth, Barry, "John Venning and Prison Reform in Russia, 1819–1830," *Slavonic and East European Review*, 48/113 (October 1970), 537–56.

Holmes, Janice, "The Role of Open-Air Preaching in the Belfast Riots of 1857," *Proceedings of the Royal Irish Academy*, 102C, no. 3 (2002), 47–66.

Hudson, Hugh D., "Urban Estate Engineering in Eighteenth-Century Russia: Catherine the Great and the Elusive *Meshchanstvo*," *Canadian-American Slavic Studies*, 18/4 (Winter 1984), 393–410.

Hughes, Lindsey, *Peter the Great: A Biography* (New Haven: Yale University Press, 2002).

—— *Russia in the Age of Peter the Great* (New Haven: Yale University Press, 1998).

Istoriia Moskvy s drevneishikh vremen do nashikh dnei, 3 vols. (Moscow: Mosgorarkhiv, 1997).

Johnson, Emily D., *How St. Petersburg Learned to Study Itself: The Russian Idea of Kraevedenie* (University Park, Pa.: Pennsylvania State University Press, 2006).

Jones, Robert E., "Jacob Sievers, Enlightened Reform and the Development of a 'Third Estate' in Russia," *Russian Review*, 36/4 (October 1977), 424–37.

—— "Getting the Goods to St. Petersburg: Water Transport from the Interior 1703–1811," *Slavic Review*, 43/3 (Autumn 1984), 413–33.

Kaganov, Grigory, *Images of Space: St. Petersburg in the Visual and Verbal Arts*, tr. Sidney Monas (Stanford, Calif.: Stanford University Press, 1997).

Kamenskii, A. B., "Akademik G.-F. Miller i russkaia istoricheskaia nauka XVIII veka," *Istoriia SSSR*, no. 1 (January 1989), 144–59.

—— "*Pod seniiu Ekateriny . . .*": *Vtoraia polovina XVIII veka* (St Petersburg: Lenizdat, 1992).

—— *Povsednevnost' russkikh gorodskikh obyvatelei: Istoricheskie anekdoty iz provintsial'noi zhizni XVIII veka* (Moscow: Rossiiskii Gosudarstvennyi Gumanitarnyi Universitet, 2006).

Kaplan, Steven L., "Note sur les commissaires de police de Paris au XVIIIe siècle," *Revue d'histoire moderne et contemporaine*, 28/4 (1981), 669–86.

Keller, Mechthild, ed., *Russen und Rußland aus deutscher Sicht—19. Jahrhundert: Von der Jahrhundertwende bis zur Reichsgründung (1800–1871)* (Munich: Wilhelm Fink, 1992).

Khristoforova, N. V., *Rossiiskie gimnazii XVIII–XX vekov: Na materiale g. Moskvy* (Moscow: Greko-latinskii kabinet Iu. A. Shichalina, 2001).

Kingston-Mann, Esther, "In the Light and Shadow of the West: The Impact of Western Economics in Pre-Emancipation Russia," *Comparative Studies in Society and History*, 33/1 (January 1991), 86–105.

—— *In Search of the True West: Culture, Economics, and Problems of Russian Development* (Princeton: Princeton University Press, 1999).

Kirsanova, Raisa Mardukhovna, *Kostium v russkoi khudozhestvenoi kul'ture 18–pervoi poloviny 20 vv.: Opyt entsiklopedii* (Moscow: Bol'shaia Rossiiskaia entsiklopediia, 1995).

Kiseleva, Liubov', "Sistema vzgliadov S. N. Glinki (1807–1812 gg.)," in *Uchenye zapiski Tartuskogo gosudarstvennogo universiteta*, vypusk 513 (1981), 52–72.

—— "S. N. Glinka i kadetskii korpus (iz istorii 'sentimental'nogo vospitaniia' v Rossii)," *Uchenye zapiski Tartuskogo gosudarstvennogo universiteta*, vypusk 604 (1982), 48–63.

—— "Zhurnal 'Zritel'" i dve kontseptsii patriotizma v russkoi literature 1800-kh gg.," in *Uchenye zapiski Tartuskogo gosudarstvennogo universiteta*, vypusk 645 (1985), 3–20.

Kivelson, Valerie A., *Cartographies of Tsardom: The Land and its Meanings in Seventeenth-Century Russia* (Ithaca, NY: Cornell University Press, 2006).

Knabe, G. S., ed., *Moskva i "moskovskii tekst" russkoi kul'tury: Sbornik statei* (Moscow: Rossiiskii Gosudarstvennyi Gumanitarnyi Universitet, 1998).

Kollmann, Nancy Shields, et al., eds., Камень Краєжгъльнъ/*Rhetoric of the Medieval Slavic World: Essays Presented to Edward L. Keenan on his Sixtieth Birthday by his Colleagues and Students*, Harvard Ukrainian Studies 19 (Cambridge, Mass.: Harvard University Press, 1995).

Konvitz, Josef W., *The Urban Millennium: The City-Building Process from the Early Middle Ages to the Present* (Carbondale, Ill.: Southern Illinois University Press, 1985).

Koshelev, A. D., ed., *Iz istorii russkoi kul'tury*, 5 vols. (Moscow: Iazyki russkoi kul'tury, 1996–2000).

Kostin, A. A. and N. D. Kochetkova, eds., *Ivan Ivanovich Dmitriev (1760–1837): Zhizn', tvorchestvo, krug obshcheniia*, Chteniia Otdela russkoi literatury XVIII veka, vypusk 6 (St Petersburg, 2011).

Kozlova, N. V., *Liudi driakhlye, bol'nye, ubogie v Moskve XVIII veka* (Moscow: ROSSPEN, 2010).

Krementsov, Nikolai, "Hormones and the Bolsheviks: From Organotherapy to Experimental Endocrinology, 1918–1929," *Isis*, 99/3 (September 2008), 486–518.

Kupriianov, A. I., *Gorodskaia kul'tura russkoi provintsii: Konets XVIII–pervaia polovina XIX veka* (Moscow: Novyi khronograf, 2007).

La Berge, Ann F., *Mission and Method: The Early Nineteenth-Century French Public Health Movement* (Cambridge: Cambridge University Press, 1992).

Lankevich, George J., *New York: A Short History* (New York: New York University Press, 1998).

Lapin, V. V., *Peterburg: Zapakhi i zvuki* (St Petersburg: Evropeiskii Dom, 2007).

LeBlanc, Ronald D., "Teniers, Flemish Art, and the Natural School Debate," *Slavic Review*, 50/3 (Fall 1991), 576–89.

LeDonne, John P., *Absolutism and Ruling Class: The Formation of the Russian Political Order, 1700–1825* (New York: Oxford University Press, 1991).

Lees, Andrew and Lynn Hollen Lees, *Cities and the Making of Modern Europe, 1750–1914* (Cambridge: Cambridge University Press, 2007).

Lehmann-Carli, Gabriela, Yvonne Drohsin, and Ulrike Klitsche-Sowitzki, eds., *Russland zwischen Ost und West? Gratwanderungen nationaler Identität* (Berlin: Frank & Timme, 2011).

Levandovskaia, Aleksandra A. and Andrei A. Levandovskii, "The 'Dark Kingdom': The Merchant Entrepreneur and his Literary Images," *Russian Studies in History*, 47/1 (Summer 2008), 72–95.

Levitt, Marcus C., "An Antidote to Nervous Juice: Catherine the Great's Debate with Chappe d'Auteroche over Russian Culture," *Eighteenth-Century Studies*, 32/1 (1998), 49–63.

—— *The Visual Dominant in Eighteenth-Century Russia* (DeKalb, Ill.: Northern Illinois University Press, 2011).

Lieven, Dominic, ed., *The Cambridge History of Imperial Russia*, vol. 2: *Imperial Russia, 1689–1917* (Cambridge: Cambridge University Press, 2006).

—— *Russia against Napoleon: The Battle for Europe, 1807 to 1814* (London: Allen Lane, 2009).

Lilly, Ian K., ed., *Moscow and Petersburg: The City in Russian Culture* (Nottingham: Astra Press, 2002).

—— "Conviviality in the Prerevolutionary 'Moscow Text' of Russian Culture," *Russian Review*, 63/3 (July 2004), 427–48.

Lincoln, W. Bruce, "N. A. Miliutin and the St. Petersburg Municipal Act of 1846: A Study in Reform under Nicholas I," *Slavic Review*, 33/1 (March 1974), 55–68.

—— *In the Vanguard of Reform: Russia's Enlightened Bureaucrats, 1825–1861* (DeKalb, Ill.: Northern Illinois University Press, 1982).

Linke, Uli, "Folklore, Anthropology, and the Government of Social Life," *Comparative Studies in Society and History*, 32 (January 1990), 117–48.

Liulevicius, Vejas Gabriel, *The German Myth of the East: 1800 to the Present* (Oxford: Oxford University Press, 2009).

Lotman, Iu. M., *Besedy o russkoi kul'ture: Byt i traditsii russkogo dvorianstva (XVIII–nachalo XIX veka)* (St Petersburg: Iskusstvo-SPB, 1994).

Madariaga, Isabel de, *Russia in the Age of Catherine the Great* (New Haven: Yale University Press, 1981).

Maiorova, Olga, *From the Shadow of Empire: Defining the Russian Nation through Cultural Mythology, 1855–1870* (Madison: University of Wisconsin Press, 2010).

Malia, Martin, *Russia under Western Eyes: From the Bronze Horseman to the Lenin Mausoleum* (Cambridge, Mass.: Belknap, 1999).

Manchester, Laurie, *Holy Fathers, Secular Sons: Clergy, Intelligentsia, and the Modern Self in Revolutionary Russia* (DeKalb, Ill.: Northern Illinois University Press, 2008).

Marker, Gary, *Publishing, Printing, and the Origins of Intellectual Life in Russia, 1700–1800* (Princeton: Princeton University Press, 1985).

Markovin, A. P., *Razvitie meditsinskoi geografii v Rossii* (St Petersburg: Nauka, 1993).

Martin, Alexander M., *Romantics, Reformers, Reactionaries: Russian Conservative Thought and Politics in the Reign of Alexander I* (DeKalb, Ill.: Northern Illinois University Press, 1997).

—— "The Family Model of Society and Russian National Identity in Sergei N. Glinka's *Russian Messenger* (1808–1812)," *Slavic Review*, 57/1 (Spring 1998), 28–49.

—— "The Response of the Population of Moscow to the Napoleonic Occupation of 1812," in Eric Lohr and Marshall Poe, eds., *The Military and Society in Russia, 1450–1917* (Leiden: Brill, 2002), 469–90.

—— "Precarious Existences: Middling Households in Moscow and the Fire of 1812," in Marsha Siefert, ed., *Extending the Borders of Russian History: Essays in Honor of Alfred J. Rieber* (Budapest: Central European University Press, 2003), 67–82.

——"Down and Out in 1812: The Impact of the Napoleonic Invasion on Moscow's Middling Strata," in Roger Bartlett et al., eds., *Eighteenth-Century Russia: Society, Culture, Economy. Papers From the VII International Conference of the Study Group on Eighteenth-Century Russia, Wittenberg 2004* (Münster: LIT-Verlag, 2007), 429–41.

—— "Sewage and the City: Filth, Smell, and Representations of Urban Life in Moscow, 1770–1880," *Russian Review*, 67/2 (April 2008), 243–74.

Matveev, N., *Moskva i zhizn' v nei nakanune nashestviia 1812 g.* (Moscow: Duma, 2008).

McCaffray, Susan P., "Confronting Serfdom in the Age of Revolution: Projects for Serf Reform in the Time of Alexander I," *Russian Review*, 64/1 (January 2005), 1–21.

McGrew, Roderick E., *Russia and the Cholera 1823–1832* (Madison: University of Wisconsin Press, 1965).

—— "Dilemmas of Development: Baron Heinrich Friedrich Storch (1766–1835) on the Growth of Imperial Russia," *Jahrbücher für Geschichte Osteuropas*, 24/1 (1976), 31–71.

McLean, Hugh, Martin E. Malia, and George Fisher, eds., *Russian Thought and Politics*, Harvard Slavic Studies vol. 4 (Cambridge, Mass.: Harvard University Press, 1957).

Melbin, Murray, "Night as Frontier," *American Sociological Review*, 43 (February 1978), 3–22.

Meshcheriakova, A. O., *F. V. Rostopchin: U osnovaniia konservatizma i natsionalizma v Rossii* (Voronezh: Izdatel'skii dom "Kitezh," 2007).

Mironov, B. N., *Russkii gorod v 1740–1860-e gody: Demograficheskoe, sotsial'noe i ekono-micheskoe razvitie* (Leningrad: Nauka, 1990).

—— "Bureaucratic or Self-Government: The Early Nineteenth Century Russian City," *Slavic Review*, 52/2 (Summer 1993), 233–55.

—— "Prestupnost' v Rossii v XIX–nachale XX veka," *Otechestvennaia istoriia*, no. 1 (1998), 24–42.

—— *Sotsial'naia istoriia Rossii perioda Imperii (XVIII–nachalo XX veka): Genezis lichnosti, demokraticheskoi sem'i, grazhdanskogo obshchestva i pravovogo gosudarstva*, 2 vols. (St Petersburg: Dmitrii Bulanin, 1999).

Monas, Sidney, *The Third Section: Police and Society in Russia under Nicholas I* (Cambridge, Mass.: Harvard University Press, 1961).

Moser, Charles A., ed., *The Cambridge History of Russian Literature* (rev. edn., Cambridge: Cambridge University Press, 1992).

Munro, George E., "The Charter to the Towns Reconsidered: The St. Petersburg Connection," *Canadian-American Slavic Studies*, 23/1 (Spring 1989), 17–35.

—— *The Most Intentional City: St. Petersburg in the Reign of Catherine the Great* (Madison, NJ: Fairleigh Dickinson University Press, 2008).

Nicassio, Susan Vandiver, *Imperial City: Rome under Napoleon* (Chicago: University of Chicago Press, 2005).

Nichols, Robert L., and Theofanis George Stavrou, eds., *Russian Orthodoxy under the Old Regime* (Minneapolis: University of Minnesota Press, 1978).

Nikolaev, P. A., ed., *Russkie pisateli 1800–1917: Biograficheskii slovar'*, 5 vols. (Moscow: Sovetskaia Entsiklopediia, 1989-).

Nikonov, V. A., *Imia i obshchestvo* (Moscow: Nauka, Glavnaia redaktsiia vostochnoi literatury, 1974).

Nilova, O. E., *Moskovskoe kupechestvo kontsa XVIII–pervoi chetverti XIX veka: Sotsial'nye aspekty mirovospriiatiia i samosoznaniia* (Moscow: Institut rossiiskoi istorii RAN, 2002).

Norris, Stephen M., "Images of 1812: Ivan Terebenev and the Russian Wartime *Lubok*," *National Identities*, 7/1 (March 2005), 1–21.

Offord, Derek, *Journeys to a Graveyard: Perceptions of Europe in Classical Russian Travel Writing* (Dordrecht: Springer, 2005).

Okenfuss, Max J., "Education and Empire: School Reform in Enlightened Russia," *Jahrbücher für Geschichte Osteuropas*, 27/1 (1979), 41–68.

Okhotin, N. G., and G. Iu. Sternin, *Nashi, spisannye s natury russkimi: Prilozhenie k faksimil'nomu izdaniiu* (Moscow: Kniga, 1986).

Ostreikovskaia, N. V., "Memuarnye zapisi Tolychevoi kak dokumental'nyi istochnik," *Vestnik Cheliabinskogo Gosudarstvennogo Universiteta*, no. 39 (177) (2009), *Filologiia, Iskusstvovedenie* (vypusk 38), 122–4 <http://www.lib.csu.ru/vch/177/024.pdf>.

O'Toole, Michael, *The Language of Displayed Art* (London: Leicester University Press, 1994).

Owen, David, *The Government of Victorian London, 1855–1889: The Metropolitan Board of Works, the Vestries, and the City Corporation* (Cambridge, Mass.: Belknap, 1982).

Paert, Irina, *Old Believers, Religious Dissent and Gender in Russia, 1760–1850* (Manchester: Manchester University Press, 2003).

Pedrocco, Filippo, *Visions of Venice: Paintings of the 18th Century*, tr. Susan Scott (London: Tauris Parke, 2002).

Phillips, Laura L., *Bolsheviks and the Bottle: Drink and Worker Culture in St. Petersburg, 1900–1929* (DeKalb, Ill.: Northern Illinois University Press, 2000).

Pinol, Jean-Luc, *Le monde des villes au XIXe siècle* (Paris: Hachette, 1991).

Pintner, Walter M., *Russian Economic Policy under Nicholas I* (Ithaca, NY: Cornell University Press, 1967).

—— "The Social Characteristics of the Early Nineteenth-Century Russian Bureaucracy," *Slavic Review*, 29/3 (September 1970), 429–43.

Pogosian, E. A., "Ot staroi Ladogi do Ekaterinoslava (mesto Moskvy v predstavleniiakh Ekateriny II o stolitse imperii)," *Lotmanovskii Sbornik*, 2 (1997), 511–20.

Poussou, Jean-Pierre and Isabelle Robin-Romero, eds., *Histoire de la famille, de la démographie et des comportements: En hommage à Jean-Pierre Bardet* (Paris: PUPS, 2007).

Proskurina, Vera, *Mify imperii: Literatura i vlast' v epokhu Ekateriny II* (Moscow: Novoe Literaturnoe Obozrenie, 2006).

Raeff, Marc, *Michael Speransky, Statesman of Imperial Russia, 1772–1839* (2nd edn., The Hague: Martinus Nijhoff, 1969).

—— *The Well-Ordered Police State: Social and Institutional Change through Law in the Germanies and Russia, 1600–1800* (New Haven: Yale University Press, 1983).

Randolph, John, *The House in the Garden: The Bakunin Family and the Romance of Russian Idealism* (Ithaca, NY: Cornell University Press, 2007).

Ransel, David L., *Mothers of Misery: Child Abandonment in Russia* (Princeton: Princeton University Press, 1988).

—— *A Russian Merchant's Tale: The Life and Adventures of Ivan Alekseevich Tolchënov, Based on his Diary* (Bloomington, Ind.: Indiana University Press, 2009).

Rashin, A. G., *Naselenie Rossii za 100 let (1811–1913 gg.): Statisticheskie ocherki* (Moscow: Gosudarstvennoe Statisticheskoe Izdatel'stvo, 1956).

Reid, Donald, *Paris Sewers and Sewermen: Realities and Representations* (Cambridge, Mass.: Harvard University Press, 1991).

Renner, Andreas, "Wissenschaftstransfer ins Zarenreich des 18. Jahrhunderts: Bemerkungen zum Forschungsstand am Beispiel der Medizingeschichte," *Jahrbücher für Geschichte Osteuropas*, 53/1 (2005), 64–85.

Rieber, Alfred J., *Merchants and Entrepreneurs in Imperial Russia* (Chapel Hill, NC: University of North Carolina Press, 1982).

Roche, Daniel, *La culture des apparences. Une histoire du vêtement (XVIIe–XVIIIe siècle)* (Paris: Arthème Fayard, 1989).

Roche, Daniel, *Le peuple de Paris. essai sur la culture populaire au XVIIIe siècle* (Paris: Arthème Fayard, 1998).

Rosen, George, *A History of Public Health*, expanded edn., ed. Elizabeth Fee and Edward T. Morman (1958; repr. Baltimore: Johns Hopkins University Press, 1993).

Roth, Andreas, *Kriminalitätsbekämpfung in deutschen Großstädten, 1850–1914: Ein Beitrag zur Geschichte des strafrechtlichen Ermittlungsverfahrens* (Berlin: Erich Schmidt, 1997).

Ruane, Christine, *The Empire's New Clothes: A History of the Russian Fashion Industry, 1700–1917* (New Haven: Yale University Press, 2009).

Ruble, Blair, *Second Metropolis: Pragmatic Pluralism in Gilded Age Chicago, Silver Age Moscow, and Meiji Osaka* (Washington, DC: Woodrow Wilson Center Press, 2001).

Rupke, Nicolaas, ed., *Medical Geography in Historical Perspective* (London: Wellcome Trust Centre for the History of Medicine at UCL, 2000).

Rustemeyer, Angela, *Dienstboten in Petersburg und Moskau, 1861–1917: Hintergrund, Alltag, soziale Rolle* (Stuttgart: F. Steiner, 1996).

Ruud, Charles A., *Fighting Words: Imperial Censorship and the Russian Press, 1804–1906* (Toronto: University of Toronto Press, 2009).

Sanders, Thomas, ed., *Historiography of Imperial Russia: The Profession and Writing of History in a Multinational State* (Armonk, NY: M. E. Sharpe, 1999).

Saunders, David, *The Ukrainian Impact on Russian Culture, 1750–1850* (Edmonton: Canadian Institute of Ukrainian Studies, 1985).

Schattenberg, Susanne, *Die korrupte Provinz? Russische Beamte im 19. Jahrhundert* (Frankfurt: Campus, 2008).

Schivelbusch, Wolfgang, "The Policing of Street Lighting," in Alice Kaplan and Kristin Ross, eds., *Everyday Life*, *Yale French Studies* 73 (New Haven: Yale University Press, 1987), 61–74.

Schleifman, Nurit, "A Russian Daily Newspaper and its Readership: *Severnaia Pchela* 1825–1840," *Cahiers du monde russe et soviétique*, 28/2 (April–June 1987), 127–44.

Schlör, Joachim, *Nights in the Big City: Paris, Berlin, London, 1840–1930*, tr. Pierre Gottfried Imhoff and Dafydd Rees Roberts (London: Reaktion, 1998).

Schmidt, Albert J., *The Architecture and Planning of Classical Moscow: A Cultural History* (Philadelphia: American Philosophical Society, 1989).

Schmidt, Christoph, *Sozialkontrolle in Moskau: Justiz, Kriminalität und Leibeigenschaft 1649–1785* (Stuttgart: Franz Steiner, 1996).

Schönle, Andreas, *Authenticity and Fiction in the Russian Literary Journey, 1790–1840* (Cambridge, Mass.: Harvard University Press, 2000).

—— *The Ruler in the Garden: Politics and Landscape Design in Imperial Russia* (Oxford: Peter Lang, 2007).

Schorske, Carl E., *Fin-de-Siècle Vienna: Politics and Culture* (New York: Vintage, 1981).

Schrader, Abby M., *Languages of the Lash: Corporal Punishment and Identity in Imperial Russia* (DeKalb, Ill.: Northern Illinois University Press, 2002).

Scott, James C., *Seeing Like a State: How Certain Schemes to Improve the Human Condition Have Failed* (New Haven: Yale University Press, 1998).

Serkov, A. I., *Russkoe masonstvo 1731–2000: Entsiklopedicheskii slovar'* (Moscow: ROSSPEN, 2001).

Shanin, Teodor, *Russia, 1905–07: Revolution as a Moment of Truth* (Houndsmills: Macmillan, 1986).

Shcherbinin, Pavel, "Zhizn' russkoi soldatki v XVIII–XIX vekakh," *Voprosy istorii*, no. 1 (2005), 79–92.

Shepelev, L. E., *Chinovnyi mir Rossii, XVIII–nachalo XX v.* (St Petersburg: Iskusstvo-SPb, 1999).

Shesgreen, Sean, ed., *The Criers and Hawkers of London: Engravings and Drawings by Marcellus Laroon* (Stanford, Calif.: Stanford University Press, 1990).

Shishkova, T., "O Bulgarine starom i novom: Osnovnye tendentsii sovremennogo bulgarinovedeniia," *Novoe Literaturnoe Obozrenie*, no. 88 (2007) <http://www.nlobooks.ru/rus/magazines/nlo/196/722/740/>.

Shoemaker, Robert, *The London Mob: Violence and Disorder in Eighteenth-Century England* (London: Hambledon Continuum, 2004).

Shovlin, John, "The Cultural Politics of Luxury in Eighteenth-Century France," *French Historical Studies*, 23/4 (Fall 2000), 578–606.

—— *The Political Economy of Virtue: Luxury, Patriotism, and the Origins of the French Revolution* (Ithaca, NY: Cornell University Press, 2006).

Shvidkovsky, Dmitry, *Russian Architecture and the West*, tr. Antony Wood (New Haven: Yale University Press, 2007).

Slezkine, Yuri, "Naturalists Versus Nations: Eighteenth-Century Russian Scholars Confront Ethnic Diversity," *Representations*, no. 47 (Summer 1994), 170–95.

Smith, Alison K., "Public Works in an Autocratic State: Water Supplies in an Imperial Russian Town," *Environment and History*, 11 (2005), 319–42.

—— *Recipes for Russia: Food and Nationhood under the Tsars* (DeKalb, Ill.: Northern Illinois University Press, 2008).

Smith, Douglas, *Working the Rough Stone: Freemasonry and Society in Eighteenth-Century Russia* (DeKalb, Ill.: Northern Illinois University Press, 1999).

—— *The Pearl: A True Tale of Forbidden Love in Catherine the Great's Russia* (New Haven: Yale University Press, 2008).

Smith, Francis Barrymore, *The People's Health, 1830–1910* (New York: Holmes & Meier, 1979).

Smith-Peter, Susan, "Defining the Russian People: Konstantin Arsen'ev and Russian Statistics before 1861," *History of Science*, 45/1 (March 2007), 47–64.

—— *The Russian Provincial Newspaper and its Public, 1788–1864*, The Carl Beck Papers in Russian & East European Studies, no. 1908 (Pittsburgh: Center for Russian and East European Studies, University of Pittsburgh, 2008).

Steigerwald, Jörn, *Die fantastische Bildlichkeit der Stadt: Zur Begründung der literarischen Fantastik im Werk E. T. A. Hoffmanns* (Würzburg: Königshausen & Neumann, 2001).

Steuer, Philipp, *Die Wasserversorgung der Städte und Ortschaften: Ihre wirtschaftliche Entwicklung und Analyse* (Berlin: Franz Siemenroth, 1912).

Stites, Richard, *Serfdom, Society, and the Arts: The Pleasure and the Power* (New Haven: Yale University Press, 2005).

Strohm, Reinhard, ed., *The Eighteenth-Century Diaspora of Italian Music and Musicians* (Turnhout: Brepols, 2001).

Sunderland, Willard, *Taming the Wild Field: Colonization and Empire on the Russian Steppe* (Ithaca, NY: Cornell University Press, 2004).

Sytin, P. B., *Iz istorii moskovskikh ulits (Ocherki)* (3rd edn., Moscow: Moskovskii rabochii, 1958).

Szabo, Franz A. J., "Changing Perpectives on the 'Revolutionary Emperor': Joseph II Biographies since 1790," *Journal of Modern History*, 83/1 (March 2011), 111–38.

Taki, Victor, "Russia on the Danube: Imperial Expansion and Political Reform in Moldavia and Wallachia, 1812–1834," Ph.D. diss., Central European University, Budapest, 2007.

Tarle, E. V., *1812 god: Izbrannye proizvedeniia* (Moscow: Pressa, 1994).

Tartakovskii, A. G., "Naselenie Moskvy v period frantsuzskoi okkupatsii," *Istoricheskie Zapiski*, 93 (1973), 356–79.

—— *1812 god i russkaia memuaristika: Opyt istochnikovedcheskogo izucheniia* (Moscow: Nauka, 1980).

Tinkler-Villani, Valeria, ed., *Babylon or New Jerusalem? Perceptions of the City in Literature* (Amsterdam: Rodopi, 2005).

Tosi, Alessandra, *Waiting for Pushkin: Russian Fiction in the Reign of Alexander I (1801–1825)* (Amsterdam: Rodopi, 2006).

Trencsényi, Balázs and Michal Kopček, *Discourses of Collective Identity in Central and Southeast Europe (1770–1945): Texts and Commentaries*, 4 vols. in 3 (Budapest: Central European University Press, 2006–10).

Tribe, Keith, "Cameralism and the Science of Government," *Journal of Modern History*, 56/2 (June 1984), 263–84.

Troitskii, N. A., *1812: Velikii god Rossii* (Moscow: Mysl', 1988).

Trubachev, O. N., ed., *Russkaia onomastka i onomastika Rossii: Slovar'* (Moscow: Shkola-Press, 1994).

Tseitlin, A. G., *Stanovlenie realizma v russkoi literature (Russkii fiziologicheskii ocherk)* (Moscow: Nauka, 1965).

Turcot, Laurent, *Le promeneur à Paris au XVIIIe siècle* (n.p.: Gallimard, 2007).

Turton, Glyn, *Turgenev and the Context of English Literature, 1850–1900* (London: Routledge, 1992).

Tydman, L. V., *Izba. Dom. Dvorets. Zhiloi inter'er Rossii s 1700 po 1840-e gody* (Moscow: Progress-Traditsiia, 2000).

Venturi, Franco, *Roots of Revolution: A History of the Populist and Socialist Movements in Nineteenth Century Russia*, tr. Francis Haskell (New York: Grosset & Dunlap, 1966).

—— *The End of the Old Regime in Europe, 1768–1776: The First Crisis*, tr. R. Burr Litchfield (Princeton: Princeton University Press, 1989).

Vishlenkova, Elena, *Vizual'noe narodovedenie imperii, ili "Uvidet' russkogo dano ne kazhdomu"* (Moscow: Novoe Literaturnoe Obozrenie, 2011).

Volkov, Solomon, *St. Petersburg: A Cultural History*, tr. Antonina W. Bouis (New York: Free Press Paperbacks, 1997).

Vries, Jan de, *The Industrious Revolution: Consumer Behavior and the Household Economy, 1650 to the Present* (Cambridge: Cambridge University Press, 2008).

Walker, Mack, *German Home Towns: Community, State, and General Estate, 1648–1871* (Ithaca, NY: Cornell University Press, 1971; repr. 1998).

Weigley, Russell F., ed., *Philadelphia: A 300-Year History* (New York: W. W. Norton, 1982).

Wesling, Molly W., *Napoleon in Russian Cultural Mythology* (New York: Peter Lang, 2001).

West, James L. and Iurii A. Petrov, eds., *Merchant Moscow: Images of Russia's Vanished Bourgeoisie* (Princeton: Princeton University Press, 1998).

Wheeler, Eileen Fabian, *Horse Stable and Riding Arena Design* (Ames, Ia.: Blackwell, 2006).

Whittaker, Cynthia Hyla, ed., *Russia Engages the World, 1453–1825* (Cambridge, Mass.: Harvard University Press, 2003).

—— *Russian Monarchy: Eighteenth-Century Rulers and Writers in Political Dialogue* (DeKalb, Ill.: Northern Illinois University Press, 2003).

Whittaker, Robert, "'My Literary and Moral Wanderings': Apollon Grigor'ev and the Changing Cultural Topography of Moscow," *Slavic Review*, 42/3 (Fall 1983), 390–407.

Wirtschafter, Elise Kimerling, *Structures of Society: Imperial Russia's "People of Various Ranks"* (DeKalb, Ill.: Northern Illinois University Press, 1994).

—— "Social Misfits: Veterans and Soldiers' Families in Servile Russia," *Journal of Military History*, 59 (April 1995), 215–36.

—— *The Play of Ideas in Russian Enlightenment Theater* (DeKalb, Ill.: Northern Illinois University Press, 2003).

—— *Russia's Age of Serfdom, 1649–1861* (Malden, Mass.: Blackwell, 2008).

Wolff, Larry, *Inventing Eastern Europe: The Map of Civilization on the Mind of the Enlightenment* (Stanford, Calif.: Stanford University Press, 1994).

Wood, Gordon S., *The Radicalism of the American Revolution* (New York: Vintage, 1993).

Woolf, Stuart, *Napoleon's Integration of Europe* (London: Routledge, 1991).

Wortman, Richard, *Scenarios of Power: Myth and Ceremony in Russian Monarchy*, 2 vols. (Princeton: Princeton University Press, 1995–2000).

Zacek, Judith C., "A Case Study in Russian Philanthropy: The Prison Reform Movement in the Reign of Alexander I," *Canadian Slavic Studies*, 1/2 (Summer 1967), 196–211.

Zaichenko, L. V., *Moskva v Otechestvennoi voine 1812 goda* (Moscow: Moskvovedenie, 2006).

Zapadov, A. V., *Istoriia russkoi zhurnalistiki XVIII–XIX vekov* (Moscow: Vysshaia Shkola, 1973).

Zhivov, Viktor, "Chuvstvitel'nyi natsionalizm: Karamzin, Rostopchin, natsional'nyi suverenitet i poiski natsional'noi identichnosti," *Novoe Literaturnoe Obozrenie*, no. 91 (2008).

Zimin, Igor', "Nochnoi sosud s pozolotoiu: Povsednevnaia zhizn' imperatorskikh dvortsov: kanalizatsiia," *Sankt-Peterburgskie Vedomosti* (28 September 2007), *Daidzhest Peterburgskoi pressy* <http://base.pl.spb.ru/FullText/spbiblio/digest_spb/SPb_v070928_3.pdf>.

Zorin, Andrei, *Kormia dvuglavogo orla . . . Literatura i gosudarstvennaia ideologiia v Rossii v poslednei treti XVIII–pervoi treti XIX veka* (Moscow: Novoe Literaturnoe Obozrenie, 2001).

—— "Pokhod v bordel' v Moskve v ianvare 1800 goda (Shiller, gonoreia, i pervorodnyi grekh v emotsional'nom mire russkogo dvorianina)," *Novoe Literaturnoe Obozrenie*, no. 92 (2008) <http://www.nlobooks.ru/rus/magazines/nlo/196/1070/1083/>.

Index

Academy of Sciences 44, 67, 77, 78, 83, 87, 91, 102, 115
Academy of the Arts 63, 87, 91
alehouses, *see* taverns
Alekseev, Fedor 67, 89–95
Alexander I, emperor of Russia 28, 90, 104, 107, 111, 113, 119, 125, 126, 145, 146, 161, 166, 169, 177, 180–9, 199, 205, 209–18, 226, 238, 247
Alexander II, emperor of Russia 193, 247, 296
Alexander School 160, 169–75, 230, 236, 237
  see also boarding schools; *institutki*
almshouses 33, 179, 258
America (North and South) 13, 19, 24, 39, 70, 98, 162–4, 248
Amvrosii, Archbishop of Moscow 14–15, 17, 80
Androssov, Vasilii, author of *A Statistical Note on Moscow* 231–3, 242–3, 258, 274–5, 279, 280, 282, 283, 293
Anna, empress of Russia 11, 19, 37, 73, 88
Arakcheev, Aleksei 183, 220
Arbat Gate 56
architects, *see* Bazhenov, Vasilii; Blank, Ivan; Geste, Vasilii; Kazakov, Matvei
architecture 1, 5, 8, 18, 66, 70, 88, 89, 91, 93, 110, 123, 125, 135, 236, 237, 266, 297
"archive youths" 135
aristocracy 10, 139, 158
  attitudes 45, 104, 118, 128–9, 132, 164–6, 175, 202, 209
  landed estates 38, 142, 144, 159, 161–2
  material conditions 40, 52, 105, 128, 132, 137, 142–4, 150, 154, 158–64, 186–8, 197, 220, 222, 267, 268
  relations with other social estates 84, 121, 124, 128, 139, 143–4, 148, 161–6, 178, 195, 288, 290, 299
  social influence and patronage 57, 114, 118, 139, 143–4, 149, 163–4, 222, 224
Arkharov, Nikolai 62
Arsen'ev, Konstantin 164, 271, 293
artisans:
  cultural and social features 29, 56, 124, 131, 153–4, 222–7, 231–5, 244, 251–5, 258, 260, 289
  guilds 28, 29, 34, 298
  statistics 29, 31, 85, 141, 148, 154, 197, 211–13, 233, 235, 243, 245, 253, 255, 258

"Asiatic," Russia described as 97–9, 108, 115, 118, 182, 286, 292, 294
  see also Moscow, described as "Asiatic"; orientalism
Atkinson, John Augustus 88
Attenhofer, Heinrich Ludwig 45–6, 275
Austria and Austrians 68, 131, 182, 202, 205, 217, 297

Baltic Germans 25, 101–4
Balzac, Honoré 100
Baroque 19, 22, 38, 92
Bashutskii, Aleksandr 278–85, 289–92
  Our People, Painted from Nature by Russians 278, 280, 282, 284
  The Panorama of St Petersburg 115, 279–80, 289
bathing 41, 49, 88, 233, 234, 236, 277
Batiushkov, Konstantin, author of "Stroll around Moscow" 97, 134–8
Bazhenov, Vasilii 23
  plans for rebuilding the Kremlin 36, 46, 80
Beccaria, Cesare 25
begging, *see* pauperism
Belinskii, Vissarion 261, 267, 284–5, 292, 293
Belousov, Ivan 244, 246
Benckendorff, Alexander von 264, 284
Benjamin, Walter, author of *The Arcades Project* 205, 286, 288
Bennigsen, Levin 182
Benois, Aleksandr 63
Bering, Vitus 77
Berlin:
  described by writers 56, 102, 112, 120–1, 123, 277
  during the Napoleonic Wars 180, 215
  urban conditions 49, 59, 61, 63, 220–1
Betskoi, Ivan 23–5, 78, 91, 138 n.130, 237
Blank, Ivan 23
Bludov, Dmitrii 135
Board of Public Welfare 33, 34
boarding schools 25, 91, 104, 165, 167–73, 197, 236, 256
  see also Alexander School; cadet schools; Catherine Institute; *institutki*
Bogatyrev, Pavel 140, 173, 231
Bolotov, Andrei 15–16, 18, 205
Bolsheviks 297
books 156, 202, 224